C   *A REFERENCE MANUAL*

C *A REFERENCE MANUAL*

Fifth Edition

Samuel P. Harbison III Texas Instruments

Guy L. Steele Jr.   Sun Microsystems

Library of Congress Cataloging-in-Publication Data

CIP data on file.

Vice President and Editorial Director, ECS: *Marcia Horton*
Senior Acquisitions Editor: *Petra J.Recter*
Vice President and Director of Production and Manufacturing, ESM: *David W.Riccardi*
Executive Managing Editor: *Vince O 'Brien*
Assistant Managing Editor: *Camille Trentacoste*
Production Editor: *Lakshmi Balasubramanian*
Cover Designer: *Bruce Kenselaar*
Manufacturing Manager: *Trudy Pisciotti*
Manufacturing Buyer: *Lisa McDowell*

© 2002 by Prentice Hall
Prentice-Hall, Inc.
Upper Saddle River, NJ 07458

Printed in the United States of America

10 9 8 7 6

ISBN 0-13-089592X

Pearson Education Ltd., *London*
Pearson Education Australia Pty. Ltd., *Sydney*
Pearson Education Singapore, Pte. Ltd.
Pearson Education North Asia Ltd., *Hong Kong*
Pearson Education Canada, Inc., *Toronto*
Pearson Educac`ýon de Mexico, S.A.de C.V.
Pearson Education —Japan, *Tokyo*
Pearson Education Malaysia, Pte.Ltd.
Pearson Education, *Upper Saddle River, New Jersey*

For Diana, Drew, and Mike Harbison.

Contents

List of Tables   xv

Preface   xvii

PART 1   The C Language   1

1 Introduction   3
    1.1   The Evolution of C 3
    1.2   Which Dialect of C Should You Use? 6
    1.3   An Overview of C Programming 7
    1.4   Conformance 8
    1.5   Syntax Notation 9

2 Lexical Elements   11
    2.1   Character Set 11
    2.2   Comments 18
    2.3   Tokens 20
    2.4   Operators and Separators 20
    2.5   Identifiers 21
    2.6   Keywords 23
    2.7   Constants 24
    2.8   C++ Compatibility 38
    2.9   On Character Sets, Repertoires, and Encodings 39
    2.10   Exercises 41

3 The C Preprocessor   43
    3.1   Preprocessor Commands 43
    3.2   Preprocessor Lexical Conventions 44
    3.3   Definition and Replacement 46
    3.4   File Inclusion 59
    3.5   Conditional Compilation 61
    3.6   Explicit Line Numbering 66
    3.7   Pragma Directive 67
    3.8   Error Directive 69
    3.9   C++ Compatibility 70
    3.10   Exercises 71

4 Declarations   **73**

    4.1   Organization of Declarations 74
    4.2   Terminology 75
    4.3   Storage Class and Function Specifiers 83
    4.4   Type Specifiers and Qualifiers 86
    4.5   Declarators 95
    4.6   Initializers 103
    4.7   Implicit Declarations 113
    4.8   External Names 113
    4.9   C++ Compatibility 116
    4.10   Exercises 119

5 Types   **123**

    5.1   Integer Types 124
    5.2   Floating-Point Types 132
    5.3   Pointer Types 136
    5.4   Array Types 140
    5.5   Enumerated Types 145
    5.6   Structure Types 148
    5.7   Union Types 160
    5.8   Function Types 165
    5.9   The Void Type 168
    5.10   Typedef Names 168
    5.11   Type Compatibility 172
    5.12   Type Names and Abstract Declarators 176
    5.13   C++ Compatibility 178
    5.14   Exercises 179

6 Conversions and Representations   **181**

    6.1   Representations 181
    6.2   Conversions 188
    6.3   The Usual Conversions 194
    6.4   C++ Compatibility 200
    6.5   Exercises 201

7 Expressions   **203**

    7.1   Objects, Lvalues, and Designators 203
    7.2   Expressions and Precedence 204
    7.3   Primary Expressions 207
    7.4   Postfix Expressions 210
    7.5   Unary Expressions 219
    7.6   Binary Operator Expressions 227
    7.7   Logical Operator Expressions 242
    7.8   Conditional Expressions 244
    7.9   Assignment Expressions 246
    7.10   Sequential Expressions 249

7.11   Constant Expressions 250
7.12   Order of Evaluation 253
7.13   Discarded Values 255
7.14   Optimization of Memory Accesses 256
7.15   C++ Compatibility 257
7.16   Exercises 258

8 Statements   **259**

8.1   General Syntactic Rules for Statements 260
8.2   Expression Statements 260
8.3   Labeled Statements 261
8.4   Compound Statements 262
8.5   Conditional Statements 264
8.6   Iterative Statements 266
8.7   Switch Statements 274
8.8   Break and Continue Statements 277
8.9   Return Statements 279
8.10   Goto Statements 280
8.11   Null Statements 281
8.12   C++ Compatibility 282
8.13   Exercises 282

9 Functions   **285**

9.1   Function Definitions 286
9.2   Function Prototypes 289
9.3   Formal Parameter Declarations 295
9.4   Adjustments to Parameter Types 298
9.5   Parameter-Passing Conventions 299
9.6   Agreement of Parameters 300
9.7   Function Return Types 301
9.8   Agreement of Return Types 302
9.9   The Main Program 303
9.10   Inline Functions 304
9.11   C++ Compatibility 306
9.12   Exercises 307

PART 2   The C Libraries   **309**

10 Introduction to the Libraries   **311**

10.1   Standard C Facilities 312
10.2   C++ Compatibility 313
10.3   Library Headers and Names 316

11 Standard Language Additions   **325**

11.1   NULL, ptrdiff_t, size_t, offsetof 325
11.2   EDOM, ERANGE, EILSEQ, errno, strerror, perror 327
11.3   bool, false, true 329

11.4   va_list, va_start, va_arg, va_end   329
11.5   Standard C Operator Macros 333

12 Character Processing   335

12.1   isalnum, isalpha, iscntrl, iswalnum, iswalpha, iswcntrl 336
12.2   iscsym, iscsymf 338
12.3   isdigit, isodigit, isxdigit, iswdigit, iswxdigit 338
12.4   isgraph, isprint, ispunct, iswgraph, iswprint, iswpunct 339
12.5   islower, isupper, iswlower, iswupper 340
12.6   isblank, isspace, iswhite, iswspace 341
12.7   toascii 341
12.8   toint 342
12.9   tolower, toupper, towlower, towupper 342
12.10   wctype_t, wctype, iswctype 343
12.11   wctrans_t, wctrans 344

13 String Processing   347

13.1   strcat, strncat, wcscat, wcsncat   348
13.2   strcmp, strncmp, wcscmp, wcsncmp 349
13.3   strcpy, strncpy, wcscpy, wcsncpy 350
13.4   strlen, wcslen 351
13.5   strchr, strrchr, wcschr, wcsrchr 351
13.6   strspn, strcspn, strpbrk, strrpbrk, wcsspn, wcscspn, wcspbrk 352
13.7   strstr, strtok, wcsstr, wcstok 354
13.8   strtod, strtof, strtold, strtol, strtoll, strtoul, strtoull 355
13.9   atof, atoi, atol, atoll 356
13.10   strcoll, strxfrm, wcscoll, wcsxfrm 356

14 Memory Functions   359

14.1   memchr, wmemchr 359
14.2   memcmp, wmemcmp 360
14.3   memcpy, memccpy, memmove, wmemcpy, wmemmove 361
14.4   memset, wmemset 362

15 Input/Output Facilities   363

15.1   FILE, EOF, wchar_t, wint_t, WEOF 365
15.2   fopen, fclose, fflush, freopen, fwide 366
15.3   setbuf, setvbuf 370
15.4   stdin, stdout, stderr 371
15.5   fseek, ftell, rewind, fgetpos, fsetpos 372
15.6   fgetc, fgetwc, getc, getwc, getchar, getwchar, ungetc, ungetwc 374
15.7   fgets, fgetws, gets 376
15.8   fscanf, fwscanf, scanf, wscanf, sscanf, swscanf 377
15.9   fputc, fputwc, putc, putwc, putchar, putwchar 385
15.10   fputs, fputws, puts 386
15.11   fprintf, printf, sprintf, snprintf, fwprintf, wprintf, swprintf 387

15.12   vfprintf, vfwprintf, vprintf, vwprintf, vsprintf, vswprintf, vfscanf, vf-
         wscanf, vscanf, vwscanf, vsscanf, vswscanf 401
15.13   fread, fwrite 402
15.14   feof, ferror, clearerr 404
15.15   remove, rename 404
15.16   tmpfile, tmpnam, mktemp 405

16 General Utilities   407
16.1   malloc, calloc, mlalloc, clalloc, free, cfree 407
16.2   rand, srand, RAND_MAX 410
16.3   atof, atoi, atol, atoll l 411
16.4   strtod, strtof, strtold, strtol, strtoll, strtoul, strtoull 412
16.5   abort, atexit, exit, _Exit, EXIT_FAILURE, EXIT_SUCCESS 414
16.6   getenv 415
16.7   system 416
16.8   bsearch, qsort 417
16.9   abs, labs, llabs, div, ldiv, lldiv 419
16.10   mblen, mbtowc, wctomb 420
16.11   mbstowcs, wcstombs 422

17 Mathematical Functions   425
17.1   abs, labs, llabs, div, ldiv, lldiv 426
17.2   fabs 426
17.3   ceil, floor, lrint, llrint, lround, llround, nearbyint, round, rint,
         trunc 427
17.4   fmod, remainder, remquo 428
17.5   frexp, ldexp, modf, scalbn 429
17.6   exp, exp2, expm1, ilogb, log, log10, log1p, log2, logb 430
17.7   cbrt, fma, hypot, pow, sqrt 432
17.8   rand, srand, RAND_MAX 432
17.9   cos, sin, tan, cosh, sinh, tanh 433
17.10   acos, asin, atan, atan2, acosh, asinh, atanh 434
17.11   fdim, fmax, fmin 435
17.12   Type-Generic Macros 435
17.13   erf, erfc, lgamma, tgamma 439
17.14   fpclassify, isfinite, isinf, isnan, isnormal, signbit 440
17.15   copysign, nan, nextafter, nexttoward 441
17.16   isgreater, isgreaterequal, isless, islessequal, islessgreater,
         isunordered 442

18 Time and Date Functions   443
18.1   clock, clock_t, CLOCKS_PER_SEC, times 443
18.2   time, time_t 445
18.3   asctime, ctime 445
18.4   gmtime, localtime, mktime 446
18.5   difftime 447

18.6   strftime, wcsftime 448

19 Control Functions   453

19.1   assert, NDEBUG 453
19.2   system, exec 454
19.3   exit, abort 454
19.4   setjmp, longjmp, jmp_buf 454
19.5   atexit 456
19.6   signal, raise, gsignal, ssignal, psignal 456
19.7   sleep, alarm 458

20 Locale   461

20.1   setlocale 461
20.2   localeconv 463

21 Extended Integer Types   467

21.1   General Rules 467
21.2   Exact-Size Integer Types 470
21.3   Least-Size Types of a Minimum Width 471
21.4   Fast Types of a Minimum Width 472
21.5   Pointer-Size and Maximum-Size Integer Types 473
21.6   Ranges of ptrdiff_t, size_t, wchar_t, wint_t, and sig_atomic_t 474
21.7   imaxabs, imaxdiv, imaxdiv_t 474
21.8   strtoimax, strtouimax 475
21.9   wcstoimax, wcstoumax 475

22 Floating-Point Environment   477

22.1   Overview 477
22.2   Floating-Point Environment 478
22.3   Floating-Point Exceptions 479
22.4   Floating-Point Rounding Modes 481

23 Complex Arithmetic   483

23.1   Complex Library Conventions 483
23.2   complex, _Complex_I, imaginary, _Imaginary_I, I 484
23.3   CX_LIMITED_RANGE 484
23.4   cacos, casin, catan, ccos, csin, ctan 485
23.5   cacosh, casinh, catanh, ccosh, csinh, ctanh 486
23.6   cexp, clog, cabs, cpow, csqrt 487
23.7   carg, cimag, creal, conj, cproj 488

24 Wide and Multibyte Facilities   489

24.1   Basic Types and Macros 489
24.2   Conversions Between Wide and Multibyte Characters 490
24.3   Conversions Between Wide and Multibyte Strings 491
24.4   Conversions to Arithmetic Types 493
24.5   Input and Output Functions 493

24.6   String Functions 493
24.7   Date and Time Conversions 494
24.8   Wide-Character Classification and Mapping Functions 494

A The ASCII Character Set   497

B Syntax   499

C Answers to the Exercises   513

Index   521

List of Tables

Table 2–1   Graphic characters   12
Table 2–2   ISO trigraphs   15
Table 2–3   Operators and separators   21
Table 2–4   Keywords in C99   23
Table 2–5   Types of integer constants   27
Table 2–6   Assignment of types to integer constants   28
Table 2–7   Character escape codes   36
Table 2–8   Additional C++ keywords   39
Table 3–1   Preprocessor commands   44
Table 3–2   Predefined macros   52
Table 4–1   Identifier scopes   75
Table 4–2   Overloading classes   78
Table 4–3   Storage class specifiers   83
Table 4–4   Default storage class specifiers   84
Table 4–5   Function declarators   101
Table 4–6   Form of initializers   104
Table 4–7   Interpretation of top-level declarations   115
Table 5–1   C types and categories   124
Table 5–2   Values defined in **limits.h**   127
Table 5–3   Values defined in **float.h**   134
Table 5–4   IEEE floating-point characteristics   135
Table 6–1   Memory models on early PCs   186
Table 6–2   Permitted casting conversions   194
Table 6–3   Allowable assignment conversions   195
Table 6–4   Conversion rank   196
Table 6–5   Usual unary conversions (choose first that applies)   197
Table 6–6   Usual binary conversions (choose first that applies)   199
Table 7–1   Nonarray expressions that can be lvalues   204
Table 7–2   Operators requiring lvalue operands   204
Table 7–3   C operators in order of precedence   205
Table 7–4   Binary operator expressions   227
Table 7–5   Conditional expression 2nd and 3rd operands (pre-Standard)   245
Table 7–6   Conditional expression 2nd and 3rd operands (Standard C)   245
Table 7–7   Assignment operands   247

Table 7–8   Operand types for compound assignment expressions   249
Table 12–1   Property names for **wctype**   344
Table 15–1   Type specifications for **fopen** and **freopen**   368
Table 15–2   Properties of **fopen** modes   368
Table 15–3   Input conversions (**scanf, fscanf, sscanf**)   380
Table 15–4   Input conversions of the **c** specifier   382
Table 15–5   Input conversions of the **s** specifier   383
Table 15–6   Output conversion specifications   393
Table 15–7   Examples of the **d** conversion   394
Table 15–8   Examples of the **u** conversion   394
Table 15–9   Examples of the **o** conversion   395
Table 15–10   Examples of the **x** and **X** conversions   395
Table 15–11   Conversions of the **c** specifier   396
Table 15–12   Examples of the **c** conversion   396
Table 15–13   Conversions of the **s** specifier   397
Table 15–14   Examples of the **s** conversion   397
Table 15–15   Examples of the **f** conversion   398
Table 15–16   Examples of **e** and **E** conversions   399
Table 17–1   Type-generic macros   437
Table 18–1   Fields in **struct tm** type   447
Table 18–2   Formatting codes for **strftime**   449
Table 19–1   Standard signals   458
Table 20–1   Predefined **setlocale** categories   462
Table 20–2   **lconv** structure components   465
Table 20–3   Examples of formatted monetary quantities   465
Table 20–4   Examples of **lconv** structure contents   466
Table 21–1   Format control string macros for integer types (N = width of type in bits)   469
Table 23–1   Domain and range of complex trigonometric functions   485
Table 23–2   Domain and range of complex hyperbolic functions   486
Table 23–3   Domain and range of complex exponential and power   487
Table 23–4   Domain and range of miscellaneous complex functions   488
Table 24–1   Wide input/output functions   494
Table 24–2   Wide-string functions   495
Table 24–3   Wide-character functions   495

Preface

This text is a reference manual for the C programming language. Our aim is to provide a complete and precise discussion of the language, the run-time libraries, and a style of C programming that emphasizes correctness, portability, and maintainability.

We expect our readers to already understand basic programming concepts, and many will be experienced C programmers. In keeping with a reference format, we present the language in a bottom-up order: lexical structure, preprocessor, declarations, types, expressions, statements, functions, and run-time libraries. We have included many cross-references in the text so that readers can begin at any point.

This Fifth Edition now includes a complete description of the latest international C standard, ISO/IEC 9899:1999 (C99). I have been careful to indicate which features of the language and libraries are new in C99 and point out how C99 differs from the previous standard, C89. This is now the only book that serves as a reference for all the major versions of the C language: traditional C, the 1989 C Standard, the 1995 Amendment and Corrigenda to C89, and now the 1999 C Standard. It also covers the Clean C subset of Standard C and Standard C++. Although there is much new material in C99, I have not changed the chapter and section organization of the book significantly, so readers familiar with previous editions will not have problems finding the information they need.

This book originally grew out of our work at Tartan, Inc. developing a family of C compilers for a range of computers—from micros to mainframes. We wanted the compilers to be well documented, provide precise and helpful error diagnostics, and generate exceptionally efficient object code. A C program that compiles correctly with one compiler must compile correctly under all the others insofar as the hardware differences allow.

In 1984, despite C's popularity, we found that there was no description of C precise enough to guide us in designing the new compilers. Similarly, no existing description was precise enough for our programmer/customers, who would be using compilers that analyzed C programs more thoroughly than was the custom at that time. In this text, we have been especially sensitive to language features that affect program clarity, object code efficiency, and the portability of programs among different environments.

WEB SITE

We encourage readers to visit the book's Web site: **CAReferenceManual.com**. We'll post example code, expanded discussions, clarifications, and links to more C resources.

ACKNOWLEDGMENTS

In preparing this Fifth Edition, I want to especially acknowledge the critical help I received from Rex Jaeschke, former chairman of NCITS J11; Antoine Trux of Helsinki, Finland; and Steve Adamczyk, the founder of Edison Design Group.

For assistance with previous editions, I would like to thank Jeffrey Esakov, Alan J. Filipski, Frank J. Wagner, Debra Martin, P. J. Plauger, and Steve Vinoski. Other help came from Aurelio Bignoli, Steve Clamage, Arthur Evans, Jr., Roy J. Fuller, Morris M. Kessan, George V. Reilly, Mark Lan, Mike Hewett, Charles Fischer, Kevin Rodgers, Tom Gibb, David Lim, Stavros Macrakis, Steve Vegdahl, Christopher Vickery, Peter van der Linden, and Dave Wilson. Also Michael Angus, Mady Bauer, Larry Breed, Sue Broughton, Alex Czajkowski, Robert Firth, David Gaffney, Steve Gorman, Dennis Hamilton, Chris Hanna, Ken Harrenstien, Rex Jaeschke, Don Lindsay, Tom MacDonald, Peter Nelson, Joe Newcomer, Kevin Nolish, David Notkin, Peter Plamondon, Roger Ray, Larry Rosler, David Spencer, and Barbara Steele.

Some of the original example programs in this book were inspired by algorithms appearing in the following works:

- Beeler, Michael, Gosper, R. William, and Schroeppel, Richard, *HAKMEM*, AI Memo 239 (Massachusetts Institute of Technology Artificial Intelligence Laboratory, February 1972);

- Bentley, Jon Louis, *Writing Efficient Programs* (Prentice-Hall, 1982);

- Bentley, Jon Louis, "Programming Pearls" (monthly column appearing in *Communications of the ACM* beginning August 1983);

- Kernighan, Brian W., and Ritchie, Dennis M., *The C Programming Language* (Prentice-Hall, 1978);

- Knuth, Donald E., *The Art of Computer Programming* Volumes 1–3 (Addison-Wesley, 1968, 1969, 1973, 1981); and

- Sedgewick, Robert, *Algorithms* (Addison-Wesley, 1983).

We are indebted to these authors for their good ideas.

The use of *I* instead of *we* in this Preface reflects that Guy Steele's work load has prevented him from being an active contributor to recent editions. The text still reflects his clear and rigorous analysis of the C language, but he cannot be held responsible for any new problems in this edition.

C: A Reference Manual is now over 17 years old. To all our readers: Thank you!

Sam Harbison
Pittsburgh, PA
harbison@CAReferenceManual.com

PART 1
The C Language

1

Introduction

Dennis Ritchie designed the C language at Bell Laboratories in the early 1970s, and its ancestry is traced from ALGOL 60 (1960), through Cambridge's CPL (1963), Martin Richards's BCPL (1967), and Ken Thompson's B language (1970) at Bell Labs. Although C is a general-purpose programming language, it has traditionally been used for systems programming. In particular, the popular UNIX operating system was originally written in C.

C's popularity is due to many factors. It is a small, efficient, yet powerful programming language with a rich run-time library. It provides precise control over the computer without a lot of hidden mechanisms. Since it has been standardized for over 10 years, programmers are comfortable with it. It is generally easy to write C programs that will be portable across different computing systems in different countries with different languages. Finally, there is a lot of legacy C code out there that is being modified and extended.

Starting in the late 1990s, C's popularity began to be eclipsed by its "big brother," C++. However, there is still a loyal following for the C language, and it continues to be popular where programmers do not need the features in C++ or where the overhead of C++ is not welcome.

C has withstood the test of time. It remains a language in which the experienced programmer can write quickly and well. Millions of lines of code testify to its usefulness.

1.1 THE EVOLUTION OF C

At the time we wrote the First Edition of this book in 1984, the C language was in widespread use, but there was no official standard or precise description of the language. The de facto standards were the C compilers being used. C became an international standard in 1989, was revised in 1994, and underwent a major revision in 1999.

Simply changing the definition of a language does not automatically alter the hundreds of millions of lines of C program code in the world. We have strived to keep this

3

book up to date so that programmers can use it as a reference for all of the dialects of C they are likely to encounter.

1.1.1 Traditional C

The original C language description is the first edition of the book, *The C Programming Language*, by Brian Kernighan and Dennis Ritchie (Prentice-Hall, 1978), usually referred to as "K&R." After the book was published, the language continued to evolve in small ways; some features were added and some were dropped. We refer to the consensus definition of C in the early 1980s as *traditional C*, the dialect before the standardization process. Of course, individual C vendors had their own extensions to traditional C, too.

1.1.2 Standard C (1989)

Realizing that standardization of the language would help C become more widespread in commercial programming, the American National Standards Institute (ANSI) formed a committee in 1982 to propose a standard for C and its run-time libraries. That committee, X3J11 (now NCITS J11), was chaired by Jim Brodie and produced a standard formally adopted in 1989 as *American National Standard X3.159-1989*, or "ANSI C."

Recognizing that programming is an international activity, an international standardization group was created as ANSI C was being completed. ISO/IEC JTC1/SC22/WG14 under P. J. Plauger turned the ANSI standard into an international standard, *ISO/IEC 9899:1990*, making only minor editorial changes. The ISO/IEC standard was thereafter adopted by ANSI, and people referred to this common standard as simply "Standard C." Since that standard would eventually be changed, we refer to it as Standard C (1989), or simply "C89."

Some of the changes from traditional C to C89 included:

- The addition of a truly standard library.
- New preprocessor commands and features.
- Function prototypes, which let you specify the argument types in a function declaration.
- Some new keywords, including **const**, **volatile**, and **signed**.
- Wide characters, wide strings, and multibyte characters.
- Many smaller changes and clarifications to conversion rules, declarations, and type checking.

1.1.3 Standard C (1995)

As a normal part of maintaining the C standard, WG14 produced two Technical Corrigenda (bug fixes) and an Amendment (extension) to C89. Taken together, these made a relatively modest change to the Standard mostly by adding new libraries. The result is what we call either "C89 with Amendment 1" or "C95." The changes to C89 included:

- three new standard library headers: **iso646.h**, **wctype.h**, and **wchar.h**,

- several new tokens and macros used as replacements for operators and punctuation characters not found in some countries' character sets,
- some new formatting codes for the **printf/scanf** family of functions, and
- a large number of new functions, plus some types and constants, for multibyte and wide characters.

1.1.4 Standard C (1999)

ISO/IEC standards must be reviewed and updated on a regular basis. In 1995, WG14 began work on a more extensive revision to the C standard, which was completed and approved in 1999. The new standard, *ISO/IEC 9899:1999*, or "C99," replaces the previous standard (and all corrigenda and amendments) and has now become the official Standard C. Vendors are updating their C compilers and libraries to conform to the new standard.

C99 adds many new features to the C89/C95 language and libraries, including:

- complex arithmetic
- extensions to the integer types, including a longer standard type
- variable-length arrays
- a Boolean type
- better support for non-English character sets
- better support for floating-point types, including math functions for all types
- C++-style comments (**//**)

C99 is a much larger change than C95 since it includes changes to the language as well as extensions to the libraries. The C99 Standard document is significantly larger than the C89 document. However, the changes are "in the spirit of C," and they do not change the fundamental nature of the language.

1.1.5 Standard C++

C++, designed by Bjarne Stroustrup at AT&T Bell Labs in the early 1980s, has now largely supplanted C for mainstream programming. Most C implementations are actually C/C++ implementations, giving programmers a choice of which language to use. C++ has itself been standardized, as *ISO/IEC 14882:1998*, or "Standard C++." C++ includes many improvements over C that programmers need for large applications, including improved type checking and support for object-oriented programming. However, C++ is also one of the most complex programming languages, with many pitfalls for the unwary.

Standard C++ is nearly—but not exactly—a superset of Standard C. Since the C and C++ standards were developed on different schedules, they could not adapt to each other in a coordinated way. Furthermore, C has kept itself distinct from C++. For example, there has been no attempt to adopt "simplified" versions of C++'s class types.

It is possible to write C code in the common subset of the Standard C and C++ languages—called *Clean C* by some—so that the code can be compiled either as a C program or a C++ program. Since C++ generally has stricter rules than Standard C, Clean C tends to be a good, portable subset in which to write. The major changes you must consider when writing Clean C are:

- Clean C programs must use function prototypes. Old-style declarations are not permitted in C++.
- Clean C programs must avoid using names that are reserved words in C++, like `class` and `virtual`.

There are several other rules and differences, but they are less likely to cause problems. In this book, we explain how to write Standard C code so that it is acceptable to C++ compilers. We do not discuss features of C++ that are not available in Standard C. (Which, of course, includes almost everything interesting in C++.)

1.1.6 What's in This Book

This book describes the three major variations of C: traditional C, C89, and C99. It calls out those features that were added in Amendment 1 to C89, and it describes the Clean C subset of C and C++. We also suggest how to write "good" C programs—programs that are readable, portable, and maintainable.

Officially, "Standard C" is C99. However, we use the term *Standard C* to refer to features and concepts of C89 that continue through C99. Features that exist only in C99 will be identified as such so that programmers using C89 implementations can avoid them.

1.2 WHICH DIALECT OF C SHOULD YOU USE?

Which dialect of C you use depends on what implementation(s) of C you have available and on how portable you want your code to be. Your choices are:

1. C99, the current version of Standard C. It has all the latest features, but some implementations may not yet support it. (That will change rapidly.)
2. C89, the previous version of Standard C. Most recent C programs and most C implementations are based on this version of C, usually with the Amendment 1 additions.
3. Traditional C, now encountered mostly when maintaining older C programs.
4. Clean C, compatible with C++.

C99 is generally upward compatible with C89, which is generally upward compatible with traditional C. Unfortunately, it is hard to write C code that is backward compatible. Consider function prototypes, for example. They are optional in Standard C, forbidden in traditional C, and required in C++. Fortunately, you can use the C preprocessor to alter your code depending on which implementation is being used—and even on whether your Standard C includes the Amendment 1 extensions. Therefore, your C programs can remain compatible with all dialects. We explain how to use the preprocessor to do this in Chapter 3. An example appears in Section 3.9.1.

If you are not limited by your compiler or an existing body of C code, you should definitely use Standard C as your base language. Standard C compilers are now almost universally available. The Free Software Foundation's GNU C (**gcc**) is a free, Standard C implementation (with many extensions).

1.3 AN OVERVIEW OF C PROGRAMMING

We expect most of our readers to be familiar with programming in a high-level language such as C, but a quick overview of C programming may be helpful to some.

A C *program* is composed of one or more *source files*, or *translation units*, each of which contains some part of the entire C program—typically some number of external functions. Common declarations are often collected into *header files* and are included into the source files with a special **#include** command (Section 3.4). One external function must be named **main** (Section 9.9); this function is where your program starts.

A C *compiler* independently processes each source file and translates the C program text into instructions understood by the computer. The compiler "understands" the C program and analyzes it for correctness. If the programmer has made an error the compiler can detect, then the compiler issues an error message. Otherwise, the output of the compiler is usually called *object code* or *an object module*.

When all source files are compiled, the object modules are given to a program called the *linker*. The linker resolves references between the modules, adds functions from the standard run-time library, and detects some programming errors such as the failure to define a needed function. The linker is typically not specific to C; each computer system has a standard linker that is used for programs written in many different languages. The linker produces a single executable program, which can then be invoked or *run*. Although most computer systems go through these steps, they may appear different to the programmer. In integrated environments such as Microsoft's Visual Studio, they may be completely hidden. In this book, we are not concerned with the details of building C programs; readers should consult their own computer system and programming documentation.

Example

Suppose we have a program to be named **aprogram** consisting of the two C source files **hello.c** and **startup.c**. The file **hello.c** might contain these lines:

```
#include <stdio.h> /* defines printf */
void hello(void)
{
    printf("Hello!\n");
}
```

Since **hello.c** contains facilities (the function **hello**) that will be used by other parts of our program, we create a header file **hello.h** to declare those facilities. It contains the line

```
extern void hello(void);
```

File **startup.c** contains the main program, which simply calls function **hello**:

```
#include "hello.h"
int main(void)
{
    hello();
    return 0;
}
```

On a UNIX system, compiling, linking, and executing the program takes only two steps:

```
% cc -o aprogram hello.c startup.c
% aprogram
```

The first line compiles and links the two source files, adds any standard library functions needed, and writes the executable program to file **aprogram**. The second line then executes the program, which prints:

Hello!

Other non-UNIX implementations may use different commands. Increasingly, modern programming environments present an integrated, graphical interface to the programmer. Building a C application in such an environment requires only selecting commands from a menu or clicking a graphical button.

1.4 CONFORMANCE

Both C programs and C implementations can *conform* to Standard C. A C program is said to be *strictly conforming* to Standard C if that program uses only the features of the language and library described in the Standard. The program's operation must not depend on any aspect of the C language that the Standard characterizes as unspecified, undefined, or implementation-defined. There are Standard C test suites available from Perennial, Inc. and Plum Hall, Inc. that help establish conformance of implementations to the standard.

There are two kinds of conforming implementations—hosted and freestanding. A C implementation is said to be a *conforming hosted implementation* if it accepts any strictly conforming program. A *conforming freestanding implementation* is one that accepts any strictly conforming program that uses no library facilities other than those provided in the header files **float.h**, **iso646.h** (C95), **limits.h**, **stdarg.h**, **stdbool.h** (C99), **stddef.h**, and **stdint.h** (C99). Chapter 10 lists the contents of these header files. Freestanding conformance is meant to accommodate C implementations for embedded systems or other target environments with minimal run-time support. For example, such systems may have no file system.

A *conforming* program is one that is accepted by a conforming implementation. Thus, a conforming program can depend on some nonportable, implementation-defined features of a conforming implementation, whereas a strictly conforming program cannot depend on those features (and so is maximally portable).

Conforming implementations may provide extensions that do not change the meaning of any strictly conforming program. This allows implementations to add library routines and define their own **#pragma** directives, but not to introduce new reserved identifiers or change the operation of standard library functions.

Compiler vendors continue to provide nonconforming extensions to which their customers have grown accustomed. Compilers enable (or disable) these extensions with special switches.

1.5 SYNTAX NOTATION

This book makes use of a stylized notation for expressing the form of a C program. When specifying the C language grammar, terminal symbols are printed in fixed type and are to appear in the program exactly as written. Nonterminal symbols are printed in italic type; they are spelled beginning with a letter and can be followed by zero or more letters, digits, or hyphens:

> *expression   argument-list   declarator*

Syntactic definitions are introduced by the name of the nonterminal being defined followed by a colon. One or more alternatives then follow on succeeding lines:

> *character* :
>> *printing-character*
>> *escape-character*

When the words *one of* follow the colon, this signifies that each of the terminal symbols following on one or more lines is an alternative definition:

> *digit* : one of
>> `0  1  2  3  4  5  6  7  8  9`

Optional components of a definition are signified by appending the suffix *opt* to a terminal or nonterminal symbol:

> *enumeration-constant-definition* :
>> *enumeration-constant   enumeration-initializer$_{opt}$*

> *initializer* :
>> *expression*
>> { *initializer-list* $_{, opt}$ }

2

Lexical Elements

This chapter describes the lexical structure of the C language—that is, the characters that may appear in a C source file and how they are collected into lexical units, or tokens.

2.1 CHARACTER SET

A C source file is a sequence of characters selected from a character set. C programs are written using the following characters defined in the Basic Latin block of ISO/IEC 10646:

1. the 52 Latin capital and small letters:

```
A B C D E F G H I J K L M N O P Q R S T
U V W X Y Z a b c d e f g h i j k l m
n o p q r s t u v w x y z
```

2. the 10 digits:

```
0 1 2 3 4 5 6 7 8 9
```

3. the SPACE,

4. the horizontal tab (HT), vertical tab (VT), and form feed (FF) control characters, and

5. the 29 graphic characters and their official names (shown in Table 2-1).

There must also be some way of dividing the source program into lines; this can be done with a character or character sequence or with some mechanism outside the source character set (e.g., an end-of-record indication).

Table 2-1 Graphic characters

Char	Name	Char	Name	Char	Name
!	EXCLAMATION MARK	+	PLUS SIGN	"	QUOTATION MARK
#	NUMBER SIGN	=	EQUALS SIGN	{	LEFT CURLY BRACKET
%	PERCENT SIGN	~	TILDE	}	RIGHT CURLY BRACKET
^	CIRCUMFLEX ACCENT	[	LEFT SQUARE BRACKET	,	COMMA
&	AMPERSAND	]	RIGHT SQUARE BRACKET	.	FULL STOP
*	ASTERISK	'	APOSTROPHE	<	LESS-THAN SIGN
(	LEFT PARENTHESIS	|	VERTICAL LINE	>	GREATER-THAN SIGN
_	LOWLINE (underscore)	\	REVERSE SOLIDUS (backslash)	/	SOLIDUS (slash, divide sign)
)	RIGHT PARENTHESIS	;	SEMICOLON	?	QUESTION MARK
-	HYPHEN-MINUS	:	COLON		

Some countries have national character sets that do not include all the graphic characters in Table 2-1. C89 (Amendment 1) defined trigraphs and token respellings to allow C programs to be written in the ISO 646-1083 Invariant Code Set.

Additional characters are sometimes used in C source programs, including:

1. formatting characters such as the backspace (BS) and carriage return (CR) characters, and

2. additional Basic Latin characters, including the characters $ (DOLLAR SIGN), @ (COMMERCIAL AT), and ` (GRAVE ACCENT).

The formatting characters are treated as spaces and do not otherwise affect the source program. The additional graphic characters may appear only in comments, character constants, string constants, and file names.

References   Basic Latin 2.9; character constants 2.7.3; comments 2.2; character encoding 2.1.3; character escape codes 2.7.6; execution character set 2.1.1; string constants 2.7.4; token respellings 2.4; trigraphs 2.1.4

2.1.1 Execution Character Set

The character set interpreted during the execution of a C program is not necessarily the same as the one in which the C program is written. Characters in the execution character set are represented by their equivalents in the source character set or by special character escape sequences that begin with the backslash (\) character.

In addition to the standard characters mentioned before, the execution character set must also include:

1. a null character that must be encoded as the value 0

2. a newline character that is used as the end-of-line marker

3. the alert, backspace, and carriage return characters

The null character is used to mark the end of strings; the newline character is used to divide character streams into lines during input/output. (It must appear to the programmer as if this newline character were actually present in text streams in the execution environment. However, the run-time library implementation is free to simulate them. For instance, newlines could be converted to end-of-record indications on output, and end-of-record indications could be turned into newlines on input.)

As with the source character set, it is common for the execution character set to include the formatting characters backspace, horizontal tab, vertical tab, form feed, and carriage return. Special escape sequences are provided to represent these characters in the source program.

These source and execution character sets are the same when a C program is compiled and executed on the same computer. However, occasionally programs are cross-compiled; that is, compiled on one computer (the host) and executed on another computer (the target). When a compiler calculates the compile-time value of a constant expression involving characters, it must use the target computer's encoding, not the more natural (to the compiler writer) source encoding.

References   character constants 2.7.3; character encoding 2.1.3; character set 2.1; constant expressions 7.11; escape characters 2.7.5; text streams Ch. 15

2.1.2 Whitespace and Line Termination

In C source programs the blank (space), end-of-line, vertical tab, form feed, and horizontal tab (if present) are known collectively as whitespace characters. (Comments, discussed next, are also whitespace.) These characters are ignored except insofar as they are used to separate adjacent tokens or when they appear in character constants, string constants, or `#include` file names. Whitespace characters may be used to lay out the C program in a way that is pleasing to a human reader.

The end-of-line character or character sequence marks the end of source program lines. In some implementations, the formatting characters carriage return, form feed, and (or) vertical tab additionally terminate source lines and are called *line break characters*. Line termination is important for the recognition of preprocessor control lines. The character following a line break character is considered to be the first character of the next line. If the first character is a line break character, then another (empty) line is terminated, and so forth.

A source line can be continued onto the next line by ending the first line with a reverse solidus or backslash (\) character or with the Standard C trigraph `??/`. The backslash and end-of-line marker are removed to create a longer, *logical source line*. This convention has always been valid in preprocessor command lines and within string constants, where it is most useful and portable. Standard C, and many non-Standard implementations, generalize it to apply to any source program line. This splicing of source lines conceptually occurs before preprocessing and before the lexical analysis of the C program, but after trigraph processing and the conversion of any multibyte character sequences to the source character set.

Example

Even tokens may be split across lines in Standard C. The two lines:

```
if (a==b) x=1; el\
se x=2;
```

are equivalent to the single line

```
if (a==b) x=1; else x=2;
```

If an implementation treats any nonstandard source characters as whitespace or line breaks, it should handle them exactly as it does blanks and end-of-line markers, respectively. Standard C suggests that an implementation do this by translating all such characters to some canonical representation as the first action when reading the source program. However, programmers should probably beware of relying on this by, for example, expecting a backslash followed by a form feed to be eliminated.

Most C implementations impose a limit on the maximum length of source lines both before and after splicing continuation lines. C89 requires implementations to permit logical source lines of at least 509 characters; C99 allows 4,095 characters.

References   character constants 2.7.3; preprocessor lexical conventions 3.2; source character set 2.1.1; string constants 2.7.4; tokens 2.3; trigraphs 2.1.4

2.1.3 Character Encoding

Each character in a computer's (execution) character set will have some conventional encoding—that is, some numerical representation on the computer. This encoding is important because C converts characters to integers, and the values of the integers are the conventional encoding of the characters. All of the standard characters listed earlier must have distinct, non-negative integer encodings.

A common C programming error is to assume a particular encoding is in use when, in fact, another one holds.

Example

The C expression `'Z'-'A'+1` computes one more than the difference between the encoding of Z and A and might be expected to yield the number of characters in the alphabet. Indeed, under the ASCII character set encoding the result is 26, but under the EBCDIC encoding, in which the alphabet is not encoded consecutively, the result is 41.

References   source and execution character sets 2.1.1

2.1.4 Trigraphs

A set of trigraphs is included in Standard C so that C programs may be written using only the ISO 646-1083 Invariant Code Set, a subset of the seven-bit ASCII code set and a code set that is common to many non-English national character sets. The trigraphs, introduced by two consecutive question mark characters, are listed in Table 2–2. Standard C also provides for respelling of some tokens (Section 2.4) and header `<iso646.h>` defines macro alternatives for some operators, but unlike trigraphs those alternatives will not be recognized in string and character constants.

Table 2–2   ISO trigraphs

Trigraph	Replaces		Trigraph	Replaces
??(	[		??)	]
??<	{		??>	}
??/	\		??!	|
??'	^		??-	~
??=	#			

The translation of trigraphs in the source program occurs before lexical analysis (tokenization) and before the recognition of escape characters in string and character constants. Only these exact nine trigraphs are recognized; all other character sequences (e.g., ??&) are left untranslated. A new character escape, \?, is available to prevent the interpretation of trigraph-like character sequences.

Example

If you want a string to contain a three-character sequence that would ordinarily be interpreted as a trigraph, you must use the backlash escape character to quote at least one of the trigraph characters. Therefore, the string constant **"What?\?!"** actually represents a string containing the characters **What??!**.

To write a string constant containing a single backslash character, you must write two consecutive backslashes. (The first quotes the second.) Then each of the backslashes can be translated to the trigraph equivalent. Therefore, the string constant **"??/??/"** represents a string containing the single character \.

References   character set 2.1; escape characters 2.7.5; **iso646.h** 11.9; string concatenation 2.7.4; token respellings 2.4

2.1.5 Multibyte and Wide Characters

To accommodate non-English alphabets that may contain a large number of characters, Standard C introduces wide characters and wide strings. To represent wide characters and strings in the external, byte-oriented world, the concept of multibyte characters is introduced. Amendment 1 to C89 expands the facilities for dealing with wide and multibyte characters.

Wide characters and strings   A *wide character* is a binary representation of an element of an *extended character set*. It has the integer type **wchar_t**, which is declared in header file **stddef.h**. Amendment 1 to C89 added the integer type **wint_t**, which must be able to represent all values of type **wchar_t** plus an additional, distinguished, nonwide character value denoted **WEOF**. Standard C does not specify any encoding for wide characters, but the value zero is reserved as a "null wide character." Wide-character constants can be specified with a special constant syntax (Section 2.7.3).

Example

> It is typical for a wide character to occupy 16 bits, so **wchar_t** could be represented as **short** or **unsigned short** on a 32-bit computer. If **wchar_t** were **short** and the value −1 were not a valid wide character, then **wint_t** could be **short** and **WEOF** could be −1. However, it is more typical for **wint_t** to be **int** or **unsigned int**.
>
> If an implementor chooses not to support an extended character set—which is common among the U.S. C vendors—then **wchar_t** can be defined as **char**, and the "extended character set" is the same as the normal character set.

A *wide string* is a contiguous sequence of wide characters ending with a null wide character. The *null wide character* is the wide character whose representation is 0. Other than this null wide character and the existence of **WEOF**, Standard C does not specify the encoding of the extended character set. Wide-string constants can be specified with special string constants (Section 2.7.4).

Multibyte characters   Wide characters may be manipulated as units within a C program, but most external media (e.g., files) and the C source program are based on byte-sized characters. Programmers experienced with extended character sets have devised *multibyte encoding*, which are locale-specific ways to map between a sequence of byte-sized characters and a sequence of wide characters.

A *multibyte character* is the representation of a wide character in either the source or execution character set. (There may be different encoding for each.) A multibyte string is therefore a normal C string, but whose characters can be interpreted as a series of multibyte characters. The form of multibyte characters and the mapping between multibyte and wide characters is implementation-defined. This mapping is performed for wide-character and wide-string constants at compile time, and the standard library provides functions that perform this mapping at run time.

Multibyte characters might use a *state-dependent encoding*, in which the interpretation of a multibyte character may depend on the occurrence of previous multibyte characters. Typically such an encoding makes use of *shift characters*—control characters that are part of a multibyte character and that alter the interpretation of the current and subsequent characters. The current interpretation within a sequence of multibyte characters is called the *conversion state* (or *shift state*) of the encoding. There is always a distinguished, *initial conversion (shift) state* that is used when starting a conversion of a sequence of multibyte characters and that frequently is returned to at the end of the conversion.

Example

> *Encoding A*—a hypothetical encoding that we use in examples—is state-dependent, with two shift states, "up" and "down." The character ↑ changes the shift state to "up" and the character ↓ changes it to "down." In the down state, which is the initial state, all nonshift characters have their normal interpretation. In the up state, each multibyte character consists of a pair of alphanumeric characters that define a wide character in a manner that we do not specify.

The following sequences of characters each contain three multibyte characters under Encoding A, beginning in the initial shift state.

   abc   ab↑e3   ↑ab↓b↑23   ↓a↓b↓c

The last string includes shift characters that are not strictly necessary. If redundant shift sequences are permitted, multibyte characters may become arbitrarily long (e.g., ↓↓...↓**x**). Unless you know what the shift state is at the start of a sequence of multibyte characters, you cannot parse a sequence like **abcdef**, which could represent either three or six wide characters.

The sequence **ab↑?x** is invalid under Encoding A because a nonalphanumeric character appears while in the up shift state. The sequence **a↑b** is invalid because the last multibyte character ends prematurely.

Multibyte characters might also use a *state-independent encoding*, in which the interpretation of a multibyte character does not depend on previous multibyte characters. (Although you may have to look at a multibyte sequence from the beginning to locate the beginning of a multibyte character in the middle of a string.) For example, the syntax of C's escape characters (Section 2.7.5) represents a state-independent encoding for type **char** since the backslash character (\) changes the interpretation of one or more following characters to form a single value of type **char**.

Example

Encoding B—another hypothetical encoding—is state-independent and uses a single special character, which we denote ∇, to change the meaning of the following non-null character. The following sequences each contain three multibyte characters under Encoding B:

   abc   ∇a∇b∇c   ∇∇∇∇∇∇   a∇bc

The sequence ∇∇∇ is not valid under Encoding B because a non-null character is missing at the end.

Standard C places some restrictions on multibyte characters:

1. All characters from the standard character set must be present in the encoding.
2. In the initial shift state, all single-byte characters from the standard character set retain their normal interpretation and do not affect the shift state.
3. A byte containing all zeroes is taken to be the null character regardless of shift state. No multibyte character can use a byte containing all zeroes as its second or subsequent character.

Together, these rules ensure that multibyte sequences can be processed as normal C strings (e.g., they will not contain embedded null characters) and a C string without special multibyte codes will have the expected interpretation as a multibyte sequence.

Source and execution uses of multibyte characters   Multibyte characters may appear in comments, identifiers, preprocessor header names, string constants, and character constants. Each comment, identifier, header name, string constant, or character constant must begin and end in the initial shift state and must consist of a valid sequence of multibyte characters. Multibyte characters in the physical representation of the source are recognized and translated to the source character set before any lexical analysis, preprocessing, or even splicing of continuation lines.

Example

> A Japanese text editing program might allow Japanese characters to be written in string constants and comments. If the text were written to a byte-stream file, then the Japanese characters would be translated to multibyte sequences, which would be acceptable to—and, in the case of string constants, understood by—Standard C implementations.

During processing, characters appearing in string and character constants are translated to the execution character set before they are interpreted as multibyte sequences. Therefore, escape sequences (Section 2.7.5) can be used in forming multibyte characters. Comments are removed from a program before this stage, so escape sequences in multibyte comments may not be meaningful.

Example

> If the source and execution character sets are the same, and if `'a'` has the value 141_8 in the execution character set, then the string constant `"∇aa"` contains the same two multibyte characters as `"∇\141\141"` (Encoding B).

> **References**   character constant 2.7.3; comments 2.2; multibyte conversion facilities 11.7, 11.8; string constants 2.7.4; **wchar_t** 11.1; **WEOF** 11.1; wide character 2.7.3; wide string 2.7.4; **wint_t** 11.1

2.2 COMMENTS

There are two ways to write a comment in Standard C. Traditionally, a comment begins with an occurrence of the two characters `/*` and ends with the first subsequent occurrence of the two characters `*/`. Comments may contain any number of characters and are always treated as whitespace.

Beginning with C99, a comment also begins with the characters `//` and extends up to (but does not include) the next line break. It is possible, but unlikely, that this change could break an older C program; it is left as an exercise to determine how this might happen.

Comments are not recognized inside string or character constants or within other comments. The contents of comments are not examined by the C implementation except to recognize (and pass over) multibyte characters and line breaks.

Example

> The following program contains four valid C comments:

```
// Program to compute the squares of
// the first 10 integers
#include <stdio.h>
void Squares( /* no arguments */ )
{
    int i;
    /*
       Loop from 1 to 10,
       printing out the squares
    */
    for (i=1; i<=10; i++)
        printf("%d //squared// is %d\n",i,i*i);
}
```

Comments are removed by the compiler before preprocessing, so preprocessor commands inside comments will not be recognized, and line breaks inside comments do not terminate preprocessor commands.

Example

The following two **#define** commands have the same effect:

```
#define ten (2*5)

#define ten /* ten:
                   one greater than nine
             */ (2*5)
```

Standard C specifies that all comments are to be replaced by a single space character for the purposes of further translation of the C program, but some older implementations do not insert any whitespace. This affects the behavior of the preprocessor and is discussed in Section 3.3.9.

A few non-Standard C implementations implement "nestable comments," in which each occurrence of **/*** inside a comment must be balanced by a subsequent ***/**. This implementation is not standard, and programmers should not depend on it. For a program to be acceptable to both implementations of comments, no comment should contain the character sequence **/*** inside it.

Example

To cause the compiler to ignore large parts of a C program, it is best to enclose the parts to be removed with the preprocessor commands

```
#if 0
...
#endif
```

rather than insert **/*** before and ***/** after the text. This avoids having to worry about **/***-style comments in the enclosed source text.

References   **#if** preprocessor command 3.5.1; preprocessor lexical conventions 3.2; whitespace 2.1

2.3 TOKENS

The characters making up a C program are collected into lexical tokens according to the rules presented in the rest of this chapter. There are five classes of tokens: operators, separators, identifiers, keywords, and constants.

The compiler always forms the longest tokens possible as it collects characters in left-to-right order, even if the result does not make a valid C program. Adjacent tokens may be separated by whitespace characters or comments. To prevent confusion, an identifier, keyword, integer constant, or floating-point constant must always be separated from a following identifier, keyword, integer constant, or floating-point constant.

The preprocessor has slightly different token conventions. In particular, the Standard C preprocessor treats **#** and **##** as tokens; they would be invalid in traditional C.

Example

Characters	C Tokens
`forwhile`	`forwhile`
`b>x`	`b, >, x`
`b->x`	`b, ->, x`
`b--x`	`b, --, x`
`b---x`	`b, --, -, x`

In the fourth example, the sequence of characters **b--x** is invalid C syntax. The tokenization **b, -, -, x** would be valid syntax, but that tokenization is not permitted.

References   comments 2.2; constants 2.7; identifiers 2.5; preprocessor tokens 3.2; keywords 2.6; token merging 3.3.9; whitespace characters 2.1

2.4 OPERATORS AND SEPARATORS

The operator and separator (punctuator) tokens in C are listed in Table 2–3. To assist programmers using I/O devices without certain U.S.–English characters, the alternate spellings <%, %>, <:, :>, %:, and %:%: are equivalent to the punctuators {, }, [,], #, ##, respectively. In addition to these respellings, the header file **iso646.h** defines macros that expand to certain operators.

In traditional C, the compound assignment operators were considered to be two separate tokens—an operator and the equals sign—that can be separated by whitespace. In Standard C, the operators are single tokens.

References   compound assignment operators 7.9.2; **iso646.h** 11.9; preprocessor tokens 3.2; trigraphs 2.1.4

Table 2–3   Operators and separators

Token class	Tokens
Simple operators	`!  %  ^  &  *  -  +  =` `~	. < > / ?`
Compound assignment operators	`+=  -=  *=  /=  %=` `<<=  >>=  &=  ^=  |=`
Other compound operators	`->  ++  --  <<  >>` `<=  >=  ==  !=  &&  ||`
Separator characters	`(  )  [  ]  {  }  ,  ;  :  ...`
Alternate token spellings	`<%  %>  <:  :>    %:  %:%:`

2.5 IDENTIFIERS

An identifier, or *name*, is a sequence of Latin capital and small letters, digits, and the underscore or LOWLINE character. An identifier must not begin with a digit, and it must not have the same spelling as a keyword.

Beginning with C99, identifiers may also contain universal character names (Section 2.9) and other implementation-defined multibyte characters. Universal characters must not be used to place a digit at the beginning of an identifier and are further restricted to be "letter-like" characters and not punctuators. An exact list is provided in the C99 standard (ISO/IEC 9899:1999, Annex D) and in ISO/IEC TR 10176-1998.

identifier :
    identifier-nondigit
    identifier   identifier-nondigit
    identifier   digit

identifier-nondigit :
    nondigit
    universal-character-name
    other implementation-defined characters

nondigit : one of
    `A   B   C   D   E   F   G   H   I   J   K   L   M`
    `N   O   P   Q   R   S   T   U   V   W   X   Y   Z`
    `a   b   c   d   e   f   g   h   i   j   k   l   m`
    `n   o   p   q   r   s   t   u   v   w   x   y   z`
    `_`

digit : one of
    `0   1   2   3   4   5   6   7   8   9`

Two identifiers are the same when they are spelled identically, including the case of all letters. That is, the identifiers **abc** and **aBc** are distinct.

In addition to avoiding the spelling of the keywords, a C programmer must guard against inadvertently duplicating a name used in the standard libraries, either in the current Standard or in the "future library directions" portion of the standard. Standard C further reserves all identifiers beginning with an underscore and followed by either an uppercase letter or another underscore; programmers should avoid using such identifiers. C implementations sometimes use these identifiers for extensions to Standard C or other internal purposes.

C89 requires implementations to permit a minimum of 31 significant characters in identifiers, and C99 raises this minimum to 63 characters. Each universal character name or multibyte sequence is considered to be a single character for this requirement.

Example

> In a pre-Standard implementation that limited the length of identifiers to eight characters, the identifiers **countless** and **countlessone** would be considered the same identifier. Longer names tend to improve program clarity and thus reduce errors. The use of underscores and mixed letter case make long identifiers more readable:
>
> ```
> averylongidentifier
> AVeryLongIdentifier
> a_very_long_identifier
> ```

External identifiers—those declared with storage class **extern**—may have additional spelling restrictions. These identifiers have to be processed by other software, such as debuggers and linkers, which may be more limited. C89 requires a minimum capacity of only six characters, *not* counting letter case. C99 raises this to 31 characters, including letter case, but allowing universal character names to be treated as 6 characters (up to \U0000FFFF) or 10 characters (\U00010000 or above). Even before C99, most implementations allowed external names of at least 31 characters.

Example

> When a C compiler permits long internal identifiers, but the target computer requires short external names, the preprocessor may be used to hide these short names. In the following code, an external error-handling function has the short and somewhat obscure name **eh73**, but the function is referred to by the more readable name **error_handler**. This is done by making **error_handler** a preprocessor macro that expands to the name **eh73**.
>
> ```
> #define error_handler eh73
> extern void error_handler();
> ...
> error_handler("nil pointer error");
> ```

Some compilers permit characters other than those specified earlier to be used in identifiers. The dollar sign (**$**) is often allowed in identifiers so that programs can access special non-C library functions provided by some computing systems.

References **#define** command 3.3; external names 4.2.9; keywords 2.6; multibyte sequence 2.1.5; reserved library identifiers 10.1.1; universal character name 2.9

2.6 KEYWORDS

The identifiers listed in Table 2–4 are keywords in Standard C and must not be used as ordinary identifiers. They can be used as macro names since all preprocessing occurs before the recognition of these keywords. The keywords **_Bool**, **_Complex**, **_Imaginary**, **inline**, and **restrict** are new to C99.

Table 2–4   Keywords in C99

auto	_Bool[a]	break	case
char	_Complex[a]	const	continue
default	restrict[a]	do	double
else	enum	extern	float
for	goto	if	_Imaginary[a]
inline	int	long	register
return	short	signed	sizeof
static	struct	switch	typedef
union	unsigned	void	volatile
while			

[a] These keywords are new in C99 and are not reserved in C++.

In addition to those listed, the identifiers **asm** and **fortran** are common language extensions. Programmers might wish to treat as reserved the macros defined in header **iso646.h** (**and**, **and_eq**, **bitand**, **bitor**, **compl**, **not**, **not_eq**, **or**, **or_eq**, **xor**, and **xor_eq**). Those identifiers are reserved in C++.

Example

The following code is one of the few cases in which using a macro with the same spelling as a keyword is useful. The definition allows the use of **void** in a program built with a non-Standard compiler.

```
#ifndef __STDC__
#define void int
#endif
```

References   **_Bool** 5.1.5; C++ keywords 2.8; **_Complex** 5.2.1; **#define** command 3.3; identifiers 2.5; **#ifndef** command 3.5; **inline** 9.10; **<iso646.h>** header 11.5; **restrict** 4.4.6; **__STDC__** 11.3; **void** type specifier 5.9

2.6.1 Predefined Identifiers

Although not a keyword, C99 introduces the concept of a *predefined identifier* and defines one such: **__func__**. Unlike a predefined macro, a predefined identifier can follow normal block scoping rules. Like keywords, predefined identifiers must not be defined by programmers.

The identifier `__func__` is implicitly declared by C99 implementations as if the following declaration appeared after the opening brace of each function definition:

```
static const char __func__[] = "function-name";
```

This identifier could be used by debugging tools to print out the name of the enclosing function, as in:

```
if (failed) printf("Function %s failed\n", __func__);
```

When translating C programs for targets with tight memory constraints, C implementations will have to be careful about getting rid of these strings if they are not needed at run time.

References   function definition 9.1; predefined macro 3.3.4; scope 4. 2.1

2.7 CONSTANTS

The lexical class of constants includes four different kinds of constants: integers, floating-point numbers, characters, and strings:

> *constant* :
>> *integer-constant*
>> *floating-constant*
>> *character-constant*
>> *string-constant*

Such tokens are called *literals* in other languages to distinguish them from objects whose values are constant (i.e., not changing) but that do not belong to lexically distinct classes. An example of these latter objects in C is enumeration constants, which belong to the lexical class of identifiers. In this book, we use the traditional C terminology of *constant* for both cases.

Every constant is characterized by a value and type. The formats of the various kinds of constants are described in the following sections.

References   character constant 2.7.3; enumeration constants 5.5; floating-point constant 2.7.2; integer constant 2.7.1; string constant 2.7.4; tokens 2.3; value 7.3

2.7.1 Integer Constants

Integer constants may be specified in decimal, octal, or hexadecimal notation:

> *integer-constant* :
>> *decimal-constant integer-suffix$_{opt}$*
>> *octal-constant integer-suffix$_{opt}$*
>> *hexadecimal-constant integer-suffix$_{opt}$*

decimal-constant :
    nonzero-digit
    decimal-constant digit

octal-constant :
    0
    octal-constant octal-digit

hexadecimal-constant :
    0x *hex-digit*
    0X *hex-digit*
    hexadecimal-constant hex-digit

digit : one of
    0   1   2   3   4   5   6   7   8   9

nonzero-digit : one of
    1   2   3   4   5   6   7   8   9

octal-digit : one of
    0   1   2   3   4   5   6   7

hex-digit : one of
    0   1   2   3   4   5   6   7   8   9
    A   B   C   D   E   F   a   b   c   d   e   f

integer-suffix :
    long-suffix   unsigned-suffix$_{opt}$
    long-long-suffix   unsigned-suffix$_{opt}$ *(C99)*
    unsigned-suffix   long-suffix$_{opt}$
    unsigned-suffix   long-long-suffix$_{opt}$ *(C99)*

long-suffix : one of
    l   L

long-long-suffix : one of   *(C99)*
    ll   LL

unsigned-suffix : one of
    u   U

These are the rules for determining the radix of an integer constant:

1. If the integer constant begins with the letters 0x or 0X, then it is in hexadecimal notation, with the characters a through f (or A through F) representing 10 through 15.

2. Otherwise, if it begins with the digit 0, then it is in octal notation.

3. Otherwise, it is in decimal notation.

An integer constant may be immediately followed by suffix letters to designate a minimum size for its type:

- letters `l` or `L` indicate a constant of type `long`

- letters `ll` or `LL` indicate a constant of type `long long` (C99)

- letters `u` or `U` indicate an **unsigned** type (`int`, `long`, or `long long`)

The **unsigned** suffix may be combined with the `long` or `long long` suffix in any order. The lowercase letter `l` can be easily confused with the digit `1` and should be avoided in suffixes.

The value of an integer constant is always non-negative in the absence of overflow. If there is a preceding minus sign, it is taken to be a unary operator applied to the constant, not part of the constant.

The actual type of an integer constant depends on its size, radix, suffix letters, and type representation decisions made by the C implementation. The rules for determining the type are complicated, and they are different in pre-Standard C, C89, and C99. All the rules are shown in Table 2–5.

If the value of an integer constant exceeds the largest integer representable in the last type within its group in Table 2–5, then the result is undefined. In C99, an implementation may instead assign an extended integer type to these large constants, following the signedness conventions in the table. (If all the standard choices are signed, then the extended type must be signed; if all are unsigned, then the extended type must be unsigned; otherwise, both signed and unsigned are acceptable.) In C89, information about the representation of integer types is provided in the header file **limits.h**. In C99, the files **stdint.h** and **inttypes.h** contain additional information.

To illustrate some of the subtleties of integer constants, assume that type **int** uses a 16-bit twos-complement representation, type **long** uses a 32-bit twos-complement representation, and type **long long** uses a 64-bit twos-complement representation. We list in Table 2–6 some interesting integer constants, their true mathematical values, their types—conventional and under the Standard C rules—and the actual C representation used to store the constant.

An interesting point to note from this table is that integers in the range 2^{15} through $2^{16}-1$ will have positive values when written as decimal constants but negative values when written as octal or hexadecimal constants (and cast to type **int**). Despite these anomalies, the programmer is rarely surprised by the values of integer constants because the representation of the constants is the same even though the type is in question.

C99 provides some portable control over the size and type of integer constants with the macros **INTN_C**, **UINTN_C**, **INTMAX_C**, and **UINTMAX_C** defined in **stdint.h**.

Example

If type **long** has a 32-bit, twos-complement representation, the following program determines the rules in effect:

Table 2–5   Types of integer constants

Constant	Original C[a]	C89[a]	C99[a,b]
dd...d	`int`	`int`	`int`
	`long`	`long`	`long`
		`unsigned long`	`long long`
0*dd...d*	`unsigned`	`int`	`int`
0X*dd...d*	`long`	`unsigned`	`unsigned`
		`long`	`long`
		`unsigned long`	`unsigned long`
			`long long`
			`unsigned long long`
dd...d **U**	*not applicable*	`unsigned`	`unsigned int`
0*dd...d* **U**		`unsigned long`	`unsigned long`
0X*dd...d* **U**			`unsigned long long`
dd...d **L**	`long`	`long`	`long`
		`unsigned long`	`long long`
0*dd...d* **L**	`long`	`long`	`long`
0X*dd...d* **L**		`unsigned long`	`unsigned long`
			`long long`
			`unsigned long long`
dd...d **UL**	*not applicable*	`unsigned long`	`unsigned long`
0*dd...d* **UL**			`unsigned long long`
0X*dd...d* **UL**			
*dd...d***LL**	*not applicable*	*not applicable*	`long long`
0*dd...d* **LL**	*not applicable*	*not applicable*	`long long`
0X*dd...d* **LL**			`unsigned long long`
dd...d **ULL**	*not applicable*	*not applicable*	`unsigned long long`
0*dd...d* **ULL**			
0X*dd...d* **ULL**			

[a] The chosen type is the first one from the appropriate group that can represent the value of the constant without overflow.

[b] If none of the listed types is large enough, an extended type may be used if it is available.

```
#define K 0xFFFFFFFF /* -1 in 32-bit, 2's compl. */
#include <stdio.h>
int main()
{
    if (0<K) printf("K is unsigned (Standard C)\n");
    else printf("K is signed (traditional C)\n");
    return 0;
}
```

References   conversions of integer types 6.2.3; extended integer types 5.1.4; integer types 5.1; **INTMAX_C** 21.5; **INT*N*_C** 21.3; **limits.h** 5.1.1; overflow 7.2.2; **stdint.h** Ch. 21; unary minus operator 7.5.3; unsigned integers 5.1.2

Table 2–6   Assignment of types to integer constants

C constant notation	True value	Traditional type	Standard C type	Actual representation
0	0	`int`	`int`	0
32767	$2^{15}-1$	`int`	`int`	0x7FFF
077777	$2^{15}-1$	`unsigned`	`int`	0x7FFF
32768	2^{15}	`long`	`long`	0x00008000
0100000	2^{15}	`unsigned`	`unsigned`	0x8000
65535	$2^{16}-1$	`long`	`long`	0x0000FFFF
0xFFFF	$2^{16}-1$	`unsigned`	`unsigned`	0xFFFF
65536	2^{16}	`long`	`long`	0x00010000
0x10000	2^{16}	`long`	`long`	0x00010000
2147483647	$2^{31}-1$	`long`	`long`	0x7FFFFFFF
0x7FFFFFFF	$2^{31}-1$	`long`	`long`	0x7FFFFFFF
2147483648	2^{31}	`long`[a]	`unsigned long` C99: `long long`	0x80000000
0x80000000	2^{31}	`long`[a]	`unsigned long`	0x80000000
4294967295	$2^{32}-1$	`long`[a]	`unsigned long` C99: `long long`	0xFFFFFFFF 0x00000000FFFFFFFF
0xFFFFFFFF	$2^{32}-1$	`long`[a]	`unsigned long`	0xFFFFFFFF
4294967296	2^{32}	undefined	undefined C99: `long long`	0x0 0x0000000100000000
0x100000000	2^{32}	undefined	undefined C99: `long long`	0x0 0x0000000100000000

[a] The type cannot represent the value exactly.

2.7.2 Floating-Point Constants

Floating-point constants may be written with a decimal point, a signed exponent, or both. Standard C allows a suffix letter (*floating-suffix*) to designate constants of types **float** and **long double**. Without a suffix, the type of the constant is **double**:

> *floating-constant :*
>   *decimal-floating-constant*
>   *hexadecimal-floating-constant*   *(C99)*

> *decimal-floating-constant :*
>   *digit-sequence exponent floating-suffix$_{opt}$*
>   *dotted-digits exponent$_{opt}$ floating-suffix$_{opt}$*

> *digit-sequence :*
>   *digit*
>   *digit-sequence digit*

dotted-digits :
      digit-sequence **.**
      digit-sequence **.** *digit-sequence*
      . *digit-sequence*

digit : one of
      0 1 2 3 4 5 6 7 8 9

exponent :
      e *sign-part*$_{opt}$ *digit-sequence*
      E *sign-part*$_{opt}$ *digit-sequence*

sign-part : one of
      + −

floating-suffix : one of
      f   F   l   L

The value of a floating-point constant is always non-negative in the absence of overflow. If there is a preceding minus sign, it is taken to be a unary operator applied to the constant, not part of the constant. If the floating-point constant cannot be represented exactly, the implementation may choose the nearest representable value *V* or the larger or smaller representative value around *V*. If the magnitude of the floating-point constant is too great or too small to be represented, then the result is unpredictable. Some compilers will warn the programmer of the problem, but most will silently substitute some other value that can be represented. In Standard C, the floating-point limits are recorded in the header file **float.h**. Special floating-point constants such as infinity and NaN (not a number) are defined in **math.h**.

In C99, a complex floating-point constant is written as a floating-point constant expression involving the imaginary constant **_Complex_I** (or **I**) defined in **complex.h**.

Example

These are valid decimal floating-point constants: **0.**, **3e1**, **3.14159**, **.0**, **1.0E-3**, **1e-3**, **1.0**, **.00034**, **2e+9**. These additional floating-point constants are valid in Standard C: **1.0f**, **1.0e67L**, **0E1L**.

An example of a C99 complex constant is **1.0+1.0*I** (if **complex.h** has been included).

C99 permits floating-point constants to be expressed in hexadecimal notation; previous versions of C had only decimal floating-point constants. The hexadecimal format uses the letter **p** to separate the fraction from the exponent because the customary letter **e** could be confused with a hexadecimal digit. The *binary-exponent* is a signed decimal number that represents a power of 2 (not a power of 10 as in the case of decimal floating-point constants, nor a power of 16 as one might guess).

hexadecimal-floating-constant: *(C99)*
      hex-prefix dotted-hex-digits   binary-exponent floating-suffix$_{opt}$
      hex-prefix hex-digit-sequence   binary-exponent floating-suffix$_{opt}$

hex-prefix:
>   `0x`
>   `0X`

dotted-hex-digits :
>   *hex-digit-sequence* **.**
>   *hex-digit-sequence* **.** *hex-digit-sequence*
>   **.** *hex-digit-sequence*

hex-digit-sequence :
>   *hex-digit*
>   *hex-digit-sequence hex-digit*

binary-exponent :
>   **p** *sign-part$_{opt}$* *digit-sequence*
>   **P** *sign-part$_{opt}$* *digit-sequence*

It may not be possible to represent a hexadecimal floating-point constant exactly if **FLT_RADIX (float.h)** is not equal to 2. If it is not representable exactly, the designated value must be correctly rounded to the nearest representable value.

References `complex.h` 23.2; `double` type 5.2; `float.h` 5.2; overflow and underflow 7.2.2; sizes of floating-point types 5.2; unary minus operator 7.5.3

2.7.3 Character Constants

A character constant is written by enclosing one or more characters in apostrophes. A special escape mechanism is provided to write characters or numeric values that would be inconvenient or impossible to enter directly in the source program. Standard C allows the character constant to be preceded by the letter **L** to specify a wide character constant.

character-constant :
>   **'** *c-char-sequence* **'**
>   **L'** *c-char-sequence* **'**   *(C89)*

c-char-sequence :
>   *c-char*
>   *c-char-sequence c-char*

c-char :
>   any source character except the apostrophe (**'**), backslash (\), or newline
>   *escape-character*
>   *universal-character-name*   *(C99)*

The apostrophe, backslash, and newline characters may be included in character constants by using escape characters, as described in Section 2.7.5. It is a good idea to use escapes for any character that might not be easily readable in the source program, such as the formatting characters. C99 allows the use of universal character names in character constants (Section 2.9).

Character constants not preceded by the letter **L** have type **int**. It is typical for such a character constant to be a single character or escape code (Section 2.7.7), and the value of the constant is the integer encoding of the corresponding character in the execution character set. The resulting integer value is computed as if it had been converted from an object of type **char**. For example, if type **char** were an eight-bit signed type, the character constant **'\377'** would undergo sign extension and thus have the value **-1**. The value of a character constant is implementation-defined if:

1. there is no corresponding character in the execution character set,
2. more than a single execution character appears in the constant, or
3. a numeric escape has a value not represented in the execution character set.

Example

Here are some examples of single-character constants along with their (decimal) values under the ASCII encoding.

Character	Value	Character	Value
`'a'`	97	`'A'`	65
`' '`	32	`'?'`	63
`'\r'`	13	`'\0'`	0
`'"'`	34	`'\377'`	255
`'%'`	37	`'\23'`	19
`'8'`	56	`'\\'`	92

Standard C wide character constants, designated by the prefix letter **L**, have type **wchar_t**, an integral type defined in the header file **stddef.h**. Their purpose is to allow C programmers to express characters in alphabets (e.g., Japanese) that are too large to be represented by type **char**. Wide character constants typically consist of a sequence of characters and escape codes that together form a single multibyte character. The mapping from the multibyte character to the corresponding wide character is implementation-defined, corresponding to the **mbtowc** function, which performs that conversion at run time. If multibyte characters use a shift-state encoding, then the wide character constant must begin and end in the initial shift state. The value of a wide character constant is implementation-defined if it contains more than a single wide character.

Multicharacter constants   Integer and wide character constants can contain a sequence of characters; after mapping that sequence to the execution character set, there may still be more than one execution character. The meaning of such a constant is implementation-defined.

One convention with older implementations was to express a four-byte integer constant as a four-character constant, such as **'gR8t'**. This usage is nonportable because some implementations may not permit it and implementations differ in the sizes of integers and in their "byte ordering" (i.e., the order in which characters are packed into words).

Example

In an ASCII implementation with four-byte integers and left-to-right packing, the value of `'ABCD'` would be 41424344_{16}. (The value of `'A'` is `0x41`, `'B'` is `0x42`, etc.) However, if right-to-left packing were used, the value of `'ABCD'` would be 44434241_{16}.

References   ASCII characters App. A; byte order 6.1.2; character encoding 2.1; **char** type 5.1.3; escape characters 2.7.5; formatting characters 2.1; **mbtowc** facility 11.7; multibyte characters 2.1.5; **wchar_t** 11.1

2.7.4 String Constants

A string constant is a (possibly empty) sequence of characters enclosed in double quotes. The same escape mechanism provided for character constants can be used to express the characters in the string. Standard C allows the string constant to be preceded by the letter **L** to specify a wide string constant.

> *string-constant* :
>   **"** *s-char-sequence*$_{opt}$ **"**
>   **L" *s-char-sequence*$_{opt}$ "**   *(C89)*
>
> *s-char-sequence* :
>   *s-char*
>   *s-char-sequence   s-char*
>
> *s-char* :
>   any source character except the double quote **"**,
>   backslash \, or newline character
>   *escape-character*
>   *universal-character-name*   *(C99)*

The double quote, backslash, and newline characters may be included in character constants by using escape characters as described in Section 2.7.5. It is a good idea to use escapes for any character that might not be easily readable in the source program, such as the formatting characters. C99 allows the use of universal character names in string constants (Section 2.9).

Example

Five string constants are listed next.

```
""
"\""
"Total expenditures: "
"Copyright 2000 \
Texas Instruments. "
"Comments begin with '/*'.\n"
```

The fourth string is the same as `"Copyright 2000 Texas Instruments."` ; it does not contain a newline character between the `0` and the `T`.

For each nonwide string constant of *n* characters, at run time there will be a statically allocated block of *n*+1 characters whose first *n* characters are the characters from the string and whose last character is the null character, `'\0'`. This block is the value of the string constant and its type is `char [n+1]`. Wide string constants similarly become *n* wide characters followed by a null wide character and have type `wchar_t [n+1]`.

Example

The `sizeof` operator returns the size of its operand, whereas the `strlen` function (Section 13.4) returns the number of characters in a string. Therefore, `sizeof("abcdef")` is 7, not 6, and `sizeof("")` is 1, not 0. `strlen("abcdef")` is 6 and `strlen("")` is 0.

If a string constant appears anywhere except as an argument to the address operator `&`, an argument to the `sizeof` operator, or as an initializer of a character array, then the usual array conversions come into play, changing the string from an array of characters to a pointer to the first character in the string.

Example

The declaration `char *p = "abcdef";` results in the pointer `p` being initialized with the address a block of memory in which seven characters are stored—`'a'`, `'b'`, `'c'`, `'d'`, `'e'`, `'f'`, and `'\0'`, respectively.

The value of a single-character string constant and the value of a character constant are quite different. The declaration `int X = (int) "A";` results in `X` being initialized with (the integer value of) a pointer to a two-character block of memory containing `'A'` and `'\0'` (if such a pointer can be represented as type `int`); but the declaration `int Y = (int) 'A';` results in `Y` being initialized with the character code for `'A'` (`0x41` in the ISO 646 encoding).

Storage for string constants   You should never attempt to modify the memory that holds the characters of a string constant since that memory may be read-only—that is, physically protected against modification. Some functions (e.g., `mktemp`) expect to be passed pointers to strings that will be modified in place; do not pass string constants to those functions. Instead, initialize a (non-`const`) array of characters to the contents of the string constant and pass the address of the first element of the array.

Example

Consider these three declarations:

```
char p1[]= "Always writable";
char *p2 = "Possibly not writable";
const char p3[] = "Never writable"; /* Standard C only */
```

The values of `p1`, `p2`, and `p3` are all pointers to character arrays, but they differ in their writability. The assignment `p1[0]='x'` will always work; `p2[0]='x'` may work or may cause a run-time error; and `p3[0]='x'` will always cause a compile-time error because of the meaning of `const`.

Do not depend on all string constants being stored at different addresses. Standard C allows implementations to use the same storage for two string constants that contain the same characters.

Example

Here is a simple program that discriminates the various implementations of strings. The assignment to **string1[0]** could cause a run-time error if string constants are allocated in read-only memory.

```
char *string1, *string2;
int main() {
    string1 = "abcd"; string2 = "abcd";
    if (string1==string2) printf("Strings are shared.\n");
    else printf("Strings are not shared.\n");
    string1[0] = '1'; /* RUN-TIME ERROR POSSIBLE */
    if (*string1=='1') printf("Strings writable\n");
    else printf("Strings are not writable\n");
    return 0;
}
```

Continuation of strings   A string constant is typically written on one source program line. If a string is too long to fit conveniently on one line, all but the final source lines containing the string can be ended with a backslash character, \, in which case the backslash and end-of-line character(s) are ignored. This allows string constants to be written on more than one line. Some older implementations may remove leading whitespace characters from the continuation line, although it is incorrect to do so.

Standard C automatically concatenates adjacent string constants and adjacent wide string constants, placing a single null character at the end of the last string. Therefore, an alternative to using the \ continuation mechanism in Standard C programs is to break a long string into separate strings. In C99, a wide string and a normal string constant can also be concatenated in this way, resulting in a wide string constant; in C89, this was not allowed.

Example

The string initializing **s1** is acceptable to Standard and pre-Standard C compilers, but the string initializing **s2** is allowed only in Standard C:

```
char s1[] = "This long string is acc\
eptable to all C compilers.";
char s2[] = "This long string is permissible "
            "in Standard C.";
```

A newline character (i.e., the end of line in the execution character set) may be inserted into a string by putting the escape sequence \n in the string constant; this should not be confused with line continuation within a string constant.

Wide strings   A string constant prefixed by the letter **L** is a Standard C wide string constant and is of type "array of **wchar_t**." It represents a sequence of wide characters from an extended execution character set, such as might be used for a language like Japanese. The characters in the wide string constant are a multibyte character string, which is mapped to a sequence of wide characters in an implementation-defined manner. (The **mbstowcs** function performs a similar function at run time.) If multibyte characters use a shift-state encoding, the wide string constant must start and end in the initial shift state.

References   array types 5.4; **const** type specifier 4.4.4; versions from array types 6.2.7; escape characters 2.7.5; initializers 4.6; **mbstowcs** facility 11.8; **mktemp** facility 15.16; multibyte characters 2.1.5; pointer types 5.3; preprocessor lexical conventions 3.2; **sizeof** operator 7.5.2; **strlen** facility 13.4; whitespace characters 2.1; usual unary conversions 6.3.3; **wchar_t** 11.1; universal character names 2.9

2.7.5 Escape Characters

Escape characters can be used in character and string constants to represent characters that would be awkward or impossible to enter in the source program directly. The escape characters come in two varieties: "character escapes," which can be used to represent some particular formatting and special characters; and "numeric escapes," which allow a character to be specified by its numeric encoding. C99 also includes universal character names as escapes.

escape-character :
    \\ *escape-code*
    universal-character-name   *(C99)*

escape-code :
    character-escape-code
    octal-escape-code
    hex-escape-code   *(C89)*

character-escape-code : one of
    n   **t**   **b**   **r**   **f**
    v   ****   **'**   **"**
    a   **?**   *(C89)*

octal-escape-code :
    octal-digit
    octal-digit *octal-digit*
    octal-digit *octal-digit* *octal-digit*

hex-escape-code :
    x *hex-digit*
    hex-escape-code *hex-digit*   *(C89)*

The meanings of these escapes are discussed in the following sections.

If the character following the backslash is neither an octal digit, the letter **x**, nor one of the character escape codes listed earlier, the result is undefined. (In traditional C, the backslash was ignored.) In Standard C, all lowercase letters following the backslash are reserved for future language extensions. Uppercase letters may be used for implementation-specific extensions.

    References   universal character name 2.9

2.7.6 Character Escape Codes

Character escape codes are used to represent some common special characters in a fashion independent of the target computer character set. The characters that may follow the backslash, and their meanings, are listed in Table 2–7.

Table 2–7   Character escape codes

Escape code	Translation	Escape code	Translation
a[a]	alert (e.g., bell)	**v**	vertical tab
b	backspace	****	backslash
f	form feed	**'**	single quote
n	newline	**"**	double quote
r	carriage return	**?**[a]	question mark
t	horizontal tab		

[a] Standard C addition.

    The code **\a** is typically mapped to a "bell" or other audible signal on the output device (e.g., ASCII control-G, whose value is 7). The **\?** escape is needed to obtain a question mark character in the rare circumstances in which it might be mistaken as part of a trigraph.

    The quotation mark (**"**) may appear without a preceding backslash in character constants, and the apostrophe (**'**) may appear without a backslash in string constants.

Example

    To show how the character escapes can be used, here is a small program that counts the number of lines (actually the number of newline characters) in the input. The function **getchar** returns the next input character until the end of the input is reached, at which point **getchar** returns the value of the macro **EOF** defined in **stdio.h**:

```
#include <stdio.h>
int main(void) /* Count the number of lines in the input. */
{
    int next_char;
    int num_lines = 0;
    while ((next_char = getchar()) != EOF)
        if (next_char == '\n')
            ++num_lines;
    printf("%d lines read.\n", num_lines);
    return 0;
}
```

References   character constants 2.7.3; EOF 15.1; getchar facility 15.6; stdio.h 15.1; string constants 2.7.4; trigraphs 2.1.4

2.7.7 Numeric Escape Codes

Numeric escape codes allow a character from the execution character set to be expressed by writing its coded value directly in octal or—in Standard C—hexadecimal notation. Up to three octal or any number of hexadecimal digits may appear, but Standard C prohibits values outside the range of **unsigned char** for normal character constants and values outside the range of **wchar_t** for wide character constants. For instance, under the ASCII encoding the character 'a' may be written as '\141' or '\x61' and the character '?' as '\77' or '\x3F'. The null character, used to terminate strings, is always written as \0. The value of a numeric escape that does not correspond to a character in the execution character set is implementation-defined.

Example

The following short code segment illustrates the use of numeric escape codes. The variable inchar has type int.

```
for (;;) {
    inchar = receive();
    if (inchar == '\0') continue;        /* Ignore */
    if (inchar == '\004') break;         /* Quit */
    if (inchar == '\006') reply('\006'); /* ACK */
    else reply('\025');                  /* NAK */
    }
```

There are two reasons for the programmer to be cautious when using numeric escapes. First, of course, the use of numeric escapes may depend on character encoding and therefore be nonportable. It is always better to hide escape codes in macro definitions so they are easy to change:

```
#define NUL '\0'
#define EOT '\004'
#define ACK '\006'
#define NAK '\025'
```

Second, the syntax for numeric escapes is delicate; an octal escape code terminates when three octal digits have been used or when the first character that is not an octal digit is encountered. Therefore, the string `"\0111"` consists of two characters, `\011` and `1`, and the string `"\090"` consists of three characters, `\0`, `9`, and `0`. Hexadecimal escape sequences also suffer from the termination problem especially since they can be of any length; to stop an Standard C hexadecimal escape in a string, break the string into pieces:

```
"\xabc"     /* This string contains one character. */
"\xab" "c"  /* This string contains two characters. */
```

Some non-Standard C implementations provide hexadecimal escape sequences that, like the octal escapes, permit only up to a fixed number of hexadecimal digits.

References   character constant 2.7.3; `#define` 3.3; macro definitions 3.3; null character 2.1; string constant 2.7.4; execution character set 2.1

2.8 C++ COMPATIBILITY

This section lists the lexical differences between C and C++.

2.8.1 Character Sets

The token respellings and trigraphs in Standard C are part of the C++ standard, but they are not common in pre-Standard C++ implementations. Both C and C++ allow universal character names with the same syntax, but only C explicitly allows other implementation-defined characters in identifiers. (One expects that C++ implementations will provide them as an extension.)

2.8.2 Comments

C99 comments are acceptable as C++ and vice versa. Before C99, the characters `//` did not introduce a comment in Standard C, and so the sequence of characters `//*` in C could be interpreted differently in C++. (The details are left as an exercise.)

2.8.3 Operators

There are three new compound operators in C++:

```
.*    ->*    ::
```

Since these combinations of tokens would be invalid in Standard C programs, there is no impact on portability from C to C++.

2.8.4 Identifiers and Keywords

The identifiers listed in Table 2–8 are keywords in C++, but not in C. However, the key-word **wchar_t** is reserved in Standard C, and the keywords **bool**, **true**, **false** are re-served in C99 as part of the standard libraries.

Table 2–8   Additional C++ keywords

asm	export	private	throw
bool	false	protected	true
catch	friend	public	try
class	mutable	reinterpret_cast	typeid
const_cast	namespace	static_cast	typename
delete	new	template	using
dynamic_cast	operator	this	virtual
explicit			wchar_t

2.8.5 Character Constants

Single-character constants have type **int** in C, but have type **char** in C++. Multicharac-ter constants—which are implementation-defined—have type **int** in both languages. In practice, this makes little difference since in C++ character constants used in integral con-texts are promoted to **int** under the usual conversions. However, **sizeof('c')** is **sizeof(char)** in C++, whereas it is **sizeof(int)** in C.

2.9 ON CHARACTER SETS, REPERTOIRES, AND ENCODINGS

The C language was originally designed at a time when the needs of an international, mul-tilingual programming community were not well understood. Standard C extends the C language to accommodate that community. This section is an informal overview of the history and problems to be addressed in Standard C to make the language more friendly to non-English users.

   Repertoires and ASCII   Every culture bases its written communication on a *char-acter repertoire* of printable letters or symbols. For U.S.–English, the repertoire consists of the usual 52 upper- and lowercase letters, the decimal digits, and some punctuation characters. There are about 100 of these characters, and they were assigned particular bi-nary values (by U.S.–English programmers and computer manufacturers) using a seven-bit encoding known as ASCII. These encoded characters appeared on standard keyboards and found their way into places such as the C language definition.

   Unfortunately, other cultures have different repertoires. For example, English speakers in the United Kingdom would rather have £ than $, but seven-bit ASCII does not contain it. Languages such as Russian and Hebrew have entirely different alphabets, and

Chinese/Japanese/Korean (CJK) cultures have repertoires with thousands of symbols. Programmers today want to build C programs that read and write text in many languages, including their native ones. They also want native language comments and variable names in their programs. Programs so written should be portable to other cultures, at least to the extent of not being invalid. (You will not be able to read a Sanskrit comment unless you understand Sanskrit and your computer can display Sanskrit characters.)

The full scope of this problem was only gradually realized, by which time several partial solutions had been devised and are still supported. For example, the ISO 646-1083 Invariant Code Set was defined as a subset of ASCII that is common across many non-English character sets, and ways were invented to replace C characters not in the smaller set, including {, }, [,], and #.

ISO/IEC 10646   The general solution for character sets is defined by the ISO/IEC standard 10646 (plus amendments), *Universal Multiple-Octet Coded Character Set (UCS)*. This defines a four-byte (or four-*octet*) encoding, UCS-4, that is capable of representing all the characters in all Earthly cultural repertoires with plenty of space left over. There is a useful 16-bit subset of UCS-4 called the Basic Multilingual Plane (UCS-2), which consists of those UCS-4 encodings whose upper two bytes are zero. UCS-2 can represent all the major cultural repertoires, including about 20,000 CJK ideograms. However, 16 bits are not quite enough in general, and no larger size less than 32 bits is convenient to manipulate on computers, which is why there is UCS-4.

The *Unicode* character set standard was originally a 16-bit encoding produced by the Unicode Consortium (**www.unicode.org**). Unicode 3.0 is now fully compatible with ISO/IEC 10646. Previous versions were compatible only with UCS-2. The Unicode Web site has a good technical introduction to character encoding.

The character set standards UCS-4, UCS-2, and Unicode are compatible with ASCII. The 16-bit characters whose high-order 8 bits are all zero are just the 8-bit extended ASCII characters, now called *Latin-1*. The original seven-bit ASCII characters, now called *Basic Latin*, are UCS-2 characters whose upper nine bits are zero.

Wide and multibyte characters   Character representations larger than the traditional eight bits are called *wide characters*. Unfortunately, the eight-bit (or seven-bit) character is not so easily eradicated. Many computers and legacy applications are based on eight-bit characters, and various schemes have been devised to represent larger character repertoires and wide characters using sequences of eight- or seven-bit characters. These are called *multibyte encodings* or *multibyte characters*. Whereas wide characters all use a fixed-size representation, multibyte characters typically use one byte for some characters, two bytes for others, three bytes for others, and so forth. One or more eight-bit characters are treated as "escape" or "shift" characters, which start multibyte sequences.

What we see today in Standard C is a combination of techniques: ways to deal with the obvious ASCII variations (trigraphs and digraphs), ways to deal with a fully modern wide character environment, ways to deal with multibyte character sequences during I/O, and, most recently, a way to represent any culturally adapted C program in a portable fashion (universal characters and locale-specific characters in identifiers).

Universal Character Names   C99 introduces a notation that allows any UCS-2 or UCS-4 character to be specified in character constants, string constants, and identifiers. The syntax is:

> *universal-character-name:*
> > \u *hex-quad*
> > \U *hex-quad hex-quad*
>
> *hex-quad:*
> > *hex-digit hex-digit hex-digit hex-digit*

Each *hex-quad* is four hexadecimal digits, which can specify a 16-bit value. The values of the *hex-quads* are specified in ISO/IEC 10646 as the four-digit and eight-digit "short identifiers" for universal characters. The character designated by \u*nnnn* is the same as the one designated by   *nnnn*.

C does not permit universal character names whose short identifier is less than **00A0** except for **0024** (**$**), **0040** (**@**), and **0060** (**`**), nor those whose short identifier lies in the range **D800** through **DFFF**. These are control characters, including DELETE, and characters reserved for UTF-16. The result of using token merging to create a universal character name is undefined.

References   identifiers and universal character names 2.5; token merging 3.3.9

2.10 EXERCISES

1. Which of the following are lexical tokens?
   (a) keywords
   (b) comments
   (c) whitespace
   (d) hexadecimal constants
   (e) trigraphs
   (f) wide string constants
   (g) parentheses

2. Assume the following strings of source characters were processed by a Standard C compiler. Which strings would be recognized as a sequence of C tokens? How many tokens would be found in each case? (Do not worry if some of the token sequences could not appear in a valid C program.)
   (a) `X++Y`
   (b) `-12uL`
   (c) `1.37E+6L`
   (d) `"String ""FOO"""`
   (e) `"String+\"FOO\""`
   (f) `x**2`
   (g) `"X??/"`
   (h) `B$C`
   (i) `A*=B`
   (j) `while##DO`

3. Eliminate all the comments from the following C program fragment.

   `/**/*/*"*/*/*"//*//**/*/`

4. A Standard C compiler must perform each of the following actions on an input program. In what order are the actions performed?
   > collecting characters into tokens
   > removing comments
   > converting trigraphs

processing line continuation

5. Some poor choices for program identifiers are shown here. What makes them poor choices?

   (a) `pipesendintake`

   (b) `Const`

   (c) `lO`

   (d) `O77U`

   (e) `SYS$input`

6. Write some simple code fragments in Standard C that would be invalid or interpreted different-ly in C++ for the reason listed:

   (a) No `//`-style comments in C89

   (b) type of constants

   (c) keyword conflicts

3

The C Preprocessor

The C preprocessor is a simple macro processor that conceptually processes the source text of a C program before the compiler proper reads the source program. In some implementations of C, the preprocessor is actually a separate program that reads the original source file and writes out a new "preprocessed" source file that can then be used as input to the C compiler. In other implementations, a single program performs the preprocessing and compilation in a single pass over the source file.

3.1 PREPROCESSOR COMMANDS

The preprocessor is controlled by special preprocessor command lines, which are lines of the source file beginning with the character #. Lines that do not contain preprocessor commands are called lines of source program text. The preprocessor commands are shown in Table 3–1.

The preprocessor typically removes all preprocessor command lines from the source file and makes additional transformations on the source file as directed by the commands, such as expanding macro calls that occur within the source program text. The resulting preprocessed source text must then be a valid C program.

The syntax of preprocessor commands is completely independent of (although in some ways similar to) the syntax of the rest of the C language. For example, it is possible for a macro definition to expand into a syntactically incomplete fragment as long as the fragment makes sense (i.e., is properly completed) in all contexts in which the macro is called.

Table 3–1 Preprocessor commands

Command	Meaning	Sec.
`#define`	Define a preprocessor macro.	3.3
`#undef`	Remove a preprocessor macro definition.	3.3.5
`#include`	Insert text from another source file.	3.4
`#if`	Conditionally include some text based on the value of a constant expression.	3.5.1
`#ifdef`	Conditionally include some text based on whether a macro name is defined.	3.5.3
`#ifndef`	Conditionally include some text with the sense of the test opposite to that of `#ifdef`.	3.5.3
`#else`	Alternatively include some text if the previous `#if`, `#ifdef`, `#ifndef`, or `#elif` test failed.	3.5.1
`#endif`	Terminate conditional text.	3.5.1
`#line`	Supply a line number for compiler messages.	3.6
`#elif`[a]	Alternatively include some text based on the value of another constant expression if the previous `#if`, `#ifdef`, `#ifndef`, or `#elif` test failed.	3.5.2
`defined`[a]	Preprocessor function that yields 1 if a name is defined as a preprocessor macro and 0 otherwise; used in `#if` and `#elif`.	3.5.5
`#` operator[b]	Replace a macro parameter with a string constant containing the parameter's value.	3.3.8
`##` operator[b]	Create a single token out of two adjacent tokens.	3.3.9
`#pragma`[b]	Specify implementation-dependent information to the compiler.	3.7
`#error`[b]	Produce a compile-time error with a designated message.	3.8

[a] Not originally part of C, but now common in ISO and non-ISO implementations.
[b] New in Standard C.

3.2 PREPROCESSOR LEXICAL CONVENTIONS

The preprocessor does not parse the source text, but it does break it up into tokens for the purpose of locating macro calls. The lexical conventions of the preprocessor are somewhat different from the compiler proper; the preprocessor recognizes the normal C tokens, and additionally recognizes as "tokens" other characters that would not be recognized as valid in C proper. This enables the preprocessor to recognize file names, the presence and absence of whitespace, and the location of end-of-line markers.

A line beginning with # is treated as a preprocessor command; the name of the command must follow the # character. Standard C permits whitespace to precede and follow the # character on the same source line, but some older compilers do not. A line whose only non-whitespace character is a # is termed a *null directive* in Standard C and is treated the same as a blank line. Older implementations may behave differently.

The remainder of the line following the command name may contain arguments for the command if appropriate. If a preprocessor command takes no arguments, then the remainder of the command line should be empty except perhaps for whitespace characters or comments. Many pre-ISO compilers silently ignore all characters following the expected arguments (if any); this can lead to portability problems. The arguments to preprocessor commands are generally subject to macro replacement.

Preprocessor lines are recognized before macro expansion. Therefore, if a macro expands into something that looks like a preprocessor command, that command will not be recognized by the preprocessors in Standard C or in most other C compilers. (Some older UNIX implementations violate this rule.)

Example

The result of the following code is *not* to include the file **math.h** in the program being compiled:

```
/* This example doesn't work as one might think! */
#define GETMATH #include <math.h>
GETMATH
```

Instead, the expanded token sequence

```
# include < math . h >
```

is merely passed through and compiled as (erroneous) C code.

As noted in Section 2.1.2, all source lines (including preprocessor command lines) can be continued by preceding the end-of-line marker by a backslash character, \. This happens before scanning for preprocessor commands.

Example

The preprocessor command

```
#define err(flag,msg)  if (flag) \
    printf(msg)
```

is the same as

```
#define err(flag,msg)  if (flag) printf(msg)
```

If the backslash character below immediately precedes the end-of-line marker, these two lines

```
#define BACKSLASH \
#define ASTERISK *
```

will be treated as the single preprocessor command

```
#define BACKSLASH #define ASTERISK *
```

As explained in Section 2.2, the preprocessor treats comments as whitespace, and line breaks within comments do not terminate preprocessor commands.

References   comments 2.2; line termination and continuation 2.1; tokens 2.3

3.3 DEFINITION AND REPLACEMENT

The **#define** preprocessor command causes a name (identifier) to become defined as a macro to the preprocessor. A sequence of tokens, called the *body* of the macro, is associated with the name. When the name of the macro is recognized in the program source text or in the arguments of certain other preprocessor commands, it is treated as a call to that macro; the name is effectively replaced by a copy of the body. If the macro is defined to accept arguments, then the actual arguments following the macro name are substituted for formal parameters in the macro body.

Example

If a macro **sum** with two arguments is defined by

```
#define sum(x,y)   x+y
```

then the preprocessor replaces the source program line

```
result = sum(5,a*b);
```

with the simple (and perhaps unintended) text substitution

```
result = 5+a*b;
```

Since the preprocessor does not distinguish reserved words from other identifiers, it is possible, in principle, to use a C reserved word as the name of a preprocessor macro, but to do so is usually bad programming practice. Macro names are never recognized within comments, string or character constants, or **#include** file names.

3.3.1 Objectlike Macro Definitions

The **#define** command has two forms depending on whether a left parenthesis immediately follows the name to be defined. The simpler, objectlike form has no left parenthesis:

#define *name sequence-of-tokens*$_{opt}$

An objectlike macro takes no arguments. It is invoked merely by mentioning its name. When the name is encountered in the source program text, the name is replaced by the body (the associated *sequence-of-tokens*, which may be empty). The syntax of the **#define** command does not require an equal sign or any other special delimiter token after the name being defined. The body starts right after the name.

The objectlike macro is particularly useful for introducing named constants into a program, so that a "magic number" such as the length of a table may be written in exactly one place and then referred to elsewhere by name. This makes it easier to change the number later.

Another important use of objectlike macros is to isolate implementation-dependent restrictions on the names of externally defined functions and variables. An example of this appears in Section 2.5.

Example

Here are some typical macro definitions:

```
#define BLOCK_SIZE 0x100
#define TRACK_SIZE (16*BLOCK_SIZE)
#define EOT '\004'
#define ERRMSG "*** Error %d: %s.\n"
```

A common programming error is to include an extraneous equal sign:

```
#define NUMBER_OF_TAPE_DRIVES = 5  /* Probably wrong. */
```

This is a valid definition, but it causes the name **NUMBER_OF_TAPE_DRIVES** to be defined as "= **5**" rather than as "**5**". If one were then to write the code fragment

```
if (count != NUMBER_OF_TAPE_DRIVES) ...
```

it would be expanded to

```
if (count != = 5) ...
```

which is syntactically invalid. For similar reasons, also be careful to avoid an extraneous semicolon:

```
#define NUMBER_OF_TAPE_DRIVES 5 ;  /* Probably wrong. */
```

References   compound assignment operators 7.9.2; operators and separators 2.4

3.3.2 Defining Macros with Parameters

The more complex, functionlike macro definition declares the names of formal parameters within parentheses separated by commas:

$$\texttt{\#define } name\texttt{(} \ identifier\text{-}list_{opt} \texttt{)} \ sequence\text{-}of\text{-}tokens_{opt}$$

where *identifier-list* is a comma-separated list of formal parameter names. In C99, an ellipsis (**...**; three periods) may also appear after *identifier-list* to indicate a variable argument list. This is discussed in Section 3.3.10; until then, we consider only fixed argument lists.

The left parenthesis must immediately follow the name of the macro with no intervening whitespace. If whitespace separates the left parenthesis from the macro name, the definition is considered to define a macro that takes no arguments and has a body beginning with a left parenthesis.

The names of the formal parameters must be identifiers, no two the same. There is no requirement that any of the parameter names be mentioned in the body (although normally they are all mentioned). A functionlike macro can have an empty formal parameter list (i.e., zero formal parameters). This kind of macro is useful to simulate a function that takes no arguments.

A functionlike macro takes as many actual arguments as there are formal parameters. The macro is invoked by writing its name, a left parenthesis, then one actual argument token sequence for each formal parameter, then a right parenthesis. The actual argument token sequences are separated by commas. (When a functionlike macro with no formal parameters is invoked, an empty actual argument list must be provided.) When a macro is invoked, whitespace may appear between the macro name and the left parenthesis or in the actual arguments. (Some older and deficient preprocessor implementations do not permit the actual argument token list to extend across multiple lines unless the lines to be continued end with a \.)

An actual argument token sequence may contain parentheses if they are properly nested and balanced, and it may contain commas if each comma appears within a set of parentheses. (This restriction prevents confusion with the commas that separate the actual arguments.) Braces and subscripting brackets likewise may appear within macro arguments, but they cannot contain commas and do not have to balance. Parentheses and commas appearing within *character-constant* and *string-constant* tokens are not counted in the balancing of parentheses and the delimiting of actual arguments.

In C99, arguments to a macro can be empty; that is, consist of no tokens.

Example

Here is the definition of a macro that multiplies its two arguments:

```
#define product(x,y)   ((x)*(y))
```

It is invoked twice in the following statement:

```
x = product(a+3,b) + product (c, d);
```

The arguments to the **product** macro could be function (or macro) calls. The commas within the function argument lists do not affect the parsing of the macro arguments:

```
return product( f(a,b), g(a,b) ); /* OK */
```

Example

The **getchar** macro has an empty parameter list:

```
#define getchar()  getc(stdin)
```

When it is invoked, an empty argument list is provided:

```
while ((c=getchar()) != EOF) …
```

(**getchar**, **stdin**, and **EOF** are defined in the standard header **stdio.h**.)

Example

We can also define a macro that takes as its argument an arbitrary statement:

```
#define insert(stmt)  stmt
```

The invocation

```
insert( {a=1; b=1;} )
```

works properly, but if we change the two assignment statements to a single statement containing two assignment expressions:

```
insert( {a=1, b=1;} )
```

then the preprocessor will complain that we have too many macro arguments for insert. To fix the problem, we would have to write:

```
insert( {(a=1, b=1);} )
```

Example

Defining functionlike macros to be used in statement contexts can be tricky. The following macro swaps the values in its two arguments, **x** and **y**, which are assumed to be of a type whose values can be converted to **unsigned long** and back without change, and to not involve the identifier **_temp**.

```
#define swap(x, y) { unsigned long _temp=x; x=y; y=_temp; }
```

The problem is that it is natural to want to place a semicolon after **swap**, as you would if **swap** were really a function:

```
if (x > y) swap(x, y); /* Whoops! */
else x = y;
```

This will result in an error since the expansion includes an extra semicolon (Section 8.1). We put the expanded statements on separate lines next to illustrate the problems more clearly:

```
if (x > y) { unsigned long _temp=x; x=y; y=_temp; }
;
else x = y;
```

A clever way to avoid the problem is to define the macro body as a `do-while` statement, which consumes the semicolon (Section 8.6.2):

```
#define swap(x, y) \
    do { unsigned long _temp=x; x=y; y=_temp; } while (0)
```

When a functionlike macro call is encountered, the entire macro call is replaced, after parameter processing, by a processed copy of the body. Parameter processing proceeds as follows. Actual argument token strings are associated with the corresponding formal parameter names. A copy of the body is then made in which every occurrence of a formal parameter name is replaced by a copy of the actual argument token sequence associated with it. This copy of the body then replaces the macro call. The entire process of replacing a macro call with the processed copy of its body is called *macro expansion*; the processed copy of the body is called the *expansion* of the macro call.

Example

Consider this macro definition, which provides a convenient way to make a loop that counts from a given value up to (and including) some limit:

```
#define incr(v,low,high)   \
    for ((v) = (low); (v) <= (high); (v)++)
```

To print a table of the cubes of the integers from 1 to 20, we could write

```
#include <stdio.h>
int main(void)
{
    int j;
    incr(j, 1, 20)
        printf("%2d %6d\n", j, j*j*j);
    return 0;
}
```

The call to the macro `incr` is expanded to produce this loop:

```
for ((j) = (1); (j) <= (20); (j)++)
```

The liberal use of parentheses ensures that complicated actual arguments are not be misinterpreted by the compiler. (See Section 3.3.6.)

References   **do** statement   8.6.2;   statement   syntax   8.1;   **unsigned long**   5.1.2; whitespace 2.1.2

3.3.3 Rescanning of Macro Expressions

Once a macro call has been expanded, the scan for macro calls resumes at the beginning of the expansion so that names of macros may be recognized within the expansion for the purpose of further macro replacement. Macro replacement is not performed on any part of a **#define** command, not even the body, at the time the command is processed and the macro name defined. Macro names are recognized within the body only after the body has been expanded for some particular macro call.

Macro replacement is also not performed within the actual argument token strings of a functionlike macro call at the time the macro call is being scanned. Macro names are recognized within actual argument token strings only during the rescanning of the expansion, assuming that the corresponding formal parameter in fact occurred one or more times within the body (thereby causing the actual argument token string to appear one or more times in the expansion).

Example

Given the following definitions:

```
#define plus(x,y)  add(y,x)
#define add(x,y)   ((x)+(y))
```

The invocation

```
plus(plus(a,b),c)
```

is expanded as shown next.

Step	Result
1. (original)	`plus(plus(a,b),c)`
2.	`add(c,plus(a,b))`
3.	`((c)+(plus(a,b)))`
4.	`((c)+(add(b,a)))`
5. (final)	`((c)+(((b)+(a))))`

Macros appearing in their own expansion—either immediately or through some intermediate sequence of nested macro expansions—are not reexpanded in Standard C. This permits a programmer to redefine a function in terms of its old definition. Older C preprocessors traditionally do not detect this recursion, and will attempt to continue the expansion until they are stopped by some system error.

Example

> The following macro changes the definition of the square root function to handle negative arguments in a different fashion than is normal:
>
> ```
> #define sqrt(x)   ((x)<0 ? sqrt(-(x)) : sqrt(x))
> ```
>
> Except that it evaluates its argument more than once, this macro would work as intended in Standard C, but might cause an error in older compilers. Similarly:
>
> ```
> #define char   unsigned char
> ```

See Section 7.4.3 for an interesting example of using a macro to trace function calls.

3.3.4 Predefined Macros

Preprocessors for Standard C are required to define certain objectlike macros (Table 3–2). The name of each begins and ends with two underscore characters. None of these predefined macros may be undefined (**#undef**) or redefined by the programmer.

The **__LINE__** and __FILE__ macros are useful when printing certain kinds of error messages. The **__DATE__** and __TIME__ macros can be used to record when a compilation occurred. The values of __TIME__ and __DATE__ remain constant throughout the compilation. The values of the __LINE__ and **__FILE__** macros are established by the implementation, but are subject to alteration by the **#line** directive (Section 3.6). The C99 predefined identifier **__func__** (Section 2.6.1) is similar in purpose to **__LINE__**, but is actually a block-scope variable, not a macro. It supplies the name of the enclosing function.

The **__STDC__** and **__STDC_VERSION__** macros are useful for writing code compatible with Standard and non-Standard C implementations. The **__STDC_HOSTED__** macro was introduced in C99 to distinguish hosted from freestanding implementations. The remaining C99 macros indicate whether the implemen-

Table 3–2 Predefined macros

Macro	Value
__LINE__ [a]	The line number of the current source program line expressed as a decimal integer constant.
__FILE__ [a]	The name of the current source file expressed as a string constant.
__DATE__	The calendar date of the translation expressed as a string constant of the form "Mmm dd yyyy". Mmm is as produced by asctime.
__TIME__	The time of the translation expressed as a string constant of the form "hh:mm:ss", as returned by asctime.
__STDC__	The decimal constant 1 if and only if the compiler is an ISO-conforming implementation.
__STDC_VERSION__	If the implementation conforms to Amendment 1 of C89, then this macro has the value 199409L. If the implementation conforms to C99, then the macro has the value 199901L. Otherwise, its value is not defined.
__STDC_HOSTED__	(C99) Defined as 1 if the implementation is a hosted implementation, 0 if it is a freestanding implementation.
__STDC_IEC_559__	(C99) Defined as 1 if the floating-point implementation conforms to IEC 60559; otherwise undefined.
__STDC_IEC_559_COMPLEX__	(C99) Defined as 1 if the complex arithmetic implementation conforms to IEC 60559; otherwise undefined.
__STDC_ISO_10646__	(C99) Defined as a long integer constant, yyyymmL to signify that wchar_t values adhere to the ISO 10646 standard with corrections and amendments as of the given year and month; otherwise undefined.

[a] These macros are common in non-ISO implementations also.

tation's floating-point and wide character facilities adhere to other relevant international standards. (Adherence is recommended, but not required.)

Implementations routinely define additional macros to communicate information about the environment, such as the type of computer for which the program is being compiled. Exactly which macros are defined is implementation-dependent, although UNIX implementations customarily predefine **unix**. Unlike the built-in macros, these macros may be undefined. Standard C requires implementation-specific macro names to begin with a leading underscore followed by either an uppercase letter or another underscore. (The macro **unix** does not meet that criterion.)

Example

The predefined macros are useful in certain kinds of error messages:

```
if (n != m)
    fprintf(stderr,"Internal error: line %d, file %s\n",
        __LINE__, __FILE__ );
```

Other implementation-defined macros can be used to isolate host or target-specific code. For example, Microsoft Visual C++ defines __WIN32 to be 1:

```
#ifdef __WIN32
   /* Code for Win32 environment */
#endif
```

The `__STDC__` and `__STDC_VERSION__` macros are useful when writing programs that must adapt to both Standard and non-Standard implementations:

```
#ifdef __STDC__
  /* Some version of Standard C */
#if defined(__STDC_VERSION__) && __STDC_VERSION__>=199901L
   /* C99 */
#elif defined(__STDC_VERSION__) && __STDC_VERSION__>=199409L
   /* C89 and Amendment 1 */
#else
   /* C89 but not Amendment 1 */
#endif
#else /* __STDC__ not defined */
  /* Not Standard C */
#endif
```

References   `asctime` facility 20.3; complex arithmetic Ch. 23; `fprintf` 15.11; free-standing and hosted implementations 1.4; `#ifdef` preprocessor command 3.5.3; `#if` preprocessor command 3.5.1; undefining macros 3.3.5; `wchar_t` 24.1

3.3.5 Undefining and Redefining Macros

The `#undef` command can be used to make a name be no longer defined:

> `#undef` *name*

This command causes the preprocessor to forget any macro definition of **name**. It is not an error to undefine a name currently not defined. Once a name has been undefined, it may then be given a completely new definition (using `#define`) without error. Macro replacement is not performed within `#undef` commands.

The benign redefinition of macros is allowed in Standard C and many other implementations. That is, a macro may be redefined if the new definition is the same, token for token, as the existing definition. The redefinition must include whitespace in the same locations as in the original definition, although the particular whitespace characters can be different. We think programmers should avoid depending on benign redefinitions. It is generally better style to have a single point of definition for all program entities, including macros. (Some older implementations of C may not allow any kind of redefinition.)

Example

In the following definitions, the redefinition of **NULL** is allowed, but neither redefinition of **FUNC** is valid. (The first includes whitespace not in the original definition, and the second changes two tokens.)

```
# define NULL 0
# define FUNC(x) x+4
# define NULL /* null pointer */ 0
# define FUNC(x) x + 4
# define FUNC(y) y+4
```

Example

When the programmer for legitimate reasons cannot tell if a previous definition exists, the **#ifndef** command can be used to test for an existing definition so that a redefinition can be avoided:

```
#ifndef MAXTABLESIZE
#define MAXTABLESIZE 1000
#endif
```

This idiom is particularly useful with implementations that allow macro definitions in the command that invokes the C compiler. For example, the following UNIX invocation of C provides an initial definition of the macro **MAXTABLESIZE** as **5000**. The C programmer would then check for the definition as shown before:

```
cc -c -DMAXTABLESIZE=5000 prog.c
```

Although disallowed in Standard C, a few older preprocessor implementations handle **#define** and **#undef** so as to maintain a stack of definitions. When a name is redefined with **#define**, its old definition is pushed onto a stack and then the new definition replaces the old one. When a name is undefined with **#undef**, the current definition is discarded and the most recent previous definition (if any) is restored.

References   **#define** command 3.3; **#ifdef** and **#ifndef** command 3.5.3

3.3.6 Precedence Errors in Macro Expansions

Macros operate purely by textual substitution of tokens. Parsing of the body into declarations, expressions, or statements occurs only after the macro expansion process. This can lead to surprising results if care is not taken. As a rule, it is safest to always parenthesize each parameter appearing in the macro body. The entire body, if it is syntactically an expression, should also be parenthesized.

Example

Consider this macro definition:

```
#define SQUARE(x) x*x
```

The idea is that **SQUARE** takes an argument expression and produces a new expression to compute the square of that argument. For example, **SQUARE(5)** expands to **5*5**. However, the expression **SQUARE(z+1)** expands to **z+1*z+1**, which is parsed as **z+(1*z)+1** rather than the expected **(z+1)*(z+1)**. A definition of **SQUARE** that avoids this problem is:

```
#define SQUARE(x)  ((x)*(x))
```

The outer parentheses are needed to prevent misinterpretation of an expression such as `(short) SQUARE(z+1)`.

References   cast expressions 7.5.1; precedence of expressions 7.2.1

3.3.7 Side Effects in Macro Arguments

Macros can also produce problems due to side effects. Because the macro's actual arguments may be textually replicated, they may be executed more than once, and side effects in the actual arguments may occur more than once. In contrast, a true function call—which the macro invocation resembles—evaluates argument expressions exactly once, so any side effects of the expression occur exactly once. Macros must be used with care to avoid such problems.

Example

Consider the macro **SQUARE** from the prior example and also a function **square** that does (almost) the same thing:

```
int square(int x) { return x*x; }
```

The macro can square integers or floating-point numbers; the function can square only integers. Also, calling the function is likely to be somewhat slower at run time than using the macro. But these differences are less important than the problem of side effects. In the program fragment

```
a = 3;
b = square(a++);
```

the variable **b** gets the value 9 and the variable **a** ends up with the value 4. However, in the superficially similar program fragment

```
a = 3;
b = SQUARE(a++);
```

the variable **b** may get the value 12 and the variable **a** may end up with the value 5 because the expansion of the last fragment is

```
a = 3;
b = ((a++)*(a++));
```

(We say that 12 and 5 may be the resulting values of **b** and **a** because Standard C implementations may evaluate the expression `((a++)*(a++))` in different ways. See Section 7.12.)

References   increment operator ++ 7.4.4

3.3.8 Converting Tokens to Strings

There is a mechanism in Standard C to convert macro parameters (after expansion) to string constants. Before this, programmers had to depend on a loophole in many C preprocessors that achieved the same result in a different way.

In Standard C, the **#** token appearing within a macro definition is recognized as a unary "stringization" operator that must be followed by the name of a macro formal parameter. During macro expansion, the **#** and the formal parameter name are replaced by the corresponding actual argument enclosed in string quotes. When creating the string, each sequence of whitespace in the argument's token list is replaced by a single space character, and any embedded quotation or backslash characters are preceded by a backslash character to preserve their meaning in the string. Whitespace at the beginning and end of the argument is ignored, so an empty argument (even with whitespace between the commas) expands to the empty string **""**.

Example

Consider the Standard C definition of macro **TEST**:

```
#define TEST(a,b) printf( #a "<" #b "=%d\n", (a)<(b) )
```

The statements **TEST(0,0xFFFF); TEST('\n',10);** would expand into

```
printf("0" "<" "0xFFFF" "=%d\n", (0)<(0xFFFF) );
printf("'\\n'" "<" "10" "=%d\n", ('\n')<(10) );
```

After concatenation of adjacent strings, these become

```
printf("0<0xFFFF=%d\n", (0)<(0xFFFF) );
printf("'\\n'<10=%d\n", ('\n')<(10) );
```

A number of non-Standard C compilers will substitute for macro formal parameters *inside* string and character constants. Standard C prohibits this.

Example

In these nonconforming C implementations, the **TEST** macro could be written this way:

```
#define TEST(a,b) printf( "a<b=%d\n", (a)<(b) )
```

The result of expanding **TEST(0,0xFFFF)** would resemble the result of stringization:

```
printf("0<0xFFFF=%d\n", (0)<(0xFFFF) );
```

However, the expansion of **TEST('\n',10)** would almost certainly be missing the extra backslash and the output of the **printf** function would be garbled with unexpected line breaks in the output:

```
printf("'\n'<10=%d\n", ('\n')<(10) );
```

The handling of whitespace in non-ISO implementations is also likely to vary from compiler to compiler—another reason to avoid depending on this feature except in Standard C implementations.

3.3.9 Token Merging in Macro Expansions

Merging of tokens to form new tokens in Standard C is controlled by the presence of a merging operator, **##**, in macro definitions. In a macro replacement list—before rescanning for more macros—the two tokens surrounding any **##** operator are combined into a single token. There must be such tokens: **##** must not appear at the beginning or end of a replacement list. If the combination does not form a valid token, the result is undefined.

```
#define TEMP(i)  temp ## i
TEMP(1) = TEMP(2 + k) + x;
```

After preprocessing, this becomes

```
temp1 = temp2 + k + x;
```

In the previous example, a curious situation can arise when expanding **TEMP()+x**. The macro definition is valid, but **##** is left with no right-hand token to combine (unless it grabs **+**, which we do not want). This problem is resolved by treating the formal parameter **i** as if it expanded to a special "empty" token just for the benefit of **##**. Thus, the expansion of **TEMP() + x** would be **temp + x** as expected.

Token concatenation must not be used to produce a universal character name.

As with the conversion of macro arguments to strings (Section 3.3.8), programmers can obtain something like this merging capability through a loophole in many non-Standard C implementations. Although the original definition of C explicitly described macro bodies as being sequences of tokens, not sequences of characters, nevertheless many C compilers expand and rescan macro bodies as if they were character sequences. This becomes apparent primarily in the case where the compiler also handles comments by eliminating them entirely (rather than replacing them with a space)—a situation exploited by some cleverly written programs.

Example

Consider the following example:

```
#define INC ++
#define TAB internal_table
#define INCTAB table_of_increments
#define CONC(x,y) x/**/y
CONC(INC,TAB)
```

Standard C interprets the body of **CONC** as two tokens, **x** and **y**, separated by a space. (Comments are converted to a space.) The call **CONC(INC,TAB)** expands to the two tokens **INC TAB**. However, some non-Standard implementations simply eliminate comments and then rescan macro bodies for tokens; these expand **CONC(INC,TAB)** to the single token **INCTAB**:

Step	Standard C expansion	Possible non-Standard expansion
1	CONC(INC,TAB)	CONC(INC,TAB)
2	INC/**/TAB	INC/**/TAB
3	INC TAB	INCTAB
4	++ internal_table	table_of_increments

References   increment operator **++** 7.5.8; universal character name 2.9

3.3.10 Variable Argument Lists in Macros

In C99, a functionlike macro can have as its last or only formal parameter an ellipsis, signifying that the macro may accept a variable number of arguments:

> #define *name*(*identifer-list*, ...) *sequence-of-tokens*$_{opt}$
> #define *name*(...) *sequence-of-tokens*$_{opt}$

When such a macro is invoked, there must be at least as many actual arguments as there are identifiers in *identifier-list*. The trailing argument(s), including any separating commas, are merged into a single sequence of preprocessing tokens called the *variable arguments*. The identifier __VA_ARGS__ appearing in the replacement list of the macro definition is treated as if it had been a macro parameter whose argument was the merged variable arguments. That is, __VA_ARGS__ is replaced by the list of extra arguments, including their comma separators. __VA_ARGS__ can only appear in a macro definition that includes ... in its parameter list.

Macros with a variable number of arguments are often used to interface to functions that take a variable number of arguments, such as **printf**. By using the **#** stringization operator, they can also be used to convert a list of arguments to a single string without having to enclose the arguments in parentheses.

Example

These directives create a macro **my_printf** that can write its arguments either to the error or standard output.

```
#ifdef DEBUG
#define my_printf(...) fprintf(stderr, __VA_ARGS__)
#else
#define my_printf(...) printf(__VA_ARGS__)
#endif
```

It can be used this way:

```
my_printf("x = %d\n", x);
```

Example

Given the definition

```
#define make_em_a_string(...) #__VA_ARGS__
```

the invocation

```
make_em_a_string(a, b, c, d)
```

expands to the string

```
"a, b, c, d"
```

3.3.11 Other Problems

Some non-Standard implementations do not perform stringent error checking on macro definitions and calls, including permitting an incomplete token in the macro body to be completed by text appearing after the macro call. The lack of error checking by certain implementations does not make clever exploitation of that lack legitimate. Standard C reaffirms that macro bodies must be sequences of well-formed tokens.

Example

For example, the following fragment in one of these non-ISO implementations:

```
#define FIRSTPART "This is a split
...
printf(FIRSTPART string."); /* Yuk! */
```

will, after preprocessing, result in the source text

```
printf("This is a split string.");
```

3.4 FILE INCLUSION

The **#include** preprocessor command causes the entire contents of a specified source text file to be processed as if those contents had appeared in place of the **#include** command. The **#include** command has the following three forms in Standard C:

```
# include < h-char-sequence >
# include " q-char-sequence "
# include   preprocessor-tokens          (Standard C)
```

h-char-sequence :
      any sequence of characters except > and end-of-line

q-char-sequence :
      any sequence of characters except " and end-of-line

preprocessor-tokens :
      any sequence of C tokens—or non-whitespace characters
        that cannot be interpreted as tokens—that does not begin with < or "

In the first two forms of **#include**, the characters between the delimiters should be a file name in some implementation-defined format. There should be only whitespace after the closing > or ". These two forms of **#include** are supported by all C compilers. The file name is subject to trigraph replacement in Standard C and source-line continuation, but no other processing of the characters occurs.

In the third form of **#include**, the *preprocessor-tokens* undergo normal macro expansion, and the result must match one of the first two forms (including the quotes or angle brackets). This form of **#include** is seen less often and may not be implemented or may be implemented in a different fashion in non-Standard compilers.

Example

Here is one way to use this third form of **#include**:

```
#if some_thing==this_thing
#    define IncludeFile "thisname.h"
#else
#    define Includefile <thatname.h>
#endif
...
#include Includefile
```

This style can be used to localize customizations, but programmers interested in compatibility with older compilers should instead place **#include** commands at the site of the **#define** commands earlier:

```
#if some_thing==this_thing
#    include "thisname.h"
#else
#    include <thatname.h>
#endif
```

File name syntax is notoriously implementation-dependent, but Standard C requires that all implementations permit file names in **#include** consisting of letters and digits (beginning with a letter), followed by a period and a single letter. C99 allows up to eight letters and digits before the period, but C89 only guaranteed up to five letters before the period. By *permit* we mean that file names in this form must be mapped to an implementation-defined file.

Files delimited by quotes and files delimited by angle brackets differ in how they are located by the C implementation. Both forms search for the file in a set of (possibly different) implementation-defined places. Typically, the form

#include < *filename* >

searches for the file in certain standard places according to implementation-defined search rules. These standard places usually contain the implementation's own header files, such as **stdio.h**. The form

#include " *filename* "

will also search in the standard places, but usually after searching some local places, such as the programmer's current directory. Often implementations have some standard way outside of the C language for specifying the set of places to search for these files. The general intent is that the **"..."** form is used to refer to header files written by the programmer, whereas the **<...>** form is used to refer to standard implementation files.

In fact, standard header files like **stdio.h** are treated as special cases in Standard C. Standard C requires that implementations recognize the standard library header names when they appear in **<>**-delimited **#include** commands, but there is no requirement that those names specify true file names. They can be handled as special cases, their contents simply "known" to the C implementation. For this reason, the Standard calls them *standard headers* and not *standard header files*. We refer to them both ways in this book.

An included file may contain **#include** commands. The permitted depth of such **#include** nesting is implementation dependent, but Standard C requires support for at least 8 levels (15 levels in C99). The location of included files can affect the search rules for nested files.

Example

Suppose that we are compiling a C program, **first.c**, in the file system directory **/near**. The file **first.c** contains the lines

```
// In /near/first.c
#include "/far/second.h"
```

which specifies that **second.h** is to be found in directory **/far**. The header file **second.h** contains the lines

```
// In /far/second.h
#include "third.h"
```

which specifies no directory. Will the implementation choose the file **/near/third.h** in the original working directory, or will it choose **/far/third.h** in the directory of the file that included it? Some UNIX C compilers would find **/far/third.h**. The original description of C seems to suggest that **/near/third.h** should be found. Most implementations let the programmer specify a list of directories to search, in order, for included files whose directories are not specified.

References   string constants 2.7.4; trigraphs 2.1.4

3.5 CONDITIONAL COMPILATION

The preprocessor conditional commands allow lines of source text to be passed through or eliminated by the preprocessor on the basis of a computed condition.

3.5.1 The #if, #else, and #endif Commands

The following preprocessor commands are used together to allow lines of source text to be conditionally included in or excluded from the compilation: **#if**, **#else**, and **#endif**. They are used in the following way:

```
#if constant-expression
    group-of-lines–1
#else
    group-of-lines–2
#endif
```

The *constant-expression* is subject to macro replacement and must evaluate to a constant arithmetic value. Restrictions on the expression are discussed in Section 7.11.1. A "group of lines" may contain any number of lines of text of any kind, even other preprocessor command lines or no lines at all. The `#else` command may be omitted, along with the group of lines following it; this is equivalent to including the `#else` command with an empty group of lines following it. Either group of lines may also contain one or more sets of `#if-#else-#endif` commands.

A set of commands such as shown before is processed in such a way that one group of lines will be passed on for compilation and the other group of lines will be discarded. First, the constant-expression in the `#if` command is evaluated. If its value is not 0, then *group-of-lines–1* is passed through for compilation and *group-of-lines–2* (if present) is discarded. Otherwise, *group-of-lines–1* is discarded; and if there is an `#else` command, then *group-of-lines–2* is passed through; but if there is no `#else` command, then no group of lines is passed through. The constant expressions that may be used in a `#if` command are described in detail in Sections 3.5.4 and 7.11.

A group of lines that is discarded is not processed by the preprocessor. Macro replacement is not performed, and preprocessor commands are ignored. The one exception is that, within a group of discarded lines, the commands `#if`, `#ifdef`, `#ifndef`, `#elif`, `#else`, and `#endif` are recognized for the sole purpose of counting them; this is necessary to maintain the proper nesting of the conditional compilation commands. This recognition in turn implies that discarded lines are scanned and broken into tokens and string constants and comments are recognized and must be properly delimited.

If an undefined macro name appears in the constant-expression of `#if` or `#elif`, it is replaced by the integer constant 0. This means that the commands "`#ifdef` *name*" and "`#if` *name*" will have the same effect as long as the macro name, when defined, has a constant, arithmetic, nonzero value. We think it is much clearer to use `#ifdef` or the defined operator in these cases, but Standard C also supports this use of `#if`.

> **References**   `defined` 3.5.5; `#elif` 3.5.2; `#ifdef` 3.5.3

3.5.2 The #elif Command

The `#elif` command is present in Standard C and in the more modern pre-ISO compilers as well. It is convenient because it simplifies some preprocessor conditionals. It is used in the following way:

```
#if  constant-expression–1          (or #ifdef or #ifndef)
    group-of-lines–1
#elif  constant-expression–2
    group-of-lines–2
...
#elif  constant-expression–n
    group-of-lines–n
#else
    last-group-of-lines
#endif
```

This sequence of commands is processed in such a way that at most one group of lines is passed on for compilation and all other groups of lines are discarded. First, the *constant-expression–1* in the **#if** command is evaluated. If its value is not 0, then *group-of-lines–1* is passed through for compilation and all other groups of lines up to the matching **#endif** are discarded. If the value of the *constant-expression–1* in the **#if** command is 0, then the *constant-expression–2* in the first **#elif** command is evaluated; if that value is not 0, then *group-of-lines–2* is passed through for compilation. In the general case, each *constant-expression–i* is evaluated in order until one produces a nonzero value; the preprocessor then passes through the group of lines following the command containing the nonzero constant expression, ignoring any other constant expressions in the command set, and discards all other groups of lines. If no *constant-expression–i* produces a nonzero value and there is an **#else** command, then the group of lines following the **#else** command is passed through; but if there is no **#else** command, then no group of lines is passed through. The constant expressions that may be used in a **#elif** command are the same as those used in a **#if** command (see Sections 3.5.4 and 7.11).

Within a group of discarded lines, **#elif** commands are recognized in the same way as **#if**, **#ifdef**, **#ifndef**, **#else**, and **#endif** commands for the sole purpose of counting them; this is necessary to maintain the proper nesting of the conditional compilation commands.

Macro replacement is performed within the part of a command line that follows an **#elif** command, so macro calls may be used in the constant-expression.

Example

Although the **#elif** command is convenient when it is appropriate, its functionality can be duplicated using only **#if**, **#else**, and **#endif**. An example is shown below.

Using **#elif**	Without **#elif**
#if *constant-expression–1*	**#if** *constant-expression–1*
group-of-lines–1	*group-of-lines–1*
#elif *constant-expression–2*	**#else**
group-of-lines–2	**#if** *constant-expression–2*
#else	*group-of-lines–2*
last-group-of-lines	**#else**
#endif	*last-group-of-lines*
	#endif
	#endif

3.5.3 The #ifdef and #ifndef Commands

The **#ifdef** and **#ifndef** commands can be used to test whether a name is defined as a preprocessor macro. A command line of the form

    #ifdef *name*

is equivalent in meaning to

```
#if 1
```

when *name* has been defined (even with an empty body) and is equivalent to

```
#if 0
```

when *name* has not been defined or has been undefined with the **#undef** command. The **#ifndef** command has the opposite sense; it is true when the *name* is not defined and false when it is.

Note that **#ifdef** and **#ifndef** test names only with respect to whether they have been defined by **#define** (or undefined by **#undef**); they take no notice of names appearing in declarations in the C program text to be compiled. (Some C implementations allow names to be defined with special compiler command-line arguments.)

Example

The **#ifndef** and **#ifdef** commands have come to be used in several stylized ways in C programs. First, it is a common practice to implement a preprocessor-time enumeration type by having a set of symbols of which only one is defined. For example, suppose that we wish to use the set of names VAX, PDP11, and CRAY2 to indicate the computer for which the program is being compiled. One might insist that all these names be defined, with one being defined to be 1 and the rest 0:

```
#define VAX 0
#define PDP11 0
#define CRAY2 1
```

One could then select machine-dependent source code to be compiled in this way:

```
#if VAX
     VAX-dependent code
#endif
#if PDP11
     PDP11-dependent code
#endif
#if CRAY2
     CRAY2-dependent code
#endif
```

However, the customary method defines only one symbol:

```
#define CRAY2 1
     /* None of the other symbols is defined. */
```

Then the conditional commands test whether each symbol is defined:

```
#ifdef VAX
     VAX-dependent code
#endif
#ifdef PDP11
     PDP11-dependent code
#endif
```

```
#ifdef CRAY2
    CRAY2-dependent code
#endif
```

Example

Another use for the **#ifdef** and **#ifndef** commands is to provide default definitions for macros. For example, a library file might provide a definition for a name only if no other definition has been provided:

```
#ifndef TABLE_SIZE
#define TABLE_SIZE 100
#endif
...
static int internal_table[TABLE_SIZE];
```

A program might simply include this file:

```
#include <table.h>
```

in which case the definition of **TABLE_SIZE** would be **100**, both within the library file and after the **#include**; or the program might provide an explicit definition first:

```
#define TABLE_SIZE 500
#include <table.h>
```

in which case the definition of **TABLE_SIZE** would be **500** throughout.

It is a common C programming error to test whether a name is defined by writing "**#if name**" instead of "**#ifdef name**" or "**#if defined(name)**". The incorrect form often works because the preprocessor replaces any name in the **#if** expression that is not defined as a macro with the constant 0. Therefore, if **name** is not defined, all three forms are equivalent. However, if **name** is defined to have the value 0, then "**#if name**" will be false even though the name is defined. Similarly, if **name** is defined with a value that is not a valid expression, then "**#if name**" will cause an error.

References **#define** 3.3; **defined** operator 3.5.5; **#include** 3.4; preprocessor lexical conventions 3.2; **#undef** 3.3

3.5.4 Constant Expressions in Conditional Commands

The expressions that may be used in **#if** and **#elif** commands are described in Section 7.11.1. They include integer constants and all the integer arithmetic, relational, bitwise, and logical operators.

C99 mandates that all preprocessor arithmetic be performed using the largest integer type found on the target computer, which is **intmax_t** or **uintmax_t** defined in **stdint.h**. Previously, Standard C did not require that the translator have the arithmetic properties of the target computer.

References **intmax_t** 21.5; **uintmax_t** 21.5

3.5.5 The defined Operator

The **defined** operator can be used in **#if** and **#elif** expressions but nowhere else. An expression in one of the two forms

>   defined *name*
>   defined (*name*)

evaluates to 1 if *name* is defined in the preprocessor and to 0 if it is not.

Example

> The **defined** command allows the programmer to write
>
>   #if defined(VAX)
>
> instead of
>
>   #ifdef VAX
>
> The **defined** operator may be more convenient to use because it is possible to build up complex expressions such as this:
>
>   #if defined(VAX) && !defined(UNIX) && debugging
>   ...

3.6 EXPLICIT LINE NUMBERING

The **#line** preprocessor command advises the C compiler that the source program was generated by another tool and indicates the correspondence of places in the source program to lines of the original user-written file from which the C source program was produced. The **#line** command may have one of two forms. The form

>   # line *n* " *filename* "

indicates that the next source line was derived from line *n* of the original user-written file named by *filename*. *n* must be a sequence of decimal digits. The form

>   # line *n*

indicates that the next source line was derived from line *n* of the user-written file last mentioned in a **#line** command. Finally, if the **#line** command does not match either of the prior forms, it is interpreted as

>   # line *preprocessor-tokens*

Macro replacement is performed on the argument token sequence, and the result must match one of the two previous forms of **#line**.

The information provided by the **#line** command is used in setting the values of the predefined macros **__LINE__** and **__FILE__**. Otherwise, its behavior is unspecified and compilers may ignore it. Typically, the information is also used in diagnostic messages. Some tools that generate C source text as output will use **#line** so that error messages can be related to the tool's input file instead of the actual C source file.

Some implementations of C allow the preprocessor to be used independently of the rest of the compiler. Indeed, sometimes the preprocessor is a separate program that is executed to produce an intermediate file that is then processed by the real compiler. In such cases, the preprocessor may generate new **#line** commands in the intermediate file; the compiler proper is then expected to recognize these even though it does not recognize any other preprocessor commands. Whether the preprocessor generates **#line** commands is implementation dependent. Similarly, whether the preprocessor passes through, modifies, or eliminates **#line** commands in the input is also implementation dependent.

Older versions of C allow simply "**#**" as a synonym for the **#line** command, allowing this form:

> **#** *n filename*

This syntax is considered obsolete and is not permitted in Standard C, but many implementations continue to support it for the sake of compatibility.

> **References**   **__FILE__** 3.3.4; **__LINE__** 3.3.4

3.7 PRAGMA DIRECTIVE

The **#pragma** command is new in Standard C. Any sequence of tokens can follow the command name:

> **# pragma** *preprocessor-tokens*

The **#pragma** directive can be used by C implementations to add new preprocessor functionality or provide implementation-defined information to the compiler. No restrictions are placed on the information that follows the **#pragma** command, and implementations should ignore information they do not understand. Except in the case of a C99 standard pragma (Section 3.7.1), whether the tokens following **#pragma** are subject to macro expansion is implementation-defined. If a nonstandard pragma is macro expanded and the expansion has the form of a standard pragma, then it is implementation-defined whether the pragma is in fact treated like a standard pragma.

There is obviously the possibility that two implementations will place inconsistent interpretations on the same information, so it is wise to use **#pragma** conditionally based on which compiler is being used.

Example

The following code checks that the proper compiler (**tcc**), computer, and standard-conforming implementation are in use before issuing the **#pragma** command:

```
#if defined(_TCC) && defined(__STDC__) && defined(vax)
#pragma builtin(abs),inline(myfunc)
#endif
```

References   **defined** 3.5.3; memory models 6.1.5; **#if** 3.5.1

3.7.1 Standard Pragmas

In C99, certain pragmas were introduced with specific meanings. To differentiate them, all standard pragmas must be preceded by the token **STDC** (before any implementation-defined macro expansion), and the following tokens must not be macro expanded. That is,

> **#pragma FENV_ACCESS ON**

is an implementation-defined pragma, but the directive

> **#pragma STDC FENV_ACCESS ON**

specifies the C99 **FENV_ACCESS** pragma. Implementations would be kind to issue a warning if a standard pragma name were used not preceded by **STDC** since this is likely to be a common error.

The only standard pragmas defined by C99 are **FP_CONTRACT**, **FENV_ACCESS**, and **CX_LIMITED_RANGE**. They all take as an argument an on-off-switch:

> *on-off-switch:*
> > **ON**
> > **OFF**
> > **DEFAULT**

The argument **DEFAULT** sets the pragma to its initial default value (on or off). The default setting for each standard pragma is implementation-defined.

References   **CX_LIMITED_RANGE** 23.2; **FENV_ACCESS** 22.2; **FP_CONTRACT** 22.5

3.7.2 Placement of Standard Pragmas

The standard pragmas must follow certain placement rules, which make it somewhat easier to process the pragmas and allow the pragmas to nest. Standard pragmas may appear in two places: at the top level of a translation unit before any external declarations, or before all explicit declarations and statements at the beginning of a compound statement.

When placed at the top level, the pragma remains in effect until the end of the translation unit or until another instance of the same pragma is encountered. This second pragma might be another one at the top level, in which case it supersedes the first, or it might be a pragma in a compound statement.

When placed at the beginning of a compound statement, the pragma remains in effect until the (lexical) end of the compound statement or until another instance of the same pragma is encountered within the compound statement. This second pragma might be at the beginning of the same compound statement, in which case it supersedes the first one, or it might be in an inner compound statement. At the end of a compound statement containing a standard pragma, the pragma is restored to its state before the compound was encountered. That is, standard pragmas nest, following normal variable scoping rules, except that they can be specified more than once at the same scope level.

References   scope 4.2.1

3.7.3 _Pragma Operator

C99 adds a **_Pragma** operator to make the pragma facility more flexible. After macro expansions, an operator expression of the form

_Pragma (*"string-literal"* **)**

is treated as if the contents of the string literal (after removing the outer quotations, changing \" to ", and changing \\ to \) were the *preprocessing-tokens* appearing in a **#pragma** directive. For example, the expression

_Pragma("STDC FENV_ACCESS ON")

would be treated as if the following pragma had appeared at that location:

#pragma STDC FENV_ACCESS ON

While **#pragma** must appear on a line by itself, and its preprocessing-tokens are not macro expanded, **_Pragma** can be surrounded by other expressions and can be produced by macro expansion.

3.8 ERROR DIRECTIVE

The **#error** directive is new in Standard C. Any sequence of tokens can follow the command name:

 # error *preprocessor-tokens*

The **#error** directive produces a compile-time error message that includes the argument tokens, which are subject to macro expansion.

Example

The **#error** directive is most useful in detecting programmer inconsistencies and violations of constraints during preprocessing. Here are some examples:

```
#if defined(A_THING) && defined(NOT_A_THING)
#error Inconsistent things!
#endif
```

```
#include "sizes.h"    /* defines SIZE */
...
#if (SIZE % 256) != 0
#error "SIZE must be a multiple of 256!"
#endif
```

In the first **#error** example, we did not use a string constant. In the second, we did because we do not want the token **SIZE** to be expanded in the output message.

References **defined** 3.5.3; **#if** 3.5.1

3.9 C++ COMPATIBILITY

C++ uses the C89 preprocessor, so there are few differences going from C to C++.

3.9.1 Predefined Macros

The macro **__cplusplus** is predefined by C++ implementations and can be used in source files meant to be used in both C and C++ environments. The name does not follow Standard C spelling conventions for predefined macros, but rather is compatible with existing C++ implementations. In Standard C++, its value is a version number, such as **199711L**.

Whether **__STDC__** is defined in C++ environments is—in the current definition of C++—implementation-defined. There are enough differences between Standard C and C++ that it is not clear whether **__STDC__** should be defined.

None of the C99-only macros in Table 3–2 are in C++.

Example

For compatibility with traditional C, Standard C, and C++, you should test the environment in this fashion:

```
#ifdef __cplusplus
    /* It's a C++ compilation */
#else
#ifdef __STDC__
    /* It's a Standard C compilation */
#else
    /* It's a non-Standard C compilation */
#endif
#endif
```

If you know that your C implementations will be Standard C conforming, this can be shortened to

```
#if defined(__cplusplus)
    /* It's a C++ compilation */
#else
    /* It's a Standard C compilation */
#endif
```

References   __STDC__ 3.3.4; __STDC_VERSION__ 3.3.4

3.10 EXERCISES

1. Which of the following Standard C macro definitions are (probably) wrong? Why? Which definitions might cause problems in traditional C?
    - (a) `#define ident (x) x`   (c) `#define PLUS +`
    - (b) `# define FIVE = 5;`   (d) `#define void int`

2. Following are some macro definitions and invocations. How would each macro invocation be expanded by Standard C and by traditional C?

Definition	*Invocation*
(a) `#define sum(a,b) a+b`	`sum(b,a)`
(b) `#define paste(x,y) x/**/y`	`paste(x,4)`
(c) `#define str(x) # x`	`str(a book)`
(d) `#define free(x )x ? free(x) : NULL`	`free(p)`

3. Two header files and a C program file are shown next. If the C preprocessor is applied to the program file, what is the result?

    ```
    /* File blue.h */        /* File red.h */          /* File test.c */
    int blue = 0;            #ifndef __red__           #include "blue.h"
    #include "red.h"         #define __red__           #include "red.h"
                            #include "blue.h"
                            int red = 0;
                            #endif
    ```

4. A friend shows you the following definition for a macro that is supposed to double its numeric argument. What is wrong with the macro? Rewrite the macro so that it operates correctly.
    ```
    #define DBL(a)    a+a
    ```

5. In the following Standard C program fragment, what is the expansion of `M(M)(A,B)`?
    ```
    #define M(x)     M ## x
    #define MM(M,y)  M = # y
    M(M)(A,B)
    ```

6. Write a sequence of preprocessor directives that will cause a Standard C program to fail to compile if the macro `SIZE` has not been defined or if it has been defined but has a value not in the range 1 through 10.

7. Give an example of a sequence of characters that is a single token to the preprocessor but not to the C compiler proper.

8. What is wrong with the following program fragment?
    ```
    if (x != 0)
        y = z/x;
    else
        # error "Attempt to divide by zero, line " __LINE__
    ```

4

Declarations

To *declare* a *name* in the C language is to associate an identifier with some C object, such as a variable, function, or type. The names that can be declared in C are

- variables
- functions
- types
- type tags

- structure and union components
- enumeration constants
- statement labels
- preprocessor macros

Except for statement labels and preprocessor macros, all identifiers are declared by their appearance in C *declarations*. Variables, functions, and types appear in *declarators* within declarations, and type tags, structure and union components, and enumeration constants are declared in certain kinds of *type specifiers* in declarations. Statement labels are declared by their appearance in a C function, and preprocessor macros are declared by the `#define` preprocessor command.

Declarations in C are difficult to describe for several reasons. First, they involve some unusual syntax that may be confusing to the novice. For example, the declaration

```
int (*f)(void);
```

declares a pointer to a function taking no arguments and returning an integer.

Second, many of the abstract properties of declarations, such as scope and extent, are more complicated in C than in other programming languages. Before jumping into the actual declaration syntax, we discuss these properties in Section 4.2.

Finally, some aspects of C's declarations are difficult to understand without a knowledge of C's type system, which is described in Chapter 5. In particular, discussions of type tags, structure and union components, and enumeration constants are left to that chapter, although some properties of those declarations are discussed here for completeness.

> **References**   enumeration type 5.5; `#define` preprocessor command 3.3; statement labels 8.3; structure types 5.6; type specifiers 4.4; union types 5.7

4.1 ORGANIZATION OF DECLARATIONS

Declarations may appear in several places in a C program, and where they appear affects the properties of the declarations. A C source file, or *translation unit*, consists of a sequence of *top-level declarations* of functions, variables, and other things. Each function has *parameter declarations* and a *body*; the body in turn may contain various *blocks*, including compound statements. A block may contain a sequence of *inner declarations*.

The basic syntax of declarations is shown next. A discussion of function definitions is deferred until Chapter 9.

> *declaration* :
>   *declaration-specifiers initialized-declarator-list* **;**
>
> *declaration-specifiers* :
>   *storage-class-specifier declaration-specifiers$_{opt}$*
>   *type-specifier declaration-specifiers$_{opt}$*
>   *type-qualifier declaration-specifiers$_{opt}$*
>   *function-specifier declaration-specifiers$_{opt}$*   *(C99)*
>
> *initialized-declarator-list* :
>   *initialized-declarator*
>   *initialized-declarator-list* **,** *initialized-declarator*
>
> *initialized-declarator* :
>   *declarator*
>   *declarator* **=** *initializer*

At most one storage class specifier and one type specifier may appear in the *declaration-specifiers*, although a single type specifier may be formed of several tokens (e.g., `unsigned long int`). In C99, a type specifier is required. Each of the type qualifiers can appear at most once in the *declaration-specifiers*. The C99 function specifier (`inline`) can appear only on function declarations. Within these constraints, type specifiers, storage class specifiers, function specifiers, and type qualifiers can appear in any order in *declaration-specifiers*.

Example

It is customary to put any storage class specifier first, followed by any type qualifiers, and finally the type specifiers. In the following declarations, `i` and `j` have the same type and storage class, but the declaration of `i` is better style.

```
unsigned volatile long extern int const j;
extern const volatile unsigned long int i;
```

References   declarators 4.5; expressions Ch. 7; function definitions Ch. 9; initializers 4.6; statements ch. 8; storage class specifiers 4.3; type specifiers and qualifiers 4.4

4.2 TERMINOLOGY

This section establishes some terminology used to describe declarations.

4.2.1 Scope

The *scope* of a declaration is the region of the C program text over which that declaration is visible. In C, identifiers may have one of the six scopes listed in Table 4–1.

Table 4–1   Identifier scopes

Kind	Visibility of declaration
Top-level identifiers	Extends from its declaration point (section 4.2.3) to the end of the source program file.
Formal parameters in function definitions	Extends from its declaration point to the end of the function body.
Formal parameters in function prototypes[a]	Extends from its declaration point to the end of the prototype.
Block (local) identifiers	Extends from its declaration point in a block to the end of the block.
Statement labels	Encompasses the entire function body in which it appears.
Preprocessor macros	Extends from the **#define** command that declares it through the end of the source program file, or until the first **#undef** command that cancels its definition.

[a] New in Standard C.

Nonpreprocessor identifiers declared within a function definition or block (including formal parameters) are often said to have *block scope* or *local scope*. Identifiers in prototypes have *prototype scope*. Statement labels have *function scope*. All other identifiers have *file scope*.

A block is most commonly a compound statement. In C99, there are also implicit blocks associated with selection and iteration statements.

The scope of every identifier is limited to the C source file in which it occurs. However, some identifiers can be declared to be *external*, in which case the declarations of the same identifier in two or more files can be linked as described in Section 4.8.

References   **#define** preprocessor command 3.3; external names 4.8; prototypes 9.2; **#undef** preprocessor command 3.3

4.2.2 Visibility

A declaration of an identifier is *visible* in some context if a use of the identifier in that context will be bound to the declaration (i.e., the identifier will be associated with that declaration). A declaration might be visible throughout its scope, but it may also be hidden by other declarations whose scope and visibility overlap that of the first declaration.

Example

In the following program, the declaration of **foo** as an integer variable is hidden by the inner declaration of **foo** as a floating-point variable. The outer **foo** is hidden only within the body of function **main**.

```
int foo = 10;    /* foo defined at the top level */
int main(void)
{
    float foo;    /* this foo hides the outer foo */
    …
}
```

In C, declarations at the beginning of a block can hide declarations outside the block. For one declaration to hide another, the declared identifiers must be the same, must belong to the same *overloading class*, and must be declared in two distinct scopes, one of which contains the other.

In Standard C, the scope of formal parameter declarations in a function definition is the same as the scope of identifiers declared at the beginning of the block that forms the function body. However, some earlier implementations of C have considered the parameter scope to enclose the block scope.

Example

The following redeclaration of **x** is an error in Standard C, but some older implementations permit it, probably allowing a troublesome programming error to go undetected.

```
int f(x)
    int x;
{
    long x = 34;    /* invalid? */
    return x;
}
```

References   block 8.4; overloading class 4.2.4; parameter declarations 9.3; top-level declarations 4.1

4.2.3 Forward References

An identifier may not normally be used before it is fully declared. To be precise, we define the *declaration point* of an identifier to be the end of the declarator that contains the identifier's lexical token. Uses of the identifier after the declaration point are permitted. In the following example, the integer variable, **intsize**, can be initialized to its own size because the use of **intsize** in the initializer comes after the declaration point:

```
static int intsize = sizeof(intsize);
```

When an identifier is used before it is completely declared, a *forward reference* to the declaration is said to occur. C permits forward references in three situations:

1. A statement label may appear in a **goto** statement before it appears as a label since its scope covers the entire function body:

   ```
   if (error) goto recover;
   ...
   recover:
       CloseFiles();
   ```

2. An incomplete structure, union, array, or enumeration type may be declared, allowing it to be used for some purposes before it is fully defined (Section 5.6.1).
3. A function can be declared separately from its definition, either with a declaration or implicitly by its appearance in a function call (Sections 4.7 and 5.8). C99 does not permit a function call to implicitly declare a function.

Example

Invalid forward references are illustrated in this example. The programmer is attempting to define a self-referential structure with a **typedef** declaration. In this case, the last occurrence of **cell** on the line is the declaration point, and therefore the use of **cell** within the structure is invalid.

```
typedef struct { int Value; cell *Next; } cell;
```

The correct way to declare such a type is by use of a structure tag, **S**, which is defined on its first appearance and then used later within the declaration:

```
typedef struct S { int Value; struct S *Next; } cell;
```

See also the later discussions of implicit declarations (Section 4.7) and duplicate declarations (Section 4.2.5).

References   duplicate declarations 4.2.5; function types 5.8; **goto** statement 8.10; implicit declarations 4.7; pointer types 5.3; structure types 5.6

4.2.4 Overloading of Names

In C and other programming languages, the same identifier may be associated with more than one program entity at a time. When this happens, we say that the name is *overloaded*, and the context in which the name is used determines the association that is in effect. For instance, an identifier might be both the name of a variable and a structure tag. When used in an expression, the variable association is used; when used in a type specifier, the tag association is used.

There are five *overloading classes* for names in C. (We sometimes refer to them as *name spaces*.) They are listed and described in Table 4–2.

Table 4–2 Overloading classes

Class	Included identifiers
Preprocessor macro names	Because preprocessing logically occurs before compilation, names used by the preprocessor are independent of any other names in a C program.
Statement labels	Named statement labels are part of statements. Definitions of statement labels are always followed by **:** (and are not part of **case** labels). Uses of statement labels always immediately follow the reserved word **goto**.
Structure, union, and enumeration tags	These tags are part of structure, union, and enumeration type specifiers and, if present, always immediately follow the reserved words **struct**, **union**, or **enum**.
Component names ("members" in Standard C)	Component names are allocated in name spaces associated with each structure and union type. That is, the same identifier can be a component name in any number of structures or unions at the same time. Definitions of component names always occur within structure or union type specifiers. Uses of component names always immediately follow the selection operators **.** and **->**.
Other names	All other names fall into an overloading class that includes variables, functions, **typedef** names, and enumeration constants.

These overloading rules differ slightly from those in the original definition of C. First, statement labels were originally in the same name space as ordinary identifiers. Second, all structure and union component names were placed in single name space instead of separate name spaces for each type.

When a name is overloaded with several associations, each association has its own scope and may be hidden by other declarations independent of other associations. For instance, if an identifier is being used both as a variable and structure tag, an inner block may redefine the variable association without altering the tag association.

C++ injects structure and union tags into the "other" name space (Section 4.9.2).

References   component names 5.6.3; duplicate definition 4.2.5; enumeration tags 5.5; **goto** statement 8.10; selection operators 7.4.2; statement labels 8.10; structure tags 5.6; structure type specifiers 5.6; **typedef** names 5.10; union tags 5.7; union type specifiers 5.7

4.2.5 Duplicate Declarations

It is invalid to make two declarations of the same name (in the same overloading class) in the same block or at the top level. Such declarations are said to *conflict*.

Example

The two declarations of **howmany**, next, are conflicting, but the two declarations of **str** are not (because they are in different name spaces).

```
extern int howmany;
extern char str[10];
typedef double howmany();
extern struct str {int a, b;} x;
```

There are two exceptions to the prohibition against duplicate declarations. First, any number of external (*referencing*) declarations for the same name may exist as long as the declarations assign the same type to the name in each instance. This exception reflects a belief that declaring the same external library function twice should not be invalid.

Second, if an identifier is declared as being external, that declaration may be followed with a *definition* (Section 4.8) of the name later in the program, assuming that the definition assigns the same type to the name as the external declaration(s). This exception allows the user to generate valid forward references to variables and functions.

Example

> We define two functions, **f** and **g**, that reference each other. Normally, the use of **f** within **g** would be an invalid forward reference. However, by preceding the definition of **g** with an external declaration of **f**, we give the compiler enough information about **f** to compile **g**. (Without the initial declaration of **f**, a one-pass compiler could not know when compiling **g** that **f** returns a value of type **double**.)

```
extern double f(double z);

double g(double x, double y)
{
    … f(x-y) …
}

double f(double z)
{
    … g(z, z/2.0) …
}
```

References   defining and referencing declarations 4.8; **extern** storage class 4.3; forward references 4.2; overloading class 4.2; **static** storage class 4.3

4.2.6 Duplicate Visibility

Because C's scoping rules specify that a name's scope begins at its declaration point rather than at the head of the block in which it is defined, a situation can arise in which two nonconflicting declarations can be referenced in different parts of the same block.

Example

> In the following code, there are two variables named **i** referenced in the block labeled **B**—the integer **i** declared in the outer block is used to initialize the variable **j**, and then a floating-point variable **i** is declared, hiding the first **i**.

```
{
    int i = 0;
    ...
    B:  {
            int j = i;
            float i = 10.0;
            ...
        }
}
```

The reference to i in the initialization of j is ambiguous. Which i was wanted? Most compilers will do what was (apparently) intended; the first use of i in block B is bound to the outer definition, and the redefinition of i then hides the outer definition for the remainder of the block. This is the Standard C rule. We consider this usage to be bad programming style; it should be avoided.

4.2.7 Extent

Variables and functions, unlike types, have an existence at run time—that is, they have storage allocated to them. The *extent* (or *lifetime*) of these objects is the period of time that the storage is allocated. Standard C calls this the *storage duration*.

An object is said to have *static extent* when it is allocated storage at or before the beginning of program execution and the storage remains allocated until program termination. In C, all functions have static extent, as do all variables declared in top-level declarations. Variables declared in blocks may have static extent depending on the declaration.

An object is said to have *local extent* when it is created on entry to a block or function and is destroyed on exit from the block or function. If a variable with local extent has an initializer, the variable is initialized each time it is created. Formal parameters have local extent, and variables declared at the beginning of blocks may have local extent depending on the declaration. A variable with local extent is called *automatic* in C.

Finally, it is possible in C to have data objects with *dynamic extent*—that is, objects that are created and destroyed explicitly at the programmer's whim. However, dynamic objects must be created through the use of special library routines such as **malloc** and are not viewed as part of the C language.

References **auto** storage class 4.3; initializers 4.6; **malloc** function 16.1; **static** storage class 4.3; storage allocation functions 16.1

4.2.8 Initial Values

Allocating storage for a variable does not necessarily establish the initial contents of that storage. Most variable declarations in C may have *initializers*—expressions used to set the initial value of a variable at the time that storage is allocated for it. If an initializer is not specified for a local variable, its value after allocation is unpredictable. (Static variables are initialized to zero by default.)

It is important to remember that a static variable is initialized only once and retains its value even when the program is executing outside that variable's scope.

Example

> In the following code, two variables, **L** and **S**, are declared at the head of a block and both are
> initialized to 0. Both variables have local scope, but **S** has static extent while **L** has local (au-
> tomatic) extent. Each time the block is entered, both variables are incremented by one and the
> new values printed.

```
{
    static int S = 0;
    auto int L = 0;
    L = L + 1;
    S = S + 1;
    printf("L = %d, S = %d\n", L, S);
}
```

> What values will be printed? If the block is executed many times, the output will be this:

```
L = 1, S = 1
L = 1, S = 2
L = 1, S = 3
L = 1, S = 4
...
```

There is one dangerous feature of C's initialization of automatic variables declared
at the beginning of blocks. The initialization is guaranteed to occur only if the block is entered normally—that is, if control flows into the beginning of the block. Through the use
of statement labels and the **goto** statement, it is possible to jump into the middle of a
block; if this is done, there is no guarantee that automatic variables will be initialized. In
fact, most Standard and non-Standard implementations do *not* initialize them. In the case
of a **switch** statement, it is normal to jump into the block that is the **switch** statement's
body to a **case** or **default** label, so automatic variables before the first such label will
not be initialized.

Example

> The initialization of variable **sum**, next, will (probably) not occur when the **goto** statement
> transfers control to label **L**. This causes **sum** to begin with an indeterminate value.

```
goto L;
...
{
    static int vector[10] = {1,2,3,4,5,6,7,8,9,10};
    int sum = 0;
L:
    /* Add up elements of "vector". */
    for ( i=0; i<10; i++ ) sum += vector[i];
        printf("sum is %d", sum);
}
```

References **goto** statement 8.10; initialization of variables 4.6; storage classes 4.3;
switch statement 8.7

4.2.9 External Names

A special case of scope and visibility is the *external* identifier, also called an identifier with *external linkage*. All instances of an external identifier among all the files making up a C program will be forced to refer to the same object or function and must be declared with compatible types in each file or else the result is undefined.

External names must be declared **extern** explicitly or implicitly, but not all names declared **extern** are external. External names are usually declared at the top level of a C program and therefore have file scope. However, non-Standard implementations differ on how external names declared within a block are handled.

Example

The following program fragment is acceptable to many C compilers; it declares an external name within a block and then uses it outside the block:

```
{
    extern int E;
    ...
}
E = 1;
```

According to normal block-scoping rules, the declaration should not be visible outside the block, but many implementations of C implicitly give **E** file scope and so compile this fragment without error. Standard C requires the declaration to have block scope, but does not state that the prior fragment should be invalid. Technically, the behavior of an implementation in this case is undefined, thus permitting a conforming implementation to accept the program. We think programmers should treat this fragment as a programming error even if the compiler accepts it and the run-time behavior is correct.

It is indisputably an error if two external declarations (in the same file or different files within the same program) specify incompatible types for the same identifier.

Example

In the following program, the two declarations of **X** do not conflict in the source file, although their behavior at run time is undefined:

```
int f() { extern int X; return X; }
double g() { extern double X; return X; }
```

References external name conventions 2.5; external name definition and reference 4.8; scope 4.2.1; type compatibility 5.11; visibility 4.2.2

4.2.10 Compile-Time Names

So far the discussion has focused mainly on variables and functions, which have an existence at run time. However, the scope and visibility rules apply equally to identifiers associated with objects that do not necessarily exist at run time: **typedef** names, type tags, and enumeration constants. When any of these identifiers are declared, their scope is the same as that of a variable defined at the same location. Macros and labels are also compile-time names, but their scopes are different.

References   enumeration constants 5.5; scope 4.2.1; structure type 5.6; `typedef` name 5.10; visibility 4.2.2

4.3 STORAGE CLASS AND FUNCTION SPECIFIERS

We now proceed to examine the pieces of declarations: storage class specifiers, type specifiers and qualifiers, function specifiers, declarators, and initializers.

A storage class specifier determines the extent of a declared object (except for `typedef`, which is special). At most one storage class specifier may appear in a declaration. It is customary for storage class specifiers (if any) to precede type specifiers and qualifiers in declarations.

> *storage-class-specifier* : one of
>   `auto   extern   register   static   typedef`

The meanings of the storage classes are given in Table 4–3. Note that not all storage classes are permitted in every declaration context.

Table 4–3   Storage class specifiers

Specifier	Usage
`auto`	Permitted only in declarations of variables within[a] blocks. It indicates that the variable has local (automatic) extent. (Because this is the default, `auto` is rarely seen in C programs.)
`extern`	May appear in declarations of external functions and variables, either at the top level or within[a] blocks. It indicates that the object declared has static extent and its name is known to the linker. See Section 4.8.
`register`	May be used for local variables or parameter declarations. It is equivalent to `auto`, except that it provides a hint to the compiler that the object will be heavily used and should be allocated in a way that minimizes access time.
`static`	May appear on declarations of functions or variables. On function definitions, it is used only to specify that the function name is not to be exported to the linker. On function declarations, it indicates that the declared function will be defined—with storage class `static`—later in the file. On data declarations, it always signifies a defining declaration that is not exported to the linker. Variables declared with this storage class have static extent (as opposed to local extent, signified by `auto`).
`typedef`	Indicates that the declaration is defining a new name for a data type, rather than for a variable or function. The name of the data type appears where a variable name would appear in a variable declaration, and the data type itself is the type that would have been assigned to the variable name (see Section 5.10).

[a] C99 permits declarations anywhere within a block. Previous versions of C permitted them only before the first statement.

Standard C allows **register** to be used with any type of variable or parameter, but it is not permitted to compute the address of such an object, either explicitly (with the **&** operator) or implicitly (e.g., by converting an array name to a pointer when subscripting the array). Many non-Standard C compilers behave differently:

- They may restrict the use of **register** to objects of scalar types.
- They may permit the use of **&** on **register** objects.
- They may implicitly widen small objects declared with **register** (e.g., treating the declaration **register char x** as if it were **register int x**).

Implementations are permitted to treat the **register** storage class specifier the same as the **auto** specifier. However, programmers can expect the use of **register** on one or two heavily used variables in a function to increase performance. Using **register** on many declarations is likely to be ineffective or counterproductive. The use of **register** with most modern compilers is likely to have less effect since those compilers already allocate variables to registers as necessary.

References   address operator **&** 7.5.6; formal parameter declarations 9.3; initializers 4.6; subscripts 7.4.1; top-level declarations 4.1; **typedef** names 5.10

4.3.1 Default Storage Class Specifiers

If no storage class specifier is supplied with a declaration, one will be assumed based on the declaration context as shown in Table 4–4.

Table 4–4   Default storage class specifiers

Location of declaration	Kind of declaration	Default storage class
Top level	All	**extern**
Function parameter	All	none (i.e., "not **register**")
Within blocks	Functions	**extern**
Within blocks	Nonfunctions	**auto**

Omitting the storage class specifier on a top-level declaration may not be the same as supplying **extern**, as discussed in Section 4.8. As a matter of good programming style, we think programmers should supply the storage class **extern** when declaring an external function inside a block. The **auto** storage class is rarely seen in C programs; it is usually defaulted.

References   blocks 8.4; parameter declarations 9.3; top-level declarations 4.1, 4.8

4.3.2 Examples of Storage Class Specifiers

An implementation of the heapsort algorithm is shown next. It is beyond the scope of this book to explain how it works in detail.

Example

The algorithm regards the array as a binary tree such that the two subtrees of element **b[k]** are elements **b[2*k]** and **b[2*k+1]**. A *heap*, as used here, is a tree such that every node contains a number that is no smaller than any of the numbers contained by that node's descendants.

```
#define SWAP(x, y) (temp = (x), (x) = (y), (y) = temp)

static void adjust (int v[], int m, register int n)
/* If v[m+1] through v[n] is already in heap form,
   this puts v[m] through v[n] into heap form. */
{
    register int *b, j, k, temp;
    b = v - 1; /* b is "1-origin", customary in heapsort,
                    i.e., v[j] is the same as b[j-1] */
    j = m;
    k = m * 2;
    while (k <= n) {
        if (k < n && b[k] < b[k+1]) ++k;
        if (b[j] < b[k]) SWAP(b[j], b[k]);
        j = k;
        k *= 2;
    }
}

/* Sort v[0]...v[n-1] into increasing order. */
void heapsort(int v[], int n)
{
    int *b, j, temp;
    b = v - 1;
    /* Put the array into the form of a heap. */
    for (j = n/2; j > 0; j--) adjust(v, j, n);
    /* Repeatedly extract the largest element and
       put it at the end of the unsorted region. */
    for (j = n-1; j > 0; j--) {
        SWAP(b[1], b[j+1]);
        adjust(v, 1, j);
    }
}
```

The auxiliary function **adjust** does not need to be externally visible, and so it is declared **static**. The speed of the **adjust** function is crucial to the performance of the sort, and so its local variables have been given storage class **register** as a hint to the compiler. The formal parameter **n** is also referred to repeatedly within **adjust**, and so it is also specified with storage class **register**. The other two formal parameters for **adjust** are defaulted to "not register."

The main function is **heapsort**; it must be visible to users of the sort package, and so it has the default storage class, namely **extern**. The local variables of function **heapsort** do not impact performance; they have been given the default storage class, **auto**.

4.3.3 Function Specifiers

Function specifiers are new to C99.

function-specifier :   *(C99)*
    `inline`

The `inline` function specifier can appear only on function declarations; such functions are then termed *inline functions*. The specifier can appear more than once with no change of meaning. The use of `inline` is a hint to the C implementation that calls on the function should be as fast as possible.

Detailed rules for inline functions are discussed in Chapter 9.

References   inline functions 9.10

4.4 TYPE SPECIFIERS AND QUALIFIERS

Type specifiers provide some of the information about the data type of the program identifiers being declared. Additional type information is supplied by the declarators. Type specifiers may also define (as a side effect) type tags, structure and union component names, and enumeration constants.

The type qualifiers `const`, `volatile`, and `restrict` specify additional properties of types that are relevant only when accessing objects of the type through lvalues:

type-specifier :
    enumeration-type-specifier
    floating-point-type-specifier
    integer-type-specifier
    structure-type-specifier
    typedef-name
    union-type-specifier
    void-type-specifier

type-qualifier :
    `const`
    `volatile`
    `restrict`   *(C99)*

Example

Here are some examples of type specifiers:

`void`	`union { int a; char b; }`
`int`	`enum {red, blue, green}`
`unsigned long int`	`char`
`my_struct_type`	`float`

The type specifiers are described in detail in Chapter 5, and we defer further discussion of particular type specifiers until then. However, a few general issues surrounding type specifiers are discussed in the following sections.

References   declarators 4.5; enumeration type specifier 5.5; floating-point type specifier 5.2; integer type specifier 5.1; lvalue 7.1; structure type specifier 5.6; type qualifiers 4.4.3; `typedef` name 5.10; union type specifier 5.7; `void` type specifier 5.9

4.4.1 Default Type Specifiers

Originally, C allowed the type specifier in a variable declaration or function definition to be omitted, in which case it defaulted to `int`. This is considered bad programming style in modern C, and in fact C99 treats it as an error. Older compilers did not implement the `void` type, so a rationale behind omitting the type specifier on function definitions was to indicate to human readers that the function did not really return a value (although the compiler had to assume that it did).

Example

In pre-Standard C, it was common to see function definitions like this:

```
/* Sort v[0]…v[n-1] into increasing order. */
sort(v, n)
    int v[], n;
{
    …
}
```

The modern, Standard C style is to declare those functions with the `void` type:

```
/* Sort v[0]…v[n-1] into increasing order. */
void sort(int v[], int n)
{
    …
}
```

Example

When using a compiler that does not implement `void`, it is much nicer to define `void` yourself and then use it explicitly than to omit the type specifier entirely:

```
/* Make "void" be a synonym for "int". */
typedef int void;
```

At least one compiler we know of actually reserves the identifier `void`, but does not implement it. For that compiler, the preprocessor definition

```
#define void int
```

is one of the few cases in which using a reserved word as a macro name is justified.

Example

The declaration syntax (Section 4.1) requires declarations to contain a storage class specifier, a type specifier, a type qualifier, or some combination of the three. This requirement avoids a syntactic ambiguity in the language. If all specifiers and qualifiers were defaulted, the declaration

```
extern int f();
```

would become simply

```
f();
```

which is syntactically equivalent to a statement consisting of a function call. We think that the best style is to always include the type specifier and allow the storage class specifier to default, at least when it is **auto**.

Example

A final note for LALR(1) grammar aficionados: both the storage class specifier and the type specifier can be omitted on a function *definition*, and this is very common in C programs, as in

```
main() { ... }
```

There is no syntactic ambiguity in this case because the declarator in a function declaration must be followed by a comma or semicolon, whereas the declarator in a function definition must be followed by a left brace.

References   declarations 4.1; function definitions 9.1; **void** type specifier 5.9

4.4.2 Missing Declarators

The following discussion deals with a subtle point of declarations and type specifiers. Type specifiers that are structure, union, or enumeration definitions define new types or enumeration constants. If you simply want to define a type, it makes sense to omit all the declarators from the declaration and write only the type specifier. Declarations in Standard C must have a declarator, define a structure or union tag, or define enumeration constants. In traditional C, nonsensical declarations were often silently ignored.

Example

The following declaration consists of a single type specifier. It defines a new structure type **S** with components **a** and **b**.

```
struct S { int a, b; }; /* Define struct S */
```

The type can be referenced later by using just the specifier

```
struct S x, y, z; /* Define 3 variables */
```

However, the following declarations are nonsensical and (in Standard C) illegal:

```
struct { int a, b; };                /* no tag */
int ;                                /* no declarator */
static struct T { int a, b; }; /* extra storage class */
```

In the first case, there is no structure tag, so it would be impossible to refer to the type later in the program. In the second case, the declaration has no effect at all. In the third case, a storage class specifier has been supplied, which will be ignored. You might think that a later declaration of the form

```
struct T x, y;
```

will cause **x** and **y** to have the storage class **static**. It will not.

References   enumeration types 5.5; declarators 4.5; structure types 5.6; type specifiers 4.4; union types 5.7

4.4.3 Type Qualifiers

The type qualifiers **const** and **volatile** were added in C89; **restrict** was added in C99. An identifier declared using any combination of these qualifiers is said to have a *qualified type*, so there are seven possible qualified *versions* of each unqualified type. (The order of type qualifiers does not matter.) None of the seven is compatible with the others or with the unqualified type. If the same qualifier appears more than once in a declaration, then the extra occurrences are ignored in C99, but cause an error in C89.

Type qualifiers specify additional properties of types that are relevant only when accessing objects through lvalues (designators) with those qualified types. When used in a context that requires a value rather than a designator, the qualifiers are eliminated from the type. That is, in the expression L=R, the type of the right operand of = always has an unqualified type even if it was declared with type qualifiers. The left operand, however, keeps its qualification since it is used in lvalue context.

In addition to their presence at the top level of declarations, type qualifiers may also appear within pointer declarators and (in C99) array declarators.

Example

When using a C compiler that does not support type qualifiers, you can supply the following macro definitions so that the use of the type qualifiers will not cause the compilation to fail. Of course, the qualifiers will also have no effect.

```
#ifndef __STDC__
#define const /*nothing*/
#define volatile /*nothing*/
#define restrict /*nothing*/
#endif
```

References **#ifndef** 3.5.3; __STDC__ 11.3; array declarators 4.5.3; pointer declarator 4.5.2; type compatibility 5.11

4.4.4 Const

An lvalue expression of a **const**-qualified type cannot be used to modify an object. That is, such an lvalue cannot be used as the left operand of an assignment expression or the operand of an increment or decrement operator. The intent is to use the **const** qualifier to designate objects whose value is unchanging, and to have the C compiler attempt to ensure that the programmer does not change the value.

Example

The following declaration specifies that `ic` is to be an integer with the constant value 37:

```
const int ic = 37;
...
ic = 5; /* Invalid */
ic++;   /* Invalid */
```

The `const` qualifier can also appear in pointer declarators to make it possible to declare both "constant pointers" and "pointers to constant data":

```
int * const const_pointer;
const int *pointer_to_const;
```

The syntax may be confusing: Constant pointers and constant integers, for example, have the type qualifier `const` in different locations. The appearance also changes when `typedef` names are used—the constant pointer `const_pointer` in the previous example may also be declared like this:

```
typedef int *int_pointer;
const int_pointer const_pointer;
```

This makes `const_pointer` look like a "pointer to constant `int_pointer`," but it is not—it is still a constant pointer to a (nonconstant) `int`. In fact, because the order of type specifiers and qualifiers does not matter, the last declaration may be written:

```
int_pointer const const_pointer;
```

You can alter a variable that has type "pointer to constant data," but the object to which it points cannot be altered. Expressions with this type can be generated by applying the address operator `&` to values of `const`-qualified types. To protect the integrity of constant data, assigning a value of type "pointer to `const` *T*" to an object of type "pointer to *T*" is allowed only by using an explicit cast.

Example

```
const int *pc; /* pointer to a constant integer */
int *p, i;
const int ic;
pc = p = &i; /* OK */
pc = &ic;       /* OK */
*p = 5;         /* OK */
*pc = 5;        /* Invalid */
```

```
pc = &i;          /* OK */
pc = p;           /* OK */
p = &ic;          /* Invalid */
p = pc;           /* Invalid */
p = (int *)&ic;   /* OK */
p = (int *)pc;    /* OK */
```

The language rules for **const** are not foolproof—that is, they may be bypassed or overridden if the programmer tries hard enough. For instance, the address of a constant object can be passed to an external function without a prototype, and that function could modify the constant object. However, implementations are permitted to allocate static objects of **const**-qualified types in read-only storage so that attempts to alter the objects could cause run-time errors.

Example

This program fragment illustrates some dangers in circumventing the **const** qualifier.

```
const int * pc;
int * p;
const int ic = 0;
...
pc = &ic;         /* OK */
p = (int *)pc;    /* Valid, but dangerous */
*p = 5;           /* Valid, but may cause a run-time error */
```

Finally, a top-level declaration that has the type qualifier **const** but no explicit storage class is considered to be **extern** in C.

References   assignment expression 7.9; increment and decrement expressions 7.4; pointer declarators 4.5.2

4.4.5 Volatile and Sequence Points

The **volatile** type qualifier informs the Standard C implementation that certain objects can have their values altered in ways not under control of the implementation. Volatile objects (i.e., any object accessed using an lvalue expression of a **volatile**-qualified type) should not participate in optimizations that assume no hidden side effects.

To be more precise, Standard C introduces the notion of *sequence points* in C programs. A sequence point exists at the completion of all expressions not part of a larger expression—that is, at the end of expression statements; after the control expressions of the **if**, **switch**, **while**, and **do** statements; after each of the three control expressions in the **for** statement; after the first operand of the logical AND (**&&**), logical OR (**||**), conditional (**?:**) and comma (**,**) operators; after **return** statement expressions; and after initializers. Additional sequence points are present at the end of a full declarator, in function calls immediately after all the arguments are evaluated, before library functions return, after the actions associated with **printf/scanf** conversion specifiers, and around calls to comparison functions supplied to **bsearch** and **qsort**.

References to and modifications of volatile objects must not be optimized across sequence points, although optimizations between sequence points are permitted. Extra references and modifications beyond those appearing in the source code are allowed by the C language standard. In our experience, however, programmers prefer that implementations access and modify volatile objects exactly "as written." It is easy enough for a programmer to copy a value out of a volatile object to encourage optimization.

Example

Consider the following program fragment, where j is assigned some value before the loop:

```
extern int f(int);
auto int i,j;
...
i = f(0);
while (i) {
    if (f(j*j)) break;
}
```

If the variable i were not used again during its lifetime, then traditional C implementations would be permitted to rewrite this program fragment as

```
if (f(0)) {
    i = j*j;
    while( !f(i) ) ;
}
```

The first assignment to i was eliminated, and i was reused as a temporary variable to hold j*j, which is evaluated once outside the loop. If the declaration of i and j were

```
auto volatile int i,j;
```

then these optimizations would not be permitted. However, we could write the loop as shown next, eliminating one reference to j before the sequence point at the end of the if statement control expression:

```
i = f(0);
while (i) {
    register int temp = j;
    if (f(temp*temp)) break;
}
```

The new syntax for pointer declarators allows the declaration of type "pointer to **volatile** ... ." References to this kind of pointer may be optimized, but references to the object to which it points cannot be. Assigning a value of type "pointer to **volatile** *T*" to an object of type "pointer to *T*" is allowed only when an explicit cast is used.

Example

Here are some examples of valid and invalid uses of **volatile** objects:

```
volatile int * pv;
int *p;
pv = p;        /* OK */
p = pv;        /* Invalid */
p = (int *)pv; /* OK */
```

The most common use of **volatile** is to provide reliable access to special memory locations used by the computer hardware or by asynchronous processes such as interrupt handlers.

Example

Consider the following typical example. A computer has three special hardware locations:

Address	Use
0xFFFFFF20	Input data buffer
0xFFFFFF24	Output data buffer
0xFFFFFF28	Control register

The control register and input data buffer can be read by a program but not written; the output buffer can be written but not read. The third least significant bit of the control register is *input available*; it is set to 1 when data have arrived from an external source, and it is set to 0 automatically when these data are read out of the input buffer by the program (after which time the contents of the buffer are undefined until "input available" becomes 1 again). The second least significant bit of the control register is called *output available*; when the external device is ready to accept data, the bit is set to 1. When data are placed in the output buffer by the program, the bit is automatically set to 0 and the data are written out. Placing data in the output buffer when the control bit is 0 causes unpredictable results.

The function **copy_data** next copies data from the input to the output until an input value of 0 is seen. The number of characters copied is returned. There is no provision for overflow or other error conditions:

```
typedef unsigned long datatype, controltype, counttype;

#define CONTROLLER \
    ((const volatile controltype * const) 0xFFFFFF28)
#define INPUT_BUF \
    ((const volatile datatype * const) 0xFFFFFF20)
#define OUTPUT_BUF \
    ((volatile datatype * const)  0xFFFFFF24)
#define input_ready ((*CONTROLLER) & 0x4)
#define output_ready ((*CONTROLLER) & 0x2)
```

```
counttype copy_data(void)
{
    counttype count = 0;
    datatype temp;
    for(;;) {
        while (!input_ready) ;      /* Wait for input */
        temp = *INPUT_BUF;
        if (temp == 0) return count;
        while (!output_ready) ;     /* Wait to do output */
        *OUTPUT_BUF = temp;
        count++;
    }
}
```

References   **bsearch** 20.5; conversion specifications 15.8.2, 15.11.2; declarators 4.5; initializers 4.6; pointer declarators 4.5.2; **qsort** 20.5

4.4.6 Restrict

The type qualifier **restrict** is new in C99. It may only be used to qualify pointers to object or incomplete types, and it serves as a "no alias" hint to the C compiler. This means that the pointer is, for the moment, the only way to access the object to which it points. Violating this assumption results in undefined behavior. The phrase "at the moment" means that in some circumstances within a function or block aliases can be created from the original restrict-qualified pointer as long as those aliases are eliminated by the end of the function or block. The C99 standard provides a precise mathematical definition of **restrict**, but here are some common situations.

1. A file-scope pointer declared using **restrict** is assumed to be the only means to access the object to which it refers. This might be an appropriate way to declare a global pointer initialized by **malloc** at run time.

   ```
   extern double * restrict ptr;
   ...
   void initialize(void)
   {
       ptr = my_malloc( sizeof(double) );
   }
   ```

2. A restricted pointer that is a function parameter is assumed to be the only way to access its object at the beginning of the function's execution, and so no other pointer not created from the parameter could be used to modify the object. For example, the **memcpy** function (unlike **memmove**) requires that its source and destination memory areas do not overlap. In C99, this expectation can now be expressed in the function prototype:

```
#include <string.h>
void *memcpy(
    void * restrict s1,
    const void * restrict s2,
    size_t n);
```

3. Two restricted pointers, or a restricted and nonrestricted pointer, can refer to the same object if the object is not modified during the lifetime of the restricted pointers. For example, consider the following function, which sums two vectors, storing the sum in a third vector:

```
void add(int n, int * restrict dest,
    int * restrict op1, int * restrict op2)
{
    int i;
    for (i = 0; i < n; i++)
        dest[i] = op1[i] + op2[i];
}
```

If **a** and **b** are disjoint arrays of length **N**, then it is all right to call **add(N, a, b, b)**, resulting in **op1** and **op2** designating array **b** because the array **b** is never modified. Of course, this depends on knowledge of the implementation of **add**; a programmer seeing only the prototype for **add** would have no way to know that such a call was safe.

4. A structure member can be a restricted pointer. The meaning is that, when an instance of the structure is created, the restricted pointer is the only way to reference the designated object.

Before **restrict** was added to the language, programmers had to rely on nonportable pragmas or compiler switches to enable the kinds of pointer optimizations that are safe when an object can only be accessed by a single pointer at a time. These optimizations can result in great speedups at run time.

Omitting **restrict** does not change the meaning of a program; a C implementation is free to ignore **restrict**. In this book, many library function prototypes are written with the **restrict** qualifier. Programmers using pre-C99 implementations should omit or disregard **restrict**.

References   malloc 16.1; **memcpy** 14.3

4.5 DECLARATORS

Declarators introduce the name being declared and also supply additional type information. No previous programming language had anything quite like C's declarators:

declarator :
    pointer-declarator
    direct-declarator

> *direct-declarator* :
>> *simple-declarator*
>> (*declarator*)
>> *function-declarator*
>> *array-declarator*

The different kinds of declarators are described in the following sections.

4.5.1 Simple Declarators

Simple declarators are used to define variables of arithmetic, enumeration, structure, and union types:

> *simple-declarator* :
>> *identifier*

Suppose that S is a type specifier and *id* is any identifier. Then the declaration

```
S id ;
```

indicates that *id* is of type S. The *id* is called a *simple declarator*.

Example

Declaration	Type of **x**
`int x;`	integer
`float x;`	floating-point
`struct S { int a; float b;} x;`	structure of two components

Simple declarators may be used in a declaration when the type specifier supplies all the typing information. This happens for arithmetic, structure, union, enumeration, and void types, and for types represented by **typedef** names. Pointer, array, and function types require the use of more complicated declarators. However, every declarator includes an identifier, and thus we say that a declarator "encloses" an identifier.

References   type specifiers 4.4; structure types 5.6; **typedef** names 5.10

4.5.2 Pointer Declarators

Pointer declarators are used to declare variables of pointer types. The *type-qualifier-list* in the following syntax is new in Standard C; in older compilers, it is omitted:

> *pointer-declarator* :
>> *pointer direct-declarator*

pointer :
> * *type-qualifier-list*$_{opt}$
> * *type-qualifier-list*$_{opt}$ *pointer*

type-qualifier-list :   *(C89)*
> *type-qualifier*
> *type-qualifer-list* *type-qualifier*

Suppose that *D* is any declarator enclosing the identifier *id* and that the declaration "*S D;*" indicates that *id* has type "... *S*." Then the declaration

    S *D ;

indicates that *id* has type "...pointer to *S*." The optional *type-qualifier-list* in pointer declarators is allowed only in Standard C. When present, the qualifiers apply to the pointer, not to the object pointed to.

Example

> In the three declarations of **x** in the following table, *id* is **x**, *S* is **int**, and "..." is, respectively, "", "array of," and "function returning." (It is harder to explain than it is to learn.)

Declaration	Type of x
`int *x;`	pointer to `int`
`int *x[];`	array of pointers to `int`
`int *x();`	function returning a pointer to `int`

Example

> In the following declarations, **ptr_to_const** is a (nonconstant) pointer to a constant **int**, whereas **const_ptr** is a constant pointer to a (nonconstant) **int**:
>
> ```
> const int * ptr_to_const;
> int * const const_ptr;
> ```

References   array declarators 4.5.3; **const** type qualifier 4.4.4; function declarators 4.5.4; pointer types 5.3; type qualifiers 4.4.3

4.5.3 Array Declarators

Array declarators are used to declare objects of array types:

array-declarator :
> *direct-declarator* **[** *constant-expression*$_{opt}$ **]**   *(until C99)*
> *direct-declarator* **[** *array-qualifier-list*$_{opt}$ *array-size-expression*$_{opt}$ **]** *(C99)*
> *direct-declarator* **[** *array-qualifier-list*$_{opt}$ ***]**   *(C99)*

constant-expression :
> *conditional-expression*

array-qualifier-list :
> *array-qualifier*
> *array-qualifier-list array-qualifier*

array-qualifier :
> `static`
> `restrict`
> `const`
> `volatile`

array-size-expression :
> *assignment-expression*
> `*`

If *D* is any declarator enclosing the identifier *id* and if the declaration "*S D;*" indicates that *id* has type "... *S*," then the declaration

> *S* (*D*) [*e*] ;

indicates that *id* has type "... array of *S*." (The parentheses may often be elided according to the precedence rules in constructing declarators; see Section 4.5.5.) Type *S* may not be an incomplete or function type.

In the most common case, an integer constant expression *e* appears within the square brackets and specifies the number of elements in the array. The number must be an integer greater than 0. C's arrays are always "0-origin." That is, the declaration `int A[3]` defines the elements `A[0]`, `A[1]`, and `A[2]`. Higher dimensioned arrays are declared as "arrays of arrays" (see Section 5.4.2).

Example

In the following three declarations, *id* is **x**, *S* is `int`, and "..." is, respectively, "", "pointer to," and "array of."

Declaration	Type of x
`int (x)[5];`	array of integers
`int (*x)[5];`	pointer to an array of integers
`int (x[5])[5];`	array of arrays of integers
`int x[5][5];`	array of arrays of integers (same)

An integer constant expression need not appear within the brackets of an array declarator. Three variations are possible: incomplete array types, variable length arrays, and the use of *array-qualifiers* (type qualifiers and `static`) inside *array-declarators*.

Incomplete array types   If the brackets are empty, then the declarator describes an incomplete array type. Objects of incomplete types cannot be created because their size is not known. You can declare pointers to incomplete types. Here are the cases in which array sizes may be omitted:

1. The array being declared is a formal parameter of a function. Since array parameters are converted to pointers, the array size is not needed. If the array has multiple dimensions, only the leftmost dimension may be omitted. For example,

   ```
   int f(int ary[]); /* array of unspecified length */
   ```

2. The declarator is accompanied by an initializer from which the length of the array can be deduced. The type is no longer incomplete after the initializer is processed. For example,

   ```
   char prompt[] = "Yes or No?";
   ```

3. The declaration is not a defining occurrence, but rather refers to an object defined elsewhere, after which the type is not incomplete. For multidimensional arrays, only the leftmost dimension may be omitted. You can create a pointer to an incomplete type. For example,

   ```
   extern int matrix[][10]; /* incomplete type */

   ...

   static int matrix[5][10]; /* no longer incomplete */
   ```

4. In C99, the last component of a structure may be a flexible array member, which is declared with no size.

The declaration of any n-dimensional array must include the sizes of the last $n-1$ dimensions so that the accessing algorithm can be determined.

Variable length arrays   In C99, if the *array-size-expression* within the *array-declarator* brackets is * or is an expression that is not constant, then the declarator describes a variable length array. The * can only appear in array parameter declarations within function prototypes that are not part of a function definition. Variable length arrays are not incomplete. See Section 5.4.5 for a discussion of variable length arrays and their use in function prototypes.

Array qualifiers   In C99, an *array-qualifier-list* within the brackets of an *array-declarator* is permitted, but only when declaring a function parameter with an array type. This is discussed in Section 9.3.

References   array types 5.4; assignment expression 7.9; conditional expression 7.8; constant expressions 7.11; flexible array member 5.6.8; formal parameters 9.3; initializers 4.6; referencing and defining declarations 4.8; type qualifiers 4.4.3 variable length arrays 5.4.5

4.5.4 Function Declarators

Function declarators are used to declare or define functions and declare types that have function pointers as components:

function-declarator :
        direct-declarator **(** *parameter-type-list* **)**   *(C89)*
        direct-declarator **(** *identifier-list$_{opt}$* **)**

parameter-type-list :
        parameter-list
        parameter-list **,** **. . .**

parameter-list :
        parameter-declaration
        parameter-list **,** *parameter-declaration*

parameter-declaration :
        declaration-specifiers declarator
        declaration-specifiers abstract-declarator$_{opt}$

identifier-list :
        identifier
        parameter-list **,** *identifier*

If D is any declarator enclosing the identifier *id* and if the declaration "S D**;**" indicates that *id* has type "... S," then the declaration

    S **(***D***)(***P***)** **;**

indicates that *id* has type "... function returning S with parameters P." The parentheses around D can be omitted in most cases according to the precedence rules in constructing declarators (Section 4.5.5). The presence of *parameter-type-list* in the declarator syntax indicates that the declarator is in Standard C prototype form. Without it, the declarator is in traditional form, which is accepted by both traditional and Standard C compilers.

Example

Some examples of function declarators are shown below:

Declaration	Type of x
`int x();`	function with unspecified parameters returning an integer
`int x(double, float);`	function taking a double and a float parameter and returning an integer (prototype)
`int x(double d, float f);`	same as the preceding declarator
`int (*x)();`	pointer to a function with unspecified parameters returning an integer
`int (*x[])(int,...);`	array of pointers to functions that take a variable number of parameters beginning with an integer and return an integer (prototype)
`int (* const x) (void)`	constant pointer to a function taking no parameters and returning an integer

Function declarators are subject to several constraints depending on whether they appear in a function definition or as part of an object or function type declaration. Table 4–5 shows the possible forms of a function declarator, indicates whether it is in traditional C form or Standard C prototype form, reveals whether it can appear in a function definition or function type declaration, and shows what parameter information is specified. In the ta-

Table 4–5 Function declarators

Syntax	Form	Appears in	Parameters specified
f()	traditional	definitions	no parameters
f()	traditional	type declarations	any number of parameters
f(x, y,..., z)	traditional	definitions	fixed[a]
f(**void**)	prototype	either	no parameters
f(T_x, T_y,..., T_z)	prototype	type declarations	fixed
f(T_x, T_y,..., T_z,...)	prototype	type declarations	fixed, plus extras[b]
f(T_x x, T_y y,..., T_z z)	prototype	either	fixed
f(T_x x, T_y y,..., T_z z,...)	prototype	either	fixed, plus extras[b]

[a] Before Standard C it was possible to have additional, unspecified parameters.
[b] The number and type of the extra parameters are unspecified.

ble, the notation T_x x refers to the syntax "*declaration-specifiers declarator*" (i.e., a parameter type declaration that includes the parameter name, x). T_x refers to

$$declaration\text{-}specifiers \quad abstract\text{-}declarator_{opt}$$

—that is, a parameter type declaration that omits the parameter name.

The declaration and use of functions are discussed in more detail in Chapter 9. Variable-length parameter lists are accessed with the facilities in the **stdarg.h** or **varargs.h** header files.

References   abstract declarator 5.12; array declarators 4.5.3; defining and referencing declarations 4.8; function types and declarations 5.8; function definitions 9.1; pointer declarators 4.5; **stdarg.h** and **varargs.h** 11.4

4.5.5 Composition of Declarators

Declarators can be composed to form more complicated types, such as "5-element array of pointers to functions returning **int**," which is the type of **ary** in this declaration:

```
int (*ary[5])();
```

The only restriction on declarators is that the resulting type must be a valid one in C. The only types that are *not* valid in C are:

1. Any type including **void** except in the form of "…function returning **void**" or (in Standard C) "pointer to **void**."

2. "Array of function of …." Arrays may contain pointers to functions, but not functions themselves.

3. "Function returning array of …." Functions may return pointers to arrays, but not arrays themselves.

4. "Function returning function of …." Functions may return pointers to other functions, but not functions themselves.

When composing declarators, the precedence of the declarator expressions is important. Function and array declarators have higher precedence than pointer declarators, so that "***x()**" is equivalent to "***(x())**" ("function returning pointer …") instead of "**(*x)()**" ("pointer to function returning …"). Parentheses may be used to group declarators properly. Early C compilers had an upper limit of 6 on the depth of declarator nesting. Standard C compilers must allow at least a depth of 12.

Although declarators can be arbitrarily complex, it is better programming style to factor them into several simpler declarators.

Example

Declaration	Type of x
`int x();`	function returning an integer
`int (*x)();`	pointer to a function returning an integer
`void (*x)();`	pointer to a function returning no result
`void *x();`	function returning "pointer to **void**"

Example

Rather than writing

```
int *(*(*(*x)())[10])();
```

write instead

```
typedef int *(*print_function_ptr)();
typedef print_function_ptr (*digit_routines)[10];
digit_routines (*x)();
```

The variable **x** is a pointer to a function returning a pointer to a 10-element array of pointers to functions returning pointers to integers, in case you wondered.

Example

The rationale behind the syntax of declarators is that they mimic the syntax of a use of the enclosed identifier. To illustrate the symmetry in the declaration and use, if you see the declaration

```
int *(*x)[4];
```

then the type of the expression

```
*(*x)[i]
```

is `int`.

References   array types 5.4; function types 5.8; pointer to **void** 5.3.2; pointer types 5.3; **void** type specifier 5.9

4.6 INITIALIZERS

The declaration of a variable may be accompanied by an initializer that specifies the value the variable should have at the beginning of its lifetime. The full syntax for initializers is

> *initializer* :
>> *assignment-expression*
>> { *initializer-list* **,** *opt* }

> *initializer-list* :
>> *initializer*
>> *initializer-list* **,** *initializer*
>> *designation initializer*   *(C99)*
>> *initializer-list* **,** *designation initializer*   *(C99)*

> *designation* :
>> *designator-list* **=**

> *designator-list* :
>> *designator*
>> *designator-list designator*

> *designator* :
>> [*constant-expression*]
>> **.** *identifier*

The optional trailing comma inside the braces does not affect the meaning of the initializer.

C99 allows *designated initializers* (Section 4.6.9), in which a programmer can name particular components of aggregates to be initialized.

The initializers permitted on a particular declaration depend on the type of the object to be initialized and on whether the declared object has static or automatic storage class. The options are listed in Table 4–6 and presented in more detail in the following sections. Declarations of external objects should have initializers only when they are defining declarations (see Section 4.8).

The shape of an initializer—the brace-enclosed lists of initializers—should match the structure of the variable being initialized. The language definition specifies that the initializers for scalar variables may optionally be surrounded by braces, although such

Table 4–6   Form of initializers

Storage	Type	Initializer expression	Default initializer
static	scalar	constant	0, 0.0, false, or null pointer
static	array[a] or structure	brace-enclosed constants (or nonconstant expressions in C99)	recursive default for each component
static	union[b]	constant (or nonconstant expression in C99)	default for the first component
automatic	scalar	any	none
automatic	array[a,b]	brace-enclosed constants	none
automatic	structure[b]	brace-enclosed constants, or a single nonconstant expression of the same structure type	none
automatic	union[b]	constant, or a single nonconstant expression of the same union type	none

[a] The array may have an unknown size; the initializer determines the size. Variable length arrays may not be initialized.
[b] Standard C; older implementations may not permit initializations of these objects.

braces are logically unnecessary. We recommend that braces be reserved to indicate aggregate initialization. There are special rules for abbreviating initializers for aggregates.

Historical note: C originally had a syntax for initializers in which the = operator was omitted, and some current C compilers accept this syntax for compatibility. Users of these compilers, when they accidentally omit a comma or semicolon in a declaration (e.g., "`int a b;`"), get an obscure error message about an invalid initializer. Standard C does not support this obsolete syntax.

The following sections explain the special requirements for each type of variable.

References   automatic and static lifetime 4.2; declarations 4.1; external objects 4.8; static storage class 4.3

4.6.1 Integers

The form of an initializer for an integer variable is

declarator = expression

The initializing expression must have a type that would be permitted in a simple assignment to the initialized variable; the usual assignment conversions are applied. If the variable is static or external, the expression must be constant. If the variable is automatic or register, any expression is permitted. The default initializer for a static integer is 0.

Example

In the following code fragment, **Count** is initialized by a constant expression, but **ch** is initialized by the result of a function call.

```
#include <stdio.h>
static int Count = 4*200;

int main(void)
{
    int ch = getchar();
    ...
}
```

References   constant expression 7.11; integer types 5.1; static and automatic extent 4.2; usual assignment conversions 6.3.2

4.6.2 Floating Point

The form of an initializer for a floating-point variable is

   declarator = *expression*

The initializing expression must have a type that would be permitted in a simple assignment to the initialized variable; the usual assignment conversions are applied. If the variable is static or external, the expression must be constant. If the variable is automatic or register, any expression is permitted.

Example

```
static void process_data(double K)
{
    static double epsilon = 1.0e-6;
    auto float fudge_factor = K*epsilon;
    ...
}
```

Standard C explicitly permits floating-point constant expressions in initializers. Some older C compilers have been known to balk at complicated floating-point constant expressions.

The default initialization of static, floating-point variables is 0.0. This value might not be represented on the target computer as an object whose bits are zero. Standard C compilers must initialize the variable to the correct representation for 0.0, but most older C compilers always initialize static storage to zero bits.

References   arithmetic types Ch. 5; constant expressions 7.11; floating-point constant 2.7.2; floating-point types 5.2; static and automatic extent 4.2; unary minus operator 7.5.3; usual assignment conversions 6.3.2

4.6.3 Pointers

The form of an initialization of a pointer variable is

   declarator = *expression*

The initializing expression must have a type that would be permitted in a simple assignment to the initialized variable; the usual assignment conversions are applied. If the variable is automatic, then any expression of suitable type is permitted.

If the variable is static or external, then the expression must be constant. Constant expressions used as initializers of a pointer type *PT* (pointer to *T*) may be formed from the following elements.

1. An integral constant expression with the value 0, or such a value cast to type **void ***. These are null pointer constants usually referred to by the name **NULL** in the standard library.

   ```
   #define NULL ((void *)0)
   double *dp = NULL;
   ```

2. The name of a static or external function of type "function returning *T*" is converted to a constant of type "pointer to function returning *T*."

   ```
   extern int f();
   static int (*fp)() = f;
   ```

3. The name of a static or external array of type "array of *T*" is converted to a constant of type "pointer to *T*."

   ```
   char ary[100];
   char *cp = ary;
   ```

4. The **&** operator applied to the name of a static or external variable of type *T* yields a constant of type "pointer to *T*."

   ```
   static short s; auto short *sp = &s;
   ```

5. The **&** operator applied to an external or static array of type "array of *T*," subscripted by a constant expression, yields a constant of type "pointer to *T*."

   ```
   float PowersOfPi[10];
   float *PiSquared = &PowersOfPi[2];
   ```

6. An integer constant cast to a pointer type yields a constant of that pointer type, although this is not portable.

   ```
   long *PSW = (long *) 0xFFFFFFF0;
   ```

   Not all compilers accept casts in constant expressions, but they are permitted in Standard C.

7. A string literal yields a constant of type "pointer to **char**" when it appears as the initializer of a variable of pointer type.

   ```
   char *greeting = "Type <cr> to begin ";
   ```

8. The sum or difference of any expression shown for Cases 3 through 7 and an integer constant expression.

   ```
   static short s;
   auto short *sp = &s + 3, *msp = &s - 3;
   ```

In general, the initializer for a pointer type must evaluate to an integer cast to a pointer type or to an address plus (or minus) an integer constant. This limitation reflects the capabilities of most linkers.

The default initialization for static pointers is the null pointer. In the (rare) case that null pointers are not represented by an object whose bits are zero, Standard C specifies that the correct null pointer value must be used. Most older C compilers simply initialize static storage to zero bits.

References   address operator **&** 7.5.6; array types 5.4; conversions involving pointers 6.2.7; function types 5.8; integer constants 2.7; pointer declarator 4.5; pointer types 5.3; string constants 2.7; usual assignment conversions 6.3.2

4.6.4 Arrays

If I_j is an expression that is an allowable initializer for objects of type T, then

```
{ I0 , I1 , ..., In-1 }
```

is an allowable initializer for type "n-element array of T." C99 permits the I_j to be nonconstant expressions, but previous versions of C required them to be constant. The initializer I_j is used to initialize element j of the array (zero origin). Multidimensional arrays follow the same pattern, with initializers listed by row. (The last subscript varies most rapidly in C.)

Example

A singly dimensioned array is initialized by listing its elements:

```
int ary[4] = { 0, 1, 2, 3 };
```

A multiply dimensioned array is initialized by each subarray:

```
int ary[4][2][3] =
            { { { 0, 1, 2}, { 3, 4, 5} },
              { { 6, 7, 8}, { 9, 10, 11} },
              { {12, 13, 14}, {15, 16, 17} },
              { {18, 19, 20}, {21, 22, 23} } };
```

Arrays of structures (Section 4.6.6) may be initialized analogously:

```
struct {int a; float b;} a[3] = { {1, 2.5},
                                  {2, 3.9},
                                  {0, -4.0} };
```

Static and external arrays may always be initialized in this way. Standard C permits the initialization of automatic arrays, but that feature was not in the original definition of C. Array initialization has a number of special rules:

1. The number of initializers may be less than the number of array elements, in which case the remaining elements are initialized to their default initialization value (the

one used in static arrays). If the number of initializers is greater than the number of elements, it is an error.

Example

The declarations

```
float ary[5] = { 1, 2, 3 };
int mat[3][3] = { {1, 2}, {3} };
```

are the same as

```
int ary[5] = { 1.0, 2.0, 3.0, 0.0, 0.0 };
int mat[3][3] = { {1, 2, 0},
                  {3, 0, 0},
                  {0, 0, 0} };
```

2. The bounds of the array need not be specified (as in an incomplete type), in which case the bounds are derived from the length of the initializer. This is true for both static and automatic initializations.

Example

The declaration

```
int squares[] = { 0, 1, 4, 9 };
```

is the same as

```
int squares[4] = { 0, 1, 4, 9 };
```

3. String literals may be used to initialize variables of type "array of **char**." In this case, the first element of the array is initialized by the first character in the string, and so forth. The string's terminating null character, `'\0'`, is stored in the array if there is room or if the size of the array is unspecified. The string may optionally be enclosed in braces. It is not an error—but it might be confusing to a reader—if the string is too long for a character array of specified size. (It is an error in C++.)

An array whose element type is compatible with **wchar_t** can be initialized by a wide string literal in the same way.

Example

The declarations

```
char  x[5]   = "ABCDE";
char  str[]  = "ABCDE";
wchar_t q[5] = L"A";
```

are the same as

```
char  x[5]   = { 'A', 'B', 'C', 'D', 'E' }; /* No '\0'! */
char  str[6] = { 'A', 'B', 'C', 'D', 'E', '\0' };
wchar_t q[5] = { L'A', L'\0', L'\0', L'\0', L'\0' };
```

4. A list of strings can be used to initialize an array of character pointers.

Example

```
char *astr[] = { "John", "Bill", "Susan", "Mary" };
```

5. Variable length arrays may not be initialized.

References   array types 5.4; character constants 2.7; character types 5.1.3; pointer types 5.3; string constants 2.7; variable length arrays 5.4.5; wide strings 2.7.4

4.6.5 Enumerations

The form of initializers for variables of enumeration type is

declarator = *expression*

The initializing expression must have a type that would be permitted in a simple assignment to the initialized variable; the usual assignment conversions are applied. If the variable is static or external, the expression must be constant. If the variable is automatic or register, any expression is permitted.

Example

Good programming style suggests that the type of the initializing expression should be the same enumeration type as the variable being initialized. For example:

```
static enum E { a, b, c } x = a;
auto enum E y = x;
```

References   cast expressions 7.5.1; constant expressions 7.11; enumeration types 5.5; usual assignment conversions 6.3.2

4.6.6 Structures

If a structure type T has n named components of types $T_j, j=1,...,n$, and if I_j is an initializer that is allowable for an object of type T_j, then

$$\{ I_1 , I_2 , ..., I_n \}$$

is an allowable initializer for type T. Unnamed bit field components do not participate in initialization. The initializers I_j need not be constant in C99, but they must be constant in previous versions of C.

Example

```
struct S {int a; char b[5]; double c; };
struct S x = { 1, "abcd", 45.0 };
```

Static and external variables of structure types can be initialized by all C compilers. Automatic and register variables of structure types can be initialized in Standard C, and either of two forms may be used. First, a brace-enclosed list of constant expressions may be used, as for static variables. Second, an initialization of the form

declarator = *expression*

may be used, where *expression* has the same type as the variable being initialized. A few older C compilers are deficient in not allowing the initialization of structures containing bit fields.

As with array initializers, structure initializers have some special abbreviation rules. In particular, if there are fewer initializers than there are structure components, the remaining components are initialized to their default initial values. If there are too many initializers for the structure, it is an error.

Example

Given the structure declaration

```
struct S1 {int a;
           struct S2 {double b;
                      char c; } b;
           int c[4]; };
```

the initialization

```
struct S1 x = { 1, {4.5} };
```

is the same as

```
struct S1 x = { 1, { 4.5, '\0' }, { 0, 0, 0, 0 } };
```

References   bit fields 5.6.5; constant expressions 7.11; structure types 5.6

4.6.7 Unions

Standard C allows the initialization of union variables. (Traditional C does not.) The initializer for a static, external, automatic, or register union variable must be a brace-enclosed constant expression that would be allowable as an initializer for an object of the type of the first component of the union. The initializer for an automatic or register union may alternatively be any single expression of the same union type. In C99, a designator may be used to initialize a component other than the first one.

Example

These two initializer forms are shown next for the union variables **x** and **y**:

```
enum Greek { alpha, beta, gamma };
union U {
        struct { enum Greek tag; int Size; } I;
        struct { enum Greek tag; float Size; } F;
        };
static union U x = {{ alpha, 42 }};
auto union U y = x;
```

The only remaining C types are function types and **void**. Since variables of these types cannot be declared, the question of initialization is moot.

> **References**   designated initializers 4.6.9; static extent 4.2; union types 5.7

4.6.8 Eliding Braces

C permits braces to be dropped from initializer lists under certain circumstances, although it is usually clearer to retain them. The general rules are listed next.

1. If a variable of array or structure type is being initialized, the outermost pair of braces may *not* be dropped.
2. Otherwise, if an initializer list contains the correct number of elements for the object being initialized, the braces may be dropped.

Example

> The most common use of these rules is in dropping inner braces when initializing a multidimensional array:

```
int matrix[2][3] = { 1, 2, 3,    4, 5, 6 };
       /* same as: { {1, 2, 3}, {4, 5, 6} } */
```

Many C compilers treat initializer lists casually, permitting too many or too few braces. We advise keeping initializers simple and using braces to make their structure explicit.

4.6.9 Designated Initializers

C99 allows you to name the components of an aggregate (structure, union, or array) to be initialized within an initializer list. Designated initializers and positional (nondesignated) initializers may be intermixed in the same initializer list.

In an initializer list for an array, the designator takes the form [*e*], where the constant expression *e* specifies an array element by index. If the array has unspecified size, then any non-negative index is allowed, and the highest explicitly initialized index determines the final size of the array. If a positional initializer follows a designated initializer, then the positional initializer begins initializing components immediately following the designated element. It is possible in this fashion for later values in a list to overwrite earlier values.

Example

> Each of the following initializations is followed by a comment that gives the resulting initial values for all the elements.

```
int a1[5] = { [2]=100, [1]=3 };
    /* {0, 3, 100, 0, 0} */
int a2[5] = { [0]=10, [2]=-2, -1, -3 };
    /* {10, 0, -2, -1, -3} */
int a3[] = { 1, 2, 3, [2]=5, 6, 7};
    /* {1, 2, 5, 6, 7} ; a3 has length 5 */
```

In an initializer list for a structure, the designator takes the form `. c`, where *c* is the name of a component of the structure. If a positional initializer follows a designated initializer, then the positional initializer begins initializing components immediately following the designated component. It is possible in this fashion for later values in a list to overwrite earlier values.

Example

> Each of the following initializations is followed by a comment that gives the resulting initial values for all the components.

```
struct S {int a; float b; char c[4]; };
struct S s1 = { .c = "abc" };
    /* {0, 0.0, "abc"} */
struct S s2 = { 13, 3.3, "xxx", .b=4.5 };
    /* {13, 4.5, "xxx"} */
struct S s3 = { .c = {'a','b','c','\0'} };
    /* {0, 0.0, "abc"} */
```

In an initializer list for a union, the designator takes the form `. c`, where *c* is one of the components of the union. This allows a union to be initialized via any of its components, not just the first one.

Example

> Each of the following initializations is followed by a comment that gives the resulting initial values for all the components.

```
union U {int a; float b; char c[4]; };
union U u1 = { .c = "abc " };
    /* u1.c is "abc\0"; other components undefined */
union U u2 = { .a = 15 };
    /* u2.a is 15; other components undefined */
union U u3 = { .b = 3.14 };
    /* u3.b is 3.14; other components undefined */
```

Nested aggregates can be initialized with designators in the corresponding fashion. Designators may be concatenated to initialize more deeply nested elements.

Example

> Each of the following initializations is followed by a comment that gives the resulting initial values for all the components.

```
struct Point {int x; int y; int z; };
typedef struct Point PointVector[4];
PointVector pv1 = {
    [0].x = 1, [0].y = 2, [0].z = 3,
    [1] = {.x = 11, .y=12, .z=13},
    [3] = {.y=3} };
    /* {{1,2,3},{11,12,13},{0,0,0},{0,3,0}} */
```

```
typedef int Vector[3];
typedef int Matrix[3][3];
struct Trio {Vector v; Matrix m; };
struct Trio t = {
    .m={[0][0]=1, [1][1]=1, [2][2]=1},
    .v={[1]=42,43} };
/* {{0,42,43},{{1,0,0},{0,1,0},{0,0,1}}} */
```

4.7 IMPLICIT DECLARATIONS

Before C99, an external function used in a function call need not have been declared previously. If the compiler sees an identifier *id* followed by a left parenthesis and if *id* has not been previously declared, then a declaration is implicitly entered in the innermost enclosing scope of the form:

```
extern int id();
```

C99 implementations issue a diagnostic if *id* is not previously declared as a function, but they are then free to continue by making the implicit declaration. Some non-Standard implementations may declare the identifier at the top level rather than in the innermost scope.

Example

Allowing functions to be declared by default is poor programming style and may lead to errors, particularly those concerning incorrect return types. If a pointer-returning function, such as **malloc** (Section 16.1), is allowed to be implicitly declared as

```
extern int malloc();
```

rather than the correct

```
extern char *malloc();  /* returns (void *) in Standard C */
```

then calls to **malloc** will probably not work if the types **int** and **char** * are represented differently. Suppose type **int** occupies two bytes and pointers occupy four bytes. When the compiler sees

```
int *p;
...
p = (int *) malloc(sizeof(int));
```

it generates code to extend what it thought was a two-byte value returned by **malloc** to the four bytes required by the pointer. The effect is that only the lower half of the address returned by **malloc** is assigned to **p**, and the program begins to fail when enough storage has been allocated to cause **malloc** to return addresses larger than **0xFFFF**.

4.8 EXTERNAL NAMES

An important issue with external names is ensuring consistency among the declarations of the same external name in several files. For instance, what if two declarations of the same external variable specified different initializations? For this and other reasons, it is useful to distinguish a single *defining declaration* of an external name within a group of files. The other declarations of the same name are then considered *referencing declarations*—that is, they reference the defining declaration.

It is a well-known deficiency in C that defining and referencing occurrences of external variable declarations are difficult to distinguish. In general, compilers use one of four models to determine when a top-level declaration is a defining occurrence.

4.8.1 The Initializer Model

The presence of an initializer on a top-level declaration indicates a defining occurrence; others are referencing occurrences. There must be a single defining occurrence among all the files in the C program. This is the model adopted by Standard C, with one additional rule discussed in the next section.

4.8.2 The Omitted Storage Class Model

In this scheme, the storage class **extern** must be explicitly included on all referencing declarations, and the storage class must be omitted from the single defining declaration for each external variable. The defining declaration can include an initializer, but it is not required to do so. It is invalid to have both an initializer and the storage class **extern** in a declaration.

In Standard C, a top-level declaration without a storage class or initializer is considered to be a *tentative definition*. That is, it is treated as a referencing declaration, but if no other declaration of the same variable with an initializer appears in the file, then the tentative definition is considered a real definition.

In C++ **extern** is ignored when an initializer is present.

4.8.3 The Common Model

This scheme is called the "common model" because it is related to the way multiple references to a **COMMON** block are merged into a single defining occurrence in implementations of the FORTRAN programming language. Both defining and referencing external declarations have storage class **extern**, whether explicitly or by default. Among all the declarations for each external name in all the object files linked together to make the program, only one may have an initializer. At link time, all external declarations for the same identifier (in all C object files) are combined and a single defining occurrence is conjured, not necessarily associated with any particular file. If any declaration specified an initializer, that initializer is used to initialize the data object. (If several declarations did, the results are unpredictable.)

This solution is the most painless for the programmer and the most demanding on system software.

4.8.4 Mixed Common Model

This model is a cross between the "omitted storage class" model and the "common" model. It is used in many versions of UNIX.

1. If **extern** is omitted and an initializer is present, a definition for the symbol is emitted. Having two or more such definitions among all the files comprising a program results in an error at link time or before.

2. If **extern** is omitted and there is no initializer, a FORTRAN **COMMON**-style definition is emitted. Any number of these definitions of the same identifier may coexist.

3. If **extern** is present, the declaration is taken to be a reference to a name defined elsewhere. It is invalid for such a declaration to have an initializer.

If no explicit initializer is provided for the external variable, the variable is initialized as if the initializer had been the integer constant 0.

4.8.5 Summary and Recommendations

Table 4–7 shows the interpretation of a top-level declaration according to the model for external references in use. To remain compatible with most compilers, we recommend

Table 4–7   Interpretation of top-level declarations

Top-level declaration	Initializer	Model			
		Omitted storage class (and C++)	Common	Mixed common	Standard C
`int x;`	Reference	Definition	Definition or reference	Definition or reference	Reference[a]
`int x = 0;`	Definition	Definition	Definition	Definition	Definition
`extern int x;`	Reference	Reference	Definition or reference	Reference	Reference
`extern int x = 0;`	Definition	(Invalid)	Definition	(Invalid)	Definition

[a] If no subsequent defining occurrence appears in the file, this becomes a defining occurrence.

following these rules:

1. Have a single definition point (source file) for each external variable; in the defining declaration, omit the **extern** storage class and include an explicit initializer:

   ```
   int errcnt = 0;
   ```

2. In each source file or header file referencing an external variable defined elsewhere, use the storage class **extern** and do not include an initializer:

   ```
   extern int errcnt;
   ```

Independent of the defining/referencing distinction, an external name should always be declared with the same type in all files making up a program. The C compiler cannot verify that declarations in different files are consistent in this fashion, and the punishment for inconsistency is erroneous behavior at run time. The **lint** program, usually supplied with the C compiler in UNIX systems, can check multiple files for consistent declarations, as can several commercial products for UNIX and Windows.

4.8.6 Unreferenced External Declarations

Although not required by the C language, it is customary to ignore declarations of external variables or functions that are never referenced. For example, if the declaration "**extern double fft();**" appears in a program, but the function **fft** is never used, then no external reference to the name **fft** is passed to the linker. Therefore, the function **fft** will not be loaded with the program, where it would take up space to no purpose.

4.9 C++ COMPATIBILITY

4.9.1 Scopes

In C++, **struct** and **union** definitions are scopes. That is, type declarations occurring within those definitions are not visible outside, whereas they are in Standard C (Section 5.6.3). To remain compatible, simply move any type declarations out of the structure. (Some C++ implementations may allow this as an anachronism, when no ambiguity can result.)

Example

In the following code, a structure **t** is defined within a structure **s**, but is referenced outside that structure. This is invalid in C++.

```
struct s {
    struct t {int a; int b;} f1; /* define t here */
} x1;
struct t x2; /* use t here; OK in C, not in C++ */
```

References   scope 4.2.1; structure components 5.6.3

4.9.2 Tag and Typedef Names

Structure and union tag names should not be used as **typedef** names except for the same tagged type. In C++, tag names are implicitly declared as **typedef** names as well as tags. (However, they can be hidden by a subsequent variable or function declaration of the same name in the same scope.) This can result in diagnostics, or—in rare cases—simply different behavior.

Example

Here are some examples that result in diagnostics in C or C++.

```
typedef struct n1 {…} n1;          /* OK in both C and C++ */
struct n2 {…}; typedef double n2; /* OK in C, not in C++ */
struct n3 {…}; n3 x; /* OK in C++, not in C */
```

However, the tag name can be used as a variable or function name without confusion. The following sequence of declarations is acceptable to both C and C++, although it would probably be better to avoid the inevitable confusion:

```
struct n4 {…};
int n4;
struct n4 x;
```

A declaration of a **struct** tag in an inner scope in C++ can hide a variable declaration from an outer scope. This can cause a C program's meaning to change without warning. In the following code, the expression **sizeof(ary)** refers to the size of the array in C, but it refers to the size of the **struct** type in C++.

```
int ary[10];
…
void f(int x)
{
    struct ary { … };/* In C++, this hides previous ary */
    …
    x = sizeof(ary);  /* Different meanings in C and C++! */
}
```

See Section 5.13.2 concerning the compatibility of **typedef** redefinitions in C++.

References   name spaces 4.2.4; redefining **typedef** names 5.10.2

4.9.3 Storage Class Specifiers on Types

Do not place storage class specifiers in type declarations. They are ignored in traditional C, but are invalid in C++ and Standard C.

Example

```
static struct s {int a; int b;}   ;   /* invalid
```

References   storage classes on types 4.4.2

4.9.4 const Type Qualifier

A top-level declaration that has the type qualifier **const** but no explicit storage class is considered to be **static** in C++ but **extern** in C. To remain compatible, examine top-level **const** declarations and provide an explicit storage class.

In C++, string constants are implicitly **const**; they are not in C.

Example

The following declaration will have different meanings in C and C++:

```
const int c1 = 10;
```

However, the following declarations will have the same meaning in C and C++:

```
static const int c2 = 11;
extern const int c3 = 12;
```

All **const** declarations—except those referencing externally-defined constants—must have initializers in C++.

References   **const** type qualifier 4.4.4

4.9.5 Initializers

In C++, when a string literal is used to initialize a fixed-size array of characters (or a wide string literal for an array of **wchar_t**), there must be enough room in the array for the entire string, including the terminating null character.

Example

```
char str[5] = "abcde"; /* valid in C, not in C++ */
char str[6] = "abcde"; /* valid in both C and C++ */
```

4.9.6 Implicit Declarations

Implicit declarations of functions (Section 4.7) are not allowed in C++ or C99. All functions must be declared before they are used.

References   implicit declarations 4.7

4.9.7 Defining and Referencing Declarations

In C++, there are no tentative definitions of top-level variables. What would be considered a tentative definition in C is considered a real definition in C++. That is, the sequence of declarations

```
int i;
...
int i;
```

would be valid in Standard C, but would cause a duplicate-definition error in C++.

Example

This rule applies to static variables also, which means that it is not possible to create mutually recursive, statically initialized variables.

```
struct cell {int val; struct cell *next;};
static struct cell a; /* tentative declaration */
static struct cell b = {0, &a};
static struct cell a = {1, &b);
```

This is not a problem for global variables: the first **static** could be replaced by **extern** and the second and third **static** could be removed. (You can declare mutually recursive, statically initialized variables in C++, but not in a way that is compatible with C.)

References   structure type reference 5.6.1; tentative declaration 4.8.2

4.9.8 Function Linkage

When calling a C function from C++, the function must be declared to have "C" linkage. This is discussed in more detail in Chapter 10.

Example

If in a C++ program you wanted to call a function **f** compiled by a C implementation, you would write the (C++) declaration as:

```
/* This is a C++ program. */
extern "C" int f(void);/* f is a C, not C++, function */
```

4.9.9 Functions With No Arguments

In C++, a function declared with an empty parameter list is assumed to take no arguments, whereas in C such a function is understood to have unspecified arguments. That is, the C++ declaration **int f()** is equivalent to the C declaration **int f(void)**.

4.10 EERCISES

1. The definition of a static function **P** is shown next. What will be the value of **P(6)** if **P** has never been called before? What will **P(6)** be the second time it is called?

    ```
    static int P(int x)
    {
        int i = 0;
        i = i+1;
        return i*x;
    }
    ```

2. The following program fragment shows a block containing various declarations of the name **f**. Do any of the declarations conflict? If so, cross out declarations until the program is valid, keeping as many different declarations of **f** as possible.

    ```
    {
        extern double f();
        int f;
        typedef int f;
        struct f {int f,g;};
        union f {int x,y;};
        enum {f,b,s};
        f: ...
    }
    ```

3. The following program fragment declares three variables named **i** with types **int**, **long**, and **float**. On which lines is each of the variables declared and used?

```
 1 int i;
 2 void f(i)
 3     long i;
 4 {
 5     long l = i;
 6     {
 7         float i;
 8         i = 3.4;
 9     }
10     l = i+2;
11 }
12 int *p = &i;
```

4. Write C declarations that express the following English statements. Use prototypes for function declarations.

   (a) **P** is an external function that has no parameters and returns no result.

   (b) **i** is a local integer variable that will be heavily used and should be optimized for speed.

   (c) **LT** is a synonym for type "pointer to character."

   (d) **Q** is an external function with two arguments and no result. The first, **i**, is an integer and the second, **cp**, is a string. The string will not be modified.

   (e) **R** is an external function whose only argument, **p**, is a pointer to a function that takes a single 32-bit integer argument, **i**, and returns a pointer to a value of type **double**. **R** returns an integer value. Assume type **long** is 32 bits wide.

   (f) **STR** is a static, uninitialized character string that should be modifiable and hold up to 10 characters, not including the terminating null character.

   (g) **STR2** is a character string initialized to the string literal that is the value of the macro **INIT_STR2**. Once initialized, the string will not be modified.

   (h) **IP** is a pointer to an integer, initialized with the address of the variable **i**.

5. The matrix **m** is declared as **int m[3][3];** the first subscript specifies the row number and the second subscript specifies the column number. Write an initializer f or **m** that places ones in the first column, twos in the second column, and threes in the third column.

6. Given the declarations

```
const int * cip;
int * const cpi;
int i;
int * ip;
```

   which of the following assignments, if any, are permitted?

   (a) `cip = ip;`

   (b) `cpi = ip;`

   (c) `*cip = i;`

   (d) `*cpi = i;`

7. Using C99 designated initializers, write the declaration and initializer for a 3x3 matrix of **int** elements named **identity**. The initializer should assign the value 1 to elements **identity[1][1]**, **identity[2][2]**, and **identity[3][3]**, and should assign zero to all other elements.

8. Write the C declarations for two structures with structure tags **left** and **right**. The **left** structure should contain a **double** field named **data** and a pointer named **link** to a **right** structure, in that order. The **right** structure should contain an **int** field named **data** and a pointer named **link** to a **left** structure, in that order.

9. You have just purchased a C99 compiler and you are recompiling your existing software using it. The software compiled without errors on your older C89 compiler, but C99 is reporting some problems. For each of the following reported errors, explain what might be causing them:

    (a)   The C99 compiler rejects a function call, reporting that the function is not defined.

    (b)   The C99 compiler rejects the local declaration **register i;** .

10. In your C program, suppose that **fm** is defined as a function-like macro and **om** is defined as an object-like macro (Section 3.3). If your program also contains the local variable declarations

    ```
    int fm;
    int om;
    ```

    will there be any conflict with between these declarations and the macros? Discuss what will happen when the program is compiled.

5

Types

A *type* is a set of *values* and a set of *operations* on those values. For example, the values of an integer type consist of integers in some specified range, and the operations on those values consist of addition, subtraction, inequality tests, and so forth. The values of a floating-point type include numbers represented differently from integers, and a set of different operations: floating-point addition, subtraction, inequality tests, and so forth.

We say a variable or expression "has type *T*" when its values are constrained to the domain of *T*. The types of variables are established by the variable's declaration; the types of expressions are given by the definitions of the expression operators. The C language provides a large number of built-in types, including integers of several kinds, floating-point numbers, pointers, enumerations, arrays, structures, unions, and functions.

It is useful to organize C's types into the categories shown in Table 5–1. The *integral types* include all forms of integers, characters, and enumerations. The *arithmetic types* include the integral and floating-point types. The *scalar types* include the arithmetic and pointer types. The *function types* are the types "function returning...." *Aggregate types* include arrays and structures. *Union types* are created with the **union** specifier. The **void** type has no values and no operations.

The **_Bool**, **_Complex**, and **_Imaginary** types are new in C99. The boolean type (**_Bool**) is an unsigned integer type, whereas the six complex types are floating-point types. C99 further classifies arithmetic types into *domains*: The six complex types are in the complex domain; all other arithmetic types are in the real domain and are *real types*.

All of C's types are discussed in this chapter. For each type, we indicate how objects of the type are declared, the range of values of the type, any restrictions on the size or representation of the type, and what operations are defined on values of the type.

References   array types 5.4; boolean type 5.1.5; character types 5.1.3; complex types 5.2.1; declarations 4.1; enumerated types 5.5; floating-point types 5.2; function types 5.8; integer types 5.1; pointer types 5.3; structure types 5.6; union types 5.7; **void** type 5.9

Table 5–1 C types and categories

C types	Type categories		
short, int, long, long long (signed and unsigned)	Integral types	Arithmetic types[a]	Scalar types
char (signed and unsigned)			
_Bool [b]			
enum {...}			
float, double, long double	Floating-point types		
float _Complex, double _Complex, long double _Complex, float _Imaginary, double _Imaginary, long double _Imaginary [b]			
T *	Pointer types		
T [...]	Array types		Aggregate types
struct {...}	Structure types		
union {...}	Union types		
T (...)	Function types		
void	Void type		

[a] All arithmetic types except the complex types are also categorized as real types.
[b] New in C99. **_Imaginary** is optional.

5.1 INTEGER TYPES

C provides more integer types and operators than do most programming languages. The variety reflects the different word lengths and kinds of arithmetic operators found on most computers, thus allowing a close correspondence between C programs and the underlying hardware. Integer types in C are used to represent:

1. signed or unsigned integer values, for which the usual arithmetic and relational operations are provided
2. bit vectors, with the operations "not," "and," "or," "exclusive or," and left and right shifts
3. boolean values, for which zero is considered "false" and all nonzero values are considered "true," with the integer 1 being the canonical "true" value
4. characters, which are represented by their integer encoding on the computer

Enumeration types are *integral*, or integerlike, types. They are considered in Section 5.5.

Standard C requires implementations to use a binary encoding of integers; this is a recognition that many low-level C operations are not describable in any portable fashion on computers with nonbinary representations.

It is convenient to divide the integer types into four classes: signed types, unsigned types, the boolean type, and characters. Each of these classes has a set of type specifiers that can be used to declare objects of the type.

> *integer-type-specifier :*
> *signed-type-specifier*
> *unsigned-type-specifier*
> *character-type-specifier*
> *bool-type-specifier*   *(C99)*

5.1.1 Signed Integer Types

C provides the programmer with four standard signed integer types denoted by the type specifiers **short**, **int**, **long**, and **long long** in nondecreasing order of size. Type **signed char** is a fifth signed integer type, but is discussed in Section 5.1.3. C99 introduced the **long long** type, as well as extended integer types (Section 5.1.4).

Each type can be named in several equivalent ways; in the following syntax, the equivalent names are shown for each of the four types.

> *signed-type-specifier* :
> **short** *or* **short int** *or* **signed short** *or* **signed short int**
> **int** *or* **signed int** *or* **signed**
> **long** *or* **long int** *or* **signed long** *or* **signed long int**
> **long long** *or* **long long int** *or* **signed long long** *or*
>   **signed long long int**

The keyword **signed** was new in C89 and can be omitted for compatibility with older C implementations. The only time the presence of **signed** might affect the meaning of a program is when it is used in conjunction with type **char** and with bit fields in structures; in that case a distinction can be made between a signed integer and a "plain integer" (i.e., one written without **signed**).

Standard C specifies the minimum precision for most integer types. Type **char** must be at least 8 bits wide, type **short** at least 16 bits wide, type **long** at least 32 bits wide, and type **long long** at least 64 bits wide. (That is, C99 requires 64-bit integer types and the full set of 64-bit arithmetic operations.) The actual ranges of the integer types are recorded in **limits.h**.

The precise range of values representable by a signed integer type depends not only on the number of bits used in the representation, but also on the encoding technique. By far the most common binary encoding technique for integers is called *twos-complement notation*, in which a signed integer represented with n bits will have a range from -2^{n-1} through $2^{n-1}-1$ encoded in the following fashion:

1. The high-order (leftmost) bit of the word is the sign bit. If the sign bit is 1, the number is negative; otherwise, the number is positive.
2. Positive numbers follow the normal binary sequence:

   $0 = 000...0000_2$
   $1 = 000...0001_2$

$2 = 000\ldots0010_2$
$3 = 000\ldots0011_2$
$4 = 000\ldots0100_2$
$\ldots$

In an n-bit word, omitting the sign bit, there are $n-1$ bits for the positive integers, which can represent the integers 0 through $2^{n-1}-1$.

3. To negate an integer, complement all the bits in the word and then add 1 to the result. Thus, to form the integer -1, start with 1 ($00\ldots0001_2$), complement the bits ($11\ldots1110_2$), and add 1 ($11\ldots1111_2 = -1$).

4. The maximum negative value, $10\ldots0000_2$ or -2^{n-1}, has no positive equivalent; negating this value produces the same value.

Other binary integer encoding techniques are *ones-complement notation*, in which negation simply complements all the bits of the word, and *sign magnitude notation*, in which negation involves simply complementing the sign bit. These alternatives have a range from $-(2^{n-1}-1)$ through $2^{n-1}-1$; they have one less negative value and two representations for zero (positive and negative). All three notations represent positive integers identically. All are acceptable in Standard C.

Standard C requires that implementations document the ranges of the integer types in the header file **limits.h**; it also specifies the maximum representable range a C programmer can assume for each integer type in all ISO-conforming implementations. The symbols that must be defined in **limits.h** are shown in Table 5–2. Implementations can substitute their own values, but they must not be less in absolute magnitude than the values shown, and they must have the same sign. Therefore, an ISO-conforming implementation cannot represent type **int** in only eight bits, nor can a strictly conforming C program depend on, say, the value $-32,768$ being representable in type **short**. (This is to accommodate computers that use a ones-complement representation of binary integers.) Programmers using non-ISO implementations can create a **limits.h** file for their implementation. The ranges documented here are not necessarily the same as the types' sizes due to the possible presence of padding bits (see Section 6.1.6).

Amendment 1 to C89 adds the symbols **WCHAR_MAX** and **WCHAR_MIN** for the maximum and minimum values represented in type **wchar_t**. However, these symbols are defined in the **wchar.h** header file, not **limits.h**. C99 adds the new header file **stdint.h**, which contains limits for additional integer types.

Example

Here are some examples of typical declarations of signed integers:

```
short i, j;
long int l;
static signed int k;
```

To keep programs as portable as possible, it is best not to depend on type **int** being able to represent integers outside the range $-32,767$ to $32,767$. Use type **long** if this range is insufficient. It is usually good style to define special integer types with **typedef** based on the needs of each particular program. For example:

Table 5–2   Values defined in `limits.h`

Name	Minimum value	Meaning
`CHAR_BIT`	8	width of **char** type, in bits
`SCHAR_MIN`	$-(2^7-1)$; -127	minimum value of **signed char**
`SCHAR_MAX`	2^7-1; 127	maximum value of **signed char**
`UCHAR_MAX`	2^8-1; 255[a]	maximum value of **unsigned char**
`SHRT_MIN`	$-(2^{15}-1)$; $-32{,}767$	minimum value of **short int**
`SHRT_MAX`	$2^{15}-1$; 32,767	maximum value of **short int**
`USHRT_MAX`	$2^{16}-1$; 65,535	maximum value of **unsigned short**
`INT_MIN`	$-(2^{15}-1)$; $-32{,}767$	minimum value of **int**
`INT_MAX`	$2^{15}-1$; 32,767	maximum value of **int**
`UINT_MAX`	$2^{16}-1$; 65,535	maximum value of **unsigned int**
`LONG_MIN`	$-(2^{31}-1)$; $-2{,}147{,}483{,}647$	minimum value of **long int**
`LONG_MAX`	$2^{31}-1$; 2,147,483,647	maximum value of **long int**
`ULONG_MAX`	$2^{32}-1$; 4,294,967,295	maximum value of **unsigned long**
`LLONG_MIN`	$-(2^{63}-1)$; $-9{,}223{,}372{,}036{,}854{,}775{,}807$	minimum value of **long long int**
`LLONG_MAX`	$2^{63}-1$; $+9{,}223{,}372{,}036{,}854{,}775{,}807$	maximum value of **long long int**
`ULLONG_MAX`	$2^{64}-1$; 18,446,744,073,709,551,615	maximum value of **unsigned long long**
`CHAR_MIN`	`SCHAR_MIN` or 0[b]	minimum value of **char**
`CHAR_MAX`	`SCHAR_MAX` or `UCHAR_MAX`[c]	maximum value of **char**
`MB_LEN_MAX`	1	maximum number of bytes in a multibyte character in any supported locale

[a] `UCHAR_MAX` must be $2^{\texttt{CHAR\_BIT}}-1$.

[b] If type **char** is signed by default, then `SCHAR_MIN`, else 0.

[c] If type **char** is signed by default, then `SCHAR_MAX`, else `UCHAR_MAX`.

```
/* invdef.h Inventory definitions for the XXX computer. */
typedef short part_number;
typedef int   order_quantity;
typedef long  purchase_order;
```

The best solution in C99 is to use one of the extended integer type names, specifying the precision needed.

```
/* invdef.h Inventory definitions for the XXX computer. */
#include <stdint.h>
typedef uint_least64_t part_number;      // at least 64 bits
typedef int_fast32_t   order_quantity;   // fast and 32 bits
typedef int32_t        purchase_order;   // exactly 32 bits
```

Example

In C, any integer type may be used to represent boolean values. The value zero represents "false" and all nonzero values represent "true." Boolean expressions evaluate to 0 if false and

1 if true. For example, `i = (a<b)` assigns to the integer variable **i** the value 1 if **a** is less than **b**, and 0 if **a** is not less than **b**. Likewise, the statement

```
if (i) statement₁; /* Do this if i is nonzero */
else statement₂;   /* Do this if i is zero */
```

results in ***statement₁*** being executed if **i** is nonzero (true), and ***statement₂*** if **i** is zero.

C99 introduces a true boolean type, **_Bool**. It also introduces a header file, **stdbool.h**, which defines the more convenient type name **bool** and the boolean values **true** and **false**. These names are consistent with the boolean type in C++, but different from the macro names traditionally used in C, **FALSE** and **TRUE**:

```
#include <stdbool.h>;
bool b;
…
b = (x < y) && (y < z);
if (b) …
```

Programmers without access to C99 can easily define **bool**, **true**, and **false**.

References   bit fields in structures 5.6.5; **_Bool** type 5.1.4; declarations 4.1; extended integer types 5.1.4; integer constants 2.7.1; **signed** type specifier 5.1.1; **stdbool.h** 11.3; **stdint.h** Ch. 21; type conversions Ch. 6; **typedef** 5.10

5.1.2 Unsigned Integer Types

For each of the signed integer types, there is a corresponding unsigned type that occupies the same amount of storage but has a different integer encoding. The unsigned type is specified by preceding the corresponding signed type specifier with the keyword **unsigned** (replacing the keyword **signed** if it were present).

> *unsigned-type-specifier* :
>   **unsigned short int**$_{opt}$
>   **unsigned int**$_{opt}$
>   **unsigned long int**$_{opt}$
>   **unsigned long long int**$_{opt}$ *(C99)*

In each case, the keyword **int** is optional but recommended. Choosing from among the unsigned types involves the same considerations already discussed for the signed integer types. C99 introduced the type **unsigned long long int** and the **_Bool** type, which is considered unsigned but is discussed separately.

All unsigned types use straight binary notation regardless of whether the signed types use twos-complement, ones-complement, or sign magnitude notation; the sign bit is treated as an ordinary data bit. Therefore, an *n*-bit word can represent the integers 0 through 2^n-1. Most computers are easily able to interpret the value in a word using either signed or unsigned notation. For example, when the twos-complement notation is used, the bit pattern $11\ldots1111_2$ (*n* bits long) can represent either -1 (using the signed notation) or 2^n-1 (using the unsigned notation). The integers from 0 through $2^{n-1}-1$ are represented identically in both signed and unsigned notations. The particular ranges of the unsigned types in a Standard C implementation are documented in the header file **limits.h**.

Whether an integer is signed or unsigned affects the operations performed on it. All arithmetic operations on unsigned integers behave according to the rules of modular (congruence) arithmetic modulo 2^n. So, for example, adding 1 to the largest value of an unsigned type is guaranteed to produce 0. The behavior of overflow is well defined.

Expressions that mix signed and unsigned integers are forced to use unsigned operations. Section 6.3.4 discusses the conversions performed, and Chapter 7 discusses the effect of each operator when its arguments are unsigned.

Example

> These conversions can be surprising. For example, because unsigned integers are always non-negative, you would expect that the following test would always be true:
>
> ```
> unsigned int u;
> …
> if (u > -1) …
> ```
>
> However, it is always false! The (signed) –1 is converted to an unsigned integer before the comparison, yielding the largest unsigned integer, and the value of **u** cannot be greater than that integer.

The original definition of C provided only a single unsigned type, **unsigned**. Most non-Standard C implementations now provide the full range of unsigned types.

References   **_Bool** type 5.1.5; integer conversions 6.2.3; constants 2.7; **limits.h** 5.1.1; signed types 5.1.1

5.1.3 Character Types

The character type in C is an integral type—that is, values of the type are integers and can be used in integer expressions:

> *character-type-specifier* :
>   **char**
>   **signed char**
>   **unsigned char**

There are three varieties of character types: signed, unsigned, and plain. Each occupies the same amount of storage, but may represent different values. The signed and unsigned representations used are the same as used for the signed and unsigned integer types. The plain character type corresponds to the absence of both **signed** and **unsigned** in the type specifier. The **signed** keyword is new in Standard C, so in C implementations not recognizing the keyword, there are only two varieties of character types: unsigned and plain. An array of characters is C's notion of a "string."

Example

> Here are some typical declarations involving characters.

```
static char greeting[7];          /* a 7-character string */
char *prompt; /* a pointer to a character */
char padding_character = '\0'; /* a single character */
```

The representation of the character types depends on the nature of the character and string processing facilities on the target computer. The character type has some special characteristics that set it apart from the normal signed and unsigned types. For example, the plain **char** type may be signed, unsigned, or a mixture of both. For reasons of efficiency, C compilers are free to treat type **char** in either of two ways:

1. Type **char** may be a signed integral type equivalent to **signed char**.

2. Type **char** may be an unsigned integral type equivalent to **unsigned char**.

In some pre-Standard implementations, type **char** was a "pseudo-unsigned" integral type—that is, it could contain only non-negative values, but it was treated as if it were a signed type when performing the usual unary conversions.

Example

If a true unsigned character type is needed, the type **unsigned char** can be specified. If a true signed type is needed, the type **signed char** can be specified. If type **char** uses an 8-bit, twos-complement representation, and given the declarations

```
unsigned char uc = -1;
signed char sc = -1;
char c = -1;
int i = uc, j = sc, k = c;
```

then **i** must have the value 255 and **j** must have the value –1 in all Standard C implementations. However, it is implementation-defined whether **k** has the value 255 or –1. If a C implementation does not recognize the keyword **signed** or does not permit **unsigned char**, you are stuck with the ambiguous plain characters.

The signedness of characters is an important issue because the standard I/O library routines, which normally return characters from files, return a negative value when the end of the file is reached. (The negative value, often –1, is specified by the macro **EOF** in the standard header files.) The programmer should always treat these functions as returning values of type **int** since type **char** may be unsigned.

Example

The following program is intended to copy characters from the standard input stream to the standard output stream until an end-of-file indication is returned from **getchar**. The first three definitions are typically supplied in the standard header file **stdio.h**:

```
extern int getchar(void);
extern void putchar(int);
#define EOF (-1) /* Could be any negative value */
```

```
void copy_characters(void)
{
    char ch; /* Incorrect! */
    while ((ch = getchar()) != EOF)
        putchar(ch);
}
```

However, this function does not work when **char** is unsigned. To see this, assume the **char** type is represented in 8 bits and the **int** type in 16 bits, and that twos-complement arithmetic is used. Then when **getchar** returns –1, the assignment **ch = getchar()** assigns the value 255 (the low-order 8 bits of –1) to **ch**. The loop test is then **255!=-1**. If type **char** is unsigned, the usual conversions will cause –1 to be converted to an unsigned integer, yielding the (unsigned) comparison **255!=65535**, which evaluates to "true." Thus, the loop never terminates. Changing the declaration of **ch** to "**int ch;**" makes everything work fine.

Example

To improve readability, you can define a "pseudo-character" type to use in these cases. For example, the following rewriting of **copy_characters** uses a new type, **character**, for characters that are represented with type **int**:

```
typedef int character;
...
void copy_characters(void)
{
    character ch;
    while ((ch = getchar()) != EOF)
        putchar(ch);
}
```

A second area of vagueness about characters is their size. In the prior example, we assumed they occupied 8 bits, and this assumption is almost always valid, although it is still unclear whether their values range from 0 to 255 or from –127 (or –128) to 127. However, a few computers may use 9 or even 32 bits. Programmers should be cautious. Standard C requires that implementations document the range of their character types in the header file **limits.h**.

References   bit fields 5.6.5; character constants 2.7.3; character set 2.1; **EOF** 15.1; **getchar** 15.6; integer types 5.1; integer conversions 6.2.3; **limits.h** 5.1.1

5.1.4 Extended Integer Types

In C99, implementations may have additional "extended" signed integer types in addition to the "standard" integer types. Each extended signed integer type must have a corresponding unsigned type. Keywords chosen for these types must be spelled beginning with two underscores or with an underscore and an uppercase letter. (Such identifiers are reserved for "any use" in Standard C.) These extended types are considered integer types, and all statements that apply to the standard integer types also apply to these extended integer types. Access to the extended integer types can be through the C99 header files **stdint.h** and **inttypes.h** described in Chapter 21.

The standard integer conversions apply to extended types. The rules are specified in the discussion of conversion rank in Chapter 6.

References   conversion rank 6.3.3; signed integer types 5.1.1

5.1.5 Boolean Type

C99 introduced the unsigned integer type **_Bool**, which can hold only the values 0 or 1 ("false" and "true," respectively). Other integer types can be used in boolean contexts (e.g., as the test in a conditional expression), but the use of **_Bool** may be clearer if the C implementation conforms to C99. When converting any scalar value to type **_Bool**, all nonzero values are converted to 1, while zero values are converted to 0.

The header file **stdbool.h** defines the macro **bool** to be a synonym for **_Bool** and defines **false** and **true** to be 0 and 1, respectively. The name **bool** is not a keyword to protect older C programs, which may have a user-defined type named **bool**. Conversions involving **_Bool** are described with the other integer conversions and promotions.

References   integer conversions 6.2.3; integer promotions 6.3.3; **stdbool.h** 11.3

5.2 FLOATING-POINT TYPES

C's floating-point numbers have traditionally come in two sizes: single and double precision, or **float** and **double**: Standard C added **long double**, and C99 adds three complex floating-point types (Section 5.2.1). The noncomplex floating-point types are also called the real floating-point types.

> *floating-point-type-specifier* :
>   **float**
>   **double**
>   **long double**   *(C89)*
>   *complex-type-specifier*   *(C99)*

The type specifier **long float** was permitted in older implementations as a synonym for **double**, but it was never popular and was eliminated in Standard C.

Example

Here are some typical declarations of objects of floating-point types:

```
double d;
static double pi;
float coefficients[10];
long double epsilon;
```

The use of **float**, **double**, and **long double** is analogous to the use of **short**, **int**, and **long**. Prior to Standard C, implementations were required to convert all values of type **float** to type **double** before any operations were performed (see Section 6.3.4), so using type **float** was not necessarily more efficient than using type **double**. In Standard C, operations can now be performed using type **float**, and there is a full set of library functions in C99 to support type **float**.

C does not dictate the sizes to be used for the floating-point types or even that they be different. The programmer can assume that the values representable in type **float** are a subset of those in type **double**, which in turn are a subset of those in type **long double**. Some C programs have depended on the assumption that **double** can accurately represent all values of type **long**—that is, converting an object of type **long** to type **double** and then back to type **long** results in exactly the original **long** value. Although this is often true, it cannot be depended on.

Standard C requires that the characteristics of the real floating-point types be documented in the header file **float.h**. Table 5–3 lists the symbols that must be defined. Symbols whose names begin with **FLT** document type **float**, names beginning with **DBL** refer to type **double**, and names beginning with **LDBL** refer to type **long double**. Also shown are the permitted magnitudes for each symbol—that is, the minimum requirements for range and precision of the floating-point types.

Most of the arithmetic and logical operations may be applied to floating-point operands. These include arithmetic and logical negation; addition, subtraction, multiplication, and division; relational and equality tests; logical AND and OR; assignment; and conversions to and from all the arithmetic types.

A real, floating-point number x—one with sign-magnitude representations and no "hidden" bits—can be written as

$$x = s \times b^e \times \sum_{k=1}^{p} f_k \times b^{-k}, e_{\min} \le e \le e_{\max}$$

where

s	is the sign (± 1)
b	is the base or radix of the representation (typically 2, 8, 10, or 16)
e	is the exponent value between some e_{min} and e_{max}
p	is the number of base-b digits in the significand
f_k	are the significand digits, $0 \le f_k < b$

A *normalized* floating-point number has $f_1 > 0$ if x is not 0. A *subnormal number* is one that is nonzero, with $e = e_{min}$ and $f_1 = 0$. An *un-normalized* number is one that is nonzero, with $e > e_{min}$ and $f_1 = 0$. (A subnormal number is too small to be normalized; an un-normalized number could be normalized, but for some reason is not.)

Floating-point types can include special values that are not floating-point numbers: *infinity* and *NaN* (Not-a-Number). A *quiet NaN* propagates through arithmetic expressions without causing an exception; the result of an expression containing a NaN is a NaN. A *signaling NaN* causes an exception when it is encountered. Infinity and NaN can be signed, and there may be different varieties of NaN. C99 extends the standard library to

Table 5–3 Values defined in **float.h**

Name	Minimum	Meaning
FLT_RADIX[a]	2	the value of the radix, b
FLT_ROUNDS[a]	*none*	rounding mode: -1: indeterminable; 0: toward 0; 1: to nearest; 2: toward $+$ infinity; 3: toward $-$ infinity[b]
FLT_EVAL_METHOD[c]	*none*	-1: indeterminable; 0: just to the range and precision of the type; 1: **float** and **double** use **double**; **long double** uses itself; 2: **long double** is used for all evaluations
FLT_EPSILON DBL_EPSILON LDBL_EPSILON	10^{-5} 10^{-9} 10^{-9}	the minimum $x>0.0$ such that $1.0 + x > 1.0$; b^{1-p}; the values shown are the maximum ones permitted
FLT_DIG DBL_DIG LDBL_DIG	6 10 10	the number of decimal digits of precision
FLT_MANT_DIG DBL_MANT_DIG LDBL_MANT_DIG	*none*	p, the number of base-b digits in the significand
DECIMAL_DIG[c]	*10*	number of decimal digits needed to represent values of the widest supported floating-point type; equal to $1 + p_{max} \log_{10} b$ if b is not a power of 10.
FLT_MIN DBL_MIN LDBL_MIN	10^{-37} 10^{-37} 10^{-37}	the minimum normalized positive number
FLT_MIN_EXP DBL_MIN_EXP LDBL_MIN_EXP	*none*	e_{min}, the minimum negative integer x such that b^{x-1} is in the range of normalized floating-point numbers
FLT_MIN_10_EXP DBL_MIN_10_EXP LDBL_MIN_10_EXP	-37 -37 -37	minimum x such that 10^x is in the range of normalized floating-point numbers
FLT_MAX DBL_MAX LDBL_MAX	10^{+37} 10^{+37} 10^{+37}	maximum representable finite number
FLT_MAX_EXP DBL_MAX_EXP LDBL_MAX_EXP	*none*	e_{max}, the maximum integer x such that b^{x-1} is a representable finite floating-point numbers
FLT_MAX_10_EXP DBL_MAX_10_EXP LDBL_MAX_10_EXP	37 37 37	maximum x such that 10^x is in the range of representable finite floating-point numbers

[a] **FLT_RADIX** and **FLT_ROUNDS** apply to all three floating-point types.
[b] Other values are implementation-defined.
[c] New in C99.

permit input and output of these special values, and provides library functions to create and test for these values (Sections 17.13 and 17.14).

Example

A common floating-point representation used by many microprocessors is given by the *IEEE Standard for Binary Floating-Point Arithmetic* (ISO/IEEE Std 754–1985). The models for 32-bit single and 64-bit double precision floating-point numbers under that standard (adjusted to the Standard C notational conventions) are

$$x_{\text{float}} = s \times 2^e \times \sum_{k=1}^{24} f_k \times 2^{-k} \qquad -125 \le e \le +128$$

$$x_{\text{double}} = s \times 2^e \times \sum_{k=1}^{53} f_k \times 2^{-k} \qquad -1021 \le e \le +1024$$

The values from `float.h` corresponding to these types are shown in Table 5–4. Floating-point constants of type `float` use the Standard C suffix `F` to denote their type. IEEE support in Standard C is optional.

References   floating-point constants 2.7.2; floating-point conversions 6.2.4; floating-point representations 6.1.1; NaN-related functions 17.14, 17.15

Table 5–4   IEEE floating-point characteristics

Name	**FLT**_*name* value	**DBL**_*name* value
`RADIX`	2	not applicable
`ROUNDS`	implementation-defined	not applicable
`EPSILON`	1.19209290E–07F or `0X1P-23F` (C99)	2.2204460492503131E–16 or `0X1P-52` (C99)
`DIG`	6	15
`MANT_DIG`	24	53
`DECIMAL_DIG`[a]	17	17
`MIN`	1.17549435E–38F or `0X1P-126F` (C99)	2.2250738585072014E–308 or `0X1P-1022` (C99)
`MIN_EXP`	–125	–1021
`MIN_10_EXP`	–37	–307
`MAX`	3.40282347E+38F or `0X1.fffffeP127F` (C99)	1.7976931348623157E+308 or `0X1.fffffffffffffP1023` (C99)
`MAX_EXP`	128	1024
`MAX_10_EXP`	38	308

[a] This name is not prefixed by `FLT_` or `DBL_`.

5.2.1 Complex Floating-Point Types

C99 adds six complex types to C: `float _Complex`, `double _Complex`, `long double _Complex`, `float _Imaginary`, `double _Imaginary`, `long double`

_Imaginary. The complex types are considered to be floating-point and arithmetic types. The noncomplex arithmetic types are termed *real types*. A freestanding implementation of C need not implement any complex types, and the pure-imaginary **_Imaginary** types are optional even in hosted implementations.

complex-type-specifier :   *(C99)*
    `float _Complex`
    `double _Complex`
    `long double _Complex`

The keyword **_Complex** was chosen to avoid conflicts with user-defined types named **complex** in existing programs. The type specifiers that precede the keyword **_Complex** designate the *corresponding real type*. The header file **complex.h** defines a macro **complex** to be a synonym for **_Complex**, so programmers without legacy problems can use the simpler name.

Each complex type is represented as a two-element array of the corresponding real type, and each has the same alignment requirements as such an array. The first element represents the real part of the complex number; the second represents the imaginary part.

A C99 implementation can optionally support pure-imaginary types, **float _Imaginary**, **double _Imaginary**, and **long double _Imaginary**. These are considered to be complex types also, but they are represented as a single element of the corresponding real type. They are convenient for some kinds of complex calculations, but not convenient enough to be an official part of the Standard.

A complex (or imaginary) value that has at least one infinite part is considered to be infinite even if the other component is a NaN. For a complex number to be finite, both parts must be finite (not infinite or NaN). A complex or imaginary number is zero if all of its parts are zero.

References   complex conversions 6.2.4; **complex.h** header file Ch. 23; usual binary conversion 6.3.4

5.3 POINTER TYPES

For any type *T*, a pointer type "pointer to *T*" may be formed. Pointer types are referred to as *object pointers* or *function pointers* depending on whether *T* is an object type or a function type. A value of pointer type is the address of an object or function of type *T*. The declaration of pointer types is discussed in Section 4.5.2.

Example

```
int *ip; /* ip: a pointer to an object of type int */
char *cp; /* cp: a pointer to an object of type char */
int (*fp)(); /* fp: a pointer to a function returning
                an integer */
```

The two most important operators used in conjunction with pointers are the address operator, &, which creates pointer values, and the indirection operator, *, which dereferences pointers to access the object pointed to.

Example

In the following example, the pointer **ip** is assigned the address of variable **i** (**&i**). After that assignment, the expression ***ip** refers to the same object denoted by **i**:

```
int i, j, *ip;
ip = &i;
i = 22;
j = *ip;     /* j now has the value 22 */
*ip = 17;    /* i now has the value 17 */
```

Other operations on pointer types include assignment, subtraction, relational and equality tests, logical AND and OR, addition and subtraction of integers, and conversions to and from integers and pointer types.

The size of a pointer is implementation-dependent and in some cases varies depending on the type of the object pointed to. For example, data pointers may be shorter or longer than function pointers (Section 6.1.5). There is not necessarily any relationship between pointer sizes and the size of any integer type, although it has been common to assume that type **long** is at least as large as any pointer type. In C99, use **intptr_t**.

In Standard C, pointer types may be qualified by the use of the type qualifiers **const**, **volatile**, and **restrict** (C99). The qualification of a pointer type (if any) can affect the operations and conversions that are possible with it and the optimizations permitted on it.

References   address operator & 7.5.6; arrays and pointers 5.4.1; assignment operators 7.9; cast expressions 7.5.1; conversions of pointers 6.2.7; **if** statement 8.5; indirection operator * 7.5.7; **intptr_t** 21.5; pointer declarators 4.5.2; type qualifiers 4.4.3

5.3.1 Generic Pointers

The need for a generic data pointer that can be converted to any object pointer type arises occasionally in low-level programming. In traditional C, it is customary to use type **char *** for this purpose, casting these generic pointers to the proper type before dereferencing them. Further details are given in Section 6.2, where pointer conversions are discussed. The problem with this use of **char *** is that the compiler cannot check that programmers always convert the pointer type properly.

Standard C introduced the type **void *** as a "generic pointer." It has the same representation as type **char *** for compatibility with older implementations, but the language treats it differently. Generic pointers cannot be dereferenced with the * or subscripting operators, nor can they be operands of addition or subtraction operators. Any pointer to an object or incomplete type (but *not* to a function type) can be converted to type **void *** and back without change. Type **void *** is considered to be neither an object pointer nor a function pointer.

Example

Some sample pointer declarations and conversions:

```
void *generic_ptr;
int *int_ptr;
char *char_ptr;
generic_ptr = int_ptr;      /* OK */
int_ptr = generic_ptr;      /* OK */
int_ptr = char_ptr;         /* Invalid in Standard C */
int_ptr = (int *) char_ptr; /* OK */
```

Generic pointers provide additional flexibility in using function prototypes. When a function has a formal parameter that can accept a data pointer of any type, the formal parameter should be declared to be of type **void ***. If the formal parameter is declared with any other pointer type, the actual argument must be of the same type since different pointer types are not assignment compatible in Standard C.

Example

The **strcpy** facility copies character strings and therefore requires arguments of type **char ***:

```
char *strcpy(char *s1, const char *s2);
```

Yet **memcpy** can take a pointer to any type and so uses **void ***:

```
void *memcpy(void *s1, const void *s2, size_t n);
```

References assignment compatibility 6.3.2; **const** type specifier 4.4; **memcpy** facility 14.3; **strcpy** facility 13.3

5.3.2 Null Pointers and Invalid Pointers

Every pointer type in C has a special value called a *null pointer*, which is different from every valid pointer of that type, which compares equal to a null pointer constant, which converts to the null pointers of other pointer types, and which has the value "false" when used in a boolean context. The *null pointer constant* in C is any integer constant expression with the value 0, or such an expression cast to type **void ***. The macro **NULL** is traditionally defined as the null pointer constant in the standard header files—**stddef.h** in Standard C and **stdio.h** in older implementations.

It is usual for all null pointers to have a representation in which all bits are zero, but that is not required. In fact, different pointer types can have different representations for their null pointers. If null pointers are not represented as zero, then an implementation must go to some lengths to be sure to properly convert null pointers and null pointer constants among the different pointer types.

Example

The statement

```
if (ip) i = *ip;
```

is a common shorthand notation for

```
if (ip != NULL) i = *ip;
```

It is good programming style to be sure that all pointers have the value **NULL** when they are not designating a valid object or function.

It is also possible to inadvertently create *invalid pointers*—that is, pointer values that are not null but also do not designate a proper object or function. An invalid pointer is most frequently created by declaring a pointer variable without initializing it to some valid pointer or to **NULL**. Any use of an invalid pointer, including comparing it to **NULL**, passing it as an argument to a function, or assigning its value to another pointer, is undefined in Standard C. Invalid pointers can also be created by casting arbitrary integer values to pointer types, by deallocating the storage for an object to which a pointer refers (as by using the **free** facility), or by using pointer arithmetic to produce a pointer outside the range of an array. An attempt to dereference an invalid pointer may cause a run-time error.

In conjunction with pointer arithmetic, C does require that the address of an object one past the last object of an array be defined, although such an address can still be invalid to dereference. This requirement makes it easier to use pointer expressions to walk through arrays.

Example

The following loop uses the address just beyond the end of an array, although it never attempts to dereference that address:

```
int array[N]; /* last object address is &array[N-1] */
int *p;
...
for (p = &array[0]; p < &array[N]; p++)
    ...
```

This requirement may restrict implementations for a few target computers that have non-contiguous addressing architectures, reducing by one object the maximum length of an array. On such computers, it may be impossible to perform arithmetic on pointers that do not fall within a contiguous area of memory, and only by allocating an array is the programmer guaranteed that the memory is contiguous.

References   **free** 16.1; integer constants 2.7.1; pointer arithmetic 7.6.2; **stddef.h** facility 11.1; **void *** type 5.3.1

5.3.3 Some Cautions With Pointers

Many C programmers assume that all pointer types (actually, all addresses) have a uniform representation. On common byte-addressed computers, all pointers are typically simple byte addresses occupying, say, one word. Conversions among pointer and integer types on these computers require no change in representation and no information is lost.

In fact, the C language does not require such nice behavior. Section 6.1 discusses the problems in more detail, but here is a brief summary:

1. Pointers are often not the same size as type **int** and sometimes not the same size as type **long**. Sometimes their size is a compiler option. In C99, type **intptr_t** is an integer type large enough to hold an object pointer.

2. Character and **void *** pointers can be larger than other kinds of pointers, and they may use a representation that is different from other kinds of pointers. For example, they may use high-order bits that are normally zero in other kinds of pointers.

3. Function pointers and data pointers may have significantly different representations, including different sizes.

The programmer should always use explicit casts when converting between pointer types, and should be especially careful that pointer arguments given to functions have the correct type expected by the function. In Standard C, **void *** can be used as a generic object pointer, but there is no generic function pointer.

References   casts 7.5.1; **intptr_t** 21.5; **malloc** function 16.1; pointer conversions 6.2.7

5.4 ARRAY TYPES

If *T* is any C type except **void**, an incomplete type, or a function type, then the type "array of *T*" may be declared. Values of this type are sequences of elements of type *T*. All arrays are 0-origin. See Section 4.5.3 for a discussion of syntax and meaning of array declarators, including incomplete and variable length array types.

Example

The array declared **int A[3];** consists of the elements **A[0]**, **A[1]**, and **A[2]**. In the following code, an array of integers (**ints**) and an array of pointers (**ptrs**) are declared, and each of the pointers in **ptrs** is set equal to the address of the corresponding integer in **ints**:

```
int ints[10], *ptrs[10], i;
for (i = 0; i < 10; i++)
    ptrs[i] = &ints[i];
```

The memory size of an array (in the sense of the **sizeof** operator) is always equal to the length of the array in elements multiplied by the memory size of an element

References   array declarators 4.5.3; **sizeof** operator 7.5.2; storage units 6.1.1; structure types 5.6; variable length arrays 5.4.5

5.4.1 Arrays and Pointers

In C there is a close correspondence between types "array of *T*" and "pointer to *T*." First, when an array identifier appears in an expression, the type of the identifier is converted from "array of *T*" to "pointer to *T*," and the value of the identifier is converted to a pointer to the first element of the array. This rule is one of the usual unary conversions. The only exceptions to this conversion rule is when the array identifier is used as an operand of the

sizeof or address (**&**) operators, in which case **sizeof** returns the size of the entire array and **&** returns a pointer to the array (not a pointer to a pointer to the first element).

Example

In the second line below, the value **a** is converted to a pointer to the first element of the array:

```
int a[10], *ip;
ip = a;
```

It is exactly as if we had written

```
ip = &a[0];
```

The value of **sizeof(a)** will be **sizeof(int)*10**, not **sizeof(int *)**.

Second, array subscripting is defined in terms of pointer arithmetic. That is, the expression **a[i]** is defined to be the same as ***((a) + (i))**, where **a** is converted to **&a[0]** under the usual unary conversions. This definition of subscripting also means that **a[i]** is the same as **i[a]**, and that any pointer may be subscripted just like an array. It is up to the programmer to ensure that the pointer is pointing into an appropriate array of elements.

Example

If **d** has type **double** and **dp** is a pointer to a **double** object, then the expression

```
d = dp[4];
```

is defined only if **dp** currently points to an element of a **double** array, and if there are at least four more elements of the array following the one pointed to.

References   address operator **&** 7.5.6; addition operator **+** 7.6.2; array declarators 4.5.3; conversions of arrays 6.3.3; indirection operator ***** 7.5.7; pointer types 5.3; **sizeof** operator 5.4.4, 7.5.2; subscripting 7.4.1; usual unary conversions 6.3.3

5.4.2 Multidimensional Arrays

Multidimensional arrays are declared as "arrays of arrays," such as in the declaration

```
int matrix[12][10];
```

which declares **matrix** to be a 12-by-10 element array of **int**. The language places no limit on the number of dimensions an array may have. The array **matrix** could also be declared in two steps to make its structure clearer:

```
typedef int vector[10];
vector matrix[12];
```

That is, **matrix** is a 12-element array of 10-element arrays of **int**. The type of **matrix** is **int [12][10]**. Multidimensional array elements are stored in row-major order. That is, those elements that only differ by one in their last subscript are stored adjacently.

The conversions of arrays to pointers happen for multidimensional arrays just as they do for singly dimensioned arrays.

Example

The elements of the array **int t[2][3]** are stored (in increasing addresses) as

t[0][0], t[0][1], t[0][2], t[1][0], t[1][1], t[1][2]

The expression **t[1][2]** is expanded to ***(*(t+1)+2)**, which is evaluated in this sequence of steps:

1. The expression **t**, a 2-by-3 array, is converted to a pointer to the first 3-element subarray.
2. The expression **t+1** is then a pointer to the second 3-element subarray.
3. The expression ***(t+1)**, the second 3-element subarray of integers, is converted to a pointer to the first integer in that subarray.
4. The expression ***(t+1)+2** is then a pointer to the third integer in the second 3-element subarray.
5. Finally, ***(*(t+1)+2)** is the third integer in the second 3-element subarray; **t[1][2]**.

In general, any expression A of type "i-by-j-by-...-by-k array of T" is immediately converted to "pointer to j-by-...-by-k array of T."

References   addition operator **+** 7.6.2; array declarators 4.5.3; indirection operator ***** 7.5.7; pointer types 5.3; subscripting 7.4.1

5.4.3 Array Bounds

Whenever storage for an array is allocated, the size of the array must be known. However, because subscripts are not normally checked to lie within declared array bounds, it is possible to omit the size (i.e., to use an incomplete array type) when declaring an external, singly dimensioned array defined in another module or when declaring a singly dimensioned array that is a formal parameter to a function (see also Section 4.5.3).

Example

The following function, **sum**, returns the sum of the first **n** elements of an external array, **a**, whose bounds are not specified:

```
extern int a[];

int sum(int n)
{
    int i, s = 0;
    for (i = 0; i < n; i++)
        s += a[i];
    return s;
}
```

The array could also be passed as a parameter, like this:

```
int sum(int a[], int n)
{
    int i, s = 0;
    for (i = 0; i < n; i++)
        s += a[i];
    return s;
}
```

The parameter **a** could be declared as **int *a** without changing the body of the function. That would more accurately reflect the implementation but less clearly indicate the intent.

When multidimensional arrays are used, it is necessary to specify the bounds of all but the first dimension so that the proper address arithmetic can be calculated:

```
extern int matrix[][10]; /* ?-by-10 array of int */
```

If such bounds are not specified, the declaration is in error. In C99, arrays may have variable length, including multidimensional arrays.

References   array declarators 4.5.3; defining and referencing declarations 4.8; indirection operator ***** 7.5.7; omitted array bounds 4.5; pointer types 5.3; subscripting 7.4.1; variable length arrays 5.4.5

5.4.4 Operations

The only operations that can be performed directly on an array value are the application of the **sizeof** and address (**&**) operators. For **sizeof**, the array must be bounded and the result is the number of storage units occupied by the array. For an n-element array of type T, the result of **sizeof** is always equal to n times **sizeof** T. The result of **&** is a pointer to (the first element of) the array.

In other contexts, such as when subscripting an array, the array value is actually treated as a pointer, and so operations on pointers may be applied to the array value.

References   array declarators 4.5.3; conversions from array to pointer 6.2.7; pointer types 5.3; **sizeof** operator 7.5.2; subscripting 7.4.1

5.4.5 Variable Length Arrays

C99 gives C programmers the ability to use variable length arrays, which are arrays whose sizes are not known until run time. A variable length array declaration is like a fixed array declaration except that the array size is specified by a nonconstant expression. When the declaration is encountered, the size expression is evaluated and the array is created with the indicated length, which must be a positive integer. Once created, a variable length array cannot change in length. Elements in the array can be accessed up to the allocated length; accessing elements beyond that length results in undefined behavior. There is no check required for such out-of-range accesses. The array is destroyed when the block containing the declaration completes. Each time the block is started, a new array is allocated.

Ignoring for the moment array parameters in functions, a variable length array must be declared at block scope and must not be **static** or **extern**. Only ordinary identifiers (not structure or union members) may be declared as variable length arrays. The scope of the array variable extends from the declaration point to the end of the innermost enclosing block. The lifetime of the array extends from the declaration until execution leaves the array's scope. In C99, this includes finishing the block, jumping out of the block, or jumping back to a location in the block before the declaration. Implementors can allocate space for the array on the execution stack when the declaration is processed.

Variably modified types include variable length arrays and other types that have a variable length array type as part of them, such as pointers to variable length arrays. Only ordinary identifiers at block scope with no linkage may be declared with variably modified types. This leaves a loophole: It is possible to use a variably modified type (that is not a variable length array) as the type of a **static** block-scope identifier. In that case, although the value of the **static** identifier is preserved across block executions, the embedded variable length array could change its dimensions each time the block is entered.

Example

In the following code fragment, **a** and **b** are variable length arrays and the pointer **c** has a variably modified type.

```
int a_size;
...
void f(int b_size)
{
    int c_size = b_size + a_size;
    int a[a_size++];
    int b[b_size][b_size];
    static int (*c)[5][c_size];
    ...
}
```

The restrictions on variable length arrays simplify the implementation of C99 while still preserving most of their usefulness. Without the restrictions, a host of complications and interactions appear. Structures might have to carry hidden type descriptors for components of variably modified types. Declaring a variable length array at file scope would require C to adopt the overhead of "elaborating" top-level declarations at run time. (C++ and other languages have such mechanisms, but they are not in the spirit of C.)

If a variable length array is used in a **typedef** declaration, then the length expression is evaluated once, when the **typedef** declaration is encountered, not each time the new type name is used.

Example

```
/* Assume n has the value 5 here */
typedef int[n] vector;
n += 1;
vector a;
int b[n];
```

The variable **a** is a five-element array of integers, reflecting the value of **n** when the **typedef** declaration was encountered. In contrast, **b** is a six-element array of integers because the value of **n** changed by the time the declaration of **b** was encountered.

Variable length array parameters   A variable length array or a variably modified type may be used as the type of a function parameter. When the array's length is also a parameter, it must necessarily appear first due to C's lexical scoping rules.

When a function with a variable length array parameter is called, the size(s) of the dimension(s) of the array argument must agree with the array parameter declaration in the function definition or else the result is undefined.

Example

The first function definition is correct. The second will either be illegal, or values of some other variables **r** and **c** will be used to compute the dimensions of **a**.

```
void f( int r, int c, int a[c][r] ) {...} /* OK */
void f( int a[c][r], int r, int c ) {...}
    /* NO: r, c are not visible to a[c][r] */
```

In a function prototype declaration (not part of a function definition), a variable length array dimension may be designated by [*]. Any nonconstant expression that appears within array brackets in such a function prototype is treated as equivalent to [*].

Example

The following prototypes are all compatible. Although the third prototype implies a square array, that constraint is not checked at compile time. The last prototype shows that the innermost (or only) dimension of a variable length array can simply be omitted.

```
void f(int, int [*][*]);
void f(int n, int [*][m]);
void f(int n, int [n][n]);
void f(int, int [][*]);
```

References   array declarators 4.5.3; function prototypes 9.2; **sizeof** operator 7.5.2

5.5 ENUMERATED TYPES

The syntax for declaring enumerated types is shown next:

enumeration-type-specifier :
      enumeration-type-definition
      enumeration-type-reference

enumeration-type-definition :
      enum *enumeration-tag$_{opt}$* { *enumeration-definition-list* }
      enum *enumeration-tag$_{opt}$* { *enumeration-definition-list* **,** } *(C99)*

enumeration-type-reference :
    enum *enumeration-tag*

enumeration-tag :
    identifier

enumeration-definition-list :
    enumeration-constant-definition
    enumeration-definition-list **,** *enumeration-constant-definition*

enumeration-constant-definition :
    enumeration-constant
    enumeration-constant **=** *expression*

enumeration-constant :
    identifier

An enumerated type in C is a set of integer values represented by identifiers called *enumeration constants*. The enumeration constants are specified when the type is defined and have type **int**. Each enumerated type is represented by an implementation-defined integer type and is compatible with that type. Thus, for the purposes of type checking, an enumerated type is just one of the integer types. When the C language permits an integer expression in some context, an enumeration constant or a value of an enumerated type can be used instead. (This is not true in C++; see Section 5.13.1.)

C99 allows a comma to be placed at the end of the *enumeration-definition-list*—a minor convenience.

Example

The declaration

```
enum fish { trout, carp, halibut } my_fish, your_fish;
```

creates an enumerated type, **enum fish**, whose values are **trout**, **carp**, and **halibut**. It also declares two variables of the enumerated type,**my_fish** and **your_fish**, which can be assigned values with the assignments

```
my_fish = halibut;
your_fish = trout;
```

Variables or other objects of the enumerated type can be declared in the same declaration containing the enumerated type definition or in a subsequent declaration that mentions the enumerated type with an "enumerated type reference."

Example

For example, the single declaration

```
enum color { red, blue, green, mauve }
    favorite, acceptable, least_favorite;
```

is exactly equivalent to the two declarations

```
enum color { red, blue, green, mauve } favorite;
enum color acceptable, least_favorite;
```

and to the four declarations

```
enum color { red, blue, green, mauve };
enum color favorite;
enum color acceptable;
enum color least_favorite;
```

The enumeration tag, **color**, allows an enumerated type to be referenced after its definition. Although the alternative declaration

```
enum { red, blue, green, mauve }
    favorite, acceptable, least_favorite;
```

declares the same variables and enumeration constants, the lack of a tag makes it impossible to introduce more variables of the type in later declarations.

Enumeration tags are in the same overloading class as structure and union tags, and their scope is the same as that of a variable declared at the same location in the source program.

Identifiers defined as enumeration constants are members of the same overloading class as variables, functions, and typedef names. Their scope is the same as that of a variable defined at the same location in the source program.

Example

In the following code, the declaration of **shepherd** as an enumeration constant hides the previous declaration of the integer variable **shepherd**. However, the declaration of the floating-point variable **collie** causes a compilation error because **collie** is already declared in the same scope as an enumeration constant.

```
int shepherd = 12;
{
    enum dog_breeds {shepherd, collie};
        /* Hides outer declaration of the name "shepherd" */
    float collie;
        /* Invalid redefinition of the name "collie" */
}
```

Enumerated types are implemented by associating integer values with the enumeration constants so that the assignment and comparison of values of enumerated types can be implemented as integer assignment and comparison. Integer values are associated with enumeration constants in the following way:

1. An explicit integer value may be associated with an enumeration constant by writing

   enumeration-constant = *expression*

   in the type definition. The expression must be a constant expression of integral type, including expressions involving previously defined enumeration constants, as in

```
enum boys { Bill = 10,
            John = Bill+2,
            Fred = John+2 };
```

2. The first enumeration constant receives the value 0 if no explicit value is specified.

3. Subsequent enumeration constants without explicit associations receive an integer value one greater than the value associated with the previous enumeration constant.

Any signed integer value representable as type **int** may be associated with an enumeration constant. Positive and negative integers may be chosen at random, and it is even possible to associate the same integer with two different enumeration constants.

Example

Given the declaration

```
enum sizes { small, medium=10, pretty_big, large=20 };
```

the values of **small, medium, pretty_big**, and **large** will be 0, 10, 11, and 20, respectively. Although the following definition is valid:

```
enum people { john=1, mary=19, bill=-4, sheila=1 };
```

its effect is to make the expression **john == sheila** true, which is not intuitive.

Although the form of an enumerated type definition is suggestive of structure and union types, with strict type checking, in fact enumerated types in Standard C (which is the definition given in this book) act as little more than slightly more readable ways to name integer constants. As a matter of style, we suggest that programmers treat enumerated types as different from integers and not mix them in integer expressions without using casts. In fact, some UNIX C compilers implement a weakly typed form of enumerations in which some conversions between enumerated types and integers are not permitted without casts.

References   cast expressions 7.5.1; identifiers 2.5; overloading classes 4.2.4; scope 4.2.1

5.6 STRUCTURE TYPES

The structure types in C are similar to the types known as *records* in other programming languages. They are collections of named *components* (also called *members* or *fields*) that can have different types. Structures can be defined to encapsulate related data objects.

structure-type-specifier :
    structure-type-definition
    structure-type-reference

structure-type-definition :
    struct *structure-tag$_{opt}$* { *field-list* }

structure-type-reference :
    struct *structure-tag*

structure-tag :
    identifier

field-list :
    component-declaration
    field-list component-declaration

component-declaration :
    type-specifier component-declarator-list **;**

component-declarator-list :
    component-declarator
    component-declarator-list **,** *component-declarator*

component-declarator :
    simple-component
    bit-field

simple-component :
    declarator

bit-field :
    declarator$_{opt}$ **:** *width*

width :
    constant-expression

Example

A programmer who wanted to implement complex numbers (before C99) might define a structure **complex** to hold the real and imaginary parts as components **real** and **imag**. The first declaration defines the new type, and the second declares two variables, **x** and **y**, of that type:

```
struct complex {
    double real;
    double imag;
};
struct complex x,y;
```

real	imag
double	double

struct complex

A function **new_complex** can be written to create a new object of the type. Note that the selection operator (**.**) is used to access the components of the structure:

```
struct complex new_complex(double r, double i)
{
    struct complex c;
    c.real = r;
    c.imag = i;
    return c;
}
```

Operations on the type, such as **complex_multiply**, can also be defined:

```
struct complex complex_multiply( struct complex a,
                                 struct complex b )
{
    struct complex product;
    product.real = a.real * b.real - a.imag * b.imag;
    product.imag = a.real * b.imag + a.imag * b.real;
    return product;
}
```

Example

The single declaration

```
struct complex { double real, imag; } x, y;
```

is equivalent to the two declarations

```
struct complex { double real, imag; };
struct complex x, y;
```

5.6.1 Structure-Type References

The use of a type specifier of the syntactic classes *structure-type-definition* or *union-type-definition* (Section 5.7) introduces the definition of a new type different from all others. If present in the definition, the structure tag is associated with the new type and can be used in a subsequent structure-type reference.

The scope of the definition (and the type tag if any) is from the declaration point to the end of the innermost block containing the specifier. The new definition explicitly overrides (hides) any definition of the type tag in an enclosing block.

The use of a type specifier of the syntactic classes *structure-type-reference* or *union-type-reference* (Section 5.7) without a preceding definition in the same or enclosing scope is allowed when the size of the structure is not required, including when declaring:

1. pointers to the structure
2. a typedef name as a synonym for the structure

The use of this kind of specifier introduces an "incomplete" definition of the type and type tag in the innermost block containing the use. For this definition to be completed, a *structure-type-definition* or *union-type-definition* must appear later in the same scope.

As a special case, a *structure-type-reference* or *union-type-reference* in a declaration with no declarators hides any definition of the type tag in any enclosing scope and establishes an incomplete type.

Example

Consider the following correct definition of two self-referential structures in an inner block:

```
{
    struct cell;
    struct header { struct cell   *first; … };
    struct cell   { struct header *head;   … };
    …
}
```

The incomplete definition "**struct cell;**" in the first line it is necessary to hide any definitions of the tag **cell** in an enclosing scope. The definition of **struct header** in the second line automatically hides any enclosing definitions, and its use of **struct cell** to define a pointer is valid. The definition of **struct cell** on the third line completes the information about **cell**.

An incomplete type declaration also exists within a *structure-type-definition* or *union-type-definition* from the first mention of the new tag until the definition is complete. This allows a single structure type to include a pointer to itself (see Figure 5–1).

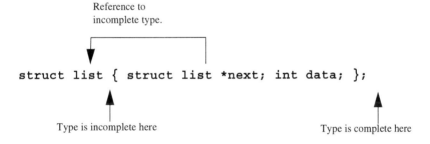

Reference to incomplete type.

```
struct list { struct list *next; int data; };
```

Type is incomplete here   Type is complete here

Figure 5–1   Incomplete structure type within a declaration

References   declarations 4.1; declarators 4.5; duplicate visibility 4.2.2; scope 4.2.1; selection operator **.** 7.4.2; type equivalence 5.11

5.6.2 Operations on Structures

The operations provided for structures may vary from compiler to compiler. All C compilers provide the selection operators **.** and **->** on structures, and newer compilers now allow structures to be assigned, passed as parameters to functions, and returned from functions. (With older compilers, assignment must be done component by component, and only pointers to structures may be passed to and from functions.)

It is not permitted to compare two structures for equality. An object of a structure type is a sequence of components of other types. Because certain data objects may be constrained by the target computer to lie on certain addressing boundaries, a structure object may contain "holes"—storage units that do not belong to any component of the structure. The holes would make equality tests implemented as a wholesale bit-by-bit comparison unreliable, and component-by-component equality tests might be too expensive. (Of course, the programmer may write component-by-component equality functions.)

In any situation where it is permitted to apply the unary address operator **&** to a structure to obtain a pointer to the structure, it is also permitted to apply the **&** operator to a component of the structure to obtain a pointer to the component. It is possible for a pointer to point into the middle of a structure. An exception to this rule occurs with components defined as bit fields. Components defined as bit fields will in general not lie on machine-addressable boundaries, and therefore it may not be possible to form a pointer to a bit field. The C language does not provide bit-field pointers.

References   address operator **&** 7.5.6; assignment 7.9; bit fields 5.6.5; equality operator **==** 7.6.5; selection operator **.** and **->** 7.4.2; type equivalence 5.11

5.6.3 Components

A component of a structure may have any object type that is not variably modified. Structures may not contain instances of themselves, although they may contain pointers to instances of themselves.

In C99, structure components may not have variably modified types. The last component in a structure may have an incomplete array type, in which case it is called a *flexible array member* (Section 5.6.8).

Example

This declaration is invalid:

```
struct S {
   int a;
   struct S next; /* invalid! */
};
```

But this one is permitted:

```
struct S {
   int a;
   struct S *next; /* OK */
};
```

The names of structure components are defined in a special overloading class associated with the structure type. That is, component names within a single structure must be distinct, but they may be the same as component names in other structures and may be the same as variable, function, and type names.

Example

Consider the following sequence of declarations:

```
int x;
struct A { int x; double y; } y;
struct B { int y; double x; } z;
```

The identifier **x** has three nonconflicting declarations: it is an integer variable, an integer component of structure **A**, and a floating-point component of structure **B**. These three declarations are used, respectively, in the expressions

```
x
y.x
z.x
```

If a structure tag is defined in one of the components, then the scope of the tag extends to the end of the block in which the enclosing structure is defined. (If the enclosing structure is defined at the top level, so is the inner tag.)

Example

In the declaration

```
struct S {
    struct T {int a, b; } x;
};
```

The tag **T** is defined from its first occurrence to the end of the scope in which **S** is defined.

Historical note: The original definition of C specified that all components in all structures were allocated out of the same overloading class, and therefore no two structures could have components with the same name. (An exception was made when the components had the same type and the same relative position in the structures!) This interpretation is now anachronistic, but you might see it mentioned in older documentation or actually implemented in some old compilers.

References   flexible array member 5.6.8; incomplete array type 5.4; overloading classes 4.2.4; scope 4.2.1; variably-modified type 5.4.5;

5.6.4 Structure Component Layout

Most programmers will be unconcerned with how components are packed into structures. However, C does give the programmer some control over the packing. C compilers are constrained to assign components increasing memory addresses in a strict order, with the first component starting at the beginning address of the structure.

Example

There is no difference in component layout between the structure

```
struct { int a, b, c; };
```

and the structure

```
struct { int a; int b, c; };
```

Both put **a** first, **b** second, and **c** last in order of increasing addresses, as pictured next:

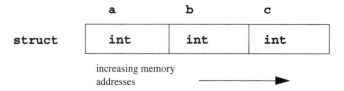

Given two pointers **p** and **q** to components within the same structure, **p < q** will be true if and only if the declaration of the component to which **p** points appears earlier within the structure declaration than the declaration of the component to which **q** points.

Example

```
struct vector3 { int x, y, z; } s;
int *p, *q, *r;
...
p = &s.x;
q = &s.y;
r = &s.z;      /* At this point p < q, q < r, and p < r. */
```

Holes or padding may appear between any two consecutive components or after the last component in the layout of a structure if necessary to allow proper alignment of components in memory. The bit patterns appearing in such holes are unpredictable and may differ from structure to structure or over time within a single structure. The space occupied by padding is included in the value returned by the **sizeof** operator. Some implementations provide pragmas or switches to control the packing of structures.

5.6.5 Bit Fields

C allows the programmer to pack integer components into spaces smaller than the compiler would ordinarily allow. These integer components are called *bit fields* and are specified by following the component declarator with a colon and a constant integer expression that indicates the width of the field in bits.

Example

The following structure has three components, **a**, **b**, and **c**, occupying four, five, and seven bits, respectively:

```
struct S {
    unsigned a:4;
    unsigned b:5, c:7;
};
```

A bit field of *n* bits can represent unsigned integers in the range 0 through 2^n-1 and signed integers in the range -2^{n-1} through $2^{n-1}-1$, assuming a twos-complement representation of signed integers. The original definition of C permitted only bit fields of type **unsigned**, but Standard C permits bit fields to be of type **unsigned int**, **signed int**, or just **int**, termed *unsigned*, *signed*, and *plain* bit fields. Like plain characters, a plain bit field may be signed or unsigned. Some C implementations allow bit fields of any integer type, including **char**. C99 allows bit fields of type **_Bool**.

Bit fields are typically used in machine-dependent programs that must force a data structure to correspond to a fixed hardware representation. The precise manner in which components (and especially bit fields) are packed into a structure is implementation-dependent but is predictable for each implementation. The intent is that bit fields should be packed as tightly as possible in a structure, subject to the rules discussed later in this section. The use of bit fields is therefore likely to be nonportable. The programmer should consult the implementation documentation if it is necessary to lay out a structure in memory in some particular fashion, and then verify that the C compiler is indeed packing the components in the way expected.

Example

> Here is an example of how bit fields can be used to create a structure that matches a predefined format. Following is the layout of a 32-bit word treated as a virtual address on a hypothetical computer. The word contains fields for the segment number, page number, and offset within a page, plus a "supervisor" bit and an unused bit.

field width (bits)   1   1   6   8   16

> To duplicate this layout, we first have to know if our computer packs bit fields left to right or right to left—that is, whether it is a "big endian" or a "little endian" (see Section 6.1.2). If packing is right to left, the appropriate structure definition is

```
typedef struct {
    unsigned Offset     : 16;
    unsigned Page       : 8;
    unsigned Segment    : 6;
    unsigned UNUSED     : 1;
    unsigned Supervisor : 1;
} virtual_address;
```

> In contrast, if packing is left to right, the appropriate structure definition is

```
typedef struct {
    unsigned Supervisor : 1;
    unsigned UNUSED     : 1;
    unsigned Segment    : 6;
    unsigned Page       : 8;
    unsigned Offset     : 16;
} virtual_address;
```

The signedness of a plain integer bit field follows the signedness of plain characters. That is, a plain integer bit field may actually be implemented as a signed or unsigned type (see Section 5.1.3). Signed and unsigned bit fields must be implemented to hold signed and unsigned values, respectively.

Example

Consider the effect of these Standard C declarations on a twos-complement computer:

```
struct S { unsigned ubf:3;
           signed sbf:3;
           int bf:3; } x = { -1, -1, -1 };
...
int i = x.ubf;
int j = x.sbf;
int k = x.bf;
```

The value of **i** must be 7 and of **j** must be –1, but the value of **k** may be either 7 or –1.

Compilers are free to impose constraints on the maximum size of a bit field and specify certain addressing boundaries that bit fields cannot cross. These alignment restrictions are usually related to the natural word size of the target computer. When a field is too long for the computer, the compiler will issue an appropriate error message. When a field would cross a word boundary, it may be moved to the next word.

An unnamed bit field may also be included in a structure to provide padding between adjacent components. Unnamed bit fields cannot be referenced, and their contents at run time are not predictable.

Example

The following structure places component **a** in the first four bits of the structure, followed by two bits of padding, followed by the component **b** in six bits. (Assuming a basic word size of 16 bits, a final four bits will also be unused at the end of the structure; see Section 5.6.7.)

```
struct S {
    unsigned a : 4;
    unsigned   : 2;
    unsigned b : 6;
};
```

Specifying a length of 0 for an unnamed bit field has a special meaning—it indicates that no more bit fields should be packed into the area in which the previous bit field, if any, was placed. *Area* here means some implementation-defined storage unit.

Example

In the following structure, the component **b** should begin on a natural addressing boundary (e.g., 16 bits) following component **a**. The new structure occupies twice as much storage as the old one:

```
struct S {
    unsigned a : 4;
    unsigned   : 0;
    unsigned b : 6;
};
```

The address operator **&** may not be applied to bit-field components since many computers cannot address arbitrary-sized fields directly.

References   address operator **&** 7.5.6; alignment restrictions 6.1.3; **_Bool** type 5.1.4; byte order 6.1.2; enumerated types 5.5; signed types 5.1.1; unsigned types 5.1.2

5.6.6 Portability Problems

Depending on packing strategies is dangerous for several reasons. First, computers differ on the alignment constraints on data types. For instance, a four-byte integer on some computers must begin on a byte boundary that is a multiple of four, whereas on other computers the integer can (and will) be aligned on the nearest byte boundary.

Second, the restrictions on bit-field widths will be different. Some computers have a 16-bit word size, which limits the maximum size of the field and imposes a boundary that fields cannot cross. Other computers have a 32-bit word size, and so forth.

Third, computers differ in the way fields are packed into a word—that is, in their "byte ordering." On the Motorola 68000 family of computers, characters are packed left to right into words, from the most significant bit to the least significant bit. On Intel 80x86 computers, characters are packed right to left, from the least significant bit to the most significant bit. As seen in the **virtual_address** example in the previous section, different structure definitions are needed for computers with different byte ordering.

We know of two situations that seem to justify the use of bit fields:

1. A predefined data structure must be matched exactly so it can be referenced in a C program. (These programs may not be portable anyway.)
2. An array of structured data must be maintained, and its large size requires that its components be packed tightly to conserve memory.

By using the C bitwise operators to do masking and shifting, it is possible to implement bit fields in a way that is not sensitive to byte ordering within a word.

Example

Consider the problem of accessing the **Page** field in the **virtual_address** structure (page 155). Since this 8-bit field is located 16 bits from the low-order end of the word, it can be accessed with the following code:

```
unsigned V;      /* formatted as a virtual_address */
int Page;
...
Page = (V & 0xFF0000) >> 16;
```

This is equivalent to the more readable structure component access **Page=V.Page**, but the mask-and-shift approach is *not* sensitive to the computer's byte ordering, as is the definition of **virtual_address**. The masking and shifting operations are demonstrated next for **V==0xb393352e** (**Page==0x93**):

```
10110011100100110011010100101110    V
00000000111111110000000000000000    0xFF0000
00000000100100110000000000000000    V & 0xFF0000
00000000000000000000000010010011    (V & 0xFF0000)>>16
```

Similar operations may be used to set the value of a bit field. There may be little difference in the run-time performance of these two access methods.

   References   alignment restrictions 6.1.3; bitwise operators 7.6.6; byte order 6.1.2; shift operators 7.6.3

5.6.7 Sizes of Structures

The size of an object of a structure type is the amount of storage necessary to represent all components of that type, including any unused padding space between or after the components. The rule is that the structure will be padded out to the size the type would occupy as an element of an array of such types. (For any type *T*, including structures, the size of an *n*-element array of *T* is the same as the size of *T* times *n*.) Another way of saying this is that the structure must terminate on the same alignment boundary on which it started—that is, if the structure must begin on an even byte boundary, it must also end on an even byte boundary. The alignment requirement for a structure type will be at least as stringent as for the component having the most stringent requirements.

Example

   On a computer that starts all structures on an address that is a multiple of four bytes, the length of the following structure will be a multiple of four (probably exactly four), even though only two bytes are actually used:

```
struct S {
    char c1;
    char c2;
};
```

c1	c2	
Bytes: 1   1   2

Example

On a computer that requires all objects of type **double** to have an address that is a multiple of 8 bytes, the length of the following structure is probably 24 bytes, even though only 18 bytes are declared:

```
struct S {
    double value;
    char name [10];
};
```

value	name	
Bytes: 8	10	6

Six extra units of padding are needed at the end to make the size of the structure a multiple of the alignment requirement, eight. If the padding were not used, then in an array of such structures not all of the structures would have the value component aligned properly to a multiple-of-eight address.

Example

Alignment requirements may cause padding to appear in the middle of a structure. If the order of the components in the previous example is reversed, the length remains 24, but the unused space appears between the components so that the value component may be aligned to an address that is a multiple of 8 bytes relative to the beginning of the structure:

```
struct S {
    char name [10];
    double value;
};
```

name		value
Bytes: 10	6	8

Any object of the structure type will be required to have an address that is a multiple of eight, and so the value component of such an object will always be properly aligned.

5.6.8 Flexible Array Members

In C99, the last component of a structure may have an incomplete array type, in which case it is called a *flexible array member*. Flexible array members were introduced to legitimize a long-standing but unsafe C programming idiom for structures whose size could vary at run time.

To use a flexible array member, declare a structure type S whose last component is a flexible array member F whose element type is E. Type S cannot contain only F; it must have at least one other named component. For example,

```
struct S { int F_len; double F[]; }; /* E is double */
```

The value of **sizeof**(S) is defined to be the size of the structure ignoring member F, except that the size must include any padding required just before F. (To determine the amount of padding needed, assume that F were declared as a fixed size array with the same element type, and use the padding, if any, that would be needed in front of F.)

When you use an lvalue of type S to access a data object, you may treat F as if it were a fixed size array with a length L that does not cause S to exceed the length of the data object. That is, if the data object has length D, then the L is the largest non-negative integer such that $\mathtt{sizeof}(S)\ +\ L\mathtt{*sizeof}(E)\ \mathtt{<=}\ D$, and you can refer to $F\mathtt{[0]}$, $F\mathtt{[1]}, \dots, F\mathtt{[}L{-}1\mathtt{]}$. If you were to simply declare a variable of type S, then you could not use the array because the data object (the variable) has no space for it. (D would be $\mathtt{sizeof}(S)$, so L would be 0.) You can always refer to $\mathtt{\&}F\mathtt{[0]}$ even if there is no room for the array.

To use type S to access a data object larger than itself, you can declare a pointer to S and assign to it the address of a larger object, or you can use a union to overlay S on a larger object.

Example

It is common to use flexible array members to define a structure to hold a variably sized vector and the vector's length.

```
struct Vec { int len; double vec[]; }
```

If the length of the vector is a constant, you can declare it statically.

```
#define N 20 /* Length of vector */
union{
    char data_object[sizeof(struct Vec) + N*sizeof(double)];
    struct S v;
} u = { .v = {N} }; /* C99 designated initializer */
```

If the length of the vector is not known until run time, use **malloc** to allocate space for it.

```
struct Vec *p;
int n; /* length of vector */
...
p = malloc( sizeof(struct Vec) + n * sizeof (double));
p->len = n;
```

Here is how you would use the vectors.

```
for (i = 0; i < u.v.len; i++) u.v.vec[i] = 0.0;
for (i = 0; i < p->len; i++) p->vec[i] = 0.0;
```

Before C99, you would have had to declare the structure as

```
struct Vec { int len; double vec[1]; }
```

and change the call to **malloc**—for example, to

```
p = malloc( sizeof(struct Vec) + (len-1)*sizeof (double));
```

Although this code usually worked, its behavior was (and still is) undefined.

5.7 UNION TYPES

The syntax for defining union types is almost identical to that for defining structure types:

union-type-specifier :
   union-type-definition
   union-type-reference

union-type-definition :
   union *union-tag*$_{opt}$ { *field-list* }

union-type-reference :
   union *union-tag*

union-tag :
   identifier

The syntax for defining components is the same as that used for structures. In traditional C, unions could not contain bit fields, but in Standard C this restriction is removed.

As with structures and enumerations, each union type definition introduces a new union type different from all others. If present in the definition, the union tag is associated with the new type and can be used in a subsequent union type reference. Forward references and incomplete definitions of union types are permitted with the same rules as structure types.

A component of a union may have any object type that is not variably modified. Also, unions may not contain instances of themselves, although they may contain pointers to instances of themselves. As with structures, the names of union components are defined in a special overload class associated with the union type. That is, component names within a single union must be distinct, but they may be the same as component names in other unions and may be the same as variable, function, and type names.

5.7.1 Union Component Layout

Each component of a union type is allocated storage starting at the beginning of the union. A union can contain only one of its component values at a time. An object of a union type will begin on a storage alignment boundary appropriate for any contained component.

Example

Here is a union with three components, all effectively overlaid in memory:

```
union U {
    double d;
    char c[2];
    int i;
};
```

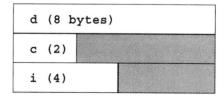

Example

If we have the following union type and object definitions:

```
static union U { …; int C; …; } object, *P = &object;
```

then the following two equalities hold:

```
(union U *) & (P->C)  ==  P
&(P->C)  ==  (int *) P
```

Furthermore, these equalities hold no matter what the type of the component C and no matter what other components in the union precede or follow C.

References   alignment restrictions 6.1.3

5.7.2 Sizes of Unions

The size of an object of a union type is the amount of storage necessary to represent the largest component of that type, plus any padding that may be needed at the end to raise the length up to an appropriate alignment boundary. The rule is that the union will be padded out to the size the type would occupy as an element of an array of such types. Recall that for any type T, including unions, the size of an n-element array of T is the same as (the size of T)·n. Another way of saying this is that the structure must terminate on the same alignment boundary on which it started. That is, if the structure had to begin on an even byte boundary, it must end on an even byte boundary.

Note that the alignment requirement for a union type will be at least as stringent as for the component having the most stringent requirements.

Example

On a computer that requires all objects of type **double** to have an address that is a multiple of 8, the length of the following union will be 16, even though the size of the longest component is only 10:

```
union U {
    double value;
    char name [10];
};
```

Six extra units of padding are needed to make the size of the union a multiple of the alignment requirement, eight. If the padding were not used, then in an array of such unions not all of the unions would have the **value** component aligned properly to a multiple-of-eight address.

5.7.3 Using Union Types

C's union type is somewhat like a "variant record" in other languages. Like structures, unions are defined to have a number of components. Unlike structures, however, a union can hold at most one of its components at a time; the components are conceptually overlaid in the storage allocated for the union. If the union is very large, or if there is a large array of the unions, then the storage savings can be significant.

Example

Suppose we want an object that can be *either* an integer or a floating-point number depending on the situation. We define union **datum**:

```
union datum {
    int i;
    double d;
};
```

and then define a variable of the union type:

```
union datum u;
```

To store an integer in the union, we write

```
u.i = 15;
```

To store a floating-point number in the union, we assign to the other component

```
u.d = 88.9e4;
```

A component of a union should be referenced only if the last assignment to the union was through the same component. C provides no way to inquire which component of a union was last assigned; the programmer can either remember or encode explicit data tags to be associated with unions. A data tag is an object associated with a union that holds an indication of which component is currently stored in the union. The data tag and union can be enclosed in a common structure.

Example

We can replace the union

```
union widget { long count; double value; char name[10];} x;
```

with

```
enum widget_tag { count_widget,
                  value_widget,
                  name_widget };

struct WIDGET {
  enum widget_tag tag;
  union { long count;
          double value;
          char name[10]; } data;
} x;

typedef struct WIDGET widget;
```

The size of the **widget** structure is 24 bytes, which is caused by the assumption that objects of type **double** must be aligned on 8-byte boundaries. A possible layout is shown next:

If, as is common, objects of type **double** can be placed on 4-byte boundaries, then **widget**'s length will be only 16 bytes.

To assign an integer to the union, we write

```
x.tag = count_widget;
x.data.count = 10000;
```

To assign a floating-point number, we write

```
x.tag = value_widget;
x.data.value = 3.1415926535897932384;
```

To assign a string, we can use the **strncpy** library function:

```
x.tag = name_widget;
strncpy(x.data.name, "Millard", 10);
```

Following is a portable function that can discriminate among the possibilities for the union. **print_widget** can be called without regard to which component was last assigned:

```
void print_widget(widget w)
{
    switch(w.tag) {
        case count_widget:
            printf("Count %ld\n", w.data.count); break;
        case value_widget:
            printf("Value %f\n", w.data.value); break;
        case name_widget:
            printf("Name \"%s\"\n", w.data.name); break;
    }
}
```

Although Standard C makes few guarantees about the layout of unions, it does make a special guarantee about unions that include a number of components of similar structure types. If the types of those structures all begin with the same initial sequence of their own components, then Standard C guarantees that those initial sequences will exactly overlay each other. This lets you place a data tag at the beginning of each structure, for example, and refer to that tag using any structure member.

References   cast expression 7.5.1; enumerations 5.5; overloading 4.2.4; scope 4.2.1; **switch** statement 8.7; **strncpy** facility 13.3; structures 5.6; **typedef** 5.10

5.7.4 (Mis)using Union Types

Unions are used in a nonportable fashion any time a union component is referenced when the last assignment to the union was not through the same component. Programmers sometimes do this to "reach under" C's type system and discover something about the computer's underlying data representation (itself a nonportable concept).

Example

To discover how a floating-point number is represented:

1. Create a union with floating-point and integer components of the same size:

float (4 bytes)
int (4 bytes)

2. Assign a value to the floating-point component.

3. Read the value of the integer component and print it out as, say, a hexadecimal number.

Here is a function that does just this, assuming types **float** and **int** have the same length:

```
void print_rep(float f)
{
    union { float f; int i } f_or_i;
    f_or_i.f = f;
    printf("The representation of %12.7e is %#010x\n",
        f_or_i.f, f_or_i.i );
}
```

When **print_rep(1.0)** is called, the output on our Motorola 68020-based workstation is

```
The representation of 1.0000000e+00 is 0x003f800000
```

Notice that a cast operation cannot be used to discover the underlying representation. The cast operator in C converts its operand to the closest value in the new representation; **(int) 1.0** is 1, not **0x003f800000**.

5.8 FUNCTION TYPES

The type "function returning T" is a function type, where T may be any type except "array of…" or "function returning…." Said another way, functions may not return arrays or other functions, although they can return pointers to arrays and functions.

Functions may be introduced in only two ways. First, a function definition can create a function, define its parameters and return value, and supply the body of the function. More information about function definitions is given in Section 9.1. Second, a function declaration can introduce a reference to a function object defined elsewhere.

Example

Here is a function definition for **square**:

```
int square(int x)
{
    return x*x;
}
```

If **square** were defined elsewhere, the following declaration would introduce its name and allow it to be called.

```
extern int square(int);
```

An external function declaration can refer to a function defined in another C source file or to a function defined later in the same source file (i.e., a "forward reference").

Example

Forward references can be used to create mutually recursive functions, such as **f** and **g**:

```
extern int f(void);
...
int g(void) { ... f(); ...}
int f(void) { ... g(); ...}
```

The same declaration style can also be used for static functions:

```
static int f();
...
static int g() { ... f(); ...}
static int f() { ... g(); ...}
```

Some non-Standard C compilers may not permit this kind of forward reference to static functions. Sometimes they compromise by allowing the first declaration to use the storage specifier **extern**, changing the storage class to **static** when the definition is seen.

Example

```
extern int f(void);   /* not really extern, see below... */
...
static int g(void) { ... f(); ...}
static int f(void) { ... g(); ...}  /* now, make f static */
```

This programming idiom is misleading at best. Standard C requires that the first declaration of a function (in fact, of any identifier) specify whether it will be external or static. This permits one-pass compilation of C programs in those cases in which an implementation must treat static and external functions differently. Standard C does not explicitly disallow the "**extern**-then-**static**" style, but it does not specify its meaning.

The only operations on an expression of function type are converting it to a function pointer and calling it.

Example

> In the following declarations, external identifiers **f**, **fp**, and **apf** have types "function return-ing **int**," "pointer to function returning **int**," and "array of pointers to functions taking a **double** parameter and returning **int**," respectively:
>
> ```
> extern int f(), (*fp)(), (*apf[])(double);
> ```
>
> The declaration of **apf** includes a Standard C prototype for the function. These identifiers can be used in function call expressions by writing
>
> ```
> int i,j,k;
> ...
> i = f(14);
> i = (*fp)(j, k);
> i = (*apf[j])(k);
> ```

When a function with no visible prototype is called, certain standard conversions are applied to the actual arguments, but no attempt is made to check the type or number of ar-guments with the type or number of formal arguments to the function if known. Argu-ments to functions with visible prototypes are converted to the indicated parameter type. In the prior example, the integer argument **k** to the function designated by ***apf[j]** will be converted to type **double**.

In Standard C and some other implementations, an expression of type "pointer to function" can be used in a function call without an explicit dereferencing; in that case, the call **(*fp)(j,k)** in the previous example can be written as **fp(j,k)**.

An expression of type "function returning..." that is not used in a function call, as the argument of the address operator, **&**, or as the argument of the **sizeof** operator is imme-diately converted to the type "pointer to function returning...." (Not performing the con-version when the function is the argument of **sizeof** ensures that the **sizeof** expression will be invalid and not just result in the size of a pointer.) The only expressions that can yield a value of type "function returning *T*" are the name of such a function and an indirec-tion expression consisting of the unary indirection operator, *****, applied to an expression of type "pointer to function returning...."

Example

> The following program assigns the same pointer value to **fp1** and **fp2**:
>
> ```
> extern int f();
> int (*fp1)(), (*fp2)();
> fp1 = f;   /* implicit conversion to pointer */
> fp2 = &f;  /* explicit manufacture of a pointer */
> ```

All the information needed to invoke a function is assumed to be encapsulated in an object of type "pointer to function returning...." Although a pointer to a function is often assumed to be the address of the function's code in memory, on some computers a func-tion pointer actually points to a block of information needed to invoke the function. Such representation issues are normally invisible to the C programmer and need concern only the compiler implementor.

References   function argument conversions 6.3.5; function call 7.4.3; function declarator 4.5.4; function definition 9.1; function prototype 9.2; indirection operator * 7.5.7; **sizeof** operator 7.5.2; usual unary conversions 6.3.3

5.9 THE VOID TYPE

The type **void** has no values and no operations.

void-type-specifier :
　　void

Type **void** is used

- as the return type of a function, signifying that the function returns no value ;
- in a cast expression when it is desired to explicitly discard a value;
- to form the type **void ***, a "universal" data pointer; and
- in place of the parameter list in a function declarator to indicate that the function takes no arguments.

Example

The declaration of **write_line** uses **void** both as a return type and in place of the parameter list.

```
extern void write_line(void);
...
write_line(); /* no value returned */
```

The declaration of **write_line2** indicates that the function returns a value, but the call uses a cast to **void** to explicitly throw away the returned value.

```
extern int write_line2(void);
...
(void) write_line2(…);     /* ignore returned value */
```

References   casts 7.5.1; discarded expressions 7.13; **void *** 5.3.2

5.10 TYPEDEF NAMES

When a declaration is written whose "storage class" is **typedef**, the type definition facility is invoked.

typedef-name :
　　identifier

An identifier enclosed in any declarator of the declaration is defined to be a name for a type (a "**typedef** name"); the type is what would have been given the identifier if the declaration were a normal variable declaration. Once a name has been declared as a type, it may appear anywhere a type specifier is permitted. This allows the use of mnemonic abbreviations for complicated types.

Example

Consider these declarations:

```
typedef int *IP;      /* IP: "pointer to int" */
typedef int (*FP)();  /* FP: "pointer to function
                            returning int" */
typedef int F(int);   /* F: "function with one int
                             parameter, returning int" */

typedef double A5[5]; /* A5: "5-element array of double" */
typedef int A[];      /* A: "array of int" */
```

After the prior declarations, the following declarations are permitted:

```
IP ip;      /* ip: pointer to an int */
IP fip();   /* fip: function returning a pointer to int */
FP fp;      /* fp: pointer to a function returning int */
F *fp2;     /* fp2: pointer to a function taking an
                 int parameter and returning an int */

A5 a5;      /* a5: 5-element double array */
A5 a25[2];  /* a25: double [2][5]: a 2-element array
                 of 5-element arrays of double */
A a;        /* a: array of int (with unspecified bounds) */
A *ap3[3];  /* ap3: 3-element array of pointers to
                 arrays of int (with unspecified bounds) */
```

Example

typedef names must not be combined with other type specifiers:

```
typedef long int bigint;
unsigned bigint x;      /* invalid */
```

Combining type qualifiers with **typedef** names is allowed and useful:

```
const bigint x;   /* OK */
```

Declarations with the **typedef** storage specifier do not introduce new types; the names are considered to be synonyms for types that could be specified in other ways.

Example

After the declaration

```
typedef struct S { int a; int b; } s1type, s2type;
```

the type specifiers **s1type**, **s2type**, and **struct S** can be used interchangeably to refer to the same type.

Although **typedef** only introduces synonyms for types that can be named in other ways, C implementations may wish to preserve the declared type names internally so that debuggers and other tools can refer to types by the names used by the programmer.

In C99, if a **typedef** declaration includes a variable length array type, then the array size expression is evaluated when the **typedef** declaration is processed, not when the **typedef** name is used to declare an array.

Example

In the following code fragment, the array **a** is a 10-element array of integers because the size of type **Array** was bound when the **typedef** was seen, not when **a** was declared.

```
{
    int n = 10;
    typedef int Array[n];
    n = 25;
    Array a;
    ...
}
```

References   type compatibility 5.11; variable length arrays 5.4.5

5.10.1 Typedef Names for Function Types

A function type may be given a **typedef** name, but functions must not inherit their "function-ness" from **typedef** names. This restricts function **typedef**s somewhat.

Example

DblFunc becomes a synonym for "function returning **double**" with this declaration:

```
typedef double DblFunc();
```

Once declared, **DblFunc** can be used to declare pointers to the function type, arrays of pointers to the function type, and so forth, using the normal rules for composing declarators:

```
extern DblFunc *f_ptr, *f_array[];
```

Abiding by the normal rules of type declarations, the programmer must not declare invalid types, such as an array of functions:

```
extern DblFunc f_array[10];    /* Invalid! */
```

However, **DblFunc** cannot be used to define functions. The following definition of **fabs** is rejected because it seems to define a function returning another function:

```
DblFunc fabs(double x)
{
    if (x<0.0) return -x; else return x;
}
```

It is not possible to get around this problem by omitting the parentheses after **fabs**, because that is where the parameter must be listed. The function definition must be written in the usual way, as if **DblFunc** did not exist:

```
double fabs(double x)
{
    if (x<0.0) return -x; else return x;
}
```

In Standard C, **typedef** names can include function prototype information, including parameter names:

```
typedef double DFuncType( double x );
typedef double (*FuncPtr)( int, float );
```

In this example, **DFuncType** is a function type and **FuncPtr** is a function pointer type.

References   function declarators 4.5; function definitions 9.1; function prototypes9.2

5.10.2 Redefining Typedef Names

The language specifies that **typedef** names may be redefined in inner blocks in the same fashion as ordinary identifiers.

Example

```
typedef int T;
T foo;
...
{
    float T; /* New definition for T */
    T = 1.0;
    ...
}
```

One restriction is that the redeclaration cannot omit the type specifiers on the assumption that the type will default to **int**. Some non-ISO compilers have been known to have problems with redeclarations of **typedef** names, probably because of the pressure **typedef** names put on the C language grammar. We now turn to this problem.

References   redefining **typedef** names in C++ 5.13.2; scope of names 4.2.1

5.10.3 Implementation Note

Allowing ordinary identifiers to be type specifiers makes the C grammar context sensitive, and hence not LALR(1). To see this, consider the program line

```
A ( *B ) ;
```

If **A** has been defined as a **typedef** name, then the line is a declaration of a variable **B** to be of type "pointer to **A**." (The parentheses surrounding "***B**" are ignored.) If **A** is not a type name, then the line is a call of the function **A** with the single parameter ***B**. This ambiguity cannot be resolved grammatically.

C compilers based on the parser-generator YACC—such as the Portable C Compiler—handle this problem by feeding information acquired during semantic analysis back to lexical analysis. All C compilers must do **typedef** processing during lexical analysis.

5.11 TYPE COMPATIBILITY

Two types in C are *compatible* if they are either the same type or "close enough" to be considered the same for many purposes. The notion of compatible types was introduced by Standard C, but for the most part it captures in a more formal way the rules that are used in traditional C. Some additional rules are necessary to handle Standard C features such as function prototypes and type qualifiers. For two types to be compatible, they either must be the same type, or must be pointers, functions, or arrays with certain properties. The specific rules are discussed in the following sections.

Associated with every two compatible types is a *composite type*, which is the common type that arises out of the two compatible types. This is similar to the way in which the usual binary conversions take two integral types and combine them to yield a common result type for some arithmetic operators. The composite type produced by two compatible types is described along with the rules for type compatibility.

References   array types 5.4; function prototypes 9.2; function types 5.8; pointer types 5.3; structure types 5.6; type qualifiers 4.4.3; union types 5.7; usual binary conversions 6.3

5.11.1 Identical Types

Two arithmetic types can be compatible only if they are the same type. If a type can be written using different combinations of type specifiers, all the alternate forms are the same type. That is, the types **short** and **short int** are the same, but the types **unsigned**, **int**, and **short** are all different. The type **signed int** is the same as **int** (and equivalently for **short** and **long**), except when they are used as the types of bit fields. The types **char**, **signed char**, and **unsigned char** are always different.

Any two types that are the same are compatible and their composite type is the same type. In Standard C, the presence of any type qualifiers changes the type: type **const int** is not the same as—nor is it compatible with—type **int**. Names declared as types in **typedef** definitions are synonyms for types, not new types.

Example

After these declarations, the types of **p** and **q** are the same; the types of **x** and **y** are the same, but neither is the same as the type of **u**; the types **TS** and **struct S** are the same; and the types of **u**, **w**, and **y** are the same.

```
char * p, *q;
struct {int a, b;} x, y;
struct S {int a, b;} u;
typedef struct S TS;
struct S w;
TS y;
```

Example

After these declarations, the type `my_int` is the same as type `int`, and the type `my_function` is the same as the type "`float *()`":

```
typedef int my_int;
typedef float *my_function();
```

Example

After these declarations, the variables **w**, **x**, **y**, and **z** all have the same type.

```
struct S { int a, b; } x;
typedef struct S t1, t2;
struct S w;
t1 y;
t2 z;
```

References   integer types 5.1; pointer types 5.3; structure types 5.6; `typedef` names 5.10

5.11.2 Enumeration Compatibility

Each enumerated type definition gives rise to a new integral type. Standard C requires each enumerated type to be compatible with the implementation-defined integer type that represents it. The compatible integer type may be different for different enumerations in the same program. The composite type is the enumerated type. No two different enumerated types defined in the same source file are compatible.

Example

In the following declarations, the types of **E1** and **E2** are not compatible, but the types of **E1** and **E3** are compatible because they are the same type.

```
enum e {a,b} E1;
enum {c,d} E2;
enum e E3;
```

Because enumerated types are generally treated as integer types, values of different enumerated types can be mixed freely regardless of type compatibility.

Example

The effect of the compatibility rule is that Standard C will reject the second function declaration below because the argument type in the prototype does not agree with the first declaration:

```
extern int f( enum {a,b} x);
extern int f( enum {b,c} x);
```

Non-Standard implementations sometimes treat enumerated types as fully compatible with **int** and with each other.

References   enumerated types 5.5

5.11.3 Array Compatibility

Two similarly qualified array types are compatible only if their element types are compatible. If both types specify constant sizes, then the sizes must also be the same. However, if only one array type specifies a constant size—or if neither do—then the two types are compatible. The composite type of two compatible array types is an array type with the composite element type and the same type qualification. If either original type specifies a constant size, then the composite type has that constant size; otherwise the size is unspecified. If two arrays are used in a context that requires them to be compatible, then the results are undefined unless the dimensions are the same at run time.

Example

The following array types are compatible as noted. **e** is a variable length array (C99).

```
extern int a[];   /* compatible with b, c, and e; not d */
int b[5]; /* compatible with a       and e only */
int c[10]; /* compatible with a      and e only */
const int d[10]; /* not compatible with other types */
int e[n]; /* compatible with a, b, and c; not d */
```

The type of **d** is not compatible with other types because its element type, **const int**, is not compatible with element type **int**. The composite type of the types of **a** and **b** is **int [5]**. At run time, using **a** and **b** in place of one another would be well defined only if the actual definition of **a** had length 5.

References   array types 5.4, array declarators 4.5.3; type qualifiers 4.4.3; variable length array 5.4.5

5.11.4 Function Compatibility

For two function types to be compatible, they must specify compatible return types. If both types are specified in traditional (nonprototype) form, that is all that is required. The composite type is a (traditional-form) function type with the composite return type.

For two function types both declared in prototype form to be compatible, the following conditions must hold:

1. The function return types must be compatible.

2. The number of parameters and the use of the ellipsis must agree.

3. The corresponding parameters must have compatible types.

It is not necessary that any parameter names agree. The composite type is a function type whose parameters have the composite parameter types, with the same use of the ellipsis, and with the composite return type.

If only one of the two function types is in prototype form, then for the two types to be compatible the following conditions must hold:

1. The return types must be compatible.

2. The prototype must not include the ellipsis terminator.

3. Each parameter type T in the prototype must be compatible with the type resulting from applying the usual argument conversions to T.

The composite type is the prototype-form function type with the composite return value.

> **References**   function prototypes 9.2; function types 5.8

5.11.5 Structure and Union Compatibility

Each occurrence of a type specifier that is a structure-type definition or union-type definition introduces a new structure or union type that is neither the same as nor compatible with any other such type in the same source file.

A type specifier that is a structure, union, or enumerated type *reference* is the same type introduced in the corresponding *definition*. The type tag is used to associate the reference with the definition, and in that sense may be thought of as the name of the type.

Example

The types of **x**, **y**, and **u** next are all different, but the types of **u** and **v** are the same:

```
struct { int a; int b; } x;
struct { int a; int b; } y;
struct S { int a; int b; } u;
struct S v;
```

> **References**   enumerations 5.5; structures 5.6; unions 5.7

5.11.6 Pointer Compatibility

Two (similarly qualified) pointer types are compatible if they point to compatible types. The composite type for two compatible pointer types is the (similarly qualified) pointer to the composite type.

5.11.7 Compatibility Across Source Files

Although structure, union, and enumerated type definitions give rise to new (noncompatible) types, a loophole must be created to allow references across separately compiled source files within the same program.

Example

Suppose a header file contains these declarations:

```
struct S {int a,b;};
extern struct S x;
```

When two source files in a program both import this header file, the intent is that the two files reference the same variable, **x**, which has the single type **struct S**. However, each file theoretically contains a definition of a different structure type that just happens to be named **struct S** in each instance.

Unless two declarations of the same type are compatible, Standard C states that the run-time behavior of the program is undefined, and therefore:

1. Two structures or unions defined in separate source files are compatible if they declare the same members in the same order and each corresponding member has a compatible type (including the width of bit fields). In C99, this rule is tightened to also require that the structure or union tags be the same (or both be omitted).

2. Two enumerations defined in separate source files are compatible if they contain the same enumeration constants (in any order), each with the same value.

In these cases, the composite type is the type in the current source file.

References   enumerated types 5.5; structure types 5.6; union types 5.7

5.12 TYPE NAMES AND ABSTRACT DECLARATORS

There are two situations in C programming when it is necessary to write the name of a type without declaring an object of that type: when writing cast expressions and when applying the **sizeof** operator to a type. In these cases, one uses a type name built from an abstract declarator. (Do not confuse "type name" with "**typedef** name.")

type-name :
    declaration-specifiers abstract-declarator$_{opt}$

abstract-declarator :
    pointer
    pointer$_{opt}$ direct-abstract-declarator

pointer:
    * *type-qualifier-list$_{opt}$*
    * *type-qualifier-list$_{opt}$ pointer*

type-qualifier-list :   *(C89)*
    type-qualifier
    type-qualifier-list type-qualifier

direct-abstract-declarator :
    (*abstract-declarator*)
    direct-abstract-declarator$_{opt}$ [*constant-expression*$_{opt}$]
    direct-abstract-declarator$_{opt}$ [*expression*]   *(C99)*
    direct-abstract-declarator$_{opt}$ [*]   *(C99)*
    direct-abstract-declarator$_{opt}$ (*parameter-type-list*$_{opt}$)

An abstract declarator resembles a regular declarator in which the enclosed identifier has been replaced by the empty string. Thus, a type name looks like a declaration from which the enclosed identifier has been omitted. In the syntax, the *declaration-specifiers* must not include storage class specifiers. The *parameter-type-list* is permitted only in Standard C, where it is used for a prototype-form type declaration.

The precedences of the alternatives of the abstract declarator are the same as in the case of normal declarators.

Example

Type name	Translation
`int`	type `int`
`float *`	pointer to `float`
`char (*)(int)`	pointer to function taking an `int` parameter and returning `char`
`unsigned *[4]`	array of 4 pointers to `unsigned`
`int (*(*)())()`	pointer to function returning pointer to function returning `int`

Type names always appear within the parentheses that form part of the syntax of the cast or `sizeof` operator. If the type specifier in the type name is a structure, union, or enumerated type *definition*, then Standard C requires an implementation to define a new type with the included type tag (if any) at that point. It is considered bad style to make use of this feature. (It is invalid in C++.)

Example

Assume that **struct S** is not defined when the following two statements are encountered. (A good C implementation should issue a warning on the first line.)

```
i = sizeof( struct S {int a,b;}); /* OK, but strange */
j = sizeof( struct S ); /* OK, struct S is now defined */
```

References   casts 7.5.1; function prototypes 9.2; **sizeof** operator 7.5.2

5.13 C++ COMPATIBILITY

5.13.1 Enumeration Types

It is good practice not to use enumerated types or enumeration constants as integer types without explicit casts. Unlike C, C++ treats enumerated types as distinct from each other and from integer types, although you can convert between them with casts. C++ also permits implicit conversions from enumeration types to integer types.

Example

```
enum e {blue, red, yellow} e_var;
int i_var;
...
i_var = red;            /* valid in both C and C++ */
e_var = 1; /* valid in C, not in C++ */
i_var = (int) red; /* valid in both C and C++ */
e_var = (enum e) 3;     /* valid in both C and C++ */
assert(sizeof(blue) == sizeof(int));
    /* always succeeds in C; may fail in C++ */
```

References   enumeration type 5.5

5.13.2 Typedef Names

As in C, **typedef** names can be redeclared as objects in inner scopes. However, in C++ it is not permitted to do so within a structure or union—which are scopes—if the original **typedef** name has been used in the structure or union already. This situation is unlikely to occur in practice.

Example

```
typedef int INT;
struct S {
   INT i;
   double INT; /* OK in C, not C++; everywhere a bad idea*/
}
```

References   redefining typedef names 5.10.2

5.13.3 Type Compatibility

C++ does not have C's notion of type compatibility. To do stricter type checking, C++ requires identical types in situations in which C would require only compatible types. In some cases, C++ will issue a diagnostic if the types are not identical. However, because C++ provides "layout compatibility" with C, a C++ program will still work correctly even if it contains undetected occurrences of nonidentical but (Standard C) compatible types.

References   type compatibility 5.11

5.14 EXERCISES

1. What C type would you choose to represent the following sets of values? Assume your main priority is portability across different compilers and computers, and your secondary priority is to minimize space consumption.

   (a) a five-digit U.S. Postal Service zip code

   (b) a phone number consisting of a three-digit area code and a seven-digit local number

   (c) the values 0 and 1

   (d) the values −1, 0, and 1

   (e) either an alphabetic character or the value −1

   (f) the balance in a bank account, in dollars and cents, up to 9,999,999.99

2. Some popular computers support an extended character set that includes the normal ASCII characters as well as additional characters whose values are in the range 128 through 255. Assume that type **char** is represented in eight bits. The following **is_up_arrow** function is supposed to return "true" if the input character represents the up-arrow key and "false" otherwise. Will this function be portable across different Standard C compilers assuming that the definition of **UP_ARROW_KEY** has the proper value for the target computer? If not, rewrite it so that it is.

   ```
   #define UP_ARROW_KEY   0x86
   ...
   int is_up_arrow(char c)
   {
       return c == UP_ARROW_KEY;
   }
   ```

3. If **vp** has type **void** * and **cp** has type **char** *, which of the following assignment statements are valid in Standard C?

   (a) **vp = cp;**   (c) ***vp = *cp;**

   (b) **cp = vp;**   (d) ***cp = *vp;**

4. If **iv** has type **int** [3] and **im** has type **int** [4] [5], rewrite the following expressions without using the subscript operator:

   (a) **iv[i]**

   (b) **im[i][j]**

5. What integer value is returned by the following function **f**? Is the cast to type **int** in the **return** statement necessary?

   ```
   enum birds {wren, robin=12, blue_jay};
   int f()
   {
       return (int) blue_jay;
   }
   ```

6. Following is the definition of a structured type and a variable of that type. Write a series of statements that assign a valid value to every component of the structure. If two components of the structure overlap, assign to only one of the overlapping components.

```
struct S {
    int i;
    struct T {
        unsigned s: 1;
        unsigned e: 7;
        unsigned m: 24;
    } F;
    union U {
        double d;
        char a[6];
        int * p;
    } U;
} x;
```

7.   Make two sketches of the structure defined in the previous problem using the same format as in
     Sections 5.6.5 and 5.7.3. Assume that the underlying computer is byte-addressed using 8 bits
     for type **char**, 32 bits for pointers and type **int**, and 64 bits for type **double**. In the first
     sketch, assume a big-endian computer with bit fields packed right to left within 32-bit words;
     in the second, assume a little-endian with bit fields packed right to left within words. In both
     cases, assume the compiler packs bit fields as tightly as possible. (Endianness is described in
     Section 6.1.2.)

8.   Write a **typedef** definition of the type "function returning pointer to integer." Write a decla-
     ration of a variable that holds a pointer to such a function and write an actual function of that
     type using the **typedef** definition where possible.

9.   Write a **stdbool.h** header file so that a programmer can use C99-style boolean types in a
     C89 implementation. Are there any limitations?

10. Rewrite the data tag example of Section 5.7.3, including the **print_widget** function, mak-
     ing a **WIDGET** be a union of three structures, each including a data tag and a data value. Is your
     implementation portable to other Standard C conforming implementations?

6

Conversions and Representations

Most programming languages try to hide the details of the language's implementation on a particular computer. For the most part, the C programmer need not be aware of these details, either, although a major attraction of C is that it allows the programmer to go below the abstract language level and expose the underlying representation of programs and data. With this freedom comes a certain amount of risk: Some C programmers inadvertently descend below the abstract programming level and build into their programs nonportable assumptions about data representations.

This chapter has three purposes. First, it discusses some characteristics of data and program representations, indicating how the choice of representations can affect a C program. Second, it discusses in some detail the conversion of values of one type to another, emphasizing the characteristics of C that are portable across implementations. Finally, it presents the "usual conversion rules" of C, which are the conversions that happen automatically when expressions are evaluated.

6.1 REPRESENTATIONS

This section discusses the representation of functions and data and how the choice of representations can affect C programs and C implementations.

6.1.1 Storage Units and Data Sizes

All data objects in C except bit fields are represented at run time in the computer's memory in an integral number of abstract *storage units*. Each storage unit is in turn made up of

some fixed number of *bits*, each of which can assume either of two values, denoted 0 and
1. Each storage unit must be uniquely addressable and is the same size as type **char**. The
number of bits in a storage unit is implementation-defined in C, but it must be large
enough to hold every character in the basic character set. The C Standard also calls storage
units *bytes*, but the term *byte* is usually understood to mean a storage unit consisting of exactly eight bits.

By definition, the *size* of a data object is the number of storage units occupied by
that data object. A storage unit is taken to be the amount of storage occupied by one character; the size of an object of type **char** is therefore 1. The number of bits in a character
(byte) is given by the value of **CHAR_BIT** in **limits.h**.

Because all data objects of a given type occupy the same amount of storage, we can
also refer to the size of a *type* as the number of storage units occupied by an object of that
type. The **sizeof** operator may be used to determine the size of a data object or type. We
say that a type is "longer" or "larger" than another type if its size is greater. Similarly, we
say that a type is "shorter" or "smaller" than another type if its size is less. Standard C requires certain minimum ranges for the integer and floating-point types and provides
implementation-defined header files **limits.h** and **float.h** that define the sizes.

Example

The following C99 program determines the sizes of the principal C data types. To be compatible with older versions of C, the length modifier **z** in **%3zd** should be replaced by a modifier
character appropriate for **size_t** (the type of **sizeof**): **l** (ell) if it is **long** and nothing if it
is **int**.

```
#include <stdio.h>
int main(void)
{
    printf("\tType sizes:\n");
    printf("char\tshort\tint\tlong\tllong\t"
           "float\tdouble\tldouble\n");
    printf("%3zd\t%3zd\t%3zd\t%3zd\t%3zd\t"
           "%3zd\t%3zd\t%3zd\n",
           sizeof(char), sizeof(short), sizeof(int),
           sizeof(long), sizeof(long long),
           sizeof(float), sizeof(double) ,
           sizeof(long double));
    return 0;
}
```

References   character types 5.1.3; **float.h** 5.2; **limits.h** 5.1.1; minimum integer
sizes 5.1.1; **sizeof** operator 7.5.2; **stdio.h** standard I/O Ch. 15

6.1.2 Byte Ordering

The addressing structure of a computer determines how storage pieces of various sizes are
named by pointers. The addressing model most natural for C is one in which each character (byte) in the computer's memory can be individually addressed. Computers using this
model are called *byte-addressable* computers. The address of a larger piece of storage—

one used to hold an integer or a floating-point number, for example—is typically the same as the address of the first character in the larger unit. The "first" character is the one with the lowest address.

Even within this simple model, computers differ in their storage "byte order"—that is, they differ in which byte of storage they consider to be the "first" one in a larger piece. In "right-to-left" or "little-endian" architectures, which include the Intel 80x86 and Pentium microprocessors, the address of a 32-bit integer is also the address of the low-order byte of the integer. In "left-to-right" or "big-endian" architectures, which include the Motorola 680x0 microprocessor family, the address of a 32-bit integer is the address of the high-order byte of the integer. Some embedded processors can be configured as either big-endian or little-endian depending on the needs of the total system.

Example

Both the Intel (little-endian) and Motorola (big-endian) architectures are byte-addressed, with 8-bit bytes and 4-byte words, which can hold 32-bit integers. The following picture shows a sequence of words on each architecture, with each word containing the 32-bit value `0x01020304`. As you can see, the two architectures look the same at this level of detail.

Big-endian,
left to right

01020304	01020304	. . .
A	A+4	A+8

Little-endian,
right to left

01020304	01020304	. . .
A	A+4	A+8

The situation changes when we look at the contents of individual bytes within a word. On the big-endian, the address of the word is the address of the leftmost (high-order) byte. Since byte addresses increase left to right, it appears consistent with the way we drew the words before. On the little-endian, however, the address of the word is the address of the rightmost (low-order) byte. You can picture this in two ways: Either the addresses in the word increase right to left or else the bytes are reversed. Both views are shown next.

Big-endian,
left to right

01	02	03	04	. . .
A	A+1	A+2	A+3	A+4

Little-endian,
right to left
(first view)

01	02	03	04	. . .
A+3	A+2	A+1	A	A+7

Little-endian,
right to left
(second view)

04	03	02	01	. . .
A	A+1	A+2	A+3	A+4

Components of a structure type are allocated in the order of increasing addresses—that is, either left to right or right to left depending on the byte order of the computer. Because bit fields are also packed following the byte order, it is natural to number the bits in a piece of storage following the same convention. Thus, in a left-to-right computer, the most significant (leftmost) bit of a 32-bit integer would be bit number 0 and the least significant bit would be bit number 31. In right-to-left computers, the least significant (rightmost) bit would be bit 0, and so forth. Programs that assume a particular byte order will not be portable.

Example

Here is a program that determines a computer's byte ordering by using a union in a nonportable fashion. The union has the same size as an object of type **long** and is initialized so that the low-order byte of the union contains a 1 and all other bytes contain zeroes. In right-to-left architectures the character component, **Char**, of the union will be overlaid on the low-order byte of the long component, **Long**, whereas in left-to-right architectures **Char** will be overlaid on the high-order byte of **Long**:

```
#include <stdio.h>
union {
    long Long;
    char Char[sizeof(long)];
} u;

int main(void)
{
    u.Long = 1;
    if (u.Char[0] == 1)
        printf("Addressing is right-to-left\n");
    else if (u.Char[sizeof(long)-1] == 1)
        printf("Addressing is left-to-right\n");
    else printf("Addressing is strange\n");
    return 0;
}
```

6.1.3 Alignment Restrictions

Some computers allow data objects to reside in storage at any address regardless of the data's type. Others impose *alignment restrictions* on certain data types, requiring that objects of those types occupy only certain addresses. It is not unusual for a byte-addressed computer, for example, to require that 32-bit (4-byte) integers be located on addresses that are a multiple of four. In this case, we say that the "alignment modulus" of those integers is four. Failing to obey the alignment restrictions can result in either a run-time error or unexpected program behavior. Even when there are no alignment restrictions per se, there may be a performance penalty for using data on unaligned addresses, and therefore a C implementation may align data purely for efficiency.

The C programmer is not normally aware of alignment restrictions because the compiler takes care to place data on the appropriate address boundaries. However, C does give the programmer the ability to violate alignment restrictions by casting pointers to different types. Uninitialized pointers may also violate alignment restrictions.

In general, if the alignment requirement for a type S is at least as stringent as that for a type D (i.e., the alignment modulus for S is no smaller than the alignment modulus for D), then converting a "pointer to type S" to a "pointer to type D" is safe. *Safe* here means that the resulting pointer to type D will work as expected if used to fetch or store an object of type D, and that a subsequent conversion back to the original pointer type will recover the original pointer. A corollary to this is that any data pointer can be converted to type **char *** or **void *** and back safely since they have the least stringent alignment requirements.

If the alignment requirement for a type S is less stringent than that for type D, then the conversion from a "pointer to type S" to a "pointer to type D" could result in either of two kinds of unexpected behavior. First, an attempt to use the resulting pointer to fetch or store an object of type D may cause an error, halting the program. Second, either the hardware or the implementation may "adjust" the destination pointer to be valid, usually by forcing it back to the nearest previous valid address. A subsequent conversion back to the original pointer type may not recover the original pointer.

References   byte ordering 6.1.2; **malloc** function 16.1; pointer types 5.3

6.1.4 Pointer Sizes

There is no requirement in C that any of the integral types be large enough to represent a pointer, although C programmers often assume that type **long** is large enough, which it is on most computers. In C99, header **inttypes.h** may define integer types **intptr_t** and **uintptr_t**, which are guaranteed large enough to hold a pointer as an integer.

Although function pointers are usually no larger than **void *** pointers, this is not guaranteed to be the case, as discussed in Section 6.1.5. Standard C treats all conversions between object and function pointers as undefined.

References   function types 5.8; pointer conversions 6.2.7; pointer types 5.3; sizes of types 6.1.1

6.1.5 Effects of Addressing Models

This section describes some ways in which a computer's memory design can impact the C programmer and implementor.

Memory models   Some smaller and special-purpose microprocessors are designed in such a way that the choice of a representation for pointers involves a time-space trade-off that may not be appropriate for all programs.These processors can make use of both "short" and "long" addresses. The smaller addresses (those within a single *segment*) are more efficient, but limit the amount of memory that can be referenced. Large programs often require access to multiple segments.

To accommodate the needs of different programs, C compilers for these computers often allow the programmer to specify a *memory model*, which establishes the time-space trade-off used in the program. Table 6–1 shows representative memory models supported by the C compilers for early PCs. Variations of these models are still found in some digital signal processors.

There are several points to note here. In all the memory models, code and data are kept in separate memory segments with their own address space. Therefore, it is possible for data and function pointers to contain the same value even though one points to an

Table 6–1 Memory models on early PCs

Memory model name	Data pointer size	Function pointer size	Characteristics
tiny	16 bits	16 bits	code, data, and stack all occupy a single segment
small	16	16	code occupies one 64K-byte segment; data and stack occupy a second 64K-byte segment
medium	16	32	code can occupy many segments; data and stack are limited to one segment
compact	32	16	code and stack are each limited to a single 64K segment; other data can occupy many segments
large	32	32	code and data can both occupy many segments; stack is restricted to one segment
huge (32-bit flat)	32	32	same as large, but single data items can exceed 64K bytes in size

object and the other to a function. In the compact and medium memory models, data and function pointers have different sizes. Some care should be used with the null pointer constant, **NULL** (Section 5.3.2), which is an object pointer. Simple uses of **NULL** in expressions involving function pointers will be properly converted, but passing **NULL** as a function pointer argument may not work correctly in the absence of a prototype. This problem can be mostly eliminated by the careful use of function prototypes in Standard C, which will cause arguments to be correctly converted.

Example

A C programmer unfamiliar with segmented architectures might suppose that a data pointer and function pointer could contain the same value only if both were null pointers, and might incorrectly use the following test. This does not work because **cp** and **fp** could point into different address spaces and accidentally have the same non-null value.

```
char *cp;
int (*fp)();
...
/* See if cp and fp are both null */
if ((int)cp == (int)fp) ...  /* Incorrect!! */
```

Example

In the following example from traditional C, the behavior of function **f** is undefined when using the compact or medium memory models because the null pointer passed as an argument is an object pointer, not a function pointer, and therefore is not the correct size:

```
extern int f(); /* no parameter information */
...
f(NULL);    /* This is NOT OK! */
...
int f( int (*fp)() ) { ... }
```

Explicit control over pointer sizes   An alternative to using a specific memory model for an entire program (or an addition to it) is to specify whether "near" or "far" pointers are to be used for specific functions or data objects. In this way, a programmer can avoid across-the-board performance penalties, although the program will be less portable and probably harder to maintain.

Example

> Several C compilers for segmented architectures define new keywords `__near` and `__far` that can be used in declarations of variables and pointers. Syntactically, they can appear where Standard C type qualifiers appear. The keywords are spelled with two leading underscores because those names are reserved for implementations (Section 10.1.1).
>
> ```
> char __near near_char, *cp;
> int __far (*fp)(), big_array[30000]
> ```
>
> The intent is that `far` pointers will occupy 32 bits, whereas `near` pointers will use 16 bits. Functions or data objects declared `far` can be placed in remote segments by the implementation, whereas `near` ones must be grouped in the "root" segment. Programmers using these language extensions must be very careful when passing the pointers to functions not declared with prototypes.

Array addressing   Regardless of whether a computer uses a segmented addressing scheme, some computers are designed in a way that makes accessing elements of an array more efficient if the array size is small—typically not bigger than 64K bytes. To use larger arrays, the programmer must supply a special compiler option or designate the large arrays in some way.

Very difficult computers   Although C has been implemented efficiently on many computers, a few computers represent data and addresses in forms that are very awkward for C implementations. A major problem can occur when the computer's natural word size is not a multiple of its natural byte size. Suppose—this was a real example—our computer has a 36-bit word and represents characters in 7 bits; each word can hold five characters with one bit remaining unused. All noncharacter data types occupy one or more full words. This memory structure will be very difficult for a C implementor because C programming relies on the ability to map any data structure onto an array of characters. That is, to copy an object of type T at address A, it should be sufficient to copy $\mathtt{sizeof}(T)$ characters beginning at A. The only alternative for the implementor on this computer would be to represent characters using some nonstandard number of bits (e.g., 9 or 36) so that they fit tightly into a word. This representation could have a significant performance penalty.

A similar problem occurs on "word-addressed" computers whose basic addressable storage unit is larger than a single character. On these computers, there may or may not be a special kind of address, a "byte pointer," that can represent characters within a word. Assuming there is such a byte pointer, it may very well be larger than a pointer to objects of noncharacter types or may use certain bits in the pointer that are ignored and normally set to zero in other kinds of pointers. A C implementor must decide whether to pay the increased overhead of representing all pointers as byte pointers, whether to use the larger format only for objects of type `char *` (and, in Standard C, `void *`), or whether to use a full word to represent each character. Having a different size for character pointers will force C programmers to be more careful about pointer conversions.

References   array types 5.4; character types 5.1.3; function argument conversions 6.3.5; function prototypes 9.2; pointer types 5.3; storage units 6.1.1

6.1.6 Type Representations

The representation of a value of some type is the particular pattern of bits in the storage area that holds object of that type; this pattern distinguishes the value of the object from other possible values of that type. It is not necessary that the type's representation use all the bits within its objects; some bits may be "padding," whose value is undefined. For example, a **short** data type may use only 16 bits but be stored in a 32-bit word. The padding bits are included in the size returned by **sizeof**. The terms *range* or *precision* are more correct when any padding is to be ignored.

It can also be the case that the same value has more than one representation in a type. There might be a representation for both **+0** and **−0** in integers, for example. Implementations have the freedom to choose among such equivalent representations at any time.

Representations belonging to one type may be incompatible with those of another type even if the types have the same size. If you were to access a **long** value as if it were of type **float**, then the result is undefined—it could even cause the program to halt.

Using a C99 term, the *effective type* of an object is the type whose representation is currently being used in the object. Normally, a data object (e.g., a variable) is declared to be of a certain type and that is always its effective type so there is no problem. Sometimes, such as when using objects allocated by **malloc**, an object has no declared type. Then the effective type of the object is the type of the lvalue expression that was last used to store a value into the object. Subsequent accesses of the object must use a type compatible with the effective type (or a qualified version of a compatible type) or else the result is undefined. Copying a value into an object with no declared type (such as with **memcpy** or by referencing the underlying **char** values of the storage object) causes the effective type of the source to be adopted by the destination.

References   lvalue 7.1; **malloc** 16.1; **memcpy** 14.3; qualified type 4.4

6.2 CONVERSIONS

The C language provides for values of one type to be converted to values of other types under several circumstances:

- A cast expression may be used to explicitly convert a value to another type.
- An operand may be implicitly converted to another type in preparation for performing some arithmetic or logical operation.
- An object of one type may be assigned to a location (lvalue) of another type, causing an implicit type conversion.

- An actual argument to a function may be implicitly converted to another type prior to the function call.

- A return value from a function may be implicitly converted to another type prior to the function return.

There are restrictions as to what types a given object may be converted. Furthermore, the set of conversions that are possible on assignment, for instance, is not the same as the set of conversions that are possible with type casts.

In the following sections, we discuss the set of possible conversions and then discuss which of these conversions are actually performed in each of the circumstances listed before.

6.2.1 Representation Changes

A conversion of a value from one type to another may or may not involve a representation change. For instance, whenever the two types have different sizes, a representation change has to be made. When integers are converted to a floating-point representation, a representation change is made even if the integer and floating-point type have the same sizes. However, when a value of type **int** is converted to type **unsigned int**, a representation change may not be necessary.

Some representation changes are very simple, involving merely discarding of excess bits or padding with extra 0 bits. Other changes may be more complicated, such as conversions between integer and floating-point representations. For each of the conversions discussed in the following sections, we describe the possible representation changes that may be required.

6.2.2 Trivial Conversions

It is always possible to convert a value from a type to another type that is the same as (or compatible with) the first type. See Section 5.11 for a discussion of when types are the same or compatible. No representation change needs to occur in this case.

Most implementations refuse to convert structure or union types to themselves because no conversions to structure or union types are normally permitted.

6.2.3 Conversions to Integer Types

Scalar types (arithmetic types and pointers) may be converted to integers.

Boolean conversions   In C99, conversions involving type **_Bool** are slightly different than those involving only the other integer types. When converting an arithmetic value to type **_Bool**, the converted value is 0 if the original value is zero; otherwise it is 1. When converting a pointer type to type **_Bool**, null pointers are converted to 0 and all other pointer values are converted to 1. When converting from type **_Bool** to an arithmetic type, the result is either 0 or 1, converted to the destination type. The rest of this section assumes the integer types are not **_Bool** unless otherwise stated.

From integer types Except for the type `_Bool`, the general rule for converting from one integer type to another is that the mathematical value of the result should equal the original mathematical value if that is possible. For example, if an unsigned integer has the value 15 and this value is to be converted to a signed type, the resulting signed value should be 15 also.

If it is not possible to represent the original value of an object of the new type, then there are two cases. If the result type is a signed type, then the conversion is considered to have overflowed and the result value is technically not defined. If the result type is an unsigned type, then the result must be that unique value of the result type that is equal (congruent) mod 2^n to the original value, where n is equal to the number of bits used in the representation of the result type. If signed integers are represented using twos-complement notation, then no change of representation is necessary when converting between signed and unsigned integers of the same size. However, if signed integers are represented in some other way, such as with ones-complement or sign-magnitude representation, then a change of representation will be necessary.

When an unsigned integer is converted to a signed integer of the same size, the conversion is considered to overflow if the original value is too large to represent exactly in the signed representation (i.e., if the high-order bit of the unsigned number is 1). However, many programmers and programs depend on the conversion being performed quietly and with no change of representation to produce a negative number.

If the destination type is longer than the source type, then the only case in which the source value will not be representable in the result type is when a negative signed value is converted to a longer, unsigned type. In that case, the conversion must necessarily behave as if the source value were first converted to a longer signed type of the same size as the destination type and then converted to the destination type.

Example

Since the constant expression **-1** has type `int`:

```
((unsigned long) -1) == ((unsigned long) ((long) -1)))
```

If the destination type is shorter than the source type and both the original and destination types are unsigned, then the conversion can be performed simply by discarding excess high-order bits from the original value. The bit pattern of the result representation will be equal to the n low-order bits of the original representation, where n is the number of bits in the destination type. This same rule of discarding works for converting signed integers in twos-complement form to a shorter unsigned type. The discarding rule is also one of several acceptable methods for converting signed or unsigned integers to a shorter signed type when signed integers are in twos-complement form. Note that this rule will not preserve the sign of the value in case of overflow, but the action on overflow is not defined in any case. When signed integers are not represented in twos-complement form, the conversions are more complicated. Although the C language does not require the twos-complement representation for signed integers, it certainly favors that representation.

When the destination type is `_Bool`, all nonzero source values are mapped to 1. Only the source value zero converts to 0.

From floating-point types   The conversion of a floating-point value to an integral value should produce a result that is (if possible) equal in value to the value of the old object. If the floating-point value has a nonzero fractional part, that fraction should be discarded—that is, conversion normally involves truncation of the floating-point value.

The behavior of the conversion is undefined if the floating-point value cannot be represented even approximately in the new type—for example, if its magnitude is much too large or if a negative floating-point value is converted to an unsigned integer type. The handling of overflow and underflow is left to the discretion of the implementor.

From pointer types   When the source value is a pointer and the destination type is not **_Bool**, the pointer is treated as if it were an unsigned integer of a size equal to the size of the pointer. Then the unsigned integer is converted to the destination type using the rules listed before. If null pointers are not represented as the value 0, then they must be explicitly converted to 0 when converting the null pointer to an integer.

C programmers used to assume that pointers could be converted to type **long** and back without loss of information. Although this was almost always true, it is not required by the language definition. In C99, the types **intptr_t** and **uintptr_t**, if defined in **stdint.h**, are signed and unsigned integer types capable of holding pointers. The problem is that some computers may have pointer representations that are longer than the largest integer type.

References   **_Bool** type 5.1.5; character types 5.1.3; floating-point types 5.2; integer types 5.1; **intptr_t** 21.5; overflow 7.2.2; pointer types 5.3; **uintptr_t** 21.5; **stdint.h** Ch. 21; unsigned types 5.1.2; **void *** type 5.3.1

6.2.4 Conversions to Floating-Point Types

Only arithmetic types may be converted to floating-point types.

When converting from **float** to **double** or from **double** to **long double**, the result should have the same value as the original value. This may be viewed as a restriction on the choice of representations for the floating-point types.

When converting from **double** to **float** or from **long double** to **double**, such that the original value is within the range of values representable in the new type, the result should be one of the two floating-point values closest to the original value. Whether the original value is rounded up or down is implementation-dependent.

If the original value is outside the range of values representable in the destination type—as when the magnitude of a **double** number is too large or too small for the representation of **float**—the resulting value is undefined, as is the overflow or underflow behavior of the program.

When converting to floating-point types from integer types, if the integer value is exactly representable in the floating-point type, then the result is the equivalent floating-point value. If the integer value is not exactly representable, but is within the range of values representable in the floating-point type, then one of the two closest floating-point values should be chosen as the result. If the integer value is outside the range of values representable in the floating-point type, the result is undefined.

Complex floating-point types (C99)   When converting from a complex type to another complex type, the real and imaginary floating-point components are each converted according to the rules for (real) floating-point conversions.

When converting a real type (integer or floating-point) to a complex type, the imaginary part of the complex value is set to zero (+0.0 if available). The conversion of the real type to the real part of the complex type follows the normal rules for converting values to (real) floating-point types.

When converting a complex type to a real type (floating-point or integer), the imaginary part is discarded and the real part is converted by the normal rules for converting from (real) floating-point types.

The `_Imaginary` types, if present, are complex types whose real part is always zero. Converting from a real type to an imaginary type, or vice versa, always results in zero—that is the only value they have in common. Converting from a `_Complex` type to an `_Imaginary` type discards the real part. Converting from an `_Imaginary` type to a `_Complex` type sets the real part of the result to zero.

> **References**   complex types 5.2.1; floating types 5.2; integer types 5.1; overflow 7.2.2

6.2.5 Conversions to Structure and Union Types

No conversions between different structure types or union types are permitted.

> **References**   structure types 5.6; union types 5.7

6.2.6 Conversions to Enumeration Types

The rules are the same as for conversions to integral types. Some permissible conversions, such as between enumeration and floating-point types, may be symptoms of a poor programming style.

> **References**   enumeration types 5.5

6.2.7 Conversions to Pointer Types

In general, pointers and integers may be converted to pointer types. There are special circumstances under which an array or a function will be converted to a pointer.

A null pointer of any type may be converted to any other pointer type, and it will still be recognized as a null pointer. The representation may change in the conversion.

A value of type "pointer to S" may be converted to type "pointer to D" for any types S and D. In Standard C, object pointers may not be converted to function pointers or vice versa. However, the behavior of the resulting pointer may be affected by representation changes or any alignment restrictions in the implementation.

The integer constant 0, or any integer constant whose value is zero, or any such constant cast to type `void *`, is a null pointer constant and may always be converted to any pointer type. The result of such a conversion is a null pointer that is different from any valid pointer. Null pointers of different pointer types may have different internal representations. Null pointers do not necessarily have all their bits equal to zero.

Integers other than the constant 0 may be converted to pointer type, but the result is nonportable. The intent is that the pointer be considered an unsigned integer (of the same size as the pointer) and the standard integer conversions then be applied to take the source type to the destination type.

An expression of type "array of T" is converted to a value of type "pointer to T" by substituting a pointer to the first element of the array. This occurs as part of the usual unary conversions (Section 6.3.3).

An expression of type "function returning T" (i.e., a function designator) is converted to a value of type "pointer to function returning T" by substituting a pointer to the function. This occurs as part of the usual unary conversions (Section 6.3.3).

References   alignment restrictions 6.1.3; array types 5.4; function calls 7.4.3; function designator 7.1; integer types 5.1; pointer types 5.3; **sizeof** operator 7.5.2; usual unary conversions 6.3.3

6.2.8 Conversions to Array and Function Types

No conversions to array or function types are possible.

Example

In particular, it is not permissible to convert between array types or between function types:

```
extern int f();
double d;
d = (( double () )f) ();      /* Invalid! */
d = (double) f();             /* OK */
d = (*(double (*)()) f)();
          /* Valid, but will have unexpected results */
```

In the last statement, the address of **f** is converted to a pointer to a function returning type **double**; that pointer is then dereferenced and the function called. This is valid, but the resulting value stored in **d** will probably be garbage unless **f** was really defined (contrary to the external declaration before) to return a value of type **double**.

6.2.9 Conversions to the Void Type

Any value may be converted to type **void**. Of course, the result of such a conversion cannot be used for anything. Such a conversion may occur only in a context where an expression value will be discarded, such as in an expression statement.

Example

The most common use of casting an expression to **void** is to ignore the result of a function call. For example, **printf** is called to write information to the standard output stream. It returns an error indication, but that indication is often ignored. It is not necessary to cast the result to **void**, but it does tell the reader that the programmer is ignoring the result on purpose.

```
(void) printf("Goodbye.\n");
```

References   discarded expressions 7.13; expression statements 8.2; **void** type 5.9

6.3 THE USUAL CONVERSIONS

6.3.1 The Casting Conversions

Any of the conversions discussed earlier in this chapter may be explicitly performed with a type cast without error. Table 6–2 summarizes the permissible casts. Note that Standard C does not permit a function pointer to be cast directly to an object pointer or vice versa, although a conversion via a suitable integer type would be possible. This restriction reflects the possibility that object and function pointers could have significantly different representations.

Table 6–2   Permitted casting conversions

Destination (cast) type	Permitted source types
any arithmetic type	any arithmetic type
any integer type	any pointer type
pointer to (object) T, or (**void ***)	(a) any integer type (b) (**void ***) (c) pointer to (object) Q, for any Q (d) pointer to (function) Q, for any Q[a]
pointer to (function) T	(a) any integer type (b) pointer to (function) Q, for any Q (c) pointer to (object) Q, for any Q[a]
structure or union	none; not a permitted cast
array of T, or function returning T	none; not a permitted cast
void	any type

[a] Not permitted in Standard C.

The presence or absence of type qualifiers does not affect the validity of the casting conversions, and some conversions could be used to circumvent the qualifiers. The allowable assignment conversions are more restrictive.

Standard C guarantees that an object pointer converted to **void *** and back to the original type will retain its original value. This is likely to be true for conversions through **char *** in other C implementations.

References   assignment conversions 6.3.2; casts 7.5.1; type qualifiers 4.4.3; **void *** 5.3.1

6.3.2 The Assignment Conversions

In a simple assignment expression, the types of the expressions on the left and right sides of the assignment operator should be the same. If they are not, an attempt will be made to convert the value on the right side of the assignment to the type on the left side. The conversions that are valid—a subset of the casting conversions—are listed in Table 6–3. Unless otherwise indicated, the presence of ISO type qualifiers does not affect the validity of the conversion, although a **const**-qualified lvalue cannot be used on the left side of the assignment.

Table 6–3   Allowable assignment conversions

Left side type	Permitted right side types
any arithmetic type	any arithmetic type
_Bool (C99)	any pointer type
a structure or union type[a]	a compatible structure or union type
(**void ***)[b]	(a) the constant 0 (b) pointer to (object) T_1[c] (c) (**void ***)
pointer to (object) T_1[b,c]	(a) the constant 0 (b) pointer to T_2, where T_1 and T_2 are compatible (c) (**void ***)
pointer to (function) F_1[b]	(a) the constant 0 (b) pointer to F_2, where F_1 and F_2 are compatible

[a] Some older C compilers do not support assigning structures or unions.
[b] The referenced type on the left must have all the qualifiers of the referenced type on the right.
[c] T_1 may be an incomplete type if the other pointer has type **void *** (Standard C).

Attempting any other conversion without an explicit cast will be rejected by ISO-conforming implementations, but traditional C compilers almost always permit the assignment of mixed pointer types and often permit any types that would be allowed in a casting conversion.

The rules governing pointer assignment impose conditions on type qualifiers because the assignment could be used to circumvent the qualification. Assigning a pointer to type **_Bool** assigns 0 if the pointer is null and otherwise assigns 1.

References   assignment operator 7.9.1; casting conversions 6.3.1; compatible types 5.11

6.3.3 The Usual Unary Conversions

The usual unary conversions determine whether and how a single operand is converted before an operation is performed. Their purpose is to reduce the large number of arithmetic types to a smaller number that must be handled by the operators. The conversions are applied automatically to operands of the unary **!**, **−**, **+**, **~**, and ***** operators, and separately to each of the operands of the binary **<<** and **>>** operators.

   Conversion rank   With the additional standard integer types in C99, including the possibility that implementations will extend the set of types, it becomes difficult to describe these implicit conversions precisely yet simply. The C99 standard introduced the concept of *conversion rank* to help explain the conversions. We use it here. For C89, simply ignore the **long long**, **_Bool**, and extended integer types. For traditional C, see the discussion later in this section.

   The conversion rank is a numeric value assigned to each integer type to specify its conversion order. Table 6–4 lists a possible assignment of ranks to the standard integer types. Enumeration types are not shown, but they have the same rank as their underlying integer type.

Table 6–4   Conversion rank

Rank	Types of that rank
60	**long long int, unsigned long long int** (C99)
50	**long int, unsigned long int**
40	**int, unsigned int**
30	**short, unsigned short**
20	**char, unsigned char, signed char**
10	**_Bool**

   The specific numbers used for ranking do not matter, but the standard types must be in the relative numeric order shown. Consecutive numbers were not chosen because C implementations may insert their own extended integer types into this table, with rank numbers between those of the standard types. Extended type ranks must follow these rules: they must be ranked below types of greater precision and below any standard types of the same precision; no two different signed integer types may have the same rank; and unsigned types must have the same rank as the signed types with the same representation.

   Given conversion ranks such as the preceding, the usual unary conversions are shown in Table 6–5. The first conversion in the table that applies is performed; if none applies, then no conversion is performed. The unary conversions applying to integers are called the *integer promotions*. The conversions of array and function types are sometimes suppressed; see Section 6.2.7 for the exceptions.

Example

   If **S** is a variable of type **unsigned short** in Standard C and its value is 1, then the expression **(−S)** has type **int** and value −1 if the range of **short** is smaller than the range of **int**, but the same expression has type **unsigned** and a large positive value if the range of **short** is the same as the range of **int**. This is because in the first instance **S** is promoted to type **int** prior to the application of the unary minus operator, whereas in the second case **S** is promoted to type **unsigned**.

Table 6–5 Usual unary conversions (choose first that applies)

If the operand has type	Standard C converts it to	Traditional C converts it to
`float`	(no conversion)	`double`
Array of T	Pointer to T	(same as Standard C)
Function returning T	Pointer to function returning T	(same as Standard C)
An integer type of rank greater or equal to `int`[a]	(no conversion)	(same as Standard C)
A signed type of rank less than `int`	`int`	(same as Standard C)
An unsigned type of rank less than `int`, all of whose values can be represented in type `int`	`int`	`unsigned int`
An unsigned type of rank less than `int`, all of whose values cannot be represented in type `int`	`unsigned int`	(same as Standard C)

[a] Bit fields of type `int`, `signed int`, or `unsigned int` are assumed to have a conversion rank *less than* `int`, which means their converted type depends on whether all their values can be represented in type `int`.

In the case of bit fields of type `int`, `signed int`, or `unsigned int`, the bit field is assumed to have a conversion rank *less than* `int`.

Traditional C implementations performed these conversions differently. First, all unsigned types of lower conversion rank were converted to `unsigned int`, thus preserving the signedness of the operand if not its value. (The programmer should be cautious of the Standard C conversions since the signedness of the result of promotion is implementation-dependent and can affect the meaning of the surrounding expression.) Second, type `float` was converted to type `double`, reducing the number of floating-point library functions needed at the possible expense of performance. This trade-off is no longer mandated, although implementations are free to continue to do the promotion.

Conversion of arrays and functions   The usual unary conversions specify that a value of array type is converted to a pointer to the first element of the array unless:

1. the array is an argument to the `sizeof` or address (`&`) operators
2. a character string literal is used to initialize a character array
3. a wide string literal is used to initialize an array of type `wchar_t`

In C99, this conversion occurs on any value of array type. Prior to C99, the conversion was performed only on lvalues of array type.

Example

```
char a[] = "abcd"; /* No conversion */
char *b = "abcd"; /* Array converted to pointer */
int i = sizeof(a); /* No conversion; size of whole array */
b = a +         1;          /* Array converted to pointer. *
```

The usual unary conversions specify that a function designator is converted to a pointer to the function unless the designator is the operand of the **sizeof** or address (**&**) operators. (If it is the operand of **sizeof**, it is also invalid.)

Example

```
extern int f();
int (*fp)();
int i;
fp = f;          /* OK, f is converted to &f */
fp = &f;         /* OK, implicit conversion suppressed */
i = sizeof(fp);  /* OK, result is the size of the pointer */
i = sizeof(f);   /* Invalid */
```

References bitwise negation operator ~ 7.5.5; extended integer types 5.1.4; function calls 7.4.3; function designator 7.1; indirection operator * 7.5.7; initializers 4.6; logical negation operator ! 7.5.4; lvalue 7.1; shift operators << and >> 7.6.3; **sizeof** 7.5.2; unary minus operator - 7.5.3; wide strings 2.7.4

6.3.4 The Usual Binary Conversions

When two values must be operated on in combination, they are first converted according to the usual binary conversions to a single common type, which is also typically the type of the result. The conversions are applied to the operands of most binary operators and to the second and third operands in a conditional expression. Together, the usual unary conversions and the usual binary conversions are called the *usual arithmetic conversions.*

An operator that performs the usual binary conversions on its two operands will first perform the usual unary conversions on each of the operands independently to widen short values and convert arrays and functions to pointers. Afterward, if either operand is not of an arithmetic type or if both have the same arithmetic type, then no further conversions are performed. Otherwise, the first applicable conversion from Table 6–6 is performed on both operands. This table assumes neither operand is complex; see the following discussion for handling complex operands.

Example

The Standard C rules differ from traditional rules when a **long** operand and an **unsigned** operand come together (and the **long** type is strictly larger than **unsigned**). Here is a program that determines which conversion occurs:

```
unsigned int UI = -1;
long int LI = 0;
int main()
{
    if (UI < LI) printf("long+unsigned==long\n");
    else printf("long+unsigned==unsigned\n");
    return 0;
}
```

Table 6–6   Usual binary conversions (choose first that applies)

If either operand has type[a]	And the other operand has type[a]	Standard C converts both to	Traditional C converts both to
`long double`	any real type	`long double`	*not applicable*
`double`	any real type	`double`	(same as Standard C)
`float`	any real type	`float`	`double`
any unsigned type	any unsigned type	the unsigned type with the greater rank	(same as Standard C)
any signed type	any signed type	the signed type with the greater rank	(same as Standard C)
any unsigned type	a signed type of less or equal rank	the unsigned type	(same as Standard C)
any unsigned type	a signed type of greater rank that can represent all values of the unsigned type	the signed type	the unsigned version of the signed type
any unsigned type	a signed type of greater rank that cannot represent all values of the unsigned type	the unsigned version of the signed type	(same as Standard C)
any other type[b]	any other type	(no conversion)	(same as Standard C)

[a] The rules assume that the usual unary conversions have already been applied to each operand.

[b] Complex operands are discussed in the text.

Complex types and the usual binary conversions   In C99, complex types must be taken into account in the usual binary conversions. In mixed real/complex operations, the operand of real type is *not* converted to a complex type for performance reasons; however, conversions are performed to bring both operands to an equivalent floating-point precision. The operation then handles mixed real/complex operands typically as if the real operand were converted to the complex type. (Of course, an implementation could actually perform the *as if* conversion if it wished to.) The result type of the operation is the type of the complex operand after the conversions.

Specifically, if both operands are complex, then the shorter operand is converted to the type of the longer, and that is the type of the result. This corresponds to what is done when combining two real floating-point operands.

When one operand is complex and the other is an integer, the integer operand is converted to the real floating-point type corresponding to the complex type. For example, if the complex operand were of type `float _Complex`, then the integer would be converted to `float`. The result is the complex type.

When one operand is complex and the other is a real floating-point type, the less precise type is converted, within its real or complex domain, to the precision of the other type. For example, when combining a `float` with a `double _Complex`, the `float` operand is promoted to `double`. When combining a `long double` with a `double _Complex`, the `double _Complex` is promoted to `long double _Complex`.

6.3.5 The Default Function Argument Conversions

If an expression appears as an argument in a function call that is not governed by a prototype, or when the expression appears as an argument in the "`...`" part of a prototype argument list, then the value of the expression is converted before being passed to the function. This default function argument conversion is the same as the usual unary conversion, except that arguments of type **float** are always promoted to type **double**, even in Standard C.

If the called function is governed by a prototype, then the arguments do not (necessarily) undergo the usual integer promotions, and arguments of type **float** are not (necessarily) promoted to **double**. An implementation is free to perform these conversions if it wishes to, but these rules allow the implementation to optimize the calling sequence. The conversions of arrays and functions to pointers do occur.

In C99 prototypes, if a formal parameter of array type has a list *L* of type qualifiers within the brackets [and], then the actual array argument is converted to an *L*-qualified pointer to the element type. This is discussed further in Section 9.3.

The **float**-to-**double** argument conversion helped previous versions of traditional and Standard C to control the number of library functions since it made it unnecessary to have versions for both types **float** and **double**. C99 specifies a full set of math functions for types **float** and **long double** as well as **double**.

> **References**   *array-qualifier-list* 4.5.3; function calls 7.4.3; math functions Ch. 17; prototypes 9.2; usual unary conversions 6.3.3

6.3.6 Other Function Conversions

The declared types of the formal parameters of a function and the type of its return value are subject to certain adjustments that parallel the function argument conversions. They are discussed in Section 9.4.

6.4 C++ COMPATIBILITY

6.4.1 Assignment Conversions

In C++, a cast must be used to convert a pointer of type **void *** to another kind of pointer. You can also use the cast in C, but it is not required in an assignment.

Example

The **malloc** function returns a **void *** pointer to a newly allocated area of memory.

```
#include <stdlib.h>
char * cp;
const int SIZE = 10 * sizeof(char);
...
cp = malloc(SIZE);              /* OK in C, not C++ */
cp = (char *) malloc(SIZE);     /* OK in both */
```

Also, only a pointer to an unqualified (not **const** or **volatile**) object may be converted to a pointer of type **void *** without a cast.

Example

```
char * cp;
const char * const_cp;
void * vp;
...
vp = cp;                  /* valid in both C and C++ */
vp = const_cp;            /* valid in C, not in C++  */
vp = (void *) const_cp;   /* valid in both C and C++ */
```

References   assignment conversions 6.3.2

6.5 EXERCISES

1. The following table lists pairs of source and destination types to be used in casting conversions. Which of the conversions are allowable in Standard C? Which in traditional C? (For traditional C, replace **void** with **char**.)

Destination type	*Source type*
(a) **char**	**int**
(b) **char ***	**int ***
(c) **int (*f) ()**	**int ***
(d) **double ***	**int**
(e) **void ***	**int (*f) ()**
(f) **int ***	**t *** (where: **typedef int t**)

2. In the table in Exercise 1, which pairs are allowable assignment conversions in Standard C? Which in traditional C? (The destination type is the left-side type; the source type is the right-side type.)

3. What is the resulting type when the usual binary conversions of traditional C are applied to the following pairs of types? In which cases is the result different under Standard C?

(a) **char** and **unsigned**	(d) **char** and **long double**
(b) **unsigned** and **long**	(e) **int []** and **int ***
(c) **float** and **double**	(f) **short ()** and **short ()**

4. Is it allowable to have a C implementation in which type **char** can represent values ranging from –2,147,483,648 through 2,147,483,647? If so, what would be **sizeof(char)** under that implementation? What would be the smallest and largest ranges of type **int**?

5. What relationship must hold between **sizeof(long double)** and **sizeof(int)**?

6. Suppose computers A and B are both byte-addressable and have a word size of 32 bits (four bytes), but computer A is a big-endian and B is a little-endian. The integer 128 is stored in a word of computer A and is then transferred to a word in computer B by moving the first byte of the word in A to the first byte of the word in B, and so on. What is the integer value stored in the word of computer B when the transfer is complete? If A were the little-endian and B the big-endian, what would be the result?

7

Expressions

The C language has an unusually rich set of operators that provide access to most of the operations provided by the underlying hardware. This chapter presents the syntax of expressions and describes the function of each operator.

7.1 OBJECTS, LVALUES, AND DESIGNATORS

An *object* is a region of memory that can be examined and stored into. An *lvalue* (pronounced "ell-value") is an expression that refers to an object in such a way that the object may be examined or altered. Only an lvalue expression may be used on the left-hand side of an assignment. An expression that is not an lvalue is sometimes called an *rvalue* (pronounced "are-value") because it can be used only on the right-hand side of an assignment. An lvalue can have an object or incomplete type, but not **void**.

As Standard C uses the term, an *lvalue* does not necessarily permit modification of the object it designates. This is true if the lvalue has an array type, an incomplete type, a **const**-qualified type, or if it has a structure or union type one of whose members (recursively applied to nested structures and unions) has a **const**-qualified type. The term *modifiable lvalue* is used to emphasize that the lvalue does permit modification of the designated object.

A *function designator* is a value of function type. It is neither an object nor an lvalue. The name of a function is a function designator, as is the result of dereferencing a function pointer. Functions and objects are often treated differently in C, and we try to be careful to distinguish between "function types" and "object types," "lvalues" and "function designators," and "function pointers" and "object pointers." The phrase "lvalue designating an object" is redundant, but we use it when appropriate to emphasize the exclusion of function designators.

The C expressions that can be lvalues are listed in Table 7–1, along with any special conditions that must apply for the expression to be an lvalue. No other form of expression can produce an lvalue, and none of the listed expressions except string literals can be lvalues if their type is "array of...." Expressions that cannot be lvalues include: array names, functions, enumeration constants, assignment expressions, casts, and function calls.

Table 7–1   Nonarray expressions that can be lvalues

Expression	Additional requirements
name	*name* must be a variable
e [*k*]	none
(*e*)	*e* must be an lvalue
e.name	*e* must be an lvalue
e->name	none
∗e	none
string-constant	none

The operators listed in Table 7–2 require certain operands to be lvalues.

Table 7–2   Operators requiring lvalue operands

Operator	Requirement
`&` (unary)	operand must be an lvalue or a function name
`++` `--`	operand must be an lvalue (postfix and prefix forms)
`= += -= *= /= %=` `<<= >>= &= ^= |=`	left operand must be an lvalue

References   address operator 7.5.6; assignment expressions 7.9; cast expression 7.5.1; component selection 7.4.2; decrement expression 7.4.4, 7.5.8; enumerations 5.5; function calls 7.4.3; increment expression 7.4.4, 7.5.8; indirection expression 7.5.7; literals 2.7, 7.3.2; names 7.3.1; string constant 2.7.4; subscripting 7.4.1

7.2 EXPRESSIONS AND PRECEDENCE

The grammar for expressions presented in this chapter completely specifies the precedence of operators in C. To summarize the information, Table 7–3 contains a concise list of the C operators in order from the highest to the lowest precedence, along with their associativity.

Table 7–3   C operators in order of precedence

Tokens	Operator	Class	Precedence	Associates
names, literals	simple tokens	primary	16	n/a
a[*k*]	subscripting	postfix	16	left-to-right
f(...)	function call	postfix	16	left-to-right
.	direct selection	postfix	16	left-to-right
->	indirect selection	postfix	16	left-to-right
++ --	increment, decrement	postfix	16	left-to-right
(*type name*) {*init*}	compound literal (C99)	postfix	16	left-to-right
++ --	increment, decrement	prefix	15	right-to-left
sizeof	size	unary	15	right-to-left
~	bitwise not	unary	15	right-to-left
!	logical not	unary	15	right-to-left
- +	arithmetic negation, plus	unary	15	right-to-left
&	address of	unary	15	right-to-left
*	indirection	unary	15	right-to-left
(*type name*)	casts	unary	14	right-to-left
* / %	multiplicative	binary	13	left-to-right
+ -	additive	binary	12	left-to-right
<< >>	left and right shift	binary	11	left-to-right
< > <= >=	relational	binary	10	left-to-right
== !=	equality/inequality	binary	9	left-to-right
&	bitwise and	binary	8	left-to-right
^	bitwise xor	binary	7	left-to-right
|	bitwise or	binary	6	left-to-right
&&	logical and	binary	5	left-to-right
||	logical or	binary	4	left-to-right
? :	conditional	ternary	3	right-to-left
= += -= *= /= %= <<= >>= &= ^= |=	assignment	binary	2	right-to-left
,	sequential evaluation	binary	1	left-to-right

7.2.1 Precedence and Associativity of Operators

Each expression operator in C has a precedence level and a rule of associativity. Where parentheses do not explicitly indicate the grouping of operands with operators, the operands are grouped with the operator having higher precedence. If two operators have the same precedence, then the operands are grouped with the left or right operator according to whether the operators are left-associative or right-associative. All operators having the same precedence level always have the same associativity.

The rules of precedence and associativity determine what an expression means, but they do not specify the order in which subexpressions within a larger expression or statement are evaluated at run time. The order of evaluation is discussed in Section 7.12.

Example

Here are some examples of the precedence and associativity rules:

Original expression	Equivalent expression	Reason for equivalence
`a*b+c`	`(a*b)+c`	`*` has higher precedence than `+`
`a+=b|=c`	`a+=(b|=c)`	`+=` and `|=` are right-associative
`a-b+c`	`(a-b)+c`	`–` and `+` are left-associative
`sizeof(int)*p`	`(sizeof(int))*p`	`sizeof` has higher precedence than cast
`*p->q`	`*(p->q)`	`->` has higher precedence than `*`

To summarize the associativity rules, the binary operators are left-associative except for the assignment operators, which are right-associative—as is the conditional operator. The unary and postfix operators are sometimes described as being right-associative, but this is needed only to express the idea that an expression such as `*x++` is interpreted as `*(x++)` rather than `(*x)++`. We prefer simply to state that the postfix operators have higher precedence than the (prefix) unary operators.

References   assignment operators 7.9; binary operators 7.6; concatenation of strings 2.7.4; conditional operator 7.8; postfix operators 7.4.4; unary + 7.5.3

7.2.2 Overflow and Other Arithmetic Exceptions

For certain operations in C, such as addition and multiplication, it may be that the true mathematical result of the operation cannot be represented as a value of the expected result type (as determined by the usual conversion rules). This condition is called overflow or, in some cases, underflow.

In general, the C language does not specify the consequences of overflow. One possibility is that an incorrect value (of the correct type) is produced. Another possibility is that program execution is terminated. A third possibility is that some sort of machine-dependent trap or exception occurs that may be detected by the program in some implementation-dependent manner.

For certain operations, the C language explicitly specifies that the effects are unpredictable for certain operand values or (more stringently) that a value is always produced, but the value is unpredictable for certain operand values. If the right-hand operand of the division operator, `/`, or the remainder operator, `%`, is zero, then the effects are unpredictable. If the right-hand operand of a shift operator, `<<` or `>>`, is too large or negative, then an unpredictable value is produced.

Traditionally, all implementations of C have ignored the question of signed integer overflow, in the sense that the result is whatever value is produced by the machine instruction used to implement the operation. (Many computers that use a twos-complement representation for signed integers handle overflow of addition and subtraction simply by producing the low-order bits of the true twos-complement result. No doubt many existing C programs depend on this fact, but such code is technically not portable.) Floating-point overflow and underflow are usually handled in whatever convenient way is supported by the machine; if the machine architecture provides more than one way to handle exceptional floating-point conditions, a library function may be provided to give the C programmer access to such options.

For unsigned integers the C language is quite specific on the question of overflow: Every operation on unsigned integers always produces a result value that is congruent modulo 2^n to the true mathematical result of the operation (where n is the number of bits used to represent the unsigned result). This amounts to computing the correct n low-order bits of the true result (of the true twos-complement result if the true result is negative, as when subtracting a big unsigned integer from a small one).

Example

As an example, suppose that objects of type unsigned are represented using 16 bits; then subtracting the unsigned value 7 from the unsigned value 4 would produce the unsigned value 65,533 (2^{16}–3) because this value is congruent modulo 2^{16} to the true mathematical result –3.

An important consequence of this rule is that operations on unsigned integers are guaranteed to be completely portable between two implementations *if* those implementations use representations having the same number of bits. It is easy to simulate the unsigned arithmetic of another implementation using some smaller number of bits.

References   division operator / 7.6.1; floating-point types 5.2; remainder operator % 7.6.1; shift operators << and >> 7.6.3; signed types 5.1.1; unsigned types 5.1.2

7.3 PRIMARY EXPRESSIONS

There are three kinds of primary expressions: names (identifiers), literal constants, and parenthesized expressions:

> *primary-expression :*
>   *identifier*
>   *constant*
>   *parenthesized-expression*

Function calls, subscript expressions, and component selection expressions were traditionally listed as primary expressions in C, but we have included them in the next section with the postfix expressions.

7.3.1 Names

The value of a name depends on its type. The type of a name is determined by the declaration of that name (if any), as discussed in Chapter 4.

The name of a variable declared to be of arithmetic, pointer, enumeration, structure, or union type evaluates to an object of that type; the name is an lvalue expression. An enumeration constant name evaluates to the associated integer value; it is not an lvalue.

Example

> In the following example, the four color names are enumeration constants. The **switch** statement (described in Section 8.7) selects one of four statements to execute based on the value of the parameter **color**:
>
> ```
> typedef enum { red, blue, green } colortype;
>
> colortype next_color(colortype color)
> {
>     switch (color) {
>         case red    : return blue;
>         case blue   : return green;
>         case green  : return red;
>     }
> }
> ```

The name of an array evaluates to that array; it is an lvalue, but not modifiable. Unless the array is the argument to **sizeof**, the argument to the address operator (**&**), or is a character array being initialized by a string constant, the array value is converted to a pointer to the first object in the array as part of the usual unary conversions.

Example

> The conversion of an array name to a pointer does not occur when the array is the argument to **sizeof**, so the result is the size of the array and not the size of a pointer.
>
> ```
> extern void PrintMatrix();
> int Matrix[10][10], total_length, row_length;
>
> total_length = sizeof Matrix;
> row_length = sizeof Matrix[0];
> PrintMatrix(Matrix); /* pointer to first
>                         element is passed */
> ```

The name of a function evaluates to that function; it is not an lvalue. Unless the function name is the argument of the address operator (**&**) or the argument to **sizeof**, the name is converted to a pointer to the function as part of the usual unary conversions. The result of **&f** is a pointer to **f**, not a pointer to a pointer to **f**, and **sizeof(f)** is invalid.

Example

> This example shows a function name used as an argument to another function:

```
extern void PlotFunction(double (*f)(double),
                         double x0, double x1);

double fn(double x) { return x * x - x; }

int main(void)
{  ...
    PlotFunction(fn, 0.01, 100.0); /* fn converts to &fn */
    ...
}
```

It is not possible for a name, as an expression, to refer to a label, **typedef** name, structure component name, union component name, structure tag, union tag, or enumeration tag. Names used for those purposes reside in name spaces separate from the names that can be referred to by a name in an expression. Some of these names may be referred to within expressions by means of special constructs. For example, structure and union component names may be referred to using the **.** or **->** operators, and **typedef** names may be used in casts and as an argument to the **sizeof** operator.

References   array types 5.4; casts 7.5.1; enumeration types 5.5; function calls 7.4.3; function types 5.8; lvalue 7.1; name space 4.2; selection operators **.** and **->** 7.4.2; **sizeof** operator 7.5.2; **typedef** names 5.10; usual unary conversions 6.3.3

7.3.2 Literals

A literal (lexical constant) is a numeric constant and, when evaluated as an expression, yields that constant as its value. Except for string constants, a literal expression is never an lvalue. See Section 2.7 for a discussion of literals and their types and values.

7.3.3 Parenthesized Expressions

A parenthesized expression consists of a left parenthesis, any expression, and then a right parenthesis:

> *parenthesized-expression* :
>   (*expression*)

The type of a parenthesized expression is identical to the type of the enclosed expression; no conversions are performed. The value of a parenthesized expression is the value of the enclosed expression and will be an lvalue if and only if the enclosed expression is an lvalue. Parentheses do not necessarily force a particular evaluation order (see Section 7.12).

The purpose of the parenthesized expression is simply to delimit the enclosed expression for grouping purposes, either to defeat the default precedence of operators or make code more readable.

Example

```
x1 = (-b + discriminant)/(2.0 * a)
```

References   lvalue 7.1

7.4 POSTFIX EXPRESSIONS

There are six kinds of postfix expressions: subscripting expressions, two forms of component selection (direct and indirect), function calls, and postfix increment and decrement expressions.

> *postfix-expression* :
>   *primary-expression*
>   *subscript-expression*
>   *component-selection-expression*
>   *function-call*
>   *postincrement-expression*
>   *postdecrement-expression*
>   *compound-literal*   *(C99)*

Function calls, subscript expressions, and component selection expressions were traditionally listed as primary expressions, but their syntax is more closely related to the postfix expressions.

7.4.1 Subscripting Expressions

A subscripting expression consists of a postfix expression, a left bracket, an arbitrary expression, and a right bracket. This construction is used for array subscripting, where the postfix expression (commonly an array name) evaluates to a pointer to the beginning of the array and the other expression to an integer offset:

> *subscript-expression* :
>   *postfix-expression* [*expression*]

In C, the expression $e_1[e_2]$ is by definition precisely equivalent to the expression $*((e_1)+(e_2))$. The usual binary conversions are applied to the two operands, and the result is always an lvalue. The indirection (*) operator must have a pointer as its operand, and the only way that the result of the + operator can be a pointer is for one of its operands to be a pointer and the other an integer. Therefore, it follows that for $e_1[e_2]$ one operand must be a pointer and the other an integer. Conventionally, e_1 is the name of an array and e_2 is an integer expression, but e_1 could alternatively be a pointer or the order of the operands could be reversed. A consequence of the definition of subscripting is that arrays use 0-origin indexing.

Multidimensional array references are formed by composing subscripting operators.

Example

```
char buffer[100], *bptr = buffer;
int i = 99;
...
buffer[0] = '\0';        /* subscripting an array */
bptr[i-1] = bptr[0];     /* subscripting a pointer */
i[bptr]   = '\0';        /* unconventional subscripting */
```

The first element allocated for the 100-element array **buffer** is referred to as **buffer[0]** and the last element as **buffer[99]**. The names **buffer** and **bptr** both point to the same place—namely, **buffer[0]**—the first element of the **buffer** array, and they can be used in identical ways within subscripting expressions. However, **bptr** is a variable (an lvalue), and thus can be made to point to some other place:

```
bptr = &buffer[6];
```

after which the expression **bptr[-4]** refers to the same place as the expression **buffer[2]**. (This illustrates the fact that negative subscripts make sense in certain circumstances.) An assignment can also make **bptr** point to no place at all:

```
bptr = NULL;    /* Store a null pointer into bptr. */
```

However, the array name **buffer** is not an lvalue and cannot be modified. Considered as a pointer, it always points to the same fixed place, as if it were declared

```
char * const buffer;
```

Example

The following code stores 1.0 in the diagonal elements of a 10-by-10 array, **matrix**, and stores 0.0 in the other elements:

```
int matrix[10][10];
...
for (i = 0; i < 10; i++)
    for (j = 0; j < 10; j++)
        matrix[i][j] = ((i == j) ? 1.0 : 0.0);
```

It is poor programming style to use a comma expression within the subscripting brackets because it might mislead a reader familiar with other programming languages to think that it means subscripting of a multidimensional array.

Example

The expression

```
commands[k=n+1, 2*k]
```

might appear to be a reference to an element of a two-dimensional array named **commands** with subscript expressions **k=n+1** and **2*k**, whereas its actual interpretation in C is as a reference to a one-dimensional array named **commands** with subscript **2*k** after **k** has been assigned **n+1**. If a comma expression is really needed (and it is hard for us to think of a plausible example), enclose it in parentheses to indicate that it is something unusual:

```
commands[(k=n+1, 2*k)]
```

It is possible to use pointers and casts to refer to a multidimensional array as if it were a one-dimensional array. This may be desirable for reasons of efficiency. It must be kept in mind that arrays in C are stored in row-major order.

Example

> The following code sets up an identity matrix—a matrix whose diagonal elements are 1 and whose other elements are zero. This method is tricky, but fast. It treats the two-dimensional matrix as if it were a one-dimensional vector with the same number of elements, which simplifies subscripting and eliminates the need for nested loops.

```
#define SIZE 10
double matrix[SIZE][SIZE];
int i;
for (i = 0; i < SIZE*SIZE; i++)
    ((double *)matrix)[i] = 0.0;    /* zero all elements */
for (i = 0; i < SIZE*SIZE; i += (SIZE + 1))
    ((double *) matrix)[i] = 1.0; /* set diagonals to 1 */
```

References   addition operator + 7.6.2; array types 5.4; comma expressions 7.10; indirection operator * 7.5.7; integral types 5.1; lvalue 7.1; pointer types 5.3

7.4.2 Component Selection

Component selection operators are used to access fields (components) of structure and union types:

> *component-selection-expression* :
> > *direct-component-selection*
> > *indirect-component-selection*

> *direct-component-selection* :
> > *postfix-expression* **.** *identifier*

> *indirect-component-selection* :
> > *postfix-expression* **->** *identifier*

A direct component selection expression consists of a postfix expression, a period (**.**), and an identifier. The postfix expression must have a structure or union type, and the identifier must be the name of a component of that type. The result of the selection expression is the named member of the structure or union.

The result of the direct component selection expression is an lvalue if the structure or union expression is an lvalue. (The only structure and union values that are not lvalues are those returned by a function.) The result is modifiable if it is an lvalue and if the selected component is not an array.

Example

```
struct S {int a,b;} x;
extern struct S f(); /* structure-returning function */
int i;
...
x = f();        /* OK */
i = f().a;      /* OK */
f().a = i;      /* Invalid; f() is not an lvalue */
```

(The last assignment, even if valid, would be nonsensical. The function **f** would return a copy of some structure, which would then have one of its components modified—just before the entire copy was discarded at the end of the statement.)

(Some non-Standard C implementations do not allow functions to return structures at all. Of those that allow it, a few do not allow a function call to have a selection operator applied to it; they would consider **f().a** to be an error.)

If the expression before the period has type qualifiers, or if the member does, then the result has the union of both sets of qualifiers.

Example

The following assignment is invalid because **x.a** has type **const int**, the **const** having been inherited from **x**:

```
const struct {int a,b;} x;
...
x.a = 5;   /* Invalid */
```

An indirect component selection expression consists of a postfix expression, the operator **->**, and a name. The value of the postfix expression must be a pointer to a structure or union type, and the name must be the name of a component of that structure or union type. The result is the named member of the union or structure and is an lvalue; it is modifiable unless the member is an array. The expression *e->name* is by definition precisely equivalent to the expression **(*e).**name*.

Example

In the following code, both components of structure **Point** are set to 0.0 in a roundabout fashion to demonstrate this equivalence:

```
struct {float x, y; } Point, *Point_Ptr;
...
Point.x = 0.0;                 /* Sets x to 0.0 */
Point_Ptr = &Point;
Point_Ptr->y = 0.0;   /* Sets y to 0.0 */
```

If the expression before the **->** has type qualifiers, or if the member does, then the result has the union of both sets of qualifiers.

Some C implementations permit the null pointer to be used on the left of the indirect selection operator. Applying the address operator **&** to the result and casting that result to an integer type yields the offset in bytes of a component within the structure. This is not explicitly permitted or prohibited by the Standard, but it often works.

Example

```
#define OFFSET(type,field)  \
    ((size_t)&((type *)0)->field)
```

This **OFFSET** macro is similar to the **offsetof** macro that appears in **stddef.h**.

References   address operator **&** 7.5.6; indirection operator ***** 7.5.7; lvalue 7.1; **offsetof** macro 11.1; **size_t** 13.1; structure types 5.6; type qualifiers 4.4.3; union types 5.7

7.4.3 Function Calls

A function call consists of a postfix expression (the function expression), a left parenthesis, a possibly empty sequence of expressions (the argument expressions) separated by commas, and then a right parenthesis:

function-call :
        postfix-expression (*expression-list*$_{opt}$)

expression-list :
        assignment-expression
        expression-list , *assignment-expression*

The type of the function expression, after the usual unary conversions, must be "pointer to function returning *T*" for some type *T*. The result of the function call has type *T* and is never an lvalue. If *T* is **void**, then the function call produces no result and may not be used in a context that requires the call to yield a result. *T* may not be an array type.

In pre-Standard compilers, the function expression is required to have type "function returning *T*," and therefore function pointers have to be explicitly dereferenced. That is, if **fp** is a function pointer, the function to which it points can be called only by writing **(*fp)** (...). An exception is sometimes made if **fp** is a formal parameter; you can write **fp** (...) in that case.

To perform the function call, the function and argument expressions are first evaluated; the order of evaluation is not specified.

Next, if the function call is governed by a Standard C prototype (Section 9.2), then the values of the argument expressions are converted to the types of the corresponding formal parameters as specified in the prototype. If such conversions are not possible, the call is in error. If the function has a variable number of arguments, then the extra arguments are converted according to the usual argument conversions (Section 6.3.5) and no further checks on the extra arguments are made.

If the function call is not governed by a prototype, the argument expressions are only converted according to the usual argument conversions and no further checks are required of the compiler. This is because, lacking a prototype, the compiler may not have any information about the formal parameters of external functions.

After the actual arguments have been evaluated and converted, they are copied into the formal parameters of the called function; thus, all arguments are passed by value. Within the called function the names of formal parameters are lvalues, but assigning to a formal parameter changes only the copied value in the formal parameter and has no effect on any actual argument that may happen to be an lvalue.

Example

Consider the following function, **square**, which returns the square of its argument:

```
double square(double y) { y = y*y; return y; }
```

Suppose **x** is a variable of type **double** with value 4.0, and we perform the function call **square(x)**. The function will return the value 16.0, but the value of **x** will remain 4.0. The assignment to **y** within **square** changes only a copy of the actual argument.

Called functions can change the caller's data only if the data are independently visible to the function (say, in a global variable) or if the caller passes a pointer to the data as an argument to the function. When a pointer is passed, the pointer is copied, but the object pointed to is not copied. Therefore, changes made indirectly through the pointer can be seen by the caller.

Example

The function **swap** below exchanges the values of two integer objects when pointers to those objects are supplied as parameters:

```
void swap(int *xp, int *yp)
{
    int t = *xp;
    *xp = *yp;
    *yp = t;
}
```

If **a** is an integer array all of whose elements are 0, and **i** is an integer variable with the value 4, then after the call **swap(&a[i],&i)**, **i** will have the value 0 and **a[4]** will have the value 4.

Formal and actual arguments of array types are always converted to pointers by C. Therefore, changes to an array formal parameter in a function will affect the actual argument, although it might not seem obvious that this is so.

Example

Consider the following function **f** which has an array parameter:

```
void f(int a[10])
{
    a[4] = 12;   /* changes caller's array */
}
```

If **vec** is an integer array, then calling **f(vec)** will set **vec[4]** to 12. The dimension **10** in the array parameter has no significance; **a** could have been declared **int a[]**.

If a function whose return type is not **void** is called in a context where the value of the function would be discarded, a compiler could issue a warning to that effect. However, it is common for non-**void** functions like **printf** to have their return values discarded, and so many programmers think that such warnings are a nuisance.

Example

The intent to discard the result of the function call may be made explicit by using a cast, as in this call to **strcat**:

```
(void) strcat(word, suffix);
```

Comma expressions may be arguments to functions if they are enclosed in parentheses so that their parts are not interpreted as separate arguments.

Example

Suppose you wish to trace all calls to a function **f** in your C program. If **f** takes a single argument, then the following macro will insert calls to **tracef** before each call to **f**.

```
#define f(x) (tracef(__FILE__, __LINE__), f((x)))
```

If a call to **f** appears as a function argument, as in **g(f(y))**, then the argument to **g** is a comma expression.

References   agreement of argument and parameters 9.6; comma operator 7.10; discarded expressions 7.13; function types 5.8; function prototypes 9.2; indirection operator * 7.5.7; lvalue 7.1; macro expansion 3.3.3; pointer types 5.3; **printf** 15.11; **strcat** 13.1; usual argument conversions 6.3.5; **void** type 5.9

7.4.4 Postfix Increment and Decrement Operators

The postfix operators **++** and **- -** are, respectively, used to increment and decrement their operands while producing the original value as a result. They are side effect-producing operators:

> *postincrement-expression :*
>   *postfix-expression* **++**

> *postdecrement-expression :*
>   *postfix-expression* **- -**

The operand of both operators must be a modifiable lvalue and may be of any real arithmetic or pointer type. The constant 1 is added to the operand in the case of **++** or subtracted from the operand in the case of **- -**, modifying the operand. The result is the old value of the operand before it was incremented or decremented. The result is not an lvalue. The usual binary conversions are performed on the operand and the constant 1 before the addition or subtraction is performed, and the usual assignment conversions are performed when storing the modified value back into the operand. The type of the result is that of the lvalue operand before conversion.

Example

> If i and j are integer variables, the statement i=j--; may be rewritten as the two statements
>
> ```
> i = j;
> j = j-1;
> ```

These operations may produce unpredictable effects if overflow occurs and the operand is a signed integer or floating-point number. The result of incrementing the largest representable value of an unsigned type is 0, and the result of decrementing the value 0 of an unsigned integer type is the largest representable value of that type.

If the operand is a pointer, say of type "pointer to T" for some type T, the effect of ++ is to move the pointer forward beyond the object pointed to, as if to move the pointer to the next element within an array of objects of type T. (On a byte-addressed computer, this means advancing the pointer by sizeof(T) bytes.) Similarly, the effect of -- is to move the pointer backward as if to the previous element within an array of objects of type T. In both cases, the value of the expression is the pointer before modification.

Example

> It is very common to use the postfix increment operator when scanning the elements of an array or string, as in this example of counting the number of characters in a string:
>
> ```
> int string_length(const char *cp)
> {
>     int count = 0;
>     while (*cp++) count++;
>     return count;
> }
> ```

References   addition 7.6.2; array types 5.4; assignment conversions 6.3.2; floating-point types 5.2; integer types 5.1; lvalue 7.1; overflow 7.2.2; pointer types 5.3; scalar types Ch. 5; signed types 5.1.1; subtraction 7.6.2; unsigned types 5.1.2; usual binary conversions 6.3.4

7.4.5 Compound Literals

C99 introduces compound literals as a way to express unnamed constants of aggregate type. A compound literal consists of a parenthesized type name followed by an initializer list contained in braces. There may be an optional trailing comma after the initializer list.

> *compound-literal :*
>   (*type-name*) { *initializer-list* $,_{opt}$}   *(C99)*

A compound literal creates an unnamed object of the designated type and returns an lvalue to that object. The type name may specify any object type or an array type with unknown size. Variable length array types may not be used in compound literals since they may not be initialized. Structure, union, array, and enumeration types would seem to be most useful in a compound literal. The format and meaning of the initializer list is the same as would be permitted in the initializer on a declaration of an object of the same type and extent. In particular, this means that uninitialized components of the compound literal are initialized to zero (see Section 4.6).

The `const` type qualifier may be used in a compound literal's type name to create a read-only literal; otherwise the literal is modifiable. If two read-only compound literals have the same type and value, then an implementation is free to reuse the same storage for them. That is, their addresses might not be different, as is the case for duplicate string literals.

Example

Make `Temp1` point to a modifiable string, and make `Temp2` point to a read-only string:

```
char *Temp1 = (char []){"/temp/XXXXXXXX"};
char *Temp2 = "/temp/XXXXXXXX";
```

Function `POW2` computes small powers of two by a table lookup:

```
inline int POW2(int n)
{
    assert( n >= 0 && n <= 7 );
    return (const int []){1, 2, 4, 8, 16, 32, 64, 128}[n];
}
```

`DrawTo` takes a point structure passed by value, whereas `DrawLine` is passed the addresses of two points.

```
DrawTo( (struct Point){.x=12, .y=n+3} );
DrawLine( &(struct Point){x,y}, &(struct Point){-x,-y} );
```

If a compound literal appears at the top level of a file, then the unnamed object has static extent—it exists throughout program execution. The initializer list in that case can contain only constant values. If the compound literal appears in a function, then it has automatic extent and scope consisting of the innermost enclosing block. The lifetime of a compound literal is important when its address is taken; the programmer must be sure that the address is not used after leaving the literal's scope.

A compound literal is allocated each time its containing block is entered, but repeated execution of the compound literal without leaving the scope merely reinitializes the storage if necessary. Such a repeated execution can only happen when a loop is constructed with a `goto` statement because in any iterative statement the compound literal would be in the scope of the iteration body, and that scope is reentered on each iteration.

Example

The following loop fills `ptrs` with pointers to a single array, and `*(ptrs[i]) == 4`.

```
int * ptrs[5]; int i = 0;
again:
    ptrs[i] = (int [1]){i};
    if (++i<5) goto again;
```

The following code fills `ptrs` with pointers to different arrays, and `*(ptr[i]) == i`.

```
int * ptrs[5]; int i = 0;
ptrs[i] = (int [1]){i++}; }
ptrs[i] = (int [1]){i++}; }
ptrs[i] = (int [1]){i++}; }
ptrs[i] = (int [1]){i++}; }
ptrs[i] = (int [1]){i++}; }
```

The following loop fills **ptrs** with undefined (dangling) pointers because each literal array was deallocated at the end of its loop iteration.

```
int *ptrs[5];
for(int i=0; i<5; i++) { ptrs[i] = (int [1]){i}; }
```

References   initializer 4.6; variable length array 5.4.5

7.5 UNARY EXPRESSIONS

There are several kinds of unary expressions discussed in the following sections.

> *cast-expression :*
> > *unary-expression*
> > (*type-name*) *cast-expression*

> *unary-expression* :
> > *postfix-expression*
> > *sizeof-expression*
> > *unary-minus-expression*
> > *unary-plus-expression*
> > *logical-negation-expression*
> > *bitwise-negation-expression*
> > *address-expression*
> > *indirection-expression*
> > *preincrement-expression*
> > *predecrement-expression*

The unary operators have precedence lower than the postfix expressions but higher than all binary and ternary operators. For example, the expression ***x++** is interpreted as ***(x++)**, not as **(*x)++**.

References   binary expressions 7.6; postfix expressions 7.4; precedence 7.2.1; unary plus operator 7.5.3

7.5.1 Casts

A cast expression consists of a left parenthesis, a type name, a right parenthesis, and an operand expression. The syntax is shown earlier, with that for *unary-expression.*

The cast causes the operand value to be converted to the type named within the parentheses. Any permissible conversion (Section 6.3.1) may be invoked by a cast expression. The result is not an lvalue.

Example

```
extern char *alloc();
struct S *p;
p = (struct S *) alloc(sizeof(struct S));
```

Some implementations of C incorrectly ignore certain casts whose only effect is to make a value "narrower" than normal.

Example

Suppose that type **unsigned short** is represented in 16 bits and type **unsigned** is represented in 32 bits. Then the value of the expression

(unsigned)(unsigned short)0xFFFFFF

should be **0xFFFF** because the cast (**unsigned short**) should cause truncation of the value **0xFFFFFF** to 16 bits, and then the cast (**unsigned**) should widen that value back to 32 bits. Deficient compilers fail to implement this truncation effect and generate code that passes the value **0xFFFFFF** through unchanged. Similarly, for the expression

(double)(float)3.1415926535897932384

deficient compilers do not produce code to reduce the precision of the approximation of π to that of a **float**, but pass through the double-precision value unchanged.

For maximum portability using non-Standard compilers, programmers should truncate values by storing them into variables or, in the case of integers, performing explicit masking operations (such as with the binary bitwise AND operator **&**) rather than relying on narrowing casts.

References   bitwise AND operator 7.6.6; type conversions Ch. 6; type names 5.12

7.5.2 Sizeof Operator

The **sizeof** operator is used to obtain the size of a type or data object:

sizeof-expression :
      sizeof (*type-name*)
      sizeof *unary-expression*

The **sizeof** expression has two forms: the operator **sizeof** followed by a parenthesized type name, or the operator **sizeof** followed by an operand expression. The result is a constant integer value and is never an lvalue. In Standard C, the result of **sizeof** has the unsigned integer type **size_t** defined in the header file **stddef.h**. Traditional C implementations often use **int** or **long** as the result type. Following the C precedence rules, `sizeof(long)-2` is interpreted as `(sizeof(long))-2` rather than as `sizeof((long)(-2))`.

Applying the `sizeof` operator to a parenthesized type name yields the size of an object of the specified type—that is, the amount of memory (measured in storage units) that would be occupied by an object of that type, including any internal or trailing padding. By definition, `sizeof` applied to any of the character types yields 1. The type name may not name an incomplete array type (one with no explicit length), a function type, or the type **void**.

Applying the `sizeof` operator to an expression yields the same result as if it had been applied to the name of the type of the expression. The `sizeof` operator does not cause any of the usual conversions to be applied to the expression in determining its type; this allows `sizeof` to be used to obtain the total size of an array without the array name being converted to a pointer. However, if the expression contains operators that do perform usual conversions, then those conversions are considered when determining the type. The operand of `sizeof` may not have an incomplete array type or function type, except that if the `sizeof` operator is applied to the name of a formal parameter declared to have array or function type, then the value returned is the size of the pointer type obtained by the normal rules for converting formal parameters of those types. In Standard C, the operand of `sizeof` may not be an lvalue that designates a bit field in a structure or union object, but some non-Standard implementations allow this and return the size of the declared type of the component (ignoring the bit-field designation).

Example

Following are some examples of the application of `sizeof`. Assume that objects of type **short** occupy 2 bytes and objects of type **int** occupy 4 bytes.

Expression	Value
`sizeof(char)`	1
`sizeof(int)`	4
`short s;… sizeof(s)`	2
`short s;… sizeof(s+0)`	4 (result of + has type **int**)
`short sa[10];… sizeof(sa)`	20
`extern int ia[]; … sizeof(ia)`	*invalid* (type is incomplete)

When `sizeof` is applied to an expression, the expression is analyzed at compile time to determine its type, but the expression is not evaluated. When the argument to `sizeof` is a type name, it is possible to declare a type as a side effect.

If a variable length array type name appears in a `sizeof` expression and the value of the array size affects the value of the `sizeof` expression, then the array size expression is always fully evaluated, including side effects. If the value of the array size does not affect the result of `sizeof`, then it is undefined whether the size expression is evaluated.

Example

In the following statements, **j** is not incremented, but **n** is. The function call **f(n)** may or may not be performed; it does not have to be because the **sizeof** expression is only computing the size of a pointer to a variable length array, which does not depend on the array's length.

```
size_t z = sizeof(j++);
size_t x = sizeof(int [n++]);
size_t y = sizeof(int (*)[f(n)]);
```

The effect of

```
sizeof(struct S {int a,b;})
```

is to create a new type in Standard C, although it would seem to be bad style to do so. The type can be referenced later in the source file. (This is invalid in C++.)

References   array types 5.4; C++ compatibility 7.15; function types 5.8; **size_t** 11.1; storage units 6.1.1; type names 5.12; unsigned types 5.1.2; usual binary conversions 6.3.4; variable length arrays 5.4.5; **void** type 5.9

7.5.3 Unary Minus and Plus

The unary minus operator computes the arithmetic negation of its operand. The unary plus operator (introduced with Standard C) simply yields the value of its operand:

unary-minus-expression :
　　- *cast-expression*

unary-plus-expression :   *(C89)*
　　+ *cast-expression*

The operands to both operators may be of any arithmetic type and the usual unary conversions are performed. The result has the promoted type and is not an lvalue.

The unary minus expression -*e* is a shorthand notation for $0 - (e)$; the two expressions perform the same computation. This computation may produce unpredictable effects if the operand is a signed integer or floating-point number and overflow occurs. For an unsigned integer operand k, the result is always unsigned and equal to $2^n - k$, where n is the number of bits used to represent the result. Because the result is unsigned, it can never be negative. This may seem strange, but note that $(-x) + x$ is equal to 0 for any unsigned integer x and for any signed integer x for which $-x$ is well defined.

The unary plus expression +*e* is a shorthand notation for $0 + (e)$.

References   floating-point types 5.2; integer types 5.1; lvalue 7.1; overflow 7.2.2; subtraction operator - 7.6.2; unsigned types 5.1.2; usual unary conversions 6.3.3

7.5.4 Logical Negation

The unary operator **!** computes the logical negation of its operand. The operand may be of any scalar type:

logical-negation-expression :
   ! *cast-expression*

The usual unary conversions are performed on the operand. The result of the ! operator is of type `int`; the result is 1 if the operand is zero (null in the case of pointers, 0.0 in the case of floating-point values) and 0 if the operand is not zero (or null or 0.0). The result is not an lvalue. The expression ! `(x)` is identical in meaning to `(x)==0`.

Example

```
#define assert(x,s) if (!(x)) assertion_failure(s)
...
assert(num_cases > 0, "No test cases.");
average = total_points/num_cases;
```

The use of the `assert` macro anticipates a problem—division by zero—that might otherwise be difficult to locate. `assertion_failure` is assumed to be a function that accepts a string and reports it as a message to the user. A similar `assert` macro appears in the standard header file `assert.h`.

References `assert` 19.1; equality operator `==` 7.6.5; floating-point types 5.2; integer types 5.1; lvalue 7.1; pointer types 5.3; scalar types Ch. 5; usual unary conversions 6.3.3

7.5.5 Bitwise Negation

The unary operator ~ computes the bitwise negation (NOT) of its operand:

bitwise-negation-expression :
   ~ *cast-expression*

The usual unary conversions are performed on the operand, which may be of any integral type. Every bit in the binary representation of ~*e* is the inverse of what it was in the (converted) operand *e*. The result is not an lvalue.

Example

If `i` is a 16-bit integer with the value `0xF0F0` (1111000011110000_2), then ~`i` has the value `0x0F0F` (0000111100001111_2).

Because different implementations may use different representations for signed integers, the result of applying the bitwise NOT operator ~ to signed operands may not be portable. We recommend using ~ only on unsigned operands for portable code. For an unsigned operand *e*, ~*e* has the value `UINT_MAX`-*e* if the converted type of *e* is `unsigned`, or `ULONG_MAX`-*e* if the converted type of *e* is `unsigned long`. The values `UINT_MAX` and `ULONG_MAX` are defined in the Standard C header file `limits.h`.

References integer types 5.1; `limits.h` 5.1.1; lvalue 7.1; signed types 5.1.1; unsigned types 5.1.2; usual unary conversions 6.3.3

7.5.6 Address Operator

The unary operator & returns a pointer to its operand:

> *address-expression* :
>   & *cast-expression*

The operand of **&** must be either a function designator or an lvalue designating an object. If it is an lvalue, the object cannot be declared with storage class **register** or be a bit field. If the type of the operand for **&** is "*T*," then the type of the result is "pointer to *T*." The usual conversions are *not* applied to the operand of the **&** operator, and its result is never an lvalue.

The address operator applied to a function designator yields a pointer to the function. Since a function designator is converted to a pointer under the usual conversion rules, the **&** operator is seldom needed for functions. In fact, some pre-Standard C implementations may not allow it.

Example

```
extern int f();
int (*fp)();
...
fp = &f;    /* OK; & yields a pointer to f */
fp = f;     /* OK; usual conversions yield a pointer to f */
```

A function pointer generated by the address operator is valid throughout the execution of the C program. An object pointer generated by the address operator is valid as long as the object's storage remains allocated. If the operand of **&** is an lvalue designating a variable with static extent, the pointer is valid throughout program execution. If the operand designates an automatic variable, the pointer is valid as long as the block containing the declaration of the variable is active. If the operand designates a dynamically allocated object (e.g., by **malloc**), the pointer is valid until that memory is explicitly freed.

The effect of the address operator in Standard C differs from its effect in traditional C in one respect. In Standard C, the address operator applied to an lvalue of type "array of *T*" yields a value of type "pointer to array of T," whereas many pre-Standard compilers treat **&a** the same as **a**—that is, as a pointer to the first element of **a**. These two interpretations are inconsistent with each other, but the Standard rule is more consistent with the interpretation of **&**.

Example

In the following Standard C program fragment, all the assignments to **p** are equivalent and all the assignments to **i** are equivalent:

```
int a[10], *p, i;
...
p = &a[0];   p = a;     p = *&a;
i = a[0];    i   = *a; i = **&a;
```

References   array type 5.4; function designator 7.1; function type 5.8; lvalue 7.1; pointer type 5.3; `register` storage class 4.3

7.5.7 Indirection

The unary operator ***** performs indirection through a pointer. The **&** and ***** operators are each the inverse of the other: If **x** is a variable, the expression ***&x** is the same as **x**.

> *indirection-expression* :
>   ***** *cast-expression*

The operand must be a pointer; if its type is "pointer to *T*," for some possibly qualified type *T*, then the type of the result is simply "*T*" (with the same qualifications). If the pointer points to an object, then the result is an lvalue referring to the object. If the pointer points to a function, then the result is a function designator.

Example

```
int i,*p;
const int *pc;
...
p   = &i;    /* p now points to variable i */
*p  = 10; /* sets value of i to 10 */
pc  = &i; /* pc now points to i, too */
*pc = 10;    /* invalid, *pc has type 'const int' */
```

The usual unary conversions are performed on the operand to the indirection operator. The only relevant conversions are from arrays and function designators to pointers. Therefore, if **f** is a function designator, the expressions ***&f** and ***f** are equivalent; in the latter case, **f** is converted to **&f** by the usual conversions.

The effect of applying the ***** operator to invalid or null pointers is undefined. In some implementations, dereferencing the null pointer will cause the program to terminate; in others, it is as if the null pointer designated a block of memory with unpredictable contents.

References   array types 5.4; function designators 7.1; function types 5.8; lvalue 7.1; pointer types 5.3; usual unary conversions 6.3.3

7.5.8 Prefix Increment and Decrement Operators

The unary operators **++** and **- -** are, respectively, used to increment and decrement their operands while producing the modified values of the operands as a result. These are side-effect-producing operations. (There are also postfix forms of these operators.)

preincrement-expression :
          ++ *unary-expression*

predecrement-expression :
          - - *unary-expression*

The operands of both operators must be modifiable lvalues and may be of any real arithmetic or pointer type. The constant 1 is added to the operand in the case of **++** and subtracted from the operand in the case of **- -**. In both cases, the result is stored back in the lvalue and the result is the new value of the operand. The result is not an lvalue. The usual binary conversions are performed on the operand and the constant 1 before the addition or subtraction is performed, and the usual assignment conversions are performed when storing the new value. The type of the result is that of the lvalue operand before conversion.

If the operand is a pointer, say of type "pointer to *T*" for some type *T*, then the effect of **++** is to move the pointer forward beyond the object pointed to, as if to move the pointer to the next object within an array of objects of type *T*. (On a byte-addressed computer, this means advancing the pointer by **sizeof**(*T*) bytes.) The effect of **- -** is to move the pointer back to the previous element within an array of objects of type *T*.

Example

The following **strrev** function copies into its second argument a reversed copy of its first argument:

```
int strrev( const char *s1, char *s2 )
{
    const char *p = s1;
    while (*p++); /* Locate end of first string. */
    --p;          /* Overshot: back up to the null. */
    /* Now copy the characters in reverse order. */
    while (p > s1)
        *s2++ = *--p;
    *s2 = '\0';   /* Terminate the result string. */
}
```

These operations may produce unpredictable effects if overflow occurs and the operand is a signed integer or floating-point number. The result of incrementing the largest representable value of an unsigned type is 0. The result of decrementing the value 0 of an unsigned integer type is the largest representable value of that type.

The expression **++***e* is identical in meaning to *e***+=1**, and **- -***e* is identical to *e***-=1**. When the value produced by the increment and decrement operators is not used, the prefix and postfix forms have the same effect. That is, the statement *e***++;** is identical to **++***e***;**, and *e***- -;** is identical to **- -***e***;**.

References   addition 7.6.2; array types 5.4; assignment conversions 6.3.2; compound assignment 7.9.2; expression statements 8.2; floating-point types 5.2; integer types 5.1; lvalue 7.1; overflow 7.2.2; pointer types 5.3; postfix increment and decrement expressions 7.4.4; scalar types ch. 5; signed types 5.1.1; subtraction 7.6.2; unsigned types 5.1.2; usual binary conversions 6.3.4

7.6 BINARY OPERATOR EXPRESSIONS

A binary operator expression consists of two expressions separated by a binary operator. The term *binary* here simply means that there are two operands; it does not have anything to do with the binary number system. The kinds of binary expressions and their operand types are listed in order of decreasing precedence in Table 7–4. All the operators are left-associative.

Table 7–4   Binary operator expressions

Expression kind	Operators	Operands	Result
multiplicative-expression	* /	arithmetic	arithmetic
	%	integer	integer
additive-expression	+	arithmetic	arithmetic
		pointer + integer or integer + pointer	pointer
	–	arithmetic	arithmetic
		pointer – integer	pointer
		pointer – pointer	integer
shift-expression	<< >>	integer	integer
relational-expression	< <= >= >	arithmetic or pointer	0 or 1
equality-expression	== !=	arithmetic or pointer	0 or 1
bitwise-and-expression	&	integer	integer
bitwise-xor-expression	^	integer	integer
bitwise-or-expression			integer	integer

For each of the binary operators described in this section, both operands are fully evaluated (but in no particular order) before the operation is performed.

References   order of evaluation 7.12; precedence 7.2.1

7.6.1 Multiplicative Operators

The three multiplicative operators, * (multiplication), / (division), and % (remainder), have the same precedence and are left-associative:

multiplicative-expression :
    cast-expression
    multiplicative-expression mult-op cast-expression

mult-op : **one of**
    * / %

References   precedence 7.2.1

Multiplication   The binary operator * indicates multiplication. Each operand may be of any arithmetic type. The usual binary conversions are performed on the operands, and the type of the result is that of the converted operands. The result is not an lvalue. For integral operands, integer multiplication is performed; for floating-point operands, floating-point multiplication is performed.

The multiplication operator may produce unpredictable effects if overflow occurs and the operands (after conversion) are signed integers or floating-point numbers. If the operands are unsigned integers, the result is congruent mod 2^n to the true mathematical result of the operation (where n is the number of bits used to represent the unsigned result).

References   arithmetic types Ch. 5; floating types 5.2; integer types 5.1; lvalue 7.1; order of evaluation 7.12; overflow 7.2.2; signed types 5.1.1; unsigned types 5.1.2; usual conversions 6.3.4

Division   The binary operator / indicates division. Each operand may be of any arithmetic type. The usual binary conversions are performed on the operands, and the type of the result is that of the converted operands. The result is not an lvalue.

For floating-point operands, floating-point division is performed. For integral operands, if the mathematical quotient of the operands is not an exact integer, then the fractional part is discarded (truncation toward zero). Prior to C99, C implementations could choose to truncate toward or away from zero if either of the operands were negative. The **div** and **ldiv** library functions were always well defined for negative operands.

The division operator may produce unpredictable effects if overflow occurs and the operands (after conversion) are signed integers or floating-point numbers. Note that overflow can occur for signed integers represented in twos-complement form if the most negative representable integer is divided by –1; the mathematical result is a positive integer that cannot be represented. Overflow cannot occur if the operands are unsigned integers.

The consequences of division by zero—integer or floating-point—are undefined.

References   arithmetic types Ch. 5; **div** 17.1; floating types 5.2; integer types 5.1; **ldiv** 17.1; lvalue 7.1; overflow 7.2.2; signed types 5.1.1; unsigned types 5.1.2; usual conversions 6.3.4

Remainder   The binary operator % computes the remainder when the first operand is divided by the second. Each operand may be of any integral type. The usual binary conversions are performed on the operands, and the type of the result is that of the converted operands. The result is not an lvalue. The library functions **div**, **ldiv**, and **fmod** also compute remainders of integers and floating-point values.

It is always true that (a/b)*b + a%b is equal to a if a/b is representable, so the behavior of the remainder operation is coupled to that of integer division. As indicated in the previous section, prior to C99 the division operator's behavior was implementation-dependent when either operand was negative. This made the remainder operator similarly implementation-dependent.

Example

The following **gcd** function computes the greatest common divisor by Euclid's algorithm. The result is the largest integer that evenly divides **x** and **y**:

```
unsigned gcd(unsigned x, unsigned y)
{
    while ( y != 0 ) {
        unsigned temp = y;
        y = x % y;
        x = temp;
    }
    return x;
}
```

The remainder operator may produce unpredictable effects if performing division on the two operands would produce overflow. Note that overflow can occur for signed integers represented in twos-complement form if the most negative representable integer is divided by −1; the mathematical result of the division is a positive integer that cannot be represented, and therefore the results are unpredictable, even though the remainder (zero) is representable. Overflow cannot occur if the operands are unsigned integers.

The effect of taking a remainder with a second operand of zero is undefined.

References   `div`, `ldiv` 17.1; `fmod` 17.3; integer types 5.1; lvalue 7.1; overflow 7.2.2; signed types 5.1.1; unsigned types 5.1.2; usual binary conversions 6.3.4

7.6.2 Additive Operators

The two additive operators, + (addition) and - (subtraction), have the same precedence and are left-associative:

additive-expression :
    multiplicative-expression
    additive-expression add-op multiplicative-expression

add-op : one of
    + -

Addition   The binary operator + indicates addition. The usual binary conversions are performed on the operands. The operands may both be arithmetic, or one may be an object pointer and the other an integer. No other operand types are allowed. The result is not an lvalue.

When the operands are arithmetic, the type of the result is that of the converted operands. For integral operands, integer addition is performed; for floating-point operands, floating-point addition is performed.

When adding a pointer p and an integer k, it is assumed that the object that p points to lies within an array of such objects or is one object beyond the last object in the array, and the result is a pointer to that object within (or just after) the presumed array that lies k objects away from the one p points to. For example, $p+1$ points to the object just after the one p points to, and $p+(-1)$ points to the object just before. If the pointers p or $p+k$ do not lie within (or just after) the array, then the behavior is undefined. It is invalid for p to be a function pointer or to have type `void *`.

Example

Suppose we are on a computer that is byte-addressable and on which the type **int** is allocated 4 bytes. Let **a** be an array of 10 integers that begins at address **0x100000**. Let **ip** be a pointer to an integer, and assign to it the address of the first element of array **a**. Finally, let **i** be an integer variable currently holding the value 6. We now have the following situation:

```
int *ip, i, a[10];
ip = &a[0];
i = 6;
```

What is the value of **ip+i**? Because integers are 4 bytes long, the expression **ip+i** becomes **0x100000+4*6**, or **0x100018**. (24_{10} is 18_{16}.)

Example

Pointers to multidimensional and variable length arrays (C99) work similarly.

```
int n = 3; int m = 5;
double rect[n][m];
double (*p)[m];
p = rect; /* same as p = &rect[0]; */
p++; /* now p == &rect[1] */
```

The identifier **p** points to an object of type **double [m]**, an array of 5 double-precision floating-point numbers, the same as a row of the matrix **rect**. The expression **p++** advances **p** to the next row of **rect**, advancing it **5*sizeof(double)** storage units.

The addition operator may produce unpredictable effects if overflow occurs and the operands (after conversion) are signed integers or floating-point numbers, or if either operand is a pointer. If the operands are both unsigned integers, then the result is congruent mod 2^n to the true mathematical result of the operation (where n is the number of bits used to represent the unsigned result).

References   array types 5.4; floating-point types 5.2; integer types 5.1; lvalue 7.1; multidimensional arrays 5.4.2; order of evaluation 7.12; overflow 7.2.2; pointer representations 5.3.2; pointer types 5.3; scalar types ch. 5; signed types 5.1.1; unsigned types 5.1.2; usual binary conversions 6.3.4; variable length arrays 5.4.5

Subtraction   The binary operator - indicates subtraction. The usual binary conversions are performed on the operands. The operands may both be arithmetic or may both be pointers to compatible object types (ignoring any type qualifiers), or the left operand may be a pointer and the other an integer. The result is not an lvalue.

If the operands are both arithmetic, the type of the result is that of the converted operands. For integral operands, integer subtraction is performed; for floating-point operands, floating-point subtraction is performed.

Example

The result of subtracting one unsigned integer from another is always unsigned and therefore cannot be negative. However, unsigned numbers always obey such identities as

```
(a+(b-a)) == b
```

and

        (a-(a-b)) == b

Subtraction of an integer from a pointer is analogous to addition of an integer to a pointer. When subtracting an integer k from a pointer p, it is assumed that the object that p points to lies within an array of such objects or is one object past the last object, and the result is a pointer to that object within (or just after) the presumed array that lies $-k$ objects away from the one p points to. For example, $p-1$ points to the object just before the one p points to, and $p-(-1)$ points to the object just after. If the pointers p or $p-k$ do not lie within (or just after) the array, then the behavior is undefined. It is invalid for p to be a function pointer or to have type **void ***.

Given two pointers p and q of the same type, the difference $p-q$ is an integer k such that adding k to q yields p. The type of the difference is the signed integer type **ptrdiff_t** defined in **stddef.h**. (In pre-Standard C, the type could be either **int** or **long** depending on the implementation.) The result is well defined and portable only if the two pointers point to objects in the same array or point to one past the last object of the array. The difference k is the difference in the subscripts of the two objects pointed to. If the pointers p or $p-q$ lie outside the array, the behavior is undefined. It is invalid for either p or q to be a function pointer or to have type **void ***.

The subtraction operator may produce unpredictable effects if overflow occurs and the operands (after conversion) are signed integers or floating-point numbers, or if either operand is a pointer. If the operands are both unsigned integers, the result is congruent mod 2^n to the true mathematical result of the operation (where n is the number of bits used to represent the unsigned result).

References   array types 5.4; floating-point types 5.2; integer types 5.1; lvalue 7.1; overflow 7.2.2; pointer representations 5.3.2; pointer types 5.3; **ptrdiff_t** 11.1; scalar types Ch. 5; signed types 5.1.1; type compatibility 5.11; type qualifiers 4.4.3; unsigned types 5.1.2; usual binary conversions 6.3.4

7.6.3 Shift Operators

The binary operator **<<** indicates shifting to the left and the binary operator **>>** indicates shifting to the right. Both have the same precedence and are left-associative:

shift-expression :
        additive-expression
        shift-expression shift-op additive-expression

shift-op : one of
        << >>

Each operand must be of integral type. The usual unary conversions are performed separately on each operand, and the type of the result is that of the converted left operand. (Pre-Standard C performed the usual binary conversions on both operands.) The result is not an lvalue.

The first operand is a quantity to be shifted, and the second operand specifies the number of bit positions by which the first operand is to be shifted. The direction of the shift operation is controlled by the operator used. The operator `<<` shifts the value of the left operand to the left; excess bits shifted off to the left are discarded, and 0-bits are shifted in from the right. The operator `>>` shifts the value of the left operand to the right; excess bits shifted off to the right are discarded. The bits shifted in from the left for `>>` depend on the type of the converted left operand: If it is unsigned (or signed and non-negative), then 0-bits are shifted in from the left; but if it is signed and negative, then at the implementor's option either 0-bits or copies of the leftmost bit of the left operand are shifted in from the left. Therefore, applying the shift operator `>>` is not portable when the left operand is a negative, signed value and the right operand is nonzero.

The result value of the shift operators is undefined if the value of the right operand is negative, so specifying a negative shift distance does not (necessarily) cause `<<` to shift to the right or `>>` to shift to the left. The result value is also undefined if the value of the right operand is greater than or equal to the width (in bits) of the value of the converted left operand. The right operand may be 0, in which case no shift occurs and the result value is identical to the value of the converted left operand.

Example

One can exploit the precedence and associativity of the operators to write expressions that are visually pleasing but semantically confusing:

```
b << 4 >> 8
```

If **b** is a 16-bit unsigned value, then this expression extracts the middle 8 bits. As always, it is better to use parentheses when there is any possibility of confusion:

```
(b << 4) >> 8
```

Example

Here is how unsigned shift operations may be used to compute the greatest common divisor of two integers by the binary algorithm. This method is more complicated than the Euclidean algorithm, but it may be faster because in some implementations of C the remainder operation is slow, especially for unsigned operands.

```
unsigned binary_gcd(unsigned x, unsigned y)
{
    unsigned temp;
    unsigned common_power_of_two = 0;
    if (x == 0) return y; /* Special cases */
    if (y == 0) return x;

    /* Find the largest power of two
       that divides both x and y. */
    while (((x | y) & 1) == 0) {
        x = x >> 1; /* or: "x >>= 1;" */
        y = y >> 1;
        ++common_power_of_two;
    }
```

```
while ((x & 1) == 0) x = x >> 1;

while (y) {
    /* x is odd and y is nonzero here. */
    while ((y & 1) == 0) y = y >> 1;
    /* x and y are odd here. */
    temp = y;
    if (x > y) y = x - y;
    else y = y - x;
    x = temp;
    /* Now x has the old value of y, which is odd.
       y is even, because it is the difference of two odd
       numbers; therefore it will be right-shifted
       at least once on the next iteration. */
}
return (x << common_power_of_two);
}
```

References   integer types 5.1; lvalue 7.1; precedence 7.2.1; signed types 5.1.1; unsigned types 5.1.2; usual unary conversions 6.3.3

7.6.4 Relational Operators

The binary operators `<`, `<=`, `>`, and `>=` are used to compare their operands:

> *relational-expression* :
>   *shift-expression*
>   *relational-expression relational-op shift-expression*

> *relational-op* : one of
>   `<    <=    >    >=`

The usual binary conversions are performed on the operands. The operands may both be of real (not complex) arithmetic types, may both be pointers to compatible types, or may both be pointers to compatible incomplete types. The presence of any type qualifiers on the pointer types does not affect the comparison. The result is always of type `int` and has the value 0 or 1. The result is not an lvalue.

The operator `<` tests for the relationship "is less than", the operator `<=` tests "is less than or equal to", the operator `>` tests "is greater than", and the operator `>=` tests "is greater than or equal to." The result is 1 if the stated relationship holds for the particular operand values and 0 if the stated relationship does not hold.

Implementations of floating-point arithmetic in Standard C may include values such as NaNs that are *unordered*. Using these values in relational expressions may raise an "invalid" exception, and the value of the relationship will be false. Section 17.16 discusses functions that are better behaved in such circumstances than are the built-in operators.

For integral operands, integer comparison is performed (signed or unsigned as appropriate). For floating-point operands, floating-point comparison is performed. For pointer operands, the result depends on the relative locations within the address space of the two objects pointed to; the result is defined only if the objects pointed to lie within the same array or structure, in which case "greater than" means "having a higher index" for arrays or "declared later in the list of components" for structures. As a special case for arrays, the pointer to the object one beyond the end of the array is well defined and compares greater than all pointers to objects strictly within the array. All pointers to members of the same union argument compare equal.

Example

> You can write an expression such as `3<x<7`. This does not have the meaning it has in usual mathematical notation, however; by left-associativity it is interpreted as `(3<x)<7`. Because the result of `(3<x)` is 0 or 1, either of which is less than 7, the result of `3<x<7` is always 1. You can express the meaning of the usual mathematical notation by using a logical AND operator, as in `3<x && x<7`.

Example

> You should exercise care when using relational operators on mixed types. A particularly confusing case is this expression:
>
> ```
> -1 < (unsigned) 0
> ```
>
> One might think that this expression would always produce 1 (true) because –1 is less than 0. However, the usual binary conversions cause the value –1 to be converted to a (large) unsigned value before the comparison, and such an unsigned value cannot be less than 0. Therefore, the expression always produces 0 (false).

Some older implementations permit relational comparisons between pointers and integers, which is actually disallowed. These older implementations may treat the comparisons as signed or unsigned.

> **References**   arithmetic types Ch. 5; array types 5.4; bitwise AND operator `&` 7.6.6; compatible types 5.11; floating-point types 5.2; incomplete types 5.4, 5.6.1; integer types 5.1; logical AND operator `&&` 7.7; lvalue 7.1; NaN 5.2; pointer types 5.3; precedence 7.2.1; signed types 5.1.1; type qualifiers 4.4.3; unsigned types 5.1.2; usual binary conversions 6.3.4

7.6.5 Equality Operators

The binary operators `==` and `!=` are used to compare their operands for equality:

> *equality-expression* :
>   *relational-expression*
>   *equality-expression equality-op relational-expression*
>
> *equality-op* : one of
>   `==`   `!=`

Several kinds of operands are permitted:

1. Both operands may be arithmetic types, including complex.
2. Both operands may be pointers to compatible types, or both may be **void *** types.

3. One operand may be a pointer to an object or incomplete type and the other may have type **void ***. The first operand will be converted to the **void *** type.

4. One of the operands may be a pointer and the other a null pointer constant (the integer constant 0).

In the case of pointer operands, the presence or absence of type qualifiers on the type pointed to does not affect whether the comparison is allowed or the result of the comparison. The usual binary conversions are performed on the arithmetic operands. The result is always of type **int** and has the value 0 or 1. The result is not an lvalue.

For integral operands, integer comparison is performed. For floating-point operands, floating-point comparison is performed. Pointer operands compare equal if and only if one of the following conditions is met:

1. Both pointers point to the same object or function.

2. Both pointers are null pointers.

3. Both pointers point one past the last element of the same array object.

The operator **==** tests for the relationship "is equal to"; **!=** tests "is not equal to." The result is 1 if the stated relationship holds for the particular operand values and 0 if the stated relationship does not hold.

For complex operands (C99), both real and imaginary parts must compare equal for the complex operands to be equal. If one operand is real and the other complex, then the comparison is performed as if the real operand were first converted to the complex type. The usual binary conversions bring both operands to the same precision.

Structures or unions cannot be compared for equality, even though assignment of these types is allowed. The gaps in structures and unions caused by alignment restrictions could contain arbitrary values, and compensating for this would impose an unacceptable overhead on the equality comparison or on all operations that modified structure and union types.

The binary equality operators both have the same precedence (but lower precedence than **<**, **<=**, **>**, and **>=**) and are left-associative.

Example

The expression **x==y==7** does not have the meaning it has in usual mathematical notation. By left-associativity, it is interpreted as **(x==y)==7**. Because the result of **(x==y)** is 0 or 1, neither of which is equal to 7, the result of **x==y==7** is always 0. You can express the meaning of the usual mathematical notation by using a logical AND operator, as in

```
x==y && y==7
```

Example

There is a bitwise XOR operator as well as bitwise AND and OR operators, but there is no logical XOR operator to go along with the logical AND and OR operators. The **!=** operator serves the purpose of a logical XOR operator: One may write **a<b != c<d** for an expression that yields 1 if exactly one of **a<b** and **c<d** yields 1 and 0 otherwise. If either of the operands might have a value other than 0 or 1, then the unary **!** operator can be applied to both operands:

`!x != !y` yields 1 if exactly one of **x** and **y** is nonzero and yields 0 otherwise. In a similar manner, `==` serves as a logical equivalence (EQV) operator.

Example

A common C programming error is to write the `=` operator (assignment) where the `==` operator (comparison) was intended. Several other programming languages use `=` for equality comparison. As a matter of style, if it is necessary to use an assignment expression in a context that will test the value of the expression against zero, it is best to write "`! = 0`" explicitly to make the intent clear. For example, it is unclear whether the following loop is correct or whether it contains a typographical error:

```
while (x = next_item()) {
/* Should this be "x==next_item()" ?? */
   ...
}
```

If the original form was correct, then the intent can be made clear in this manner:

```
while ((x = next_item()) != 0) {
   ...
}
```

References   alignment restrictions 5.6.4, 6.1.3; bitwise operators 7.6.6; compatible types 5.11; logical operators 7.5.4, 7.7; lvalue 7.1; null pointer 5.3.2; pointer types 5.3; precedence 7.2.1; assignment operator = 7.9.1; type qualifiers 4.4.3; usual binary conversions 6.3.4; **void *** 5.3.1

7.6.6 Bitwise Operators

The binary operators **&**, **^**, and **|** designate the bitwise "and," "exclusive-or," and "or" functions, respectively. Individually, they are left-associative; together their different precedences determine the expression evaluation order. Their operands must be integral and are subject to the usual binary conversions. The type of the result is that of the converted operands; the result is not an lvalue:

     bitwise-or-expression :
         bitwise-xor-expression
         bitwise-or-expression | *bitwise-xor-expression*

     bitwise-xor-expression :
         bitwise-and-expression
         bitwise-xor-expression   ^   *bitwise-and-expression*

     bitwise-and-expression :
         equality-expression
         bitwise-and-expression   **&**   *equality-expression*

Each bit of the result of these operators is equal to a boolean function of the two corresponding bits of the two (converted) operands:

- The **&** (and) function yields a 1-bit if both arguments are 1-bits and otherwise a 0-bit.

- The **^** (exclusive-or) function yields a 1-bit if one argument is a 1-bit and the other is a 0-bit, and yields a 0-bit if both arguments are 1-bits or both are 0-bits.

- The **|** (or) function yields a 1-bit if either argument is a 1-bit and otherwise a 0-bit.

This behavior is summarized next:

a	b	a&b	a^b	a|b
0	0	0	0	0
0	1	0	1	1
1	0	0	1	1
1	1	1	0	1

Each of the bitwise operators is commutative and associative, and the compiler is permitted to rearrange an expression containing the operators subject to the restrictions discussed in Section 7.12.

For portable code, we recommend using the bitwise operators only on unsigned operands. Signed operands will cause no problems among the majority of computers that use the twos-complement representation for signed integers, but they may cause failures on other computers.

Programmers should be careful not to accidentally use the bitwise operators **&** and **|** in place of the logical AND and OR operators, **&&** and **||**. The bitwise operators give the same result as the corresponding logical operators only if the arguments have no side effects and are known to be boolean (0 or 1). Also, the bitwise operators always evaluate both their operands, whereas the logical operators do not evaluate their right-hand operand if the value of the left operand is sufficient to determine the final result of the expression.

Example

If **a** is 2 and **b** is 4, then **a&b** is 0 (false) whereas **a&&b** is 1 (true).

7.6.7 Set of Integers Example

The following pages show the use, declaration, and definition, respectively, of a "set of integers" package. It uses the bitwise operators to implement sets as bit vectors. The example includes a sample program (**testset.c**), the test program's output, the package header file (**set.h**), and the implementation of the functions in the package (**set.c**).

References   integer types 5.1; logical operators **&&** and **||** 7.7; lvalue 7.1; order of evaluation 7.12; relational operators 7.6.4; signed types 5.1.1; unsigned types 5.1.2; usual binary conversions 6.3.4

```
#include "set.h"
int main(void)
{
    print_k_of_n(0, 4);
    print_k_of_n(1, 4);
    print_k_of_n(2, 4);
    print_k_of_n(3, 4);
    print_k_of_n(4, 4);
    print_k_of_n(3, 5);
    print_k_of_n(3, 6);
    return 0;
}
```

Sample usage of the SET package: file `testset.c`

```
All the size-0 subsets of {0, 1, 2, 3}:
{}
The total number of such subsets is 1.

All the size-1 subsets of {0, 1, 2, 3}:
{0}  {1}  {2}  {3}
The total number of such subsets is 4.

All the size-2 subsets of {0, 1, 2, 3}:
{0, 1}  {0, 2}  {1, 2}  {0, 3}  {1, 3}  {2, 3}
The total number of such subsets is 6.

All the size-3 subsets of {0, 1, 2, 3}:
{0, 1, 2}  {0, 1, 3}  {0, 2, 3}  {1, 2, 3}
The total number of such subsets is 4.

All the size-4 subsets of {0, 1, 2, 3}:
{0, 1, 2, 3}
The total number of such subsets is 1.

All the size-3 subsets of {0, 1, 2, 3, 4}:
{0, 1, 2}  {0, 1, 3}  {0, 2, 3}  {1, 2, 3}
{0, 1, 4}  {0, 2, 4}  {1, 2, 4}  {0, 3, 4}
{1, 3, 4}  {2, 3, 4}
The total number of such subsets is 10.

All the size-3 subsets of {0, 1, 2, 3, 4, 5}:
{0, 1, 2}  {0, 1, 3}  {0, 2, 3}  {1, 2, 3}
{0, 1, 4}  {0, 2, 4}  {1, 2, 4}  {0, 3, 4}
{1, 3, 4}  {2, 3, 4}  {0, 1, 5}  {0, 2, 5}
{1, 2, 5}  {0, 3, 5}  {1, 3, 5}  {2, 3, 5}
{0, 4, 5}  {1, 4, 5}  {2, 4, 5}  {3, 4, 5}

The total number of such subsets is 20.
```

The SET package: output from file `testset.c`

```
/* set.h
A set package, suitable for sets of small integers in the
range 0 to N-1, where N is the number of bits in an unsigned
int type. Each integer is represented by a bit position; bit
i is 1 if and only if i is in the set. The low-order bit is
bit 0. */

#include <limits.h> /* defines CHAR_BIT */

/* Type SET is used to represent sets. */

typedef unsigned int SET;

/* SET_BITS: Maximum bits per set. */

#define SET_BITS                (sizeof(SET)*CHAR_BIT)

/* check(i): True if i can be a set element. */

#define check(i)                (((unsigned) (i)) < SET_BITS)

/* emptyset: A set with no elements. */

#define emptyset ((SET) 0)

/* add(s,i): Add a single integer to a set. */

#define add(set,i)              ((set) | singleset (i))

/* singleset(i): Return a set with one element in it. */

#define singleset(i)(((SET) 1) << (i))

/* intersect: Return intersection of two sets. */

#define intersect(set1,set2 )((set1) & (set2))

/* union: Return the union of two sets. */

#define union(set1,set2     )((set1) | (set2))

/* setdiff: Return a set of those elements in set1 or set2,
   but not both. */

#define setdiff(set1,set2   )((set1) ^ (set2))

/* element: True if i is in set. */

#define element(i,set       )(singleset((i)) & (set))
```

The SET package: file set.h (1 of 2   )

```
/* forallelements:  Perform the following statement once for
   every element of the set s, with the variable j set to
   that element. To print all the elements in s, just write
   int j;
   forallelements(j, s)
      printf("%d ", j);
*/

#define forallelements(j,s) \
   for ((j)=0; (j)<SET_BITS; ++(j)) if (element((j),(s)))

/* first_set_of_n_elements(n): Produce a set of size n whose
   elements are the integers from 0 through n-1.  This
   exploits the properties of unsigned subtractions. */

#define first_set_of_n_elements(n)(SET)((1<<(n))-1)

/* next_set_of_n_elements(s): Given a set of n elements,
   produce a new set of n elements.  If you start with the
   result of first_set_of_n_elements(k), and then at each
   step apply next_set_of_n_elements to the previous result,
   and keep going until a set is obtained containing m as a
   member, you will have obtained a set representing all
   possible ways of choosing k things from m things. */

extern SET next_set_of_n_elements (SET x);

/* printset(s): Print a set in the form "{1, 2, 3, 4}". */

extern void printset(SET z);

/* cardinality(s): Return the number of elements in s. */

extern int cardinality(SET x);

/* print_k_of_n(k,n): Print all the sets of size k having
   elements less than n.  Try to print as many as will fit
   on each line of the output.  Also print the total number
   of such sets; it should equal n!/(k!(n-k)!)
   where n! = 1*2*…*n. */

extern void print_k_of_n(int k, int n);
```

The SET package: file set.h (2 of 2)

```
#include <stdio.h>
#include "set.h"

int cardinality(SET x)
{
/* The following loop body is executed once for every 1-bit
   in the set x.  Each iteration, the smallest remaining
   element is removed and counted. The expression (x & -x)
   is a set containing only the smallest element in x, in
   twos-complement arithmetic. */

    int count = 0;
    while (x != emptyset) {
        x ^= (x & -x);
        ++count;
    }
    return count;
}

SET next_set_of_n_elements(SET x)
{
/* This code exploits many unusual properties of unsigned
   arithmetic.  As an illustration:
      if x == 001011001111000, then
      smallest          == 000000000001000
      ripple            == 001011010000000
      new_smallest      == 000000010000000
      ones              == 000000000000111
      the returned value == 001011010000111
   The overall idea is that you find the rightmost
   contiguous group of 1-bits. Of that group, you slide the
   leftmost 1-bit to the left one place, and slide all the
   others back to the extreme right.
   (This code was adapted from HAKMEM.) */

    SET smallest, ripple, new_smallest, ones;
    if (x == emptyset) return x;
    smallest     = (x & -x);
    ripple       = x + smallest;
    new_smallest = (ripple & -ripple);
    ones         = ((new_smallest / smallest) >> 1) - 1;
    return (ripple | ones);
}
```

The SET package: file `set.c` **(1 of 2   )**

7.7 LOGICAL OPERATOR EXPRESSIONS

A logical operator expression consists of two expressions separated by one of the logical operators `&&` or `||`. These operators are sometimes called "conditional AND" and "conditional OR" in other languages because their second operand is not evaluated if the value of the first operand provides sufficient information to determine the value of the expression:

> *logical-or-expression* :
> > *logical-and-expression*
> > *logical-or-expression* `||` *logical-and-expression*

> *logical-and-expression* :
> > *bitwise-or-expression*
> > *logical-and-expression* `&&` *bitwise-or-expression*

The logical operators accept operands of any scalar type. There is no connection between the types of the two operands—each is independently subject to the usual unary conversions. The result, of type `int`, has the value 0 or 1 and is not an lvalue.

AND   The left operand of `&&` is fully evaluated first. If the left operand is equal to zero (in the sense of the `==` operator), then the right operand is not evaluated and the result value is 0. If the left operand is not equal to zero, then the right operand is evaluated. The result value is 0 if the right operand is equal to zero, and is 1 otherwise.

OR   The left operand of `||` is fully evaluated first. If the value of the left operand is not equal to zero (in the sense of the `!=` operator), then the right operand is not evaluated and the result value is 1. If the left operand is equal to zero, then the right operand is evaluated. The result value is 1 if the right operand is not equal to zero, and is 0 otherwise.

Example

The assignment `r = a && b` is equivalent to

```
if (a == 0) r = 0;
else {
    if (b == 0) r = 0;
    else r = 1;
}
```

The assignment `r = a || b` is equivalent to

```
if (a != 0) r = 1;
else {
    if (b != 0) r = 1;
    else r = 0;
}
```

```c
void printset(SET z)
{
    int first = 1;
    int e;
    forallelements(e, z) {
        if (first) printf("{");
        else printf(", ");
        printf("%d", e);
        first = 0;
    }
    if (first) printf("{");  /* Take care of emptyset */
    printf("}");             /* Trailing punctuation */
}



#define LINE_WIDTH 54

void print_k_of_n(int k, int n)
{
    int count = 0;
    int printed_set_width = k * ((n > 10) ? 4 : 3) + 3;
    int sets_per_line = LINE_WIDTH / printed_set_width;
    SET z = first_set_of_n_elements(k);
    printf("\nAll the size-%d subsets of ", k);
    printset (first_set_of_n_elements(n));
    printf(":\n");
    do {      /* Enumerate all the sets. */
        printset(z);
        if ((++count) % sets_per_line) printf (" ");
        else printf("\n");
        z = next_set_of_n_elements(z);
    }while ((z != emptyset) && !element(n, z));
    if ((count) % sets_per_line) printf ("\n");
    printf("The total number of such subsets is %d.\n",
        count);
}
```

The SET package: file set.c (2 of 2   )

Example

Here are some examples of the logical operators:

a	b	a && b	Is b evaluated?	a || b	Is b evaluated?
1	0	0	yes	1	no
0	34.5	0	no	1	yes
1	"Hello\n"	1	yes	1	no
'\0'	0	0	no	0	yes
&x	y=2	1	yes	1	no

Both of the logical operators are described as being syntactically left-associative, although this does not matter much to the programmer because the operators happen to be fully associative semantically and no other operators have the same levels of precedence. The operator && has higher precedence than ||, although it often makes programs more readable to use parentheses liberally around logical expressions.

Example

The expression

    a<b || b<c && c<d || d<e

is the same as (and is more clearly written as):

    a<b || (b<c && c<d) || d<e

References   bitwise operators & and | 7.6.6; equality operators == and != 7.6.5; lvalue 7.1; pointer types 5.3; precedence 7.2.1; scalar types Ch. 5; usual unary conversions 6.3.3

7.8 CONDITIONAL EXPRESSIONS

The ? and : operators introduce a conditional expression, which has lower precedence than the binary expressions and differs from them in being right-associative:

> *conditional-expression :*
>   *logical-or-expression*
>   *logical-or-expression* **?** *expression* **:** *conditional-expression*

A conditional expression has three operands. The first operand must be of a scalar type. The second and third operands can be of various types and they are subject to the usual unary conversions—if they are evaluated at all. The type of the result depends on the types of the second and third operands. Table 7–5 shows the permissible operand types for traditional C, and Table 7–6 shows the permissible operand types for Standard C. Conditional expressions are right-associative with respect to their first and third operands. The result is not an lvalue, although some pre-Standard C compilers did make the result an lvalue.

Table 7–5   Conditional expression 2nd and 3rd operands (pre-Standard)

One operand type	The other operand type	Result type
arithmetic	arithmetic	type after usual binary conversions
structure or union[a]	the same structure or union	the structure or union type
pointer	the same pointer type, or 0	the pointer type

[a] These operand types may not be permitted in somepre-Standard compilers.

Table 7–6   Conditional expression 2nd and 3rd operands (Standard C)

One operand type	The other operand type	Result type
arithmetic	arithmetic	type after usual binary conversions
structure or union	compatible structure or union	the structure or union type
`void`	`void`	`void`
pointer to qualified or unqualified version of type T_1	pointer to qualified or unqualified version of type T_2, if types T_1 and T_2 are compatible	composite pointer type[a]
pointer to type T[b]	qualified or unqualified `void *`	`void *`[a]
any pointer type	null pointer constant	the pointer type[a]

[a] The type pointed to by the result has all the qualifiers of the types pointed to by both operands.
[b] T must be an object or incomplete type.

The execution of the conditional expression proceeds as follows:

1. The first operand is fully evaluated and tested against zero.
2. If the first operand is not equal to zero, then the second operand is evaluated and its value, converted to the result type, becomes the value of the conditional expression. The third operand is not evaluated.
3. If the first operand is equal to zero, then the third operand is evaluated and its value, converted to the result type, becomes the value of the conditional expression. The second operand is not evaluated.

Example

The expression `r=a?b:c` is equivalent to

```
if (a != 0) r = b;
else r = c;
```

The expression

```
a ? b : c ? d : e ? f : g
```

is interpreted as

```
a ? b : (c ? d : (e ? f : g))
```

Example

In this example, the nesting of conditional expressions seems useful—the **signum** function, which returns 1, –1, or 0 depending on whether its argument is positive, negative, o rzero:

```
int signum(int x){ return (x > 0) ? 1 : (x < 0) ? -1 : 0; }
```

Anything more complicated than this is probably better done with one or more **if** statements. As a matter of style, it is a good idea to enclose the first operand of a conditional expression in parentheses, but this is not required.

References   arithmetic types Ch. 5; array types 5.4; floating-point types 5.2; integer types 5.1; lvalue 7.1; pointer types 5.3; precedence 7.2.1; scalar types Ch. 5; signed types 5.1.1; structure types 5.6; union types 5.7; unsigned types 5.1.2; usual binary conversions 6.3.4; usual unary conversions 6.3.3; **void** type 5.9

7.9 ASSIGNMENT EXPRESSIONS

Assignment expressions consist of two expressions separated by an assignment operator; they are right-associative. The operator = is called the simple assignment operator; all the others are compound assignment operators:

> *assignment-expression* :
>   *conditional-expression*
>   *unary-expression assignment-op assignment-expression*

> *assignment-op* : one of
>   =   +=   -=   *=   /=   %=   <<=   >>=   &=   ^= |=

Assignment operators are all of the same level of precedence and are right-associative (all other operators in C that take two operands are left-associative).

Example

For example, the expression **x*=y=z** is treated as **x*=(y=z)**, not as **(x*=y)=z**; similarly, the expression **x=y*=z** is treated as **x=(y*=z)**, not as **(x=y)*=z**.

The right-associativity of assignment operators allows multiple assignment expressions to have the "obvious" interpretation. That is, the expression **a=b=d+7** is interpreted as **a=(b=(d+7)**, and therefore assigns the value of **d+7** to **b** and then to **a**.

Every assignment operator requires a modifiable lvalue as its left operand and modifies that lvalue by storing a new value into it. The operators are distinguished by how they compute the new value. The result of an assignment expression is never an lvalue.

References   modifiable lvalue 7.1; precedence 7.2.1

7.9.1 Simple Assignment

The single equal sign, =, indicates simple assignment. The value of the right operand is converted to the type of the left operand and is stored into that operand. The permitted operand types are given in Table 7–7.

Table 7–7   Assignment operands

Left operand type	Right operand type
arithmetic	arithmetic
structure or union	compatible structure or union
pointer to T	pointer to T', where T and T' are compatible
void *	pointer to T[a]
pointer to T[a]	**void ***
any pointer	null pointer constant

[a] In Standard C, T must be an object or incomplete type.

The original definition of C did not permit the assignment of structures and unions. A few older compilers may still have this restriction.

In Standard C, there are additional restrictions on the operands having to do with type qualifiers. First, the left operand can never have a **const**-qualified type. In addition:

1. If the operands are arithmetic, they can be qualified or unqualified.
2. If the operands are structures or unions, they must be qualified or unqualified versions of compatible types. This means, for example, that their members must be identically qualified.
3. If the operands are both object or function pointers, they must be qualified or unqualified versions of pointers to compatible types, and the type pointed to by the left operand must have all the qualifiers of the type pointed to by the right operand. This prevents a **const int *** pointer from being assigned to an **int *** pointer, after which the constant integer could be modified.
4. If one operand is a qualified or unqualified version of **void ***, the other must be a pointer to an object or incomplete type. The type pointed to by the left operand must have all the qualifiers of the type pointed to by the right operand. The reason is the same as for the previous case.

The type of the result of the assignment operator is equal to the (unconverted and unqualified) type of the left operand. The result is the value stored into the left operand. The result is not an lvalue. When the two operands are of arithmetic types, the usual assignment conversions are used to convert the right operand to the type of the left operand before assignment.

The simple assignment operator cannot be used to copy the entire contents of one array into another. The name of an array is not a modifiable lvalue and so cannot appear on the left-hand side of an assignment. Also, the name of an array appearing on the right-hand side of an assignment is converted (by the usual conversions) to be a pointer to the first element, and so the assignment would copy the pointer, not the contents of the array.

Example

The = operator can be used to copy the address of an array into a pointer variable:

```
int a[20], *p;
...
p = a;
```

In this example, **a** is an array of integers and **p** is of type "pointer to integer." The assignment causes **p** to point to (the first element of) the array **a**.

It is possible to get the effect of copying an entire array by embedding the array within a structure or union because simple assignment can copy an entire structure or union:

```
struct matrix {double contents[10][10]; };
struct matrix a, b;
...
{
    /* Clear the diagonal elements. */
    for (j = 0; j < 10; j++)
        b.contents[j][j] = 0;
    /* Copy whole 10x10 array from b to a. */
    a = b;
}
```

The implementation of the simple assignment operator assumes that the right-hand value and the left-hand object do not overlap in memory (unless they exactly overlap, as in the assignment **x=x**). If overlap does occur, the behavior of the assignment is undefined.

References   arithmetic types 5.1–2; array types 5.4; usual assignment conversions 6.3.2; lvalue 7.1; null pointer 5.3.2; pointer types 5.3; structure types 5.6; type compatibility 5.11; union types 5.7

7.9.2 Compound Assignment

The compound assignment operators may be informally understood by taking the expression "*a op= b*" to be equivalent to "*a = a op b*," with the proviso that the expression *a* is evaluated only once. The permitted types of the operands depend on the operator being used. The possibilities are listed in Table 7–8.

More precisely, the left and right operands of *op=* are evaluated, and the left operand must be a modifiable lvalue. The operation indicated by the operator *op* is then applied to the two operand values, including any "usual conversions" performed by the operator. The resulting value is then stored into the object designated by the left operand after performing the usual assignment conversions.

For the compound assignment operators, as for the simple assignment operator, the type of the result is equal to the (unconverted) type of the left operand. The result is the value stored into the left operand and is not an lvalue.

Table 7–8 Operand types for compound assignment expressions

Assignment operator	Left operand	Right operand
`*=  /=`	arithmetic	arithmetic
`%=`	integer	integer
`+=  -=`	arithmetic	arithmetic
`+=  -=`	pointer	integer
`<<=  >>=`	integer	integer
`&=`	integer	integer
`^=`	integer	integer
`|=`	integer	integer

In the earliest versions of C, the compound assignment operators were written in the reverse form, with the equal sign preceding the operation. This led to syntactic ambiguities; `x=-1` could be interpreted as either `x=(-1)` or `x=x-1`. The newer form eliminates these difficulties. Some non-Standard C compilers continue to support the older forms for the sake of compatibility and will mistake `x=-1` as `x=x-1` unless a blank appears between the equal and minus signs.

References   arithmetic types Ch. 5; assignment conversions 6.3.2; floating-point types 5.2; integer types 5.1; pointer types 5.3; signed types 5.1.1; unsigned types 5.1.2; usual binary conversions 6.3.4; usual unary conversions 6.3.3

7.10 SEQUENTIAL EXPRESSIONS

A comma expression consists of two expressions separated by a comma. The comma operator is described here as being syntactically left-associative, although this does not matter much to the programmer because the operator happens to be fully associative semantically. Note that the *comma-expression* is at the top of the C expression syntax tree:

comma-expression :
    assignment-expression
    comma-expression **,** *assignment-expression*

expression :
    comma-expression

The left operand of the comma operator is fully evaluated first. It need not produce any value; if it does produce a value, that value is discarded. The right operand is then evaluated. The type and value of the result of the comma expression are equal to the type and value of the right operand, after the usual unary conversions. The result is not an lvalue. Thus, the statement "`r=(a,b,…,c);`" (notice that the parentheses are required) is equivalent to "`a;b;… r=c;`". The difference is that the comma operator may be used in expression contexts, such as in loop control expressions.

Example

> In the `for` statement the comma operator allows several assignment expressions to be combined into a single expression for the purpose of initializing or stepping several variables in a single loop:
>
> ```
> for( x=0, y=N; x<N && y>0; x++, y--) …
> ```

The comma operator is associative, and one may write a single expression consisting of any number of expressions separated by commas; the subexpressions will be evaluated in order, and the value of the last one will become the value of the entire expression.

Example

> The overuse of the comma operator can be confusing, and in certain places it conflicts with other uses of the comma. For example, the expression
>
> ```
> f(a, b=5,2*b, c)
> ```
>
> is always treated as a call to the function `f` with four arguments. Any comma expressions in the argument list must be surrounded by parentheses:
>
> ```
> f(a, (b=5,2*b), c)
> ```

Other contexts where the comma operator may not be used without parentheses include field-length expressions in structure and union declarator lists, enumeration value expressions in enumeration declarator lists, and initialization expressions in declarations and initializers. The comma is also used as a separator in preprocessor macro calls.

While the comma operator guarantees that its operands will be evaluated in left-to-right order, other uses of the comma character do not make this guarantee. For example, the argument expressions in a function invocation need not be evaluated left to right.

References discarded expressions 7.13; enumeration types 5.5; `for` statement 8.6.3; function calls 7.4.3; initializers 4.6; lvalue 7.1; macro calls 3.3; structure types 5.6; union types 5.7

7.11 CONSTANT EXPRESSIONS

In several contexts, the C language permits an expression to be written that must evaluate to a constant at compile time. Each context imposes slightly different restrictions on what forms of expression are permitted. There are three classes of constant expressions:

1. *preprocessor constant expressions*, which are used as the tested value in the `#if` and `#elif` preprocessor control statements

2. *integral constant expressions*, which are used for array bounds, the length of a bit field in a structure, explicit enumerator values, and the values in `case` labels in `switch` statements

3. *initializer constant expressions*, which are used as the initializers for static and external variables and (prior to C99) for automatic variables of aggregate types

No constant expression may contain assignment, increment, decrement, function call, or comma expressions unless they are contained within the operand of a **sizeof** operator. Otherwise any literal or operator can appear subject to the additional restrictions discussed in the following sections for each expression class. These restrictions are imposed in Standard C; traditional implementations may have somewhat looser requirements in individual cases.

7.11.1 Preprocessor Constant Expressions

Preprocessor constant expressions must be evaluated at compile time and are subject to some relatively strict constraints. Such expressions must have integral type and can involve only integer constants, character constants, and the special **defined** operator. In C99, all arithmetic is done using host types equivalent to the target types **intmax_t** or **uintmax_t** as appropriate to the signedness of the operands. These types are defined in **stdint.h** and are at least 64 bits long. Prior to C99, Standard C only required all arithmetic to be done using the host's own types **long** or **unsigned long**, which is problematic when the host and target computers are significantly different.

Preprocessor expressions must not perform any environmental inquiries except by reference to macros defined in **float.h**, **limits.h**, **stdint.h**, and so on. Casts are not permitted, nor is the **sizeof** operator. No program variables are visible to the preprocessor even if declared with the **const** qualifier.

Example

This code incorrectly attempts to see if type **int** on the target computer is larger than 16 bits:

```
#if 1<<16
/* Target integer has more than 16 bits (NOT!)*/
...
#endif
```

In fact, the code is only testing the representation of type **long** on the *host* computer (in C89) or the representation of type **intmax_t** on the target computer (in C99). Here is the correct way to test the sizes of target types.

```
#include <limits.h>
...
#if UINT_MAX > 65535
    /* target integer has more than 16 bits */
    ...
#endif
```

The preprocessor must recognize escape sequences in character constants, but is allowed to use either the source or target character sets in converting character constants to integers. This means that the expressions **'\n'** or **'z'-'a'** might have different values in a preprocessor expression than they would appearing in, say, an **if** statement. Programmers using cross-compilers in which the host and target character sets are different should beware of this license.

After macro expansion, if the preprocessor constant expression contains any remaining identifiers, they are each replaced by the constant 0. This is probably a bad rule because the presence of such identifiers is almost certainly a programming error. A better way to test whether a name is defined in the preprocessor is to use the **defined** operator or **#ifdef** and **#ifndef** commands.

Compilers are free to accept additional forms of preprocessor constant expressions, but programs making use of these extensions are not portable.

References   cast expressions 7.5.1; character constants 2.7.3; character sets 2.1; **defined** operator 3.5.5; enumeration constants 5.5; escape characters 2.7.5; **float.h** 5.2; **#ifdef** and **#ifndef** 3.5.3; **intmax_t** 21.5; **limits.h** 5.1; **sizeof** operator 7.5.2; **stdint.h** Ch. 21

7.11.2 Integral Constant Expressions

An integral constant expression is used for array bounds, the length of a bit field in a structure, explicit enumerator values, and the values in **case** labels in **switch** statements. An integral constant expression must have an integral type and can include integer constants, character constants, and enumeration constants. The **sizeof** operator can be used and can have any operand. Cast expressions may be used, but only to convert arithmetic types to integer types (unless they are part of the operand to **sizeof**). A floating-point constant is permitted only if it is the immediate operand of a cast or is part of the operand of **sizeof**.

Constant expressions not appearing in preprocessor commands should be evaluated as they would be on the target computer, including the values of character constants.

Compilers are free to accept additional forms of integral constant expressions, including more general floating-point expressions that are converted to an integer type, but programs making use of these extensions are not portable. Some pre-Standard compilers do not permit casts of any kind in constant expressions. Programmers concerned with portability to these compilers might be wise to avoid casts in constant expressions.

References   bit fields 5.6.5; cast expressions 7.5.1; enumeration types 5.5; floating-point constants 2.7.2; **sizeof** operator 7.5.2; switch statement 8.7

7.11.3 Initializer Constant Expressions

The constant expression in an initializer can include arithmetic constant expressions and address constant expressions.

Arithmetic constant expressions include the integral constant expressions, but can also include floating-point constants generally (not just those cast to integers or in **sizeof**) and casts to any arithmetic type (including the floating-point types). If a floating-point expression is evaluated at compile time in a constant expression, the implementation may use a representation that provides more precision or a greater range than the target environment. Therefore, the value of a floating-point expression may be slightly different at compile time than it would be if evaluated during program execution. This rule reflects the difficulty of exactly simulating a foreign floating-point implementation. Other than this case, the expressions should be evaluated just as they would be on the target computer.

An *address constant expression* can be the null pointer constant—for example, **(void *)0**—or the address of a static or external object or function, or the address of a static or external object plus or minus an integer constant expression. In forming addresses, the address (**&**), indirection (*****), subscript (**[]**), and the component selection operators (**.** and **->**) may be used, but no attempt must be made to access the value of any object. Casts to pointer types may also be used.

Compilers are free to accept additional forms of initializer constant expressions, such as more complicated addressing expressions involving several addresses, but programs making use of these extensions are not portable.

Standard C states that an implementation is free to perform initializations at run time, and so could avoid floating-point arithmetic at compile time. However, it might be difficult to do this initialization before executing any code that accesses the initialized variable.

Example

Examples of address constant expressions are shown below in the initializers for **p** and **pf**:

```
static int a[10];
static struct { int f1, f2; } s;
extern int f();
int i = 3;
...
int *p[] = { &i, a, &a[0],
             (int *)((char *)&a[0]+sizeof(a)),
             &s.f2 };
int (*pf)() = &f;
```

References   address operator **&** 7.5.6; array types 5.4; initializers 4.6; **sizeof** operator 7.5.2; structure types 5.6

7.12 ORDER OF EVALUATION

The value of an expression is defined abstractly by Standard C according to the associative rules of Table 7–3: The value of **a+b+c+d** is defined to be **(((a+b)+c)+d)**, for example. A Standard C implementation can reorder an expression only if it can guarantee that the result of evaluating the reordered expression will be the same as the original expression for all possible values of the operands, including the effects of overflow or underflow. For example, the operators **&**, **^**, and **|** on unsigned operands are commutative and associative, and so expressions involving them can often be reordered. This effectively means that programmers can depend on their expressions being evaluated as written, without resorting to extraneous parentheses or the use of temporary variables. However, parentheses can make a complicated expression more readable.

Traditional C did in fact permit reordering that could change the value of an expression. Traditional C compilers were free, for example, to evaluate **(a+b)+(c+d)** as **(a+d)+(b+c)**. This reordering was disallowed in Standard C.

Example

Traditional C programs introduced temporary variables to attempt to force the evaluation of expressions in a certain order, but this was not reliable and is not necessary in Standard C:

```
int temp1, temp2;
...
/* Traditional C: Compute q=(a+b)+(c+d) as written(?!) */
temp1 = a+b;
temp2 = c+d;
q = temp1 + temp2;
```

Example

In the following example, the two expressions are not equivalent, and the compiler is not free to substitute one for the other despite the fact that one is obtained from the other "merely by rearranging the additions":

```
(1.0 + -3) + (unsigned) 1; /* Result is -1.0 */
1.0 + (-3 + (unsigned) 1); /* Result is large */
```

The first assignment is straightforward and produces the expected result. The second produces a large result because the usual binary conversions cause the signed value -3 to be converted to a large unsigned value 2^n-3, where n is the number of bits used to represent an unsigned integer. This is then added to the unsigned value 1, the result converted to floating-point representation and added to 1.0, resulting in the value 2^n-1 in a floating-point representation. Now this result may or may not be what the programmer intended, but the compiler must not confuse the issue further by capriciously rearranging the additions.

The order in which a floating-point expression is evaluated can have a significant impact on the accuracy of the result depending on the particular values of the operands. This further restricts the implementation's freedom in reordering expressions. In C99, implementations may contract a floating-point expression to make use of more efficient computer instructions, but the programmer can control such contraction with the standard pragma **FP_CONTRACT** (Section 22.5).

When evaluating the actual arguments in a function call, the order in which the arguments and the function expression are evaluated is not specified; but the effect will be as if it chose one argument, evaluated it fully, then chose another argument, evaluated it fully, and so on until all arguments were evaluated. A similar freedom and restriction holds for each operand to a binary expression operand to a binary expression operatooperator and for *a* and *i* in the expression *a[i]*.

Example

In this example, the variable **x** is an array of pointers to characters and is to be regarded as an array of strings. The variable **p** is a pointer to a pointer to a character and is to be regarded as a pointer to a string. The purpose of the **if** statement is to determine whether the string pointed to by **p** (call it **s1**) and the next string after that one (call it **s2**) are equal (and, in passing, to step the pointer **p** beyond those two strings in the array).

```
char *x[10], **p=x;
...
if ( strcmp(*p++, *p++) == 0 ) printf("Same.");
```

It is, of course, bad programming style to have two side effects on the same variable in the same expression because the order of the side effects is not defined; but this all-too-clever programmer has reasoned that the order of the side effects does not matter because the two strings in question may be given to **strcmp** in either order.

7.12.1 Sequence Points

In Standard C, if a single object is modified more than once between successive sequence points, the result is undefined. A *sequence point* is a point in the program's execution sequence at which all previous side effects of execution are to have taken place and at which no subsequent side effects will have occurred. Sequence points occur:

- at the end of a full expression—that is, an initializer, an expression statement, the expression in a **return** statement, and the control expressions in a conditional, iterative, or **switch** statement (including each expression in a **for** statement)

- after the first operand of a **&&**, **||**, **?:**, or comma operator

- after the evaluation of the arguments and function expression in a function call

According to this rule, the value of the expression **++i*++i** is undefined as is the prior **strcmp** example.

> **References**   addition operator **+** 7.6.2; binary operators 7.6; bitwise AND operator **&** 7.6.6; bitwise OR operator **|** 7.6.8; bitwise XOR operator **^** 7.6.7; comma operator 7.10; conditional expression **?:** 7.8; conditional statement 8.5; expression statement 8.2; function calls 7.4.3; initializers 4.6; iterative statements 8.6; logical and **&&** and or **||** 7.7; multiplication operator ***** 7.6.1; **return** statement 8.9; **strcmp** function 13.2; usual binary conversions 6.3.4

7.13 DISCARDED VALUES

There are three contexts in which an expression can appear but its value is not used:

1. an expression statement

2. the first operand of a comma expression

3. the initialization and increment expressions in a **for** statement

In these contexts, we say that the expression's value is discarded.

When the value of an expression without side effects is discarded, the compiler may presume that a programming error has been made and issue a warning. Side effect-producing operations include assignment and function calls. The compiler may also issue a warning message if the main operator of a discarded expression has no side effect.

Example

```
extern void f();
f(x);      /* These expressions do not */
i++;       /* justify any warning about */
a = b;     /* discarded values.  */
```

These statements, although valid, may elicit warning messages:

```
extern int g();
g(x);              /* The result of g is discarded. */
x + 7;             /* Addition has no defined side effects. */
x + (a *= 2);      /* The result of the last operation to be
                      performed, "+", is discarded. */
```

The programmer can avoid warnings about discarded values by using a cast to type **void** to indicate that the value is purposely being discarded:

```
extern int g();
(void) g(x);       /* Returned value is purposely discarded */
(void)(x + 7);     /* This is pretty silly, but presumably
                      the programmer has a purpose. */
```

C compilers typically do not issue warnings when the value of a function call is discarded because traditionally functions that returned no result had to be declared of type "function returning **int**." Although Standard C gives compilers more information, vendors try to be compatible with old code.

If a compiler determines that the main operator of a discarded expression has no side effect, it may choose not to generate code for that operator (whereupon its operands become discarded values and may be recursively subjected to the same treatment).

References   assignments 7.9; casts 7.5.1; comma operator 7.10; **for** statement 8.6.3; function calls 7.4.3; expressions statements 8.2; **void** type 5.9

7.14 OPTIMIZATION OF MEMORY ACCESSES

As a general rule, a compiler is free to generate any code equivalent in computational behavior to the program as written. The compiler is explicitly granted certain freedoms to rearrange code, as described in Section 7.12. It may also generate no code for an expression when the expression has no side effects and its value is discarded, as described in Section 7.13.

Example

Some compilers may also reorganize the code in such a way that it does not always refer to memory as many times, or in the same order, as specified in the program. For example, if a certain array element is referred to more than once, the compiler may cleverly arrange to fetch it only once to gain speed; in effect, it might rewrite this code:

```
int x,a[10];
...
x = a[j] * a[j] * a[j];    /* Cube the table entry. */
```

causing it to be executed as if it had been written like this:

```
int x,a[10];
register int temp;
...
temp = a[j];
x = temp * temp * temp;  /* Cube the table entry. */
```

For most applications, including nearly all portable applications, such optimization techniques are a very good thing because the speed of a program may be improved by a factor of two or better without altering its effective computational behavior. However, this may be a problem when writing interrupt handlers and certain other machine-dependent programs in C. In this case, the programmer should use the Standard C type qualifier **volatile** to control some memory accesses.

References   **volatile** 4.4.5

7.15 C++ COMPATIBILITY

7.15.1 Changes in sizeof Expressions

In C++, it is invalid to declare types in expressions, such as casts or **sizeof**. Also, the values of some **sizeof** expressions can be different in C and C++ for reasons of scoping changes and the type of character literals.

Example

```
i = sizeof(struct S { ... }); /* OK in C, not in C++ */
```

Example

The value of **sizeof(T)** could be different in some cases in which **T** is redefined.

The value of **sizeof('a')** will be **sizeof(int)** in C, but it will be **sizeof(char)** in C++.

The value of **sizeof(e)**, for an enumeration constant **e**, will be **sizeof(int)** in C, but it may be different in C++.

References   character literals 2.8.5; enumeration types 5.13.1; scoping differences 4.9.2; **sizeof** 7.5.2

7.16 EXERCISES

1. Which of the following expressions are valid in traditional C? For the ones that are valid, what type does the expression have? Assume that **f** is of type **float**, **i** is of type **int**, **cp** is of type **char ***, and **ip** is of type **int ***.

   (a) `cp+0x23`   (f) `f==0`

   (b) `i+f`   (g) `!ip`

   (c) `++f`   (h) `cp && cp`

   (d) `ip[i]`   (i) `f%2`

   (e) `cp?i:f`   (j) `f+=i`

2. Assume **p1** and **p2** have type **char ***. Rewrite the following two statements without using the increment or decrement operators.

   (a) `*++p1=*++p2;`

   (b) `*p1--=*p2--;`

3. A "bit mask" is an integer consisting of a specified sequence of binary zeroes and ones. Write macros that produce the following bit masks. If the macro arguments are constants, the result should also be a constant. You can assume a twos-complement representation for integers, but your macros should not depend on how many bits are in an integer or whether the computer is a big-endian or little-endian.

   (a) `low_zeroes(n)`, a word in which the low-order *n* bits are zeroes and all other bits are ones.

   (b) `low_ones(n)`, a word whose low-order *n* bits are ones and all other bits are zeroes.

   (c) `mid_zeroes(width,offset)`, a word whose low-order *offset* bits are ones, whose next higher *width* bits are zeroes, and all other bits are ones.

   (d) `mid_ones(width,offset)`, a word whose low-order *offset* bits are zeroes, whose next higher *width* bits are ones, and all other bits are zeroes

4. Is `j++==++j` a valid expression? What about `j++&&++j`? If **j** begins with the value 0, what is the result of each of the expressions?

5. The following table lists pairs of types of the left- and right-hand sides of a simple assignment expression. Which of the combinations are allowable in Standard C?

	Left-side type	Right-side type
(a)	`short`	`signed short`
(b)	`char *`	`const char *`
(c)	`int (*)[5]`	`int (*)[]`
(d)	`short`	`const short`
(e)	`int (*)()`	`signed (*)(int x, float d)`
(f)	`int *`	`t *` (where: `typedef int t`)

6. If the variable **x** has the type `struct{int f;}` and the variable **y** has a separately defined type `struct{int f;}`, is `x=y` valid in Standard C?

8

Statements

The C language provides the usual assortment of statements found in most algebraic programming languages, including conditional statements, loops, and the ubiquitous "goto." We describe each in turn after some general comments about syntax:

statement :
        expression-statement
        labeled-statement
        compound-statement
        conditional-statement
        iterative-statement
        switch-statement
        break-statement
        continue-statement
        return-statement
        goto-statement
        null-statement

conditional-statement :
        if-statement
        if-else-statement

iterative-statement :
        do-statement
        while-statement
        for-statement

8.1 GENERAL SYNTACTIC RULES FOR STATEMENTS

Although C statements will be familiar to programmers used to ALGOL-like languages, there are a few syntactic differences that often cause confusion and errors.

As in Pascal or Ada, semicolons typically appear between consecutive statements in C. However, in C, the semicolon is not a statement separator, but rather simply a part of the syntax of certain statements. The only C statement that does not require a terminating semicolon is the compound statement (or block), which is delimited by braces ({}) instead of **begin** and **end** keywords:

```
a = b;
{ b = c; d = e; }
x = y;
```

Another rule for C statements is that "control" expressions appearing in conditional and iterative statements must be enclosed in parentheses. There is no special keyword following control expressions, such as "then," "loop," or "do"; the remainder of the statement immediately follows the expression:

```
if (a<b) x=y;
while (n<10) n++;
```

Finally, the assignment statement in other languages is an assignment *expression* in C. It can appear as part of more complicated expressions or can be followed by a semicolon allowing it to stand by itself:

```
if ((x=y)>3) a=b;
```

References   assignment expression 7.9; compound statement 8.4; conditional statements 8.5; iterative statements 8.6

8.2 EXPRESSION STATEMENTS

Any expression can be treated as a statement by writing the expression followed by a semicolon:

> *expression-statement* :
>   *expression* **;**

The statement is executed by evaluating the expression and then discarding the resulting value if any.

An expression statement is useful only if evaluation of the expression involves a side effect, such as assigning a value to a variable or performing input or output. Usually the expression is an assignment, an increment or decrement operation, or a function call.

Example

```
speed = distance / time;   /* assign a quotient */
++event_count;             /* Add 1 to event_count.*/
printf("Again?");          /* Call the function printf.*/
pattern &= mask;           /* Remove bits from pattern */
(x<y) ? ++x : ++y;         /* Increment smaller of x and y */
```

The last statement, although valid, might be written more clearly with an **if** statement:

```
if (x < y) ++x;
else ++y;
```

The compiler is not obligated to evaluate an expression, or a portion of an expression, that has no side effects and whose result is discarded (see Section 7.13).

References   assignment expressions 7.9; discarded expressions 7.13; expressions Ch. 7; function call 7.4.3; increment expressions 7.5.8, 7.4.4

8.3 LABELED STATEMENTS

A label can be used to mark any statement so that control may be transferred to the statement by a **goto** or **switch** statement. There are three kinds of labels. A named label may appear on any statement and is used in conjunction with the **goto** statement. A **case** label or **default** label may appear only on a statement within the body of a **switch** statement:

labeled-statement :
    label **:** *statement*

label :
    named-label
    case-label
    default-label

A label cannot appear by itself, but must always be attached to a statement. If it is desired to place a label by itself (e.g., at the end of a compound statement), it may be attached to a null statement. In C99, which allows statements and declarations to be intermixed, the label cannot be applied directly to a declaration; it must be attached to a null statement before the declaration.

Named labels are discussed further in the description of the **goto** statement. The **case** and **default** labels are discussed with the **switch** statement.

References   **goto** statement 8.10; null statement 8.11; **switch** statement 8.7

8.4 COMPOUND STATEMENTS

A compound statement consists of a brace-enclosed list of zero or more declarations and statements. In C99, declarations and statements may be intermixed. In previous versions of C, declarations must precede statements.

> *compound-statement* :
>   { *declaration-or-statement-list$_{opt}$* }
>
> *declaration-or-statement-list* :
>   *declaration-or-statement*
>   *declaration-or-statement-list*   *declaration-or-statement*
>
> *declaration-or-statement* :
>   *declaration*
>   *statement*

A compound statement may appear anywhere a statement does. It brings into existence a new scope, or block, which affects any declarations or compound literals appearing within it. A compound statement is normally executed by processing each declaration and statement in order one at a time. Execution ceases when the last declaration or statement has been executed. It is possible to jump out of a compound statement before its end by using a **goto**, **return**, **continue**, or **break** statement. It is also possible to enter a compound statement other than at its beginning by using a **goto** or **switch** statement to jump to a label within the compound statement. Jumping into or out of a compound statement may affect declarations within it; this is discussed in the next section.

> **References**   **auto** storage class 4.3; **break** and **continue** statements 8.8; declarations Ch. 4; **goto** statement 8.10; **register** storage class 4.3; **return** statement 8.9; scope 4.2.1

8.4.1 Declarations Within Compound Statements

An identifier declared within a compound statement or other block is called a block-level identifier and the declaration is called a block-level declaration. A block-level identifier has a scope that extends from its declaration point to the end of the block. The identifier is visible throughout that scope except when hidden by a declaration of the same identifier in an inner block. Declaring identifiers in blocks is usually a good programming practice because limiting the scope of variables makes programs easier to understand.

An identifier declared in a block without a storage class specifier is assumed to have storage class **extern** if the identifier has a function type, and it is assumed to have storage class **auto** in all other cases. It is invalid for an identifier of function type to have any storage class except **extern** when it is declared in a block.

If a variable or function is declared in a block with storage class **extern**, no storage is allocated and no initialization expression is permitted. The declaration refers to an external variable or function defined elsewhere, either in the same or different source file.

If a variable other than a variable length array is declared in a block with storage class **auto** or **register**, then it is allocated with an undefined value every time the block is entered and is deallocated every time the block is exited. That is, the variable's lifetime extends over the entire block, not just from the declaration point. If there is an initialization expression with the variable's declaration, then the initializer is evaluated and the variable initialized every time the declaration is encountered in the flow of execution. This normally happens only once, but in C99 it might happen multiple times if a **goto** statement transfers control from within the compound statement backward to a place before the declaration. If a **goto** or **switch** statement is used to jump into a compound statement to a place following the declaration, then the initializer may not be evaluated and the variable's value may be left undefined. The value of an automatic block-level identifier does not carry over from one execution of the block to the next.

In C99, a variable length array declared in a block is not allocated at block entry, as are other automatic variables. It is allocated when its declaration is encountered and its size expression is evaluated, and it is deallocated when control leaves the block. Therefore, its lifetime and scope are the same. Variable length arrays cannot be initialized. It is illegal to jump into the array's scope (i.e., after the declaration) from outside the scope. It is permitted to jump from within the scope backward to a place before the declaration. In this case, the array is deallocated and reallocated, possibly with a new size. All variable length arrays in a block obey a last-allocated, first-deallocated discipline, so they can be allocated on the procedure call stack.

If a variable is declared in a block with storage class **static**, then it is effectively allocated once, prior to program execution, just like any other static variable. If there is an initialization expression with the declaration, then the initializer (which must be constant) is evaluated only once, prior to program execution, and the variable retains its value from one execution of the compound statement to the next. In C99, the initializer must also be constant.

Example

The following code fragment is unlikely to work if the statement labeled **L:** is the target of a jump from outside the compound statement because the variable sum will not be initialized. Furthermore, it is not possible to tell if any such jump does occur without examining the entire body of the enclosing function:

```
{
        extern int a[100];
        int i, sum = 0;
        ...
    L:
        for (i = 0; i < 100; i++)
            sum += a[i];
        ...
}
```

Example

An unlabeled compound statement used as the body of a **switch** statement cannot be executed normally, but only through transfer of control to labeled statements within it. Therefore, initializations of **auto** and **register** variables at the beginning of such a compound statement never occur and their presence is *a priori* an error.

```
switch (i) {
        int sum = 0; /* ERROR! sum is NOT set to 0 */
case 1: return sum;
default: return sum+1;
}
```

References **auto** storage class 4.3; **extern** storage class 4.3; **goto** statement 8.10; initial values 4.2.8; initializers 4.6; **register** storage class 4.3; scope 4.2.1; **static** storage class 4.3; **switch** statement 8.7; variable length array 5.4.5; visibility 4.2.2

8.5 CONDITIONAL STATEMENTS

There are two forms of conditional statement: with and without an **else** clause. C does not use the keyword **then** as part of the syntax of its **if** statement:

> *conditional-statement* :
>   *if-statement*
>   *if-else-statement*

> *if-statement* :
>   **if** (*expression*) *statement*

> *if-else-statement* :
>   **if** (*expression*) *statement* **else** *statement*

For each form of **if** statement, the expression within parentheses is first evaluated. If this value is nonzero (Section 8.1), then the statement immediately following the parentheses is executed. If the value of the control expression is zero and there is an **else** clause, then the statement following the keyword **else** is executed instead; but if the value of the control expression is zero and there is no **else** clause, then execution continues immediately with the statement following the conditional statement.

In C99, the entire **if** statement forms its own block scope, as do the substatements even if they are not compound statements. This serves to restrict the scope of objects and types that might be created as a side effect of using compound literals or type names.

References compound literals 7.4.5; control expression 8.1; type names 5.12

8.5.1 Multiway Conditional Statements

A multiway decision can be expressed as a cascaded series of **if-else** statements, where each **if** statement but the last has another **if** statement in its **else** clause. Such a series looks like this:

```
if (expression₁)
    statement₁
else if (expression₂)
    statement₂
else if (expression₃)
    statement₃
...
else
    statementₙ
```

Example

Here is a three-way decision: the function **signum** returns –1 if its argument is less than zero, 1 if its argument is greater than zero, and otherwise 0:

```
int signum(int x)
{
    if (x > 0) return 1;
    else if (x < 0) return -1;
    else return 0;
}
```

Compare this with the version of **signum** that uses conditional expressions shown in Section 7.8.

The **switch** statement handles the specific kind of multiway decision where the value of an expression is to be compared against a fixed set of constants.

References   **switch** statement 8.7

8.5.2 The Dangling-Else Problem

An ambiguity arises because a conditional statement may contain another conditional statement. In some situations, it may not be apparent to which of several conditional statements an **else** might belong. The ambiguity is resolved in an arbitrary but customary way: An **else** part is always assumed to belong to the innermost **if** statement possible.

Example

To illustrate the ambiguity, the following example is indented in a misleading fashion:

```
if ((k >= 0) && (k < TABLE_SIZE))
    if (table[k] >= 0)
        printf("Entry %d is %d\n", k, table[k]);
else printf("Error: index %d out of range.\n",k);
```

A casual reader might assume that the **else** part was intended to be an alternative to the outer **if** statement. That is, the error message should be printed when the test

```
(k >= 0) && (k < TABLE_SIZE)
```

is false. However, if we change the wording of the last error message to

```
else printf("Error: entry %d is negative.\n", k);
```

then it might appear that the programmer intended the **else** part to be executed when the test **table[k] >=0** is false. The second interpretation of the prior code fragment will work as intended, whereas the first will not. The first interpretation can be made to work by introducing a compound statement:

```
if (k >= 0 && k < TABLE_SIZE) {
    if (table[k] >= 0)
        printf("Entry %d is %d\n", k, table[k]);
}
else printf("Error: index %d out of range.\n", k);
```

To reduce confusion, the second interpretation could also use a compound statement:

```
if (k >= 0 && k < TABLE_SIZE) {
    if (table[k] >= 0)
        printf("Entry %d is %d\n", k, table[k]);
    else printf("Error: entry %d is negative.\n",k);
}
```

Confusion can be eliminated entirely if braces are always used to surround statements controlled by an **if** statement. However, this conservative rule can clutter a program with unnecessary braces. It seems to us that a good stylistic compromise between confusion and clutter is to use braces with an **if** statement whenever the statement controlled by the **if** is anything but an expression or null statement.

References   compound statement 8.4; expression statement 8.2; null statement 8.11

8.6 ITERATIVE STATEMENTS

Three kinds of iterative statements are provided in C:

iterative-statement :
    while-statement
    do-statement
    for-statement

The **while** statement tests an exit condition before each execution of a statement. The **do** statement tests an exit condition after each execution of a statement. The **for** statement provides a special syntax that is convenient for initializing and updating one or more control variables as well as testing an exit condition. The statement embedded within an iteration statement is sometimes called the *body* of the iterative statement.

In C99, each iterative statement forms its own block scope, as do the substatements even if they are not compound statements. This serves to restrict the scope of objects and types that might be created as a side effect of using compound literals or type names.

References   compound literals 7.4.5; control expression 8.1; type names 5.12

8.6.1 While Statement

C does not use the keyword **do** as part of the syntax of its **while** statement:

> *while-statement* :
>   **while** (*expression*) *statement*

The **while** statement is executed by first evaluating the control expression. If the result is true (not zero), then the statement is executed. The entire process is then repeated, alternately evaluating the expression and then, if the value is true, executing the statement. The value of the expression can change from time to time because of side effects in the statement or expression.

The execution of the **while** statement is complete when the control expression evaluates to false (zero) or when control is transferred out of the body of the **while** statement by a **return, goto**, or **break** statement. The **continue** statement can also modify the execution of a **while** statement.

Example

The following function uses a **while** loop to raise an integer **base** to the power specified by the non-negative integer **exponent** (with no checking for overflow). The method used is that of repeated squaring of the base and decoding of the exponent in binary notation to determine when to multiply the base into the result.

To see why this works, note that the **while** loop maintains the invariant condition that the correct answer is **result** times **base** raised to the **exponent** power. When eventually **exponent** is 0, this condition degenerates to stating that **result** has the correct value.

```
int pow(int base, int exponent)
{
    int result = 1;
    while (exponent > 0) {
        if ( exponent % 2 ) result *= base;
        base *= base;
        exponent /= 2;
    }
    return result;
}
```

Example

A **while** loop may usefully have a null statement for its body:

```
while ( *char_pointer++ );
```

In this code, a character pointer is advanced along by the **++** operator until a null character is found, and it is left pointing to the character after the null. This is a compact idiom for locating the end of a string. (Notice that the test expression is interpreted as ***(char_pointer++)**, not as **(*char_pointer)++**, which would increment the character pointed to by **char_pointer**.)

Example

Another common idiom uses two pointers to copy a character string:

```
while ( *dest_pointer++ = *source_pointer++ );
```

Characters are copied until the terminating null character is found (and also copied). Of course in writing this, the programmer should have reason to believe that the destination area will be large enough to contain all the characters to be copied.

References **break** and **continue** statements 8.8; control expression 8.1; **goto** statement 8.10; null statement 8.11; **return** statement 8.9

8.6.2 Do Statement

The **do** statement differs from the **while** statement in that the **do** statement always executes the body at least once, whereas the **while** statement may never execute its body:

> *do-statement* :
>   do *statement* **while** (*expression*) ;

The **do** statement is executed by first executing the embedded statement. Then the control expression is evaluated; if the value is true (not zero), then the entire process is repeated, alternately executing the statement, evaluating the control expression, and then, if the value is true, repeating the process.

The execution of the **do** statement is complete when the control expression evaluates to zero or when control is transferred out of the body of the **do** statement by a **return**, **goto**, or **break** statement. Also, the **continue** statement can modify the execution of a **do** statement.

The C **do** statement is similar in function to the "repeat-until" statement in Pascal. The C **do** statement is unusual in that it terminates execution when the control expression is false, whereas a Pascal repeat-until statement terminates if its control expression is true. C is more consistent in this regard: All iteration constructs in C (**while, do**, and **for**) terminate when the control expression is false.

Example

This program fragment reads and processes characters, halting after a newline character has been processed:

```
int ch;
do
    process( ch = getchar());
while (ch != '\n');
```

The same effect could have been obtained by moving the computations into the control expression of a **while** statement, but the intent would be less clear:

```
int ch;
while( ch = getchar(ch),
       process(ch),
       ch != '\n' ) /*empty*/ ;
```

Example

It is possible to write a **do** statement whose body is a null statement:

```
do ; while (expression );
```

However, it is more common to write this loop using a **while** statement:

```
while ( expression );
```

References break and **continue** statements 8.8; control expression 8.1; **goto** statement 8.10; null statement 8.11; **return** statement 8.9; **while** statement 8.6.1

8.6.3 For Statement

C's **for** statement is considerably more general than the "increment and test" statements found in most other languages. After explaining the execution of the **for** statement, we give several examples of how it can be used:

for-statement :
    for *for-expressions statement*

for-expressions :
    (*initial-clause*$_{opt}$; *expression*$_{opt}$; *expression*$_{opt}$)

initial-clause:
    expression
    declaration   *(C99)*

A **for** statement consists of the keyword **for**, followed by three expressions separated by semicolons and enclosed in parentheses, followed by a statement. Each of the three expressions within the parentheses is optional and may be omitted, but the two semicolons separating them and the parentheses surrounding them are mandatory.

Typically, the first expression is used to initialize a loop variable, the second tests whether the loop should continue or terminate, and the third updates the loop variable (e.g., by incrementing it). However, in principle, the expressions may be used to perform any computation that is useful within the framework of the **for** control structure. The **for** statement is executed as follows:

1. If the *initial-clause* is an expression, then it is evaluated and the value is discarded. If the *initial-clause* is a declaration (C99), then the declared variables are initialized. If the *initial-clause* is not present, then no action occurs.
2. If present, the second expression is evaluated like a control expression. If the result is zero, then execution of the **for** statement is complete. Otherwise (if the value is not zero or if the second expression was omitted), proceed to Step 3.
3. The body of the **for** statement is executed.
4. If present, the third expression is evaluated and the value is discarded.
5. Return to Step 2.

The execution of a **for** statement is terminated when the second (control) expression evaluates to zero or when control is transferred outside the **for** statement by a **return**, **goto**, or **break** statement. The execution of a **continue** statement within the body of the **for** statement has the effect of causing a jump to Step 4.

In C99, the **for** statement forms its own block scope, as does the substatement even if it is not a compound statement. This serves to restrict the scope of objects and types that might be created as a side effect of using compound literals or type names. Also, the first expression in the **for** loop may be replaced by a declaration, which can declare and initialize one or more loop control variables. The scope of such variables extends to the end of the **for** statement and includes the second and third expressions in the loop control. It is common when writing **for** loops to want such control variables, and restricting their scope allows the C compiler more optimization latitude.

References **break** and **continue** statements 8.8; compound literals 7.4.5; control expression 8.1; discarded expressions 7.13; **goto** statement 8.10; **return** statement 8.9; type names 5.12; **while** statement 8.6.1

8.6.4 Using the for Statement

Example

Typically, the first expression in a **for** statement is used to initialize a variable, the second expression to test the variable in some way, and the third to modify the variable toward some goal. For example, to print the integers from 0 to 9 and their squares, one might write

```
int j;
...
for (j = 0; j < 10; j++)
    printf("%d %d\n", j, j*j);
```

Here the first expression initializes **j**, the second expression tests whether it has reached 10 yet (if it has, the loop is terminated), and the third expression increments **j**.

In C99, the variable **j** can be declared in the loop and its scope thereby limited to the loop:

```
for (int j = 0; j < 10; j++)
    printf("%d %d\n", j, j*j);
```

Example

There are two common ways in C to write a loop that "never terminates" (sometimes known as a "do forever" loop):

```
for (;;) statement
```

```
while (1) statement
```

The loops can be terminated by a **break**, **goto**, or **return** statement within the body.

Example

The **pow** function used earlier to illustrate the **while** statement can be rewritten using a **for** statement:

```
int pow(int base, int exponent)
{
    int result = 1;
    for (; exponent > 0; exponent /= 2) {
        if ( exponent % 2 )
            result *= base;
        base *= base;
    }
    return result;
}
```

This form stresses that the loop is controlled by the variable **exponent** as it progresses toward 0 by repeated divisions by 2. Note that the loop variable **exponent** still had to be declared outside the **for** statement. The **for** statement does not include the declaration of any variables. A common programming error is to forget to declare a variable such as **i** or **j** used in a **for** statement, only to discover that some other variable named **i** or **j** elsewhere in the program is inadvertently modified by the loop.

Example

Here is a simple sorting routine that uses the insertion sort algorithm.

```
void insertsort(int v[], int n)
{
    register int i, j, temp;
    for (i = 1; i < n; i++) {
        temp = v[i];
        for (j = i-1; j >= 0 && v[j] > temp; j--)
            v[j+1] = v[j];
        v[j+1] = temp;
    }
}
```

The outer **for** loop counts **i** up from 1 (inclusive) to **n** (exclusive). At each step, elements **v[0]** through **v[i-1]** have already been sorted, and elements **v[i]** through **v[n-1]** remain to be sorted. The inner loop counts **j** down from **i-1**, moving elements of the array up one at a time until the right place to insert **v[i]** has been found. (That is why this is called *insertion sort*.) This algorithm is not a good method for very large unordered arrays, because in the worst case the time to perform the sort is proportional to **n*n** (i.e., it is $O(n^2)$).

Example

The insertion sort can be improved from $O(n^2)$ to $O(n^{1.25})$ by simply wrapping a third loop around the first two and introducing **gap** in a few places where **insertsort** used the constant 1. The following sort function, using the shell sort algorithm, is similar to one called **shell** that appeared as an example in Kernighan and Ritchie's *The C Programming Language*, but we have modified it here in three ways, two of them suggested by Knuth and Sedgewick (see the Preface), to make it faster:

```
void shellsort(register int v[], int n)
{
    register int gap, i, j, temp;
    gap = 1;
    do (gap = 3*gap + 1); while (gap <= n);
    for (gap /= 3; gap > 0; gap /= 3)
        for (i = gap; i < n; i++) {
            temp = v[i];
            for (j=i-gap; (j>=0)&&(v[j]>temp); j-=gap)
                v[j+gap] = v[j];
            v[j+gap] = temp;
        }
}
```

The improvements are: (1) In the original **shell** function, the value of **gap** started at **n/2** and was divided by two each time through the outer loop. In this version, **gap** is initialized by finding the smallest number in the series (1, 4, 13, 40, 121, …) that is not greater than **n**, and **gap** is divided by three each time through the outer loop. This makes the sort run 20%–30% faster. (This choice of the initial value of **gap** has been shown to be superior to using **n** as the initial value.) (2) The assignments in the inner loop were reduced from three to one. (3) The **register** and **void** storage classes were added. In some implementations, **register** declarations can improve performance dramatically (40% in one case).

Example

The **for** statement need not be used only for counting over integer values. Here is an example of scanning down a linked chain of structures where the loop variable is a pointer:

```
struct intlist {
    struct intlist *link;
    int data;
};

void print_duplicates(struct intlist *p)
{
    for (; p; p = p->link) {
        struct intlist *q;
        for (q = p->link; q; q = q->link)
            if (q->data == p->data) {
                printf("Duplicate data %d", p->data);
                break;
            }
    }
}
```

The structure **intlist** is used to implement a linked list of records, each record containing some data. Given such a linked list, the function **print_duplicates** prints the data for every redundant record in the list. The first **for** statement uses the formal parameter **p** as its loop variable—it scans down the given list. The loop terminates when a null pointer is encountered. For every record, all the records following it are examined by the inner **for** statement, which scans a pointer **q** along the list in the same fashion.

References   pointer types 5.3; **register** storage class 4.3; selection operator —> 7.4.2; structure types 5.6; **void** type 5.9

8.6.5 Multiple Control Variables

Sometimes it is convenient to have more than one variable controlling a **for** loop. In this connection, the comma operator is especially useful because it can be used to group several assignment expressions into a single expression.

Example

The following function reverses a linked list by modifying the links:

```
struct intlist { struct intlist *link; int data; };

struct intlist *reverse(struct intlist *p)
{
    struct intlist *here, *previous, *next;
    for (here = p, previous = NULL ;
        here != NULL ;
        next = here->link, here->link = previous,
           previous = here, here = next) /*empty*/ ;
    return previous;
}
```

Example

The following function **string_equal** accepts two strings and returns 1 if they are equal and 0 otherwise.

```
int string_equal(const char *s1, const char *s2)
{
    char *p1, *p2;
    for (p1=s1, p2=s2; *p1 && *p2; p1++, p2++)
        if (*p1 != *p2) return 0;
    return *p1 == *p2;
}
```

The **for** statement is used to scan two pointer variables in parallel down the two strings. The expression **p1++, p2++** causes each of the two pointers to be advanced to the next character. If the strings are found to differ, the return statement is used to terminate execution of the entire function and return 0. If a null character is found in either string, as determined by the expression ***p1 && *p2**, then the loop is terminated normally, whereupon the second **return** statement determines whether both strings ended with a null character in the same place. (The function would still work correctly if the expression ***p1** were used instead of ***p1 && *p2**. It would also be a bit faster, although not as pleasantly symmetrical.)

References **break** and **continue** statements 8.8; comma operator 7.10; pointer types 5.3; selection operator —> 7.4.2; structure types 5.6

8.7 SWITCH STATEMENTS

The **switch** statement is a multiway branch based on the value of a control expression. In use, it is similar to the "case" statement in Pascal or Ada, but it is implemented more like the FORTRAN "computed goto" statement:

switch-statement :
      switch (*expression*) *statement*

case-label :
      case *constant-expression*

default-label :
      default

The control expression that follows the keyword **switch** must have an integral type and is subject to the usual unary conversions. The expression following the keyword **case** must be an integral constant expression (Section 7.11.2). The statement embedded within a **switch** statement is sometimes called the *body* of the **switch** statement; it is usually a compound statement, but need not be.

A **case** label or **default** label is said to belong to the innermost **switch** statement that contains it. Any statement within the body of a **switch** statement—or the body itself—may be labeled with a **case** label or a **default** label. In fact, the same statement may be labeled with several **case** labels and a **default** label. A **case** or **default** label is not permitted to appear other than within the body of a **switch** statement, and no two **case** labels belonging to the same **switch** statement may have constant expressions with the same value. At most one **default** label may belong to any one **switch** statement. A **switch** statement is executed as follows:

1. The control expression is evaluated.

2. If the value of the control expression is equal to that of the constant expression in some **case** label belonging to the **switch** statement, then program control is transferred to the point indicated by that **case** label as if by a **goto** statement.

3. If the value of the control expression is not equal to any **case** label, but there is a **default** label that belongs to the **switch** statement, then program control is transferred to the point indicated by that **default** label.

4. If the value of the control expression is not equal to any **case** label and there is no **default** label, no statement of the body of the **switch** statement is executed; program control is transferred to whatever follows the **switch** statement.

When comparing the control expression and the **case** expressions, the **case** expressions are converted to the type of the control expression (after the usual unary conversions).

The order in which the control expression is compared against each **case** expression is not defined, and the way in which the comparisons are implemented may depend on the number and values of the **case** expressions. Programmers often assume that the

switch statement is implemented as a sequence of **if** statements in the same order as the **case** expressions, but this may not be true.

When control is transferred to a **case** or **default** label, execution continues through successive statements, ignoring any additional **case** or **default** labels that are encountered, until the end of the **switch** statement is reached or until control is transferred out of the **switch** statement by a **goto**, **return**, **break**, or **continue** statement.

Although Standard C allows the control expression to be of any integer type, some older compilers do not permit it to be of type **long** or **unsigned long**. Standard C also permits an implementation to limit the number of separate **case** labels in a **switch** statement. The limit is 257 in C89 and 1,023 in C99—more than enough to handle all values of a typical (eight-bit) **char** type, for example.

In C99, if any object of variably modified type is visible at any **case** or **default** label, then that object's scope must cover the entire **switch** statement. That is, no object of variably modified type can have a scope that encompasses only part of the **switch** statement unless that scope is entirely contained within a **case** or **default** arm. Stated another way, you cannot "bury" a **case** or **default** label in a block containing an object of a variably modified type.

References **break** and **continue** statements 8.8; constant expressions 7.11; **goto** statement 8.10; integer types 5.1; labeled statement 8.3; **return** statement 8.9; variably modified type 5.4.5

8.7.1 Use of switch Statements

Normally, the body of a **switch** statement is a compound statement whose inner, top-level statements have **case** and/or **default** labels. It should be noted that **case** and **default** labels do not alter the flow of program control; execution proceeds unimpeded by such labels. The **break** statement can be used within the body of a **switch** statement to terminate its execution.

Example

```
switch (x) {
    case 1: printf("*");
    case 2: printf("**");
    case 3: printf("***");
    case 4: printf("****");
}
```

In the prior **switch** statement, if the value of **x** is 2, then nine asterisks will be printed. The reason for this is that the **switch** statement transfers control to the **case** label with the expression 2. The call to **printf** with argument **"**"** is executed. Next the call to **printf** with argument **"***"** is executed, and finally the call to **printf** with argument **"****"** is executed. If it is desired to terminate execution of the **switch** body after a single call to **printf** in each case, then the **break** statement should be used:

```
switch (x) {
   case 1: printf("*");
           break;
   case 2: printf("**");
           break;
   case 3: printf("***");
           break;
   case 4: printf("****");
           break;
}
```

Although the last **break** statement in this example is logically unnecessary, it is a good thing to put in as a matter of style. It will help prevent program errors in the event that a fifth **case** is later added to the **switch** statement.

We recommend sticking to this simple rule of style for **switch** statements: The body should always be a compound statement, and all labels belonging to the **switch** statement should appear on top-level statements within that compound statement. (The same stylistic guidelines apply as for **goto** statements.) Furthermore, every **case** (or **default**) label but the first should be preceded by one of two things: either a **break** statement that terminates the code for the previous **case** or a comment noting that the previous code is intended to drop in.

Although this is considered good style, the language definition does not require that the body be a compound statement, that **case** and **default** labels appear only at the "top level" of the compound statement, or that **case** and **default** labels appear in any particular order or on different statements.

Example

In the following code fragment, the comment tells the reader that the lack of   **break** statement after case **fatal** is intentional.

```
...
case fatal:
   printf("Fatal ");
   /* Drops through. */
case error:
   printf("Error");
   ++error_count;
   break;
...
```

Example

Here is an example of how good intentions can lead to chaos. The intent was to implement this simple program fragment as efficiently as possible:

```
if (prime(x)) process_prime(x);
else process_composite(x);
```

The function **prime** returns 1 if its argument is a prime number and 0 if the argument is a composite number. Program measurements indicated that most of the calls to **prime** were being made with small integers. To avoid the overhead of calls to **prime**, the code was changed to use a **switch** statement to handle the small integers, leaving the **default** label to handle larger numbers. By steadily compressing the code, the following was produced:

```
switch (x)
    default:
    if (prime(x))
        case 2: case 3: case 5: case 7:
            process_prime(x);
    else
        case 4: case 6: case 8: case 9: case 10:
            process_composite(x);
```

This is frankly the most bizarre **switch** statement we have ever seen that still has pretenses to being purposeful.

8.8 BREAK AND CONTINUE STATEMENTS

The **break** and **continue** statements are used to alter the flow of control inside loops and—in the case of **break**—in **switch** statements. It is stylistically better to use these statements than to use the **goto** statement to accomplish the same purpose:

break-statement :
    break;

continue-statement :
    continue;

Execution of a **break** statement causes execution of the smallest enclosing **while**, **do**, **for**, or **switch** statement to be terminated. Program control is immediately transferred to the point just beyond the terminated statement. It is an error for a **break** statement to appear where there is no enclosing iterative or **switch** statement.

A **continue** statement terminates the execution of the *body* of the smallest enclosing **while**, **do**, or **for** statement. Program control is immediately transferred to the end of the body, and the execution of the affected iterative statement continues from that point with a reevaluation of the loop test (or the increment expression, in the case of the **for** statement). It is an error for a **continue** statement to appear where there is no enclosing iterative statement.

The **continue** statement, unlike **break**, has no interaction with **switch** statements. A **continue** statement may appear within a **switch** statement, but it will only affect the smallest enclosing iterative statement, not the **switch** statement.

Example

The **break** and **continue** statements can be explained in terms of the **goto** statement. Consider the statements affected by a **break** or **continue** statement:

```
while ( expression ) statement
do statement while ( expression );
for (expression₁; expression₂; expression₃) statement
switch ( expression ) statement
```

Imagine that all such statements were to be rewritten in this manner:

```
{ while (expression) {statement C:;} B:;}
{ do {statement C:;} while (expression); B:;}
{ for (expression₁; expression₂; expression₃) {statement C:;} B:;}
{ switch (expression) statement B:;  }
```

where in each case **B** and **C** are labels that appear nowhere else in the enclosing function. Then any occurrence of a **break** statement within the body of any of these statements is equivalent to "**goto B;**" and any occurrence of a **continue** statement within the body of any of these statements (except **switch**, where it is not permitted) is equivalent to "**goto C;**". This assumes that the loop bodies do not contain yet another loop containing the **break** or **continue**.

Example

The **break** statement is frequently used in two important contexts: to terminate the processing of a particular **case** within a **switch** statement, and to terminate a loop prematurely. The first use is illustrated in conjunction with **switch** in Section 8.7. The second use is illustrated by this example of filling an array with input characters, stopping when the array is full or when the input is exhausted:

```
#include <stdio.h>
static char array[100];
int i, c;
…
for (i = 0; i < 100; i++) {
    c = getchar();
    if (c == EOF) break;    /* Quit if end-of-file. */
    array[i] = c;
}
/* Now i is the actual number of characters read. */
```

Note how **break** is used to handle the abnormal case. It is generally better style to handle the normal case in the loop test.

Example

Here is an example of the use of a **break** statement within a "do forever" loop. The idea is to find the smallest element in the array **a** (whose length is **N**) as efficiently as possible. It is assumed that the array may be modified temporarily:

```
int temp = a[0];
register int smallest = a[0];
register int *ptr = &a[N];   /* just beyond end of a */
...
for (;;) {
    while (*--ptr > smallest) ;
    if (ptr == &a[0]) break;
    a[0] = smallest = *ptr;
}
a[0] = temp;
```

The point is that most of the work is done by a tight **while** loop that scans the pointer **ptr** backward through the array, skipping elements that are larger than the smallest one found so far. (If the elements are in a random order, then once a reasonably small element has been found, most elements will be larger than that and so will be skipped.) The **while** loop cannot fall off the front of the array because the smallest element so far is also stored in the first array element. When the **while** loop is done, if the scan has reached the front of the array, then the **break** statement terminates the outer loop. Otherwise **smallest** and **a[0]** are updated and the **while** loop is entered again.

Example

Compare the prior code with a simpler, more obvious approach:

```
register int smallest = a[0];
register int j;
...
for (j = 1; j < N; ++j)
    if (a[j] < smallest) smallest = a[j];
```

This version is certainly easier to understand. However, on every iteration of the loop, an explicit check (**j<n**) must be made for falling off the end of the array, as opposed to the implicit check made by the more clever code. Under certain circumstances where efficiency is paramount, the more complicated code may be justified; otherwise the simpler, clearer loop should be used.

References   **do** statement 8.6.2; **for** statement 8.6.3; **goto** statement 8.10; **switch** statement 8.7; **while** statement 8.6.1

8.9 RETURN STATEMENTS

A **return** statement is used to terminate the current function, perhaps returning a value:

return-statement :
        return *expression*$_{opt}$ **;**

Execution of a **return** statement causes execution of the current function to be terminated; program control is transferred to the caller of the function at the point immediately following the call.

If no expression appears in the **return** statement, then the return type of the function must be **void** in C99 or else the statement is invalid. C89 permitted the expression to be omitted in non-**void** functions, but stated that the behavior was undefined if a value from the function call was expected.

If an expression appears in the **return** statement, then the return type of the function must not be **void** or else the statement is invalid. The return expression is converted as if by assignment to the return type of the function; if such conversion is not possible, then the **return** statement is invalid.

If program control reaches the end of a function body without encountering a **return** statement, then the effect is as if a **return** statement with no expression were executed. If the function has a non-**void** return type, then the behavior is undefined.

Example

Many programmers put parentheses around the expression in a **return** statement, although this is not necessary. It is probably a habit developed after putting parentheses around the expressions following **switch**, **if**, **while**, and so on.

```
int twice(int x) { return (2*x); }
```

References   discarded values 7.13; function call 7.4.3; function definition 9.1; function return type agreement 9.8

8.10 GOTO STATEMENTS

A **goto** statement may be used to transfer control to any statement within a function:

goto-statement :
    goto *named-label* **;**

named-label :
    identifier

The identifier following the keyword **goto** must be the same as a named label on some statement within the current function. Execution of the **goto** statement causes an immediate transfer of program control to the point in the function indicated by the label; the statement labeled by the indicated name is executed next.

References   labeled statement 8.3

8.10.1 Using the goto Statement

C permits a **goto** statement to transfer control to any other statement within a function, but certain kinds of branching can result in confusing programs, and the branching may hinder compiler optimizations. For these reasons, we recommend that you do not branch: into the "then" or "else" arm of an **if** statement from outside the **if** statement, from the "then" arm to the "else" arm or back, into the body of a **switch** or iteration statement from outside the statement, or into a compound statement from outside. Such branches should be avoided not only when using the **goto** statement, but also when placing **case** and **default** labels in a **switch** statement. Branching into the middle of a compound statement from outside bypasses the initialization of any variables declared at the top of the compound statement. It is good programming style to use the **break**, **continue**, and **return** statements in preference to **goto** whenever possible.

Example

Despite the cautions, the **goto** is useful at times. In the following example, a two-dimension array **a** is searched for a value **v**. If found, a **goto** is used to branch out of a doubly nested loop, preserving the values of the loop variables **i** and **j**.

```
#include <stdio.h>
int i, j, v, a[N][M];
...
for (i=0; i++; i<N)
  for (j=0; j++; j<M)
    if (a[i][j] == v) goto found;
printf("a does not contain %d\n", v);
...
found:
  printf("a[%d][%d]==%d\n", i, j, v);
```

References **break** and **continue** statements 8.8; control expression 8.1; **if** statement 8.5; labeled statement 8.3; **return** statement 8.9; **switch** statement 8.7

8.11 NULL STATEMENTS

The null statement consists simply of a semicolon:

null-statement :
    ;

The null statement is useful primarily in two situations. In the first case, a null body is used as the body of an iterative statement (**while**, **do**, or **for**). The second case is where a label is desired just before the right brace that terminates a compound statement. A label cannot simply precede the right brace, but must always be attached to a statement.

Example

The following loop needs no body because the control expression does all the work:

```
char *p;
...
while ( *p++ ); /* find the end of the string */
```

Example

The label **L** is placed on a null statement:

```
if (e) {
    ...
    goto L; /* terminate this arm of the 'if' */
    ...
    L:;}
else ...
```

References do statement 8.6.2; **for** statement 8.6.2; labeled statement 8.3; **while** statement 8.6.1

8.12 C++ COMPATIBILITY

8.12.1 Compound Statements

C++ does not allow jumping into a compound statement in a way that would skip declarations with initializers.

Example

```
goto L; /* Valid but unwise in C; invalid in C++ */
{
    int i = 10;
L:
    ...
}
```

References jumping into compound statements 8.4.2

8.12.2 Declarations in Loops

C99 allows variables to be declared in the *initial-clause* of a **for** loop; their scope ends at the end of the loop body. This is consistent with Standard C++. Some earlier versions of C++ extended the scope of such variables past the end of the loop into the enclosing compound statement or function.

8.13 EXERCISES

1. Rewrite the following statements without using **for**, **while**, or **do** statements.
    (a) `for(n=A;n<B;n++) sum+=n;`
    (b) `while(a<b) a++;`
    (c) `do sum+=*p; while (++p < q);`
2. What is the value of **j** at the end of the following program fragment?

```
{   int j=1;
    goto L;
    {
        static int i = 3;
    L:
        j = i;
    }
}
```

3.   What is the value of **sum** after the following program fragment is executed?

```
int i,sum = 0;
for(i=0;i<10;i++) {
    switch(i) {
    case 0: case 1: case 3: case 5: sum++;
    default: continue;
    case 4: break;
    }
    break;
}
```

9

Functions

This chapter discusses the use of functions, and the details of declaring and defining functions, specifying formal parameters and return types, and calling functions. Some information on functions appears previously in this book: Function declarators are described in Section 4.5.4, and function types and declarations are discussed in Section 5.8.

The description of functions has become more complicated since the original definition of C. Standard C introduced a new (better) way of declaring functions using function *prototypes* that specify more information about a function's parameters. The operation of a function call when a prototype has appeared is different from its operation without a prototype. Although the prototype and nonprototype forms are individually easy to understand, there are complicated rules for deciding what should happen when these two forms are mixed for the same function. (In C++, prototypes must be used.)

The presence of a function prototype is determined by the syntax of a function declarator (Section 4.5.4). Briefly, in traditional C and when a prototype is *not* used:

1. Function arguments undergo automatic promotions (the usual argument conversions) before a call.
2. No checking of the type or number of arguments occurs.
3. Any function can potentially take a variable number of arguments.

In contrast to this, when prototypes *are* used:

1. Function arguments are converted, as if by assignment, to the declared types of the formal parameters.
2. The number and types of the arguments must match the declared types, or else the program is in error.
3. Functions taking a variable number of arguments are designated explicitly, and the unspecified arguments undergo the default argument conversions.

Whether to use prototypes in C programs is a tricky portability issue. To remain compatible with non-Standard implementations, you must avoid them. To remain compatible with C++, you must use them. You could write both forms using conditional compilation directives to decide which to include, but that is awkward too. The following sections discuss both prototype-form and nonprototype-form function declarations, and they also discuss some portability options.

9.1 FUNCTION DEFINITIONS

A function definition introduces a new function and provides the following information:

1. the type of the value returned by the function, if any

2. the type and number of the formal parameters

3. the visibility of the function outside the file in which it is defined

4. the code that is to be executed when the function is called

The syntax for a function definition is shown next. Function definitions can appear only at the top level of a C source file or *translation unit*.

translation-unit :
      top-level-declaration
      translation-unit   top-level-declaration

top-level-declaration :
      declaration
      function-definition

function-definition :
      function-def-specifier   compound-statement

function-def-specifier :
      declaration-specifiers$_{opt}$ declarator declaration-list$_{opt}$

declaration-list :
      declaration
      declaration-list   declaration

The syntax for other top-level declarations was discussed in Chapter 4. Prior to C99, if no type specifier appeared in the *declaration-specifiers$_{opt}$* of a function definition, then **int** was assumed. In C99, a type specifier is required.

Within a *function-def-specifier*, the declarator must contain a *function-declarator* that specifies the function identifier immediately before the left parenthesis. The syntax of a function declarator was shown in Section 4.5.4 and is repeated next for convenience:

function-declarator :
  direct-declarator (*parameter-type-list*)   (C89)
  direct-declarator (*identifier-list$_{opt}$*)

parameter-type-list :
  parameter-list
  parameter-list , **...**

parameter-list :
  parameter-declaration
  parameter-list , parameter-declaration

parameter-declaration :
  declaration-specifiers declarator
  declaration-specifiers abstract-declarator$_{opt}$

identifier-list :
  identifier
  identifier-list , identifier

If the function declarator that names the defined function includes a *parameter-type-list*, then the function definition is said to be in prototype form; otherwise it is in nonprototype, or traditional, form. In prototype form, the parameter names and types are declared in the *declarator*, and the *declaration-list* following the declarator must be empty. All C function definitions should be written in prototype form as a matter of good style.

In the pre-Standard traditional form, the parameter names are listed in the *declarator* and the types are specified (in any order) in the *declaration-list$_{opt}$* following the declarator. All parameters should be declared in the *declaration-list*, but prior to C99 omitted parameter declarations defaulted to type **int**. C99 lists the traditional form of function definitions as an obsolescent feature, which means it may not be supported in the future.

Example

```
int f(int i, long j) { … }        /* prototype form */
int f(i,j) int i; long j; { … }   /* traditional form */
```

There are several constraints on the form of the *function-def-specifier*. The identifier declared in a function definition must have a function type, as indicated by the declarator portion of the definition. That is, the declarator must contain a *function-declarator* that specifies the function identifier immediately before the left parenthesis. It is not allowed for the identifier to inherit its "functionness" from a typedef name.

The function return type cannot be an array or function type.

The declarator must specify the function's parameter names. If the declarator is in prototype form, the *parameter-declarations* must include a *declarator* as opposed to an *abstract-declarator*. If the declarator is not in prototype form, it must include *identifier-list* unless the function takes no arguments. To avoid an ambiguity between an identifier list and a parameter type list, it is invalid to have a parameter name that is the same as a visible **typedef** name. (This restriction is usually not present in older compilers.)

The only storage class specifier allowed in a parameter declaration is `register`.

The *declaration-list_opt* is permitted only with nonprototype definitions and can include only declarations of parameter identifiers. Some traditional C compilers will permit additional declarations (e.g., structures or typedefs), but the meaning of such declarations is problematic and are better placed in the function body.

Example

To illustrate these rules, the following are valid function definitions:

Definition	Explanation
`void f()` `{...}`	f is a function taking no parameters and returning no value (traditional form)

`int g(x, y)`
`   int x, y;`
`{...}`
	g is a function taking two integer parameters and returning an integer result (traditional)

`int h(int x, int y)` `{...}`	h is a function taking two integer parameters and returning an integer result (prototype form)
`int (*f(int x))[]` `{...}`	f is a function taking an integer parameter and returning a pointer to an array of integers (prototype form)

The following are not valid function definitions for the reasons given. Assume the typedef name `T` was declared as "`typedef int T();`".

Definition	Explanation
`int (*q)() {...}`	q is a pointer, not a function
`T r {...}`	r cannot inherit "functionness" from a `typedef` name
`T s() {...}`	declares s as a function returning a function
`void t(int, double)` `{...}`	t's parameter names do not appear in the declarator

`void u(int x, y)`
`   int y;`
`{...}`
	parameter declarations are only partially in prototype form

The only storage class specifiers that may appear in a function definition are `extern` and `static`. `extern` signifies that the function can be referenced from other files—that is, the function name is exported to the linker. The specifier `static` signifies that the function cannot be referenced from other files—that is, the name is *not* exported to the linker. If no storage class appears in a function definition, **extern** is assumed. In any case, the function is always visible from the definition point to the end of the file. In particular, it is visible within the body of the function.

References declarators 4.5; **extern** storage class 4.3; function declarations 5.8; initialized declaration 4.1; **static** storage class 4.3; type specifiers 4.4

9.2 FUNCTION PROTOTYPES

A function prototype is a function declaration written in the prototype syntax (the *parameter-type-list*) or a function definition written in that syntax. Like a traditional function declaration, a function prototype declares the return type of a function. Unlike a traditional function declaration, a function prototype also declares the number and type of the function's formal parameters. All modern C code should be written using prototypes. C99 characterizes the older, nonprototype form as obsolescent.

There are three basic kinds of prototypes depending on whether a function has no parameters, a fixed number of parameters, or a variable number of parameters:

1. A function that has no parameters must have a parameter type list consisting of the single type specifier **void**. In a function definition, an empty parameter list means the same as **void**, but this is an obsolescent notation that should be avoided.

Example

```
extern int random_generator(void);
static void do_nothing(void) { }   /* void is optional */
```

2. A function that has a fixed number of parameters indicates the types of those parameters in the parameter type list. If the prototype appears in a function declaration, parameter names may be included, as desired. (We think they help in documenting the function.) Parameter names must appear in function definitions.

Example

```
double square(double x) { return x*x; }
extern char *strncpy(char *, const char *, size_t);
```

3. A function that has a variable number of parameters or parameters of varying types indicates the types of any fixed parameters as before and follows them by a comma and an ellipsis (. . .). There must be at least one fixed parameter or else the parameter list cannot be referenced using the standard library facilities from **stdarg.h**.:

Example

This is a declaration for a function that has a variable number of parameters. The parameter names are spelled in a way reserved for implementors as required in the standard library.

```
extern int fprintf( FILE *__file,
    const char *__format, ... );
```

Example

Prototypes may be used in any function declarator, including those used to form more complicated types. The Standard C declaration of **signal** (Section 19.6) is

```
void (*signal(int sig, void (*func)(int siga)))(int siga);
```

This declares **signal** to be a function that takes two arguments: **sig**, an integer, and **func**,
a pointer to a **void** function of a single integer argument, **siga**. The function **signal** returns
a pointer of the same type as its second parameter (i.e., a pointer to a **void** function taking a
single integer argument). A clearer way to write the declaration of **signal** is

```
typedef void sig_handler(int siga);
sig_handler *signal(int sig, sig_handler *func);
```

However, when actually defining a signal handler function, the **sig_handler** typedef name
cannot be used by the rules for function definitions. Instead, the type must be repeated:

```
void new_signal_handler(int sig a) {…}
```

It is possible to use prototypes for some declarators and not for others in the same declaration.
If we were to declare **signal2** as

```
typedef void sig_handler2();   /* not a prototype */
sig_handler2 *signal2(int sig, sig_handler2 *func);
```

then the second argument of the **signal2** function would not be in prototype form, although
signal2 still has the prototype form.

References   function declarator 4.5.4; function declarations 5.8; function definitions 9.1;
void type 5.9

9.2.1 When Is a Prototype Present?

To predict how a function call will be performed, it is important that the programmer
know whether the function (or function type) being called is governed by a prototype. A
function call is governed by a prototype when:

1. a declaration for the function (or type) is visible and the declaration is in prototype
   form, or
2. the function definition is visible and that definition is in prototype form.

Note that the visibility of *any* prototype for the function is all that is required; there may be
other nonprototype declarations or definitions visible.

   If there are two or more prototype declarations of the same function or function
type, or a prototype declaration and a prototype definition, then the declarations and definition must be compatible using the rules in Section 5.11.4.

References   compatible and composite types 5.11

9.2.2 Mixing Prototype and Nonprototype Declarations

Although mixing prototype and nonprototype declarations for the same function is not recommended, Standard C specifies conditions under which the two kinds of declarations are compatible (see Section 5.11.4).

The behavior of a function call is undefined if the call supplies arguments that do not "match" the function definition. In traditional C, the programmer assumes all responsibility for making sure the call matches the definition; the language helps by converting arguments and parameters to a smaller and perhaps more manageable set of types. In Standard C, through the use of prototype declarations, the compiler can check at the call site that the arguments match the prototype.

Depending on where function declarations appear, it is possible that some function calls will be governed by prototype declarations, some by traditional declarations, and some by the actual function definition. The calls and definition may be in a single source file or many files. Whenever some calls are not governed by a prototype, the programmer must assume the additional responsibility in being sure that the arguments in those calls match the function definition.

Example

In general, there are many different prototypes that are individually compatible with a nonprototype declaration. For example, suppose the nonprototype declaration

```
extern int f();
```

appeared somewhere in a C program. Here are some compatible and incompatible prototype declarations.

Prototype	Compatible with `int f()`?	Reason
`extern double f(void);`	no	the parameter list is OK, but the return types are not compatible
`extern int f(int, float);`	no	`float` changes to `double` under the usual argument conversions; the two types are not compatible
`extern int f(double x);`	yes	parameter type does not change on conversion
`extern int f(int i, ...);`	no	the prototype must not contain ellipses
`extern int f(float *);`	yes	the argument is a pointer that is not converted

In general, there is only one prototype that matches a nonprototype function definition; this prototype is sometimes referred to as the function's *Miranda prototype* since it is "appointed" to a function definition that otherwise would not have one.

In Standard C, functions taking a variable number of arguments must be governed by prototypes. This means that any pre-Standard declarations of functions that take a variable number of arguments (e.g., **printf**) must be rewritten with a prototype before they are used by a Standard C implementation.

Example

For example, suppose the following (nonprototype) definition appeared in a C program:

```
int f(x,y)
    float x;
    int y;
{...}
```

Here are some compatible and incompatible prototype declarations for this definition.

Prototype	Compatible?	Reason
`extern double` `    f(double x, int y);`	no	the parameter list is OK, but the return types are not compatible
`extern int` `    f(float, int);`	no	the first parameter must have type **double**
`extern int` `    f(float, int, ...);`	no	the prototype must not contain ellipses
`extern int` `    f(double a, int b);`	yes	this is the only compatible prototype; the parameter names do not matter

References   compatible types 5.11; **printf** 15.11

9.2.3 Using Prototypes Wisely

Argument checking with prototypes is not foolproof. In a C program divided into many source files, the compiler cannot check that all calls to a function are governed by a prototype, that all the prototypes for the same function are compatible, or that all the prototypes match the function definition.

However, if the programmer follows some simple rules, the loopholes can be eliminated for all practical purposes:

1. Every external function should have a single prototype declaration in a header file. By having a single prototype, the possibility of incompatible prototypes for the same function is eliminated.

2. Every source file that has in it a call to the function should include the header file with the prototype. This ensures that all calls to the function will be governed by the same prototype and allows the compiler to check the arguments at the call sites.

3. The source file containing the definition of the function should also include the header file. This allows the compiler to check that the prototype and the declaration match, and, by transitivity, that all calls match the definition.

It is not necessary that the function definition be in prototype form.

The use of static functions should follow similar rules. Be sure a prototype-form declaration of the static function appears before any calls to the function and before the function's definition.

9.2.4 Prototypes and Calling Conventions

This section is primarily useful to compiler implementors, although it may give other programmers some insight into the rules for function prototypes. One advantage to function prototypes is that they can permit a compiler to generate more efficient calling sequences for some functions.

Example

> For example, under traditional C rules, even if a function were defined to take a parameter of type **float**, the compiler had no choice but convert argument to type **double**, call the function, convert the argument back to **float** inside the function, and store it in the parameter. In Standard C, if the compiler sees a function call governed by the prototype
>
> ```
> extern int f(float);
> ```
>
> then the compiler is free to *not* convert the argument to type **double**, assuming it makes the corresponding assumption on the other side when it implements the definition of **f**:
>
> ```
> int f(float x) {…}
> ```

The subtle point here is that the compiler does not have to remain compatible with calls that are not governed by a prototype in this case because no nonprototype declarations (or definition) of **f** could possibly be compatible with the indicated prototype. Hence, Standard C does not define what should happen if a call to **f** is made without the prototype visible. The compiler is free to pass the argument in a register even if the nonprototype convention is to pass all arguments on a stack.

On the other hand, if a prototype declaration *could* be a Miranda prototype for a function declared or defined in the traditional way, then the compiler must use a compatible calling convention.

Example

> A call to a function **g** governed by either of the following declarations would have to be implemented in a compatible way:
>
> ```
> extern short g();
> extern short g(int,double);   /* Could be g's Miranda */
> ```
>
> Stated another way, if a compiler for Standard C sees the function call
>
> ```
> process( a, b, c, d );
> ```
>
> where no prototype is visible and where the types of the actual arguments are
>
> ```
> short a;
> struct {int a,b;} b;
> float *c;
> float d;
> ```

then the function call must be implemented the same as if this prototype were in effect:

```
int process(int, struct {int a,b;}, float *, double);
```

This rule does not actually establish a prototype that might affect later calls. Should a second call on **process** appear later in the program or in another source file, at which time the arguments to **process** are three values of type **double**, then that second call must be implemented as if the prototype were

```
int process( double, double, double );
```

even though the two calls will probably be incompatible at execution time.

To summarize the rules, a compiler is allowed to depend on *all* calls to a function being governed by a prototype only if it sees a call of the function that is governed by a prototype and that prototype

1. includes an argument type that is not compatible with the usual argument conversions (**char**, **short**, their unsigned variants, or **float**), or
2. includes ellipses, indicating a variable argument list.

Since the conversions of **char** and **short** to **int** have minimal cost on most computers, the first rule is useful mainly with arguments of type **float**.

The second rule indicates that the compiler's standard calling convention need not support variable argument lists, as it must in traditional C. For example, a Standard compiler could elect in its standard convention to use registers for the first four (fixed) argument words to any function, with the remainder of the arguments passed on the stack. This convention would probably not be appropriate in traditional C because some functions taking variable arguments depend on all the arguments being passed contiguously on the stack. Any traditional C functions that take a variable number of arguments (e.g., **printf**) must be rewritten to have a prototype before they are compiled by a Standard C implementation.

The storage class **register** is ignored when it appears in a prototype declaration. This means that **register** cannot be used to alter the calling convention of the function; it can only be used as a hint within the function body.

9.2.5 Compatibility With Standard and Traditional C

Standard C is now common enough that prototypes are recommended for all C programs. In the unusual case requiring compatibility with implementations that do not provide prototypes, you can remain compatible with both traditional and Standard C by not using them. However, you will give up the additional type checking when using a Standard C compiler. Here is a way around the problem using a macro **PARMS**:

```
#ifdef __STDC__
#define PARMS(x) x
#else
#define PARMS(x) ()
#endif
```

Then instead of the prototype declaration

```
extern int f(int a, double b, char c);
```

write this declaration (note the doubled parentheses):

```
extern int f PARMS((int a, double b, char c));
```

When compiled by a traditional implementation, the preprocessor expands this line to

```
extern int f ();
```

But a Standard C implementation expands it to:

```
extern int f (int a, double b, char c);
```

The **PARMS** macro does not work correctly in function definitions, so you must write the corresponding function definitions using the traditional syntax, which is also accepted by Standard C:

```
int f(a, b, c)
    int a; double b; long c;
{
    ...
}
```

A traditional definition in Standard C does not cause a problem as long as a prototype declaration for the function appears earlier in the source file.

References   __STDC__ predefined macro 3.3. 4

9.3 FORMAL PARAMETER DECLARATIONS

In function definitions, formal parameters are declared either in the prototype syntax or in the traditional syntax.

The only storage class specifier that may be present in a parameter declaration is **register**, which is a hint to the compiler that the parameter will be used heavily and might better be stored in a register after the function has begun executing. The normal restrictions as to what types of parameters may be marked register apply (see Section 4.3).

In Standard C, formal parameters have the same scope as identifiers declared at the top level of the function body, and therefore they cannot be hidden or redeclared by declarations in the body. Some current C implementations allow such a redeclaration, which is almost invariably a programming error.

Example

In the following function definition, the declaration **double x;** would be an error if compiled by a Standard-conforming compiler. However, some non-Standard compilers permit it, and thereby make the parameter **x** inaccessible within the function body.

```
int f(x)
    int x;
{
    double x;  /* hides parameter!? */
    ...
}
```

In Standard C, a parameter may be declared to be of any type except **void**. However, if a parameter is declared to have a type "function returning T" it is implicitly rewritten to have type "pointer to function returning T," and if a parameter is declared to have type "array of T" it is rewritten to have type "pointer to T." The array type in the parameter declaration can be incomplete. These adjustments are made regardless of whether a prototype or traditional definition is used and parallel the default argument conversions at the call site (Section 6.3.5). The programmer need not be aware of this change of parameter types in most cases since the parameters can be used within the function as if they had the declared type.

Example

Suppose the function **FUNC** were defined as

```
void FUNC(int f(void), int (*g)(void), int h[], int *j)
{
    int i;
    i = f();   /* OK */
    i = g();   /* OK */
    i = h[3];  /* OK */
    i = j[3];  /* OK */
    ...
}
```

Suppose moreover that the following call were made to **FUNC**:

```
extern int a(void), b[20];
...
FUNC( a, a, b, b );
```

Within **FUNC** the expression **f** would be equivalent to **g**, and **h** would be equivalent to **j**.

Some pre-Standard implementations reject declarations of parameters of type "function returning T," requiring instead that they be explicitly declared as "pointer to function returning T."

C99 extends the syntax for declaring formal array parameters. An *array-qualifier-list* may appear within the top-level brackets ([]) of the array declarator. The array qualifiers (type qualifiers) **const**, **volatile**, and **restrict** support the equivalence of array and pointer types. That is, parameter declarations of the form

```
T A[qualifier-list e]
```

are treated as equivalent to

```
T * qualifier-list A
```

Example

Given these C99 declarations

```
extern int f(int x[const 10]);
extern int g(const y[10]);
```

Then in function **f** the parameter **x** is treated as if it had type **int * const** (a constant pointer to **int**), whereas in **g** the parameter **y** is treated as if it had type **const int *** (a pointer to a constant **int**).

The **static** array qualifier is also permitted within array brackets in C99. It is an optimization hint to the C implementation, asserting that the actual array argument will be non-null and will have the declared size and type upon entry to the function. Without this qualifier, a null pointer could be passed as the actual argument for an array parameter, which makes it difficult for an implementation to know that it is safe, for example, to prefetch the contents of an input parameter array upon entry to the function.

Finally, for a C99 formal array parameter declaration in a prototype (not part of a function definition), the size may be replaced by an asterisk, signifying that the actual argument will be a variable-length array. Any nonconstant expression as the array size in a prototype declaration is treated the same as the asterisk. The function definition must supply a nonconstant expression for the size.

A formal parameter is treated just like a local variable of the specified (or rewritten) type into which is copied the value of the corresponding argument passed to the function. The parameter can be assigned to, but the assignment only changes the local argument value, not the argument in the calling function. Parameter names declared to have function or array types are lvalues due to the rewriting rules, even though identifiers with those types are not normally lvalues.

It is permissible in traditional C implementations to include **typedef**, structure, union, or enumeration type declarations in the parameter declaration section. In Standard C, the only names that can be defined in the parameter declaration section are the formal parameter names, and all of them must be defined. (Prior to C99, definitions of parameters of type **int** were optional.) If parameters are declared using the prototype syntax, then the parameter declaration section must be empty.

Example

```
int process_record(r)
    struct { int a; int b; } *r; /* not Standard C */
{
    ...
}
```

It is generally bad programming style to do this in traditional C. If the declarations involve the parameters, the declarations should be moved outside the function where the caller can also use them. If the declarations do not involve the parameters, they should be moved into the function body.

References *array-qualifier-list* 4.5.3 ; enumeration types 5.5; function declarator 4.5.4; function prototype 9.2; incomplete types 5.4; register storage class 4.3; storage class specifiers 4.3; structure types 5.6; **typedef** 5.10; union types 5.7; variable length array 5.4.5; **void** type 5.9

9.4 ADJUSTMENTS TO PARAMETER TYPES

This section applies only when function prototypes are not used in Standard and traditional C. Without a prototype, certain conversions (promotions) of the values of function arguments must be made. These conversions, which are designed to simplify and regularize function arguments, are called the usual argument conversions (or promotions) and are listed in Section 6.3.5. Expecting these argument conversions by the caller, C functions arrange for the promoted argument values to be converted to the declared parameter types before the function body is executed. For example, if a function **F** were declared to take a parameter, **x**, of type **short**, and a call to **F** specified a value of type **short**, then the call would be implemented as if the following sequence of events occurred:

1. The caller widens the argument of type **short** to become a value of type **int**.
2. The value of type **int** is passed to **F**.
3. **F** narrows the **int** value to type **short**.
4. **F** stores the value of type **short** in the parameter **x**.

Fortunately, the conversions that occur have little, if any, overhead—at least for integers. The argument types affected by the conversions include **char**, **short**, **unsigned char**, **unsigned short**, and **float**.

Example

Programmers should be aware that some pre-Standard compilers fail to perform the required narrowing operations on entry to a function. Consider the following function, which has a parameter of type **char**:

```
int pass_through(c)
    char c;
{
    return c;
}
```

Some compilers will implement this function as if it were defined with an **int** parameter:

```
int pass_through(c)
    int c;
{
    return c;
}
```

A consequence of this incorrect implementation is that the argument value is not narrowed to type **char**. That is, **pass_through(0x1001)** would return the value **0x1001** instead of **1**. The correct implementation of the function would resemble this:

```
int pass_through(anonymous)
    int anonymous;
{
    char c = anonymous;
    return c;
}
```

References   array types 5.4; floating-point types 5.2; function argument conversions 6.3.5; function definition 9.1; function prototypes 9.2; function types 5.8; integer types 5.1; lvalue 7.1; pointer types 5.3

9.5 PARAMETER-PASSING CONVENTIONS

C provides only call-by-value parameter passing. This means that the values of the actual parameters are conceptually copied into a storage area local to the called function. It is possible to use a formal parameter name as the left side of an assignment, for instance, but in that case only the local copy of the parameter is altered. If the programmer wants the called function to alter its actual parameters, the addresses of the parameters must be passed explicitly.

Example

Function **swap** below will not work correctly because **x** and **y** are passed by value:

```
void swap(x, y)
/* swap: exchange the values of x and y */
/* Incorrect version! */
    int x, y;
{
    int temp;
    temp = x; x = y; y = temp;
}
...
swap(a, b); /* Fails to swap a and b. */
```

A correct implementation of the function requires that addresses of the arguments be passed:

```
void swap(x, y)
/* swap - exchange the values of *x and *y */
/* Correct version */
    int *x, *y;
{
    int temp;
    temp = *x; *x = *y; *y = temp;
}
...
swap(&a, &b); /* Swaps contents of a and b. */
```

The local storage area for parameters is usually implemented on a pushdown stack. However, the order of pushing parameters on the stack is not specified by the language, nor does the language prevent the compiler from passing parameters in registers. It is valid to apply the address operator **&** to a formal parameter name (unless it was declared with storage class **register**), thereby implying that the parameter in question would have to be in addressable storage when the address was taken. (Note that the address of a formal parameter is the address of the copy of the actual parameter, not the address of the actual parameter.)

When writing functions that take a variable number of arguments, programmers should use the **varargs** or **stdarg** facilities for maximum portability.

> **References**   address operator **&** 7.5.6; function prototype 9.2; **register** storage class 4.3; **stdarg** facility 11.4; **varargs** facility 11.4.1

9.6 AGREEMENT OF PARAMETERS

Most modern programming languages such as Pascal and Ada check the agreement of formal and actual parameters to functions—that is, both the number of arguments and the types of the individual arguments must agree. This checking is also performed in Standard C when a function is declared with a prototype.

Example

In the following example, the call to the function **sqrt** is not governed by a prototype; therefore, the C compiler is not required to warn the programmer that the actual parameter to **sqrt** is of type **long**, whereas the formal parameter is declared to have type **double**. (In fact, if the call and definition were in different source files, then the compiler would be unable to do so.) The function will simply return an incorrect value:

```
double sqrt( x )      /* not a prototype */
    double x;
{
    ...
}
```

```
long hypotenuse(x,y)
    long x,y;
{
    return sqrt(x*x + y*y);
}
```

When a call is governed by a prototype in Standard C, the actual arguments are converted to the corresponding formal parameter type. Only if this conversion is impossible, or if the number of arguments does not agree with the number of formal parameters, will the C compiler reject the program.

Example

By adding a prototype to the definition of **sqrt** above, the example will work correctly: The **long** argument will be converted to **double** without the programmer's knowledge:

```
double sqrt( double x )      /* prototype */
{
    ...
}

long hypotenuse(x,y)
    long x,y;
{
    return sqrt(x*x + y*y);
}
```

As a matter of good style, we recommend using explicit casts to convert arguments to the expected parameter type unless that conversion is just duplicating the usual argument conversions. That is, we would write the return statement in the example above like this:

```
return  sqrt( (double) (x*x + y*y) );
```

Some C functions, such as **fprintf**, are written to take arguments that vary in number and type. In traditional C, the **varargs** library facility has evolved to provide a fairly reliable way of writing such functions, although the usage is not portable since different implementations have slightly different forms of **varargs**. In Standard C a similar library mechanism, **stdarg**, was created to provide portability and reliability. Functions using **stdarg** must be declared with a prototype that uses the ellipsis notation, "**, ...**", before any call, thus giving the compiler an opportunity to prepare a suitable calling mechanism.

References   conversion of actual parameters 9.4; function argument conversions 6.3.5; function prototypes 9.2; **fprintf** 15.11

9.7 FUNCTION RETURN TYPES

A function may be defined to return a value of any type except "array of T" or "function returning T." These two cases must be handled by returning pointers to the array or function. There is no automatic rewriting of the return type as there is for formal parameters.

The value returned by the function is specified by an expression in the **return** statement that causes the function to terminate. The rules governing the expression are discussed in Section 9.8.

The value returned by a function is not an lvalue (the return is "by value"), and therefore a function call cannot appear as the outermost expression on the left side of an assignment operator.

Example

```
f() = x;    /* Invalid */
*f() = x;   /* OK if f returns a pointer of suitable type */
f().a = x;  /* Invalid--not an lvalue ( Section 7.4.2) */
```

References   array types 5.4; function calls 7.4.3; function parameters 9.4; function types 5.8; lvalue 7.1; pointer types 5.3; **void** type 5.9

9.8 AGREEMENT OF RETURN TYPES

If a function has a declared return type T that is not **void**, then the type of any expression appearing in a **return** statement must be convertible to type T by assignment, and that conversion in fact happens on return in both Standard and traditional C.

Example

In a function with declared return type **int**, the statement

```
return 23.1;
```

is equivalent to

```
return (int) 23.1;
```

which is the same as

```
return 23;
```

If a function has a declared return type of **void**, it is an error to supply an expression in any **return** statement in the function. It is also an error to call the function in a context that requires a value. With older compilers that do not implement **void**, it is the custom to omit the type specifier on those functions that return no value:

```
process_something()       /* probably returns nothing */
{
    ...
}
```

It is also possible to define your own **void** type to improve readability (Section 4.4.1).

If a function has a non-**void** return type, C89 permits a **return** statement with no expression—that is, simply "**return;**". (C99 prohibits such a **return**, as does C++.) This rule is to provide backward compatibility with compilers that do not implement

void. When a function has a non-**void** return type and a **return** statement with no arguments is executed, then the value actually returned is undefined. It is therefore unwise to call the function in a context that requires a value.

References   adjustments to formal parameters 9.4; default type specifiers 4.4.1; lvalue 7.1; **return** statement 8.9; **void** type 5.9

9.9 THE MAIN PROGRAM

All C programs must define a single external function named **main**. That function will become the entry point of the program—that is, the first function executed when the program is started. Returning from this function terminates the program, and the returned value is treated as an indication of program success or failure, as if it had been used in a call to the library function **exit**. If the end of the body of **main** is reached without returning, it is treated as if **return 0;** were executed.

Standard C permits **main** to be defined with either zero or two parameters:

```
int main(void) { ... }
int main() { ... } /* also OK, but not recommended */
int main( int argc, char *argv[] ) { ... }
```

When no parameters are declared, no arguments are available to the main program from the environment, although library functions such as **getenv** or **system** may be used to obtain other information from the environment.

Prior to C99, the return type of **main** was often omitted, defaulting to **int**. This is no longer allowed.

When arguments are declared, those arguments are set up by the execution environment and are not directly under control of the C programmer. The parameter **argc** is the count of the number of "program arguments" or "options" supplied to the program when it was invoked by a user or another program. The parameter **argv** is a vector of pointers to strings representing the program arguments. The first string, **argv[0]**, is the name of the program; if the name is not available, **argv[0][0]** must be **'\0'**. The string **argv**[i], for $i=1, \ldots,$ **argc**-1, is the ith program argument. Standard C requires that **argv[argc]** be a null pointer, but it is not so in some older implementations. The vector **argv** and the strings to which it points must be modifiable, and their values must not be changed by the implementation or host system during program execution. If the implementation does not support mixed-case strings, then the strings stored in **argv** must be in lower case.

Freestanding C environments and certain software frameworks (e.g., Microsoft Windows MFC) may have special conventions for how C programs are started.

Example

The following short program prints out its name and arguments.

```
#include <stdio.h>
int main(int argc, char *argv[])
{
    int i;
    printf("Name: %s\n", argv[0]);
    printf("Arguments: ");
    for( i=1; i<argc; i++)
        printf("%s ", argv[i]);
    printf("\n");
    return 0;
}
```

Some implementations permit a third argument to **main**, **char * envp[]**, which points to a null-terminated vector of "environment values," each one a pointer to a null-terminated string of the form **"name=value"**. When the environment pointer is not a parameter to **main**, it might be found in a global variable. Some UNIX implementations use the global variable **environ** to hold the environment pointer. However, it is more portable to use the Standard C facility **getenv** to access the environment.

Example

Assuming **envp** holds the environment pointer, this code prints out the environment contents:

```
for(i=0; envp[i] != NULL; i++)
    printf("%s\n", envp[i]);
```

References   **exit** 16.5; **getenv** 16.6; **system** 16.7

9.10 INLINE FUNCTIONS

Inline functions are new to C99 and are designated by the appearance of the function specifier **inline** on a function declaration or definition. The **inline** designation is only a hint to the translator, suggesting that calls to the inline function should be as fast as possible. The name comes from a compiler optimization called *inline expansion*, whereby a call to a function is replaced by a copy of the function's body. This eliminates the overhead of the function call. Many C translators prior to C99 had extended C to provide inline functions, and C++ provides them as well. There are three important principles for inline expansion:

1. *Visible definition.* To expand a function call inline, the translator must know the definition of the function when the call is translated. In C99, if a function is declared **inline**, then the function's definition must be visible in that translation unit.

2. *Free choice.* Translators are never obligated to perform inline expansion. If there are four calls to an inline function, it is perfectly all right to expand two of the calls inline and generate two normal function calls for the other two. A C program must never depend on whether a call is expanded.

3. *Same meaning*. Whenever a translator expands one or more calls inline, it must ensure that the program behaves as if the function had been called normally. Inline expansion is only an optimization; it does not change the meaning of the program.

Any static function can be designated `inline` because all the calls and the definition are limited to a single translation unit.

External functions are another matter because in the usual case the call is in one unit and the definition is in another unit. Since the definition must be visible where any inline declaration is visible, it would seem that an inline declaration of an external function could only appear in the translation unit that defined the function. What we would like is a way to give other translation units a "peek" at the definition of the external function, just in case the translator would like to expand calls to the external function in those units.

The "peek" is called an *inline definition*. If *all* the top-level declarations of a function in a translation unit include `inline` and do not include `extern`, then the definition of that function in that unit is called an inline definition. (It follows that there must be such a definition, and it must be `inline` and not `extern`.) An inline definition does not provide an external definition for the function; another external definition must be provided in some other translation unit. Rather, the internal definition is an alternative to making an external call, and the translator can use the alternative to perform inline expansion. If the translator chooses not to use the alternative, then it just generates a normal function call, treating the inline definition as a normal `extern` declaration. If all the inline definitions and the single external definition of a function are not equivalent, then the program's behavior is undefined. One way to use inline definitions is to alter a header file to replace the declaration of a function with an inline definition.

Example

The function `square` returns the square of its argument. The header file `square.h` provides an inline definition for any translation unit that includes it. The inline definition also serves as a declaration of the external function if the translator chooses not to expand a call or needs to take the address of the function. A translation unit named `square.c` includes the inline definition, but also supplies an `extern` declaration; this makes the definition in `square.h` become the external function definition.

```
// File: square.h
// Inline definition:
inline double square(double x) { return x*x; }

// File square.c
#include "square.h"
// Force an external definition using the inline code
extern inline square(double x);
```

Standard library headers in general cannot make use of `inline` definitions of the standard functions because programs are permitted to redeclare those functions (macros) in some circumstances. However, implementations are always free to use their own, nonportable mechanisms to inline or treat specially in some other fashion standard library facilities.

Problems can arise if an external inline function includes the definition of a static object. There is no easy way to link the static object appearing in an inline definition with the static object appearing in the external definition in another unit. Therefore, C99 prohibits any (nonstatic) inline function from defining a modifiable static object and from containing a reference to an identifier with internal linkage. Constant static objects can be defined, but each inline definition may create its own object.

References   `inline` function specifier 4.3.3

9.11 C++ COMPATIBILITY

9.11.1 Prototypes

To be compatible with C++, all functions must be declared with prototypes. In fact, the nonprototype form has a different meaning in C++—an empty parameter list signifies a function that takes no parameters in C++, whereas it signifies a function that takes an unknown number of parameters in C.

Example

```
int f(); /* Means int f(void) in C++, int f(...) in C */
int g(void); /* Means the same in both C and C++ */
...
x = f(2);    /* valid in C, not in C++ */
```

9.11.2 Type Declarations in Parameter and Return Types

Do not place type declarations in parameter lists or return type declarations; they are not permitted in C++.

Example

```
struct s { ... } f1(int i); /* OK in C, not in C++ */
void f2(enum e{...} x); /* OK in C, not in C++ */
```

9.11.3 Agreement of Return Types

In C++ and C99, you must return a value of appropriate type from a function that has a non-**void** return type. C89 permits not returning a value for backward compatibility.

Example

```
int f(void)
{
    ...
    return ; /* Valid but unpredictable in C;
                invalid in C++ */
}
```

References   agreement of return types 9.8

9.11.4 Main

In C++, the **main** function must not be called recursively, nor can its address be taken. C++ imposes more restrictions on program start-up, so implementations may handle **main** as a special case. If you need to manipulate the **main** function, simply create a second function, call it from **main**, and use it in place of **main** in your program.

In C++, if control reaches the end of **main**, then it is as if an implicit **return 0;** were executed. In C, prior to C99, the return value would be undefined. In C99 and in all C++ functions except **main**, it is illegal to omit the return statement in nonvoid functions.

9.11.5 Inline

The C99 rules for inline definitions of functions are less strict than those for C++, which requires all inline definitions and the external definition to be "exactly" the same and not merely equivalent. C99 permits inline definitions in some translation units to be specialized and puts the responsibility for equivalence on the programmer. C++ also requires an inline function to be declared inline in all translation units, which C99 does not. For portability, you have to follow the stricter C++ rules.

9.12 EXERCISES

1. Which of the following declarations serve as Standard C prototypes?

    (a) **short f(void);**   (d) **int f(i,j);**
    (b) **int f();**   (e) **int *f(float);**
    (c) **double f(...);**   (f) **int f(i) int i; {…}**

2. Declarations and definitions of functions are shown next. Which pairs are compatible in Standard C?

Declaration	*Definition*
(a) **extern int f(short x);**	**int f(x) short x; {…}**
(b) **extern int f();**	**int f(short x) {…}**
(c) **extern f(short x);**	**int f(short int y) {…}**
(d) **extern void f(int x);**	**void f(int x,...) {…}**
(e) **extern f();**	**int f(x,y) short x,y; {…}**
(f) **extern f();**	**f(void) {…}**

3. Declarations and invocations of functions are shown next. In each case, indicate whether the invocation is valid in Standard C and, if so, what conversions will be applied to each actual parameter. Assume **s** has type **short** and **ld** has type **long double**.

Declaration	*Invocation*
(a) **extern int f(int *x);**	**f(&s)**
(b) **extern int f();**	**f(s,ld)**
(c) **extern f(short x);**	**f(ld)**
(d) **extern void f(short,...);**	**f(s,s,ld)**
(e) **int f(x) short x; {…}**	**f(s)**
(f) **int f(x) short x; {…};**	**f(ld)**

4. In the following program fragment, is the invocation of **P** governed by a prototype? Why?

```
extern void P(void);
...
int Q()
{
    extern P();
    P();
    ...
}
```

5. If the declared return type of a function is **short**, which of the following types of expressions appearing in a **return** statement would be allowable and would produce a predictable value at the call site?
    (a) **int**
    (b) **long double**
    (c) **void** (e.g., the invocation of a function returning **void**)
    (d) **char ***

6. Explain the ways in which this macro definition of **square** differs from the inline version in Section 9.10:

```
#define square(x)  ((x)*(x))
```

PART 2
The C Libraries

10

Introduction to the Libraries

Standard C comprises both a language standard and a set of standard libraries. These libraries support characters and strings, input and output, mathematical functions, date and time conversions, dynamic storage allocation, and other features. The facilities (types, macros, functions) in each library are defined by standard header files; to use a library's facilities, add a preprocessor `#include` command that references the header for that library.

Example

> In the following program fragment, the header file **math.h** gives the program access to the cosine function, **cos**.
>
> ```
> #include <math.h>
> double x, y;
> ...
> x = cos(y);
> ```

Some implementations of traditional C do not use header files for all library functions, so some must be declared by the programmer.

For those library facilities that are defined as functions, Standard C permits implementations to provide a function-like macro of the same name in addition to the true function. The macro might provide a faster implementation of a simple function or it might call a function of a different name. The macro will take care to evaluate each argument expression exactly once, just as a function would. If you truly need to access the function, regardless whether a macro exists, you must bypass the macro as shown in the following example.

Example

Suppose you were worried that there was a macro shadowing **cos** in **math.h**. Here are two ways to reference the underlying function. Both depend on there not being an opening parenthesis immediately after the possible macro name; this prevents any function-like macro named **cos** from expanding.

```
#include <math.h>
double a, b, (*p) (double);

...
p= &cos; a = (*p) (b); /* calls function cos, always */
a = (cos) (b);              /* calls function cos, always */
```

Alternatively, you can simply remove any shadowing macro:

```
#include <math.h>
#undef cos

...
a = cos(b);                 /* calls function cos, always */
```

References   **#include** 3.4; macros with parameters 3.3.2; **#undef** 3.3.5

10.1 STANDARD C FACILITIES

Section 10.3 summarizes the standard library facilities by listing for each library header the names defined in the header and the chapter or section in this book that describes the facilities. If you are looking for a particular library facility name and do not know which header it is in, then look up the name in the index at the back of the book.

In the individual chapters and sections, each facility is described in its Standard C form. Except where noted in the text, the traditional C library function definitions may be obtained from the Standard C definitions by rewriting them as follows.

1. Eliminate any functions that use Standard C types such as **long long** or **_Complex**, or which are identified as new in Standard C (C89 or C99).
2. Drop qualifiers **const**, **restrict**, and **volatile**. Drop **static** when used inside array declarator brackets.
3. Change type **void *** to **char ***. Change type **size_t** to **int**.

Library facilities and header files in Standard C are special in many ways mostly to protect the integrity of implementations:

1. Library names are in principle reserved. Programmers may not define external objects whose names duplicate the names of the standard library.
2. Library header files or file names may be "built in" to the implementation, although they still must be included for their names to become visible. That is, **stdio.h** might not actually correspond to a **#include** file named "**stdio.h**."
3. Programmers may include library header files in any order any number of times. (This may not be true in traditional C implementations.)

Example

Here is a typical way that library headers ensure that they are not included multiple times:

```
/* Header stddef.h */
#ifndef _STDDEF            /* Don't try to redeclare */
#define _STDDEF 1
typedef int ptrdiff_t;
… /* other definitions */
#endif
```

10.1.1 Reserved Library Identifiers

Standard C reserves certain identifiers for its own use in current and future versions of C. The rules are complicated, but here is a safe superset of them.

Programmers and C implementors should avoid identifiers reserved for the language and libraries: C keywords; identifiers used in any of the present libraries; identifiers beginning with **is**, **to**, **str**, **mem**, or **wcs** and a lowercase letter; identifiers beginning with **PRI** or **SCN** and either a lowercase letter or **X**; identifiers beginning **LC_**, **SIG**, or **SIG_** and an uppercase letter; identifiers beginning **int** or **uint** and ending with **_t**; identifiers beginning **INT** or **UINT** and ending with **_MAX**, **_MIN**, or **_C**; identifiers beginning with **E** and either a digit or an uppercase letter; identifiers **cerf**, **cerfc**, **cexp2**, **cexpm1**, **clog10**, **clog1p**, **clog2**, **clgamma**, and **ctgamma**, optionally suffixed by **f** or **l** (ell); identifiers beginning **__STDC_**; lowercase letters as I/O conversion specifiers or as character escape sequences; and pragmas whose first preprocessing token is **STDC**.

The identifiers that are reserved for C implementations to use include: for local or file scope variables, identifiers beginning with _; for macros, keywords, or global variables, identifiers beginning with _ and either a second _ or an uppercase letter (except **__STDC_**....); and for I/O conversion specifiers or as character escape sequences, uppercase letters.

C programmers can use any identifier not listed above. To remain maximally compatible with C++, you should also consider avoiding C++ keywords and library facilities.

You cannot write your own replacements for standard library functions. Attempting to replace the **sqrt** function has undefined results. This restriction gives C implementations more freedom in packaging and using internally the standard library functions.

10.2 C++ COMPATIBILITY

The C++ language includes the Standard C run-time library, but adds a number of C++-specific libraries. None of the additional libraries has names ending in ".h," so they are unlikely to conflict with your C libraries.

C++ uses a different convention for calling its functions, which means that, in general, it is not possible to call a C++ function from a C program. However, C++ does provide a way to call C functions from C++. There are two requirements on the declarations of the C functions:

1. The function declarations must use Standard C prototypes. C++ requires prototypes.

2. The external C declarations must be explicitly labeled as having C linkage by including the string **"C"** after the storage class **extern** in the C++ declaration.

Example

If you were calling a C function from another C function, it would be declared as, for example

```
extern int f(void);
```

However, if called from a C++ program, the declaration would have to be

```
extern "C" int f(void);
```

If a group of C functions were to be declared in C++, you can apply the linkage specification to all of them:

```
extern "C" {
    double sqrt(double x);
    int f(void);
    ...
}
```

When writing a header file for a library that might be called from C or C++, you must choose whether to specify the C linkage within the header file or whether you will require C++ programs to supply the linkage declaration in the file that includes the header.

Example

Suppose a header file **library.h** is to be called from C or C++ programs. The first possibility is to include the **extern "C"** declarations inside the header file, conditional on the **__cplusplus** macro, which indicates that this is a C++ program.

```
/* File library.h */
#ifdef __cplusplus
extern "C" {
#endif

...
/* C declarations */
...
#ifdef __cplusplus
}
#endif
```

The second alternative is to write the header file using normal C declarations and simply require that C++ users wrap the linkage declaration around the **#include** command:

```
extern "C" {
#include "library.h"
}
```

The second alternative in the previous example must be used when calling libraries that were written before C++ became a consideration. There is no harm in nesting the **extern "C" { }** declarations.

References   __cplusplus macro 3.9.1

10.3 LIBRARY HEADERS AND NAMES

10.3.1 assert.h

See Chapter 19.

```
assert                  NDEBUG
```

10.3.2 complex.h

See Chapter 23. This header file was added in C99.

```
cabs          catan         clog          csinf
cabsf         catanf        clogf         csinh
cabsl         catanh        clogl         csinhf
cacos         catanhf       complex       csinhl
cacosf        catanhl       _Complex_I    csinl
cacosh        catanl        conj          csqrt
cacoshf       ccos          conjf         csqrtf
cacoshl       ccosf         conjl         csqrtl
cacosl        ccosh         cpow          ctan
carg          ccoshf        cpowf         ctanf
cargf         ccoshl        cpowl         ctanh
cargl         ccosl         cproj         ctanhf
casin         cexp          cprojf        ctanhl
casinf        cexpf         cprojl        ctanl
casinh        cexpl         creal         CX_LIMITED_RANGE
casinhf       cimag         crealf        I
casinhl       cimagf        creall        imaginary
casinl        cimagl        csin          _Imaginary_I
```

10.3.3 ctype.h

See Chapter 12.

```
isalnum            isgraph            isupper
isalpha            islower            isxdigit
isblank            isprint            tolower
iscntrl            ispunct            toupper
isdigit            isspace
```

10.3.4 errno.h

See Chapter 11.

```
EDOM               ERANGE
EILSEQ             errno
```

10.3.5 fenv.h

See Chapter 22. This header file was added in C99.

FE_ALL_EXCEPT	FE_TONEAREST	fegetround	fesetround
FE_DFL_ENV	FE_TOWARDZERO	feholdexcept	fetestexcept
FE_DIVBYZERO	FE_UNDERFLOW	FENV_ACCESS	feupdateenv
FE_DOWNWARD	FE_UPWARD	fenv_t	fexcept_t
FE_INEXACT	feclearexcept	feraiseexcept	
FE_INVALID	fegetenv	fesetenv	
FE_OVERFLOW	fegetexceptflag	fesetexceptflag	

10.3.6 float.h

See Table 5–3.

DBL_DIG	DBL_MIN_EXP	FLT_MAX_EXP	LDBL_MANT_DIG
DBL_EPSILON	DECIMAL_DIG	FLT_MIN	LDBL_MAX
DBL_MANT_DIG	FLT_DIG	FLT_MIN_10_EXP	LDBL_MAX_10_EXP
DBL_MAX	FLT_EPSILON	FLT_MIN_EXP	LDBL_MAX_EXP
DBL_MAX_10_EXP	FLT_EVAL_METHOD	FLT_RADIX	LDBL_MIN
DBL_MAX_EXP	FLT_MANT_DIG	FLT_ROUNDS	LDBL_MIN_10_EXP
DBL_MIN	FLT_MAX	LDBL_DIG	LDBL_MIN_EXP
DBL_MIN_10_EXP	FLT_MAX_10_EXP	LDBL_EPSILON	

10.3.7 inttypes.h

See Chapter 21. This header file was added in C99.

CNiLEASTN	PRIoMAX	PRIxPTR	SCNuFASTN
imaxabs	PRIoN	PRIXPTR	SCNuLEASTN
imaxdiv	PRIoPTR	SCNdFASTN	SCNuMAX
imaxdiv_t	PRIuFASTN	SCNdLEASTN	SCNuN
PRIdFASTN	PRIuLEASTN	SCNdMAX	SCNuPTR
PRIdLEASTN	PRIuMAX	SCNdN	SCNxFASTN
PRIdMAX	PRIuN	SCNdPTR	SCNxLEASTN
PRIdN	PRIuPTR	SCNiFASTN	SCNxMAX
PRIdPTR	PRIxFASTN	SCNiMAX	SCNxN
PRIiFASTN	PRIXFASTN	SCNiN	SCNxPTR
PRIiLEASTN	PRIxLEASTN	SCNiPTR	strtoimax
PRIiMAX	PRIXLEASTN	SCNoFASTN	strtoumax
PRIiN	PRIxMAX	SCNoLEASTN	wcstoimax
PRIiPTR	PRIXMAX	SCNoMAX	wcstoumax
PRIoFASTN	PRIxN	SCNoN	
PRIoLEASTN	PRIXN	SCNoPTR	

10.3.8 iso646.h

See Section 11.5. This header file was added in Amendment 1 to C89.

and	bitor	not_eq	xor
and_eq	compl	or	xor_eq
bitand	not	or_eq	

10.3.9 limits.h

See Table 5–2.

CHAR_BIT	LLONG_MAX	SCHAR_MAX	UINT_MAX
CHAR_MAX	LLONG_MIN	SCHAR_MIN	ULLONG_MAX
CHAR_MIN	LONG_MAX	SHRT_MAX	ULONG_MAX
INT_MAX	LONG_MIN	SHRT_MIN	USHRT_MAX
INT_MIN	MB_LEN_MAX	UCHAR_MAX	

10.3.10 locale.h

See Chapter 20.

LC_ALL	LC_MONETARY	lconv	setlocale
LC_COLLATE	LC_NUMERIC	localeconv	
LC_CTYPE	LC_TIME	NULL	

10.3.11 math.h

See Chapter 17.

acos	coshl	fmin	isinf
acosf	cosl	fminf	isless
acosh	double_t	fminl	islessequal
acoshf	erf	fmod	islessgreater
acoshl	erfc	fmodf	isnan
acosl	erfcf	fmodl	isnormal
asin	erfcl	FP_CONTRACT	isunorderedldex
asinf	erff	FP_FAST_FMA	p
asinh	erfl	FP_FAST_FMAF	ldexpf
asinhf	exp	FP_FAST_FMAL	ldexpl
asinhl	exp2	FP_ILOGB0	lgamma
asinl	exp2f	FP_ILOGBNAN	lgammaf
atan	exp2l	FP_INFINITE	lgammal
atan2	expf	FP_NAN	llrint
atan2f	expl	FP_NORMAL	llrintf
atan2l	expm1	FP_SUBNORMAL	llrintl
atanf	expm1f	FP_ZERO	llround
atanh	expm1l	fpclassify	llroundf
atanhf	fabs	frexp	llroundllog
atanhl	fabsf	frexpf	log10
atanl	fabsl	frexpl	log10f
cbrt	fdim	HUGE_VAL	log10l
cbrtf	fdimf	HUGE_VALF	log1p
cbrtl	fdiml	HUGE_VALL	log1pf
ceil	float_t	hypot	log1pl
ceilf	floor	hypotf	log2
ceill	floorf	hypotl	log2f
copysign	floorl	ilogb	log2l
copysignf	fma	ilogbf	logb
copysignl	fmaf	ilogbl	logbf
cos	fmal	INFINITY	logbl
cosf	fmax	isfinite	
cosh	fmaxf	isgreater	
coshf	fmaxl	isgreaterequal	

`math.h` continued.

logf	nanl	remquol	sinhl
logl	nearbyint	rint	sinl
lrint	nearbyintf	rintf	sqrt
lrintf	nearbyintl	rintl	sqrtf
lrintl	nextafter	round	sqrtl
lround	nextafterf	roundf	tan
lroundf	nextafterl	roundl	tanf
lroundl	nexttoward	scalbln	tanh
MATH_ERREXCEPT	nexttowardf	scalblnf	tanhf
math_	nexttowardl	scalblnl	tanhl
errhandling	pow	scalbn	tanl
MATH_ERRNO	powf	scalbnf	tgamma
modf	powl	scalbnl	tgammaf
modff	remainder	signbit	tgammal
modfl	remainderf	sin	trunc
NAN	remainderl	sinf	truncf
nan	remquo	sinh	truncl
nanf	remquof	sinhf	

10.3.12 setjmp.h

See Section 19.4.

```
jmp_buf              longjmp              setjmp
```

10.3.13 signal.h

See Section 19.6.

```
raise                SIG_ERR              SIGFPE               signal
sig_atomic_t         SIG_IGN              SIGILL               SIGSEGV
SIG_DFL              SIGABRT              SIGINT               SIGTERM
```

10.3.14 stdarg.h

See Section 11.4.

```
va_arg               va_end               va_start
va_copy              va_list
```

10.3.15 stdbool.h

See Section 11.3.

```
bool                              false
__bool_true_false_are_defined     true
```

10.3.16 stddef.h

See Section 11.1.

```
NULL                 ptrdiff_t            wchar_t
offsetof             size_t
```

10.3.17 stdint.h

See Chapter 21. This header file was added in C99.

INT_FASTN_MAX	INTN_C	SIG_ATOMIC_MIN	UINTN_MAX
INT_FASTN_MIN	INTN_MAX	SIZE_MAX	uintN_t
int_fastN_t	INTN_MIN	UINT_FASTN_MAX	UINTPTR_MAX
INT_LEASTN_MAX	intN_t	uint_fastN_t	uintptr_t
INT_LEASTN_MIN	INTPTR_MAX	UINT_LEASTN_MAX	WCHAR_MAX
int_leastN_t	INTPTR_MIN	uint_leastN_t	WCHAR_MIN
INTMAX_C	intptr_t	UINTMAX_C	WINT_MAX
INTMAX_MAX	PTRDIFF_MAX	UINTMAX_MAX	WINT_MIN
INTMAX_MIN	PTRDIFF_MIN	uintmax_t	
intmax_t	SIG_ATOMIC_MAX	UINTN_C	

10.3.18 stdio.h

See Chapter 15.

BUFSIZ	fputs	printf	stderr
clearerr	fread	putc	stdin
EOF	freopen	putchar	stdout
fclose	fscanf	puts	TMP_MAX
feof	fseek	remove	tmpfile
ferror	fsetpos	rename	tmpnam
fflush	ftell	rewind	ungetc
fgetc	fwrite	scanf	vfprintf
fgetpos	getc	SEEK_CUR	vfscanf
fgets	getchar	SEEK_END	vprintf
FILE	gets	SEEK_SET	vscanf
FILENAME_MAX	_IOFBF	setbuf	vsnprintf
fopen	_IOLBF	setvbuf	vsprintf
FOPEN_MAX	_IONBF	size_t	vsscanf
fpos_t	L_tmpnam	snprintf	
fprintf	NULL	sprintf	
fputc	perror	sscanf	

10.3.19 stdlib.h

See Chapter 16.

abort	_Exit	MB_CUR_MAX	strtof
abs	EXIT_FAILURE	mblen	strtol
atexit	EXIT_SUCCESS	mbstowcs	strtold
atof	free	mbtowc	strtoll
atoi	getenv	NULL	strtoul
atol	labs	qsort	strtoull
atoll	ldiv	rand	system
bsearch	ldiv_t	RAND_MAX	wchar_t
calloc	llabs	realloc	wcstombs
div	lldiv	size_t	wctomb
div_t	lldiv_t	srand	
exit	malloc	strtod	

10.3.20 string.h

See Chapter 13.

memchr	size_t	strcspn	strpbrk
memcmp	strcat	strerror	strrchr
memcpy	strchr	strlen	strspn
memmove	strcmp	strncat	strstr
memset	strcoll	strncmp	strtok
NULL	strcpy	strncpy	strxfrm

10.3.21 tgmath.h

See Section 17.12. This header file was added in C99.

acos	cproj	hypot	nexttoward
acosh	creal	ilogb	pow
asin	erf	ldexp	remainder
asinh	erfc	lgamma	remquo
atan	exp	llrint	rint
atan2	exp2	llround	round
atanh	expm1	log	scalbln
carg	fabs	log10	scalbn
cbrt	fdim	log1p	sin
ceil	floor	log2	sinh
cimag	fma	logb	sqrt
conj	fmax	lrint	tan
copysign	fmin	lround	tanh
cos	fmod	nearbyint	tgamma
cosh	frexp	nextafter	trunc

10.3.22 time.h

See Chapter 18.

asctime	ctime	mktime	struct tm
clock	difftime	NULL	time
clock_t	gmtime	size_t	time_t
CLOCKS_PER_SEC	localtime	strftime	

10.3.23 wchar.h

See Chapter 24. This header file was added in Amendment 1 to C89.

btowc	putwchar	wcschr	wcstok
fgetwc	size_t	wcscmp	wcstol
fgetws	swprintf	wcscoll	wcstold
fputwc	swscanf	wcscpy	wcstoll
fputws	tm	wcscspn	wcstoul
fwide	ungetwc	wcsftime	wcstoull
fwprintf	vfwprintf	wcslen	wcsxfrm
fwscanf	vfwscanf	wcsncat	wctob
getwc	vswprintf	wcsncmp	WEOF
getwchar	vswscanf	wcsncpy	wint_t
mbrlen	vwprintf	wcspbrk	wmemchr
mbrtowc	vwscanf	wcsrchr	wmemcmp
mbsinit	WCHAR_MAX	wcsrtombs	wmemcpy
mbsrtowcs	WCHAR_MIN	wcsspn	wmemmove
mbstate_t	wchar_t	wcsstr	wmemset
NULL	wcrtomb	wcstod	wprintf
putwc	wcscat	wcstof	wscanf

10.3.24 wctype.h

See Chapter 24. This header file was added in Amendment 1 to C89.

iswalnum	iswgraph	iswxdigit	wctype
iswalpha	iswlower	towctrans	wctype_t
iswblank	iswprint	towlower	WEOF
iswcntrl	iswpunct	towupper	wint_t
iswctype	iswspace	wctrans	
iswdigit	iswupper	wctrans_t	

11

Standard Language Additions

Certain Standard C libraries can be considered part of the language. They provide standard definitions and parameterization that help make C programs more portable. They must be provided by freestanding implementations even when the other libraries are not provided. These core libraries consist of the header files **float.h**, **iso646.h**, **limits.h**, **stdarg.h**, **stdbool.h**, **stddef.h**, and **stdint.h**. The facilities in **float.h** and **limits.h** were described in Chapter 5. The **stdint.h** library is described in Chapter 21. The other libraries are described in this chapter.

This chapter also describes the facilities in **errno.h**, although that library is not considered to be a language addition. Despite its name, the header file **stdlib.h** is also not considered a language addition; it is described in Chapter 16.

11.1 *NULL, ptrdiff_t, size_t, offsetof*

Synopsis

```
#include <stddef.h>

#define NULL …

typedef ... ptrdiff_t;
typedef ... size_t;
typedef ... wchar_t;

#define offsetof( type, member-designator )…
```

These are the facilities defined in the header file **stddef.h**.

The value of the macro **NULL** is the traditional null pointer constant. Many implementations define it to be simply the integer constant 0 or 0 cast to type **void ***. In Standard C the macro is defined in many different header files for convenience.

Type **ptrdiff_t** is an implementation-defined signed integral type that is the type of the result of subtracting two pointers; most implementations have used **long** for this type. Type **size_t** is the unsigned integral type of the result of the **sizeof** operator; most implementations have used **unsigned long** for this type. Pre-Standard implementations sometimes used the (signed) type **int** for **size_t**. The minimum and maximum values for **ptrdiff_t** and **size_t** are defined in **stdint.h** in C99.

As processors become larger and more powerful, memory sizes are becoming too large for 32-bit pointers. C implementations may use the C99 type **long long** for **ptrdiff_t** and **unsigned long long** for **size_t**. This may cause problems for older C code, which assumes **sizeof(size_t) = sizeof(ptrdiff_t) = sizeof(long)**.

The macro **offsetof** expands to an integral constant expression (of type **size_t**) that is the offset in bytes of member *member-designator* within structure type *type*. If the member is a bit field, the result is unpredictable. If **offsetof** is not defined (in a non-Standard implementation), it is often possible to define it as follows:

```
#define offsetof(type,memb)  ((size_t)&((type *)0)->memb)
```

If the implementation does not permit the use of the null pointer constant in this fashion, it may be possible to compute the offset by using a predefined, non-null pointer and subtracting the member's address from the structure's base address.

Example

At the end of the following program fragment, the value of **diff** will be 1 and the values of **size** and **offset** will be equal. [For a byte-addressed computer on which **sizeof(int)** is 4, **size** and **offset** will both be equal to 4.]

```
#include <stddef.h>
struct s {int a; int b; } x;
size_t size, offset;
ptrdiff_t diff;
...

diff = &x.b - &x.a;
size = sizeof(x.a);
offset = offsetof(struct s,b);
```

Type **wchar_t** is defined in **stddef.h**, but we defer its description to the chapter on the **wchar.h** header file in Chapter 24.

References   conversion of integers to pointers 6.2.7; null pointers 5.3.2; pointer types 5.3; **sizeof** operator 7.5.2; **stdint.h** Ch. 21; subtraction of pointers 7.6.2; **wchar_t** 24.1

11.2 *EDOM, ERANGE, EILSEQ, errno, strerror, perror*

Synopsis

`#include <errno.h>`
`extern int errno;`
or `#define errno ...`
`#define EDOM    ...`
`#define ERANGE ...`
`#define EILSEQ ...`

`#include <stdio.h>` `void perror(const char *s)`
`#include <string.h>` `char *strerror(int errnum)`

These are the facilities defined in **errno.h** and other headers, which support error reporting in the standard libraries.

The external variable **errno** is used to hold implementation-defined error codes from library routines, traditionally defined as macros spelled beginning with **E** in **errno.h**. All error codes are positive integers, and library routines should never clear **errno**. In Standard C, **errno** need not be a variable; it can be a macro that expands to any modifiable lvalue of type **int**.

Example

It would be possible to define **errno** this way:

```
extern int *_errno_func();
#define errno (*_errno_func())
```

Example

The typical way of using **errno** is to clear it before calling a library function and check it afterward:

```
errno = 0;
x = sqrt(y);
if (errno) {
    printf("?sqrt failed, code %d\n", errno);
    x = 0;
}
```

C implementations generally define a standard list of error codes that can be stored in **errno**. The standard codes defined in **errno.h** are

EDOM	An argument was not in the domain accepted by a mathematical function. An example of this is giving a negative argument to the **log** function.
ERANGE	The result of a mathematical function is out of range; the function has a well-defined mathematical result, but cannot be represented because

of the limitations of the floating-point format. An example of this is trying to use the **pow** function to raise a large number to a very large power.

EILSEQ   An encoding error was encountered when translating a multibyte character sequence. This error is ultimately detected by **mbrtowc** or **wcrtomb**, which are in turn called by other wide character functions. (Amendment 1 to C89)

The function **strerror** returns a pointer to an error message string whose contents are implementation-defined; the string is not modifiable and may be overwritten by a subsequent call to the **strerror** function.

The function **perror** prints the following sequence on the standard error output stream: the argument string **s**, a colon, a space, a short message concerning the error whose error code is currently in **errno**, and a newline. In Standard C, if **s** is the null pointer or points to a null character, then only the error message is printed; the prefix string, colon, and space are not printed.

Example

The previous **sqrt** example could be rewritten to use **perror** in this way:

```
#include <math.h>
#include <errno.h>
...
errno = 0;
x = sqrt(y);
if (errno) {
    perror("sqrt failed");
    x = 0;
}
```

If the call to **sqrt** failed, the output might be:

```
sqrt failed: domain error
```

It is not part of the C Standard, but in some systems the error messages corresponding to values of **errno** may be stored in a vector of string pointers, typically called **sys_errlist**, which can be indexed by the value in **errno**. The variable **sys_nerr** contains the maximum integer that can be used to index **sys_errlist**; this should be checked to ensure that **errno** does not contain a nonstandard error number.

References   encoding error 2.1.5; **mbrtowc** 11.7; **wcrtomb** 11.7

11.3 *bool, false, true*

Synopsis

```
#include <stdbool.h>

#define bool _Bool
#define false 0
#define true 1
#define __bool_true_false_are_defined 1
```

The **stdbool.h** header file is new in C99 and contains just the declarations shown previously. These names for the Boolean type and values are consistent with C++.

Although it is normally not allowed to **#undefine** macros defined in the standard header files, C99 does permit the programmer to **#undefine** and, if desired, redefine the macros **bool**, **false**, and **true**.

      References   _Bool type 5.1.5

11.4 *va_list, va_start, va_arg, va_end*

Synopsis

```
#include <stdarg.h>

typedef ... va_list;

#define va_start( a_list ap, type LastFixedParm) ...
#define va_arg( va_list ap, type) ...

void va_end(va_list ap);
void va_copy(va_list dest, va_list src);
```

The **stdarg.h** facility gives programmers a portable way to access variable argument lists, as is needed in functions such as **fprintf** (implicitly) and **vfprintf** (explicitly).

C originally placed no restrictions on the way arguments were passed to functions, and programmers consequently made nonportable assumptions based on the behavior of one computer system. Eventually the **varargs.h** facility arose in traditional C to promote portability, and Standard C adopts a similar facility defined in **stdarg.h**. The usage of **stdarg.h** differs from **varargs.h** because Standard C allows a fixed number of parameters to precede the variable part of an argument list, whereas previous implementations force the entire argument list to be treated as variable-length.

The meanings of the defined macros, functions, and types are listed next. This facility is stylized, making few assumptions about the implementation:

    va_list   This type is used to declare a local state variable, uniformly called **ap** in this exposition, which is used to traverse the parameters.

    va_start   This macro initializes the state variable **ap** and must be called before

any calls to **va_arg** or **va_end**. In traditional C, **va_start** sets
the internal pointer in **ap** to point to the first argument passed to the
function; in Standard C, **va_start** takes an additional parameter—
the last fixed parameter name—and sets the internal pointer in **ap** to
point to the first variable argument passed to the function.

va_arg   This macro returns the value of the next parameter in the argument
list and advances the internal argument pointer (in **ap**) to the next argument (if any). The type of the next argument (after the usual argument conversions) must be specified (by *type*) so that **va_arg** can
compute its size on the stack. The first call to **va_arg** after calling
va_start will return the value of the first variable parameter.

va_end   This function or macro should be called after all the arguments have
been read with **va_arg**. It performs any necessary cleanup operations on **ap** and **va_alist**.

va_copy   (C99) This macro duplicates the current state of **src** in **dest**, creating a second pointer into the argument list. **va_arg** may then be applied to **src** and **dest** independently. **va_end** must be called on
dest just as it must be on **src**.

The type name *type* used in the **va_arg** macro call must be written in such a way
that suffixing "*****" to it will produce the type "pointer to *type*."

The new C99 macro **va_copy(saved_ap, ap)** can be used to retain a pointer
into the argument list while **va_arg(ap,** *type*) is used to advance further down the list.
If needed, **va_arg(saved_ap,** *type*) can be used to look back at the earlier position.

Example

We show how to write a variable-arguments function in Standard C. The next section will show
the implementation in traditional C. The function, **printargs**, takes a variable number of
arguments of different types and prints their values on the standard output. The first argument
to **printargs** is an array of integers that indicates the number and types of the following
arguments. The array is terminated by a zero element. Here is an example of how
printargs is used. This example is valid in both traditional and Standard C:

```
#include "printargs.h"
int arg_types[] = { INTARG, DBLARG, INTARG, DBLARG, 0 };
int main()
{
    printargs( &arg_types[0], 1, 2.0, 3, 4.0 );
    return 0;
}
```

The declaration of **printargs** and the values of the integer type specifiers are kept in file
printargs.h:

```
/* file printargs.h; Standard C */
#include <stdarg.h>
#define INTARG   1      /* codes used in argtypep[] */
#define DBLARG 2
…
void printargs(int *argtypep, ...);
```

The corresponding definition of **printargs** in Standard C is shown next.

```
#include <stdio.h>
#include "printargs.h"
void printargs( int *argtypep, ...)      /* Standard C */
{  va_list ap; int argtype;
   va_start(ap, argtypep);

   while ( (argtype = *argtypep++) != 0 ) {
      switch (argtype) {
      case INTARG:
         printf("int: %d\n", va_arg(ap, int) );
         break;

      case DBLARG:
         printf("double: %f\n", va_arg(ap, double) );
         break;
      /* … */
      }
   } /*while*/
   va_end(ap);
}
```

11.4.1 Traditional Facilities: varargs.h

Traditional C synopsis

```
#include <varargs.h>
#define va_alist ...
#define va_dcl ...

typedef ... va_list;

void va_start( va_list ap );

type va_arg( va_list ap, type);

void va_end(va_list ap);
```

In traditional C, variable arguments are implemented using the header file **varargs.h**.
It has two new macros and a change in the definition of **va_start**:

va_alist   This macro replaces the parameter list in the definition of a function
taking a variable number of arguments.

va_dcl   This macro replaces the parameter declarations in the function definition. It should not be followed by a semicolon to allow for it to be empty.

`va_start`   This macro initializes the state variable **ap**, and must be called before any calls to **va_arg** or **va_end**. In traditional C, **va_start**
sets the internal pointer in **ap** to point to the first argument passed to
the function; it takes one fewer argument than the Standard C version.

Example

Here is the declaration of **printargs** in traditional C.

```
/* file printargs.h; Traditional C */
#define INTARG    1      /* codes used in argtypep[] */
#define DBLARG 2

...
#include <varargs.h>
printargs( va_alist );
```

The traditional C implementation of **printargs** is shown next. The only differences are in
the function argument list and in the call to **va_start**.

```
#include <stdio.h>
#include "printargs.h"
printargs( va_alist           )/* Traditional C */
    va_dcl
{   va_list ap; int argtype, *argtypep;
    va_start(ap);

    argtypep = va_arg(ap, int *);
    while ( (argtype = *argtypep++) != 0 ) {
        switch (argtype) {
        case INTARG:
            printf("int: %d\n", va_arg(ap, int) );
            break;
        case DBLARG:
            printf("double: %f\n", va_arg(ap, double) );
            break;
        /* ... */
        }
    }
    va_end(ap);
}
```

11.5 *Standard C Operator Macros*

Synopsis

```
#include <iso646.h>
#define and      &&
#define and_eq   &=
#define bitand   &
#define bitor    |
#define compl    ~
#define not      !
#define not_eq   !=
#define or       ||
#define or_eq    |=
#define xor      ^
#define xor_eq   ^=
```

Amendment 1 to C89 adds the header file **iso646.h**, which contains definitions of macros that can be used in place of certain operator tokens. Those tokens could be inconvenient to write in a restricted source character set (such as ISO 646). In C++, these identifiers are keywords.

Example

Each of the following three **if** statements has the same effect.

```
#include <iso646.h>
...
if (*p || q != 0)      *p ^= q;      /* customary */
if (*p ??!??! q != 0) *p ??'= q;     /* trigraphs */
if (*p or q != 0)      *p xor_eq q;  /* iso646.h*/
```

Amendment 1 also provides for the respelling of punctuator tokens such as **{** and **}** using other characters that are more common in foreign alphabets.

References   keywords 2.6; token respelling 2.4.1; trigraphs 2.1.4

—

12

Character Processing

There are two kinds of facilities for handling characters: classification and conversion. Every character classification facility has a name beginning with **is** and returns a value of type **int** that is nonzero (true) if the argument is in the specified class and zero (false) if not. Every character conversion facility has a name beginning with **to** and returns a value of type **int** representing a character or **EOF**. Standard C reserves names beginning with **is** and **to** for more conversion and classification facilities that may be added to the library in the future. The character-related facilities described here are declared by the library header file **ctype.h**.

Amendment 1 to C89 defines a parallel set of classification and conversion facilities that operate on wide characters. These facilities have names beginning with **isw** and **tow**, with the remainder of the name matching the corresponding character-based facility. The wide character classification facilities accept arguments of **wint_t** and return a truth value of type **int**. The conversion facilities map between values of type **wint_t**. There are also generalized classification functions **wctrans** and **iswctrans** and generalized conversion functions **wctrans** and **towctrans** since extended character sets may have special classifications. These facilities are all defined in the header file **wctype.h**.

The negative integer **EOF** is a value that is not an encoding of a "real character." (**WEOF** serves the same purpose for wide characters.) For example, **fgetc** (Section 15.6) returns **EOF** when at end-of-file because there is no "real character" to be read. It must be remembered, however, that the type **char** may be signed in some implementations, and so **EOF** is not necessarily distinguishable from a "real character" if nonstandard character values appear. (Standard character values are always non-negative even if the type **char** is signed.) All of the facilities described here operate properly on all values representable as type **char** or type **unsigned char**, and also on the value **EOF**, but are undefined for all other integer values unless the individual description states otherwise. **WEOF** serves the same purpose for **wchar_t** as **EOF** does for char, but **WEOF** does not have to be negative.

The formulation of these facilities in Standard C takes into account the possibility that several locales will be supported; in general it tries to make as few assumptions as possible about character encodings or concepts such as "letter." The traditional C version of these functions is roughly equivalent to the Standard C formulation for the "C" locale except that any ASCII-dependencies (such as **isascii** and **toascii**) are also removed.

Warning: Some non-Standard implementations of C let the type **char** be signed and also support a type **unsigned char**, yet the character-handling facilities fail to operate properly on all values representable by type **unsigned char**. In some cases, the facilities even fail to operate properly on all values representable by type **char**, but handle only "standard" character values and **EOF**.

References   EOF 11.1; WEOF 11.1; wide character 2.1.4; **wchar_t** 11.1; **wint_t** 11.1

12.1 isalnum, isalpha, iscntrl, iswalnum, iswalpha, iswcntrl

Synopsis

```
#include <ctype.h>

int isalnum(int c);
int isalpha(int c);
int iscntrl(int c);
int isascii(int c); /* Common extension */
```

```
#include <wctype.h>

int iswalnum(wint_t c);
int iswalpha(wint_t c);
int iswcntrl(wint_t c);
```

The **isalnum** function tests whether **c** is an alphanumeric character—that is, one of the following in the C locale:

```
0 1 2 3 4 5 6 7 8 9
A B C D E F G H I J K L M N O P Q R S T U V W X Y Z
a b c d e f g h i j k l m n o p q r s t u v w x y z
```

This function is by definition equivalent to

```
isalpha(c) || isdigit(c)
```

The **isalpha** function tests whether **c** is an alphabetic character—that is, one of the following for the C locale:

```
A B C D E F G H I J K L M N O P Q R S T U V W X Y Z
a b c d e f g h i j k l m n o p q r s t u v w x y z
```

In any locale, this function is true whenever **islower(c)** or **isupper(c)** is true, and it is false whenever **iscntrl(c)**, **isdigit(c)**, **ispunct(c)**, or **isspace(c)** is true, but otherwise it is implementation-defined.

The function **iscntrl** tests whether **c** is a "control character." If the standard 128-character ASCII set is in use, the control characters are those with values 0 through 31 (37_8 or $1F_{16}$) and also 127 (177_8 or $7F_{16}$). The **isprint** function (Section 12.4) is the complementary function at least for standard ASCII implementations.

The function **isascii** is not part of Standard C, but it is a common extension in C libraries. It tests whether the value of **c** is in the range 0 through 127 (177_8 or $7F_{16}$)—the range of the standard 128-character ASCII character set. Unlike most of the character classification functions in traditional C, **isascii** operates properly on any value of type **int** (and its argument is of type **int** even in traditional C).

In traditional C, these functions take an argument of type **char**, but they return **int**.

Example

> The following function **is_id** returns **TRUE** if the argument string **s** is a valid C identifier; otherwise it returns **FALSE**. The current locale must be C for this function to work correctly.

```
#include <ctype.h>
#define TRUE 1
#define FALSE 0

int is_id(const char *s)
{
    char ch;
    if ((ch = *s++) == '\0') return FALSE; /*empty string*/
    if (!(isalpha(ch) || ch == '_')) return FALSE;
    while ((ch = *s++) != '\0') {
        if (!(isalnum(ch) || ch == '_')) return FALSE;
    }
    return TRUE;
}
```

12.1.1 Wide-Character Facilities

Header **wctype.h**, defined in Amendment 1 of C89, provides three additional functions.

The **iswalnum** function is equivalent to **iswalpha(c)** || **iswdigit(c)**.

The **iswalpha** function tests whether **c** is a locale-specific set of "alphabetic" wide characters. In any locale, this function is true whenever **iswlower(c)** or **iswupper(c)** is true, and it is false whenever **iswcntrl(c)**, **iswdigit(c)**, **iswpunct(c)**, or **iswspace(c)** is true, but otherwise it is implementation-defined.

The function **iswcntrl** returns a nonzero value if **c** is the code for a member of a locale-specific set of *control wide characters*. A control wide character cannot be a printing wide character as classified by **iswprint** (Section 12.4).

12.2 iscsym, iscsymf

Non-Standard synopsis

```
#include <ctype.h>

int iscsym(char c);
int iscsymf(char c);
```

These functions are not found in Standard C. The `iscsym` function tests whether `c` is a character that may appear in a C identifier. `iscsymf` tests whether `c` is the code for a character that may additionally appear as the first character of an identifier.

The `iscsymf` function is true for at least the 52 upper- and lowercase letters and the underscore character. `iscsym` will additionally be true for at least 10 decimal digits. These functions may be true for other characters as well depending on the implementation.

12.3 isdigit, isodigit, isxdigit, iswdigit, iswxdigit

Synopsis

```
#include <ctype.h>

int isdigit(int c);
int isxdigit(int c)
```

```
#include <wctype.h>

int iswdigit(wint_t c);
int iswxdigit(wint_t c);
```

The `isdigit` function tests whether `c` is one of the 10 decimal digits. The `isxdigit` function tests whether `c` is one of the 22 hexadecimal digits—that is, one of the following:

```
0 1 2 3 4 5 6 7 8 9 A B C D E F a b c d e f
```

In pre-Standard C, these functions took an argument of type **char**, but they returned **int**. Also, you may see a non-Standard `isodigit` function, which tests whether `c` is the code for one of the 8 octal digits.

12.3.1 Wide-Character Facilities

The `iswdigit` function (C89 Amendment 1) tests whether `c` corresponds to one of the decimal-digit characters. The `iswxdigit` function tests whether `c` corresponds to one of the hexadecimal-digit characters.

12.4 *isgraph, isprint, ispunct, iswgraph, iswprint, iswpunct*

Synopsis

```
#include <ctype.h>

int isgraph(int c);
int ispunct(int c);
int isprint(char c);
```
```
#include <wctype.h>

int iswgraph(wint_t c);
int iswpunct(wint_t c);
int iswprint(wint_t c);
```

The **isprint** function tests whether **c** is a *printing character*—that is, any character that is not a control character. A space is always considered to be a printing character. The **isgraph** function tests whether **c** is the code for a "graphic character"—that is, any printing character other than space. The **isprint** and **isgraph** functions differ only in how they handle the space character; **isprint** is the opposite of **iscntrl** in most implementations, but this need not be so for every locale in Standard C. In traditional C, these functions take an argument of type **char**, but they return **int**.

Example

If the standard 128-character ASCII set is in use, the printing characters are those with codes **040** through **0176**—that is, space plus the following:

```
! " # $ % & ' ( ) * + , - . /
0 1 2 3 4 5 6 7 8 9 : ; < = > ?
@ A B C D E F G H I J K L M N O P Q R S T U V W X Y Z
[ \ ] ^ _
` a b c d e f g h i j k l m n o p q r s t u v w x y z
{ | } ~
```

The graphic characters are the same, but space is omitted.

The function **ispunct** tests whether **c** is the code for a "punctuation character"—a printing character that is neither a space nor any character for which **isalnum** is true.

Example

If the standard 128-character ASCII character set is in use, the punctuation characters are space plus the following:

```
! " # $ % & ' ( ) * + , - . / : ; < = >
? @ [ \ ] ^ _ ` { | } ~
```

12.4.1 Wide-Character Facilities

The `iswprint` function (C89 Amendment 1) tests whether **c** is a *printing wide charac-ter*—that is, a locale-specific wide character that occupies at least one position on a display device and is not a control wide character.

The `iswgraph` function is equivalent to `iswprint(c) && !iswspace(c)`. The function `iswpunct` tests whether **c** is a local-specific wide character for which:

```
iswprint(c) && !(iswalnum(c) || iswspace(c))
```

12.5 islower, isupper, iswlower, iswupper

Synopsis

```
#include <ctype.h>
int islower(int c);
int isupper(int c);
```

```
#include <wctype.h>
int iswlower(wint_t c);
int iswupper(wint_t c);
```

In the C locale, the `islower` function tests whether **c** is one of the 26 lowercase letters, and the `isupper` function tests whether **c** is one of the 26 uppercase letters. In other lo-cales, the functions may return true for other characters as long as they satisfy:

```
!iscntrl(c) && !isdigit(c) && !ispunct(c) && !isspace(c)
```

In traditional C, these functions take an argument of type **char**, but they return **int**.

12.5.1 Wide-Character Facilities

The `iswlower` function (C89 Amendment 1) tests whether **c** corresponds to a lowercase letter or is another of a local-specific set of wide characters that satisfies:

```
!iswcntrl(c) && !iswdigit(c) &&
!iswpunct(c) && !iswspace(c)
```

The `iswupper` function tests whether **c** corresponds to an uppercase letter or is an-other of a locale-specific set of wide characters that satisfies the same logical condition as `iswlower`.

12.6 *isblank, isspace, iswhite, iswspace*

Synopsis
| ```
#include <ctype.h>
int isblank(int c);
int isspace(int c);
``` |
| ```
#include <wctype.h>
int iswspace(wint_t c);
``` |

The `isspace` function tests whether `c` is the code for a whitespace character. In the C locale, `isspace` returns true for only the tab (`'\t'`), carriage return (`'\r'`), newline (`'\n'`), vertical tab (`'\v'`), form feed (`'\f'`), and space (`' '`) characters. Many other library facilities use `isspace` as the definition of whitespace.

The `isblank` function tests whether `c` is the code for a character used to separate words within a line of text. This always includes the standard blank characters, space (`' '`) and horizontal tab (`'\t'`), and it may include additional locale-specific characters for which `isspace` is true. The `"C"` locale has no additional blank characters.

Some implementations of C provide a variant of `isspace` called `iswhite`. In traditional C, these functions take an argument of type `char`, but they return `int`.

12.6.1 Wide-Character Facilities

The `iswspace` function (C89 Amendment 1) tests whether `c` is a locale-specific wide character that satisfies:

```
!iswalnum(c) && !iswgraph(c) && !ispunct(c)
```

12.7 *toascii*

Non-Standard Synopsis
| ```
#include <ctype.h>
int toascii(int c);
``` |

The non-Standard `toascii` function accepts any integer value and reduces it to the range of valid ASCII characters (codes 0 through 127 [177_8 or $3F_{16}$]) by discarding all but the low-order seven bits of the value. If the argument is already a valid ASCII code, the result is equal to the argument.
```

12.8 toint

Non-Standard synopsis

```
#include <ctype.h>
int toint(char c);
```

The non-Standard **toint** function returns the "weight" of a hexadecimal digit: 0 through 9 for the characters **'0'** through **'9'**, respectively, and 10 through 15 for the letters **'a'** through **'f'** (or **'A'** through **'F'**), respectively. The function's behavior if the argument is not a hexadecimal digit is implementation-defined.

Example

> This facility is not present in Standard C, but it is easily implemented. This implementation assumes that certain characters are contiguous in the target encoding:
>
> ```
> int toint( int c )
> {
>     if (c >= '0' && c <= '9') return c - '0';
>     if (c >= 'A' && c <= 'F') return c - 'A' + 10;
>     if (c >= 'a' && c <= 'f') return c - 'a' + 10;
>     /* c is not a hexadecimal digit */
>     return 0;
> }
> ```

12.9 tolower, toupper, towlower, towupper

Synopsis

```
#include <ctype.h>
int tolower(int c);
int toupper(int c);
```

```
#include <wctype.h>
wint_t towlower(wint_t c);
wint_t towupper(wint_t c);
```

If **c** is an uppercase letter, then **tolower** returns the corresponding lowercase letter. If **c** is a lowercase letter, then **toupper** returns the corresponding uppercase letter. In all other cases, the argument is returned unchanged. In some locales, there may be uppercase letters without corresponding lowercase letters or vice versa; in these cases, the functions return their arguments unchanged.

The functions **towlower** and **towupper** are defined in Amendment 1 to C89. If **c** is a wide character for which **iswupper(c)** is true and if **d** is a wide character corresponding to **c** for which **iswlower(d)** is true, then **towlower(c)** returns **d** and **towupper(d)** returns **c**. Otherwise, the two functions return their arguments unchanged.

When using non-Standard implementations, you should be wary of the value returned by **tolower** when its argument is not an uppercase letter and of the value returned by **toupper** when its argument is not a lowercase letter. Many older implementations work correctly only when the argument is a letter of the proper case. Implementations that allow more general arguments to **tolower** and **toupper** may provide faster versions of these—macros named **_tolower** and **_toupper**. These macros require more restrictive arguments and are correspondingly faster. The non-Standard signatures are

```
#include <ctype.h>
int tolower(char c);
int toupper(char c);
#define _tolower(c) …
#define _toupper(c) …
```

Example

If the version of **tolower** in your C library is not well behaved for arbitrary arguments, the following function **safe_tolower** acts like **tolower**, but is safe for all arguments. It is difficult to write **safe_tolower** as a macro because the argument is evaluated more than once (by **isupper**, **tolower**, and the **return** statement):

```
#include <ctype.h>
int safe_tolower(int c)
{
    if (isupper(c)) return tolower(c);
    else return c;
}
```

12.10 wctype_t, wctype, iswctype

Synopsis

```
#include <wctype.h>

typedef … wctype_t;
wctype_t wctype(const char *property);
int iswctype(wint_t c, wctype_t desc);
```

The functions **wctype** and **iswctype** are defined in Amendment 1 to C89. They implement an extensible, locale-specific, wide-character classification facility.

The type **wctype_t** must be scalar; it holds values representing locale-specific wide-character classifications. The **wctype** function constructs a value of type **wctype_t** that represents a class of wide characters. The class is specified by the string name **property**, which is specific to the value of the **LC_CTYPE** category of the current locale. All locales must permit **property** to have any of the string names in Table 12–1, with the listed meaning.

The **iswctype** function tests whether **c** is a member of the class represented by the value **desc**. The setting of the **LC_CTYPE** category when **iswctype** is called must

Table 12–1   Property names for **wctype**

property name	specifies the class for which
"alnum"	**iswalnum(c)** is true
"alpha"	**iswalpha(c)** is true
"cntrl"	**iswcntrl(c)** is true
"digit"	**iswdigit(c)** is true
"graph"	**iswgraph(c)** is true
"lower"	**iswlower(c)** is true
"print"	**iswprint(c)** is true
"punct"	**iswpunct(c)** is true
"space"	**iswspace(c)** is true
"upper"	**iswupper(c)** is true
"xdigit"	**iswxdigit(c)** is true

be the same as the setting of **LC_CTYPE** when the value **desc** was determined by **wctype**.

Example

> The expression **iswctype(c, wctype("alnum"))** has the same truth value as **iswalnum(c)** for any wide character **c** and any locale setting. The same holds for the other property strings and their corresponding classification functions.

> **References**   **LC_CTYPE** 11.5; locale 11.5

12.11 wctrans_t, wctrans

Synopsis

```
#include <wctype.h>

typedef ... wctrans_t;
wctrans_t wctrans( const char *property );
wint_t towctrans( wint_t c, wctrans_t desc );
```

The facilities in this section are defined in Amendment 1 to C89. They implement an extensible, locale-specific, wide-character mapping facility.

The type **wctrans_t** must be scalar; it holds values representing locale-specific wide-character mappings. The **wctrans** function constructs a value of type **wctrans_t** that represents a mapping between wide characters. The mapping is specified by the string name **property**, which is specific to the value of the **LC_CTYPE** category of the current locale. All locales must permit **property** to have any of the following string values with the listed meaning:

property value	specifies the same mapping as performed by
`"tolower"`	`towlower(c)`
`"toupper"`	`towupper(c)`

(Note that the property names are different from the function names.)

The **towctrans** function maps **c** to another wide character as specified by the value **desc**. The setting of the **LC_CTYPE** category when **towctrans** is called must be the same as the setting of **LC_CTYPE** when the value **desc** was determined by **wctrans**.

Example

> The expression **towctrans(c, wctrans("tolower"))** has the same value as **towlower(c)** for any wide-character **c** and any locale setting. The same holds for the other property string and its corresponding mapping function.

References   **LC_CTYPE** 11.5; locale 11.5

13

String Processing

By convention, strings in C are arrays of characters ending with a null character (`'\0'`). The compiler automatically supplies an extra null character after all string constants, but it is up to the programmer to make sure that strings created in character arrays end with a null character. All of the string-handling facilities described here assume that strings are terminated by a null character.

All the characters in a string, not counting the terminating null character, are together called the *contents* of the string. An empty string contains no characters and is represented by a pointer to a null character. Note that this is not the same as a null character pointer (**NULL**), which is a pointer that points to no character at all.

When characters are transferred to a destination string, often no test is made for overflow of the destination. It is up to the programmer to make sure that the destination area in memory is large enough to contain the result string, including the terminating null character.

Most of the facilities described here are declared by the library header file `string.h`; some Standard C conversion facilities are provided by `stdlib.h`. In Standard C, string parameters that are not modified are generally declared to have type **const char *** instead of **char ***; integer arguments or return values that represent string lengths have type **size_t** instead of **int**.

Amendment 1 to C89 adds a set of wide-string functions that parallel the normal string functions. The differences are that the wide-string functions take arguments of type **wchar_t *** instead of **char ***, and the names of the wide-string functions are derived from the string functions by replacing the initial letters **str** with **wcs**. Wide strings are terminated with a wide null character. When comparing wide strings, the integral values of the **wchar_t** elements are compared. The wide characters are not interpreted, and no encoding errors are possible.

Other string facilities are provided by the memory functions (Chapter 14), `sprintf` (Section 15.11), and `sscanf` (Section 15.8).

References   `wchar_t` 11.1; wide character 2.1.4

13.1 *strcat, strncat, wcscat, wcsncat*

Synopsis

```
#include <string.h>

char *strcat( char *dest, const char *src );
char *strncat( char *dest, const char *src, size_t n );

#include <wchr.h>

wchar_t *wcscat( wchar_t *dest, const wchar_t *src );
wchar_t *wcsncat( wchar_t *dest, const wchar_t *src, size_t n );
```

The function `strcat` appends the contents of the string `src` to the end of the string `dest`. The value of `dest` is returned. The null character that terminates `dest` (and perhaps other characters following it in memory) is overwritten with characters from `src` and a new terminating null character. Characters are copied from `src` until a null character is encountered in `src`. The memory area beginning with `dest` is assumed to be large enough to hold both strings.

`wcscat` is the same as `strcat` except for the types of the arguments and result.

Example

The following statements append three strings to `D`; at the end, `D` contains the string `"All for one. "`:

```
#include <string.h>
char D[20];
...
D[0] = '\0';        /* Set string to empty */
strcat(D,"All ");
strcat(D,"for ");
strcat(D,"one.");
```

The `strncat` function appends up to `n` characters from the contents of `src` to the end of `dest`. If the null character that terminates `src` is encountered before `n` characters have been copied, then the null character is copied but no more. If no null character appears among the first `n` characters of `src`, then the first `n` characters are copied and a null character is supplied to terminate the destination string; that is, `n+1` characters in all are written. If the value of `n` is zero or negative, then calling `strncat` has no effect. The function always returns `dest`. In traditional C, the last argument to `strncat` has type `int`.

`wcsncat` is like `strncat` except for the types of the arguments and result.

The behavior of all these functions is undefined if the strings overlap in memory.

13.2 *strcmp, strncmp, wcscmp, wcsncmp*

Synopsis

```
#include <string.h>

int strcmp( const char *s1, const char *s2 );
int strncmp( const char *s1, const char *s2, size_t n );
```

```
#include <wchr.h>

int wcscmp( const wchar_t *s1, const wchar_t *s2 );
int wcsncmp( const wchar_t *s1, const wchar_t *s2, size_t n );
```

The function **strcmp** lexicographically compares the contents of the null-terminated string **s1** with the contents of the null-terminated string **s2**. It returns a value of type **int** that is less than zero if **s1** is less than **s2**, equal to zero if **s1** is equal to **s2**, and greater than zero if **s1** is greater than **s2**.

Example

To check only whether two strings are equal, you negate the return value from **strcmp**:

```
if (!strcmp(s1,s2)) printf("Strings are equal\n");
else printf("Strings are not equal\n");
```

Two strings are equal if their contents are identical. String **s1** is lexicographically less than string **s2** under either of two circumstances:

1. The strings are equal up to some character position, and at that first differing character position the character value from **s1** is less than the character value from **s2**.

2. The string **s1** is shorter than the string **s2**, and the contents of **s1** are identical to those of **s2** up to length of **s1**.

wcscmp (Amendment 1) is like **strcmp** except for the types of the arguments.

The function **strncmp** is like **strcmp** except that it compares up to **n** characters of the null-terminated string **s1** with up to **n** characters of the null-terminated string **s2**. In comparing the strings, the entire string is used if it contains fewer than **n** characters; otherwise the string is treated as if it were **n** characters long. If the value of **n** is zero or negative, then both strings are treated as empty and therefore equal, and zero is returned. In traditional C, the argument **n** has type **int**.

wcsncmp is like **strncmp** except for the types of the arguments.

The function **memcmp** (Section 14.2) provides similar functionality to **strcmp**. The **strcoll** function (Section 13.10) provides locale-specific comparison facilities.

13.3 strcpy, strncpy, wcscpy, wcsncpy

Synopsis

```
#include <string.h>

char *strcpy( char *dest, const char *src );
char *strncpy( char *dest, const char *src, size_t n );
```

```
#include <wchar.h>

wchar_t *wcscpy( wchar_t *dest, const wchar_t *src );
wchar_t *wcsncpy( wchar_t *dest, const wchar_t *src, size_t n );
```

The function **strcpy** copies the contents of the string **src** to the string **dest**, overwriting the old contents of **dest**. The entire contents of **src** are copied, plus the terminating null character, even if **src** is longer than **dest**. The argument **dest** is returned.

wcscpy (C89 Amendment 1) is like **strcpy** except for the types of its arguments.

Example

The **strcat** function (Section 13.1) can be implemented with the **strcpy** and **strlen** (Section 13.4) functions as follows:

```
#include <string.h>
char *strcat(char *dest, const char *src)
{
    char *s = dest + strlen(dest);
    strcpy(s, src);
    return dest;
}
```

The function **strncpy** copies exactly **n** characters to **dest**. It first copies up to **n** characters from **src**. If there are fewer than **n** characters in **src** before the terminating null character, then null characters are written into **dest** as padding until exactly **n** characters have been written. If there are **n** or more characters in **src**, then only **n** characters are copied, and so only a truncated copy of **src** is transferred to **dest**. It follows that the copy in **dest** is terminated with a null by **strncpy** only if the length of **src** (not counting the terminating null) is less than **n**. If the value of **n** is zero or negative, then calling **strncpy** function has no effect. The value of **dest** is always returned. In traditional C, the argument **n** has type **int**.

wcsncpy (Amendment 1) is like **strcpy** except for the types of its arguments.

The functions **memcpy** and **memccpy** (Section 14.3) provide similar functionality to **strcpy**. The results of both **strcpy**, **strncpy**, and their wide-string equivalents are unpredictable if the two string arguments overlap in memory. The functions **memmove** and **wmemmove** (Section 14.3) are provided in Standard C for cases in which overlap may occur.

13.4 strlen, wcslen

Synopsis
`#include <string.h>`
`size_t strlen(const char *s);`
`#include <wchar.h>`
`size_t wcslen(const wchar_t *s);`

The function **strlen** returns the number of characters in **s** preceding the terminating null character. An empty string has a null character as its first character and therefore its length is zero. In some older implementations of C, this function is called **lenstr**.

wcslen (C89 Amendment 1) is like **strlen** except for the type of its argument.

13.5 strchr, strrchr, wcschr, wcsrchr

Synopsis
`#include <string.h>`
`char *strchr( const char *s, int c );`
`char *strrchr( const char *s, int c );`
`#include <wchar.h>`
`wchar_t *wcschr( const wchar_t *s, wchar_t c );`
`wchar_t *wcsrchr( const wchar_t *s, wchar_t c );`

The functions in this section all search for a single character **c** within a null-terminated string **s**. In the Standard C functions, the terminating null character of **s** is considered to be part of the string. That is, if **c** is the null character (0), the functions will return the position of the terminating null character of **s**. In Standard C, the argument **c** has type **int**; in traditional C, it has type **char**. The return value of these function is pointer to non-**const**, but in fact the object designated will be **const** if the first argument points to a **const** object. In that case, storing a value into the object designated by the return pointer will result in undefined behavior.

The function **strchr** searches the string **s** for the first occurrence of the character **c**. If the character **c** is found in the string, a pointer to the first occurrence is returned. If the character is not found, a null pointer is returned.

The function **wcschr** (C89 Amendment 1) is like **strchr** except for the types of its arguments and return value.

The function **strrchr** is like **strchr** except that it returns a pointer to the last occurrence of the character **c**. If the character is not found, a null pointer is returned.

The function **wcsrchr** (C89 Amendment 1) is like **strrchr** except for the types of its arguments and return value.

The traditional C function **strpos** is like **strchr** except that the return value has type **int** and position of the first occurrence of **c** is returned, where the first character of **s** is considered to be at position 0. If the character is not found, the value –1 is returned. The function **strrpos** is like **strpos** except that the position of the last occurrence of **c** is returned. Neither **strpos** nor **strrpos** is provided by Standard C.

The functions **memchr** and **wmemchr** (Section 14.1) provide similar functionality to **strchr** and **wcschr**. In some implementations of C, **strchr** and **strrchr** are called **index** and **rindex**, respectively. Some implementations of C provide the function **scnstr**, which is a variant of **strpos**.

Example

The following function **how_many** uses **strchr** to count the number of times a specified nonnull character appears in a string. The parameter **s** is repeatedly updated to point to the portion of the string just after the last-found character:

```
int how_many(const char *s, int c)
{
    int n = 0;
    if (c == 0) return 0;
    while(s) {
        s = strchr(s, c);
        if (s) n++, s++;
    }
    return n;
}
```

13.6 strspn, strcspn, strpbrk, strrpbrk, wcsspn, wcscspn, wcspbrk

Synopsis

```
#include <string.h>

size_t strspn( const char *s, const char *set );
size_t strcspn( const char *s, const char *set );
char *strpbrk( const char *s, const char *set );
```

```
#include <wchar.h>

size_t wcsspn( const wchar_t *s, const wchar_t *set );
size_t wcscspn( const wchar_t *s, const wchar_t *set );
wchar_t *wcspbrk( const wchar_t *s, const wchar_t *set );
```

The functions in this section all search a null-terminated string **s** for occurrences of characters specified by whether they are included in a second null-terminated string **set**. The second argument is regarded as a set of characters; the order of the characters, or whether there are duplications, does not matter.

The function **strspn** searches the string **s** for the first occurrence of a character that is not included in the string **set**, skipping over ("spanning") characters that are in set. The value returned is the length of the longest initial segment of **s** that consists of characters found in **set**. If every character of **s** appears in **set**, then the total length of **s** (not counting the terminating null character) is returned. If **set** is an empty string, then the first character of **s** will not be found in it, and so zero will be returned.

The function **strcspn** is like **strspn** except that it searches **s** for the first occurrence of a character that is included in the string **set**, skipping over characters that are not in **set**.

The function **strpbrk** is like **strcspn** except that it returns a pointer to the first character found from **set** rather than the number of characters skipped over. If no characters from **set** are found, a null pointer is returned.

The non-Standard function **strrpbrk** has the same signature as **strpbrk** but it returns a pointer to the last character from **set** found within **s**. If no character within **s** occurs in **set**, then a null pointer is returned.

The **wcsspn**, **wcscspn**, and **wcspbrk** functions (C89 Amendment 1) are the same as their **str** counterparts except for the types of their arguments and result.

Rarely, **strspn** and **strcspn** are called **notstr** and **instr**.

Example

The function **is_id** determines whether the input string is a valid C identifier. **strspn** is used to see whether all the string's characters are letters, digits, or the underscore character. If so, a final test is made to be sure the first character is not a digit. Compare this solution with the one given in Section 12.1:

```
#include <string.h>
#define TRUE (1)
#define FALSE (0)

int is_id(const char *s)
{
    static char *id_chars =
            "abcdefghijklmnopqrstuvwxyz"
            "ABCDEFGHIJKLMNOPQRSTUVWXYZ"
            "0123456789_";
    if (s == NULL) return FALSE;
    if (strspn(s,id_chars) != strlen(s)) return FALSE;
    return !isdigit(*s);
}
```

13.7 strstr, strtok, wcsstr, wcstok

Synopsis

```
#include <string.h>

char *strtok( char *str, const char *set );
char *strstr( const char *src, const char *sub );
```

```
#include <wchar.h>

wchar_t *wcstok(
    wchar_t *str, const wchar_t *set,wchar_t **ptr );
wchar_t *wcsstr(
    const wchar_t *src, const wchar_t *sub );
```

The function **strstr** is new in Standard C. It locates the first occurrence of the string **sub** in the string **src** and returns a pointer to the beginning of the first occurrence. If **sub** does not occur in **src**, a null pointer is returned. The **wcsstr** function (C89 Amendment 1) is the same as **strstr** except for the types of its arguments and result.

The function **strtok** may be used to separate a string **str** into tokens separated by characters from the string **set**. A call is made on **strtok** for each token, possibly changing the value of **set** in successive calls. The first call includes the string **str**; subsequent calls pass a null pointer as the first argument, directing **strtok** to continue from the end of the previous token. (The original string **str** must not be modified while **strtok** is being used to find more tokens in the string.)

More precisely, if **str** is not null, then **strtok** first skips over all characters in **str** that are also in **set**. If all the characters of **str** occur in **set**, then **strtok** returns a null pointer, and an internal state pointer is set to a null pointer. Otherwise, the internal state pointer is set to point to the first character of **str** not in **set**, and execution continues as if **str** had been null.

If **str** and the internal state pointer are null, then **strtok** returns a null pointer, and the internal state pointer is unchanged. (This handles extra calls to **strtok** after all the tokens have been returned.) If **str** is null, but the internal state pointer is not null, then the function searches beginning at the internal state pointer for the first character contained in **set**. If such a character is found, the character is overwritten with '\0', **strtok** returns the value of the internal state pointer, and the internal state pointer is adjusted to point to the character immediately following inserted null character. If no such character is found, **strtok** returns the value of the internal state pointer, and the internal state pointer is set to null.

Library facilities in Standard C are not permitted to alter the internal state of **strtok** in any way that the programmer could detect. That is, the programmer does not have to worry about a library function using **strtok** and thereby interfering with the programmer's own use of the function.

The **wcstok** function (C89 Amendment 1) is the same as **strtok**, except for the types of its arguments and result. Also, the additional **ptr** parameter indirectly designates a pointer that is used as the "internal state pointer" of **strtok**. That is, the caller of **wcstok** provides a holder for the internal state.

If the first argument to **strstr** or **wcsstr** is a pointer to a constant string, then so will be the returned value, although it is not declared as pointer to **const**.

Example

The following program reads lines from the standard input and uses **strtok** to break the lines into "words"—sequences of characters separated by spaces, commas, periods, quotation marks, and/or question marks. The words are printed on the standard output:

```
#include <stdio.h>
#include <string.h>
#define LINELENGTH 80
#define SEPCHARS " .,?\"\n"
int main(void)
{
    char line[LINELENGTH];
    char *word;

    while(1) {
        printf("\nNext line?  (empty line to quit)\n");
        fgets(line,LINELENGTH,stdin);
        if (strlen(line) <= 1) break;   /* exit program */
        printf("That line contains these words:\n");
        word = strtok(line,SEPCHARS);/* find first word */
        while (word != NULL) {
            printf("\"%s\"\n",word);
            word = strtok(NULL,SEPCHARS);/*find next word*/
        }
    }
}
```

Here is a sample execution of the program:

```
Next line?  (empty line to quit)
"My goodness," she said, "Is that right?"
That line contains these words:
"My"
"goodness"
"she"
"said"
"Is"
"that"
"right"

Next line?  (empty line to quit)
```

13.8 strtod, strtof, strtold, strtol, strtoll, strtoul, strtoull

See Section 16.4.

13.9 atof, atoi, atol, atoll

See Section 16.3.

13.10 strcoll, strxfrm, wcscoll, wcsxfrm

Synopsis

```
#include <string.h>

int strcoll( const char *s1, const char *s2 );
size_t strxfrm(
    char *dest, const char *src, size_t len );
```

```
#include <wchar.h>

int wcscoll(const wchar_t *s1, const wchar_t *s2);
size_t wcsxfrm(
    wchar_t *dest, const wchar_t *src, size_t len);
```

The **strcoll** and **strxfrm** functions provide locale-specific string-sorting facilities. The **strcoll** function compares the strings **s1** and **s2** and returns an integer greater than, equal to, or less than zero depending on whether the string **s1** is greater than, equal to, or less than the string **s2**. The comparison is computed according to the locale-specific collating conventions (**LC_COLLATE** with **setlocale**, Section 11.5). In contrast, the **strcmp** and **wcscmp** functions (Section 13.2) always compare two strings using the normal collating sequence of the target character set (**char** or **wchar_t**).

The function **wcscoll** (C89 Amendment 1) is the same as **strcoll** except for the types of its arguments.

The **strxfrm** function transforms (in a way described later) the string **src** into a second string that is stored in the character array **dest**, which is assumed to be at least **len** characters long. The number of characters needed to store the string (excluding the terminating null character) is returned by **strxfrm**. Thus, if the value returned by **strxfrm** is greater than or equal to **len**, or if **src** and **dest** overlap in memory, the final contents of **dest** is undefined. Additionally, if **len** is 0 and **dest** is a null pointer, **strxfrm** simply computes and returns the length of the transformed string corresponding to **src**.

The **strxfrm** function transforms strings in such a way that the **strcmp** function can be used on the transformed strings to determine the correct sorting order. That is, if **s1** and **s2** are strings, and **t1** and **t2** are the transformed strings produced by **strxfrm** from **s1** and **s2**, then

- **strcmp(t1,t2) > 0**   if **strcoll(s1,s2) > 0**
- **strcmp(t1,t2) == 0** if **strcoll(s1,s2) == 0**
- **strcmp(t1,t2) < 0**   if **strcoll(s1,s2) < 0**

The function **wcsxfrm** (C89 Amendment 1) is like **strxfrm** except for the types of its arguments. The **wcscmp** function must be used to compare the transformed wide string.

The functions **strcoll** and **strxfrm** have different performance trade-offs. The **strcoll** function does not require the programmer to supply extra storage, but it may have to perform string transformations internally each time it is called. Using **strxfrm** may be more efficient when many comparisons must be done on the same set of strings.

Example

The following function **transform** uses **strxfrm** to create a transformed string corresponding to the argument **s**. Space for the string is dynamically allocated:

```
#include <string.h>
#include <stdlib.h>

char *transform( char *s )
/* Return the result of applying strxfrm to s */
{
    char *dest; /* Buffer to hold transformed string */
    size_t length; /* Buffer length required */
    length = strxfrm(NULL,s,0) + 1;
    dest = (char *) malloc(length);
    strxfrm(dest,s,length);
    return dest;
}
```

14

Memory Functions

The facilities in this chapter give the C programmer efficient ways to copy, compare, and set blocks of memory. In Standard C, these functions are considered part of the string functions and are declared in the library header file **string.h**. In older implementations, they are declared in their own header file, **memory.h**.

Blocks of memory are designated by a pointer of type **void *** in Standard C and **char *** in traditional C. In Standard C, memory is interpreted as an array of objects of type **unsigned char**; in traditional C, this is not explicitly stated, and either **char** or **unsigned char** might be used. These functions do not treat null characters any differently than other characters.

Amendment 1 to C89 added five new functions for manipulating wide-character arrays, which are designated by pointers of type **wchar_t ***. These functions are defined in header **wchar.h**, and their names all begin with the letters **wmem**. The ordering of wide characters is simply the ordering of integers in the underlying integer type **wchar_t**. No interpretation of the wide characters is made, so no encoding errors are possible.

References wchar_t 11.1; wide character 2.1.4

14.1 *memchr, wmemchr*

Synopsis
`#include <string.h>`
`void *memchr( const void *ptr, int val, size_t len );`
`#include <wchar.h>`
`wchar_t *wmemchr( const wchar_t *ptr, wchar_t val, size_t len );`

The function **memchr** searches for the first occurrence of **val** in the first **len** characters beginning at **ptr**. It returns a pointer to the first character containing **val**, if any, or returns a null pointer if no such character is found. Each character **c** is compared to **val** as if by the expression **(unsigned char) c == (unsigned char) val**. See also **strchr** (Section 13.5). Although the returned pointer is declared to be a pointer to a non-**const** object, in fact it may point into a **const** object if the first argument was such.

The **wmemchr** function (C89 Amendment 1) finds the first occurrence of **val** in the **len** wide characters beginning at **ptr**. A pointer to the found wide character is returned. If no match is found, a null pointer is returned.

In traditional C, the signature of **memchr** is

```
#include <memory.h>
char *memchr(char *ptr, int val, int len );
```

14.2 memcmp, wmemcmp

Synopsis

```
#include <string.h>
int memcmp( const void *ptr1, const void *ptr2, size_t len );
```

```
#include <wchar.h>
int wmemcmp(
    const wchar_t *ptr1, const wchar_t *ptr2, size_t len );
```

The function **memcmp** compares the first **len** characters beginning at **ptr1** with the first **len** characters beginning at **ptr2**. If the first string of characters is lexicographically less than the second, then **memcmp** returns a negative integer. If the first string of characters is lexicographically greater than the second, then **memcmp** returns a positive integer. Otherwise **memcmp** returns 0. See also **strcmp** (Section 13.2).

The **wmemcmp** function (C89 Amendment 1) performs the same comparison on wide-character arrays. The ordering function on wide characters is simply the integer ordering on the underlying integral type **wchar_t**. The value returned is negative, zero, or positive according to whether the wide characters at **ptr1** are less than, equal to, or greater than, respectively, the sequence of wide characters at **ptr2**.

Older C implementations may include the function **bcmp**, which also compares two strings of characters, but returns 0 if they are the same and nonzero otherwise. No comparison for less or greater is made. The traditional C signatures of **bcmp** and **memcmp** are:

```
#include <memory.h>
int bcmp( char *ptr1, char *ptr2, int len );
int memcmp( char *ptr1, char *ptr2, int len );
```

14.3 memcpy, memccpy, memmove, wmemcpy, wmemmove

Synopsis

```
#include <string.h>

void *memcpy (void *dest, const void *src, size_t len);
void *memmove(void *dest, const void *src, size_t len);

#include <wchar.h>

wchar_t *wmemcpy(
   wchar_t *dest, const wchar_t *src, size_t len);
wchar_t * wmemmove(
   wchar_t *dest, const wchar_t *src, size_t len);
```

The functions **memcpy** and **memmove** (Standard C) both copy **len** characters from **src** to **dest** and return the value of **dest**. The difference is that **memmove** will work correctly for overlapping memory regions—that is, **memmove** acts as if the source area were first copied to a separate temporary area and then copied back to the destination area. (In fact, no temporary areas are needed to implement **memmove**.) The behavior of **memcpy** is undefined when the source and destination overlap, although some versions of **memcpy** do implement the copy-to-temporary semantics. If both versions are available, the programmer should expect **memcpy** to be faster. See also **strcpy** (Section 13.3).

The functions **wmemcpy** and **wmemmove** (C89 Amendment 1) are analogous to **memcpy** and **memmove**, respectively, but they operate on wide-character arrays. They both return **dest**.

Older C implementations may use the functions **memccpy** and **bcopy** in addition to **memcpy**. The function **memccpy** also copies **len** characters from **src** to **dest**, but it will stop immediately after copying a character whose value is **val**. When all **len** characters are copied, **memccpy** returns a null pointer; otherwise it returns a pointer to the character following the copy of **val** in **dest**. The function **bcopy** works like **memcpy**, but the source and destination operands are reversed. The traditional C signatures of these functions are

```
#include <memory.h>

char *memcpy( char *dest, char *src, int len );
char *memccpy(char *dest, char *src, int val, int len);
char *bcopy( char *src, char *dest, int len );
```

14.4 memset, wmemset

Synopsis

```
#include <string.h>

void *memset( void *ptr, int val, size_t len );
```

```
#include <wchar.h>

wchar_t *wmemset( wchar_t *ptr, int val, size_t len );
```

The function **memset** copies **val** into each of **len** characters beginning at **ptr**. The characters designated by **ptr** are considered to be of type **unsigned char**. The function returns the value of **ptr**.

The function **wmemset** (C89 Amendment 1) is analogous to **memset**, but it fills an array of wide characters.

Older C implementations may include the more restricted function **bzero**, which copies 0 into each of **len** characters at **ptr**. The traditional C signatures are

```
#include <memory.h>
char *memset( char *ptr, int val, int len );
void bzero( char *ptr,int len );
```

15

Input/Output Facilities

C has a rich and useful set of I/O facilities based on the concept of a stream, which may be a file or some other source or consumer of data, including a terminal or other physical device. The data type **FILE** (defined in **stdio.h** along with the rest of the I/O facilities) holds information about a stream. An object of type **FILE** is created by calling **fopen**, and a pointer to it (a *file pointer*) is used as an argument to most of the I/O facilities described in this chapter.

Among the information included in a **FILE** object is the current position within the stream (the *file position*), pointers to any associated buffers, and indications of whether an error or end of file has occurred. Streams are normally buffered unless they are associated with interactive devices. The programmer has some control over buffering with the **setvbuf** facility, but in general streams can be implemented efficiently, and the programmer should not have to worry about performance.

There are two general forms of streams: text and binary. A text stream consists of a sequence of characters divided into lines; each line consists of zero or more characters followed by (and including) a newline character, `'\n'`. Text streams are portable when they consist only of complete lines made from characters from the standard character set. The hardware and software components underlying a particular C run-time library implementation may have different representations for text files (especially for the end-of-line indication), but the run-time library must map those representations into the standard one. Standard C requires implementations to support text stream lines of at least 254 characters including the terminating newline.

Binary streams are sequences of data values of type **char**. Because any C data value may be mapped onto an array of values of type **char**, binary streams can transparently record internal data. Implementations do not have to distinguish between text and binary streams if it is more convenient not to do so.

When a C program begins execution, there are three text streams predefined and open: *standard input* (**stdin**), *standard output* (**stdout**), and *standard error* (**stderr**).

> **References** **fopen** 15.2; **setvbuf** 15.3; standard character set 2.1

Wide-character input and output   Amendment 1 to C89 adds a wide-character I/O facility to C. The new *wide-character input/output functions* in header file **wchar.h** correspond to older *byte input/output functions*, except the underlying program data type (and stream element) is the wide character (**wchar_t**) instead of the character (**char**). In fact, the implementation of these wide-character I/O functions may translate the wide characters to and from multibyte sequences held on external media, but this is generally transparent to the programmer.

Instead of creating a new stream type for wide-character I/O, Amendment 1 adds an *orientation* to existing text and binary streams. After a stream is opened and before any input/output operations are performed on it, a stream has no orientation. The stream becomes *wide-oriented* or *byte-oriented* depending on whether the first input/output operation is from a wide-character or byte function. Once a stream is oriented, only I/O functions of the same orientation may be used or else the result is undefined. The **fwide** function (Section 15.2) may be used to set and/or test the orientation of a stream.

When the external representation of a file is a sequence of multibyte characters, some rules for multibyte character sequences are relaxed in the files:

1. Multibyte encodings in a file may contain embedded null characters.

2. Files do not need to begin or end in the initial conversion state.

Different files may use different multibyte character encodings of wide characters. The encoding for a file, which is logically part of the internal conversion state, is established by the setting of the **LC_CTYPE** category of the locale when that internal conversion state is first *bound*, not later than after the first wide-character input/output function is called. After the conversion state (and the encoding rule) of a file is bound, the setting of **LC_CTYPE** no longer affects the conversions on the associated stream.

Because the conversion between wide character and multibyte character may have state associated with it, a hidden **mbstate_t** object is associated with every wide-oriented stream. Conversion during input/output conceptually occurs by calling **mbrtowc** or **wcrtomb** using the hidden conversion state. The **fgetpos** and **fsetpos** functions must record this conversion state with the file position. Conversion during wide-character input/output can fail with an encoding error, in which case **EILSEQ** is stored in **errno**. When multiple encodings of files are permitted, the encoding for a stream will probably be part of the **mbstate_t** object or at least recorded with it.

> **References**   conversion state 2.1.5; **EILSEQ** 11.2; **fgetpos** and **fsetpos** 15.5; **mbrtowc** 11.7; **mbstate_t** 11.1; multibyte character 2.1.5; orientation 15.2.2; **wcrtomb** 11.7; wide characters 2.1.5

15.1 FILE, EOF, wchar_t, wint_t, WEOF

Synopsis

```
#include <stdio.h>

typedef ... FILE ...;
#define EOF (-n)
#define NULL ...
#define size_t ...
```

```
#include <wchar.h>

typedef ... wchar_t;
typedef ... wint_t;
#define WEOF ...
#define WCHAR_MAX ...
#define WCHAR_MIN ...
#define NULL ...
#define size_t ...
```

Type **FILE** is used throughout the standard I/O library to represent control information for a stream. It is used for reading from both byte- and wide-character-oriented files.

The value **EOF** is conventionally used as a value that signals *end of file*—that is, the exhaustion of input data. It has the value –1 in most traditional implementations, but Standard C requires only that it be a negative integral constant expression. Because **EOF** is sometimes used to signal other problems, it is best to use the **feof** facility (Section 15.14) to determine whether end of file has indeed been encountered when **EOF** is returned. The macro **WEOF** (Amendment 1) is used in wide-character I/O for the same purpose as **EOF** in byte I/O; it is a value of type **wint_t** (not necessarily **wchar_t**) and need not be a negative value. **WCHAR_MAX** is the largest value representable by type **wchar_t**, and **WCHAR_MIN** is the smallest.

The type **size_t** and the null pointer constant **NULL** are defined in the header files **stdio.h** and **wchar.h** for convenience. In Standard C, they are also defined in **stddef.h**, and it does no harm to use more than one header file.

References   wchar_t 2.1.5, 11.1; wint_t 2.1.5, 11.1

15.2 fopen, fclose, fflush, freopen, fwide

Synopsis

```
#include <stdio.h>

FILE *fopen(
    const char * restrict filename, const char * restrict mode);
int fclose(FILE * restrict stream);
int fflush(FILE * restrict stream);
FILE *freopen(
    const char * restrict filename,
    const char * restrict mode,
    FILE * restrict stream);

#define FOPEN_MAX …
#define FILENAME_MAX …
```

```
#include <wchar.t>

int fwide(FILE * restrict stream, int orient);
```

The function **fopen** takes as arguments a file name and a mode; each is specified as a character string. The file name is used in an implementation-specified manner to open or create a file and associate it with a stream. (The value of the macro **FILENAME_MAX** is the maximum length for a file name or an appropriate length if there is no practical maximum.) A pointer of type **FILE** * is returned to identify the stream for other input/output operations. If any error is detected, **fopen** stores an error code into **errno** and returns a null pointer. The number of streams that may be open simultaneously is not specified; in Standard C, it is given by the value of the macro **FOPEN_MAX**, which must be at least eight, including the three predefined streams. (The number of open streams allowed may depend on current resource consumption in the operating system.)

Under C89 Amendment 1, the stream returned by **fopen** has no orientation, and either byte or wide-character input/output (but not both) may be performed on it.

The function **fclose** closes an open stream in an appropriate and orderly fashion, including any necessary emptying of internal data buffers. The function **fclose** returns **EOF** if an error is detected; otherwise it returns zero.

Example

Here are some functions that open and close normal text files. They handle error conditions and print diagnostics as necessary, and their return values match those of **fopen** and **fclose**:

```
#include <errno.h>
#include <stdio.h>

FILE *open_input(const char *filename)
    /* Open filename for input; return NULL if problem */
{
    FILE *f;
    errno = 0;
    /* Functions below might choke on a NULL filename. */
    if (filename == NULL) filename = "";
    f = fopen(filename,"r");    /* "w" for open_output */
    if (f == NULL)
        fprintf(stderr,
                "open_input(\"%s\") failed: %s\n",
                filename, strerror(errno));
    return f;
}

int close_file(FILE *f)
    /* Close file f */
{
    int s  = 0;
    if (f == NULL) return 0; /* Ingore this case */
    errno = 0;
    s = fclose(f);
    if (s == EOF) perror("Close failed");
    return s;
}
```

The function **fflush** empties any buffers associated with the output or update stream argument. The stream remains open. If any error is detected, **fflush** returns **EOF**; otherwise it returns 0. **fflush** is typically used only in exceptional circumstances; **fclose** and **exit** normally take care of flushing output buffers.

The function **freopen** takes a file name, a mode, and an open stream. It first tries to close **stream** as if by a call to **fclose**, but any error while doing so is ignored. Then **filename** and **mode** are used to open a new file as if by a call to **fopen**, except that the new stream is associated with **stream** rather than getting a new value of type **FILE ***. The function **freopen** returns **stream** if it is successful; otherwise (if the new open fails) a null pointer is returned. One of the main uses of **freopen** is to reassociate one of the standard input/output streams **stdin**, **stdout**, and **stderr** with another file. Under Amendment 1 to C89, **freopen** removes any previous orientation from the steam.

References   **EOF** 15.1; **exit** 19.3; **stdin** 15.4

15.2.1 File Modes

The values shown in Table 15–1 are permitted for the mode specification in the functions **fopen** and **freopen**.

Table 15–1   Type specifications for **fopen** and **freopen**

Mode[a]	Meaning
"r"	Open an existing file for input.
"w"	Create a new file or truncate an existing one for output.
"a"	Create a new file or append to an existing one for output.
"r+"	Open an existing file for update (both reading and writing) starting at the beginning of the file.
"w+"	Create a new file or truncate an existing one for update.
"a+"	Create a new file or append to an existing one for update.

[a] All modes can have the letter **b** appended to them, signifying that the stream is to hold binary rather than character data.

When a file is opened for update (**+** is present in the mode string), the resulting stream may be used for both input and output. However, an output operation may not be followed by an input operation without an intervening call to **fsetpos**, **fseek**, **rewind**, or **fflush**, and an input operation may not be followed by an output operation without an intervening call to **fsetpos**, **fseek**, **rewind**, or **fflush** or an input operation that encounters end of file. (These operations empty any internal buffers.)

Standard C allows any of the types listed in Table 15–1 to be followed by the character **b** to indicate a "binary" (as opposed to "text") stream is to be created. (The distinction under UNIX was blurred because both kinds of files are handled the same; other operating systems are not so lucky.) Standard C also allows any of the "update" file types to assume binary mode; the **b** designator may appear before or after the **+** in the stream mode specification.

In Standard C, the mode string may contain other characters after the modes listed earlier. Implementations may use these additions to specify other attributes of streams; for example,

```
f = fopen("C:\\work\\dict.txt","r,access=lock");
```

Table 15–2 lists some properties of each of the stream modes.

Table 15–2   Properties of **fopen** modes

Property	Mode					
	r	w	a	r+	w+	a+
Named file must already exist	yes	no	no	yes	no	no
Existing file's contents are lost	no	yes	no	no	yes	no
Read from stream permitted	yes	no	no	yes	yes	yes
Write to stream permitted	no	yes	yes	yes	yes	yes
Write begins at end of stream	no	no	yes	no	no	yes

15.2.2 File Orientation

The **fwide** function (C89 Amendment 1) is used to test and/or set the orientation of a stream. The function returns a positive, negative, or zero value according to whether **stream** is wide-oriented, byte-oriented, or has no orientation, respectively, after the call. The **orient** argument determines whether **fwide** will first attempt to set the orientation. If **orient** is 0, no attempt to set the orientation is made, and the return value reflects the orientation at the time of the call. If **orient** is positive, then **fwide** attempts to set wide orientation; if **orient** is negative, then **fwide** attempts to set byte orientation. These attempts can only be successful if the stream previously had no orientation—that is, if it had just been opened by **fopen** or **freopen**. Otherwise, the orientation remains unchanged.

Example

> When using wide-oriented streams, it is a good idea to use **fwide** to establish the orientation at the time fopen is called. Here is a function that opens a specified file in a specified mode and sets it to be wide-oriented in a given locale. If successful, the function returns a file pointer; otherwise, it returns **NULL**.

```
FILE *fopen_wide(
    const char *filename, /* file to open */
    const char *mode,     /* mode for open */
    const char *locale)/* locale for encoding */
{
    FILE *f = fopen(filename, mode);
    if (f != NULL) {
        char *old_locale = setlocale(LC_CTYPE, locale);
        if (old_locale == NULL || fwide(f, 1) <= 0) {
            fclose(f);   /* setlocale or fwide failed */
            f = NULL;
        }
        /* return locale to its original value */
        setlocale(LC_CTYPE, old_locale);
    }
    return f;
}
```

The multibyte encoding used (if any) is determined when the orientation of the stream is established. It will be affected by the **LC_CTYPE** category of the current locale at the time the orientation is established.

15.3 setbuf, setvbuf

Synopsis

```
#include <stdio.h>

int setvbuf(
   FILE * restrict stream,
   char *b restrict uf,
   int bufmode,
   size t size );
void setbuf(
   FILE * restrict stream,
   char * restrict buf );

#define BUFSIZ ...
#define _IOFBF ...
#define _IOLBF ...
#define _IONBF ...
```

These functions allow the programmer to control the buffering strategy for streams in those rare instances in which the default buffering is unsatisfactory. The functions must be called after a stream is opened and before any data are read or written.

The function **setvbuf** is the more general function adopted from UNIX System V. The first argument is the stream being controlled; the second (if not null) is a character array to use in place of the automatically generated buffer; **bufmode** specifies the type of buffering, and **size** specifies the buffer size. The function returns zero if it is successful and nonzero if the arguments are improper or the request cannot be satisfied.

The macros **_IOFBF**, **_IOLBF**, and **_IONBF** expand to values that can be used for **bufmode**. If **bufmode** is **_IOFBF**, the stream is fully buffered; if **bufmode** is **_IOLBF**, the buffer is flushed when a newline character is written or when the buffer is full; if **bufmode** is **_IONBF**, the stream is unbuffered. If buffering is requested and if **buf** is not a null pointer, then the array specified by **buf** should be **size** bytes long and will be used in place of the automatically generated buffers. The constant **BUFSIZ** is an "appropriate" value for the buffer size.

The function **setbuf** is a simplified form of **setvbuf**. The expression

```
setbuf(stream,buf)
```

is equivalent to the expression

```
((buf==NULL) ?
   (void) setvbuf(stream,NULL,_IONBF,0) :
   (void) setvbuf(stream,buf,_IOFBF,BUFSIZ))
```

References   EOF 15.1; fopen 15.2; size_t 11.1

15.4 *stdin, stdout, stderr*

Synopsis

`#include <stdio.h>`
 	
`#define stderr ...`
`#define stdin  ...`
`#define stdout ...`

The expressions **stdin**, **stdout**, and **stderr** have type **FILE ***, and their values are established prior to the start of an application program to certain standard text streams. **stdin** points to an input stream that is the "normal input" to the program, **stdout** to an output stream for the "normal output", and **stderr** to an output stream for error messages and other unexpected output from the program. In an interactive environment, all three streams are typically associated with the terminal used to start the program and, except **stderr**, are buffered.

These expressions are not usually lvalues, and in any case they should not be altered by assignment. The **freopen** function (Section 15.2) may be used to change them.

Example

The expressions **stdin**, **stdout**, and **stderr** are often defined as addresses of static or global stream descriptors:

```
extern FILE __iob[FOPEN_MAX];
...
#define stdin (&__iob[0])
#define stdout (&__iob[1])
#define stderr (&__iob[2])
```

UNIX systems in particular provide convenient ways to associate these standard streams with files or other programs when the application is launched, making them powerful when used according to certain standard conventions.

Under C89 Amendment 1, **stdin**, **stdout**, and **stderr** have no orientation when a C program is started. Therefore, those streams can be used for wide-character input/output by calling **fwide** (Section 15.2) or using a wide-character input/output function on them.

15.5 fseek, ftell, rewind, fgetpos, fsetpos

Synopsis

```
#include <stdio.h>

int fseek(
   FILE * restrict stream, long int offset, int wherefrom);
long int ftell(FILE * restrict stream);
void rewind(FILE * restrict stream);
#define SEEK_SET 0
#define SEEK_CUR 1
#define SEEK_END 2

typedef ... fpos_t ...;
int fgetpos( FILE * restrict stream, fpos_t *pos );
int fsetpos( FILE * restrict stream, const fpos_t *pos );
```

The functions in this section allow random access within text and binary streams—typically, streams associated with files.

15.5.1 fseek and ftell

The function `ftell` takes a stream that is open for input or output and returns the position in the stream in the form of a value suitable for the second argument to `fseek`. Using `fseek` on a saved result of `ftell` will result in resetting the position of the stream to the place in the file at which `ftell` had been called.

For binary files, the value returned will be the number of characters preceding the current file position. For text files, the value returned is implementation-defined. The returned value must be usable in `fseek`, and the value `0L` must be a representation—not necessarily the only one—of the beginning of the file.

If `ftell` encounters an error, it returns `-1L` and sets `errno` to an implementation-defined, positive value. Since `-1L` could conceivably be a valid file position, `errno` must be checked to confirm the error. Conditions that can cause `ftell` to fail include an attempt to locate the position in a stream attached to a terminal or an attempt to report a position that cannot be represented as an object of type `long int`.

The function `fseek` allows random access within the (open) `stream`. The second two arguments specify a file position: `offset` is a signed (long) integer specifying (for binary streams) a number of characters, and `wherefrom` is a "seek code" indicating from what point in the file `offset` should be measured. The stream is positioned as indicated next, and `fseek` returns zero if successful or a nonzero value if an error occurs. (The value of `errno` is not changed.) Any end of file indication is cleared and any effect of `ungetc` is undone. Standard C defines the constants `SEEK_SET`, `SEEK_CUR`, and `SEEK_END` to represent the values of `wherefrom`; programmers using non-Standard implementations must use the integer values specified or define the macros.

When repositioning a binary file, the new position is given by the following table:

If **wherefrom** is:	Then the new position is:
SEEK_SET or 0	**offset** characters from the beginning of the file
SEEK_CUR or 1	**offset** characters from the current position in the file
SEEK_END or 2	**offset** characters from the end of the file (Negative values specify positions before the end; positive values extend the file with unspecified contents.)

Standard C does not require implementations to "meaningfully" support a **where-from** value of **SEEK_END** for binary streams. The following, more limited set of calls is permitted on text streams by Standard C:

A call of the form	Positions (text) stream
fseek(stream,0L,SEEK_SET)	at the beginning of the file
fseek(stream,0L,SEEK_CUR)	at the same location (i.e., the call has no effect)
fseek(stream,0L,SEEK_END)	at the end of the file
fseek(stream,*ftell-pos*,SEEK_SET)	at a position returned by a previous call to **ftell** for **stream**

These limitations recognize that a position within a text file may not map directly onto the file's internal representation. For example, a position may require a record number and an offset within the record. (However, Standard C requires that implementations support the call **fseek(stream,0L,SEEK_END)** for text files, whereas they do not have to "meaningfully" support it for binary streams.)

Under Amendment 1 of C89, file positioning operations performed on wide-oriented streams must satisfy all restrictions applicable to either binary or text files. The **fseek** and **ftell** functions are in general not powerful enough to support wide-oriented streams, even for the simplest positioning operations such as the beginning or end of the stream. The **fgetpos** and **fsetpos** functions described in the next section should be used for wide-oriented streams.

The function **rewind** resets a stream to its beginning. By Standard C definition, the call **rewind(stream)** is equivalent to

```
(void) fseek(stream, 0L, SEEK_SET)
```

15.5.2 fgetpos and fsetpos

The functions **fgetpos** and **fsetpos** are new to Standard C. They were added to handle files that are too large for their positions to be representable within an integer of type **long int** (as in **ftell** and **fseek**).

The **fgetpos** function stores the current file position in the object pointed to by **pos**. It returns zero if successful. If an error is encountered, it returns a nonzero value and stores an implementation-defined, positive value in **errno**.

The **fsetpos** function sets the current file position according to the value in ***pos**, which must be a value returned earlier by **fgetpos** on the same stream. **fsetpos** undoes any effect of **ungetc** or **ungetwc**. It returns zero if successful. If an error is encountered, it returns a nonzero value and stores an implementation-defined, positive value in **errno**.

Under C89 Amendment 1, the file position object used by **fgetpos** and **fsetpos** will have to include a representation of the hidden conversion state associated with the wide-oriented stream (i.e., a value of type **mbstate_t**). That state, in addition to the position in the file, is needed to interpret the following multibyte characters after a repositioning operation.

In wide-oriented output streams, using **fsetpos** to set the output position and then writing one or more multibyte characters will cause any following multibyte characters in the file to become undefined. This is because the output could partially overwrite an existing multibyte character or could change the conversion state in such a way that later multibyte characters could not be properly interpreted.

References   mbstate_t 11.1; ungetc 15.6

15.6 fgetc, fgetwc, getc, getwc, getchar, getwchar, ungetc, ungetwc

Synopsis

```
#include <stdio.h>

int fgetc(FILE *stream);
int getc(FILE *stream);
int getchar(void);
int ungetc(int c, FILE *stream);
```

```
#include <stdio.h>
#include <wchar.h>

wint_t fgetwc(FILE *stream);
wint_t getwc(FILE *stream);
wint_t getwchar(void);
wint_t ungetwc(wint_t c, FILE *stream);
```

The function **fgetc** takes an input stream as its argument. It reads the next character from the stream and returns it as a value of type **int**. The internal stream position indicator is advanced. Successive calls to **fgetc** will return successive characters from the input stream. If an error occurs or if the stream is at end of file, then **fgetc** returns **EOF**. The **feof** and/or **ferror** facilities should be used in this case to determine whether end of file has really been reached.

The function **getc** is identical to **fgetc** except that **getc** is usually implemented as a macro for efficiency. The **stream** argument should not have any side effects because it may be evaluated more than once.

The function **getchar** is equivalent to **getc(stdin)**. Like **getc**, **getchar** is often implemented as a macro.

In C89 Amendment 1, the functions **fgetwc**, **getwc**, and **getwchar** are analogous to their byte-oriented counterparts—including probable macro implementations—but they read and return the next wide character from the input stream. **WEOF** is returned to indicate error or end of file; if the error is an encoding error, **EILSEQ** is stored in **errno**. Reading a wide character involves a conversion from a multibyte character to a wide character; this is performed as if by a call to **mbrtowc** using the stream's internal conversion state.

The function **ungetc** causes the character **c** (converted to **unsigned char**) to be pushed back onto the specified input stream so that it will be returned by the next call to **fgetc**, **getc**, or **getchar** on that stream. If several characters are pushed, they are returned in the reverse order of their pushing (i.e., last character first). **ungetc** returns **c** when the character is successfully pushed back, **EOF** if the attempt fails. A successful file-positioning command on the stream (**fseek**, **fsetpos**, or **rewind**) discards all pushed-back characters. After reading (or discarding) all pushed-back characters, the file position is the same as immediately before the characters were pushed.

One character of pushback is guaranteed provided the stream is buffered and at least one character has been read from the stream since the last **fseek**, **fopen**, or **freopen** operation on the stream. An attempt to push the value **EOF** back onto the stream as a character has no effect on the stream and returns **EOF**. A call to **fsetpos**, **rewind**, **fseek**, or **freopen** erases all memory of pushed-back characters from the stream without affecting any external storage associated with the stream.

The function **ungetc** is useful for implementing input-scanning operations such as **scanf**. A program can "peek ahead" at the next input character by reading it and then putting it back if it is unsuitable. (However, **scanf** and other library functions are not permitted to preempt the use of **ungetc** by the programmer—that is, the programmer is guaranteed to have at least one character of pushback even after a call to **scanf** or similar function.)

The function **ungetwc** (C89 Amendment 1) is analogous to **ungetc**.

References   **EOF** 15.1; **feof** 15.14; **fseek** 15.5; **fopen** 15.2; **freopen** 15.2; **scanf** 15.8; **stdin** 15.4

15.7 fgets, fgetws, gets

Synopsis

```
#include <stdio.h>

char *fgets(char *s, int n, FILE *stream);
char *gets(char *s);
```

```
#include <stdio.h>
#include <wchar.h>

wchar_t *fgetws(wchar_t *s, int n, FILE *stream);
```

The function **fgets** takes three arguments: a pointer **s** to the beginning of a character array, a count **n**, and an input stream. Characters are read from the input stream into **s** until a newline is seen, end of file is reached, or **n**–1 characters have been read without encountering end of file or a newline character. A terminating null character is then appended to the array after the characters read. If the input is terminated because a newline was seen, the newline character will be stored in the array just before the terminating null character. The argument **s** is returned on successful completion.

If end of file is encountered before any characters have been read from the stream, then **fgets** returns a null pointer and the contents of the array **s** are unchanged. If an error occurs during the input operation, then **fgets** returns a null pointer and the contents of the array **s** are indeterminate. The **feof** facility (Section 15.14) should be used to determine whether end of file has really been reached when **NULL** is returned.

The function **gets** reads characters from the standard input stream, **stdin**, into the character array **s**. However, unlike **fgets**, when the input is terminated by a newline character **gets** discards the newline and does not put it into **s**. The use of **gets** can be dangerous because it is always possible for the input length to exceed the storage available in the character array. The function **fgets** is safer because no more than **n** characters will ever be placed in **s**.

The function **fgetws** (C89 Amendment 1) is analogous to **fgets**, but it operates on wide-oriented input streams and stores wide characters into **s**, including a null wide character at the end. There is no wide-character function corresponding to **gets**—another hint that **gets** is to be avoided.

References   feof 15.14; stdin 15.4

15.8 *fscanf, fwscanf, scanf, wscanf, sscanf, swscanf*

Synopsis

```
#include <stdio.h>

int fscanf(
   FILE * restrict stream, const char * restrict format, ...);
int scanf(
   const char * restrict format, ...);
int sscanf(
   char *s, const char * restrict format, ...);
```

```
#include <stdio.h>
#include <wchar.h>

int fwscanf(
   FILE * restrict stream,
   const wchar_t * restrict format, ...);
int wscanf(
   const wchar_t *format, ...);
int swscanf(
   wchar_t *s, const wchar_t *format, ...);
```

The function **fscanf** parses formatted input text, reading characters from the stream specified as the first argument and converting sequences of characters according to the control string format. Additional arguments may be required depending on the contents of the control string. Each argument after the control string must be a pointer; converted values read from the input stream are stored into the objects designated by the pointers.

The functions **scanf** and **sscanf** are like **fscanf**. In the case of **scanf**, characters are read from the standard input stream **stdin**. In the case of **sscanf**, characters are read from the string **s**. When **sscanf** attempts to read beyond the end of the string **s**, it operates as **fscanf** and **scanf** when end of file is reached.

The input operation may terminate prematurely because the input stream reaches end of file or because there is a conflict between the control string and a character read from the input stream. The value returned by these functions is the number of successful assignments performed before termination of the operation for either reason. If the input reaches end of file before any conflict or assignment is performed, then the functions return **EOF**. When a conflict occurs, the character causing the conflict remains unread and will be processed by the next input operation.

Amendment 1 to C89 defines a set of wide-character formatted input functions corresponding to **fscanf**, **scanf**, and **sscanf**. The new **wscanf** "family" of functions use wide-character control strings and expect the input to be a sequence of wide characters. Any conversions from underlying multibyte sequences in the external file are transparent to the programmer. In the descriptions that follow, the byte-oriented functions are described. The behavior of the wide-oriented functions can be derived by substituting "wide character" for "character" or "byte" unless otherwise noted.

Amendment 1 also extends Standard C's formatting strings, permitting the **l** size specifier to be added to the **s**, **c**, and **[** conversion operations to indicate that the associated argument is a pointer to a wide string or character. See the description of those conversion operations for more information.

15.8.1 Control String

The control string is a picture of the expected form of the input. In Standard C, it is a multibyte character sequence beginning and ending in its initial shift state for the **scanf** family, and it is a sequence of wide characters for the **wscanf** family. One may think of these functions as performing a simple matching operation between the control string and the input stream. The contents of the control string may be divided into three categories:

1. *Whitespace characters.* A whitespace character in the control string causes whitespace characters to be read and discarded. The first input character encountered that is not a whitespace character remains as the next character to be read from the input stream. Note that if several consecutive whitespace characters appear in the control string, the effect is the same as if only one had appeared. Thus, any sequence of consecutive whitespace characters in the control string will match any sequence of consecutive whitespace characters, possibly of different length, from the input stream.

2. *Conversion specifications.* A conversion specification begins with a percent sign, **%**; the remainder of the syntax for conversion specifications is described in detail next. The number of characters read from the input stream depends on the conversion operation. As a rule of thumb, a conversion operation processes characters until: (a) end of file is reached, (b) a whitespace character or other inappropriate character is encountered, or (c) the number of characters read for the conversion operation equals the specified maximum field width. The processed characters are normally converted (e.g., to a numeric value) and stored in a place designated by a pointer argument following the control string.

3. *Other characters.* Any character other than a whitespace character or a percent sign must match the next character of the input stream. If it does not match, a conflict has occurred; the conversion operation is terminated, and the conflicting input character remains in the input stream to be read by the next input operation on that stream.

There should be exactly the right number of pointer arguments, each of exactly the right type, to satisfy the conversion specifications in the control string. If there are too many arguments, the extra ones are ignored; if there are too few, the results are undefined. If any conversion specification is malformed, the behavior is likewise undefined. There is a sequence point after the actions performed by each conversion specification.

15.8.2 Conversion Specifications

A conversion specification begins with a percent sign, **%**. After the percent sign, the following conversion specification elements should appear in this order:

1. An optional *assignment suppression flag*, written as an asterisk,*****. If this is present for a conversion operation that normally performs an assignment, then characters are read and processed from the input stream in the usual way for that operation, but no assignment is performed and no pointer argument is consumed.

2. An optional *maximum field width* expressed as a positive decimal integer.

3. An optional *size specification* expressed as one of the character sequences **hh**, **h**, **l** (ell), **ll** (ell-ell), **j**, **z**, **t**, or **L**. The conversion operations to which these may be applied are listed in Table 15–3. The **hh**, **ll**, **j**, **z**, and **t** size specifications are new in C99.

4. A required *conversion operation* (or *conversion specifier*) expressed (with one exception) as a single character: **a**, **c**, **d**, **e**, **f**, **g**, **i**, **n**, **o**, **p**, **s**, **u**, **x**, **%**, or **[**. The exception is the **[** operation, which causes all following characters up to the next **]** to be part of the conversion specification.

The conversion specifications for **fscanf** are similar in syntax and meaning to those for **fprintf**, but there are certain differences. It is best to regard the control string syntax for **fprintf** and **fscanf** as being only vaguely similar; do not use the documentation for one as a guide to the other.

Example

Here are some of the differences between the conversions in **fscanf** and **fprintf**:

The **[** conversion operation is peculiar to **fscanf**.

fscanf does not admit any precision specification of the kind accepted by **fprintf**, nor any of the flag characters **-**, **+**, *space*, **0**, and **#** that are accepted by **fprintf**.

An explicitly specified field width is a minimum for **fprintf**, but a maximum for **fscanf**.

Whereas **fprintf** allows a field width to be specified by a computed argument, indicated by using an asterisk for the field width, **fscanf** uses the asterisk for another purpose—namely, assignment suppression; this is perhaps the most glaring inconsistency of all.

Except as noted, all conversion operations skip over any initial whitespace before conversion. This initial whitespace is not counted toward the maximum field width. None of the conversion operations normally skips over trailing whitespace characters as a matter of course. Trailing whitespace characters (such as the newline that terminates a line of input) will remain unread unless explicitly matched in the control string. (Doing this may be tricky because a whitespace character in the control string will attempt to match many whitespace characters in the input, resulting in an attempt to read beyond a newline.)

It is not possible to determine directly whether matches of literal character in the control string succeed or fail. It is also not possible to determine directly whether conversion operations involving suppressed assignments succeed or fail. The value returned by these functions reflects only the number of successful assignments performed.

The conversion operations are complicated. A brief summary is presented in Table 15–3 and discussed in detail next.

Table 15–3　Input conversions (`scanf`, `fscanf`, `sscanf`)

Conversion letter	Size specifier	Argument type	Input format
d i[a]	none hh h l ll[e] j z t	int * char * short * long * long long * intmax_t * size_t * ptrdiff_t *	[−|+]dd...d [−|+][0[x]]dd...d[b]
u o x	none hh h l ll[e] j z t	unsigned * unsigned char * unsigned short * unsigned long * unsigned long long * uintmax_t * size_t * ptrdiff_t *	[−|+]dd...d$_c$ [−|+]dd...d$_c$ [−|+][0x]dd...d[d]
c	none l[a]	char * wchar_t *	a fixed-width sequence of characters; must be multibytes if **l** is used
s	none l[a]	char * wchar_t *	a sequence of non-whitespace characters; must be multibytes if **l** is used
p[a]	none	void **	a sequence of characters such as output with %p in **fprintf**.
n[a]	none hh h l ll[e] j z t	int * char * short * long * long long * intmax_t * size_t * ptrdiff_t *	none; the number of characters read is stored in the argument
a[e], f, e, g	none l L[a]	float * double * long double *	any floating-point constant or decimal integer constant, optionally preceded by − or +
[	none l[a]	char * wchar_t *	a sequence of characters from a scanning set; must be multibytes if **l** is used

[a] C89 addition.

[b] The base of the number is determined by the first digits in the same way as for C constants.

[c] The number is assumed to be octal.

[d] The number is assumed to be hexadecimal regardless of the presence of **0x**.

[e] C99 addition.

The d conversion　Signed decimal conversion is performed. One argument is consumed; it should be of type `int *`, `short *`, or `long *` depending on the size specification.

The format of the number read is the same as expected for the input to the **strtol** function (**wcstol** for **wscanf**) with the value 10 for the **base** argument—that is, a sequence of decimal digits optionally preceded by – or +. If the value expressed by the input is too large to be represented as a signed integer of the appropriate size, then the behavior is undefined.

The i conversion   Signed integer conversion is performed. One argument is consumed; it should be of type **int ***, **short ***, or **long *** depending on the size specification.

The format of the number read is the same as expected for the input to the **strtol** function (**wcstol** for **wscanf**) with the value 0 for the **base** argument—that is, a C *integer-constant,* without suffix, and optionally preceded by – or +, and **0** (octal) or **0x** (hexadecimal) prefixes. If the value expressed by the input is too large to be represented as a signed integer of the appropriate size, then the behavior is undefined.

The u conversion   Unsigned decimal conversion is performed. One argument is consumed; it should be of type **unsigned ***, **unsigned short ***, or **unsigned long *** depending on the size specification.

The format of the number read is the same as expected for the input to the **strtoul** function (**wcstoul** for **wscanf**) with the value 10 for the **base** argument—that is, a sequence of decimal digits optionally preceded by – or +. If the value expressed by the input is too large to be represented as an unsigned integer of the appropriate size, then the behavior is undefined.

The o conversion   Unsigned octal conversion is performed. One argument is consumed; it should be of type **unsigned ***, **unsigned short ***, or **unsigned long *** depending on the size specification.

The format of the number read is the same as expected for the input to the **strtoul** function (**wcstoul** for **wscanf**) with the value 8 for the **base** argument—that is, a sequence of octal digits optionally preceded by – or +. If the value expressed by the input is too large to be represented as an unsigned integer of the appropriate size, then the behavior is undefined.

The x conversion   Unsigned hexadecimal conversion is performed. One argument is consumed; it should be of type **unsigned ***, **unsigned short ***, or **unsigned long *** depending on the size specification.

The format of the number read is the same as expected for the input to the **strtoul** function (**wcstoul** for **wscanf**) with the value 16 for the **base** argument—that is, a sequence of hexadecimal digits optionally preceded by – or +. The operation accepts all of the characters **0123456789abcdefABCDEF** as valid hexadecimal digits. If the value expressed by the input is too large to be represented as an unsigned integer of the appropriate size, then the behavior is undefined.

Some non-Standard C implementations accept the letter **X** as an equivalent conversion operation.

The c conversion   One or more characters are read. One pointer argument is consumed; it must be of type `char *` or, if the `l` size specification is present, `wchar_t *`. The `c` conversion operation does not skip over initial whitespace characters. The conversions applied to the input character(s) depend on whether the `l` size specifier is present and whether `scanf` or `wscanf` is used. The possibilities are listed in Table 15–4.

Table 15–4   Input conversions of the `c` specifier

Function	Size specifier	Argument type	Input	Conversions
`scanf`	none	`char *`	character(s)	none; characters are copied
	`l`	`wchar_t *`	multibyte character(s)	to wide character(s), as if by one or more calls to `mbrtowc`
`wscanf`	none	`char *`	wide character(s)	to multibyte character(s), as if by one or more calls to `wcrtomb`
	`l`	`wchar_t *`	wide character(s)	none; wide characters are copied

If no field width is specified, then exactly one character is read unless the input stream is at end of file, in which case the conversion operation fails. The character value is assigned to the location indicated by the next pointer argument.

If a field width is specified, then the pointer argument is assumed to point to the beginning of an array of characters, and the field width specifies the number of characters to be read; the conversion operation fails if end of file is encountered before that many characters have been read. The characters read are stored into successive locations of the array. No extra terminating null is appended to the characters that are read.

The s conversion   A string is read. One pointer argument is consumed; it must be of type `char *` or, if the `l` size specification is present (C89 Amendment 1), `wchar_t *`. The `s` conversion operation always skips initial whitespace characters.

Characters are read until end of file is reached, until a whitespace character is seen (in which case that character remains unread), or (if a field width was specified) until the maximum number of characters has been read. If end of file is encountered before any nonwhitespace character is seen, the conversion operation is considered to have failed. Conversions may be applied to the input characters depending on whether the `l` size specifier is present and on whether `scanf` or `wscanf` is used (see Table 15–5). In the case of the `l` specifier used with `scanf`, the input is terminated by the first whitespace character; this occurs before the input characters are interpreted as multibyte characters.

A terminating null is always appended to the stored characters. The `s` conversion operation can be dangerous if no maximum field width is specified because it is always possible for the input length to exceed the storage available in the character array.

The `s` operation with an explicit field width differs from the `c` operation with an explicit field width. The `c` operation does not skip over whitespace characters and will read exactly as many characters (or wide characters) as were specified unless end of file is encountered. The `s` operation skips over initial whitespace characters, will be terminated by

Table 15–5   Input conversions of the **s** specifier

Func-tion	Size specifier	Argument type	Input	Conversion
scanf	none	**char ***	characters	none; characters are copied
	l	**wchar_t ***	multibyte characters	to wide characters, as if by calls to **mbrtowc**
wscanf	none	**char ***	wide characters	to multibyte characters, as if by calls to **wcrtomb**
	l	**wchar_t ***	wide characters	none; wide characters are copied

a whitespace character after reading in some number of characters (or wide characters) that are not whitespace, and will append a null character to the stored characters.

The p conversion   Pointer conversion is performed. One argument is consumed; it should be of type **void ****. The format of the pointer value read is implementation-specified, but it will usually be the same as the format produced by the **%p** conversion in the **printf** family. The interpretation of the pointer is also implementation-defined, but if you write out a pointer and later read it back, all during the same program execution, then the pointer read in will compare equal to the pointer written out. The **p** conversion is new with Standard C.

The n conversion   No conversion is performed and no characters are read. Instead, the number of characters processed so far by the current call of the **scanf**-family function is written to the argument, which must be of type **int ***, **short ***, or **long *** depending on the size specification. The **n** conversion is new with Standard C.

The a, f, e, and g conversions   Signed decimal floating-point conversion is performed. In C99, the **a** conversion is allowed and is identical to **f**, **e**, and **g** for input. One pointer argument is consumed; it must be of type **float ***, **double ***, or **long double *** depending on the size specification.

The format of the number read is the same as expected for the input to the **strtod** function (**wcstod** for **wscanf**)—that is, a sequence of decimal or hexadecimal digits optionally preceded by – or + and optionally containing a decimal point and signed exponent part. (An integer with no decimal point is acceptable.) The input strings **INF**, **INFINITY**, **NAN**, and **NAN(...)**, ignoring case, denote special floating-point numbers. Acceptance of hexadecimal floating-point input is new in C99.

The characters read are interpreted as a floating-point number representation and converted to a floating-point number of the specified size. If no digits are read, or at least no digits are read before the exponent part is seen, then the value is zero. If no digits are seen after the letter introducing the exponent, then the exponent part of the representation is assumed to be zero. If the value expressed by the input is too large or too small to be represented as a floating-point number of the appropriate size, then the value **HUGE_VAL** is returned (with the proper sign) and the value **ERANGE** is stored in **errno**. (In implementations that do not conform to Standard C, the return value and setting of **errno** are unpredictable.) If the value expressed by the input is not too large or too small, but nevertheless cannot be represented exactly as a floating-point number of the appropriate size, then some form of rounding or truncation occurs.

The **a**, **f**, **e**, and **g** conversion operations are completely identical; any one of them will accept any style of floating-point representation. Some implementations may accept **G** and **E** as floating-point conversion letters.

The % conversion   A single percent sign is expected in the input. Because a percent sign is used to indicate the beginning of a conversion specification, it is necessary to write two of them to have one matched. No pointer argument is consumed. The assignment suppression flag, field width, and size specification are not relevant to the **%** conversion operation.

The [conversion   A string is read and one pointer argument of type **char *** or **wchar_t *** (if the **l** size specifier is present) is consumed. The **[** conversion operation does not skip over initial whitespace characters. The conversion specification indicates exactly what characters may be read as part of the input field. The **[** must be followed in the control string by more characters, terminated by **]**. All the characters up to the **]** are part of the conversion specification, called the *scanset*. If the character immediately following the **[** is the circumflex **^**, it has a special meaning as a negation flag, and the scanset consists of all characters *not* appearing between **^** and **]**. The characters in the scanset are regarded as a set in the mathematical sense.

Any **[** between the initial **[** and the terminating **]** is treated as any other character. Similarly, any **^** that does not immediately follow the initial **[** is treated as any other character. In Standard C, if **]** immediately follows the initial **[**, then it is in the scanset and the *next* **]** will terminate the conversion specification. If **]** immediately follows the negation flag **^**, then the **]** is *not* in the scanset and the next **]** will terminate the scanset. Older implementations might not support this special treatment of **]** at the beginning of the conversion specification.

Example

If the conversion is...	Then the scanset is...
%[abca]	the three characters **a**, **b**, and **c**
%[^abca]	all characters except **a**, **b**, and **c**
%[[]	the single character **[**
%[]]	the single character **]**
%[,\t]	the characters space, comma, and horizontal tab

Characters are read until end of file is reached, until a character not in the scanset is seen (in which case that character remains unread), or (if a field width was specified) until the maximum number of characters has been read. Then if the assignment is not suppressed by *****, the input characters are stored into the object designated by the argument pointer, just as for the **s** conversion operation, including any conversions to or from multibyte characters (see Table 15–5). Then an extra terminating null character is appended to the stored characters. Size specification is not relevant to the [conversion operation.

Like the **s** conversion, the [conversion operation can be dangerous if no maximum field width is specified because it is always possible for the input length to exceed the storage available in the character array.

References   **EOF** 15.1; **fprintf** 15.11; **stdin** 15.4;

15.9 fputc, fputwc, putc, putwc, putchar, putwchar

<table>
<tr><td align="center">Synopsis</td></tr>
<tr><td>

```
#include <stdio.h>

int fputc(int c, FILE *stream);
int putc(int c, FILE *stream);
int putchar(int c);
```
</td></tr>
<tr><td>

```
#include <stdio.h>
#include <wchar.h>

wint_t fputwc(wchar_t c, FILE *stream);
wint_t putwc(wchar_t c, FILE *stream);
wint_t putwchar(wchar_t c);
```
</td></tr>
</table>

The function **fputc** takes as arguments a character value and an output stream. It writes the character to the stream at its current position and also returns the character as a value of type **int**. Successive calls to **fputc** will write the given characters successively to the output stream. If an error occurs, **fputc** returns **EOF** instead of the character that should have been written.

The function **putc** operates like **fputc**, but it is usually implemented as a macro. The argument expressions must not have any side effects because they may be evaluated more than once.

The function **putchar** writes a character to the standard output stream **stdout**. Like **putc**, **putchar** is usually implemented as a macro and is quite efficient. The call **putchar(c)** is equivalent to **putc(c, stdout)**.

Amendment 1 to C89 added the wide-character functions **fputwc**, **putwc**, and **putwchar**, which correspond to the byte-oriented functions. The value **WEOF** is returned on error. If an encoding error occurs, **EILSEQ** is also stored into **errno**.

References   **EOF** 15.1; **stdout** 15.4

15.10 fputs, fputws, puts

Synopsis
```#include <stdio.h>```
```int fputs(const char *s, FILE *stream);```   ```int puts(const char *s);```
```#include <stdio.h>```   ```#include <wchar.h>```
```int fputws(const wchar_t *s, FILE *stream);```

The function **fputs** takes as arguments a null-terminated string and an output stream. It writes to the stream all the characters of the string, not including the terminating null character. If an error occurs, **fputs** returns **EOF**; otherwise it returns some other, non-negative value.

The function **puts** is like **fputs** except that the characters are always written to the stream **stdout**; after the characters in **s** are written out, an additional newline character is written (regardless of whether **s** contained a newline character).

Several non-Standard UNIX implementations of **fputs** have an error that causes the return value to be indeterminate if **s** is the empty string. Programmers might be alert for that boundary case.

Amendment 1 to C89 added the function **fputws**, which is analogous to **fputs**. The function returns **EOF** (not **WEOF**) on error, and **EILSEQ** is stored in **errno** if the error was an encoding error.

References   **EOF** 15.1; **stdout** 15.4

15.11 *fprintf, printf, sprintf, snprintf, fwprintf, wprintf, swprintf*

Synopsis

```
#include <stdio.h>

int fprintf(
  FILE * restrict stream, const char * restrict format, ... );
int printf(
  const char * restrict format, ...);
int sprintf(
  char * restrict s,
  const char * restrict format, ...);
int snprintf(
  char * restrict s, size_t n,
  const char * restrict format, ...);       // C99
```

```
#include <stdio.h>
#include <wchar.h>

int fwprintf(
  FILE * restrict stream,
  const wchar_t * restrict format, ... );
int wprintf(
  const wchar_t * restrict format, ...);
int swprintf(
  wchar_t *s, size_t n, const wchar_t *format, ...);
```

The function **fprintf** performs output formatting, sending the output to the stream specified as the first argument. The second argument is a format control string. Additional arguments may be required depending on the contents of the control string. A series of output characters is generated as directed by the control string; these characters are sent to the specified stream.

The **printf** function is related to **fprintf**, but sends the characters to the standard output stream **stdout**.

The **sprintf** function causes the output characters to be stored into the string buffer **s**. A final null character is output to **s** after all characters specified by the control string have been output. It is the programmer's responsibility to ensure that the **sprintf** destination string area is large enough to contain the output generated by the formatting operation. However, the **swprintf** function, unlike **sprintf**, includes a count of the maximum number of wide characters (including the terminating null character) to be written to the output string **s**. In C99, **snprintf** was added to provide the count for the nonwide function.

The value returned by these functions is **EOF** if an error occurred during the output operation; otherwise the result is some value other than **EOF**. In Standard C and most current implementations, the functions return the number of characters sent to the output stream if no error occurs. In the case of **sprintf**, the count does not include the terminating null character. (Standard C allows these functions to return any negative value if an error occurs.)

C89 (Amendment 1) specifies three wide-character versions of these functions; **fwprintf**, **wprintf**, and **swprintf**. The output of these functions is conceptually a wide string, and they convert their additional arguments to wide strings under control of the conversion operators. We denote these functions as the **wprintf** family of functions, or just *wprintf functions*, to distinguish them from the original byte-oriented *printf functions*. Under Amendment 1 also, the **l** size specifier may be applied to the **c** and **s** conversion operators in both the **printf** and **wprintf** functions.

C99 introduces the **a** and **A** conversion operators for hexadecimal floating-point conversions and the **hh**, **ll**, **j**, **z**, and **t** length modifiers.

References **EOF** 15.1; hexadecimal floating-point format 2.7.2; **scanf** 15.8; **stdout** 15.4; wide characters 2.1.4

15.11.1 Output Format

The control string is simply text to be copied verbatim, except that the string may contain conversion specifications. In Standard C, the control string is an (uninterpreted) multibyte character sequence beginning and ending in its initial shift state. In the **wprintf** functions, it is a wide-character string.

A conversion specification may call for the processing of some number of additional arguments, resulting in a formatted conversion operation that generates output characters not explicitly contained in the control string. There should be exactly the right number of arguments, each of exactly the right type, to satisfy the conversion specifications in the control string. Extra arguments are ignored, but the result from having too few arguments is unpredictable. If any conversion specification is malformed, then the effects are unpredictable. The conversion specifications for output are similar to those used for input by **fscanf** and related functions; the differences are discussed in Section 15.8.2. There is a sequence point just after the actions called for by each conversion specification.

The sequence of characters or wide characters output for a conversion specification may be conceptually divided into three elements: the *converted value* proper, which reflects the value of the converted argument; the *prefix*, which, if present, is typically **+**, **−**, or a space; and the *padding*, which is a sequence of spaces or zero digits added if necessary to increase the width of the output sequence to a specified minimum. The prefix always precedes the converted value. Depending on the conversion specification, the padding may precede the prefix, separate the prefix from the converted value, or follow the converted value. Examples are shown in the following figure; the enclosing boxes show the extent of the output governed by the conversion specification.

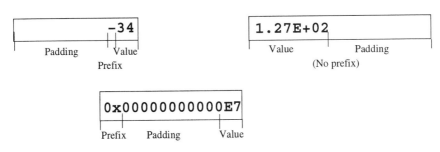

15.11.2 Conversion Specifications

In what follows, the terms *characters*, *letters*, and so on are to be understood as normal characters or letters (bytes) in the case of the **printf** functions and wide characters or letters in the case of the **wprintf** functions. For example, in **wprintf**, conversion specifications begin with the wide-character percent sign, **%**.

A conversion specification begins with a percent sign character, **%**, and has the following elements in order:

1. Zero or more *flag characters* (-, +, 0, #, or space), which modify the meaning of the conversion operation.
2. An optional *minimum field width* expressed as a decimal integer constant.
3. An optional *precision specification* expressed as a period optionally followed by a decimal integer.
4. An optional *size specification* expressed as one of the letters **11, 1, L, h, hh, j, z,** or **t**.
5. The *conversion operation*, a single character from the set **a, A, c, d, e, E, f, g, G, i, n, o, p, s, u, x, X,** and **%**.

The size specification letters **L** and **h**, and the conversion operations **i, p,** and **n**, were introduced in C89. The size specification letters **11, hh, j, z,** and **t**, and the conversion operations **a** and **A**, were introduced in C99.

The conversion letter terminates the specification. The conversion specification **%-#012.4hd** is shown next broken into its constituent elements:

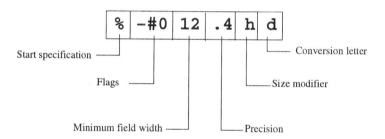

15.11.3 Conversion Flags

The optional flag characters modify the meaning of the main conversion operation:

-	Left-justify the value within the field width.
0	Use 0 for the pad character rather than space.
+	Always produce a sign, either + or -.
space	Always produce either the sign - or a space.
#	Use a variant of the main conversion operation.

The effects of the flag characters are described in more detail now.

The – flag   If a minus-sign flag is present, then the converted value will be left-justified within the field—that is, any padding will be placed to the right of the converted value. If no minus sign is present, the converted value will be right-justified within the field. This flag is relevant only when an explicit minimum field width is specified and the converted value is smaller than that minimum width; otherwise the value will fill the field without padding.

The 0 flag   If a 0 (zero) flag is present, then 0 will be used as the pad character if padding is to be placed to the left of the converted value. The 0 flag is relevant only when an explicit minimum field width is specified and the converted value is smaller than that minimum width. In integer conversions, this flag is superseded by the precision specification.

If no zero-digit flag is present, then a space will be used as the pad character. Space is always used as the pad character if padding is to be placed to the right of the converted value even if the - flag character is present.

The + flag   If a + flag is present, then the result of a signed conversion will always begin with a sign—that is, an explicit + will precede a converted positive value. (Negative values are always preceded by – regardless of whether a plus-sign flag is specified.) This flag is only relevant for the conversion operations a, A, d, e, E, f, g, G, and i.

The space flag   If a *space* flag is present and the first character in the converted value resulting from a signed conversion is not a sign (+ or –), then a space will be added before the converted value. The adding of this space on the left is independent of any padding that may be placed to the left or right under control of the - flag character. If both the *space* and + flags appear in a single conversion specification, the *space* flag is ignored because the + flag ensures that the converted value will always begin with a sign. This flag is relevant only for the conversion operations a, A, d, e, E, f, g, G, and i.

The # flag   If a # flag is present, then an alternate form of the main conversion operation is used. This flag is relevant only for the conversion operations a, A, e, E, f, g, G, i, o, x, and X. The modifications implied by the # flag are described in conjunction with the relevant conversion operations.

15.11.4 Minimum Field Width

An optional minimum field width, expressed as a decimal integer constant, may be specified. The constant must be a nonempty sequence of decimal digits that does not begin with a zero digit (which would be taken to be the 0 flag). If the converted value (including prefix) results in fewer characters than the specified field width, then pad characters are used to pad the value to the specified width. If the converted value results in more characters than the specified field width, then the field is expanded to accommodate it without padding.

The field width may also be specified by an asterisk, *, in which case an argument of type `int` is consumed and specifies the minimum field width. The result of specifying a negative width is unpredictable.

Example

The following two calls to `printf` result in the same output:

```
int width=5, value;
...
printf("%5d", value);
printf("%*d", width, value);
```

15.11.5 Precision

An optional precision specification may be specified and expressed as a period followed by an optional decimal integer. The precision specification is used to control:

1. the minimum number of digits to be printed for **d**, **i**, **o**, **u**, **x**, and **X** conversions
2. the number of digits to the right of the decimal point in **e**, **E**, and **f** conversions
3. the number of significant digits in the **g** and **G** conversions
4. the maximum number of characters to be written from a string in the **s** conversion

If the period appears but the integer is missing, then the integer is assumed to be zero, which usually has a different effect than omitting the entire precision specification.

The precision may also be specified by an asterisk following the period, in which case an argument of type **int** is consumed and specifies the precision. If both the field width and precision are specified with asterisks, then the field width argument precedes the precision argument.

15.11.6 Size Specification

An optional size modifier, one of the letter sequences **ll** (ell-ell), **l** (ell), **L**, **h**, **hh**, **j**, **z**, or **t**, may precede some conversion operations.

The letter **l**, in conjunction with the conversion operations **d**, **i**, **o**, **u**, **x**, and **X**, indicates that the conversion argument has type **long** or **unsigned long**. In conjunction with the n conversion, it specifies that the argument has type **long ***. In C89, the modifier **l** may also be used with **c**, in which case the argument is of type **wint_t**, or with **s**, in which case it specifies that the argument has type **wchar_t ***. The modifier **l** has no effect when used with **a**, **A**, **e**, **E**, **f**, **F**, **g**, and **G**; compare this with the **L** modifier and be careful which you use.

The modifier **ll**, in conjunction with the conversion operations **d**, **i**, **o**, **u**, **x**, and **X**, indicates that the conversion argument has type **long long int** or **unsigned long long int**. In conjunction with the n conversion, the **ll** modifier specifies that the argument has type **long long int ***. The **ll** size modifier was introduced in C99.

The letter **h**, in conjunction with the conversion operations **d**, **i**, **o**, **u**, **x**, and **X**, indicates that the conversion argument has type **short** or **unsigned short**. That is, although the argument would have been converted to **int** or **unsigned** by the argument promotions, it should be converted to **short** or **unsigned short** before conversion. In conjunction with the **n** conversion, the **h** modifier specifies that the argument has type **short ***. The **h** size modifier was introduced in C89.

The modifier **hh**, in conjunction with the conversion operations **d**, **i**, **o**, **u**, **x**, and **X**, indicates that the conversion argument has type **char** or **unsigned char**. That is, although the argument would have been converted to **int** or **unsigned** by the argument promotions, it should be converted to **char** or **unsigned char** before conversion. In conjunction with the **n** conversion, the **hh** modifier specifies that the argument has type **signed char** *. The **hh** size modifier is available in C99.

The letter **L**, in conjunction with the conversion operations **a**, **A**, **e**, **E**, **f**, **F**, **g**, and **G**, indicates that the argument has type **long double**. The **L** size modifier was introduced in C89. Be careful to use **L** and not **l** for **long double** since **l** has no effect on these operations.

The modifier **j**, in conjunction with the conversion operations **d**, **i**, **o**, **u**, **x**, and **X**, indicates that the conversion argument has type **intmax_t** or **uintmax_t**. In conjunction with the **n** conversion, the **j** modifier specifies that the argument has type **intmax_t** *. The **j** size modifier was introduced in C99.

The modifier **z**, in conjunction with the conversion operations **d**, **i**, **o**, **u**, **x**, and **X**, indicates that the conversion argument has type **size_t**. In conjunction with the **n** conversion, the **z** modifier specifies that the argument has type **size_t** *. The **z** size modifier was introduced in C99.

The modifier **t**, in conjunction with the conversion operations **d**, **i**, **o**, **u**, **x**, and **X**, indicates that the conversion argument has type **ptrdiff_t**. In conjunction with the **n** conversion, the **t** modifier specifies that the argument has type **ptrdiff_t** *. The **t** size modifier was introduced in C99.

15.11.7 Conversion Operations

The conversion operation is expressed as a single character: **a**, **A**, **c**, **d**, **e**, **E**, **f**, **g**, **G**, **i**, **n**, **o**, **p**, **s**, **u**, **x**, **X**, or **%**. The specified conversion determines the permitted flag and size characters, the expected argument type, and how the output looks. Table 15–6 summarizes the conversion operations. Each operation is then discussed individually.

The d and i conversions Signed decimal conversion is performed. The argument should be of type **int** if no size modifier is used, type **short** if **h** is used, or type **long** if **l** is used. The **i** operator is present in Standard C for compatibility with **fscanf**; it is recognized on output for uniformity, where it is identical to the **d** operator.

The converted value consists of a sequence of decimal digits that represents the absolute value of the argument. This sequence is as short as possible, but not shorter than the specified precision. The converted value will have leading zeros if necessary to satisfy the precision specification; these leading zeros are independent of any padding, which might also introduce leading zeros. If the precision is 1 (the default), then the converted value will not have a leading 0 unless the argument is 0, in which case a single 0 is output. If the precision is 0 and the argument is 0, then the converted value is empty (the null string).

The prefix is computed as follows. If the argument is negative, the prefix is a minus sign. If the argument is non-negative and the **+** flag is specified, then the prefix is a plus sign. If the argument is non-negative, the *space* flag is specified, and the **+** flag is not specified, then the prefix is a space. Otherwise, the prefix is empty. The **#** flag is not relevant to the **d** and **i** conversions. Table 15–7 shows examples of the **d** conversion.

Table 15–6   Output conversion specifications

Conversion	Defined flags - + # 0 *space*	Size modifier	Argument type	Default precision[a]	Output
d, i[b]	- + 0 *space*	*none* h l	int short long	1	dd...d –dd...d +dd...d
u	- + 0 *space*	*none* h l	unsigned int unsigned short unsigned long	1	dd...d
o	- + # 0 *space*	*none* h l	unsigned int unsigned short unsigned long	1	oo...o 0oo...o
x, X	- + # 0 *space*	*none* h l	unsigned int unsigned short unsigned long	1	hh...h 0xhh...h 0Xhh...h
f	- + # 0 *space*	*none* l L	double double long double	6	d...d.d...d –d...d.d...d +d...d.d...d
e, E	- + # 0 *space*	*none* l L	double double long double	6	d.d...de+dd –d.d...dE-dd
g, G	- + # 0 *space*	*none* l L	double double long double	6	*like* e, E, *or* f
a, A[c]	- + # 0 *space*	*none* l L	double double long double	6	0xh.h...hp+dd –0Xh.h...hP- dd
c	-	*none* l[d]	int wint_t	1	c
s	-	*none* l[c]	char * wchar_t *	×	cc...c
p[b]	*impl. defined*	*none*	void *	1	*impl. defined*
n[b]		*none* h l	int * short * long *	n/a	*none*
%		*none*	*none*	n/a	%

[a] Default precision, if none is specified.

[b] Introduced in C89. The conversions **i** and **d** are equivalent on output.

[c] Introduced in C99

[d] Introduced in C89 (Amendment 1).

The u conversion   Unsigned decimal conversion is performed. The argument should be of type **unsigned** if no size modifier is used, type **unsigned short** if **h** is used, or type **unsigned long** if **l** is used.

The converted value consists of a sequence of decimal digits that represents the value of the argument. This sequence is as short as possible, but not shorter than the specified

Table 15-7   Examples of the **d** conversion

Sample format	Sample output Value = 45	Sample output Value = –45
%12d	45	-45
%012d	000000000045	-00000000045
% 012d	00000000045	-00000000045
%+12d	+45	-45
%+012d	+00000000045	-00000000045
%-12d	45	-45
%- 12d	45	-45
%-+12d	+45	-45
%12.4d	0045	-0045
%-12.4d	0045	-0045

precision. The converted value will have leading zeros if necessary to satisfy the precision specification; these leading zeros are independent of any padding, which might also introduce leading zeros. If the precision is 1 (the default), then the converted value will not have a leading 0 unless the argument is 0, in which case a single 0 is output. If the precision and argument are 0, then the converted value is empty (the null string). The prefix is always empty. The **+**, *space*, and **#** flags are not relevant to the **u** conversion operation. Table 15-8 shows examples of the **u** conversion.

Table 15-8   Examples of the **u** conversion

Sample format	Sample output Value = 45	Sample output Value = –45
%14u	45	4294967251
%014u	00000000000045	00004294967251
%#14u	45	4294967251
%#014u	00000000000045	00004294967251
%-14u	45	4294967251
%-#14u	45	4294967251
%14.4u	0045	4294967251
%-14.4u	0045	4294967251

The o conversion   Unsigned octal conversion is performed. The argument should be of type **unsigned** if no size modifier is used, type **unsigned short** if **h** is used, or type **unsigned long** if **l** is used.

The converted value consists of a sequence of octal digits that represents the value of the argument. This sequence is as short as possible, but not shorter than the specified precision. The converted value will have leading zeros if necessary to satisfy the precision specification; these leading zeros are independent of any padding, which might also introduce leading zeros. If the precision is 1 (the default), then the converted value will not have a leading 0 unless the argument is 0, in which case a single 0 is output. If the precision is 0 and the argument is 0, then the converted value is empty (the null string). If the **#**

flag is present, then the prefix is 0. If the **#** flag is not present, then the prefix is empty. The **+** and *space* flags are not relevant to the **o** conversion operation. Table 15–9 shows examples of the **o** conversion.

Table 15–9   Examples of the **o** conversion

Sample format	Sample output Value = 45	Sample output Value = –45
%14o	55	37777777723
%014o	00000000000055	00037777777723
%#14o	055	037777777723
%#014o	00000000000055	00037777777723
%-14o	55	37777777723
%-#14o	055	037777777723
%14.4o	0055	37777777723
%-#14.4o	00055	037777777723

The x and X conversions   Unsigned hexadecimal conversion is performed. The argument should be of type **unsigned** if no size modifier is used, type **unsigned short** if **h** is used, or type **unsigned long** if **l** is used.

The converted value consists of a sequence of hexadecimal digits that represents the value of the argument. This sequence is as short as possible, but not shorter than the specified precision. The **x** operation uses **0123456789abcdef** as digits, whereas the **X** operation uses **0123456789ABCDEF**. The converted value will have leading zeros if necessary to satisfy the precision specification; these leading zeros are independent of any padding, which might also introduce leading zeros. If the precision is 1, then the converted value will not have a leading 0 unless the argument is 0, in which case a single 0 is output. If the precision is 0 and the argument is 0, then the converted value is empty (the null string). If no precision is specified, then a precision of 1 is assumed.

If the **#** flag is present, then the prefix is **0x** (for the **x** operation) or **0X** (for the **X** operation). If the **#** flag is not present, then the prefix is empty. The **+** and *space* flags are not relevant. Table 15–10 shows examples of **x** and **X** conversions.

Table 15–10   Examples of the **x** and **X** conversions

Sample format	Sample output Value = 45	Sample output Value = –45
%12x	2d	ffffffd3
%012x	00000000002d	0000ffffffd3
%#12X	0X2D	0XFFFFFFD3
%#012X	0X000000002D	0X00FFFFFFD3
%-12x	2d	ffffffd3
%-#12x	0x2d	0xffffffd3
%12.4x	002d	ffffffd3
%-#12.4x	0x002d	ffffffd3

The c conversion   The argument is printed as a character or wide character. One argument is consumed. The **+**, *space*, and **#** flags, and the precision specification, are not relevant to the **c** conversion operation. The conversions applied to the argument character depend on whether the **l** size specifier is present and whether **printf** or **wprintf** is used. The possibilities are listed in Table 15–13. Table 15–12 shows examples of the **c** conversion.

Table 15–11   Conversions of the **c** specifier

Func-tion	Size specifier	Argument type	Conversion
printf	none	**int**	argument is converted to **unsigned char** and copied to the output
	l	**wint_t**	argument is converted to **wchar_t**, converted to a multibyte characters as if by **wcrtomb**[a], and output
wprintf	none	**int**	argument is converted to a wide character as if by **btowc** and copied to the output
	l	**wint_t**	argument is converted to **wchar_t** and copied to the output

[a] The conversion state for the **wcrtomb** function is set to zero before the character is converted.

Table 15–12   Examples of the **c** conversion

Sample format	Sample output Value = '*'
%12c	*
%012c	00000000000*
%-12c	*

The s conversion   The argument is printed as a string. One argument is consumed. If the **l** size specifier is not present, the argument must be a pointer to an array of any character type. If **l** is present, the argument must have type **wchar_t *** and designate a sequence of wide characters. The prefix is always empty. The **+**, *space*, and **#** flags are not relevant to the **s** conversion.

If no precision specification is given, then the converted value is the sequence of characters in the string argument up to but not including the terminating null character or null wide character. If a precision specification *p* is given, then the converted value is the first *p* characters of the output string or up to but not including the terminating null character, whichever is shorter. When a precision specification is given, the argument string need not end in a null character as long as it contains enough characters to yield the maximum number of output characters. When writing multibyte characters (**printf**, with **l**), in no case will a partial multibyte character be written, so the actual number of bytes written may be less than *p*.

The conversions that occur on the argument string depend on whether the **1** size specifier is present and whether the **printf** or **wprintf** functions are used. The possibilities are listed in Table 15–13. Table 15–14 shows examples of the **s** conversion.

Table 15–13   Conversions of the **s** specifier

Function	Size specifier	Argument type	Conversion
printf	none	**char ***	characters from the argument string are copied to the output
	1	**wchar_t ***	wide characters from the argument string are converted to multibyte characters as if by **wcrtomb**[a]
wprintf	none	**char ***	multibyte characters from the argument string are converted to wide characters as if by **mbrtowc**[a]
	1	**wchar_t ***	wide characters from the argument string are copied to the output

[a] The conversion state for the **wcrtomb** or **mbrtowc** function is set to zero before the first character is converted. Subsequent conversions use the state as modified by the preceding characters.

Table 15–14   Examples of the **s** conversion

Sample format	Sample output Value = **"zap"**	Sample output Value = **"longish"**
%12s	zap	longish
%12.5s	zap	longi
%012s	000000000zap	00000longish
%-12s	zap	longish

The p conversion   The argument must have type **void ***, and it is printed in an implementation-defined format. For most computers, this will probably be the same as the format produced by the **o**, **x**, or **X** conversions. This conversion operator is found in Standard C, but is otherwise uncommon.

The n conversion   The argument must have type **int *** if no size modifier is used, type **long *** if the **1** specifier is used, or type **short *** if the **h** specifier is used. Instead of outputting characters, this conversion operator causes the number of characters output so far to be written into the designated integer. This conversion operator is found in Standard C, but is otherwise uncommon.

The f and F conversions   Signed decimal floating-point conversion is performed. One argument is consumed, which should be of type **double** if no size modifier is used or type **long double** if **L** is used. If an argument of type **float** is supplied, it is converted to type **double** by the usual argument promotions, so it does work to use **%f** to print a number of type **float**.

The converted value consists of a sequence of decimal digits, possibly with an embedded decimal point, that represents the approximate absolute value of the argument. At least one digit appears before the decimal point. The precision specifies the number of digits to appear after the decimal point. If the precision is 0, then no digits appear after the decimal point. Moreover, the decimal point also does not appear unless the # flag is present. If no precision is specified, then a precision of 6 is assumed.

If the floating-point value cannot be represented exactly in the number of digits produced, then the converted value should be the result of rounding the exact floating-point value to the number of decimal places produced. (Some C implementations do not perform correct rounding in all cases.)

In C99, if the floating-point value represents infinity, then the converted value using the f operator is one of **inf**, **-inf**, **infinity**, or **-infinity**. (Which one is chosen is implementation-defined.) If the floating-point value represents NaN, then the converted value using the f operator is one of **nan**, **-nan**, **nan(...)**, or **-nan(...)**, where "..." is an implementation-defined sequence of letters, digits, or underscores. The **F** operator converts infinity and NaN using uppercase letters. The # and 0 flags have no effect on conversion of infinity or NaN.

The prefix is computed as follows. If the argument is negative, the prefix is a minus sign. If the argument is non-negative and the + flag is specified, then the prefix is a plus sign. If the argument is non-negative, the *space* flag is specified, and the + flag is not specified, then the prefix is a space. Otherwise, the prefix is empty. Table 15–15 shows examples of the f conversion.

Table 15–15   Examples of the **f** conversion

Sample format	Sample output Value = 12.678	Sample output Value = –12.678
%10.2f	12.68	-12.68
%010.2f	000000012.68	-00000012.68
% 010.2f	00000012.68	-00000012.68
%+10.2f	+12.68	-12.68
%+010.2f	+00000012.68	-00000012.68
%-10.2f	12.68	-12.68
%- 10.2f	12.68	-12.68
%-+10.4f	+12.6780	-12.6780

The e and E conversions   Signed decimal floating-point conversion is performed. One argument is consumed, which should be of type **double** if no size specifier is used or type **long double** if L is used. An argument of type **float** is permitted, as for the **f** conversion. The **e** conversion is described; the **E** conversion differs only in that the letter **E** appears whenever **e** appears in the e conversion.

The converted value consists of a decimal digit, then possibly a decimal point and more decimal digits, then the letter **e**, then a plus or minus sign, then finally at least two more decimal digits. Unless the value is zero, the part before the letter **e** represents a value between 1.0 and 9.99.... The part after the letter **e** represents an exponent value as a signed decimal integer. The value of the first part, multiplied by 10 raised to the value of the second part, is approximately equal to the absolute value of the argument. The number of exponent digits is the same for all values and is the maximum number needed to represent the range of the implementation's floating-point types. Table 15–16 shows examples of e and E conversions.

Table 15–16   Examples of e and E conversions

Sample format	Sample output Value = 12.678	Sample output Value = –12.678
%10.2e	1.27e+01	-1.27e+01
%010.2e	00001.27e+01	-0001.27e+01
% 010.2e	0001.27e+01	-0001.27e+01
%+10.2E	+1.27E+01	-1.27E+01
%+010.2E	+0001.27E+01	-0001.27E+01
%-10.2e	1.27e+01	-1.27e+01
%- 10.2e	1.27e+01	-1.27e+01
%-+10.2e	+1.27e+01	-1.27e+01

The precision specifies the number of digits to appear after the decimal point; if not supplied, then 6 is assumed. If the precision is 0, then no digits appear after the decimal point. Moreover, the decimal point also does not appear unless the # flag is present. If the floating-point value cannot be represented exactly in the number of digits produced, then the converted value is obtained by rounding the exact floating-point value. The prefix is computed as for the f conversion. Values of infinity or NaN are converted as specified for the f and F conversions.

The g and G conversions   Signed decimal floating-point conversion is performed. One argument is consumed, which should be of type **double** if no size specifier is used, or type **long double** if L is used. An argument of type **float** is permitted, as for the f conversion. Only the g conversion operator is discussed later; the G operation is identical except that wherever g uses e conversion, G uses E conversion. If the specified precision is less than 1, then a precision of 1 is used. If no precision is specified, then a precision of 6 is assumed.

The g conversion begins the same as either the f or e conversions; which one is selected depends on the value to be converted. The Standard C specification says that the e conversion is used only if the exponent resulting from the e conversion is less than –4 or greater than or equal to the specified precision. Some other implementations use the e conversion if the exponent is less than –3 or strictly greater than the specified precision.

The converted value (whether by f or e) is then further modified by stripping off trailing zeros to the right of the decimal point. If the result has no digits after the decimal point, then the decimal point is also removed. If the # flag is present, this stripping of zeros and the decimal point does not occur.

The prefix is computed as for the f and e conversions. Values of infinity or NaN are converted as specified for the f and F conversions.

The a and A conversions   These conversions are new in C99. Signed hexadecimal floating-point conversion is performed. One argument is consumed, which should be of type **double** if no size specifier is used or type **long double** if L is used. An argument of type **float** is permitted, as for the other floating-point conversions. The **a** conversion is described; the **A** conversion differs by using uppercase letters for the hexadecimal digits, the prefix (**0X**), and the exponent letter (**P**).

The converted value consists of a hexadecimal digit, then possibly a decimal point and more hexadecimal digits, then the letter **p**, then a plus or minus sign, then finally one or more decimal digits. Unless the value is zero or denormalized, the leading hexadecimal digit is nonzero. The part after the letter **p** represents a binary exponent value as a signed decimal integer.

The precision specifies the number of hexadecimal digits to appear after the decimal point; if not supplied, then enough digits appear to distinguish values of type **double**. (If **FLT_RADIX** is 2, then the default precision is enough to exactly represent the values.) If the precision is 0, then no digits appear after the decimal point; moreover, the decimal point also does not appear unless the **#** flag is present. If the floating-point value cannot be represented exactly in the number of hexadecimal digits produced, then the converted value is obtained by rounding the exact floating-point value. The prefix is computed as for the **f** conversion.

Values of infinity or NaN are converted as specified for the **f** and **F** conversions.

The % conversion   A single percent sign is printed. Because a percent sign is used to indicate the beginning of a conversion specification, it is necessary to write two of them to have one printed. No arguments are consumed, and the prefix is empty.

Standard C does not permit any flag characters, minimum width, precision, or size modifiers to be present; the complete conversion specification must be **%%**. However, other C implementations perform padding just as for any other conversion operation; for example, the conversion specification **%05%** prints **0000%** in these implementations. The **+**, *space*, and **#** flags, the precision specification, and the size specifications are never relevant to the **%** conversion operation.

Example

The following two-line program is known as a *quine*—a self-reproducing program. When executed, it will print a copy of itself on the standard output. (The first line of the program is too long to fit on a printed line in this book, so we have split it after **%cmain()** by inserting a backslash and a line break.)

```
char*f="char*f=%c%s%c,q='%c',n='%cn',b='%c%c';%cmain()\
{printf(f,q,f,q,q,b,b,b,n,n);}%c",q='"',n='\n',b='\\';
main(){printf(f,q,f,q,q,b,b,b,n,n);}
```

The following one-line program is almost a quine. (We have split it after **";main()** by inserting a backslash and a line break since it does not fit on a printed line.) We leave it to the reader to discover why it is not exactly a quine.

```
char*f="char*f=%c%s%c;main(){printf(f,34,f,34);}";main()\
{printf(f,34,f,34);}
```

15.12 *v[x]printf, v[x]scanf*

Synopsis

```
#include <stdarg.h>
#include <stdio.h>

int vfprintf(FILE * restrict stream,
  const char * restrict format, va_list arg);
int vprintf(
  const char * restrict format, va_list arg);
int vsprintf(char *s,
  const char * restrict format, va_list arg);
int vfscanf(FILE * restrict stream,
  const char * restrict format, va_list arg); // C99
int vscanf(
  const char * restrict format, va_list arg); // C99
int vsscanf(const char * restrict s,
  const char * restrict format, va_list arg); // C99
```

```
#include <stdarg.h>
#include <stdio.h>
#include <wchar.h>

int vfwprintf(FILE * restrict stream,
  const wchar_t * restrict format, va_list arg);
int vwprintf(
  const wchar_t * restrict format, va_list arg);
int vswprintf(wchar_t * restrict s,
  size_t n, const wchar_t * restrict format, va_list arg);
int vfwscanf(FILE * restrict stream,
  const wchar_t * restrict format, va_list arg); // C99
int vswscanf(const wchar_t * restrict s,
  const wchar_t * restrict format, va_list arg); // C99
int vwscanf(
  const wchar_t * restrict format, va_list arg); // C99
```

The functions **vfprintf**, **vprintf**, and **vsprintf** are the same as the functions
fprintf, **printf**, and **sprintf**, respectively, except that the extra arguments are
given as a variable argument list as defined by the **varargs** (or **stdarg**) facility (Section 11.4). The argument **arg** must have been initialized by the **va_start** macro and
possibly subsequent **va_arg** calls. These functions are useful when the programmer
wants to define his or her own variable-argument functions that use the formatted output
facilities. The functions do not invoke the **va_end** facility.

Amendment 1 to C89 added the functions **vfwprintf**, **vwprintf**, and
vswprintf, which are analogous to **fwprintf**, **wprintf**, and **swprintf**,
respectively. C99 added the corresponding input functions, **vfscanf**, **vscanf**, and
vsscanf, and their wide versions **vfwscanf**, **vwscanf**, and **vswscanf**.

Example

Suppose you want to write a general function, `trace`, that prints the name of a function and its arguments. Any function to be traced would begin with a call to `trace` of the form:

```
trace(name,format,parm1,parm2,…,parmN)
```

where `name` is the name of the function being called and `format` is a format string suitable for printing the argument values `parm1`, `parm2`, ..., `parmN`. For example:

```
int f(int x, double y)  /* Trace this function. */
{
    trace("f","x=%d, y=%f", x, y);
    …
}
```

A possible implementation of `trace` is given next for traditional C:

```
#include <varargs.h>
#include <stdio.h>
void trace(va_alist)
    va_dcl
{
    va_list args;
    char *name;
    char *format;
    va_start(args);
    name = va_arg(args,char *);
    format = va_arg(args,char *);
    fprintf(stderr,"--> entering %s(", name);
    vfprintf(stderr, format, args);
    fprintf(stderr,")\n");
    va_end(args);
}
```

15.13 fread, fwrite

Synopsis

```
#include <stdio.h>
size_t fread(
    void * restrict ptr, size_t element_size, size_t count,
    FILE * restrict stream);
size_t fwrite(
    const void * restrict ptr, size_t element_size, size_t count,
    FILE * restrict stream);
```

The functions `fread` and `fwrite` perform input and output, respectively, to binary files. In both cases, `stream` is the input or output stream and `ptr` is a pointer to an array of `count` elements, each of which is `element_size` characters long.

The function **fread** reads up to **count** elements of the indicated size from the input stream into the specified array. The actual number of items read is returned by **fread**; it may be less than **count** if end of file is encountered. If an error is encountered, zero is returned. The **feof** or **ferror** facilities may be used to determine whether an error or an immediate end of file caused zero to be returned. If either **count** or **element_size** is zero, no data are transferred and zero is returned.

Example

The following program reads an input file containing objects of a structure type and prints the number of such objects read. The program depends on **exit** closing the input file:

```
/* Count the number of elements
    of type "struct S" in file "in.dat" */
#include <stdio.h>
static char *FileName = "in.dat";
struct S { int a,b; double d; char str[103]; };

int main(void)
{
    struct S buffer;
    int items_read = 0;
    FILE *in_file = fopen(FileName,"r");
    if (in_file == NULL)
    { fprintf(stderr,"?Couldn't open %s\n",FileName);
      exit(1); }

    while (fread((char *) &buffer,
           sizeof(struct S), 1, in_file) == 1)
      items_read++;

    if (ferror(in_file))
       { fprintf(stderr,"?Read error, file %s record %d\n",
          FileName,items_read+1); exit(1); }
    printf("Finished; %d elements read\n",items_read);
    return 0;
}
```

The function **fwrite** writes **count** elements of size **element_size** from the specified array. The actual number of items written is returned by **fwrite**; it will be the same as **count** unless an error occurs.

In traditional C, the **element_size** arguments have type **unsigned**, **ptr** arguments have type **char ***, and **count** arguments have type **int**.

References   exit 19.3; feof, ferror 15.14; fseek, ftell 15.5

15.14 feof, ferror, clearerr

Synopsis

```
#include <stdio.h>

int feof(FILE *stream);
int ferror(FILE *stream);
void clearerr(FILE *stream);
```

The function **feof** takes as its argument an input stream. If end of file has been detected while reading from the input stream, then a nonzero value is returned; otherwise zero is returned. Note that even if there are no more characters in the stream to be read, **feof** will not signal end of file unless and until an attempt is made to read "past" the last character. The function is normally used after an input operation has signaled a failure.

The function **ferror** returns the error status of a stream. If an error has occurred while reading from or writing to the stream, then **ferror** returns a nonzero value; otherwise zero is returned. Once an error has occurred for a given stream, repeated calls to **ferror** will continue to report an error unless **clearerr** is used to explicitly reset the error indication. Closing the stream, as with **fclose**, will also reset the error indication.

The function **clearerr** resets any error and end of file indication on the specified stream; subsequent calls on **ferror** will report that no error has occurred for that stream unless and until another error occurs.

15.15 remove, rename

Synopsis

```
#include <stdio.h>

int rename(
   const char *oldname, const char *newname);
int remove(const char *filename);
```

The **remove** function removes or deletes the named file; it returns zero if the operation succeeds and a nonzero value if it does not. The string pointed to by **filename** is not altered. Implementations may differ in the details of what "remove" or "delete" actually mean, but it should not be possible for a program to open a file that it has deleted. If the file is open or does not exist, then the action of **remove** is implementation-defined. This function is not present in traditional C; instead, a UNIX-specific **unlink** function is commonly provided.

The **rename** function changes the name of **oldname** to **newname**; it returns zero if the operation succeeds and a nonzero value if it does not. The strings pointed to by **oldname** and **newname** are not altered. If **oldname** names an open or nonexistent file, or if **newname** names a file that already exists, then the action of **rename** is implementation-defined.

15.16 *tmpfile, tmpnam, mktemp*

Synopsis

```
#include <stdio.h>

FILE *tmpfile(void);
char *tmpnam(char *buf);
#define L_tmpnam ...
#define TMP_MAX ...
```

The function **tmpfile** creates a new file and opens it using **fopen** mode **"w+b"** (**"w+"** in traditional C). A file pointer for the new file is returned if the operation succeeds or a null pointer if it fails. The intent is that the new file be used only during the current program's execution. The file is deleted when it is closed or on program termination. After writing data to the file, the programmer can use the **rewind** function to reposition the file at its beginning for reading.

The function **tmpnam** is used to create new file names that do not conflict with other file names currently in use; the programmer can then open a new file with that name using the full generality of **fopen**. The files so created are not "temporary"; they are not deleted automatically on program termination. If **buf** is **NULL**, **tmpnam** returns a pointer to the new file name string; the string may be altered by subsequent calls to **tmpnam**. If **buf** is not **NULL**, it must point to an array of not less than **L_tmpnam** characters; **tmpnam** will copy the new file name string into that array and return **buf**. If **tmpnam** fails, it returns a null pointer. Standard C defines the value **TMP_MAX** to be the number of successive calls to **tmpnam** that will generate unique names; it must be at least 25.

The traditional C function **mktemp** has the same signature as **tmpnam**, but **buf** (the "template") must point to a string with six trailing **X** characters, which will be overwritten with other letters or digits to form a unique file name. The value **buf** is returned. Successive calls to **mktemp** should specify different templates to ensure unique names. UNIX implementations often substitute the program's process identification for **XXXXXX**. **mktemp** is not in Standard C.

Example

A common but poor programming practice in C is to write

```
ptr = fopen(mktemp("/tmp/abcXXXXXX"),"w+");
```

This idiom will fail if the string constant is not modifiable. The programmer also loses the ability to reference the file name string. It is better and no less efficient to write

```
char filename[]="/tmp/abcXXXXXX";
ptr = fopen(mktemp(filename),"w+");
```

Security note   The use of **tmpnam**, **tmpfile**, and **mktemp** have been identified as security problems on many computers because the files may be accessible to other users. You should consider using more secure versions of these functions, such as **mkstemp** found in FreeBSD UNIX.

16

General Utilities

The facilities in this chapter are declared by the header file **stdlib.h**. They fall into several general categories:

- Storage allocation
- Random number generation
- Numeric conversions and integer arithmetic
- Environment communication
- Searching and sorting
- Multibyte, wide-character, and string conversions

16.1 malloc, calloc, mlalloc, clalloc, free, cfree

Synopsis

```
#include <stdlib.h>
void *malloc(size_t size);
void *calloc(size_t elt_count, size_t elt_size);
void *realloc(void *ptr, size_t size);
void free(void *ptr);
```

The function **malloc** allocates a region of memory large enough to hold an object whose size (as measured by the **sizeof** operator) is **size**. A pointer to the first element of the region is returned, and it is guaranteed to be properly aligned for any data type. The caller may then use a cast operator to convert this pointer to another pointer type. If it is impossible for some reason to perform the requested allocation, then a null pointer is returned. If the requested size is 0, then the Standard C functions will return either a null pointer or a non-null pointer that nonetheless must not be used to access an object. The allocated memory is not initialized in any way, so the caller cannot depend on its contents. Since every allocated region from **malloc** must be aligned for any type, each region will effectively occupy a block of memory that is a multiple of the alignment size: usually four or eight bytes.

Example

> The caller of an allocation routine will typically assign the result pointer to a variable of the appropriate type. Herein, we assume that **T** is some object type that we wish to allocate dynamically; it might be a structure, array, or character.

```
T *NewObject(void)
{
    T *objptr = (T *) malloc(sizeof(T));
    if (objptr==NULL) printf("NewObject: failed!\n");
    return objptr;
}
```

> The cast (**T ***) is not strictly necessary in Standard C because **malloc** returns a pointer of type **void *** and the implicit conversion on assignment to **objptr** is allowed. In traditional C, the return type of **malloc** is **char *** and an implicit conversion may provoke a warning message. The cast is needed for C++ compatibility.

The function **calloc** allocates a region of memory large enough to hold an array of **elt_count** elements, each of size **elt_size** (typically given by the **sizeof** operator). The region of memory is cleared bitwise to zero, and a pointer to the first element of the region is returned. If for some reason it is impossible to perform the requested allocation, or if **elt_count** or **elt_size** is zero, then the return value is the same as for **malloc**. Note that memory cleared bitwise to zero might not have the same representation as a floating-point zero or a null pointer.

The function **realloc** takes a pointer to a memory region previously allocated by one of the standard functions and changes its size while preserving its contents. If necessary, the contents are copied to a new memory region. A pointer to the (possibly new) memory region is returned. If the request cannot be satisfied, a null pointer is returned and the old region is not disturbed. If the first argument to **realloc** is a null pointer, then the function behaves like **malloc**. If **ptr** is not null and **size** is zero, then **realloc** returns either a null pointer or a pointer that must not be used (like **malloc**), and the old region is deallocated. If the new size is smaller than the old size, then some of the old contents at the end of the old region will be discarded. If the new size is larger than the old size, then all of the old contents are preserved and new space is added at the end; the new space is not initialized in any way, and the caller must assume that it contains garbage information. Whenever **realloc** returns a pointer that is different from its first argument, the programmer should assume that the old region of memory was freed and should not be used.

Example

> The following shows a typical use of **realloc** to expand the dynamic array designated by the pointer **samples**. (The elements of such an array must be referenced using subscript expressions; any pointers into the array could be invalidated by the call to **realloc**.)

```
#include <stdlib.h>
#define SAMPLE_INCREMENT 100
int sample_limit = 0; /* Max size of current array */
int sample_count = 0; /* Number of elements in array */
double *samples = NULL; /* Will point to array */

int AddSample( double new_sample )
   /* Add an element to the end of the array */
{
   if (sample_count < sample_limit) {
      samples[sample_count++] = new_sample;
   } else {
      /* Allocate a new, larger array. */
      int new_limit = sample_limit + SAMPLE_INCREMENT;
      double *new_array =
         realloc(samples, new_limit * sizeof(double));
      if (new_array == NULL) {
         /* Can't expand; leave samples untouched. */
         fprintf(stderr,"?AddSample: out of memory\n");
      } else {
         samples = new_array;
         sample_limit = new_limit;
         samples[sample_count++] = new_sample;
      }
   }
   return sample_count;
}
```

The function **free** deallocates a region of memory previously allocated by **malloc**, **calloc**, or **realloc**. The argument to **free** must be a pointer that is the same as a pointer previously returned by one of the allocation functions. If the argument is a null pointer, then the call has no effect. Once a region of memory has been freed, it must not be used for any other purpose. The use of any pointer into the region—a "dangling pointer"—will have unpredictable effects. Likewise, allocating a region of storage once but freeing it more than once, has unpredictable effects.

In a freestanding implementation with limited memory, the programmer may have direct control over how much memory is made available for allocations by **malloc** and the other functions. This memory is generally called the *heap*. In many C programs for freestanding environments, **malloc** is never used and so no heap is necessary. How the size of the heap is specified is implementation-dependent.

References   assignment conversions 6.3.2

16.1.1 Traditional Storage-Allocation Facilities

Traditional and alternate facilities synopsis

```
char *malloc (unsigned       size);
char *mlalloc(unsigned long size);
char *calloc (unsigned       elt_count, unsigned       elt_size);
char *clalloc(unsigned long elt_count, unsigned long elt_size);
void  free (char *ptr);
void  cfree(char *ptr);
char *realloc (char *ptr, unsigned       size);
char *relalloc(char *ptr, unsigned long size);
```

In traditional C implementations, there is typically no header file to declare these facilities, so the programmer must declare them.

The **size** arguments to the storage-allocation functions originally had type **unsigned int**. Since that type could be too small to express large storage areas, new versions of the allocation functions appeared whose size arguments had type **unsigned long**. The return types are **char ***, and the result pointer should be explicitly cast to the type of the object pointer.

The traditional version of **free** deallocates memory previously allocated by **malloc**, **mlalloc**, **realloc**, or **relalloc**. The **cfree** function deallocates memory previously allocated by **calloc** or **clalloc**. Passing a null pointer to a traditional **free** or **cfree** function has implementation-defined behavior in traditional implementations.

16.2 rand, srand, RAND_MAX

Synopsis

```
#include <stdlib.h>
int rand(void);
void srand(unsigned seed);
#define RAND_MAX …
```

Successive calls to **rand** return integer values in the range from 0 to the largest representable positive value of type **int** (inclusive) that are the successive results of a pseudorandom-number generator. In Standard C, the upper bound of the range of **rand** is given by **RAND_MAX**, which will be at least 32,767.

The function **srand** may be used to initialize the pseudorandom-number generator that is used to generate successive values for calls to **rand**. After a call to **srand**, successive calls to **rand** will produce a certain series of pseudorandom numbers. If **srand** is called again with the same argument, then after that point successive calls to **rand** will produce the same series of pseudorandom numbers. Successive calls made to **rand** before

srand is ever called in a user program will produce the same series of pseudo-random numbers that would be produced after **srand** is called with argument 1.

Standard C library facilities will not call **rand** or **srand** in any way that affects the programmer's observed sequence of pseudorandom numbers.

16.3 atof, atoi, atol, atoll l

<table>
<tr><td align="center">Synopsis</td></tr>
</table>

```
#include <stdlib.h>
double    atof ( const char *str );
int       atoi ( const char *str );
long      atol ( const char *str );
long long atoll( const char *str );   // C99
```

These functions, which convert the initial portion of the string **str** to numbers, are found in many UNIX implementations. In Standard C, they are present for compatibility, but are defined in terms of the **strtox** functions in Section 16.4, which are preferred. If the functions in this section are unable to convert the input string, then their behavior is undefined.

Except for their behavior on error, these functions are defined in terms of the more general ones as follows:

```
#include <stdlib.h>

double atof(const char *str) {
    return strtod(str, (char **) NULL);
}

int atoi(const char *str) {
    return (int) strtol(str, (char **) NULL, 10);
}

long atol(const char * str) {
    return strtol(str, (char **) NULL, 10);
}

long long atoll(const char * str) {
    return strtoll(str, (char **) NULL, 10);
}
```

16.4 strtod, strtof, strtold, strtol, strtoll, strtoul, strtoull

Synopsis

```
#include <stdlib.h>

double strtod(
    const char * restrict str, char ** restrict ptr );
float strtof(
    const char * restrict str, char ** restrict ptr );
long double strtold(
    const char * restrict str, char ** restrict ptr );

long strtol(
    const char * restrict str, char ** restrict ptr, int base );
long long strtoll(
    const char * restrict str, char ** restrict ptr, int base );
unsigned long strtoul(
    const char * restrict str, char ** restrict ptr, int base );
unsigned long long strtoull(
    const char * restrict str, char ** restrict ptr, int base );
```

The string-to-number conversion functions **strtod** and **strtol** originated in System V UNIX and were adopted by Standard C. The **strtoul** function was added to C89 for completeness. The **strtof**, **strtold**, **strtoll**, and **strtoull** functions were added in C99. In general, these functions provide more control over conversions than, say, the corresponding facilities of **sscanf**. C99 also has **strto[u]imax** functions (Section 21.8).

For all of these functions, **str** points to the string to be converted, and **ptr** (if not null) designates a **char **** pointer that is set by the functions to point to the first character in **str** immediately following the converted part of the string. If **ptr** is null, then it is ignored. If **str** begins with whitespace characters (as defined by the **isspace** function), then those whitespace characters are skipped before conversion is attempted.

There are wide-character versions of these functions (see Sections 24.4 and 21.9).

Floating-point number conversion The floating-point conversion functions **strtod**, **strtof**, and **strtold** expect the number to be converted to consist of an optional plus or minus sign followed by one of the following:

1. a sequence of decimal digits possibly containing a single decimal point, followed by an optional exponent part as defined in Section 2.7.2;
2. the characters **0x** or **0X**, followed by a nonempty sequence of hexadecimal digits, followed by an optional binary exponent as defined in Section 2.7.2;
3. the string **INF** or **INFINITY**, ignoring case; or
4. the string **NAN** or **NAN(...)**, ignoring case, where "..." may be any sequence of letters, digits, or underscore characters.

The longest sequence of characters matching one of these models is converted to a floating-point number, which is returned. The return type depends on which function is chosen. The format for the expected number differs from C's own floating-point constant syntax (Section 2.7.2) in that an optional **-** or **+** may appear, no decimal point is needed, the decimal point might not be a period (based on locale), and no floating suffix (**f**, **F**, **l**, or **L**) may appear.

If no conversion is possible because the string does not match the expected number model (or is empty), then zero is returned, ***ptr** is set to the value of **str**, and **errno** is set to **ERANGE**. If the number converted would cause overflow, then **HUGE_VAL**, **HUGE_VALF**, or **HUGE_VALL** (with the correct sign) is returned. If the number converted would cause underflow, then zero is returned. For both overflow and underflow, **errno** is set to **ERANGE**. According to this definition, an invalid number is indistinguishable from one that causes underflow, except perhaps by the value set in ***ptr**. Some traditional implementations may set **errno** to **EDOM** when the string does not match the number model.

Conversion of hexadecimal floating-point numbers, infinity, and NaN with **strtod** is new in C99. The strings **INF** and **INFINITY** are interpreted as infinity. If infinity is not representable in the return type, then those inputs are treated as if they caused overflow. The strings **NAN** and **NAN(**...**)** denote a quiet NaN. If NaN is not representable in the return type, then those inputs are treated as if they could not be converted.

If the locale is not **"C"**, additional floating-point input formats may be accepted.

Integer conversions   The integer conversion functions **strtol**, **strtoll**, **strtoul**, and **strtoull** convert the initial portion of the argument string to an integer of type **long int**, **long long int**, **unsigned long int**, or **unsigned long long int**, respectively. The expected format of the number—which changes with the value of **base**, the expected radix—is the same in all cases and can include an optional **-** or **+** sign. No integer suffix (**l**, **L**, **u**, or **U**) may appear.

If **base** is zero, then the number (after the optional sign) should have the format of a *decimal-constant*, *octal-constant*, or *hexadecimal-constant*. The number's radix is deduced from its format. If **base** is between 2 and 36, inclusive, the number must consist of a nonzero sequence of letters and digits representing an integer in the specified base. The letters **a** through **z** (or **A** through **Z**) represent the values 10 through 35, respectively. Only those letters representing values less than **base** are permitted. As a special case, if **base** is 16, then the number may begin (after any sign) with **0x** or **0X**, which is ignored.

If no conversion can be performed, then the functions return zero, ***ptr** is set to the value of **str**, and **errno** is set to **ERANGE**. If the number to be converted would cause an overflow, then the functions return **LONG_MAX**, **LONG_MIN**, **LLONG_MAX**, **LLONG_MIN**, **ULONG_MAX**, or **ULLONG_MAX** (depending on the function's return type and the sign of the value); **errno** is set to **ERANGE**.

If the locale is not **"C"**, then additional integer input formats may be accepted.

References   *decimal-constant* 2.7; **errno** 11.2; *floating-constant* 2.7; *hexadecimal-constant* 2.7; **HUGE_VAL** Ch. 17; *integer-constant* 2.7; **isspace** function 12.6; **LONG_MAX**, **LONG_MIN**, **ULONG_MAX** 5.1.1; NaN 5.2 ; *octal-constant* 2.7; *type-marker* 2.7

16.5 abort, atexit, exit, _Exit, EXIT_FAILURE, EXIT_SUCCESS

Synopsis

```
#include <stdlib.h>
#define EXIT_FAILURE ...
#define EXIT_SUCCESS ...
void exit (int status);
void _Exit(int status);                    // C99
void abort(void);
int atexit(void (*func)(void));
```

The **exit**, **_Exit**, and **abort** functions cause the program to terminate. Control does not return to the caller of these functions.

The function **exit** terminates a program normally with these cleanup actions:

1. (Standard C only) All functions registered with the **atexit** function are called in the reverse order of their registration as many times as they were registered.
2. Open output streams are flushed. All open streams are closed.
3. Files created by the **tmpfile** function are removed.
4. Control is returned to the host environment with a status value.

By convention in many systems, a **status** value of 0 signifies successful program termination, and nonzero values are used to signify various kinds of abnormal termination. In Standard C the value 0 and the value of the macro **EXIT_SUCCESS** will signify successful termination, and the value of the macro **EXIT_FAILURE** will signify unsuccessful termination; the meaning of other values is implementation-defined. Returning an integer value from the function **main** acts like calling **exit** with the same value.

The function **_Exit** differs from **exit** in that it does not call exit handlers registered by **atexit** nor signal handlers registered by **signal**. Whether other cleanup operations are performed, such as closing open streams, is implementation-defined. **_Exit** is new in C99; traditionally some implementations provided similar functionality under the name **_exit**.

The **abort** function causes "abnormal" program termination. Functions registered with **atexit** are not called. Whether **abort** causes cleanup actions is implementation-defined. The status value returned to the host system is implementation-defined, but must denote "unsuccessful." In Standard C and many traditional implementations, the call to **abort** is translated to a special signal (**SIGABRT** in Standard C) that can be caught. If the signal is ignored or if the handler returns, then Standard C implementations will still terminate the program, but other implementations may allow the **abort** function to return to the caller. Assertion failures (Section 19.1) also call **abort**.

The **atexit** function is new in Standard C. It "registers" a function so that the function will be called when **exit** is called or when the function **main** returns. The functions are not called when the program terminates abnormally, as with **abort** or **raise**. Implementations must allow at least 32 functions to be registered. The **atexit** function returns zero if the registration succeeds and returns a nonzero value otherwise. There is no way to unregister a function. The registered functions are called in the reverse order of their registration before any standard cleanup actions are performed by **exit**. Each function is called with no arguments and should have return type **void**. A registered function should not attempt to reference any objects with storage class **auto** or **register** (e.g., through a pointer) except those it defines. Registering the same function more than once will cause the function to be called once for each registration. Some Traditional C implementations implemented similar functionality under the name **onexit**.

Example

In the following example, the **main** function opens a file and then registers the **cleanup** function that will close the file in case **exit** is called. (In fact, **exit** closes all files, but perhaps the programmer wants to close this one first.)

```
#include <stdlib.h>
#include <stdio.h>
#include <assert.h>
FILE *Open_File;

void cleanup(void) {
    if (Open_File != NULL) fclose(Open_File);
}

int main(void)
{
    int status;
    ...
    Open_File = fopen("out.dat","w");
    status = atexit(cleanup);
    assert(status == 0);
    ...
}
```

References   **assert** 19.1; **fflush** 15.2; **atexit** 19.5; **main** function 9.9; **raise** 19.6; **return** statement 8.9; **signal** 19.6; **tmpfile** 15.16; **void** type 5.9

16.6 getenv

Synopsis
`#include <stdlib.h>` `char * getenv( const char *name );`

The **getenv** function takes as its single argument a pointer to a string that is interpreted in some implementation-defined manner as a name understood by the execution environment. The function returns a pointer to another string, which is the "value" of the argument **name**. If the indicated name has no value, a null pointer is returned. The returned string should not be modified by the programmer, and it may be overwritten by a subsequent call to **getenv**.

In traditional C, the set of (*name*, *value*) bindings may also be made available to the **main** function as a non-Standard third parameter to **main** named **env** (Section 9.9). Functions **setenv** or **putenv**, if available, can be used to set an environment variable.

16.7 system

Synopsis

```
#include <stdlib.h>
int system( const char *command );
```

The function **system** passes its string argument to the operating system's *command processor* (or *shell*) for execution in some implementation-defined way. The behavior and value returned by **system** is implementation-defined, but the return value is usually the completion status of the command. In Standard C, **system** may be called with a null argument, in which case 0 is returned if there is no command processor provided in the implementation and a nonzero value is returned if there is.

16.7.1 exec

Traditional C synopsis

```
execl (char *name, char *argi, ..., NULL);
execlp(char *name, char *argi, ..., NULL);
execle(char *name, char *argi, ..., NULL, char *envp[]);
execv (char *name, char *argv[]);
execvp(char *name, char *argv[]);
execve(char *name, char *argv[], char *envp[]);
```

The various forms of **exec** are not part of Standard C—they are found mainly in UNIX systems. In all cases, they transform the current *process* into a new process by executing the program in file **name**. They differ in how arguments are supplied for the new process:

1. The functions **execl**, **execlp**, and **execle** take a variable number of arguments, the last of which must be a null pointer. By convention, the first argument should be the same as **name**—that is, it should be the name of the program to be executed.

2. The functions **execv**, **execvp**, and **execve** supply a pointer to a null-terminated vector of arguments, such as is provided to function **main**. By convention, **argv[0]** should be the same as **name**—that is, it should be the name of the program to be executed.

3. The functions **execle** and **execve** also pass an explicit "environment" to the new process. The parameter **envp** is a null-terminated vector of string pointers. Each string is of the form **"name=value"**. (In the other versions of **exec**, the environment pointer of the calling process is implicitly passed to the new process.)

4. The functions **execlp** and **execvp** are the same as **execl** and **execv**, respectively, except that the system looks for the file in the set of directories normally containing commands (usually the value of the environment variable **path** or **PATH**).

When the new process is started, the arguments supplied to **exec** are made available to the new process's **main** function (Section 9.9).

16.8 bsearch, qsort

Synopsis

```
#include <stdlib.h>

void *bsearch(
    const void *key,
    const void *base,
    size_t count,
    size_t size,
    int (*compar)(const void *the_key, const void *a_value));

void qsort(
    void *base,
    size_t count,
    size_t size,
    int (*compar)(const void *element1, const void *element2) );
```

The function **bsearch** searches an array of **count** elements whose first element is pointed to by **base**. The size of each element in characters is **size**. **compar** is a function whose arguments are a pointer to the key and a pointer to an array element; it returns a negative, zero, or positive value depending on whether the key is less than, equal to, or greater than the element, respectively. The array must be sorted in ascending order (according to **compar**) at the beginning of the search. **bsearch** returns a pointer to an element of the array that matches the **key** or a null pointer if no such element is found.

The function **qsort** sorts an array of **count** elements whose first element is pointed to by **base**. The size of each element in characters is specified by **size**. **compar** is a function that takes as arguments pointers to two elements and returns –1 if the first element is "less than" the second, 1 if the first element is "greater than" the second, and 0 if the two elements are "equal." The array will be sorted in ascending order (according to **compar**) at the end of the sort.

There is a sequence point before and after each call to **compar** within these functions.

Example

The following function **fetch** uses **bsearch** to search **Table**, a sorted array of structures. The function **key_compare** is supplied to test the key values. Notice that **fetch** first embeds the key in a dummy element (**key_elem**); this allows **key_compare** to be used with both **bsearch** and **qsort** (Section 20.6):

```
#include <stdlib.h>
#define COUNT 100
struct elem {int key; int data; } Table[COUNT];

int key_compare(const void * e1, const void * e2)
{
    int v1 = ((struct elem *)e1)->key;
    int v2 = ((struct elem *)e2)->key;
    return (v1<v2) ? -1 : (v1>v2) ? 1 : 0;
}

int fetch(int key)
/* Return the data item associated with key in
   the table, or 0 if no such key exists. */
{
    struct elem *result;
    struct elem key_elem;
    key_elem.key = key;
    result = (struct elem *)
            bsearch(
                (void *) &key_elem, (void *) &Table[0],
                (size_t) COUNT, sizeof(struct elem),
                key_compare);
    if (result == NULL)
        return 0;
    else
        return result->data;
}
```

Example

The following function **sort_table** uses **qsort** to sort the table in theprior example. The same function, **key_compare**, is used to compare table elements:

```
void sort_table(void)
/* Sorts Table according to the key values */
{
    qsort(
        (void *)Table,
        (size_t) COUNT,
        sizeof(struct elem),
        key_compare );
}
```

16.8.1 Traditional C Forms

The signatures of **bsearch** and **qsort** in traditional C are:

```
char *bsearch(
    char *key,
    char *base,
    unsigned count,
    int size,
    int (*compar)(
        char *the_key,
        char *a_value));

void qsort(
    char *base,
    unsigned count,
    int size,
    int (*compar)(
        char *element1,
        char *element2));
```

16.9 abs, labs, llabs, div, ldiv, lldiv

Synopsis

```
#include <stdlib.h>

int       abs(int        x);
long      labs(long int  x);
long long llabs(long long int x);         // C99
typedef …   div_t;
typedef …   ldiv_t;
typedef … lldiv_t;                        // C99
div_t     div(int     n, int       d);
ldiv_t    ldiv(long   n, long      d);
lldiv_t lldiv(long long n, long long d);  // C99
```

The functions in this section are integer arithmetic functions defined in **stdlib.h** in Standard C and in **math.h** in traditional C. The functions **abs**, **labs**, and (in C99) **llabs** all return the absolute value of their arguments. They differ only in the types of their arguments and results. A floating-point version is provided by the **fabs** functions in **math.h**, and a maximum-sized integer version is provided by **imaxabs** in **inttypes.h** (Section 21.7). The absolute-value functions are so easy to implement that some compilers may treat them as built-in functions; this is permitted in Standard C.

The three division functions **div**, **ldiv**, and (in C99) **lldiv** compute simultaneously the quotient and remainder of the division of **n** by **d**. They differ only in the type of their arguments and results. The types **div_t**, **ldiv_t**, and (C99) **lldiv_t** are structures containing two components, **quot** and **rem** (in unspecified order), of type **int**, **long int**, and **long long int**, respectively. The returned quotient **quot** is the same as

n/d, and the remainder **rem** is the same as **n%d**. The behavior of the functions when **d** is zero, or when the quotient or remainder cannot be represented in the return types, is undefined (not necessarily a domain error) to allow for the most efficient implementation. A maximum-sized integer division function is provided by **imaxdiv** in **inttypes.h**.

The division functions are provided because most computers can compute the quotient and remainder at the same time. Therefore, using this function—which could be expanded inline—is faster than using **/** and **%** separately.

        References   **fabs** 17.2; **imaxabs** 21.7; **imaxdiv** 21.7

16.10 mblen, mbtowc, wctomb

Synopsis

```
#include <stdlib.h>
typedef ... wchar_t;
#define MB_CUR_MAX ...
int mblen(const char *s, size_t n);
int mbtowc(wchar_t *pwc, const char *s, size_t n);
int wctomb(char *s, wchar_t wchar);
```

The Standard C language handles extended locale-specific character sets that are too large for each character to be represented within a single object of type **char**. For such character sets, Standard C provides both an internal and external representation scheme. Internally, an extended character code is assumed to fit in a wide character, an object of the implementation-defined integral type **wchar_t**. Strings of extended characters—wide strings—can be represented as objects of type **wchar_t[]**. Externally, a single wide character is assumed to be representable as a sequence of normal characters—a *multibyte character* corresponding to the wide character. See the discussion of multibyte and wide characters in Section 2.1.5 and of character sets and encoding in Section 2.9.

The functions in this section for converting characters were enhanced in C89 Amendment 1 by the addition of new "restartable" facilities, including **mbrlen**, **btowc**, **wctob**, **mbrtowc**, and **wcrtomb**. The new functions are more flexible, and their behavior is more completely specified. They are defined in **wchar.h** and described in Section 24.2.

16.10.1 Encodings and Conversion States

This section discusses some characteristics of conversions between multibyte characters and wide characters. The terminology applies to many of the functions in this chapter.

No particular representation for wide or multibyte characters is mandated or excluded, but the single null character, **'\0'**, must act as a terminator in both normal and multibyte character sequences. Multibyte encodings are in general state-dependent, employing sequences of shift characters to alter the meaning of subsequent characters.

The original Standard C functions in this chapter retain internal conversion state information from the multibyte character they last processed. The new functions in Amendment 1 provide an explicit type, **mbstate_t**, to hold the conversion state, which allows several strings to be processed in parallel. However, if the new state argument is null, each function uses its own internal state. No other standard library calls are permitted to affect these internal shift states.

The maximum number of bytes used in representing a multibyte character in the current locale is given by the (nonconstant) expression **MB_CUR_MAX**. Most functions that take as an argument a pointer **s** to a multibyte character also take an integer **n** that specifies the maximum number of bytes at **s** to consider. There is no reason for **n** to be larger than **MB_CUR_MAX**, but it could be smaller to restrict the conversion.

Given a current conversion state, a pointer **s** to a multibyte character, and a length **n**, there are several possibilities:

1. The first **n** or fewer bytes at **s** could form a *valid multibyte character*, which therefore corresponds to a single wide character **wc**. The conversion state would be updated accordingly. If **wc** happens to be the null wide character, we say that **s** *yields* the null wide character.

2. All **n** bytes at **s** could form the beginning of a valid multibyte character, but not be a complete one in themselves. No corresponding wide character can be computed. In this case, we call **s** an *incomplete multibyte character.* (If **n** is at least **MB_CUR_MAX**, this result might occur if **s** contains redundant shift characters.)

3. The **n** bytes at **s** could form an *invalid multibyte character.* That is, it might be impossible for them to form a valid, or incomplete, multibyte character in the current encoding.

Changing the **LC_CTYPE** category of the locale (Section 11.5) may change the character encodings and leave the shift state indeterminate. The value of **MB_CUR_MAX** will include enough space for shift characters.

References mbstate_t 11.1

16.10.2 Length Functions

The **mblen** function inspects up to **n** bytes from the string designated by **s** to see whether those characters represent a valid multibyte character relative to the current shift state. If so, the number of bytes making up the multibyte character is returned. The value –1 is returned if **s** is invalid or incomplete. If **s** is a null pointer, **mblen** returns a nonzero value if the locale-specific encoding of multibyte characters is state-dependent; as a side effect, such a call resets any internal state to a predefined "initial" condition.

16.10.3 Conversions to Wide Characters

The **mbtowc** function converts a multibyte character **s** to a wide character according to its internal conversion state. The result is stored in the object designated by **pwc** if **pwc** is not a null pointer. The return value is the number of characters that made up the multibyte character. If **s** is an invalid or incomplete multibyte character, then –1 is returned. If **s** is a null pointer, **mbtowc** returns a nonzero value if the locale-specific encoding of multibyte characters is state-dependent; as a side effect, the conversion state is reset to the initial state.

Example

Here is an implementation of **mbstowcs** (Section 16.11) using the **mbtowc** function:

```
#include <stdlib.h>
size_t mbstowcs(wchar_t *pwcs, const char *pmbs, size_t n)
{
    size_t i = 0; /* index into output array */
    (void) mbtowc(NULL,NULL,0); /* Initial shift state */
    while (*pmbs && i < n) {
        int len = mbtowc(&pwcs[i++],pmbs,MB_CUR_MAX);
        if (len == -1) return (size_t) -1;
        pmbs += len;    /* to next multibyte character */
    }
    return i;
}
```

References **mbstate_t** 11.1; multibyte characters 2.1.5; **size_t** 11.1; **WEOF** 11.1

16.10.4 Conversions From Wide Characters

The **wctomb** function converts the wide character **wc** to multibyte representation (according to its current shift state) and stores the result in the character array designed by **s**, which should be at least **MB_CUR_MAX** characters long. The conversion state is updated. A null character is not appended. The number of characters stored at **s** is returned if **wc** is a valid character encoding; otherwise –1 is returned. If **s** is a null pointer, **wctomb** returns a nonzero value if the locale-specific encoding of multibyte characters is state-dependent; as a side effect, such a call resets any internal state to a predefined "initial" condition.

16.11 mbstowcs, wcstombs

Synopsis

```
#include <stdlib.h>
size_t mbstowcs(wchar_t *pwcs, const char *s, size_t n);
size_t wcstombs(char *s, const wchar_t *pwcs, size_t n);
```

The Standard C functions in this section convert between wide strings and sequences of multibyte characters. "Restartable" versions of these functions, **mbsrtowcs** and **wcsr-tombs**, were added in C89 Amendment 1 and are defined in **wchar.h**; see Section 24.3.

16.11.1 Conversions to Wide Strings

The function **mbstowcs** converts a sequence of multibyte characters in the null-terminated string **s** to a corresponding sequence of wide characters, storing the result in the array designated by **pwcs**. The multibyte characters in **s** must begin in the initial shift state and be terminated by a null character. Each multibyte character, up to and including the terminating null character, is converted as if by a call to **mbtowc**. The conversion stops when **n** elements have been stored into the wide character array, when the end of **s** is reached (in which case a null wide character is stored in the output), or when a conversion error occurs (whichever occurs first). The function returns the number of wide characters stored (not including the terminating null wide character, if any) or –1 (cast to **size_t**) if a conversion error occurred.

The output pointer **pwcs** may be the null pointer, in which case no output wide characters are stored and the length argument **n** is ignored.

The conversion of the input multibyte string will stop before the terminating null character is converted if **n** output wide characters have been written to **pwcs** (and **pwcs** is not a null pointer). In this case, the pointer designated by **src** is set to point just after the last-converted multibyte character. The conversion state is updated—it will not necessarily be the initial state—and **n** is returned.

The conversion of the input multibyte string will also stop prematurely if a conversion error occurs. In this case, the pointer designated by **src** is updated to point to the multibyte character whose attempted conversion caused the error. The function returns –1 (cast to **size_t**), **EILSEQ** is stored in **errno**, and the conversion state will be indeterminate.

16.11.2 Conversions From Wide Strings

The function **wcstombs** converts a sequence of wide characters beginning with the value designated by **pwcs** to a sequence of multibyte characters, storing the result into the character array designated by **s**. Each wide character is converted as if by a call to **wctomb**. The sequence of input wide characters must be terminated by a null wide character. The output multibyte character sequence will begin in the initial shift state. The conversion stops when **n** characters have been written to **s**, when the end of **pwcs** is reached (in which case a null character is appended to **s**), or when a conversion error occurs (whichever occurs first). The function returns the number of characters written to **s**, not counting the terminating null character (if any). If a conversion error occurs, the function returns –1 (cast to **size_t**).

The output pointer **s** may be the null pointer, in which case no output bytes are stored and the length argument **n** is ignored.

The conversion of the input wide string will stop before the terminating null wide character is converted if **n** output bytes have been written to **s** (and **s** is not a null pointer). In this case, the pointer designated by **src** is set to point just after the last-converted wide character. The conversion state is updated—it will not necessarily be the initial state—and **n** is returned.

The conversion of the input wide string will also stop prematurely if a conversion error occurs. In this case, the pointer designated by **src** is updated to point to the wide character whose attempted conversion caused the error. The function returns −1 (cast to `size_t`), `EILSEQ` is stored in **errno**, and the conversion state will be indeterminate.

Example

The following statements read in a multibyte character string (**mbs**), convert it to a wide-character string (**wcs**), and then convert it back to a multibyte character string (**mbs2**). We consider it to be an error if the conversion functions completely fill the destination arrays because then the converted strings will not be null-terminated:

```
#include <stdlib.h>
#include <stdio.h>
#define MAX_WCS 100
#define MAX_MBS (100*MB_CUR_MAX)
wchar_t wcs[MAX_WCS+1];
char mbs[MAX_MBS], mbs2[MAX_MBS];
size_t len_wcs, len_mbs;

/* Read in multibyte string; check for error */
if (!fgets(mbs, MAX_MBS, stdin))
    abort();

/* Convert to wide character string; check for error */
len_wcs = mbstowcs(wcs, mbs, MAX_WCS);
if (len_wcs == MAX_WCS || len_wcs == (size_t)-1)
    abort();

/* Convert back to multibyte string; check for error */
len_mbs = wcstombs(mbs2, wcs, MAX_MBS);
if (len_mbs == MAX_MBS || len_mbs == (size_t)-1)
    abort();
```

References   conversion state 2.1.5; multibyte character 2.1.5; wide character 2.1.5

17

Mathematical Functions

The facilities described in this section are declared by the library header file **math.h**. In Standard C, a few more math facilities are in **stdlib.h**. Complex mathematical functions are declared by **complex.h** in C99.

Here are some general rules about the math facilities in this chapter.

Argument types   Prior to C99, all of the C library operations on floating-point numbers were defined only for arguments of type **double**. This was adequate even when using type **float** because of the automatic conversion of **float** arguments to type **double** before the call. C99 now defines parallel sets of mathematical functions for arguments of type **float** and **long double**, created by suffixing the letters **f** and **l** (ell), respectively, to the names of the original functions.

Distinctly named mathematical functions for each floating-point argument type give the programmer control over performance and type conversions, but at the cost of program portability. For example, changing a variable's type from **double** to **long double** will force you to edit many function names or else you will silently suffer precision problems as **long double** arguments are converted to **double** according to the **double** functions' prototypes. Therefore, C99 defines a set of *type-generic macros* in the header file **tgmath.h** (Section 17.12). These macros, which have the same names as the original type-**double** library functions, will call the proper function based on the type of the argument(s), just as the built-in additive and multiplicative operators do. The programmer can **#undef** these macros (or simply not include **tgmath.h**) if access to the original function is needed. The macros must be built into C99 implementations because it is not possible to write type-generic macros in C.

Error handling   Two general kinds of errors are possible with the mathematical functions, although older C implementations may not handle them consistently. When an input argument lies outside the domain over which the function is defined, or when an argument has a special value such as infinity or NaN, then a *domain error* occurs. **errno** (Section 11.2) is set to the value **EDOM** and the function returns an implementation-defined value. Zero was the traditional error return value, but some implementations may have better choices, such as special "not a number" values.

If the result of a function cannot be represented as a value of the function's return type, then a *range error* occurs. When this happens, **errno** should be set to the value **ERANGE**, and the function should return the largest representable floating-point value with the same sign as the correct result. In C89, this is the value of the macro **HUGE_VAL**; in C99, the macros **HUGE_VALF** and **HUGE_VALL** are available. C99 allows considerable flexibility in controlling which situations represent errors and which simply continue with infinite or NaN values.

If the result of a function is too small in magnitude to be represented, then the function should return zero; whether **errno** is also set to **ERANGE** is left to the discretion of the implementation.

17.1 *abs, labs, llabs, div, ldiv, lldiv*

These functions are defined in **stdlib.h** (see Section 16.9).

17.2 *fabs*

Synopsis
| ```
#include <math.h>
double      fabs (double x);
float       fabsf(float x); // C99
long double fabsl(long double x);    // C99
``` |

The **fabs** functions return the absolute value of their argument. Integer absolute value functions (**abs**, **labs**, and **llabs**) are defined in **stdlib.h**.

References **abs**, **labs**, **llabs** 16.9; type-generic macros 17.12
```

17.3 ceil, floor, lrint, llrint, lround, llround, nearbyint, round, rint, trunc

Synopsis
`#include <math.h>`   `// All new to C99 except ceil, floor`

```
double     ceil  (double x);
float      ceilf (float x);
long double ceill (long double x);

double     floor  (double x);
float      floorf (float x);
long double floorl (long double x);

double     nearbyint  (double x);
float      nearbyintf (float x);
long double nearbyintl (long double x);

double     rint  (double x);
float      rintf (float x);
long double rintl (long double x);

long int lrint  (double x);
long int lrintf (float x);
long int lrintl (long double x);

long long int llrint  (double x);
long long int llrintf (float x);
long long int llrintl (long double x);

double     round  (double x);
float      roundf (float x);
long double roundl (long double x);

long int lround  (double x);
long int lroundf (float x);
long int lroundl (long double x);

long long int llround  (double x);
long long int llroundf (float x);
long long int llroundl (long double x);

double     trunc  (double x);
float      truncf (float x);
long double truncl (long double x);
```

All these functions calculate integers that are "nearby" their floating-point argument. Many functions have floating-point return types even though the values returned are integers because the integers may be too large in magnitude to represent using the integer types. All the functions in this section except **ceil** and **floor** are new in C99. They all have type-generic macros. Those functions having floating-point return types will return infinity (with the correct sign) if their argument is infinite.

- The **ceil** functions return the smallest integer not less than **x**.

- The **floor** functions return the largest integer not greater than **x**.

- The **round** functions return the nearest integer to **x**; if **x** lies halfway between two integers, the **round** functions return the integer larger in absolute value (i.e., they round away from zero).

- The **trunc** functions return the nearest integer to **x** in the direction of zero. They are **floor(x)** for positive numbers and **ceil(x)** for negative numbers.

- The **nearbyint** functions return the nearest integer to **x** according to the current rounding direction (see **fenv.h**).

- The **lrint** and **llrint** functions are the same as **nearbyint** except that they return the rounded value as an integer type. If the rounded value cannot be represented as that integer type, then the result is undefined.

- The **rint** functions are the same as **nearbyint** except that the "inexact" floating-point exception will be raised if the value of the result differs from the argument (i.e., if the argument was not already an integer).

References   rounding direction 22.4; type-generic macros 17. 12

17.4 fmod, remainder, remquo

Synopsis

```
#include <math.h>   // All new to C99 except fmod

double       fmod  (double x,        double y);
float        fmodf (float x, float y);
long double fmodl (long double x, long double y);

double       remainder   (double x, double y);
float        remainderf (float x, float y);
long double remainderl (long double x, long double y);

double       remquo (double x, double y, int *quo); C99
float        remquof(float x, float y, int *quo); C99
long double remquol(long double x, long double y, int *quo);
```

These functions return an approximation to the floating-point remainder of **x/y**—that is, an approximation to the mathematical value $r = x - n*y$ for some integer n. They differ in how n is chosen, but in all cases the absolute value of r is less than the absolute value of y. All of these functions are new in C99 except **fmod** and have type-generic macros.

- The **fmod** functions choose n as **trunc** (x/y). This means that r will have the same sign as x.

- The **remainder** and **remquo** functions choose n to be **round** (x/y), except that if x/y is midway between two integers, then the even integer is chosen. The sign of r may not be the same as the sign of x.

The **remquo** functions return the same value as the **remainder** functions. In addition, they store in *$*$quo* a value whose sign is the same as x/y and whose magnitude is congruent modulo 2^k to the magnitude of the integral quotient of x/y. The value k is an implementation-defined integer greater than or equal to 3. That is, *$*$quo* is set to some "low-order bits" of the integer quotient x/y. This can be of some use in certain argument reduction calculations, which are beyond the scope of the C library.

If **y** is zero, then a Standard C-conforming implementation may generate a domain error or may return 0 from these functions. In some older C implementations, **x** is returned in this case. Although the remainder is mathematically defined in terms of x/y, the value **x/y** need not be representable for the remainder to be well defined.

The function **fmod** should not be confused with **modf** (Section 17.5)—a function that extracts the fractional and integer parts of a floating-point number.

References   **round** 17.4; **trunc** 17.4; type-generic macros 17.12

17.5 frexp, ldexp, modf, scalbn

Synopsis
```#include <math.h>   // All new to C99 except frexp```

```
double       frexp (double x, int *nptr);
float        frexpf(float x, int *nptr);
long double  frexpl(long double x, int *nptr);

double       ldexp (double x, int n);
float        ldexpf(float x, int n);
long double  ldexpl(long double x, int n);

double       modf (double x, double *nptr);
float        modff(float x, float *nptr);
long double  modfl(long double x, long double *nptr);

double       scalbn (double x, int n);
float        scalbnf(float x, int n);
long double  scalbnl(long double x, int n);

double       scalbln (double x, long int n);
float        scalblnf(float x, long int n);
long double  scalblnl(long double x, long int n);
```

The functions in this section are mostly new in C99, and they have type-generic macros.

The **frexp** functions split a floating-point number **x** into a fraction f and an exponent n, such that either f is 0.0 or $0.5 \le |f| < 1.0$, and $f*2^n$ is equal to **x**. The fraction f is returned, and as a side effect the exponent n is stored into the place pointed to by **nptr**. If **x** is zero, then both returned values are zero. If **x** is not a floating-point number, then the results are undefined.

The **ldexp** functions are the inverse of **frexp**; they compute the value $x*2^n$. A range error may occur.

The **modf** functions split a floating-point number into a fractional part f and an integer part n, such that $|f| < 1.0$ and $f+n$ is equal to **x**. Both f and n will have the same sign as **x**. The fractional part f is returned, and as a side effect the integer part n is stored into the object pointed to by **nptr**. The name **modf** is a misnomer; the value it computes is properly called a remainder. The function **modf** should not be confused with **fmod** (Section 17.3), a function that computes the remainder from dividing one floating-point number by another. Some older C implementations are reported to define **modf** differently; check your local library documentation. In C99, **modf** does *not* have a type-generic macro.

The **scalbn** and **scalbln** functions scale a floating-point number **x** by multiplying it by b^n, where b is **FLT_RADIX**. They are expected to do this calculation more efficiently than actually computing b^n and multiplying it by **x**. A range error can occur.

17.6 exp, exp2, expm1, ilogb, log, log10, log1p, log2, logb

Synopsis

```
#include <math.h>       // All new in C99 except exp, log, log10
double      exp (double x);
float       expf(float x);
long double expf(long double x);

double      exp2 (double x);
float       exp2f(float x);
long double exp2l(long double x);

double      expm1 (double x);
float       expm1f(float x);
long double expm1l(long double x);

double      log (double x);
float       logf(float x);
long double logl(long double x);

double      log10 (double x);
float       log10f(float x);
long double log10l(long double x);

double      log1p (double x);
float       log1pf(float x);
long double log1pl(long double x);

double      log2 (double x);
float       log2f(float x);
long double log2l(long double x);

int ilogb (double x);
int ilogbf(float x);
int ilogbl(long double x);
```

The functions in this section are mostly new in C99 and have type-generic macros.

The **exp** functions compute e^x, where e is the base of the natural logarithms. The **exp2** functions compute 2^x. The **expm1** functions compute $e^x - 1$. (If **x** is small in magnitude, then **expm1(x)** should be more accurate than **exp(x)-1**.) In all cases, a range error can occur for large arguments. Only the **exp** function was present before C99.

The **log** functions compute the natural logarithm function of **x**. The **log10** functions compute the base-10 logarithm, and the **log2** functions compute the base-2 logarithm. If **x** is negative, a domain error occurs. If **x** is zero or close to zero, a range error may occur (toward $-\infty$), or the value $-\infty$ may be returned without error. Some older C implementations treat zero as a domain error and may name the **log** function **ln**. Only the **log** and **log10** functions were present before C99.

The **logb** and **ilogb** functions extract the exponent from the representation of the floating-point argument, **x**. Recall that the letter b is used for the radix of the floating-point representation in the standard model and is available as **FLT_RADIX** in **float.h**. The argument **x** need not be normalized. The **logb** functions return the (integer) exponent as a floating-point number; if **x** is 0 then a domain error may occur. The **ilogb** functions return the exponent as an integer, as if casting the result of **logb** to type **int**, except for the following cases: If **x** is 0, then **ilogb** returns **FP_ILOGB**; if **x** is ∞ or $-\infty$, then **ilogb** returns **INT_MAX**; and if **x** is a NaN, then **ilogb** returns **FP_ILOGBNAN**.

References   floating-point model 5.2; **FLT_RADIX** 5.2; type-generic macros 17.12

17.7 cbrt, fma, hypot, pow, sqrt

Synopsis

```
#include <math.h>        // All new in C99 except pow, sqrt

double      cbrt (double x);
float       cbrtf(float x);
long double cbrtl(long double x);

double      hypot (double x, double y);
float       hypotf(float x, float y);
long double hypotl(long double x, long double y);

double      fma (double x, double y, double z);
float       fmaf(float x, float y, float z);
long double fmal(long double x, long double y, long double z);

double      pow( double x, double y);
float       powf(float x, float y);
long double powl(long double x, long double y);

double      sqrt (double x);
float       sqrtf(float x);
long double sqrtl(long double x);
```

The **pow** functions compute x^y. When **x** is nonzero and **y** is zero, the result is 1.0. When **x** is zero and **y** is positive, the result is zero. Domain errors occur if **x** is negative and **y** is not an exact integer, or if **x** is zero and **y** is nonpositive. Range errors may also occur.

The **hypot** functions compute the square root of $x^2 + y^2$. C99 requires that **hypot** compute its result without undue overflow or underflow, such as would result by writing **sqrt(x*x+y*y)**.

The **fma** functions compute $(x * y) + z$. They do this calculation as if by using infinite precision and then rounding the final result once to the return type.

The **sqrt** functions compute the non-negative square root of **x**. A domain error occurs if **x** is negative.

The **cbrt** functions compute the cube root of x.

References   type-generic macros 17.12

17.8 rand, srand, RAND_MAX

These functions are defined in **stdlib.h** (see Section 16.2).

17.9 cos, sin, tan, cosh, sinh, tanh

Synopsis

```
#include <math.h>

double      cos (double x);
float       cosf(float x); // C99
long double cosl(long double x);      // C99

double      sin (double x);
float       sinf(float x); // C99
long double sinl(long double x);      // C99

double      tan (double x);
float       tanf(float x); // C99
long double tanl(long double x);      // C99

double      cosh (double x);
float       coshf(float x); // C99
long double coshl(long double x);     // C99

double      sinh (double x);
float       sinhf(float x); // C99
long double sinhl(long double x);     // C99

double      tanh (double x);
float       tanhf(float x); // C99
long double tanhl(long double x);     // C99
```

The **cos** functions compute the trigonometric cosine function of **x**, which is taken to be in radians. No domain or range errors are possible, but the programmer should be aware that the result may have little significance for large values of **x**.

The **sin** and **tan** functions compute the trigonometric sine and tangent functions, respectively. A range error may occur in the **tan** function if the argument is close to an odd multiple of $\pi/2$. The same caution about large-magnitude arguments applies to **sin** and **tan**.

The **cosh**, **sinh**, and **tanh** functions compute the hyperbolic cosine, hyperbolic sine, and hyperbolic tangent function of **x**, respectively. A range error can occur if the absolute value of the argument to **sinh** or **cosh** is large.

References   type-generic macros 17.12

17.10 acos, asin, atan, atan2, acosh, asinh, atanh

Synopsis

```
#include <math.h>    // New in C99 except acos, asin, atan, atan2
double      acos (double x);
float       acosf(float x);
long double acosl(long double x);

double      asin (double x);
float       asinf(float x);
long double asinl(long double x);

double      atan (double x);
float       atanf(float x);
long double atanl(long double x);

double      atan2(double y, double x);
float       atan2f(float y, float x);
long double atan2l(long double y, long double x);

double      acosh (double x);
float       acoshf(float x);
long double acoshl(long double x);

double      asinh (double x);
float       asinhf(float x);
long double asinhl(long double x);

double      atanh (double x);
float       atanhf(float x);
long double atanhl(long double x);
```

The **acos** functions compute the principal value of the trigonometric arc cosine function of **x**. The result is in radians and lies between 0 and π. (The range of these functions is approximate because of the effect of round-off errors.) A domain error occurs if the argument is less than -1.0 or greater than 1.0.

The **asin** functions compute the principal value of the trigonometric arc sine function of **x**. The result is in radians and lies between $-\pi/2$ and $\pi/2$. A domain error occurs if the argument is less than -1.0 or greater than 1.0.

The **atan** functions compute the principal value of the arc tangent function of **x**. The result is in radians and lies between $-\pi/2$ and $\pi/2$. No range or domain errors are possible. In some older implementations of C, this function is called **arctan**.

The **atan2** functions compute the principal value of the trigonometric arc tangent function of the value **y/x**. The signs of the two arguments are taken into account to determine quadrant information. Viewed in terms of a Cartesian coordinate system, the result is the angle between the positive x-axis and a line drawn from the origin through the point (**x**, **y**). The result is in radians and lies between $-\pi$ and π. If **x** is zero, then the result is either $\pi/2$ or $-\pi/2$ depending on whether **y** is positive or negative. A domain error occurs if both **x** and **y** are zero.

The **acosh** functions compute the (non-negative) arc hyperbolic cosine of **x**. A domain error occurs if **x**<1.

The **asinh** functions compute the arc hyperbolic sin of **x**.

The **atanh** functions compute the arc hyperbolic tangent of **x**. A domain error occurs if **x** < −1 or **x** > 1. A range error may occur if **x** is −1 or 1.

References   type-generic macros 17.11

17.11 fdim, fmax, fmin

Synopsis

```
#include <math.h>                    // All new in C99
double      fdim (double x, double y);
float       fdimf(float x, float y);
long double fdiml(long double x, long double y);

double      fmax (double x, double y);
float       fmaxf(float x, float y);
long double fmaxl(long double x, long double y);

double      fmin (double x, double y);
float       fminf(float x, float y);
long double fminl(long double x, long double y);
```

The **fdim** functions compute the positive difference between **x** and **y**. That is, they return $x - y$ if $x > y$ and +0 if $x \le y$.

The **fmax** functions return the larger (toward +∞) of the two arguments; the **fmin** functions return the smaller (toward −∞) of the arguments. In both instances, if one argument is a number and the other is a NaN, then the number is returned.

References   NaN 5.2; type-generic macros 17.12

17.12 TYPE-GENERIC MACROS

C99 defines a set of type-generic macros that can improve the portability of C programs that use mathematical and/or complex functions. These macros expand to calls on particular library functions depending on the type of their argument(s). The macros may be used by including the library header **tgmath.h**, which includes the library headers **math.h** and **complex.h**.

Table 17–1 lists the type-generic macros using a prototype notation in which **T** stands for the generic type: **float**, **double**, **long double**, **float complex**, **double complex**, or **long double complex**. The notation **REAL(T)** denotes the real type of the same size as the complex generic type. Although most functions take a single, generic argument, some functions take more than one generic argument and some functions take additional arguments of specific (nongeneric) types; those argument types will be the same regardless of the generic type. The table also lists the real and/or complex functions that are actually called depending on the argument type. The functions are named using consistent rules based on the name of the original **double** version of the C library function: Complex functions are prefixed by the letter **c**, functions taking **float** or **float complex** arguments are suffixed by the letter **f**, and functions taking **long double** or **long double complex** arguments are suffixed by the letter **l**.

Example

> Implementations are free to treat the type-generic macros specially, but as an example the **sqrt** macro might also be implemented as:

```
#define sqrt(x) \
  ((sizeof(x) == sizeof(float)) ? sqrt(x) :
   (sizeof(x) == sizeof(double)) ? sqrtf(x) : sqrtl(x))
```

If you "call" a type-generic macro from Table 17–1 with generic argument(s) of certain type(s), then the following rules are used to determine which function is selected to be called. Once that function is selected, all arguments are converted to the appropriate types for that function, following the normal rules for converting arguments when function prototypes are present.

1. If any of the generic arguments have type **long double complex**, then the **long double complex** version of the function is called. If there is no such function, then the result is undefined.

2. Otherwise, if any of the generic arguments have type **double complex**, then the **double complex** version of the function is called. If there is no such function, then the result is undefined.

3. Otherwise, if any of the generic arguments have type **float complex**, then the **float complex** version of the function is called. If there is no such function, then the result is undefined.

4. Otherwise, if any of the generic arguments have type **long double**, then the **long double** version of the function is called. If there is no such function, but there is a **long double complex** version of the function, then that complex function is called.

5. Otherwise, if any of the generic arguments have type **double** or any generic argument has an integral type, then the **double** version of the function is called. If there is no such function, but there is a **double complex** version of the function, then that complex function is called.

6. Otherwise, the **float** version of the function is called. (All generic arguments would have to have type **float** for this rule to be reached.) If there is no such function, but there is a **float complex** version of the function, then that complex function is called.

Table 17–1   Type-generic macros

Type-generic macros (`tgmath.h`)	Real functions (`math.h`)	Complex functions (`complex.h`)
`T acos(T x)`	`acos, acosf, acosl`	`cacos, cacosf, cacosl`
`T acosh(T x)`	`acosh, acoshf, acoshl`	`cacosh, cacoshf, cacoshl`
`T asin(T x)`	`asin, asinf, asinl`	`casin, casinf, casinl`
`T asinh(T x)`	`asinh, asinhf, asinhl`	`casinh, casinhf, casinhl`
`T atan(T x)`	`atan, atanf, atanl`	`catan, catanf, catanl`
`T atan2(T y, T x)`	`atan2, atan2f, atan2l`	
`T atanh(T x)`	`atanh, atanhf, atanhl`	`catanh, catanhf, catanhl`
`T carg(T x)`		`carg, cargf, cargl`
`T cbrt(T x)`	`cbrt, cbrtf, cbrtl`	
`T ceil(T x)`	`ceil, ceilf, ceill`	
`REAL(T) cimag(T x)`		`cimag, cimagf, cimagl`
`T conj(T x)`		`conj, conjf, conjl`
`T copysign(T x, T y)`	`copysign, copysignf, copysignl`	
`T cos(T x)`	`cos, cosf, cosl`	`ccos, ccosf, ccosl`
`T cosh(T x)`	`cosh, coshf, coshl`	`ccosh, ccoshf, ccoshl`
`T cproj(T x)`		`cproj, cprojf, cprojl`
`REAL(T) creal(T x)`		`creal, crealf, creall`
`T erf(T x)`	`erf, erff, erfl`	
`T erfc(T x)`	`erfc, erfcf, erfcl`	
`T exp(T x)`	`exp, expf, expl`	`cexp, cexpf, cexpl`
`T exp2(T x)`	`exp2, exp2f, exp2l`	
`T expm1(T x)`	`expm1, expm1f, expm1l`	
`T fabs(T x)`	`fabs, fabsf, fabsl`	`cabs, cabsf, cabsl`
`T fdim(T x, T y)`	`fdim, fdimf, fdiml`	
`T floor(T x)`	`floor, floorf, floorl`	
`T fma(T x, T y, T z)`	`fma, fmaf, fmal`	
`T fmax(T x, T y)`	`fmax, fmaxf, fmaxl`	
`T fmin(T x, T y)`	`fmin, fminf, fminl`	
`T fmod(T x, T y)`	`fmod, fmodf, fmodl`	
`T frexp(T value, int *exp)`	`frexp, frexpf, frexpl`	
`T hypot(T x, T y)`	`hypot, hypotf, hypotl`	
`int ilogb(T x)`	`ilogb, ilogbf, ilogbl`	
`T ldexp(T x, int exp)`	`ldexp, ldexpf, ldexpl`	

Table 17–1   Type-generic macros

Type-generic macros (`tgmath.h`)	Real functions (`math.h`)	Complex functions (`complex.h`)
`T lgamma(T x)`	`lgamma, lgammaf, lgammal`	
`long long int llrint(T x)`	`llrint, llrintf, llrintl`	
`long long int llround(T x)`	`llround, llroundf, llroundl`	
`T log(T x)`	`log, logf, logl`	`clog, clogf, clogl`
`T log10(T x)`	`log10, log10f, log10l`	
`T log1p(T x)`	`log1p, log1pf, log1pl`	
`T log2(T x)`	`log2, log2f, log2l`	
`T logb(T x)`	`logb, logbf, logbl`	
`long int lrint(T x)`	`lrint, lrintf, lrintl`	
`long int lround(T x)`	`lround, lroundf, lroundl`	
none	`modf, modff, modfl`	
`T nearbyint(T x)`	`nearbyint, nearbyintf, nearbyintl`	
`T nextafter(T x)`	`nextafter, nextafterf, nextafterl`	
`T nexttoward(T x, long double y)`	`nexttoward, nexttowardf, nexttowardl`	
`T pow(T x, T y)`	`pow, powf, powl`	`cpow, cpowf, cpowl`
`T remainder(T x, T y)`	`remainder, remainderf, remainderl`	
`T remquo(T x, Ty, int *quo)`	`remquo, remquof, remquol`	
`T rint(T x)`	`rint, rintf, rintl`	
`T round(T x)`	`round, roundf, roundl`	
`T scalbln(T x, long int n)`	`scalbln, scalblnf, scalblnl`	
`T scalbn(T x, int n)`	`scalbn, scalbnf, scalbnl`	
`T sin(T x)`	`sin, sinf, sinl`	`csin, csinf, csinl`
`T sinh(T x)`	`sinh, sinhf, sinhl`	`csinh, csinhf, csinhl`
`T sqrt(T x)`	`sqrt, sqrtf, sqrtl`	`csqrt, csqrtf, csqrtl`
`T tan(T x)`	`tan, tanf, tanl`	`ctan, ctanf, ctanl`

Table 17–1 Type-generic macros

Type-generic macros (`tgmath.h`)	Real functions (`math.h`)	Complex functions (`complex.h`)
`T tanh(T x)`	`tanh, tanhf, tanhl`	`ctanh, ctanhf, ctanhl`
`T tgamma(T x)`	`tgamma, tgammaf,` `tgammal`	
`T trunc(T x)`	`trunc, truncf, truncl`	

17.13 erf, erfc, lgamma, tgamma

Synopsis

```
#include <math.h>        // All new in C99 but common in UNIX
double      erf (double x);
float       erff(float x);
long double erfl(long double x);

double      erfc (double x);
float       erfcf(float x);
long double erfcl(long double x);

double      lgamma (double x);
float       lgammaf(float x);
long double lgammal(long double x);

double      tgamma (double x);
float       tgammaf(float x);
long double tgammal(long double x);
```

The **erf** functions compute the error function

$$\frac{2}{\sqrt{\pi}} \cdot \int_0^x e^{-t^2} dt$$

The **erfc** functions compute **1-erf(x)**, which is

$$\frac{2}{\sqrt{\pi}} \cdot \int_x^\infty e^{-t^2} dt$$

The **lgamma** functions compute the natural logarithm of the gamma function of the magnitude of **x**:

$$\log|\Gamma(x)|$$

The **tgamma** functions compute the gamma function of **x**,

$$\Gamma(x)$$

17.14 *fpclassify, isfinite, isinf, isnan, isnormal, signbit*

Synopsis

```
#include <math.h>          // All new in C99
int fpclassify(real-floating-type x);
#define FP_INFINITE ...
#define FP_NAN ...
#define FP_NORMAL ...
#define FP_SUBNORMAL ...
#define FP_ZERO ...

int isfinite(real-floating-type x);

int isinf(real-floating-type x);

int isnan(real-floating-type x);

int isnormal(real-floating-type x);

int signbit(real-floating-type x);
```

The macros in this section whose arguments are listed as *real-floating-type* are type-generic; their argument can be an expression of any real floating-point type. Since floating-point expressions may be evaluated using a greater precision than their actual "semantic" type, these macros must take care to convert the argument expression to the correct type representation before inspecting it. As the C standard points out, a normalized number in **long double** format could become subnormal in **double** format and could become zero in **float** format.

The **fpclassify** macro returns one of the values **FP_INFINITE**, **FP_NAN**, **FP_NORMAL**, **FP_SUBNORMAL**, or **FP_ZERO**. Each of these macros is a distinct integer constant expression. Additional classification macros beginning with **FP_** and a capital letter may be specified by C implementations.

The **isfinite** macro returns a nonzero value if and only if its argument is neither infinite nor a NaN. Subnormal numbers are finite.

The **isinf** macro returns a nonzero value if and only if its argument is infinite (with any sign).

The **isnan** macro returns a nonzero value if and only if its argument is a NaN.

The **isnormal** macro returns a nonzero value if and only if its argument is normal. The macro returns zero for zero, subnormal, infinite, and NaN values.

The **signbit** macro returns a nonzero value if and only if its argument is negative.

17.15 *copysign, nan, nextafter, nexttoward*

<table>
<tr><td colspan="2" align="center">Synopsis</td></tr>
<tr><td colspan="2">

```
#include <math.h>      // All new in C99
double      copysign (double x, double y);
float       copysignf(float x, float y);
long double copysignl(long double x, long double y);

double      nan (const char *tagp);
float       nanf(const char *tagp);
long double nanl(const char *tagp);

double      nextafter (double x, double y);
float       nextafterf(float x, float y);
long double nextafterl(long double x, long double y);

double      nexttoward (double x, long double y);
float       nexttowardf(float x, long double y);
long double nexttowardl(long double x, long double y);
```
</td></tr>
</table>

The functions in this section manipulate floating-point values.

The **copysign** functions return **x** with the sign of **y**.

The **nan** functions return a "quiet" NaN with content indicated by the string designated by **tagp** if the C implementation provides quiet NaNs. Otherwise **nan** returns zero. The calls

```
nan("char-sequence")
nan("")
nan(NULL)
```

are equivalent to the calls

```
strtod("NAN(char-sequence)", (char **) NULL)
strtod("NAN()", (char **) NULL)
strtod("NAN", (char **) NULL)
```

respectively. Calls to **nanf** and **nanl** map to corresponding calls on **strtof** and **strtodl**.

The **nextafter** functions return the next representable floating-point value to **x** in the direction of **y**. A range error can occur if there is no such finite value. If **x** and **y** are equal, then **y** is returned. Care must be taken that the arguments and return value are in fact converted to the formal parameter and return types, even in a macro implementation, because the exact floating-point representations are important.

The **nexttoward** functions are equivalent to the **nextafter** functions except that the type of **y** is always long double.

References quiet NaN 5.2; **strtod** 13.8

17.16 isgreater, isgreaterequal, isless, islessequal, islessgreater, isunordered

Synopsis

```
#include <math.h>          // All new in C99

int isgreater( real-floating-type x, real-floating-type y);

int isgreaterequal(real-floating-type x, real-floating-type y);

int isless(real-floating-type x, real-floating-type y);

int islessequal( real-floating-type x, real-floating-type y);

int islessgreater( real-floating-type x, real-floating-type y);

int isunordered( real-floating-type x, real-floating-type y);
```

Two floating-point values are *unordered* if one or both of them are NaNs. Using C's comparison operators on unordered values will normally cause the "invalid" floating-point exception to be raised. The type-generic comparison macros in this section will not raise the exception and so are useful for certain kinds of careful floating-point programming. If the C implementation does not raise the invalid exception on the comparison operators, then those operators behave as these macros do.

The `isunordered` macro returns true if and only if its arguments are unordered.

The `isgreater` macro returns 0 if its arguments are unordered and otherwise returns $(x) > (y)$.

The `isgreaterequal` macro returns 0 if its arguments are unordered and otherwise returns $(x) >= (y)$.

The `isless` macro returns 0 if its arguments are unordered and otherwise returns $(x) < (y)$.

The `islessequal` macro returns 0 if its arguments are unordered and otherwise returns $(x) <= (y)$.

The `islessgreater` macro returns 0 if its arguments are unordered and otherwise returns $(x) < (y) \;||\; (x) > (y)$ (without evaluating its arguments twice).

References   NaN 5.2

18

Time and Date Functions

The facilities in this section give the C programmer ways to retrieve and use the (calendar) date and time, and the process time—that is, the amount of processing time used by the running program.

Calendar time may be used to record the date that a program was run or a file was written, or to compute a date in the past or future. Calendar time is represented in two forms: a simple arithmetic value returned by the time function and a broken-down, structured form computed from the arithmetic value by the **gmtime** and **localtime** functions. Locale-specific formatting is provided by the Standard C function **strftime**.

Process time is often used to measure how fast a program or part of a program executes. Process time is represented by an arithmetic value (usually integral) returned by the **clock** function.

18.1 *clock, clock_t, CLOCKS_PER_SEC, times*

Synopsis

```
#include <time.h>

typedef ... clock_t;
#define CLOCKS_PER_SEC ...
clock_t clock(void);
```

The **clock** function returns an approximation to the processor time used by the current process. The units in which the time is expressed vary with the implementation; microseconds are customary. The Standard C version of **clock** allows the implementor freedom to use any arithmetic type, **clock_t**, for the process time. The number of time units ("clock ticks") per second is defined by the macro **CLOCKS_PER_SEC**. If the processor time is not available, the value –1 (cast to be of type **clock_t**) will be returned.

Programmers should be aware of "wrap-around" in the process time. For instance, if type `clock_t` is represented in 32 bits and `clock` returns the time in microseconds, the time returned will "wrap around" to its starting value in about 36 minutes.

Example

Here is how the `clock` function can be used to time a Standard C program:

```
#include <time.h>
clock_t start, finish;
...
start = clock();
process();
finish = clock();
printf("process() took %f seconds to execute\n",
        ((double) (finish - start)) / CLOCKS_PER_SEC );
```

The cast to type `double` allows `clock_t` and `CLOCKS_PER_SEC` to be either floating-point or integral.

In traditional C, the return type of `clock` is `long`, but the value returned is really of type `unsigned long`; the use of `long` predates the addition of `unsigned long` to the language. Unsigned arithmetic should always be used when computing with process times. The `times` function is also found in some non-Standard implementations instead of `clock`; it returns a structured value that reports various components of the process time, each typically measured in units of 1/60 of a second. The signatures are:

```
#include <sys/types.h>
#include <sys/times.h>
long clock(void);
void times(struct tms *);
struct tms { ... };
```

Example

A rough equivalent to the (Standard C) `clock` function can be written using (non-Standard) `times`:

```
#include <sys/types.h>
#include <sys/times.h>
#define CLOCKS_PER_SEC 60
long clock(void)
{
    struct tms tmsbuf;
    times(&tmsbuf);
    return (tmsbuf.tms_utime + tmsbuf.tms_stime);
}
```

There is a type, `time_t`, used in the prior structure; it is a "process time" unit and therefore is not the same as the "calendar time" type `time_t` defined in Standard C.

References `time` 18.2; `time_t` 18.2

18.2 time, time_t

Synopsis

```
#include <time.h>

typedef ... time_t;
time_t time(time_t *tptr);
```

The Standard C function `time` returns the current calendar time encoded in a value of type `time_t`, which can be any arithmetic type. If the parameter `tptr` is not null, the return value is also stored at `*tptr`. If errors are encountered, the value –1 (cast to type `time_t`) is returned.

Typically, the value returned by `time` is passed to the function `asctime` or `ctime` to convert it to a readable form, or it is passed to `localtime` or `gmtime` to convert it to a more easily processed form. Computing the interval between two calendar times can be done by the Standard C function `difftime`; in other implementations, the programmer must either work with the broken-down time from `gmtime` or depend on a customary representation of the time as the number of seconds since some arbitrary past date. (January 1, 1970 seems to be popular.)

In traditional implementations, type `long` is used in place of `time_t`, but the value returned is logically of type `unsigned long`. When errors occur, `-1L` is returned. In System V UNIX, `errno` is also set to `EFAULT`.

References `asctime` 18.3; `ctime` 18.3; `difftime` 18.5; `errno` 11.2; `gmtime` 18.4; `localtime` 18.4

18.3 asctime, ctime

Synopsis

```
#include <time.h>

char *asctime( const struct tm *ts );
char *ctime( const time_t *timptr );
```

The `asctime` and `ctime` functions both return a pointer to a string that is a printable date and time of the form

```
"Sat May 15 17:30:00 1982\n"
```

The `asctime` function takes as its single argument a pointer to a structured calendar time; such a structure is produced by `localtime` or `gmtime` from the arithmetic time that is returned by `time`. The `ctime` function takes a pointer to the value returned by `time`, and therefore `ctime(tp)` is equivalent to `asctime(localtime(tp))`.

In most implementations—including many Standard C-conforming implementations—the functions return a pointer to a static data area, and therefore the returned string should be printed or copied (with `strcpy`) before any subsequent call to either function.

In traditional C, type `long` is used in place of `time_t` and the functions may be found in the header file `sys/time.h`.

Example

Many programs need to print the current date and time. Here is how to do it using `time` and `ctime`:

```
#include <time.h>
#include <stdio.h>
time_t now;
...
now = time(NULL);
printf("The current date and time is: %s",ctime(&now));
```

References   `gmtime` 18.4; `localtime` 18.4; `strcpy` 13.3; `struct tm` 18.4; `time` 18.2

18.4 gmtime, localtime, mktime

Synopsis
`#include <time.h>`

`struct tm { ... };`
`struct tm *gmtime( const time_t *t );`
`struct tm *localtime( const time_t *t );`
`time_t mktime( struct tm *tmptr );`

The functions `gmtime` and `localtime` convert an arithmetic calendar time returned by `time` to a "broken-down" form of type `struct tm`. The `gmtime` function converts to Greenwich mean time (GMT) while `localtime` converts to local time, taking into account the time zone and possible Daylight Savings Time. The functions return a null pointer if they encounter errors and are portable across UNIX systems and Standard C. The structure `struct tm` includes the fields listed in Table 18–1. All fields have type `int`.

In most implementations—including many Standard ones—`gmtime` and `localtime` return a pointer to a single static data area overwritten on every call. Therefore, the returned structure should be used or copied before any subsequent call to either function.

The function `mktime` (Standard C) constructs a value of type `time_t` from the broken-down local time specified by the argument `tmptr`. The values of

Table 18-1 Fields in **struct tm** type

Name	Units	Range
tm_sec	seconds after the minute	0..61[a]
tm_min	minutes after the hour	0..59
tm_hour	hours since midnight	0..23
tm_mday	day of month	1..31
tm_mon	month since January	0..11
tm_year	years since 1900	
tm_wday	day since Sunday	0..6
tm_yday	day since January 1	0..365
tm_isdst	daylight saving time flag	>0 if daylight saving time; 0 if not; <0 if don't know

[a] This allows up to two leap-seconds (C89), although C99 only requires one.

tmptr->tm_wday and **tmptr->tm_yday** are ignored by **mktime**. If successful, **mktime** returns the new time value and adjusts the contents of ***tmptr**, setting the **tm_wday** and **tm_yday** components. If the indicated calendar time cannot be represented as a value of **time_t**, then **mktime** returns the value **-1** (cast to **time_t**). Section 18.5 shows an example.

The traditional C signatures of the time functions are

```
#include <sys/time.h>
struct tm { ... };
struct tm *gmtime(long *t);
struct tm *localtime(long *t);
```

18.5 difftime

Synopsis

```
#include <time.h>
double difftime( time_t t1, time_t t0 );
```

The **difftime** function is only found in Standard C. It subtracts calendar time **t0** from calendar time **t1**, returning the difference in seconds as a value of type **double**. Programmers cannot assume that calendar time is encoded in **time_t** as a scalar value (such as a number of microseconds), and so **difftime** must be used rather than simply subtracting two values of type **time_t**.

Example

The following function returns the number of seconds between midnight on April 15, 1990 and the current date and time.

```
#include <time.h>
...
double Secs_Since_Apr_15(void)
{
    struct tm Apr_15_struct = {0}; /* Set all fields to 0 */
    time_t Apr_15_t;
    Apr_15_struct.tm_year = 90;
    Apr_15_struct.tm_mon  = 3;
    Apr_15_struct.tm_mday = 15;
    Apr_15_t = mktime(&Apr_15_struct);
    if (Apr_15_t == (time_t)-1)
        return 0.0; /* error */
    else
        return difftime( time(NULL), Apr_15_t);
}
```

References   time_t 18.2

18.6 strftime, wcsftime

Synopsis

```
#include <time.h>

size_t strftime(
   char *s, size_t maxsize,
   const char *format,
   const struct tm *timeptr);
```

```
#include <wchar.h>

size_t wcsftime(
   wchar_t *s, size_t maxsize,
   const wchar_t *format,
   const struct tm *timeptr);
```

These functions are only found in Standard C. Like **sprintf** (Section 15.11), **strftime** stores characters into the character array pointed to by the parameter **s** under control of the multibyte string **format**. However, **strftime** only formats a single date and time quantity specified by **timeptr** (Section 18.4), and the formatting codes in **format** are interpreted differently from **sprintf**. No more than **maxsize** characters (including the terminating null character) are placed into the array designated by **s**. The actual number of characters stored (not including the terminating null character) is returned. If **maxsize** is not large enough to hold the entire formatted string, then zero is returned and the content of the output string is undefined. The formatting of **strftime** is locale-specific using the **LC_TIME** category (see **setlocale**, Section 20.1).

Amendment 1 to C89 adds the **wcsftime** function for formatting the date and time as a wide string. The function is analogous to **wsprintf** (Section 15.11).

18.6.1 Formatting Codes

The **format** string consists of an arbitrary mixture of conversion specifications and other multibyte characters. In the formatting process, the conversion specifications are replaced by other characters as indicated in Table 18–2, and the other multibyte characters are simply copied to the output. A conversion specification consists of the character **%**, optionally followed by one of the modifier letters **E** or **O** (uppercase oh), followed by a single character that specifies the conversion.

Table 18–2 Formatting codes for **strftime**

Ltr	Replaced by	`timeptr` fields used
a	abbreviated weekday name; in the **"C"** locale it is always the first three letters of **%A**, **"Mon"** (etc.)	`tm_wday`
A	full weekday name; in the **"C"** locale **"Monday"** (etc.)	`tm_wday`
b	abbreviated month name; in **"C"** locale, it is always the first three letters of **%B:"Feb"** (etc.)	`tm_mon`
B	full month name; in **"C"** locale **"February"** (etc.)	`tm_mon`
c	locale-specific date and time; in the **"C"** locale, it is the same as **%a %b %e %T %Y**	any or all
C	(C99) the last two digits of the year (00–99)	`tm_year`
d	day of the month as a decimal integer (01–31)	`tm_mday`
D	equivalent to **%m/%d/%y**	`tm_mon, tm_mday, tm_year`
e	the day of the month (1–31), with single digits preceded by a space	`tm_mday`
F	ISO 8601 date format: **%Y-%m-%d**	`tm_mon, tm_mday, tm_year`
g	the last two digits of the week-based year (00–99)[a]	`tm_year, tm_wday, tm_yday`
G	the week-based year (0000–9999)	`tm_year, tm_wday, tm_yday`
h	same as **%b**	`tm_mon`
H	the hour (24-hour clock) as a decimal integer (00–23)	`tm_hour`
I	the hour (12-hour clock) as a decimal integer (01–12)	`tm_hour`
j	day of the year as a decimal number (001–366)	`tm_yday`
m	month as a decimal number (01–12)	`tm_mon`

Table 18–2 Formatting codes for `strftime`

Ltr	Replaced by	`timeptr` fields used
M	minute as a decimal number (00–59)	`tm_min`
n	(C99) replaced by a newline character	none
p	the locale's equivalent of AM/PM designation for 12-hour clock; in the `"C"` locale, it is **AM** or **PM**	`tm_hour`
r	(C99) the locale's 12-hour clock time; in the `"C"` locale, it is `%I:%M:%S %p`	`tm_hour`, `tm_min`, `tm_sec`
R	(C99) same as `%H:%M`	`tm_hour`, `tim_min`
S	second as a decimal number (00–60)[b]	`tm_sec`
t	(C99) replaced by a horizontal tab character	none
T	(C99) ISO 8601 time format: `%H:%M:%S`	`tm_hour`, `tim_min`, `tm_sec`
u	(C99) ISO 8601 weekday number (1–7), with Monday being 1	`tm_wday`
U	week number of the year (00–53)[c]	`tm_year`, `tm_wday`, `tm_yday`
V	(C99) ISO 8601 week number (01–53) in the week-based year	`tm_year`, `tm_wday`, `tm_yday`
w	weekday as a decimal number (0–6, with Sunday = 0)	`tm_wday`
W	week number of the year (00–53)[d]	`tm_year`, `tm_wday`, `tm_yday`
x	locale-specific date; in the `"C"` locale, it is `%m/%d/%y`	any or all
X	local-specific time; in the `"C"` locale, it is `%T`	any or all
y	last two digits of the year (00–99)	`tm_year`
Y	year with century as a decimal number (e.g., **1952**)	`tm_year`
z	(C99) ISO 8601 offset of time zone from UTC, or nothing; **-530** means 5 hours 30 minutes behind (west of) Greenwich	`tm_isdst`
Z	time zone name or abbreviation, or nothing if no time zone is known; in the `"C"` locale it is implementation-defined	`tm_isdst`
%	a single %	none

[a] See the definition of *week-based year* in the text.
[b] Allows for a leap-second (60).
[c] Week number 1 has the first Sunday; previous days are week 0.
[d] Week number 1 has the first Monday; previous days are week 0.

The modifier and many of the conversion letters are new in C99. The modifier **E** may be applied to the conversions **c**, **C**, **x**, **X**, **y**, and **Y**; it specifies that the locale's alternative representation (not specified) is to be used. The modifier **O** may be applied to **d**, **e**, **H**, **I**, **M**, **m**, **s**, **u**, **U**, **V**, **w**, **W**, and **y**; it specifies that the locale's alternative numeric symbols (not specified) are to be used. In the `"C"` locale, the modifiers are ignored.

Some of the C99 conversion letters specify conversions according to the ISO 8601 week-based year. In this system, weeks begin on Monday, and week 1 of the year is the week containing January 4 (equivalently, the first week to contain at least 4 days of the new year). This means that January 1, 2, or 3 could be considered part of the last week of the preceding year, or that December 29, 30, or 31 could be considered part of the first week of the following year. For example, Saturday, January 2, 1999 is in week 53 of year 1998. Contrast this with **%U** and **%W**, which introduce a partial "week 0" if needed.

Example

A plausible implementation of **asctime** (Section 18.3) using **strftime** is shown below. Since the formatting is locale-specific, the length of the output string (including the terminating null character) is not easily predictable (which is the case for the output from **asctime**):

```
#include <time.h>
#define TIME_SIZE 80  /* hope this is big enough */
char *asctime2( const struct tm *tm )
{
    static char time_buffer[TIME_SIZE];
    size_t len;
    len = strftime( time_buffer, TIME_SIZE,
        "%a %b %d %H:%M:%S %Y\n", tm);
    if (len == 0)
        return NULL;  /* time_buffer is too short */
    else
        return time_buffer;
}
```

19

Control Functions

The facilities in this chapter provide extensions to the standard flow of control in C programs. They are provided in the header files **assert.h**, **setjmp.h**, and **signal.h**. A few control functions described in this chapter in earlier editions of the book have been moved to Chapter 16, including **system** and the **exit**-related functions.

19.1 *assert, NDEBUG*

Synopsis

```
#include <assert.h>

#ifndef NDEBUG
void assert( int expression );
#else
#define assert(x)  ((void)0)
#endif
```

The macro **assert** takes as its single argument a value of any integer type. (Many implementations permit any scalar type.) If that value is 0 and if the macro **NDEBUG** is not defined, then **assert** will print a diagnostic message on the standard output stream and halt the program by calling **abort** (in Standard C) or **exit** (in traditional C). The **assert** facility is always implemented as a macro, and the header file **assert.h** must be included in the source file to use the facility. The diagnostic message will include the text of the argument, the file name (__FILE__), and the line number (__LINE__). C99 implementations can also use the function name (__func__).

If the macro **NDEBUG** is defined when the header file **assert.h** is read, the **assert** facility is disabled usually by defining **assert** to be the empty statement. No diagnostic messages are printed, and the argument to **assert** is not evaluated.

Example

The **assert** facility is typically used during program development to verify that certain conditions are true at run time. It provides reliable documentation to people reading the program and can greatly aid in debugging. When a program is operational, assertions can easily be disabled, after which they have no run-time overhead. In the following example, the assertion is better documentation than the English comment, which can be misinterpreted:

```
#include <assert.h>
int f(int x)
{
    /* x should be between 1 and 10 */    /* !? */
    assert(x>0 && x<10);
    ...
}
```

References   abort 19.3; exit 19.3; __func__ 2.6.1; __LINE__ 3.3.4

19.2 system, exec

See Section 16.7.

19.3 exit, abort

See Section 16.5.

19.4 setjmp, longjmp, jmp_buf

Synopsis
`#include <setjmp.h>`

`typedef ... jmp_buf;`
`int setjmp( jmp_buf env );`
`void longjmp( jmp_buf env, int status );`

The **setjmp** and **longjmp** functions implement a primitive form of nonlocal jumps, which may be used to handle abnormal or exceptional situations. This facility is traditionally considered more portable than **signal** (Section 19.6), but the latter has also been incorporated into Standard C.

The macro **setjmp** records its caller's environment in the "jump buffer" **env**, an implementation-defined array, and returns 0 to its caller. (The type **jmp_buf** must be implemented as an array type so that a pointer to **env** is actually passed to **setjmp**.)

The function **longjmp** takes as its arguments a jump buffer previously filled by calling **setjmp** and an integer value, **status**, that is usually nonzero. The effect of calling **longjmp** is to cause the program to return from the call to **setjmp** again, this time returning the value **status**. Some implementations, including Standard C, do not permit **longjmp** to cause 0 to be returned from **setjmp** and will return 1 from **setjmp** if **longjmp** is called with status 0.

The **setjmp** and **longjmp** functions are notoriously difficult to implement, and the programmer would do well to make minimal assumptions about them. When **setjmp** returns with a nonzero value, the programmer can assume that static variables have their proper value as of the time **longjmp** was called. Automatic variables local to the function containing **setjmp** are guaranteed to have their correct value in Standard C only if they have a **volatile**-qualified type or if their values were not changed between the original call to **setjmp** and the corresponding **longjmp** call. Furthermore, Standard C requires that the call to **setjmp** either be an entire expression statement (possibly cast to **void**), the right-hand side of a simple assignment expression, or be used as the controlling expression of an **if**, **switch**, **do**, **while**, or **for** statement in one of the following forms:

> (setjmp(…))
> (!setjmp(…))
> (*exp relop* setjmp(…))
> (setjmp(…) *relop exp*)

where *exp* is an integer constant expression and *relop* is a relational or equality operator. C89 required that **longjmp** operate correctly in unnested signal (interrupt) handlers, but C99 dropped that requirement. Interrupt handlers should be considered implementation-defined.

If the jump buffer argument to **longjmp** is not set by **setjmp**, or if the function containing **setjmp** is terminated before the call to **longjmp**, the behavior is undefined.

Example

```
#include <setjmp.h>
jmp_buf ErrorEnv;
…

int guard(void)
    /* Return 0 if successful; else longjmp code. */
{
    int status = setjmp(ErrorEnv);
    if ( status != 0) return status;   /* error */
    process();
    return 0;
}

int process(void)
{   …
    if (error_happened) longjmp(ErrorEnv, error_code);
    …
}
```

The **longjmp** function is to be called when an error is encountered in function **process**. The function **guard** is the "backstop," to which control will be transferred by **longjmp**. The function **process** should be called directly or indirectly from **guard**; this ensures that **longjmp** cannot be called after **guard** returns, and that no attempt is made to depend on the values of local variables in the function **process** containing **longjmp**. (This is a conservative policy.) Note that the return value from **setjmp** must be tested to determine if the return was caused by **longjmp** or not.

19.5 atexit

See Section 16.5.

19.6 signal, raise, gsignal, ssignal, psignal

Synopsis

```
#include <signal.h>

#define SIG_IGN …
#define SIG_DFL …
#define SIG_ERR …
#define SIGxxx …

…
void (*signal( int sig, void (*func)(int) )) (int);
int raise( int sig );
typedef … sig_atomic_t;


/* Non-Standard extensions: */
int kill( int pid, intsig );
int (*ssignal( int softsig, int (*func)(int) )) (int);
int gsignal( int softsig );
void psignal( int sig, char *prefix );
```

Signals are (potentially) asynchronous events that may require special processing by the user program or by the implementation. Signals are named by integer values, and each implementation defines a set of signals in header file **signal.h**, spelled beginning with the letters **SIG**. Signals may be triggered or *raised* by the computer's error-detection mechanisms, by the user program via **kill** or **raise**, or by actions external to the program. Software signals used by the functions **ssignal** and **psignal** are user-defined, with values generally in the range 1 through 15; otherwise they operate like regular signals.

A signal handler for signal **sig** is a user function invoked when signal **sig** is "raised." The handler function is expected to perform some useful action and then return, generally causing the program to resume at the point it was interrupted. Handlers may also call **exit** or (if permitted by the implementation) **longjmp**. Signal handlers are normal C functions taking one argument, the raised signal:

```
void my_handler(int the_signal) { ... }
```

Some non-Standard implementations may pass extra arguments to handlers for certain predefined signals.

The function **signal** is used to associate signal handlers with specific signals. In the normal case, **signal** is passed a signal value and a pointer to the signal handler for that signal. If the association is successful, then **signal** returns a pointer to the previous signal handler; otherwise it returns the value –1 (**SIG_ERR** in Standard C) and sets **errno**.

Example

```
void new_handler(int sig) { ... }
void (*old_handler)();
...
/* Set new handler, saving old handler */
old_handler = signal( sig, &new_handler );
if (old_handler==SIG_ERR)
    fprintf(stderr, "?Couldn't establish new handler.\n");
...
/* Restore old handler */
if (signal(sig,old_handler)==SIG_ERR)
    fprintf(stderr, "?Couldn't put back old handler.\n");
```

The function argument to **signal**—and the returned value—may also have two special values, **SIG_IGN** and **SIG_DFL**. A call to **signal** of the form **signal(sig, SIG_IGN)** means that signal **sig** is to be ignored. A call to **signal** of the form **signal(sig, SIG_DFL)** means that signal **sig** is to receive its "default" handling, which usually means ignoring some signals and terminating the program on other signals.

The **ssignal** function (found in UNIX System V) works exactly like **signal**, but is only used in conjunction with **gsignal** for user-defined software signals. Handlers supplied to **ssignal** return integer values that become the return value of **gsignal**.

The **raise** and **gsignal** functions cause the indicated signal (or software signal) to be raised in the current process. The **kill** function causes the indicated signal to be raised in the specified process; it is less portable.

When a signal is raised for which a handler has been established by **signal** or **gsignal**, the handler is given control. Standard C (and most other implementations) either reset the associated handler to **SIG_DFL** before the handler is given control or in some other way block the signal; this is to prevent unwanted recursion. (Whether this happens for the signal **SIGILL** is implementation-defined for historical and performance reasons.) The handler may return, in which case execution continues at the point of interruption with the following caveats:

1. If the signal were raised by **raise** or **gsignal**, then those functions return to their caller.

2. If the signal were raised by **abort**, then Standard C programs are terminated. Other implementations may return to the caller of **abort**.

3. If the handled signal were **SIGFPE** or another implementation-defined computational signal, then the behavior on return is undefined.

Signal handlers should refrain from calling library functions other than **signal**, since some signals could arise from library functions and library functions (other than **signal**) are not guaranteed to be reentrant.

Standard C defines the macros listed in Table 19–1 to stand for certain standard signals. These signals are common to many implementations of C.

Table 19–1   Standard signals

Macro name	Signal meaning
SIGABRT	abnormal termination, such as is caused by the **abort** facility
SIGFPE	an erroneous arithmetic operation, such as an attempt to divide by zero
SIGILL	an error caused by an invalid computer instruction
SIGINT	an attention signal, as from an interactive user striking a special keystroke
SIGSEGV	an invalid memory access
SIGTERM	a termination signal from a user or another program

The **psignal** function (not in Standard C) prints on the standard error output the string **prefix** (which is customarily the name of the program) and a brief description of signal **sig**. This function may be useful in handlers about to call **exit** or **abort**.

References   **exit** 19.3; **longjmp** 19.4

19.7 sleep, alarm

```
                       Non-Standard synopsis
void sleep( unsigned seconds );
unsigned alarm( unsigned seconds );
```

These functions are not part of Standard C. The **alarm** function sets an internal system timer to the indicated number of seconds and returns the number of seconds previously on the timer. When the timer expires, the signal **SIGALRM** is raised in the program. If the argument to **alarm** is 0, then the effect of the call is to cancel any previous **alarm** request. The **alarm** function is useful for escaping from various kinds of deadlock situations.

The **sleep** function suspends the program for the indicated number of seconds, at which time the sleep function returns and execution continues. Sleep is typically implemented using the same timer as **alarm**. If the sleep time exceeds the time already on the **alarm** timer, **sleep** will return immediately after the **SIGALRM** signal is handled. If the sleep time is shorter than the time already on the **alarm** timer, then **sleep** will reset the timer just before it returns so that **SIGALRM** will be received when expected.

Implementations will generally terminate **sleep** when any signal is handled; some supply the number of unslept seconds as the return value of **sleep** (of type **unsigned**).

Some implementations may define these functions as taking arguments of type **unsigned long**.

References   **signal** 19.6

20

Locale

Standard C was designed for an international community whose members have different alphabets and different conventions for formatting numbers, monetary quantities, dates, and time. The language standard allows implementations to adjust the behavior of the run-time library accordingly while still permitting reasonable portability across national boundaries.

The set of conventions for nationality, culture, and language is termed the *locale*, and facilities for it are defined in the header file `locale.h`. The locale affects such things as the format of decimal and monetary quantities, the alphabet and collation sequence (as for the character handling facilities in Chapter 12), and the format of date and time values. The "current locale" can be changed at run time by choosing from an implementation-defined set of locales. Standard C defines only the "C" locale, which specifies a minimal environment consistent with the original definition of C.

20.1 setlocale

Synopsis

```
#include <locale.h>
#define LC_ALL ...
#define LC_COLLATE ...
#define LC_CTYPE ...
#define LC_MONETARY ...
#define LC_NUMERIC ...
#define LC_TIME ...
char *setlocale( int category, const char *locale );
```

The `setlocale` function is used to change locale-specific features of the run-time library. The first argument, `category`, is a code that specifies the behavior to be changed. The permitted values for `category` include the values of the macros in Table 20–1, possibly augmented by additional implementation-defined categories spelled beginning with the letters **LC_**.

Table 20–1   Predefined **setlocale** categories

Name	Behavior affected
LC_ALL	all behavior
LC_COLLATE	behavior of **strcoll** and **strxfrm** facilities
LC_CTYPE	character handling functions (Chapter 12)
LC_MONETARY	monetary information returned by **localeconv**
LC_NUMERIC	decimal-point and nonmonetary information returned by **localeconv**
LC_TIME	behavior of **strftime** facility

The second argument, **locale**, is an implementation-defined string that names the locale whose conventions are to be used for the behavior designated by **category**. The only predefined values for **locale** are **"C"** for the Standard C locale, and the empty string, **""**, which by convention means an implementation-defined native locale. The run-time library always uses the C locale until it is explicitly changed with **setlocale**.

If the **locale** argument to **setlocale** is a null pointer, the function does not change the locale, but instead returns a pointer to a string that is the name of the current locale for the indicated category. This name is such that if **setlocale** were to be later called using the same value for **category** and the returned string as the value for **locale**, the effect would be to change the behavior to the one in effect when **setlocale** was called with the null **locale**. For example, a programmer who was about to change locale-specific behavior might first call **setlocale** with arguments **LC_ALL** and **NULL** to get a value for the current locale that could be used later to restore the previous locale-specific behavior. The string returned must not be altered, and may be overwritten by subsequent calls to **setlocale**.

If the **locale** argument to **setlocale** is not null, **setlocale** changes the current locale and returns a string that names the new locale. A null pointer is returned if **setlocale** cannot honor the request for any reason. The string returned must not be altered and may be overwritten by subsequent calls to **setlocale**.

Example

The function **original_locale** below returns a description of the current locale so that it can be later restored if necessary. There is no fixed maximum length for the string returned by **setlocale**, so space for it must be dynamically allocated.

```
#include <locale.h>
#include <string.h>
#include <stdlib.h>
```

```
char *original_locale(void)
{
    char *temp, *copy;
    temp = setlocale(LC_ALL, NULL);
    if (temp == NULL) return NULL;   /* setlocale() failed */
    copy = (char *)malloc(strlen(temp)+1);
    if (copy == NULL) return NULL;   /* malloc() failed */
    strcpy(copy,temp);
    return copy;
}
```

The following code uses **original_locale** to change and then restore the locale:

```
#include <locale.h>
extern char *original_locale(void);
char *saved_locale;
...
saved_locale = original_locale();
setlocale(LC_ALL,"");              /* Change to native locale */
setlocale(LC_ALL,saved_locale);/* Restore former locale    */
```

References malloc 16.1; localeconv 20.2; **strcoll** 13.10; **strcpy** 13.3;
strftime 18.6; **strlen** 13.4; **strxfrm** 13.10

20.2 localeconv

Synopsis

```
#include <locale.h>
struct lconv {...};
struct lconv *localeconv(void);
```

The **localeconv** function is used to obtain information about the conventions for formatting numeric and monetary quantities in the current locale. This allows a programmer to implement application-specific conversion and formatting routines with some portability across locales and avoids the necessity of adding locale-specific conversion facilities to Standard C. The **localeconv** function returns a pointer to an object of type **struct lconv**, whose components must include at least those in Table 20–2. The returned structure must not be altered by the programmer, and it may be overwritten by a subsequent call to **localeconv**. In **struct lconv**, string components whose value is the empty string and character components whose value is **CHAR_MAX** should be interpreted as "don't know."

Example

The following function uses **localeconv** to print a floating-point number with the correct decimal point character:

```
#include <locale.h>
#include <stdio.h>
...
void P(int int_part, int fract_part, int fract_digits)
{
    struct lconv *lconv = localeconv();
    char *pt = lconv->decimal_point;
    /* If *pt is the empty string, use "." */
    if (!*pt) pt = ".";
    printf("%d%s%0*d\n",
        int_part, pt, fract_digits, fract_part);
}
```

Other contents of **struct lconv** are listed in Table 20–2 and discussed herein.

Digit groupings   The **grouping** and **mon_grouping** components of **struct lconv** are sequences of integer values of type **char**. Although they are described as strings, the string is just a way to encode a sequence of small integers. Each integer in the sequence specifies the number of digits in a group. The first integer corresponds to the first group to the left of the decimal point, the second integer corresponds to the next group moving leftward, and so on. The integer 0 (the null character at the end of the string) means that the previous digit group is to be repeated; the integer **CHAR_MAX** means that no further grouping is to be performed. The conventional grouping by thousands would be specified by **"\3"**—three digits in the first group repeated for subsequent groups—and the string **"\1\2\3\127"** would group **1234567890** as **1234 567 89 0** (**CHAR_MAX** is assumed to be 127).

Sign positions   The **p_sign_posn** and **n_sign_posn** components of **struct lconv** determine where **positive_sign** and **negative_sign**, respectively, are placed. The possible values and their meaning are

0	Parentheses surround the number and **currency_symbol**.
1	The sign string precedes the number and **currency_symbol**.
2	The sign string follows the number and **currency_symbol**.
3	The sign string immediately precedes the **currency_symbol**.
4	The sign string immediately follows the **currency_symbol**.

Complete examples of monetary formatting are shown in Tables 20–3 and 20–4, which were taken from the Standard C standard. Table 20–3 shows typical monetary formatting in four countries. Table 20–4 shows the values of the components of **struct lconv** that would specify the formatting illustrated in Table 20–3.

Table 20–2   **lconv** structure components

Type	Name	Use	Value in C locale
char *	decimal_point	Decimal point character (nonmonetary)	"."
char *	thousands_sep	Nonmonetary digit group separator character(s)	""
char *	grouping	Nonmonetary digit groupings	""
char *	int_curr_symbol	The three-character international currency symbol, plus the character used to separate the international symbol from the monetary quantity	""
char *	currency_symbol	The local currency symbol for the current locale	""
char *	mon_decimal_point	Decimal point character (monetary)	""
char *	mon_thousands_sep	Monetary digit group separator character(s)	""
char *	mon_grouping	Monetary digit groupings	""
char *	positive_sign	Sign character(s) for non-negative monetary quantities	""
char *	negative_sign	Sign character(s) for negative monetary quantities	""
char	int_frac_digits	Digits shown to the right of the decimal point for international monetary formats	CHAR_MAX
char	frac_digits	Digits shown to the right of the decimal point for other than international monetary formats	CHAR_MAX
char	p_cs_precedes	1 if **currency_symbol** precedes non-negative monetary values; 0 if it follows	CHAR_MAX
char	p_sep_by_space	1 if **currency_symbol** is separated from non-negative monetary values by a space or else 0	CHAR_MAX
char	n_cs_precedes	Like **p_cs_precedes** for negative values	CHAR_MAX
char	n_sep_by_space	Like **p_sep_by_space** for negative values	CHAR_MAX
char	p_sign_posn	The positioning of **positive_sign** for a non-negative monetary quantity (plus its **currency_symbol**)	CHAR_MAX
char	n_sign_posn	The positioning of **negative_sign** for a negative monetary quantity (plus its **currency_symbol**)	CHAR_MAX

Table 20–3   Examples of formatted monetary quantities

Country	Format		
	Positive	Negative	International
Italy	L.1.234	-L.1.234	ITL.1.234
The Netherlands	F 1.234,56	F -1.234,56	NLG 1.234,56
Norway	kr1.234,56	kr1.234,56-	NOK 1.234,56
Switzerland	SFrs.1,234.56	SFrs.1,234.56C	CHF 1,234.56

Table 20–4   Examples of `lconv` structure contents

Component	Italy	The Netherlands	Norway	Switzerland
`int_curr_symbol`	`"ITL."`	`"NLG "`	`"NOK "`	`"CHF "`
`currency_symbol`	`"L."`	`"F"`	`"kr"`	`"SFrs."`
`mon_decimal_point`	`""`	`","`	`","`	`"."`
`mon_thousands_sep`	`"."`	`"."`	`"."`	`","`
`mon_grouping`	`"\3"`	`"\3"`	`"\3"`	`"\3"`
`positive_sign`	`""`	`""`	`""`	`""`
`negative_sign`	`"-"`	`"-"`	`"-"`	`"C"`
`int_frac_digits`	0	2	2	2
`frac_digits`	0	2	2	2
`p_cs_precedes`	1	1	1	1
`p_sep_by_space`	0	1	0	0
`n_cs_precedes`	1	1	1	1
`n_sep_by_space`	0	1	0	0
`p_sign_posn`	1	1	1	1
`n_sign_posn`	1	4	2	2

21

Extended Integer Types

The C99 facilities of this section provide additional declarations for integer types having various characteristics. The facilities are provided by the headers **stdint.h** and **inttypes.h**. The **stdint.h** header contains basic definitions of integer types of certain sizes and is required in both hosted and freestanding implementations. The **inttypes.h** header file includes **stdint.h** and adds portable formatting and conversion functions; it is only required in hosted implementations.

The "spirit of C" is to leave the choice of the sizes for the standard types up to the implementor. Unfortunately, this makes it hard to write portable code. The facilities in this chapter address portability, but the number of definitions in these headers is somewhat daunting.

References hosted and freestanding implementations 1.4

21.1 GENERAL RULES

These libraries contain a large number of types, macros, and functions all constructed in a regular fashion. This section discusses the general rules that apply to the libraries.

21.1.1 Type Kinds

The libraries contain a number of different "kinds" of integer types and macros, some parameterized by the width N of the types. N must be an unsigned decimal integer with no leading zeros and represents a type's width in bits.

Example

> The exact-size 8-bit integer types are named **int8_t** and **uint8_t** (not **int08_t** and **uint08_t**). The fastest integer types that are at least 8 bits wide are named **int_fast8_t** and **uint_fast8_t**. "Exact-sized" and "fastest" are two different "kinds" of types.

21.1.2 Define All or None

Which types are defined (i.e., for which values of N) is implementation-defined in some cases. However, if a particular kind of type for some value of N is defined, then both signed and unsigned types and all the macros for that kind and size of type must be defined. If a particular kind and size of type is optional and the implementation chooses not to define it, then none of the associated types or macros is defined.

Example

> If the implementation has an exact-size 16-bit integer type, then the types **int16_t** and **uint16_t** and the macros **INT16_MIN**, **INT16_MAX**, **UINT16_MAX**, **PRId16**, **PRIi16**, **PRIo16**, **PRIu16**, **PRIx16**, **PRIX16**, **SCNd16**, **SCNi16**, **SCNo16**, **SCNu16**, and **SCNx16** must all be defined. If the implementation does not have an exact-size 16-bit integer type, then none of these macros or types is defined.

21.1.3 MIN and MAX Limits

The ...**MIN** and ...**MAX** macros define the ranges of the defined types by specifying maximum and minimum values representable in those types, just as do the ...**MIN** and ...**MAX** macros in **limits.h** for the standard types. In most cases, the minimum magnitudes of the ranges are specified by C99.

Example

> Types **int16_t** and **uint16_t** are exact-size 16-bit integer types. Their ranges are:
>
> ```
> #define INT16_MIN -32768
> #define INT16_MAX 32767
> #define UINT16_MAX 65535
> ```
>
> **References**   **limits.h** Table 5–2

21.1.4 PRI... and SCN... Format String Macros

The macros **PRI**c*KN* and **SCN**c*KN* are format control strings for the **printf** and **scanf** families of functions, respectively. The c stands for a particular conversion operator letter: **d**, **i**, **o**, **u**, **x**, or **X**. The K represents the kind of type: empty or **LEAST**, **FAST**, **PTR**, or **MAX**. The N is the width in bits. The full set of macros is listed in Table 21–1.

The **PRI**... macros expand to string literals containing the **printf** conversion operation character c (**d**, **i**, **o**, **u**, **x**, or **X**) preceded by an optional size specification suitable for outputting values of the particular kind and size of type. The **SCN**... macros similarly expand to string literals containing the **scanf** conversion operation character c (**d**, **i**, **o**, **u**, or **x**) preceded by an optional size specification suitable for converting numeric input and storing it in objects designated by pointers to types of the particular kind and size.

Example

The smallest integer types at least 64-bits wide are named **int_least64_t** and **uint_least64_t** (the kind, K, is **LEAST**). If these types are defined to be **long** and **unsigned long**, respectively, then you would expect to find in **inttypes.h** the definitions

```
#define PRIdLEAST64 "ld"
#define PRIiLEAST64 "li"
#define PRIoLEAST64 "lo"
#define PRIuLEAST64 "lu"
#define PRIxLEAST64 "lx"
#define PRIXLEAST64 "lX"
#define SCNdLEAST64 "ld"
#define SCNiLEAST64 "li"
#define SCNoLEAST64 "lo"
#define SCNuLEAST64 "lu"
#define SCNxLEAST64 "lx"
```

Now suppose that variable **a** has type **long** and **b** has type **int_least64_t**. The following two statements show two ways of printing these values. The second way is more portable in that it works regardless of which integer type is assigned to **int_least64_t**.

```
printf("a=%25ld\n", a); /* usual */
printf("b=%25" PRIdLEAST64 "\n", b); /* portable */
```

References   **limits.h** Table 5–2; **printf** conversions 15.11.7; **scanf** conversions 15.8.2

Table 21–1   Format control string macros for integer types (N = width of type in bits)

	Exact-size kind	Least-size kind	Fast-size kind	Pointer kind	Maximum kind
Signed **printf** formats	PRIdN PRIiN	PRIdLEASTN PRIiLEASTN	PRIdFASTN PRIiFASTN	PRIdPTR PRIiPTR	PRIdMAX PRIiMAX
Unsigned **printf** formats	PRIoN PRIuN PRIxN PRIXN	PRIoLEASTN PRIuLEASTN PRIxLEASTN PRIXLEASTN	PRIoFASTN PRIuFASTN PRIxFASTN PRIXFASTN	PRIoPTR PRIuPTR PRIxPTR PRIXPTR	PRIoMAX PRIuMAX PRIxMAX PRIXMAX
Signed **scanf** formats	SCNdN SCNiN	SCNdLEASTN SCNiLEASTN	SCNdFASTN SCNiFASTN	SCNdPTR SCNiPTR	SCNdMAX SCNiMAX
Unsigned **scanf** formats	SCNoN SCNuN SCNxN	SCNoLEASTN SCNuLEASTN SCNxLEASTN	SCNoFASTN SCNuFASTN SCNxFASTN	SCNoPTR SCNuPTR SCNxPTR	SCNoMAX SCNuMAX SCNxMAX

21.2 EXACT-SIZE INTEGER TYPES

Synopsis

```
#include <stdint.h>                // All C99
typedef ... intN_t
typedef ... uintN_t
#define   INTN_MIN    -2^{N-1}
#define   INTN_MAX    2^{N-1}-1
#define  UINTN_MAX    2^{N}-1

#include <inttypes.h>
#define PRIcN "..."
#define SCNcN "..."
```

These types and macros define integer types having certain exact sizes with no padding bits. The ...**MIN** and ...**MAX** macros must have the exact values shown.

These types are optional in **stdint.h**, except that if the implementation has integer types of exact widths 8, 16, 32, or 64 bits, then the corresponding types and macros must be defined. An implementation is free to define additional exact-width integer types.

Example

The following definitions would be expected in many C implementations for byte-addressed computers:

```
#include <limits.h> /* SCHAR_MIN, SCHAR_MAX, UCHAR_MAX */
typedef signed char              int8_t;
typedef unsigned char uint8_t;
typedef short int16_t;
typedef unsigned short           uint16_t;
typedef int int32_t;
typedef unsigned int             uint32_t;
typedef long long int int64_t;
typedef unsigned long long int uint64_t;
#define INT8_MIN SCHAR_MIN
#define INT8_MAX SCHAR_MAX
#define UINT8_MAX UCHAR_MAX
#define PRId8 "hhd"
#define SCNo64 "llo"
// etc.
```

As computer word sizes increase in the future, we might expect **long** to be named **int64_t** and **long long int** to be named **int128_t**.

21.3 LEAST-SIZE TYPES OF A MINIMUM WIDTH

Synopsis

```
#include <stdint.h>                // All C99
typedef ...  int_leastN_t
typedef ... uint_leastN_t
#define   INT_LEASTN_MIN
#define   INT_LEASTN_MAX
#define  UINT_LEASTN_MAX
#define   INTN_C(constant)   ...
#define  UINTN_C(constant)   ...

#include <inttypes.h>
#define PRICLEASTN "..."
#define SCNcLEASTN "..."
```

$-(2^{N-1}-1)$

$2^{N-1}-1$

$2^{N}-1$

These types and macros define integer types that are the smallest having certain minimum sizes. The ...**MIN** and ...**MAX** macros must have the same sign and at least the magnitude of the values shown. Since these types must be the smallest having the designated width, it follows that if an exact-width type (Section 21.2) exists for a certain N, then that exact-width type must also be the least-sized type for the same value of N.

All C99 implementations must define these types and macros for N=8, 16, 32, and 64. Definitions for other values of N are optional, but if any other N is provided, then all the types and macros for that value of N must be defined.

Example

> A C implementation for a 32-bit word-addressed computer might define **char**, **short** and **int** to be all 32-bit types. In that case, the exact-width types **int8_t** and **int16_t** (and their unsigned counterparts) would not be defined, and the least-width types **int8_t** and **int16_t** would have to be defined as one of the 32-bit type, such as **int**.

Macro **INTN_C** takes as an argument a decimal, hexadecimal, or octal constant and expands to a signed integer constant of type **int_least$N$_t** with the same value. Macro **UINTN_C** expands to an unsigned integer constant of type **uint_least$N$_t**. The macros add the appropriate suffix letter to the constant.

Example

> If **int_least64_t** is defined to be **long long int**, then **INT64_C(1)** would be **1LL** and **UINT64_C(1)** would be **1ULL**.

21.4 FAST TYPES OF A MINIMUM WIDTH

Synopsis

```
#include <stdint.h>                     // All C99
typedef ...  int_fastN_t
typedef ... uint_fastN_t
#define   INT_FASTN_MIN   -(2^(N-1)-1)
#define   INT_FASTN_MAX   2^(N-1)-1
#define  UINT_FASTN_MAX   2^N-1

#include <inttypes.h>
#define PRIcFASTN "..."
#define SCNcFASTN "..."
```

These types and macros define integer types that are the fastest having certain minimum sizes. The ...**MIN** and ...**MAX** macros must have the same sign and at least the magnitude of the values shown. All C99 implementations must define these types and macros for $N=8$, 16, 32, and 64. Definitions for other values of N are optional, but if any other N is provided, then all the types and macros for that value of N must be defined.

Determining which type is "fastest" might be a judgment call on the part of the implementor, and it might not be correct for all possible uses of a type. For example, the fastest type for scalar arithmetic might not be the fastest type for accessing array elements.

Example

On a byte-addressed computer optimized for 32-bit arithmetic, a C implementation might choose to recommend 32-bit types even if fewer bits were needed. Here is a possible set of definitions from **stdint.h**. Only the signed types are shown in this example.

```
typedef char    int8_t;
typedef char    int_least8_t;
typedef int     int_fast8_t;

typedef short   int16_t;
typedef short   int_least16_t;
typedef int     int_fast16_t;

typedef int     int32_t;
typedef int     int_least32_t;
typedef int     int_fast32_t;
```

21.5 POINTER-SIZE AND MAXIMUM-SIZE INTEGER TYPES

	Synopsis

```
#include <stdint.h>              // All C99
typedef ... intptr_t;
typedef ... uintptr_t;
#define  INTPTR_MIN   -(2^15-1)
#define  INTPTR_MAX    2^15-1
#define UINTPTR_MA X    2^16-1


typedef ...  intmax_t;
typedef ... uintmax_t;
#define  INTMAX_MIN    -(2^63-1)
#define  INTMAX_MAX     2^63-1
#define UINTMAX_MA X    2^64-1
#define  INTMAX_C (constant) ...
#define UINTMAX_C (constant) ...


#include <inttypes.h>
#define PRIcPTR "..."
#define SCNcPTR "..."
#define PRIcMAX "..."
#define SCNcMAX "..."
```

The types `intptr_t` and `uintptr_t` are signed and unsigned integer types, respectively, that can hold any object pointer. That is, if P is a value of type **void ***, P can be converted to `intptr_t` or `uintptr_t` and then converted back to **void ***, and the result is the original pointer P. The ...**MIN** and ...**MAX** macros must have the same sign and at least the magnitude of the values shown. These types are optional because it is possible (but unusual) for there to be no such integer type.

Types `intmax_t` and `uintmax_t` are the largest signed and unsigned integer types defined in the implementation, respectively. These types must be defined by all C implementations. Since C99 implementations are permitted to provide extended integer types, the `intmax_t` type might not be one of the standard C types, such as **long long int**. The ...**MIN** and ...**MAX** macros must have the same sign and at least the magnitude of the values shown.

The **INTMAX_C** macro takes a decimal, hexadecimal, or octal constant and expands it to an integer constant of type `intmax_t` with the same value. The **UINTMAX_C** macro expands to an integer constant of type `uintmax_t`.

References   `limits.h` Table 5–2

21.6 Ranges of ptrdiff_t, size_t, wchar_t, wint_t, and sig_atomic_t

Synopsis

```
#include <stdint.h>
#define PTRDIFF_MIN    ...                      // All C99
#define PTRDIFF_MAX    ...
#define SIZE_MAX       ...
#define WCHAR_MIN      ...
#define WCHAR_MAX      ...
#define WINT_MIN       ...
#define WINT_MAX       ...
#define SIG_ATOMIC_MIN ...
#define SIG_ATOMIC_MAX ...
```

The macros in this section expand to preprocessor constant expressions that are the numeric ranges of various types defined in **stddef.h** and **wchar.h**. They must all be defined by all implementations.

PTRDIFF_MIN and **PTRDIFF_MAX** specify the range of type **ptrdiff_t**, which must be a signed type of at least 16 bits.

SIZE_MAX is the largest value that can be represented in type **size_t**.

WCHAR_MIN and **WCHAR_MAX** specify the range of **wchar_t**, which can be a signed or unsigned type of at least 8 bits.

WINT_MIN and **WINT_MAX** specify the range of **wint_t**, which can be a signed or unsigned type of at least 16 bits.

SIG_ATOMIC_MIN and **SIG_ATOMIC_MAX** specify the range of **sig_atomic_t**, which can be a signed or unsigned type of at least 8 bits.

References ptrdiff_t 11.1; **sig_atomic_t** 19.6; **size_t** 11.1; **wchar_t** 24.1; **wint_t** 24.1

21.7 imaxabs, imaxdiv, imaxdiv_t

Synopsis

```
#include <inttypes.h>
typedef ... imaxdiv_t;                          // All C99
intmax_t imaxabs( intmax_t x );
imaxdiv_t imaxdiv( intmax_t n, intmax_t d );
```

The facilities in this section support basic arithmetic on maximum-size integer types, similar to the **abs** and **div** functions defined in **stdlib.h**. The **imaxabs** function computes the absolute value of its argument. If the absolute value is not representable, then the result is undefined.

The `imaxdiv` function computes both `n / d` and `n % d` in a single operation. The results are stored in the `quot` and `rem` components, respectively, of the structure type `imaxdiv_t`. The order of the components in `imaxdiv_t` is not specified.

References   `abs` 16.9; `div` 16.9

21.8 strtoimax, strtouimax

Synopsis

```
#include <inttypes.h>
intmax_t strtoimax(
   const char * restrict str,
   char ** restrict ptr,
   int base);
uintmax_t strtoumax(
   const char * restrict str,
   char ** restrict ptr,
   int base);
```

These functions convert strings to maximum-size integers in the same way as the `strtol` and `strtoul` functions in `stdlib.h`. If the result would cause overflow, then one of `INTMAX_MAX`, `INTMAX_MIN`, or `UINTMAX_MAX`, as appropriate, is returned and `errno` is set to `ERANGE`.

References   `errno` and `ERANGE` 11.2; `strtol` and `strtoul` 16.4

21.9 wcstoimax, wcstoumax

Synopsis

```
#include <stddef.h>       // wchar_t
#include <inttypes.h>
intmax_t wcstoimax(
   const wchar_t * restrict str,
   wchar_t ** restrict ptr,
   int base);
uintmax_t wcstoumax(
   const wchar_t * restrict str,
   wchar_t ** restrict ptr,
   int base);
```

These functions convert wide strings to maximum-size integers in the same way as the `wcstol` and `wcstoul` functions in `wchar.h`. If the result would cause overflow, then one of **INTMAX_MAX**, **INTMAX_MIN**, or **UINTMAX_MAX**, as appropriate, is returned and **errno** is set to **ERANGE**.

References   **errno** and **ERANGE** 11.2; **wcstol** and **wcstoul** Ch. 24

22

Floating-Point Environment

The facilities of this section are new in C99 and supplement the information in `float.h`. They provide access to the floating-point environment for those applications that require a high degree of control over the precision or performance of floating-point operations. The facilities are provided in the header file `fenv.h`.

References `float.h` Table 5–3

22.1 Overview

Programmers who code high-precision floating-point algorithms need control over various aspects of the floating-point environment: how rounding of results occurs; how floating-point expressions can be simplified or transformed; and whether certain floating-point events like underflow are ignored or cause a program error. Control is exerted by setting floating-point *control modes*, which affect how floating-point operations are carried out. The operations communicate back to the programmer by causing *floating-point exceptions*, which can interrupt the flow of control in the C program and which are also recorded in *status flags* that the programmer can read. The C99 programmer can also control floating-point behavior by using the specialized floating-point math functions listed in Chapter 17.

Floating-point operations can be performed at two times. When the C program is translated, constant (compile-time) floating-point operations are performed, whereas when the C program runs dynamic (execution-time) floating-point operations may be performed. The C99 standard provides explicit control over run-time operations only. Implementations may provide their own facilities to control translation-time arithmetic.

The international floating-point standard referenced by C99 is IEC 60559:989, *Binary floating-point arithmetic for microprocessor systems, second edition.* Previous designations of this standard were IEC 559:1989 and ANSI/IEEE 754-1985, *IEEE Standard for Binary Floating-point Arithmetic.* (The IEEE 754 was later generalized to remove dependencies on radix and word length in ANSI/IEEE 854-1987, *IEEE Standard for Radix-Independent Floating-point Arithmetic*.) Appendix F of the C99 standard details the mapping of the C language to IEC 60559, which is optional unless the C implementation defines the macro `__STDC_IEC_559__`.

22.1.1 Programming Conventions

The facilities to control floating-point behavior are dynamic. That is, once changed during program execution by the functions in this chapter, the changes persist until another explicit change is made. How a particular function performs floating-point operations will depend on what functions from `fenv.h` were most recently called and so cannot be determined when the C program is compiled. This is all right when the underlying hardware uses global control registers to control floating-point arithmetic; it is more difficult to implement if the actual opcodes emitted by the compiler control the behavior.

The C99 standard recommends that programmers always assume that any called function will expect the default floating-point behavior unless it is documented otherwise. Likewise, called functions should not alter the environment unless they are documented to do so. That is, a function should not depend on any status flags nor alter the flags in effect when called. It can (if needed) expect the default control mode to be in effect, and it should not change the caller's mode. Any function may raise a floating-point exception.

22.2 Floating-Point Environment

Synopsis

```
#include <fenv.h>
#pragma STDC FENV_ACCESS     on-off-switch
typedef ... fenv_t;
#define FE_DEFL_ENV ...
int fegetenv(fenv_t *envp);
int fesetenv(fenv_t *envp);
int feholdexcept(fenv_t *envp);
int feupdateenv(const fenv_t *envp);
```

The standard pragma **FENV_ACCESS** is used to indicate whether the C program will set floating-point control modes, test status flags, or even run under nondefault control modes. The behavior of those actions when **FENV_ACCESS** is "off" is undefined. The pragma is provided in case such knowledge makes a significant difference in how the C program is translated or optimized. The default setting is implementation-defined, so the programmer concerned with portability should always assume it is "off." The **FENV_ACCESS** pragma follows the normal placement rules for standard pragmas.

The **fenv_t** type is implementation-defined to hold the entire floating-point state, including control modes and exception status bits.

The **FE_DEFL_ENV** macro expands to specify the default floating-point environment as a value of type **fenv_t***. C implementations may define additional environment macros spelled beginning with **FE_** and an uppercase letter. Programmers should treat these macros as designating read-only objects.

The **fegetenv** function retrieves the current floating-point environment and stores it in the object pointed to by **envp**. It returns zero if successful and otherwise returns a nonzero value.

The **fesetenv** function replaces the current floating-point environment with the environment pointed to by **envp**. That environment must have previously been set by **fegetenv** or **feholdexcept**, or it must be a predefined environment such as **FE_DEFL_ENV**. It returns zero if successful and otherwise returns a nonzero value.

The **feholdexcept** function is typically used to turn off floating-point exceptions for a period of time. The function saves the current floating-point environment in the object pointed to by **envp** and then installs an environment that ignores all floating-point exceptions. The function returns zero if such a "nonstop" environment was successfully installed; otherwise it returns a nonzero value. Some implementations may not be able to ignore all exceptions.

The **feupdateenv** function saves the currently raised floating-point exceptions in some local storage, stores the environment pointed to by **envp** as the new environment, and finally raises the saved exceptions. It returns zero if successful and otherwise returns a nonzero value.

References   pragmas and placement rules 3.7; raising floating-point exceptions 22.3

22.3 *Floating-Point Exceptions*

Synopsis

```
#include <fenv.h>

macro FE_DIVBYZERO ...
macro FE_INEXACT ...
macro FE_INVALID ...
macro FE_OVERFLOW ...
macro FE_UNDERFLOW ...
...
macro FE_ALL_EXCEPT ...

typedef ... fexcept_t;
int fegetexceptflag(fexcept_t *flagp, int excepts);
int fesetexceptflag(const fexcept_t *flagp, int excepts);
int fetestexcept(int excepts);
int feraiseexcept(int excepts);
int feclearexcept(int excepts);
```

A floating-point exception is a side effect of certain floating-point operations. All exceptions set a status flag indicating that the exception has occurred. Whether the exception also interrupts the program's flow of control depends on the floating-point control mode settings.

The **fexcept_t** type is implementation-defined to hold all the floating-point status flags supported by the implementation. This is often an integer type whose bits represent the different exceptions, but it could be more elaborate. For example, **fexcept_t** could hold information about where the status flags were raised.

C implementations may support different floating-point exceptions. For each supported exception, the implementation must define a macro such as **FE_DIVBYZERO**, **FE_INEXACT**, **FE_INVALID**, **FE_OVERFLOW**, and **FE_UNDERFLOW**. Unsupported exceptions must be left undefined (e.g., not just defined as zero). Each defined macro expands to an integer constant expression, and it must be possible to bitwise-or these values together to represent any subset of the exceptions. Typically the macros each expand to a different power of two. The macro **FE_ALL_EXCEPT** is the bitwise-or of all the supported exceptions. It follows from the signatures of the functions in this section that there cannot be more exceptions than there are bits in type **int**, which contains at least 16 bits.

The **fegetexceptflag** function stores the current setting of the floating-point status flags into the object pointed to by **flagp**. Not all the status flags are stored into **flagp***; rather, only those exceptions listed in **excepts** argument are set; the others remain unchanged in **flagp***. The **excepts** argument acts as a mask of "interesting" exceptions. The function returns zero if successful and otherwise returns a nonzero value.

The **fesetexceptflag** function sets the current floating-point status flags to the values held in the object pointed to by **flagp**. Not all the status flags are set; rather only those exceptions listed in **excepts** argument are set; the others remain unchanged. The **excepts** argument acts as a mask of "interesting" exceptions. The function returns zero if all specified flags were set to the appropriate state and otherwise returns a nonzero value.

The **fetestexcept** returns the bitwise-or of the exception macros corresponding to the exception flags, which are currently set in the environment *and* which are present in the **excepts** argument. Thus, **fetestexcept** returns the subset of the exceptions in **excepts** that are currently set.

The **feraiseexcept** function raises the exceptions represented in the **excepts** argument. The order in which the exceptions are raised is not specified, and it is possible that some exceptions will, as a side effect, raise other exceptions. **FE_INEXACT**, for example, is often combined with other exceptions.

The **feclearexcept** function clears the current exception status flags corresponding to the exceptions represented in **excepts**. It returns zero if all of the exceptions in **excepts** were cleared and otherwise returns a nonzero value.

22.4 Floating-Point Rounding Modes

Synopsis

```
#include <fenv.h>

macro FE_DOWNWARD ...
macro FE_UPWARD ...
macro FE_TONEAREST ...
macro FE_TOWARDZERO ...
```

```
int fegetround(void);
int fetestround(int rounds);
```

C99 implementations must define macros such as **FE_DOWNWARD**, **FE_UPWARD**, **FE_TONEAREST**, or **FE_TOWARDZERO** for each rounding direction that can be set and gotten by the functions in this section. The macros expand to distinct non-negative integer constant expressions representable in type **int**. Unsupported rounding directions will not have their corresponding macros defined.

The **fegetround** function returns the current rounding direction, represented as one of the values of the rounding direction macros. Similarly, the **fesetround** function sets the current rounding direction and returns zero if successful. The functions return a negative value if they cannot get or set, respectively, the rounding direction.

22.5 Floating-Point Expression Contraction

Synopsis

```
#pragma STDC FP_CONTRACT on-off-switch              // C99
```

C99 allows floating-point expressions to be optimized (or *contracted*) to take advantage of fast computer instructions that combine multiple operators. Some of these instructions, such as the multiply-add instruction often found in digital signal processors, might differ in their rounding or other behavior compared to the requirements of the C abstract machine. Contraction is controlled with the standard pragma **FP_CONTRACT**: If *on-off-switch* has the value **ON**, then contraction is permitted; if it has the value **OFF**, then contraction is forbidden. The default setting of this pragma is implementation-defined. The pragma follows the normal placement rules for standard pragmas (Section 3.7.2).

References   *on-off-switch* 3.7.2; standard pragma 3.7.2

23

Complex Arithmetic

The facilities of this section support complex arithmetic. They are defined in the C99 header file `complex.h`.

23.1 COMPLEX LIBRARY CONVENTIONS

All angular measurements are in radians. The complex number z is also written as $x+yi$, where x and y are real numbers. Similarly, $w = u+vi$ and $c = a+bi$.

For complex functions having branch cuts across which the functions are discontinuous, one of the following implementation-defined conventions should be adopted. If the implementation has a signed zero, the sign of zero distinguishes the two sides of the branch cut. Otherwise the library implementation should treat the cut so that the functions are continuous when approaching the cut counter-clockwise around the finite end of the branch cut.

References complex types 5.2.1

23.2 complex, _Complex_I, imaginary, _Imaginary_I, I

Synopsis

```
#include <complex.h>                    // All C99
#define complex _Complex
#define imaginary _Imaginary
#define _Complex_I    ...
#define _Imaginary_I ...
#define I ...
```

If complex types are supported, then the macro **complex** is defined as a synonym for the keyword **_Complex**. If the imaginary types are supported, then the macro **imaginary** is defined as a synonym for the keyword **_Imaginary**. If their respective types are supported, then the macros **_Complex_I** and **_Imaginary_I** are defined as constant expressions of type **const float _Complex** and **const float _Imaginary**, respectively, whose values are the imaginary unit, $\sqrt{(-1)}$ or i.

If complex types are supported, then the macro **I** expands to **_Complex_I**. If the imaginary type is defined, **I** may alternatively expand to **_Imaginary_I**.

Because the identifiers **complex**, **imaginary**, and **I** may be used in programs written before C99, it is permitted to **#undefine** and possibly redefine these macros.

References   complex types 5.2.1

23.3 CX_LIMITED_RANGE

Synopsis

```
#include <complex.h>                    // All C99
#pragma STDC CX_LIMITED_RANGE on-or-off-switch
```

The standard pragma **CX_LIMITED_RANGE**, if "on," informs the implementation that using the "obvious" implementations of complex multiply, divide, and absolute value is acceptable. The default state of the pragma is "off." The **CX_LIMITED_RANGE** pragma follows the placement rules for standard pragmas. The "obvious" implementations are:

multiplication: $z * w = (x+iy)\,(u+iv) = (x\,u-y\,v) + i(y\,u+x\,v)$

division: $z/w = (x+iy)\,/\,(u+iv) = ((x\,u+y\,v) + i\,(y\,u-x\,v))\,/\,(u^2+v^2)$

absolute value: $|z| = |\,x+iy\,| = \sqrt{(x^2+y^2)}$

These implementations are "numerically challenged" because of their potential for unnecessary underflow and overflow and because they do not handle infinities well. However, they may be faster, if the programmer knows that they are safe in the current program.

References   standard pragmas, *on-off-switch*, and placement rules 3.7

23.4 *cacos, casin, catan, ccos, csin, ctan*

Synopsis

```
#include <complex.h>                          // All C99

double complex cacos (double complex z);
float complex cacosf(float complex z);
long double complex cacosl(long double complex z);

double complex casin (double complex z);
float complex casinf(float complex z);
long double complex casinl(long double complex z);

double complex catan (double complex z);
float complex catanf(float complex z);
long double complex catanl(long double complex z);

double complex ccos (double       complex z);
float complex ccosf(float complex z);
long double complex caosl(long double complex z);

double complex csin (double       complex z);
float complex csinf(float complex z);
long double complex csinl(long double complex z);

double complex ctan (double       complex z);
float complex ctanf(float complex z);
long double complex ctanl(long double complex z);
```

The domain and range of the functions are listed in Table 23–1 assuming the notation $(a + bi) = f(x + yi)$.

Table 23–1   Domain and range of complex trigonometric functions

C name	Function	Branch cuts	Range
cacos	complex arc cosine	$y = 0, x > +1$ and $y = 0, x < -1$	$0 \le a \le \pi$
casin	complex arc sine	$y = 0, x > +1$ and $y = 0, x < -1$	$-\pi/2 \le a \le +\pi/2$
catan	complex arc tangent	$x = 0, y > +1$ and $x = 0, y < -1$	$-\pi/2 \le a \le +\pi/2$
ccos	complex cosine		
csin	complex sine		
ctan	complex tangent		

23.5 *cacosh, casinh, catanh, ccosh, csinh, ctanh*

Synopsis

```
#include <complex.h>                          // All C99

double complex cacosh (double complex z);
float complex cacoshf(float complex z);
long double complex cacoshl(long double complex z);

double complex casinh (double complex z);
float complex casinhf(float complex z);
long double complex casinhl(long double complex z);

double complex catanh (double complex z);
float complex catanhf(float complex z);
long double complex catanhl(long double complex z);

double complex ccosh (double complex z);
float complex ccoshf(float complex z);
long double complex ccoshl(long double complex z);

double complex csinh (double complex z);
float complex csinhf(float complex z);
long double complex csinhl(long double complex z);

double complex ctanh (double complex z);
float complex ctanhf(float complex z);
long double complex ctanhl(long double complex z);
```

The domain and range of the functions are listed in Table 23–2 assuming the notation $(a + bi) = f(x + yi)$.

Table 23–2   Domain and range of complex hyperbolic functions

C name	Function	Branch cuts	Range
cacosh	complex arc hyperbolic cosine	$y = 0, x < +1$	$0 \le a, -\pi \le b \le +\pi$
casinh	complex arc hyperbolic sine	$x = 0, y > +1$ and $x = 0, y < -1$	$-\pi / 2 \le b \le +\pi / 2$
catanh	complex arc hyperbolic tangent	$y = 0, x > +1$ and $y = 0, x < -1$	$-\pi / 2 \le b \le +\pi / 2$
ccosh	complex hyperbolic cosine		
csinh	complex hyperbolic sine		
ctanh	complex hyperbolic tangent		

23.6 cexp, clog, cabs, cpow, csqrt

	Synopsis

```
#include <complex.h>                            // All C99

double     complex cexp (double complex z);
float      complex cexpf(float      complex z);
long double complex cexpl(long double complex z);

double     complex clog (double complex z);
float      complex clogf(float      complex z);
long double complex clogl(long double complex z);

double           cabs (double complex z);
float            cabsf(float      complex z);
long double cabsl(long double complex z);

double     complex cpow (
    double complex z,
    double complex u);
float      complex cpowf(
    float complex z,
    float complex u);
long double complex cpowl(
    long double complex z,
    long double complex u);

double     complex csqrt (double complex z);
float      complex csqrtf(float complex z);
long double complex csqrtl(long double complex z);
```

The domain and range of the functions are listed in Table 23–3 assuming the notation

$(a + bi) = f(z) = f(x + yi)$ or

$(a + bi) = f(z, w) = f(x + yi, u + vi)$.

Table 23–3 Domain and range of complex exponential and power

C name	Function	Branch cuts	Range
cexp	e^z		
clog	$\ln z$	$y = 0, x < 0$	$-\pi \le b \le +\pi$
cabs	absolute value $a = \mathbf{sqrt}(x^2 + y^2)$		
cpow	z^w	$y = 0, x < 0$	
csqrt	square root	$y = 0, x < 0$	

23.7 carg, cimag, creal, conj, cproj

Synopsis

```
#include <complex.h>                      // All C99
double       carg (double complex z);
float        cargf(float        complex z);
long double  cargl(long double complex z);

double       cimag (double complex z);
float        cimagf(float        complex z);
long double  cimagl(long double complex z);

double       creal (double complex z);
float        crealf(float        complex z);
long double  creall(long double complex z);

double complex conj (double       complex z);
float complex conjf(float complex z);
long double complex conjl(long double complex z);

double complex cproj (double complex z);
float complex cprojf(float complex z);
long double complex cprojl(long double complex z);
```

The domain and range of the functions are listed in Table 23–4 assuming the notation

$(a + bi) = f(x + yi)$ or

$(a + bi) = f(x + yi, u + vi)$.

Table 23–4 Domain and range of miscellaneous complex functions

C name	Function	Branch cuts	Range
carg	argument (also called phase angle)	$y = 0, x < 0$	$[-\pi, +\pi]$
cimag	imaginary part of z: y		
creal	real part of z: x		
conj	$a = x, b = -y$		
cproj	projection onto Riemann sphere		

The value of **carg(z)** is the angle on the complex plane from the positive real axis to the line from the origin to **z**.

The value of **cproj(z)** is **z** if **z** is not infinite. If **z** is infinite, then **cproj(z)** is positive real infinity expressed as a complex number. If the implementation supports signed zeroes and **z** is infinite, then the (zero) imaginary part of **cproj(z)** will have the same sign as the imaginary part of **z**. For **z** to be infinite, it is sufficient that either component of **z** be infinite even if the other component is NaN.

24

Wide and Multibyte Facilities

The facilities of this section support wide characters and strings, and multibyte characters and strings. Character classification and mapping facilities are found in header file **wctype.h**, and the remaining character and string facilities are found in **wchar.h**. For the most part, the facilities duplicate those for traditional characters and strings found in **ctype.h**, **string.h**, and **stdio.h**, changing the argument and return types in an obvious fashion.

24.1 Basic Types and Macros

Synopsis

```
#include <wchar.h>
typedef ... wchar_t;
typedef ... wint_t;
typedef ... mbstate_t;
typedef ... size_t;

#define WEOF ...
#define WCHAR_MIN ...
#define WCHAR_MAX ...
```

Type **wchar_t** (the wide-character type) is an integral type that can represent all distinct values for any execution-time extended character set in the supported locales. It may be a signed or unsigned type, and it is also defined in **stddef.h**. The macros **WCHAR_MIN** and **WCHAR_MAX** give the numerical limits of the **wchar_t** type; their values do not have to correspond to extended characters.

Type **wint_t** is also an integral type that can hold all the values of **wchar_t** and, in addition, at least one additional value that is not a member of the extended character set.

That constant value is given by the macro **WEOF** and is used to designate "end of input" and other exceptional conditions. The **wint_t** type is one that is not altered under the usual argument promotions.

Type **mbstate_t** is a nonarray object type that can represent the state of a conversion between sequences of multibyte characters and wide strings.

Type **size_t** is the same type defined in **stddef.h**.

References   **size_t** 11.1; **wchar_t** 11.1; wide characters 2.7.3

24.2 Conversions Between Wide and Multibyte Characters

<table>
<tr><td align="center">Synopsis</td></tr>
</table>

```
#include <wchar.h>
size_t mbrlen(const char *s, size_t n, mbstate_t *ps);
wint_t btowc(int c);
size_t mbrtowc(wchar_t *pwc, const char *s, size_t n,
    mbstate_t *ps);
int wctob(wint_t c);
size_t wcrtomb(char *s, wchar_t wc, mbstate_t *ps);
int mbsinit(const mbstate_t *ps);
```

The conversion functions in this section are extended versions of the basic functions defined in **stdlib.h**: **mblen**, **mbtowc**, and **wctomb** (Section 16.10). These functions, added in C89 Amendment 1, are more flexible, and their behavior is more completely specified.

The **mbrlen** function inspects up to **n** bytes from the string designated by **s** to see if those characters represent a valid multibyte character relative to the conversion state held in **ps**. If **ps** is null, then the function uses its own internal state object, initialized at program startup to the initial state. If **s** is a null pointer, the call is treated as if **s** were **""** and **n** were 1. If **s** is valid and corresponds to the null wide character, then 0 is returned (regardless of how many bytes make up the multibyte character). If **s** is any other valid multibyte character, then the number of bytes making up that character is returned (i.e., the value returned is in the range 1 through **n**). If **s** is an incomplete multibyte character, then –2 is returned. If **s** is an invalid multibyte character, then –1 is returned, and **errno** is set to **EILSEQ**. The conversion state is updated when the return value is non-negative, it is undefined when –1 is returned, and it is unchanged if –2 is returned.

The **btowc** function returns the wide character corresponding to the byte **c**, which is treated as a one-byte multibyte character in the initial conversion state. If **c** (cast to **unsigned char**) does not correspond to a valid multibyte character, or if **c** is **EOF**, then **btowc** returns **WEOF**.

The **mbrtowc** function converts a multibyte character **s** to a wide character according to conversion state **ps**. (If **ps** is null, then an internal state object is used, set at program startup to the initial state.) The result is stored in the object designated by **pwc** if **pwc** is not a null pointer. If **s** is a null pointer, then the call to **mbrtowc** is equivalent to

mbrtowc(NULL, "", 1, ps). That is, **s** is treated as the empty string and the values of **pwc** and **n** are ignored. If **s** is a valid character corresponding to the null wide character, then 0 is returned (regardless of how many bytes in s were used). Otherwise, if **s** is a valid multibyte character, then the number of bytes used is returned. If **s** is an incomplete multibyte character, then –2 is returned. Finally, if **s** is an invalid multibyte character, then –1 is returned. The conversion state specified by **ps** (or the internal conversion state if **ps** is the null pointer) is updated when a valid conversion occurs. The conversion state is unchanged if **s** is incomplete and is undefined if **s** is invalid.

The **wctob** function (C89 Amendment 1) returns the single-byte, multibyte character corresponding to the wide character **c** in the initial conversion state. If no such single byte exists, **EOF** is returned.

The **wcrtomb** function converts a wide-character **wc** to a multibyte character relative to the conversion state designated by **ps**. (If **ps** is null, then an internal conversion state object is used.) The multibyte character is stored into the array whose first element is designated by **s** and that must be at least **MB_CUR_MAX** characters long. The conversion state is updated. If **wc** is a null wide character, then a null byte is stored, preceded by any shift sequence needed to restore to the initial conversion state. The function returns the number of characters stored into **s**. If **s** is a null pointer, then **wc** is ignored, and the effect of calling **wcrtomb** is simply to restore the initial conversion state and return 1 (as if **L'\0'** had been converted into a hidden buffer). If **wc** is not a valid wide character, then **EILSEQ** is stored into **errno** and –1 is returned.

The **mbsinit** function returns a nonzero value if **ps** is either null or points to an object that represents an initial conversion state. Otherwise it returns zero.

> **References**   **EILSEQ** 11.2; **errno** 11.2; multibyte characters 2.1.5; **mbstate_t** 11.1; **size_t** 11.1; **wchar_t** 11.1; **wint_t** 11.1

24.3 Conversions Between Wide and Multibyte Strings

Synopsis

```
#include <wchar.h>
size_t mbsrtowcs(wchar_t *pwcs, const char **src, size_t n,
    mbstate_t *ps);
size_t wcsrtombs(char *s, const wchar_t **src, size_t n,
    mbstate_t *ps);
```

The functions in this section are "restartable" versions of **mbstowcs** and **wcstombs**, which are defined in **stdlib.h** (see Section 16.11). These functions were added in Amendment 1 to C89.

The **mbsrtowcs** function converts a sequence of multibyte characters in the null terminated string **s** to a corresponding sequence of wide characters, storing the result in the array designated by **pwcs**. The initial conversion state is specified by **ps**, and the input sequence of multibyte characters is specified indirectly by **src**. In normal operation, each multibyte character, up to and including the terminating null character, is converted as if by a call to **mbrtowc**, with the output wide characters being placed in the character array designated by **pwcs**. After the conversion, the pointer designated by **src** is set to the null pointer to indicate that the entire input string was converted, and the number of wide characters stored into **pwcs** (not counting the terminating null wide character) is returned. The conversion state will be updated to be initial shift state—a consequence of converting the null character at the end of the input multibyte string. The output pointer **pwcs** may be the null pointer, in which case **mbsrtowcs** simply calculates the length of the output wide string required for the conversion.

The conversion of the input multibyte string will also stop prematurely if a conversion error occurs. In this case, the pointer designated by **src** is updated to point to the multibyte character whose attempted conversion caused the error. The function returns –1, **EILSEQ** is stored in **errno**, and the conversion state will be indeterminate.

The function **wcsrtombs** converts a sequence of wide characters beginning with the value designated by **pwcs** to a sequence of multibyte characters, storing the result into the character array designated by **s**. The initial conversion state is specified by **ps**, and the input wide string is specified indirectly by **src**. In normal operation, each wide character, up to and including the terminating null wide character, is converted as if by a call to **wcrtomb**, with the output multibyte characters being placed in the character array designated by **s**. After the conversion, the pointer designated by **src** is set to the null pointer to indicate that the entire input string was converted, and the number of bytes stored into **s** (not counting the terminating null character) is returned. The conversion state will be updated to be initial shift state—a consequence of converting the null wide character at the end of the input wide string. The output pointer **s** may be the null pointer, in which case **wcsrtombs** simply calculates the length of the output character array that would be needed for the conversion.

The conversion of the input wide string will stop before the terminating null wide character is converted if **n** output bytes have been written to **s** (and **s** is not a null pointer). In this case, the pointer designated by **src** is set to point just after the last-converted wide character. The conversion state is updated—it will not necessarily be the initial state—and **n** is returned.

The conversion of the input wide string will also stop prematurely if a conversion error occurs. In this case, the pointer designated by **src** is updated to point to the wide character whose attempted conversion caused the error. The function returns –1, **EILSEQ** is stored in **errno**, and the conversion state is indeterminate.

References conversion state 2.1.5; multibyte character 2.1.5; wide character 2.1.5

24.4 Conversions to Arithmetic Types

Synopsis

```
#include <wchar.h>

double wcstod(
  const wchar_t * restrict str,
  wchar_t ** restrict ptr );
float wcstof(
  const wchar_t * restrict str,
  wchar_t ** restrict ptr );
long double wcstold(
  const wchar_t * restrict str,
  wchar_t ** restrict ptr );

long wcstol(
  const wchar_t * restrict str,
  wchar_t ** restrict ptr, int base );
long long wcstoll(
  const wchar_t * restrict str,
  wchar_t ** restrict ptr, int base );
unsigned long wcstoul(
  const char * restrict str,
  wchar_t ** restrict ptr, int base );
unsigned long strtoull(
  const char * restrict str,
  wchar_t ** restrict ptr, int base );
```

The **wcsto**... functions in this section are the same as their corresponding **strto**... functions in Section 16.4, except for the types of their arguments, the use of the **iswspace** function to detect whitespace, and the use of the decimal-point wide character in place of the period. These wide-string conversion functions can accept implementation-defined input strings in addition to the strings accepted by **strto**....

The functions **wcstod**, **wcstol**, and **wcstoul** functions were added in (C89 Amendment 1); the remaining ones are new in C99.

24.5 Input and Output Functions

The functions for input and output of wide character strings are listed in Table 24–1 along with their byte counterparts and the section in this book that discusses both the byte and wide-character functions.

24.6 String Functions

Table 24–2 lists the functions supporting wide strings along with their byte counterparts and the section in this book that discusses both the byte- and wide-string functions.

Table 24–1   Wide input/output functions

Wide-character function	Section	Byte-character function
fgetwc	15.6	fgetc
fgetws	15.7	fgets
fputwc	15.9	fputc
fputws	15.10	fputs
fwide	15.2	
fwprintf	15.11	fprintf
fwscanf	15.8	fscanf
getwc	15.6	getc
getwchar	15.6	getchar
putwc	15.9	putc
putwchar	15.9	putchar
swprintf	15.11	sprintf
swscanf	15.8	sscanf
ungetwc	15.6	ungetc
vfwprintf	15.12	vfprintf
vfwscanf	15.12	vfscanf
vswprintf	15.12	vsprintf
vswscanf	15.12	vsscanf
vwprintf	15.12	vprintf
vwscanf	15.8	vscanf
wprintf	15.11	printf
wscanf	15.8	scanf

24.7 Date and Time Conversions

The **wcsftime** wide function corresponds to the **strftime** byte function.

References   **strftime** 18.6

24.8 Wide-Character Classification and Mapping Functions

Table 24–3 lists the wide-character classification and mapping functions, along with the corresponding character function and the section in this book that describes it.

The wide-character function **towctrans** has no parallel function. Its signature is:

```
#include <wctype.h>
wint_t towctrans( wint_t wc, wctrans_t desc );
```

The **towctrans** function maps the wide-character **wc** to a new value, which it returns. The mapping is specified by a value of type **wctrans_t**, which can be obtained by calling the **wctrans** function (Section 12.11). The **LC_CTYPE** locale category must be

Table 24–2   Wide-string functions

Wide-string function	Section	Byte-string function
wcscat	13.1	strcat
wcschr	13.5	strchr
wcscmp	13.2	strcmp
wcscoll	13.10	strcoll
wcscpy	13.3	strcpy
wcscspn	13.6	strcspn
wcslen	13.4	strlen
wcsncat	13.1	strncat
wcsncmp	13.2	strncmp
wcsncpy	13.3	strncpy
wcspbrk	13.6	strpbrk
wcsrchr	13.5	strrchr
wcsspn	13.6	strspn
wcsstr	13.7	strstr
wcstok	13.7	strtok
wcsxfrm	13.10	strxfrm
wmemchr	14.1	memchr
wmemcmp	14.1	memcmp
wmemcpy	14.3	memcpy
wmemmove	14.3	memmove
wmemset	14.4	memset

Table 24–3   Wide-character functions

Wide-character function	Section	Byte-character function
iswalnum	12.1	isalnum
iswalpha	12.1	isalpha
iswblank	12.	isblank
iswcntrl	12.1	iscntrl
iswctype	12.	isctype
iswdigit	12.3	isdigit
iswgraph	12.4	isgraph
iswlower	12.5	islower
iswprint	12.4	isprint
iswpunct	12.4	ispunct
iswspace	12.6	isspace
iswupper	12.5	isupper
iswxdigit	12.3	isxdigit
towlower	12.9	tolower
towupper	12.9	toupper
wctrans	12.11	ctrans

the same during the call to **towctrans** as it was during the call to **wctrans_t**, which produced the value of **desc**.

A

The ASCII Character Set

Hex.	Octal	Dec.	Char.	Name	Dec.	Char.	Dec.	Char.	Dec.	Char.
		0			0x20		0x40		0x60	
		0			040		0100		0140	
0	0	0	^@	NUL	32	SP	64	@	96	`
1	1	1	^A	SOH	33	!	65	A	97	a
2	2	2	^B	STX	34	"	66	B	98	b
3	3	3	^C	ETX	35	#	67	C	99	c
4	4	4	^D	EOT	36	$	68	D	100	d
5	5	5	^E	ENQ	37	%	69	E	101	e
6	6	6	^F	ACK	38	&	70	F	102	f
7	7	7	^G	BEL, \a	39	'	71	G	103	g
8	010	8	^H	BS, \b	40	(	72	H	104	h
9	011	9	^I	TAB, \t	41	)	73	I	105	i
0xA	012	10	^J	LF, \n	42	*	74	J	106	j
0xB	013	11	^K	VT, \v	43	+	75	K	107	k
0xC	014	12	^L	FF, \f	44	,	76	L	108	l
0xD	015	13	^M	CR, \r	45	-	77	M	109	m
0xE	016	14	^N	SO	46	.	78	N	110	n
0xF	017	15	^O	SI	47	/	79	O	111	o
0x10	020	16	^P	DLE	48	0	80	P	112	p
0x11	021	17	^Q	DC1	49	1	81	Q	113	q
0x12	022	18	^R	DC2	50	2	82	R	114	r
0x13	023	19	^S	DC3	51	3	83	S	115	s
0x14	024	20	^T	DC4	52	4	84	T	116	t
0x15	025	21	^U	NAK	53	5	85	U	117	u
0x16	026	22	^V	SYN	54	6	86	V	118	v
0x17	027	23	^W	ETB	55	7	87	W	119	w
0x18	030	24	^X	CAN	56	8	88	X	120	x
0x19	031	25	^Y	EM	57	9	89	Y	121	y
0x1A	032	26	^Z	SUB	58	:	90	Z	122	z
0x1B	033	27	^[	ESC	59	;	91	[	123	{
0x1C	034	28	^\	FS	60	<	92	\	124	|
0x1D	035	29	^]	GS	61	=	93	]	125	}
0x1E	036	30	^^	RS	62	>	94	^	126	~
0x1F	037	31	^_	US	63	?	95	_	127	DEL

B

Syntax

abstract-declarator :
> *pointer*
> *pointer$_{opt}$ direct-abstract-declarator*

additive-expression :
> *multiplicative-expression*
> *additive-expression add-op multiplicative-expression*

add-op : one of
> **+ -**

address-expression :
> **&** *cast-expression*

array-declarator :

direct-declarator **[** *constant-expressionopt* **]**		*(until C99)*
direct-declarator **[** *array-qualifier-list$_{opt}$ array-size-expression$_{opt}$* **]**		*(C99)*
direct-declarator **[** *array-qualifier-list$_{opt}$* ***]**		*(C99)*

array-qualifier :
> **static**
> **restrict**
> **const**
> **volatile**

array-qualifier-list :
> *array-qualifier*
> *array-qualifier-list array-qualifier*

array-size-expression :
> *assignment-expression*
> *****

assignment-expression :

        conditional-expression

        unary-expression assignment-op assignment-expression

assignment-op : one of

        =   +=   -= *= /= %= <<= >>= &= ^= |=

binary-exponent :

        p *sign-part$_{opt}$ digit-sequence*

        P *sign-part$_{opt}$ digit-sequence*

bit-field :

        declarator$_{opt}$ **:** *width*

bitwise-and-expression :

        equality-expression

        bitwise-and-expression **&** *equality-expression*

bitwise-negation-expression :

        ~ *cast-expression*

bitwise-or-expression :

        bitwise-xor-expression

        bitwise-or-expression **|** *bitwise-xor-expression*

bitwise-xor-expression :

        bitwise-and-expression

        bitwise-xor-expression **^** *bitwise-and-expression*

break-statement :

        break;

case-label :

        case *constant-expression*

cast-expression :

        unary-expression

        (*type-name* **)** *cast-expression*

c-char :

        any source character except the apostrophe (**'**), backslash (****), or newline

        escape-character

        universal-character-name   *(C99)*

c-char-sequence :

        c-char

        c-char-sequence c-char

character-constant :

        ' *c-char-sequence* **'**

        L' *c-char-sequence* **'**   *(C89)*

character-escape-code : one of

        n t b r f

        v \\ ' "

        a ?   *(C89)*

character-type-specifier :
>   **char**
>   **signed char**
>   **unsigned char**

comma-expression :
>   *assignment-expression*
>   *comma-expression* **,** *assignment-expression*

complex-type-specifier :   *(C99)*
>   **float _Complex**
>   **double _Complex**
>   **long double _Complex**

component-declaration :
>   *type-specifier component-declarator-list* **;**

component-declarator :
>   *simple-component*
>   *bit-field*

component-declarator-list :
>   *component-declarator*
>   *component-declarator-list* **,** *component-declarator*

component-selection-expression :
>   *direct-component-selection*
>   *indirect-component-selection*

compound-literal :
>   **(** *type-name* **)** **{** *initializer-list* **,** *opt***}*   *(C99)*

compound-statement :
>   **{** *declaration-or-statement-list*$_{opt}$ **}**

conditional-expression :
>   *logical-or-expression*
>   *logical-or-expression* **?** *expression* **:** *conditional-expression*

conditional-statement :
>   *if-statement*
>   *if-else-statement*

constant :
>   *integer-constant*
>   *floating-constant*
>   *character-constant*
>   *string-constant*

constant-expression :
>   *conditional-expression*

continue-statement :
>   **continue;**

decimal-constant :
>   *nonzero-digit*
>   *decimal-constant digit*

decimal-floating-constant :
>   *digit-sequence exponent floating-suffix$_{opt}$*
>   *dotted-digits   exponent$_{opt}$ floating-suffix$_{opt}$*

declaration :
>   *declaration-specifiers initialized-declarator-list* **;**

declaration-list :
>   *declaration*
>   *declaration-list declaration*

declaration-or-statement :
>   *declaration*
>   *statement*

declaration-or-statement-list :
>   *declaration-or-statement*
>   *declaration-or-statement-list   declaration-or-statement*

declaration-specifiers :
>   *storage-class-specifier   declaration-specifiers$_{opt}$*
>   *type-specifier   declaration-specifiers$_{opt}$*
>   *type-qualifier   declaration-specifiers$_{opt}$*
>   *function-specifier declaration-specifiers$_{opt}$*   *(C99)*

declarator :
>   *pointer-declarator*
>   *direct-declarator*

default-label :
>   **default**

designation :
>   *designator-list* **=**

designator :
>   **[** *constant-expression* **]**
>   **.** *identifier*

designator-list :
>   *designator*
>   *designator-list designator*

digit : one of
>   **0   1   2   3   4   5   6   7   8   9**

digit-sequence :
>   *digit*
>   *digit-sequence digit*

direct-abstract-declarator :
>   **(** *abstract-declarator* **)**
>   *direct-abstract-declarator$_{opt}$* **[** *constant-expressionopt* **]**

$\qquad$ *direct-abstract-declarator*$_{opt}$ [*expression*]   *(C99)*
$\qquad$ *direct-abstract-declarator*$_{opt}$ [*]   *(C99)*
$\qquad$ *direct-abstract-declaratoropt* (*parameter-type-listopt*)

direct-component-selection :
$\qquad$ *postfix-expression* . *identifier*

direct-declarator :
$\qquad$ *simple-declarator*
$\qquad$ (*declarator*)
$\qquad$ *function-declarator*
$\qquad$ *array-declarator*

do-statement :
$\qquad$ **do** *statement* **while** (*expression*) ;

dotted-digits :
$\qquad$ *digit-sequence* .
$\qquad$ *digit-sequence* . *digit-sequence*
$\qquad$. *digit-sequence*

dotted-hex-digits :
$\qquad$ *hex-digit-sequence* .
$\qquad$ *hex-digit-sequence* . *hex-digit-sequence*
$\qquad$. *hex-digit-sequence*

enumeration-constant :
$\qquad$ *identifier*

enumeration-constant-definition :
$\qquad$ *enumeration-constant*
$\qquad$ *enumeration-constant* **=** *expression*

enumeration-definition-list :
$\qquad$ *enumeration-constant-definition*
$\qquad$ *enumeration-definition-list* **,** *enumeration-constant-definition*

enumeration-tag :
$\qquad$ *identifier*

enumeration-type-definition :
$\qquad$ **enum** *enumeration-tag*$_{opt}$ { *enumeration-definition-list* }
$\qquad$ **enum** *enumeration-tag*$_{opt}$ { *enumeration-definition-list* **,** }   *(C99)*

enumeration-type-reference :
$\qquad$ **enum** *enumeration-tag*

enumeration-type-specifier :
$\qquad$ *enumeration-type-definition*
$\qquad$ *enumeration-type-reference*

equality-expression :
$\qquad$ *relational-expression*
$\qquad$ *equality-expression equality-op relational-expression*

equality-op : one of
$\qquad$ **== !=**

escape-character :
        \ *escape-code*
        universal-character-name   *(C99)*

escape-code :
        character-escape-code
        octal-escape-code
        hex-escape-code   *(C89)*

exponent :
        e *sign-part$_{opt}$* *digit-sequence*
        E *sign-part$_{opt}$* *digit-sequence*

expression :
        comma-expression

expression-list :
        assignment-expression
        expression-list **,** *assignment-expression*

expression-statement :
        expression **;**

field-list :
        component-declaration
        field-list component-declaration

floating-constant :
        decimal-floating-constant
        hexadecimal-floating-constant   *(C99)*

floating-point-type-specifier :
        float
        double
        long double   *(C89)*
        complex-type-specifier   *(C99)*

floating-suffix : one of
        f **F** **l** **L**

for-expressions :
        (*initial-clause$_{opt}$* **;** *expression$_{opt}$* **;** *expression$_{opt}$*)

for-statement :
        for *for-expressions statement*

function-call :
        postfix-expression (*expression-list$_{opt}$*)

function-declarator :
        direct-declarator (*parameter-type-list*)   *(C89)*
        direct-declarator (*identifier-list$_{opt}$*)

function-definition :
        function-def-specifier compound-statement

function-def-specifier :
        declaration-specifiers$_{opt}$ declarator declaration-list$_{opt}$

function-specifier :   (C99)

        inline

goto-statement :

        goto *named-label* **;**

h-char-sequence :

        any sequence of characters except > and end-of-line

hexadecimal-constant :

        0x *hex-digit*

        0X *hex-digit*

        hexadecimal-constant hex-digit

hexadecimal-floating-constant: (C99)

        hex-prefix dotted-hex-digits   binary-exponent   floating-suffix$_{opt}$

        hex-prefix hex-digit-sequence   binary-exponent   floating-suffix$_{opt}$

hex-digit : one of

        0   1   2   3   4   5   6   7   8   9

        A   B   C   D   E   F   a   b   c   d   e   f

hex-digit-sequence :

        hex-digit

        hex-digit-sequence   hex-digit

hex-escape-code :

        x *hex-digit*

        hex-escape-code hex-digit   (C89)

hex-prefix:

        0x

        0X

hex-quad:

        hex-digit hex-digit hex-digit hex-digit

identifier :

        identifier-nondigit

        identifier identifier-nondigit

        identifier digit

identifier-list :

        identifier

        parameter-list **,** *identifier*

identifier-nondigit :

        nondigit

        universal-character-name

        other implementation-defined characters

if-else-statement :

        if (*expression*) *statement* **else** *statement*

if-statement :

        if (*expression*) *statement*

indirect-component-selection :
> *postfix-expression* -> *identifier*

indirection-expression :
> * *cast-expression*

initial-clause:
> *expression*
> *declaration*   *(C99)*

initialized-declarator :
> *declarator*
> *declarator* = *initializer*

initialized-declarator-list :
> *initialized-declarator*
> *initialized-declarator-list* , *initialized-declarator*

initializer :
> *assignment-expression*
> { *initializer-list* ,$_{opt}$ }

initializer-list :
> *initializer*
> *initializer-list* , *initializer*
> *designation initializer*   *(C99)*
> *initializer-list* , *designation initializer*   *(C99)*

integer-constant :
> *decimal-constant integer-suffix$_{opt}$*
> *octal-constant integer-suffix$_{opt}$*
> *hexadecimal-constant integer-suffix$_{opt}$*

integer-suffix :
> *long-suffix unsigned-suffix$_{opt}$*
> *long-long-suffix unsigned-suffix$_{opt}$*   *(C99)*
> *unsigned-suffix long-suffix$_{opt}$*
> *unsigned-suffix long-long-suffix$_{opt}$*   *(C99)*

integer-type-specifier :
> *signed-type-specifier*
> *unsigned-type-specifier*
> *character-type-specifier*
> *bool-type-specifier*   *(C99)*

iterative-statement :
> *while-statement*
> *do-statement*
> *for-statement*

label :
> *named-label*
> *case-label*
> *default-label*

labeled-statement :
    label **:** *statement*

logical-and-expression :
    bitwise-or-expression
    logical-and-expression **&&** *bitwise-or-expression*

logical-negation-expression :
    ! *cast-expression*

logical-or-expression :
    logical-and-expression
    logical-or-expression **||** *logical-and-expression*

long-long-suffix : one of   *(C99)*
    ll LL

long-suffix : one of
    l L

multiplicative-expression :
    cast-expression
    multiplicative-expression mult-op cast-expression

mult-op **: one of**
    * / %

named-label :
    identifier

nondigit : one of

A	**B**	**C**	**D**	**E**	**F**	**G**	**H**	**I**	**J**	**K**	**L**	**M**
N	**O**	**P**	**Q**	**R**	**S**	**T**	**U**	**V**	**W**	**X**	**Y**	**Z**
a	**b**	**c**	**d**	**e**	**f**	**g**	**h**	**i**	**j**	**k**	**l**	**m**
n	**o**	**p**	**q**	**r**	**s**	**t**	**u**	**v**	**w**	**x**	**y**	**z**
_												

nonzero-digit : one of
    1 2 3 4 5 6 7 8 9

null-statement :
    ;

octal-constant :
    0
    octal-constant octal-digit

octal-digit : one of
    0 1 2 3 4 5 6 7

octal-escape-code :
    octal-digit
    octal-digit octal-digit
    octal-digit octal-digit octal-digit

on-off-switch:
> **ON**
> **OFF**
> **DEFAULT**

parameter-declaration :
> *declaration-specifiers declarator*
> *declaration-specifiers abstract-declarator*$_{opt}$

parameter-list :
> *parameter-declaration*
> *parameter-list* **,** *parameter-declaration*

parameter-type-list :
> *parameter-list*
> *parameter-list* **,** **. . .**

parenthesized-expression :
> **(** *expression* **)**

pointer :
> ***** *type-qualifier-list*$_{opt}$
> ***** *type-qualifier-list*$_{opt}$ *pointer*

pointer-declarator :
> *pointer direct-declarator*

postdecrement-expression :
> *postfix-expression* **- -**

postfix-expression :
> *primary-expression*
> *subscript-expression*
> *component-selection-expression*
> *function-call*
> *postincrement-expression*
> *postdecrement-expression*
> *compound-literal*   *(C99)*

postincrement-expression :
> *postfix-expression* **++**

predecrement-expression :
> **- -** *unary-expression*

preincrement-expression :
> **++** *unary-expression*

preprocessor-tokens :
> *any sequence of C tokens—or non-whitespace characters*
> *that cannot be interpreted as tokens—that does not begin with* **<** *or* **"**

primary-expression :
> *identifier*
> *constant*
> *parenthesized-expression*

q-char-sequence :

        any sequence of characters except **"** *and* end-*of-line*

relational-expression :

        shift-expression
        relational-expression relational-op shift-expression

relational-op : one of

        <   <=   >   >=

return-statement :

        return *expressionopt* **;**

s-char :

        any source character except the double quote **"**,
          backslash ****, *or newline character*
        escape-character
        universal-character-name   *(C99)*

s-char-sequence :

        s-char
        s-char-sequence s-char

shift-expression :

        additive-expression
        shift-expression shift-op additive-expression

shift-op : one of

        << >>

signed-type-specifier :

        short *or* **short int** *or* **signed short** *or* **signed short int**
        int *or* **signed int** *or* **signed**
        long *or* **long int** *or* **signed long** *or* **signed long int**
        long long *or* **long long int** *or* **signed long long** *or*
          signed long long int

sign-part : one of

        +   -

simple-component :

        declarator

simple-declarator :

        identifier

sizeof-expression :

        sizeof **(** *type-name* **)**
        sizeof *unary-expression*

statement :

        expression-statement
        labeled-statement
        compound-statement
        conditional-statement
        iterative-statement
        switch-statement

        break-statement
        continue-statement
        return-statement
        goto-statement
        null-statement

storage-class-specifier : one of
        auto   extern   register   static   typedef

string-constant :
        " *s-char-sequence*opt **"**
        L" *s-char-sequence*opt **"**   *(C89)*

structure-tag :
        identifier

structure-type-definition :
        struct *structure-tag*opt **{** *field-list* **}**

structure-type-reference :
        struct *structure-tag*

structure-type-specifier :
        structure-type-definition
        structure-type-reference

subscript-expression :
        postfix-expression **[** *expression* **]**

switch-statement :
        switch (*expression*) *statement*

top-level-declaration :
        declaration
        function-definition

translation-unit :
        top-level-declaration
        translation-unit top-level-declaration

typedef-name :
        identifier

type-name :
        declaration-specifiers abstract-declarator$_{opt}$

type-qualifier :
        const
        volatile
        restrict   *(C99)*

type-qualifier-list :   *(C89)*
        type-qualifier
        type-qualifer-list type-qualifier

type-specifier :
        enumeration-type-specifier
        floating-point-type-specifier

       integer-type-specifier
       structure-type-specifier
       typedef-name
       union-type-specifier
       void-type-specifier

unary-expression :
       postfix-expression
       sizeof-expression
       unary-minus-expression
       unary-plus-expression
       logical-negation-expression
       bitwise-negation-expression
       address-expression
       indirection-expression
       preincrement-expression
       predecrement-expression

unary-minus-expression :
       - *cast-expression*

unary-plus-expression :   *(C89)*
       + *cast-expression*

union-tag :
       identifier

union-type-definition :
       union *union-tagopt* { *field-list* }

union-type-reference :
       union *union-tag*

union-type-specifier :
       union-type-definition
       union-type-reference

universal-character-name:
       \u *hex-quad*
       \U *hex-quad hex-quad*

unsigned-suffix : one of
       u   U

unsigned-type-specifier :
       unsigned short int$_{opt}$
       unsigned int$_{opt}$
       unsigned long int$_{opt}$
       unsigned long long int$_{opt}$ *(C99)*

void-type-specifier :
       void

while-statement :
       while (*expression*) *statement*

width :

       constant-expression

C

Answers to the Exercises

This appendix contains solutions to the exercises in Chapters 2 to 9.

CHAPTER 2 ANSWERS

1. Reserved words, hexadecimal constants, wide string constants, and parentheses are lexical tokens. Comments and whitespace serve only to separate tokens. Trigraphs are removed before
   token recognition.

2. The number of tokens for each string is:

   (a) 3 tokens

   (b) 2 tokens; - is an operator,
       not part of the constant

   (c) 1 token

   (d) 3 tokens; the second one is `"FOO"`

   (e) 1 token

   (f) 4 tokens; `**` is not a single operator

   (g) not a token; same as `"X\"`, which is
       an unterminated string constant

   (h) not a token; identifiers cannot have `$`

   (i) 3 tokens; `*=` is an operator

   (j) either none or 3; `##` is not a lexical token,
       but it happens to be a preprocessor token

3. The result is `***/`; the comments are identified next between parentheses. Quotation marks
   inside a comment do not have to balance.

   ```
   /**/*/*"*/*/*"//*//**/*/
   (--) (---) (-----) (--)
   ```

4. The order is:
   1. converting trigraphs
   2. processing line continuation
   3. removing comments
   4. collecting characters into tokens

5. Some possible objections:

   (a) difficult to identify (read) the multiple words in the identifier;
       use uppercase or underscores

   (b) the identifier's spelling is close to a reserved word

(c) lowercase **l** ("ell") and uppercase **O** ("oh") are easily mistaken for **1** (one) and **0** (zero)

(d) closely resembles a numeric literal (the first letter is an "oh")

(e) if the compiler accepted this identifier, it would be an extension

6. (a) For example: **x = a //*divide*/ b;**

(b) Assuming a Standard C implementation that distinguished only the first 31 characters of identifiers, a Standard C program that spelled the same identifier differently after the 31st character would be flagged as an error in C++.

(c) For example, the declaration: **int class = 0;**

(d) The expression **sizeof('a')==sizeof(char)** will be different in C and C++ assuming **sizeof(char)!=sizeof(int)**.

CHAPTER 3 ANSWERS

1. (a) The space before the left parenthesis is not permitted in Standard or traditional C. Instead of a macro with one parameter, **ident** will be a macro with no parameters that expands to "**(x) x**".

(b) The **=** and **;** characters are not necessary and are probably wrong. In some traditional C compilers, the space after **#** might cause problems.

(c) This definition is all right.

(d) This definition is all right; you can define reserved words as macros.

2.   *Standard C*   *Traditional C*

(a) **b+a**   **b+a**

(b) **x 4** (two tokens)   **x4** (one token)

(c) **"a book"**   **# a book**

(d) **p?free(p):NULL**   **p?p?p?...:NULL:NULL:NULL** (infinitely)

3. The result after preprocessing (ignoring whitespace) is these three lines:

```
int blue = 0;
int blue = 0;
int red = 0;
```

4. Because the arguments and body are not parenthesized, the result of expanding the macro could be misinterpreted in a larger expression. A safer definition would be

```
#define DBL(a)    ((a)+(a))
```

5. The macro is expanded in the following steps:

```
M(M)(A,B)
MM(A,B)
A = "B"
```

6. This solution depends on the presence of **defined** and **#error**:

```
#if !defined(SIZE) || (SIZE<1) || (SIZE>10)
#error "SIZE not properly defined "
#endif
```

7. In the preprocessor command **#include </a/file.h>**, the sequence **/a/file.h** is considered a token (a single file name); it would not be a token to the compiler.

8. Presumably the programmer wishes to print an error when **x==0**. However, **x==0** is a run-time test, whereas **#error** is a compile-time command. If this program were compiled, the error message would always appear and halt compilation regardless of the value of **x**.

CHAPTER 4 ANSWERS

1. The function will return the value of its argument each time it is called. Only if the **static** storage class specifier is used on the declaration of **i** inside **P** will the return value change in successive calls.

2. The declarations of **f** as a function, integer variable, type name, and enumeration constant all conflict with each other; eliminate all but one of those declarations. The use of **f** as both a structure tag and a union tag conflict; eliminate the union so that **f** is also declared as a structure component. The use of **f** as a label does not conflict with any other declarations except in a few older C implementations.

3.

Code	int i;	long i;	float i;
1 `int i;`	(declared)		
2 `void f(i)`		(declared)	
3 `   long i;`		(declared)	
4 `{`			
5 `   long l = i;`		(used)	
6 `   {`			
7 `      float i;`			(declared)
8 `      i = 3.4;`			(used)
9 `   }`			
10 `   l = i+2;`		(used)	
11 `}`			
12 `int *p = &i;`	(used)		

4. (a) `extern void P(void);`
    (b) `register int i;`
    (c) `typedef char *LT;`
    (d) `extern void Q(int i, const char *cp);`
    (e) `extern int R( double *(*p)(long i) );`
    (f) `static char STR[11];` (Note: leave room for the null character.)
    (g) `const char STR2[] = INIT_STR2;` Braces around **INIT_STR2** are optional.
        Also acceptable would be: `const char *STR2=INIT_STR2;` (No braces.)
    (h) `int *IP = &i;`

5. `int m[3][3] = {{1,2,3},{1,2,3},{1,2,3}};`

CHAPTER 5 ANSWERS

1. Note that none of these types should involve type **int** since the size of **int** might be no larger than **short** anyway.
    (a) **long** or **unsigned long** (**unsigned short** might not handle 99999)
    (b) a structure containing two components: type **short** (for the area code) and type **long** (for the local number) (or the unsigned versions of these types)
    (c) **char** (any variant)
    (d) **signed char** in Standard C; **short** in other implementations (**char** might be unsigned)
    (e) **signed char** in Standard C; **short** in other implementations (**char** might be unsigned)
    (f) **double** would work, but less space would be occupied by using type **long** and storing

the balance as a number of cents

2. The type of **UP_ARROW_KEY** is **int** and has the value **0x86** (134). If the computer uses a **signed** type for **char**, the values for the extended characters will be negative, so if the argument to **is_up_arrow** really is **0x86**, the **return** statement test will be **-122==134**, which is false instead of true. The correct way to write the function is to coerce the character code to be of type **char** or coerce the argument to be of type **unsigned char**. That is, use one of the following return statements:

```
return c == (char) UP_ARROW_KEY;
return (unsigned char) c == UP_ARROW_KEY;
```

The first solution is probably better since it allows the most freedom in defining a value for **UP_ARROW_KEY**.

3. (a) legal
    (b) legal
    (c) illegal; cannot dereference a **void** * pointer
    (d) illegal; cannot dereference a **void** * pointer

4. (a) ***(iv + i)**
    (b) ***(*(im+i)+j)**

5. 13. The cast is not necessary in Standard C, but it makes the intent clearer and may be needed in some older compilers.

6.
```
x.i =  0;
x.F.s = 0;                          (0 and 1 are the only legal values.)
x.F.e = 0; x.F.m = 0;
x.U.d = 0 . 0;                      (or x.U.p = NULL; ,
                                    but not x.U.a[0] = '\0';,
                                    which leaves some elements of a undefined)
```

7. The sketches are shown next. The number of bits occupied by each field is indicated, and markers along the bottom indicate word boundaries. Note particularly the order of the bit fields.

Big-endian, right-to-left bit packing

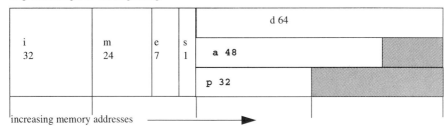

increasing memory addresses ⟶

Little-endian, right-to-left bit packing

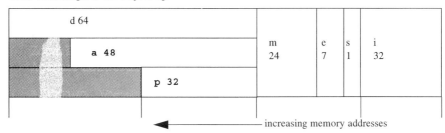

⟵ increasing memory addresses

8.  ```
    typedef int *fpi(); /* type definition */
    fpi *x; /* variable declaration */
    int *fpi() /* function; can't use typedef in header */
    {
        return (fpi *)0;
    }
    ```

CHAPTER 6 ANSWERS

1. All the casts are permitted in Standard and traditional C except (c) and (e), which are disallowed in Standard C.

2. In this solution, we assume the traditional C compiler allows mixed pointer assignments but otherwise follows Standard rules. However, for some traditional C compilers, the answers will be the same as for Question 1.
    (a) Permitted in Standard and traditional C.
    (b) Disallowed in Standard C, permitted in traditional C.
    (c) Disallowed in Standard C, permitted in traditional C.
    (d) Disallowed in Standard and traditional C.
    (e) Disallowed in Standard C, permitted in traditional C.
    (f) Permitted in Standard and traditional C.

3. (a) **unsigned**
    (b) **unsigned long** in traditional C; **long** or **unsigned long** in Standard C
    ```

(c) `double`

(d) `long double` in Standard C;

(e) `int *` (the usual unary conversions are applied to `int []`)

(f) `short (*)()`, because the usual unary conversions are applied first. Here is a plausible situation in which this could happen:

```
extern short f1(), f2(), (*pf)();
extern int i;
pf = (i>0 ? f1 : f2);   /* binary conv on f1 and f2 */
```

4. It is permitted (if wasteful) for an implementation to use 32 bits to represent type **char**. Regardless of the representation, the value of `sizeof(char)` is always 1. The range of type `int` cannot be smaller than that of type `char`; it can be the same or it can be arbitrarily larger.

5. There is not necessarily any relationship between them. They could be the same or one could be larger than the other.

6. The value 128 can be expressed as the 32-bit hexadecimal number 00000080_{16}. Since computer A is a big-endian, the bytes are stored in the order 00_{16}, 00_{16} 00_{16}, 80_{16}. On the little-endian computer, the bytes are reassembled from the low-order end, yielding 80000000_{16} or –2,147,483,648. The result is the same if A is the little-endian and B is the big-endian.

CHAPTER 7 ANSWERS

1. (a) `char *`

(b) `float` (`double` in traditional C)

(c) `float`

(d) `int`

(e) `float` (`double` in traditional C)

(f) `int`

(g) `int`

(h) `int`

(i) illegal

(j) `float`

2. (a) `p1+=1; p2+=1; *p1=*p2;`

(b) `*p1=*p2; p1-=1; p2-=1;`

3. (a) `#define low_zeroes(n)  (-1<<n)` (if `n` is not greater than the width of type `int`)

(b) `#define low_ones(n) (~low_zeroes(n))`

(c) `#define mid_zeroes(width,offset) \`
     `        (low_zeroes(width+offset) | low_ones(offset))`
   (The `+` operator could be used in place of `|`.)

(d) `#define mid_ones(width,offset (~mid_zeroes(width,offset))`

4. The expression `j++==++j` is legal, but its result is undefined in Standard C because `j` is modified twice in the same expression. Depending on which operand of `==` is evaluated first, the result could be 0 or 1, although the final value of `j` is likely to be 2. However, `j++&&++j` is legal and defined; its result is 0, and `j` has the value 1 at the end of the expression.

5. (a) allowed since the types are compatible

(b) not allowed (the referenced type on the left does not have enough qualifiers)

(c) allowed since only one type specifies a size

(d) allowed since qualification is irrelevant if the right side is not an lvalue

    (e)   not allowed only because **float** is not compatible with its promoted type (**double**)

    (f)   allowed since the referenced types are compatible

6.   No. The assignment is illegal because each structure definition creates a new type. If the definitions are in different source files, the types are compatible, but this is a technicality that permits programs compiled in separate pieces to have well-defined behavior.

CHAPTER 8 ANSWERS

1.   (a)
```
n = A;
L1:
if (n>=B) goto L2;
sum+=n;
n++;
goto L1;
L2:;
```
    (b)
```
L:
if (a<b) {
    a++;
    goto L;
}
```
    (c)
```
L:
sum += *p;
if (++p < q) goto L;
```

2.   The value of **j** is 3. "**j** is undefined" is incorrect; although the program jumps into a block, the fact that **i** has storage class **static** means that it will be properly initialized before the program begins.

3.   The value of **sum** is 3. **i** takes on the values 0, 1, … each time around the loop. When **i** is 0, 1, and 3, **sum** is incremented and the **continue** statement causes another loop iteration. When **i** is 2, **sum** is not altered, but the loop is continued. However, when **i** is 4, the **break** within the **switch** causes control to reach the **break** statement in the loop, which causes termination of the loop. Therefore, **case 5:** is never executed.

CHAPTER 9 ANSWERS

1.   (a)   valid prototype

    (b)   legal declaration, but not a prototype; must have a parameter type list within parentheses

    (c)   illegal declaration; must have at least one parameter declaration before ellipsis

    (d)   illegal declaration; must have at least one type specifier, storage class specifier, or type qualifier before each parameter name

    (e)   valid prototype; parameter name is not necessary

    (f)   legal definition, but not a prototype; must have parameter types within parentheses

2.   (a)   not compatible; prototype's parameter type is not compatible with the usual argument conversions, which is required when the definition is not in prototype form

    (b)   not compatible; it does not matter that the prototype appears in the definition

    (c)   compatible; the parameter names do not have to be the same

    (d)   not compatible; the two prototypes do not agree in the use of the ellipsis

      (e)   compatible; neither is a prototype, so promoted argument types are passed

      (f)   compatible

3.   (a)   not legal; cannot convert **short** * to **int** * under the assignment conversions

      (b)   legal; **s** will be converted to type **int** and **ld** will be unchanged

      (c)   legal; **ld** will be converted to type **short**

      (d)   legal; the first parameter is unchanged, the second is converted to type **int**, and the third is unchanged

      (e)   legal; the parameter is converted to type **int** before the call, and back to type **short** at the beginning of the called function

      (f)   legal, but probably wrong; the parameter is unchanged but will be interpreted as being of type **int** by the caller

4.   The call is governed by the prototype appearing on the first line. The latter declaration does not hide the former, because **P** has external linkage.

5.   (a)   OK; the value will be converted to type **short** before being returned

      (b)   OK; the value will be converted to type **short** before being returned

      (c)   illegal; the expression cannot be converted to the type of the return value

      (d)   illegal; the expression cannot be converted under the assignment conversion rules

Index

-- decrement operator 204, 216, 225

- subtraction operator 229

- unary-minus operator 222

! logical-negation operator 222, 333

!= not-equal operator 234, 333

preprocessor token 55

preprocessor token 56

$ dollar sign 22

% remainder operator 228

%= assign-remainder operator 249

& address operator 84, 106, 137, 224

& bitwise-and operator 236, 333

&& logical-and operator 333

&= assign-bitwise-and operator 249, 333

() cast operator 219

() function-call operator 204, 214

() grouping 204, 209

* indirection operator 137, 204, 225

* multiplication operator 228

*= assign-product operator 249

+ addition operator 229

+ unary-plus operator 222

++ increment operator 204, 216, 225

+= assign-sum operator 249

. component-selection operator 204, 212

.* C++ operator 38

/ division operator 228

/= assign-quotient operator 249

: statement label separator 261

:: C++ operator 38

; statement terminator 260

< less-than operator 233

<< left-shift operator 231

<<= assign-shifted operator 249

<= less-or-equal operator 233

-= assign-difference operator 249

= assignment operator 204

== equal-to operator 234

-> component-selection operator 204, 212

> greater-than operator 233

->* C++ operator 38

>= greater-or-equal operator 233

>> right-shift operator 231

>>= assign-shifted operator 249

??x trigraphs 15

[] subscripting operator 204, 210

\ backslash 13, 35

^ bitwise-xor operator 236, 333

^= assign-bitwise-xor operator 249, 333

_ underscore (lowline) character 22

{} compound statements 262

| bitwise-or operator 236, 333

|= assign-bitwise-or operator 249, 333

|| logical-or operator 333

~ bitwise-negation 223, 333

A

abort facility 414

abs facility 419

absolute value functions 419

abstract data type 149

abstract declarators 176

acknowledgments xviii

acos facility 434

acosh facility 435

Ada 260, 274, 300

addition 229

address constant expression 253

address operator 84, 106, 137, 152, 224

addressing structure 183, 185

alarm facility 458

alert character 13, 36

ALGOL 60 3

alignment
   bit fields 154
   restrictions 184
   structure components 152
   structures 158
   unions 162

Amendment 1 to C89 4

and macro 333

and_eq macro 333

answers to exercises 513–520

arctan function 434

arithmetic types 123

array qualifiers 99, 296

arrays
   bounds 142

conversions to pointers 106, 140, 193
declarators 97
function parameters 99
incomplete 98, 108
initializers 107
multidimensional 98, 141, 210, 230
operations on 143
size of 140, 143
sizeof 221
subscripting 141, 210
type compatibility 174
type of 140
value of name 208
variable length 99, 109, 143, 170, 217, 230, 263
ASCII 14, 31, 39, 497
asctime facility 445
asin facility 434
asinh facility 435
assert facility 453
assert.h header file 453
assignment
    compatibility 195
    conversions during 195
    expressions 246
associativity of operators 205
atan facility 434
atan2 facility 434
atanh facility 435
atexit facility 414
atof facility 411
atoi facility 411
atol facility 411
atoll facility 411
auto storage class 83
automatic variables 80

B

B language 3
backslash character 12, 14, 34, 35, 36
backspace character 13, 36
Basic Latin 40
bcmp facility 360
bcopy function 361
BCPL 3

Beeler, Michael xviii
Bell Laboratories 3
Bentley, Jon Louis xviii
big-endian computers 183
binary expressions 227
binary streams 363
bit fields 154, 197
bitand macro 333
bitor macro 333
bitwise expressions 157, 223, 236
blank 11
blocks 74, 262
bool C++ keyword 39
bool macro 132, 329

_bool_true_false_are _defined macro 329
_Bool type specifier 132
Boolean type 127, 132
    conversion 189
    values 124
bounds of arrays 142
branch cut 483
break statement 277
Brodie, Jim 4
bsearch facility 417
btowc function 490
buffered I/O 363, 370
BUFSIZ value 370
byte 182
byte input/output functions 364
byte order 183
byte-oriented stream 364
bzero function 362

C

C++ compatibility
    calling C functions 313
    character sets 38
    const type qualifier 117
    constants 39
    defining declarations 118
    enumeration types 178
    expressions 257
    identifiers 39
    implicit declarations 118
    initializers 118
    keywords 39

operators 38
parameter declarations 306
prototypes 306
return types 306
scopes 116
sizeof 257
statements 282
tag names 116
type compatibility 178
type declarations 117
typedef names 116, 178
C89 4
C95 4
C99 5
cabs function 487
cacos function 485
cacosh function 486
calendar time conversions 446
call
    function 214
    macro 49
call-by-value 299
calloc facility 408, 410
carg function 488
carriage return 36
carriage return character 13
case labels 274
casin function 485
casinh function 486
cast expressions 176, 219
    conversions during 194
    use of **void** 168
catan function 485
catanh function 486
catch C++ keyword 39
cbrt facility 432
ccos function 485
ccosh function 486
ceil facility 427
cexp function 487
cfree facility 410
CHAR_BIT 127
CHAR_MAX 127
CHAR_MIN 127
character set 11, 497
characters
    constants 30, 39
    encoding 14, 39, 497
    escape 13, 35, 38

formatting 31
integer values 124
library functions 335–345
line break 13
macro parameters in 55
multibyte 40
operator 20
pseudo-unsigned 130
repetoire 39
separator 20
signed and unsigned 130, 336
size of 131, 182
standard 11
type 129
universal 41
whitespace 13
wide 40
cimag function 488
circumflex accent 12
CJK 40
clalloc facility 410
class C++ keyword 39
Clean C 5
clearerr facility 404
clock facility 443
clock_t type 443
CLOCKS_PER_SEC 443
clog function 487
comma expression 211, 216, 249
comments 18
    preprocessor 19, 57
COMMON 114
compatible types 172
compiler 7
compiler optimizations 237, 256
compile-time objects 83
compiling a C program 8
compl macro 333
_Complex_I macro 484
complex macro 484
_Complex type specifier 135
complex types 135
    constants 29
    conversions 192, 199
    corresponding real type 136
complex.h header file 484
components 149
    overloading class 78, 153, 161
    selection 212, 214

structure 149
unions 161
composite types 172
compound statements 262, 282
concatenation of strings 34
conditional compilation 61
conditional expressions 244
conditional statement 264
    dangling-else problem 265
conformance to C standard 8
conj function 488
const type qualifier 89
const_cast C++ keyword 39
constant expressions 250
    in initializers 106
    in preprocessor 251
constants 24–38
    character 30, 39
    complex 29
    enumeration 146
    floating-point 29
    integer 25
    lexical 24
    value of 209
continuation
    of preprocessor commands 45
    of source lines 14
    of string constants 34
continue statement 277
control expressions 260
control functions 453–459
control wide character 337
conversion
    of Boolean type 189
conversion specifier 379
conversion state 16
conversions 188–200
    argument 128, 214
    array 193
    array to pointer 106, 140, 193
    assignment 195
    binary 198
    casting 194
    complex 192, 199
    floating-point 191
    function 193
    functions to pointers 106
    integer to floating-point 191
    integer to integer 190

integer to pointer 106, 193
pointer to array 140
pointer to integer 191
pointer to pointer 140, 192
rank 196
representation changes 189
string to pointer 106
trivial 189
void 193
copysign facility 441
corresponding type 136
cos facility 433
cosh facility 433
CPL 3
__cplusplus macro 70
cpow function 487
cproj function 488
Cray Research, Inc. 187
creal function 488
csin function 485
csinh function 486
csqrt function 487
ctan function 485
ctanh function 486
ctime facility 445
ctype.h header file 335
CX_LIMITED_RANGE
    pragma 484

D

dangling-else problem 265
data representation 181
data tags 163
date facilities 443–451
__DATE__ facility 51
DBL_DIG 134
DBL_EPSILON 134
DBL_MANT_DIG 134
DBL_MAX 134
DBL_MAX_10_EXP 134
DBL_MAX_EXP 134
DBL_MIN 134
DBL_MIN_10_EXP 134
DBL_MIN_EXP 134
decimal point 29, 465
DECIMAL_DIG 134
declarations 73–120
    blocks, at head of 84

conflicting 78
default 113
defining 114
duplicate 78, 79
extent 80
function 165
hidden 76
implicit 113
in compound statements 262
inner 74
parameter 84, 99, 295
point of 76
referencing 114
storage classes 84
structure 148
tentative 114
top-level 74, 84
union 160
visibility 76
declarators 73, 95
abstract 176
array 97
compostion of 101
function 99
illegal 101
missing 88
pointer 96
precedence of 102
simple 96
decrement expression 216, 225
default
declarations 113
initializer 103
storage class 84
type specifier 87
default labels 274
#define preprocessor
command 46
defined preprocessor
command 66
defining declaration 114
delete C++ keyword 39
designated initializers 103, 111
difftime facility 447
discarded expressions 250, 255,
261, 269
div facility 419
divide by 0 206, 228, 229
do statement 268

dollar sign character 22
domain error 425
domain, real and complex 123,
199
double type 132
duplicate declarations 78, 79, 151
dynamic_cast C++
keyword 39

E

EBCDIC 14
EDOM error code 327, 425
effective type 188
EILSEQ error code 328
#elif command 62
else (See conditional statement)
#else command 61
encoding of characters 14, 16, 39,
497
#endif preprocessor
command 61
end-of-file 363
end-of-line 11, 13, 34
entry point of programs (See
main)
enumeration constants
in expressions 208
overloading class 78
value of 147
enumerations
compatibility 173
constants 83, 146
declaration syntax 145
definition 145
initializers 109
overloading class 147
scope 147
tags 83, 145
type of 145
EOF facility 335, 365
equality expressions 234
ERANGE error code 327, 426
erf facility 439
erfc facility 439
errno facility 327, 425
errno.h header file 325, 327
error indication in files 363

#error preprocessor
command 69
escape characters 35
Euclid's GCD algorithm 228
evaluation order 253
exceptions (arithmetic) 206
exec facility 416
executable program 7
_Exit facility 414
exit facility 414
exp facility 431
exp2 facility 431
expansion of macros 49
explicit C++ keyword 39
expm1 facility 431
export C++ keyword 39
exported identifiers 82
expressions 203–258
addition 229
address 224
assignment 246
associativity 205
binary 227
bitwise and 157, 236
bitwise or 236
bitwise xor 236
cast 219
comma 211, 216, 249
component selection 212, 214
conditional 244
constant 250
control 260
conversions 198
decrement 216, 225
designators 203
discarded 250, 255, 261, 269
division 228
equality 234
function call 214
increment 216, 225
indirection 225
logical and 242
logical or 242
lvalues 203
minus 222
multiplication 228
negation (arithmetic) 222
negation (bitwise) 223
negation (logical) 222

objects 203
order of evaluation 253, 256
parenthesized 209
plus 222
postfix 210
precedence 206
primary 207
relational 233
remainder 228
sequential 249
shift 231
sizeof 220
statements, as 260
subscript 210
subtraction 230
unary 219
extended character set 15
extended integer types 131
extent of declarations 80
extern storage class 83
external names 22, 75, 82, 114
advice on defining 115

F

fabs facility 426
false C++ keyword 39
false macro 329
far pointers 187
fclose facility 366
fdim facility 435
FE_ALL_EXCEPT macro 480
FE_DEFL_ENV macro 478
FE_DIVBYZERO macro 480
FE_DOWNWARD macro 481
FE_INEXACT macro 480
FE_INVALID macro 480
FE_OVERFLOW macro 480
FE_TONEAREST macro 481
FE_TOWARDZERO macro 481
FE_UNDERFLOW macro 480
FE_UPWARD macro 481
feclearexcept function 480
fegetenv function 479
fegetexceptflag 480
fegetround function 481
feholdexcept function 479
FENV_ACCESS macro 478
fenv_t type 478

feof facility 365, 404
feraiseexcept function 480
ferror facility 404
fesetenv function 479
fesetexceptflag
function 480
fesetround function 481
fetestexcept function 480
feupdateenv function 479
fexcept_t type 480
fflush facility 366
fgetc facility 374
fgetpos facility 372
fgets facility 376
fgetwc function 375
fgetws function 376
fields (See components)
__FILE__ facility 51
file inclusion 59
file names 59, 366
file pointer 363
file position 363, 372
FILE type 363
FILENAME_MAX macro 366
flexible array component 159
float type specifier 132
float.h header file 8, 134
floating-point
complex 135
constants 29
control modes 477
domain 199
exception 479
exceptions 477
expressions 254
IEC 60559 477
IEEE standard 135
imaginary 136
infinity 133
initializers 105
NaN 442
normalized 133
real 136
representation 165
size of 133
status flags 477
subnormal 133
types 132
unnormalized 133

unordered 442
floor facility 428
FLT 134
FLT_DIG 134
FLT_EPSILON 134
FLT_EVAL_METHOD 134
FLT_MANT_DIG 134
FLT_MAX 134
FLT_MAX_10_EXP 134
FLT_MAX_EXP 134
FLT_MIN 134
FLT_MIN_10_EXP 134
FLT_MIN_EXP 134
FLT_RADIX 134
FLT_ROUNDS 134
fma facility 432
fmax facility 435
fmin facility 435
fmod facility 428
fopen facility 366
FOPEN_MAX macro 366
for statement 269
form feed character 11, 13, 36
formal parameters 295
adjustments to type 298
declarations 84
passing conventions 299
type checking 300
FORTRAN 114, 274
forward references 76, 150
FP_CONTRACT pragma 481
FP_INFINITE facility 440
FP_NAN facility 440
FP_NORMAL facility 440
FP_SUBNORMAL facility 440
FP_ZERO facility 440
fpclassify facility 440
fpos_t type 372
fprintf facility 301, 387
fputc facility 385
fputs facility 386
fputwc function 385
fputws function 386
fread facility 402
free facility 409, 410
freestanding implementation 8
freestanding implementations 325
freopen facility 366, 371
frexp facility 429

friend C++ keyword 39
fscanf facility 377
fseek facility 372
fsetpos facility 372
ftell facility 372
full stop character 12
__func__ predefined
    identifier 23, 51, 453
function-like macros 47
functions 285–308
    agreement of parameters 300
    agreement of return values 302
    argument conversions 128,
        214
    calling 214, 299
    conversion to pointers 106,
        193
    declaration of 165
    declarators for 99
    definition 74, 165, 286
    designators 203, 224, 225
    main 303
    operations on 167
    parameters 99, 295, 298, 299
    pointer arguments 215
    pointers to 136, 167
    prototypes 100, 214, 285,
        289–295
    return statement 279
    return types 301
    returning structures 213
    returning **void** 214
    storage classes 84, 288
    type of 165, 289
    typedef names for 170
    value of name 208
fwprintf function 388
fwrite facility 402

G

GCD (Greatest Common
    Divisor) 228
getc facility 374
getchar facility 36, 130, 374
getenv facility 415
gets facility 376
getwc function 375
getwchar function 375

gmtime facility 446
goto statement 77, 280, 282
    effect on initialization 81
graphic characters 12
gsignal facility 456

H

header files 7, 312
    assert.h 453
    complex.h 484
    ctype.h 335
    errno.h 325, 327
    float.h 8, 134
    in Amendment 1 to ISO C 4
    in freestanding
        implementations 8
    inttypes.h 467
    iso646.h 4, 8, 325, 333
    limits.h 8, 126
    locale.h 461
    math.h 425
    memory.h 359
    setjmp.h 453
    signal.h 453
    stdarg.h 8, 325, 329
    stdbool.h 8, 132, 325
    stddef.h 8, 325, 477, 483
    stdint.h 8, 325, 467
    stdio.h 363
    stdlib.h 325, 347, 407,
        410, 425
    string.h 347
    sys/times.h 443
    sys/types.h 443
    tgmath.h 425
    time.h 443
    varargs.h 331
    wchar.h 4, 359, 364, 489
    wctype.h 4, 489
heap sort 85
heapsort algorithm 84
hexadecimal escape 35
hexadecimal numbers 25
hidden declarations 76
holes (in structures) 152
horizontal tab character 13, 36
host computer 13
hosted implementation 8

HUGE_VAL macro 383, 426
HUGE_VALF 426
HUGE_VALL 426
hyperbolic functions 433
hypot facilities 432

I

identifiers
    creating with preprocessor 57
    declaration 73
    enclosed by declarators 96
    enumeration constants 147
    external 22, 75, 82
    in expressions 208
    naming conventions 22
    overloading 77
    reserved 313
    spelling rules 21
    visibility 76
IEC 60559
    1989 floating-point
        standard 477
IEEE floating-point standard 135
if (See conditional statement)
#if preprocessor command 61
#ifdef preprocessor
    command 63
#ifndef preprocessor
    command 63
ilogb 431
_Imaginary_I macro 484
imaginary macro 484
_Imaginary type 192
imaginary type 136
_Imaginary type specifier 135,
    136
imaxabs function 474
imaxdiv function 475
imaxdiv_t function 475
implicit declarations 113
implicit **int** 87
#include preprocessor
    command 59
incomplete array 98
incomplete type 137, 151
increment expression 216, 225
index facility 352
indirection operator 137, 210, 225

INF input string 383
infinity 133, 136
INFINITY input string 383
initializers 80, 103
   arrays 107
   automatic variables 103
   constant expressions 250
   default 103
   designated 103, 111
   enumerations 109
   floating-point 105
   in compound statements 263
   integer 104
   pointer 105
   static variables 103
   structures 109
   unions 110
inner declarations 74
input/output functions 363–??
insertion sort 271
instr 353
instr facility 353
int type specifier 125, 128
INT_FASTN_MAX macro 472
INT_FASTN_MIN macro 472
int_fastN_t type 472
INT_LEASTN_MAX macro 471
INT_LEASTN_MIN macro 471
int_leastN_t type 471
INT_MAX 127
INT_MIN 127
integer promotions 196
integers
   constants 25
   conversion to pointer 106
   initializers 104
   pointer conversions 193
   size of 128
   unsigned 128
integral types 124
Intel 80x86 185
INTMAX_C macro 473
INTMAX_MAX macro 473
INTMAX_MIN macro 473
intmax_t type 251
intmaxr_t type 473
INTN_C macro 471
INTN_MAX macro 470
INTN_MIN macro 470

intN_t type 470
INTPTR_MAX macro 473
INTPTR_MIN macro 473
intptr_t type 191, 473
inttypes.h header file 467
invalid pointer 139
_IOFBF value 370
_IOLBF value 370
_IONBF value 370
isalnum facility 336
isalpha facility 336
isascii facility 337
iscntrl facility 337
iscsymf facility 338
isdigit facility 338
isfinite facility 440
isgraph facility 339
isgreater facility 442
isgreaterequal facility 442
isinf facility 440
isless facility 442
islessequal facility 442
islessgreater facility 442
islower function 340
isnan facility 440
isnormal facility 440
ISO 646-1083 Invariant Code
   Set 14, 40
ISO 8601 451
ISO C 6
ISO/IEC 10646 Universal Multiple-Octet Coded Character
   Set 40
ISO/IEC 14882
   1998 5
ISO/IEC 9899
   1990 4
   1999 5
iso646.h 14, 23
iso646.h header file 4, 8, 325,
   333
isodigit facility 338
isprint facility 339
ispunct facility 339
isspace function 341
isunordered facility 442
isupper facility 340, 348
iswalnum facility 337
iswalpha facility 337

iswcntrl facility 337
iswctype function 343
iswgraph function 340
iswhite facility 341
iswlower 340
iswprint function 340
iswpunct 340
iswspace function 341
iswupper 340
iswxdigit facility 338
isxdigit facility 338
iterative statements 266

J

jmp_buf facility 454

K

Kernighan, Brian xviii, 4
keywords 23, 39
Knuth, Donald xviii

L

L_tmpnam macro 405
labels
   case 274
   default 274
   overloading class 78
   statement 77, 78, 261, 280
labs facility 419
LALR(1) grammar 88, 171
Latin-1 40
LC_*x* locale macros 462
lconv structure 463
LDBL_DIG 134
LDBL_EPSILON 134
LDBL_MANT_DIG 134
LDBL_MAX 134
LDBL_MAX_10_EXP 134
LDBL_MAX_EXP 134
LDBL_MIN 134
LDBL_MIN_10_EXP 134
LDBL_MIN_EXP 134
ldexp facility 430
ldiv facility 419
length (See **sizeof**, **strlen**)
lenstr facility 351

lexical structure 11–42
lgamma facility 439
library functions 309–324
    character processing 335–345
    control 453–459
    input/output 363–??
    mathematical functions 425–433
    memory 359–362
    storage allocation 407–410
    string processing 347–357
    time and date 443–451
lifetime 80
limits.h file 8, 126
line break characters 13
#line command 66
line continuation
    in macro calls 48
    in preprocessor commands 45
    in strings 34
    __LINE__ facility 51
linkage 82
linker 7
lint program 115
literal (See constant)
little-endian computers 183
LLONG_MAX 127
LLONG_MIN 127
llrint facility 428
ln facility 431
locale 413
locale.h header file 461
localeconv facility 463
localtime facility 446
log facility 431
log10 facility 431
log2 431
logb 431
logical expressions 242
logical negation 222
long double type 132
long float type 132
long type 125, 128
LONG_MAX 127
LONG_MIN 127
longjmp facility 454
loops (See iterative statements)
lowline character 12
lrint facility 428

lvalues 197, 203

M

macros 46–59
    body 46
    calling 49
    defining 46, 47, 73
    expansion 49
    function-like 47
    object-like 46
    overloading class 78
    parameters 47
    pitfalls 47, 54
    precedence 54
    predefined 51, 64
    redefining 53
    replacement 50, 63, 66
    side effects 55
    simple 46
    undefining 53
main program 7, 303, 414
malloc facility 113, 185, 407, 410
math.h header file 425
mathematical functions 425–433
MB_CUR_MAX macro 491
MB_LEN_MAX 127
mblen facility 421
mbrlen function 490
mbrtowc function 490
mbsinit function 491
mbsrtowcs function 491
mbstate_t type 490
mbstowcs facility 35
mbstowcs function 423
mbtowc facility 421
members (See components)
memccpy function 361
memchr function 359
memcmp facility 360
memcpy function 361
memmove function 361
memory accesses 256
memory alignment (See alignment)
memory functions 359–362
memory models 185
memory.h header file 359

memset function 362
merging of tokens 55, 57
Microsoft C 185
minus operator 222
Miranda prototype 291, 293
mktemp facility 405
mktime facility 446
mlalloc facility 410
modf facility 430
modifiable lvalue 203
monetary formats 463
multibyte character 21, 40
multibyte characters 16, 31, 420
multibyte strings 422
multidimensional arrays 141, 210
multiplicative expressions 227
mutable C++ keyword 39

N

name space (See overloading class)
names 73, 208
namespace C++ keyword 39
NaN 133, 136, 442
nan facility 441
NAN input string 383
NDEBUG facility 453
near pointers 187
nearbyint facility 428
new C++ keyword 39
newline character 12, 36
nextafter 441
nexttoward 441
normalized floating-point number 133
not macro 333
not_eq macro 333
notation (See representation)
notstr 353
notstr facility 353
null character 12
NULL macro 138, 325
null pointer 106, 138, 191, 192, 225, 325
null preprocessor command 44, 67
null statement 281
null wide character 16

O

object code (module) 7
object pointer 136
object-like macro 46
objects 203
octal numbers 25
octet 40
offsetof facility 326
onexit facility 415
on-off-switch 68
operator C++ keyword 39
operators (See expressions)
optimizations
    compiler 237
    memory access 92, 256
or macro 333
or_eq macro 333
order of evaluation 253
orientation of streams 364, 369,
    371
overflow 206
    floating-point conversion 191
    integer conversions 190
overlapping assignment 248
overloading 76, 78, 209
    component names 152
    of identifiers 77
    union components 161

P

padding bits 188
parameters (See formal parameters)
parenthesized expressions 209
PARMS macro 294
Pascal 260, 268, 274, 300
Perennial, Inc 8
perror facility 328
Plauger, P. J. 4
Plum Hall, Inc. 8
plus operator 222
pointers
    addition 229
    and arrays 140
    arithmetic 139, 229
    comparison 234, 235
    conversions between 140

conversions to arrays 140
declarators for 96
function arguments 215
functions 167
initializers 105
integer conversions 193
invalid 139
near and far 187
null 138, 191
representation of 140
size of 185, 193
subscripting 141
subtraction 231
type compatibility 175
types 136
portability 181, 220
    bit fields 155, 157
    bitwise expressions 223, 237
    byte order 184
    character sets 22
    comments 19
    compound assignment 249
    constant expressions 251, 252
    external names 22, 82
    floating-point types 133
    generic pointers 185
    input/output 363
    integer arithmetic 207
    integer types 126
    pointer arithmetic 139, 231,
        234
    pointers and integers 106, 193
    string constants 33
    union types 165
    variable argument lists 289,
        301
position in file (See file position)
postfix expressions 210
pow facility 432
_Pragma operator 69
#pragma preprocessor
    command 67
pragmas
    #pragma directive 67
    placement 68
    standard 68
precedence of operators 205
predefined identifier 23
predefined macros 51, 64

prefix expressions 225
preprocessor 43–71
    commands 43
    comments 19, 57
    constant expressions 250
    defined 66
    #elif 62
    #else 61
    #endif 61
    #error 69
    #if 61
    #ifdef 63
    #ifndef 63
    #include 59
    lexical conventions 44
    #line 66
    pitfalls 47, 54
    #pragma 67
    stringization 55
    token merging 55, 57
    #undef 53, 64
PRIcKN macros 468
primary expressions 207
printf facility 387
printing character 339
printing wide character 340
private C++ keyword 39
process time 443
program 7, 74
protected C++ keyword 39
prototype 100, 214, 285, 289–295
pseudo-unsigned characters 130
psignal facility 456
PTRDIFF_MAX macro 474
PTRDIFF_MIN macro 474
ptrdiff_t facility 326
public C++ keyword 39
punctuator 20
putc facility 385
putchar facility 385
puts facility 386
putwc function 385
putwchar function 385

Q

qsort facility 417
qualifiers (See type qualifiers)
quiet NaN 133

quine (self-reproducing program) 400

R

raise facility 456
rand facility 410
RAND_MAX macro 410
range 188
range error 426
rank, conversion 196
real type 136
realloc facility 408, 410
referencing declarations 114
register storage 83, 224
reinterpret_cast C++ keyword 39
relalloc facility 408, 410
relational expressions 233
remainder 228, 419, 428, 430
remainder 428
remove facility 404
remquo facilities 428
rename facility 404
repetoire, character 39
representation of data 165, 181–188
reserved identifiers 22, 23, 313
restrict type qualifier 94
return statement 279, 302
reverse solidus character 12
rewind facility 372
Richards, Martin 3
rindex facility 352
rint facility 428
Ritchie, Dennis xviii, 3, 4
round facility 428
rvalue 203

S

scalar types 123
scalbln 430
scalbn 430
scanf facility 377
scanset 384
SCHAR_MAX 127
SCHAR_MIN 127
SCN*cKN* macros 468

scnstr facility 352
scope 75, 83
Sedgewick, Robert xviii
SEEK_CUR macro 372
SEEK_END macro 372
SEEK_SET macro 372
selection of components 149, 152, 212, 214
semantic type 440
semicolons, use of in statements 260
sequence point 91, 255, 378, 388, 417
sequential expressions 249
set of integers example 237
setbuf facility 370
setenv function 416
setjmp facility 454
setjmp.h header file 453
setlocale facility 461
setvbuf facility 370
shell sort 271
shift expressions 231
shift state 16, 420
short type specifier 125, 128
SHRT_MAX 127
SHRT_MIN 127
SIG_ATOMIC_MAX macro 474
SIG_ATOMIC_MIN macro 474
sign magnitude notation 126
signal facility 456
signal.h header file 453
signaling NaN 133
signbit facility 440
sin facility 433
single quote 36
sinh facility 433
size
    arrays 140, 143
    bit fields 156
    characters 182
    data objects 182
    enumerations 147
    floating-point objects 133
    pointers 193
    storage units 182
    structures 158
    types 182
    unions 162

SIZE_MAX macro 474
size_t facility 326, 365
sizeof operator 182, 188, 193, 220
    applied to arrays 141, 143
    applied to functions 167
    type name arguments 176
sleep facility 458
snprintf facility 387
solidus character 12
sorting
    heap sort 85
    insertion sort 271
    library facilities 417
    shell sort 271
source files 7, 175
space character 11
sprintf facility 387
sqrt facility 432
srand facility 410
sscanf facility 377
ssignal facility 456
Standard 132
Standard C 4, 6
standard headers 61
standard I/O functions 363
state-dependent encoding 16
statement labels 77, 78, 261, 280
statements 259–283
    assignment 246
    block 262
    break 277
    compound 262, 282
    conditional 264
    continue 277
    do 268
    expression 260
    for 269
    goto 280, 282
    if 264
    iterative 266
    labeled 261, 280
    null 281
    return 279, 302
    switch 274
    while 267
static storage class 98
    array parameters 297

static storage class
  specifier 83
static_cast C++ keyword 39
stdarg.h header file 8, 325,
  329
stdbool.h header file 8, 132,
  325
__STDC__ facility 51
__STDC_IEC_559__
  macro 478
stddef.h header file 8, 325
stderr facility 371
stdin facility 371
stdint.h header file 8, 325,
  467
stdio.h header file 130
stdlib.h header file 325, 347,
  407, 410, 425
stdout facility 371
storage allocation 407–410
storage class
  static 98
storage class specifier 83
  auto 83
  default 84, 88
  extern 83
  register 83, 224
  static 83
  typedef 83
storage duration 80
storage units 182
strcat facility 348
strchr facility 351
strcmp facility 349
strcoll facility 356
strcpy facility 350
strcspn facility 353
streams 363
strerror facility 328
strftime facility 448
string.h header file 347
stringization of tokens 55
strings
  concatenation 34, 348
  constants 32
  conversions to pointer 106
  library functions 347–357
  macro parameters in 55
  multibyte 34

type 129
  used to initialize array of
    char 108
  wide 34
  writing into 33
strlen facility 351
strncat facility 348
strncmp facility 349
strncpy facility 350
Stroustrup, Bjarne 5
strpbrk facility 353
strpos facility 351
strrchr facility 351
strrpbrk facility 353
strrpos facility 352
strspn facility 352
strstr facility 354
strtod facility 412
strtof facility 412
strtoimax function 475
strtok facility 354
strtol facility 412
strtold facility 412
strtoll facility 412
strtoul facility 412
strtoull facility 412
strtoumax function 475
structures
  alignment of 158
  bit fields 154
  compatibility 175
  components 83, 149, 152
  declaration of 148
  flexible array member 159
  holes in 152
  initializers 109
  operations on 152
  packing of components 152,
    153
  portability problems 157
  returning from functions 213
  selection of components 149
  self-referential 151
  size of 158
  tags 83, 148
  type of 149
strxfrm facility 356
subnormal 440

subnormal floating-point
  number 133
subscripting 84, 141, 210
switch statement 274
  body 263
  effect on initialization 81
  use 275
swprintf function 388
syntax notation 9
sys/times.h header file 443
sys/types.h header file 443
sys_errlist facility 328
system facility 416

T

tags
  data 163
  enumeration 145
  overloading class 78
  structure 148
  union 160
tan facility 433
tanh facility 433
target computer 13
Technical Corrigenda to C89 4
template C++ keyword 39
tentative definition 114
test suites 8
text streams 363
tgamma facility 440
tgmath.h 425, 435
this C++ keyword 39
Thompson, Ken 3
throw C++ keyword 39
tilde character 12
__TIME__ facility 51
time facility 445
time.h header file 443
time_t type 445
time-of-day facilities 443–451
times facility 443
tm structure 446
TMP_MAX macro 405
tmpfile facility 405
tmpnam facility 405
toascii facility 341
toint facility 342
tokens (lexical) 20

converting to strings 55
merging by preprocessor 41,
    55, 57
top-level declarations 74, 84
toupper facility 342
towctrans function 345
towlower function 342
towupper function 342
traditional C 4
    converting library
        descriptions 312
translation units 7, 74, 175
trigonometric functions 433, 434
trigraphs 14, 59, 333
true C++ keyword 39
true macro 329
trunc facility 428
try C++ keyword 39
twos-complement
    representation 125, 190
type (See types)
type checking
    of function parameters 300
    of function return values 302
type names 176
    in cast expression 219
    in **sizeof** expression 221
type qualifiers 89, 98, 213, 247,
    296
    restrict 94
type specifiers 73, 86
    _Bool 132
    char 129
    _Complex 135
    default 87
    double 132
    enumeration 145
    float 132
    _Imaginary 136
    int 125, 128
    integer 125
    long 128
    long double 132
    long float 132
    short 125, 128
    signed 125
    structure 148
    typedef names 168
    union 160

unsigned 128, 129
void 87
    without declarators 88
typedef names 168–172
    equivalence of 173
    LALR(1) grammar 171
    overloading class 78
    redefining 171
    scope 83
typedef storage class 83, 168
type-generic macros 425, 435
typeid C++ keyword 39
typename C++ keyword 39
types 123–180
    arithmetic 123
    array 140
    Boolean 132
    categories of 123
    character 129
    compatible 172–176
    complex 135
    composite 172
    conversions 188
    corresponding 136
    domain 123
    effective 188
    enumerated 145, 173
    extended 131
    floating-point 132
    functions 165, 289
    imaginary 136
    integer 124
    pointer 136, 175
    real 136
    representation of 188
    same 172
    scalar 123
    semantic 440
    signed 125
    structure 149, 175
    unions 162, 175
    unsigned 128
    user defined 168
    variably modified 144
    void 168

U

UCHAR_MAX 127

UCS-2 40
UCS-4 40
UINT_FASTN_MAX macro 472
uint_fastN_t type 472
UINT_LEASTN_MAX macro 471
uint_leastN_t type 471
UINT_MAX 127
UINTMAX_C macro 473
UINTMAX_MAX macro 473
uintmax_t type 473
UINTN_C macro 471
UINTN_MAX macro 470
uintN_t type 470
UINTPTR_MAX macro 473
uintptr_t type 191, 473
ULLONG_MAX 127
ULONG_MAX 127
unary expressions 219
#undef preprocessor
    command 53, 64
underflow 206
    floating-point conversion 191
underscore character 22
ungetc facility 372, 374
ungetwc function 375
Unicode 40
union type 160
unions
    alignment of 162
    compatibility 175
    components 83, 161
    data tags 163
    declaration of 160
    initializers 110
    packing of components 161
    portability of 165
    size of 162
    tags 83, 160
    type of 162
universal character name 21, 41
UNIX 3, 52, 115, 172
unix macro 52
unnormalized floating-point
    number 133
unordered 442
unsigned integers
    arithmetic rules 207
    conversions 190
unsigned type specifier 128

user-defined type (See **typedef**)
USHRT_MAX 127
using C++ keyword 39
usual arithmetic conversions 198
usual conversions
    argument 128, 214
    assignment 195
    binary 198
    casts 194

V

__VA_ARGS__ macro
    parameter 58
va_x_ variable-argument
    facilities 329
varargs.h header file 331
variable length arrays 99, 109,
    143, 170, 174, 217, 221, 230,
    263
variables
    automatic 80
    declarators for 96
    in expressions 208
    static 80
variably modified type 144
vax macro 52
VAX-11 52
vertical tab character 11, 13, 36
vfprintf function 401
vfscanf facility 401
vfwprintf function 401
vfwscanf facility 401
virtual C++ keyword 39
visibility 76, 151
void type specifier 87, 168
    defining your own 23
    discarded expressions 256
    function result 214
    function return type 302
    in casts 168
volatile type qualifier 91
vprintf function 401
vscanf facility 401
vsprintf function 401
vsscanf facility 401
vswprintf function 401
vswscanf facility 401
vwprintf function 401

vwscanf facility 401

W

wchar.h file 4, 359, 364
wchar.h header file 489
WCHAR_MAX 126, 365, 474, 489
WCHAR_MIN 126, 365, 474, 489
wchar_t C++ keyword 39
wchar_t type 15, 31, 108, 326,
    489
wcrtomb function 491
wcscat function 348
wcschr function 351
wcscmp function 349
wcscoll function 356
wcscpy function 350
wcscspn function 353
wcsftime function 448
wcslen function 351
wcsncat function 348
wcsncmp function 349
wcsncpy function 350
wcspbrk function 353
wcsrchr function 351
wcsrtombs function 492
wcsspn function 353
wcsstr function 354
wcstod function 493
wcstof function 493
wcstoimax function 475
wcstok function 354
wcstol function 493
wcstold function 493
wcstoll function 493
wcstombs function 423
wcstoul function 493
wcstoull function 493
wcstoumax function 475
wcsxfrm function 357
wctob function 491
wctomb facility 422
wctrans function 344
wctrans_t type 344
wctype function 343
wctype.h header file 4, 489
wctype_t type 343
WEOF macro 490
WG14 (C) 4

while statement 267
whitespace 13
wide character 40
wide characters 15, 31, 34, 420
    input/output 364
wide string 16, 34, 108, 422
wide-oriented stream 364
WINT_MAX macro 474
WINT_MIN macro 474
wint_t type 15, 365, 489
wmemchr function 360
wmemcmp function 360
wmemcpy function 361
wmemmove function 361
wmemset function 362
wprintf function 388

X

X3J11 (C) 4
xor macro 333
xor_eq macro 333

Y

YACC 172